Contemporary Authors®

ISSN 0010-7468

Contemporary Authors®

A Bio-Bibliographical Guide to
Current Writers in Fiction, General Nonfiction,
Poetry, Journalism, Drama, Motion Pictures,
Television, and Other Fields

volume **258**

THOMSON

GALE

Detroit • New York • San Francisco • New Haven, Conn. • Waterville, Maine • London

Contemporary Authors, Vol. 258

Project Editor
Amy Elisabeth Fuller

Editorial
Michelle Kazensky, Lisa Kumar, Mary Ruby,
Rob Russell, Amanda Sams

Permissions
Margaret Gaston-Chamberlain, Lisa Kinkade,
Tracie Richardson

Imaging and Multimedia
Lezlie Light

Composition and Electronic Capture
Gary Oudersluys

Manufacturing
Drew Kalasky

LIBRARY OF CONGRESS CATALOG CARD NUMBER 62-52046

ISBN-13: 978-0-7876-7887-6
ISBN-10: 0-7876-7887-2
ISSN 0010-7468

This title is also available as an e-book.
ISBN-13: 978-1-4144-2907-6
ISBN-10: 1-4144-2907-X
Contact your Gale Group sales representative for ordering information.

Printed in the United States of America
10 9 8 7 6 5 4 3 2 1

Contents

Indexing note: All *Contemporary Authors* entries are indexed in the *Contemporary Authors* cumulative index, which is published separately and distributed twice a year.

As always, the most recent Contemporary Authors cumulative index continues to be the user's guide to the location of an individual author's listing.

Preface

Contemporary Authors (*CA*) provides information on approximately 130,000 writers in a wide range of media, including:

- Current writers of fiction, nonfiction, poetry, and drama whose works have been issued by commercial publishers, risk publishers, or university presses (authors whose books have been published only by known vanity or author-subsidized firms are ordinarily not included)

- Prominent print and broadcast journalists, editors, syndicated cartoonists, graphic novelists, screenwriters, television scriptwriters, and other media people

- Notable international authors

- Literary greats of the early twentieth century whose works are popular in today's high school and college curriculums and continue to elicit critical attention

A *CA* listing entails no charge or obligation. Authors are included on the basis of the above criteria and their interest to *CA* users. Sources of potential listees include trade periodicals, publishers' catalogs, librarians, and other users of the series.

How to Get the Most out of *CA*: Use the Index

The key to locating an author's most recent entry is the *CA* cumulative index, which is published separately and distributed twice a year. It provides access to *all* entries in *CA* and *Contemporary Authors New Revision Series* (*CANR*). Always consult the latest index to find an author's most recent entry.

For the convenience of users, the *CA* cumulative index also includes references to all entries in these The Gale Group literary series: *Authors and Artists for Young Adults, Authors in the News, Bestsellers, Black Literature Criticism, Black Literature Criticism Supplement, Black Writers, Children's Literature Review, Concise Dictionary of American Literary Biography, Concise Dictionary of British Literary Biography, Contemporary Authors Autobiography Series, Contemporary Authors Bibliographical Series, Contemporary Dramatists, Contemporary Literary Criticism, Contemporary Novelists, Contemporary Poets, Contemporary Popular Writers, Contemporary Southern Writers, Contemporary Women Poets, Dictionary of Literary Biography, Dictionary of Literary Biography Documentary Series, Dictionary of Literary Biography Yearbook, DISCovering Authors, DISCovering Authors: British, DISCovering Authors: Canadian, DISCovering Authors: Modules* (including modules for Dramatists, Most-Studied Authors, Multicultural Authors, Novelists, Poets, and Popular/Genre Authors), *DISCovering Authors 3.0, Drama Criticism, Drama for Students, Feminist Writers, Hispanic Literature Criticism, Hispanic Writers, Junior DISCovering Authors, Major Authors and Illustrators for Children and Young Adults, Major 20th-Century Writers, Native North American Literature, Novels for Students, Poetry Criticism, Poetry for Students, Short Stories for Students, Short Story Criticism, Something about the Author, Something about the Author Autobiography Series, St. James Guide to Children's Writers, St. James Guide to Crime & Mystery Writers, St. James Guide to Fantasy Writers, St. James Guide to Horror, Ghost & Gothic Writers, St. James Guide to Science Fiction Writers, St. James Guide to Young Adult Writers, Twentieth-Century Literary Criticism, 20th Century Romance and Historical Writers, World Literature Criticism,* and *Yesterday's Authors of Books for Children.*

A Sample Index Entry:

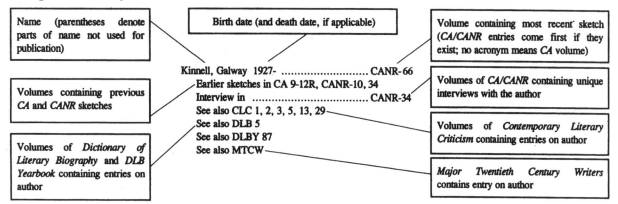

How Are Entries Compiled?

The editors make every effort to secure new information directly from the authors; listees' responses to our questionnaires and query letters provide most of the information featured in *CA*. For deceased writers, or those who fail to reply to requests for data, we consult other reliable biographical sources, such as those indexed in The Gale Group's *Biography and Genealogy Master Index*, and bibliographical sources, including *National Union Catalog, LC MARC*, and *British National Bibliography*. Further details come from published interviews, feature stories, and book reviews, as well as information supplied by the authors' publishers and agents.

An asterisk (*) at the end of a sketch indicates that the listing has been compiled from secondary sources believed to be reliable but has not been personally verified for this edition by the author sketched.

What Kinds of Information Does An Entry Provide?

Sketches in *CA* contain the following biographical and bibliographical information:

- **Entry heading:** the most complete form of author's name, plus any pseudonyms or name variations used for writing

- **Personal information:** author's date and place of birth, family data, ethnicity, educational background, political and religious affiliations, and hobbies and leisure interests

- **Addresses:** author's home, office, or agent's addresses, plus e-mail and fax numbers, as available

- **Career summary:** name of employer, position, and dates held for each career post; resume of other vocational achievements; military service

- **Membership information:** professional, civic, and other association memberships and any official posts held

- **Awards and honors:** military and civic citations, major prizes and nominations, fellowships, grants, and honorary degrees

- **Writings:** a comprehensive, chronological list of titles, publishers, dates of original publication and revised editions, and production information for plays, television scripts, and screenplays

- **Adaptations:** a list of films, plays, and other media which have been adapted from the author's work

- **Sidelights:** a biographical portrait of the author's development; information about the critical reception of the author's works; revealing comments, often by the author, on personal interests, aspirations, motivations, and thoughts on writing

- **Interview:** a one-on-one discussion with authors conducted especially for *CA*, offering insight into authors' thoughts about their craft

- **Autobiographical essay:** an original essay written by noted authors for *CA*, a forum in which writers may present themselves, on their own terms, to their audience

- **Photographs:** portraits and personal photographs of notable authors

- **Biographical and critical sources:** a list of books and periodicals in which additional information on an author's life and/or writings appears

- **Obituary Notices** in *CA* provide date and place of birth as well as death information about authors whose full-length sketches appeared in the series before their deaths. The entries also summarize the authors' careers and writings and list other sources of biographical and death information.

Related Titles in the *CA* Series

Contemporary Authors Autobiography Series complements *CA* original and revised volumes with specially commissioned autobiographical essays by important current authors, illustrated with personal photographs they provide. Common topics include their motivations for writing, the people and experiences that shaped their careers, the rewards they derive from their work, and their impressions of the current literary scene.

Contemporary Authors Bibliographical Series surveys writings by and about important American authors since World War II. Each volume concentrates on a specific genre and features approximately ten writers; entries list works written by and about the author and contain a bibliographical essay discussing the merits and deficiencies of major critical and scholarly studies in detail.

Available in Electronic Formats

GaleNet. *CA* is available on a subscription basis through GaleNet, an online information resource that features an easy-to-use end-user interface, powerful search capabilities, and ease of access through the World-Wide Web. For more information, call 1-800-877-GALE.

Licensing. *CA* is available for licensing. The complete database is provided in a fielded format and is deliverable on such media as disk, CD-ROM, or tape. For more information, contact The Gale Group's Business Development Group at 1-800-877-GALE, or visit us on our website at www.galegroup.com/bizdev.

Suggestions Are Welcome

The editors welcome comments and suggestions from users on any aspect of the *CA* series. If readers would like to recommend authors for inclusion in future volumes of the series, they are cordially invited to write the Editors at *Contemporary Authors*, The Gale Group, 27500 Drake Rd., Farmington Hills, MI 48331-3535; or call at 1-248-699-4253; or fax at 1-248-699-8054.

Contemporary Authors Product Advisory Board

The editors of *Contemporary Authors* are dedicated to maintaining a high standard of excellence by publishing comprehensive, accurate, and highly readable entries on a wide array of writers. In addition to the quality of the content, the editors take pride in the graphic design of the series, which is intended to be orderly yet inviting, allowing readers to utilize the pages of *CA* easily and with efficiency. Despite the longevity of the *CA* print series, and the success of its format, we are mindful that the vitality of a literary reference product is dependent on its ability to serve its users over time. As literature, and attitudes about literature, constantly evolve, so do the reference needs of students, teachers, scholars, journalists, researchers, and book club members. To be certain that we continue to keep pace with the expectations of our customers, the editors of *CA* listen carefully to their comments regarding the value, utility, and quality of the series. Librarians, who have firsthand knowledge of the needs of library users, are a valuable resource for us. The *Contemporary Authors* Product Advisory Board, made up of school, public, and academic librarians, is a forum to promote focused feedback about *CA* on a regular basis. The six-member advisory board includes the following individuals, whom the editors wish to thank for sharing their expertise:

- **Anne M. Christensen,** Librarian II, Phoenix Public Library, Phoenix, Arizona.

- **Barbara C. Chumard,** Reference/Adult Services Librarian, Middletown Thrall Library, Middletown, New York.

- **Eva M. Davis,** Youth Department Manager, Ann Arbor District Library, Ann Arbor, Michigan.

- **Adam Janowski, Jr.,** Library Media Specialist, Naples High School Library Media Center, Naples, Florida.

- **Robert Reginald,** Head of Technical Services and Collection Development, California State University, San Bernadino, California.

- **Stephen Weiner,** Director, Maynard Public Library, Maynard, Massachusetts.

International Advisory Board

Well-represented among the 130,000 author entries published in *Contemporary Authors* are sketches on notable writers from many non-English-speaking countries. The primary criteria for inclusion of such authors has traditionally been the publication of at least onetitle in English, either as an original work or as a translation. However, the editors of *Contemporary Authors* came to observe that many important international writers were being overlooked due to a strict adherence to our inclusion criteria. In addition, writers who were publishing in languages other than English were not being covered in the traditional sources we used for identifying new listees. Intent on increasing our coverage of international authors, including those who write only in their native language and have not been translated into English, the editors enlisted the aid of a board of advisors, each of whom is an expert on the literature of a particular country or region. Among the countries we focused attention on are Mexico, Puerto Rico, Germany, Luxembourg, Belgium, the Netherlands, Norway, Sweden, Denmark, Finland, Taiwan, Singapore, Spain, Italy, South Africa, Israel, and Japan, as well as England, Scotland, Wales, Ireland, Australia, and New Zealand. The sixteen-member advisory board includes the following individuals, whom the editors wish to thank for sharing their expertise:

- **Lowell A. Bangerter,** Professor of German, University of Wyoming, Laramie, Wyoming.

- **Nancy E. Berg,** Associate Professor of Hebrew and Comparative Literature, Washington University, St. Louis, Missouri.

- **Frances Devlin-Glass,** Associate Professor, School of Literary and Communication Studies, Deakin University, Burwood, Victoria, Australia.

- **David William Foster,** Regent's Professor of Spanish, Interdisciplinary Humanities, and Women's Studies, Arizona State University, Tempe, Arizona.

- **Hosea Hirata,** Director of the Japanese Program, Associate Professor of Japanese, Tufts University, Medford, Massachusetts.

- **Jack Kolbert,** Professor Emeritus of French Literature, Susquehanna University, Selinsgrove, Pennsylvania.

- **Mark Libin,** Professor, University of Manitoba, Winnipeg, Manitoba, Canada.

- **C. S. Lim,** Professor, University of Malaya, Kuala Lumpur, Malaysia.

- **Eloy E. Merino,** Assistant Professor of Spanish, Northern Illinois University, DeKalb, Illinois.

- **Linda M. Rodríguez Guglielmoni,** Associate Professor, University of Puerto Rico—Mayagüez, Puerto Rico.

- **Sven Hakon Rossel,** Professor and Chair of Scandinavian Studies, University of Vienna, Vienna, Austria.

- **Steven R. Serafin,** Director, Writing Center, Hunter College of the City University of New York, New York City.

- **David Smyth,** Lecturer in Thai, School of Oriental and African Studies, University of London, England.

- **Ismail S. Talib,** Senior Lecturer, Department of English Language and Literature, National University of Singapore, Singapore.

- **Dionisio Viscarri,** Assistant Professor, Ohio State University, Columbus, Ohio.

- **Mark Williams,** Associate Professor, English Department, University of Canterbury, Christchurch, New Zealand.

CA Numbering System and Volume Update Chart

Occasionally questions arise about the *CA* numbering system and which volumes, if any, can be discarded. Despite numbers like "29-32R," "97-100" and "258," the entire *CA* print series consists of only 348 physical volumes with the publication of *CA* Volume 258. The following charts note changes in the numbering system and cover design, and indicate which volumes are essential for the most complete, up-to-date coverage.

CA First Revision
- 1-4R through 41-44R (11 books)
  Cover: Brown with black and gold trim.
  There will be no further First Revision volumes because revised entries are now being handled exclusively through the more efficient *New Revision Series* mentioned below.

CA Original Volumes
- 45-48 through 97-100 (14 books)
  Cover: Brown with black and gold trim.
  101 through 258 (158 books)
  Cover: Blue and black with orange bands.
  The same as previous *CA* original volumes but with a new, simplified numbering system and new cover design.

CA Permanent Series
- *CAP*-1 and *CAP*-2 (2 books)
  Cover: Brown with red and gold trim.
  There will be no further Permanent Series volumes because revised entries are now being handled exclusively through the more efficient *New Revision Series* mentioned below.

CA New Revision Series
- CANR-1 through CANR-163 (163 books)
  Cover: Blue and black with green bands.
  Includes only sketches requiring significant changes; **sketches are taken from any previously published CA, CAP, or CANR volume.**

If You Have:	You May Discard:
CA First Revision Volumes 1-4R through 41-44R and *CA Permanent Series* Volumes 1 and 2	*CA* Original Volumes 1, 2, 3, 4 Volumes 5-6 through 41-44
CA Original Volumes 45-48 through 97-100 and 101 through 258	**NONE:** These volumes will not be superseded by corresponding revised volumes. Individual entries from these and all other volumes appearing in the left column of this chart may be revised and included in the various volumes of the *New Revision Series*.
CA New Revision Series Volumes *CANR*-1 through *CANR*-163	**NONE:** The *New Revision Series* does not replace any single volume of *CA*. Instead, volumes of *CANR* include entries from many previous *CA* series volumes. All *New Revision Series* volumes must be retained for full coverage.

A Sampling of Authors and Media People Featured in This Volume

Paula Deen

Celebrity chef Deen is the author of numerous cookbooks, the owner of two restaurants, and the host of the Food Network cooking shows *Paulas's Home Cooking* and *Paula's Party*. Deen's career took off when The Lady and Sons, her restaurant in Savannah, Georgia, received an award for best meal from *USA Today* and was featured on the *Oprah Winfrey Show*. Known for her simple, Southern cooking, Deen began her career as a restaurant owner and went on to establish a food, broadcasting, and publishing empire now known as Lady Enterprises, Inc. She relays her colorful life experiences, which include being robbed at gunpoint and battling agoraphobia, in *Paula Deen: It Ain't All about the Cookin'*.

Ina Garten

The popular television host of the Food Network program *The Barefoot Contessa,* Garten is also known for her series of best-selling cookbooks, which offer easy recipes that are ideal for small parties with friends. She began her career as a budget analyst for the White House, where she helped prepare budgets concerning the nation's nuclear energy policies. In 1978, however, her love of food prompted her to buy a specialty food store in East Hampton, New York. She later built her media presence around the name of the store, The Barefoot Contessa. Her first book, *The Barefoot Contessa Cookbook: Secrets from the Legendary Specialty Food Store for Simple Food and Party Platters You Can Make at Home* sold nearly two hundred thousand copies soon after it was released in 1999.

Brian Kennedy

Kennedy first rose to prominence as a singer/songwriter in his native Ireland. Between 1996 and 2006, he released a number of highly successful solo albums that garnered global attention. He has performed for former U.S. president Bill Clinton, starred in *Riverdance* on Broadway, and hosted a music television show. Also a writer, Kennedy has published two novels, *The Arrival of Fergal Flynn* and *Roman Song*.

Natsuo Kirino

Kirino is an acclaimed Japanese crime writer whose controversial novel *Out* won the Mystery Writers of Japan Award, the country's top award for mysteries. Several of her novels have been adapted for film, including *Tenshi ni misuterareta yoru, Yawaraka na hou, Out,* and *Tamamoe! Out,* which presents a social critique of Japan, was translated and published in English in 2003.

Howard Marks

Once one of the world's most notorious marijuana smugglers, Marks has now garnered fame through more conventional means, including television and film appearances, one-man stage plays, and books. His memoir, *Mr. Nice: An Autobiography,* details how, with the aid of his classmates at Oxford University, Marks moved hundreds of tons of marijuana throughout the western world before being arrested and serving seven years in Terre Haute Penitentiary. He has since been an advocate for the legalization of marijuana, speaking out against what he calls "selective enforcement" of antidrug laws by local police. Marks's other books include *The Howard Marks Book of Dope Stories* and *101 Uses of a Dead Roach.*

Kit Reed

Reed is a prolific author of award-winning short stories and novels for adults and teenage readers. While she has written in a variety of genres, including science fiction, fantasy, and mainstream fiction, much of her work is character-driven. Among her most popular titles are *The Ballad of T. Rantula, Captain Grownup,* and *Thinner Than Thou.* An autobiographical essay by Reed is included in this volume of *CA.*

Anthony Swofford

Born into a military family, former U.S. Marine Swofford served in the Gulf War as part of the Surveillance and Target Acquisition/Scout-Sniper platoon. His account of the experience, *Jarhead: A Marine's Chronicle of the Gulf War and Other Battles,* was adapted into a major motion picture directed by Sam Mendes and starring Jake Gyllenhal, Peter Sarsgaard, and Jamie Foxx. In 2007, Swofford followed *Jarhead* with the novel *Exit A.*

Russell Taylor

Though he has never bought a stock share or even worked in an office, Taylor, with artist partner Charles Peattie, created a cartoon strip character that York *Evening Press* contributor Chris Titley called "Britain's most famous stockbroker." The character, Alex Masterley, is the centerpiece of Taylor and Peattie's comic strip "Alex," which enjoyed an immensely popular sixteen-year run in major British newspapers, including the London *Daily News, Independent,* and *Daily Telegraph.* With illustrator Peattie, Taylor created more than four thousand strips, which have been collected in some seventeen "Alex" books.

Acknowledgments

Grateful acknowledgment is made to those publishers, photographers, and artists whose work appear with these authors's essays. Following is a list of the copyright holders who have granted us permission to reproduce material in this volume of *CA*. Every effort has been made to trace copyright, but if omissions have been made, please let us know.

Photographs/Art Reed, Kit: All photographs courtesy of Kit Reed. Reproduced by permission.

A

ABUNIMAH, Ali 1971-

PERSONAL: Born 1971, in Washington, DC. *Education:* Princeton University, B.A., 1993; University of Chicago, M.A., 1995.

ADDRESSES: Home—Chicago, IL. *E-mail*—abunimah01@yahoo.com; ahabunim@midway.uchicago.edu.

CAREER: Writer, commentator. University of Chicago, Chicago, IL, researcher in social policy; Arab-American Action Network, vice president; *Electronic Intifada* and *Electronic Iraq* founder, publisher, and editor.

WRITINGS:

One Country: A Bold Proposal to End the Israeli-Palestinian Impasse, Metropolitan Books (New York, NY), 2006.

Contributor to collections, including *Iraq under Siege: The Deadly Impact of Sanctions and War,* South End Press (Cambridge, MA), 2000; *The New Intifada: Resisting Israel's Apartheid,* edited by Roane Carey, Verso (New York, NY), 2001; and *The Anti-Capitalism Reader,* edited by Joel Schalit, Akashic Books (New York, NY), 2001; contributor to periodicals, including the *New York Times, Los Angeles Times, Financial Times, Chicago Tribune, Jordan Times, Philadelphia Inquirer, Ha'aretz,* and *Daily Star* (Lebanon).

SIDELIGHTS: Ali Abunimah is the American-born son of Palestinian refugees, a media analyst whose goal is fair coverage of the conflict in the Middle East. A *Tikkun* interviewer wrote: "In every possible sense of the word, Abunimah is a revolutionary. Even if you don't agree with all of his political opinions, his intelligence, wit, and capacity to engage in serious dialogue with those who consider him their opponent is worthy of the utmost respect."

Abunimah contacted National Public Radio in 1996 to complain that their coverage of the Israeli bombing of Lebanon was not balanced. He was then asked to contribute commentary on the United States bombing of Sudan and Afghanistan. Since that time Abunimah has appeared as a guest on many radio and television news programs, particularly National Public Radio and the Public Broadcasting System. Abunimah is the founder, publisher, and editor of two Web sites that provide coverage of the Middle East.

A contributor to books by others, Abunimah published his debut *One Country: A Bold Proposal to End the Israeli-Palestinian Impasse,* in which he argues that the most frequently proposed plan to establish a Palestinian state is not the ideal, but rather that the region should be united as one state. He is not the first to offer this approach, but as Brendan Driscoll noted in *Booklist,* Abunimah's approach "is fresh, energetic." Abunimah suggests that both sides not forget, but rather put aside, the past in order to reach a peaceful union. *Middle East* contributor Remi Kanazi wrote: "*One Country* is an inspiring message of hope and reconciliation, and presents an intricate and well-crafted path for two peoples that deserve not only reconciliation, but also a prosperous future."

BIOGRAPHICAL AND CRITICAL SOURCES:

PERIODICALS

Booklist, January 1, 2007, Brendan Driscoll, review of *One Country: A Bold Proposal to End the Israeli-Palestinian Impasse,* p. 43.

Kirkus Reviews, October 15, 2006, review of *One Country,* p. 1051.

Middle East, January 18, 2007, Remi Kanazi, review of *One Country.*

Middle East Policy, winter, 2006, Clayton E. Swisher, review of *One Country,* p. 174.

Tikkun, May-June, 2006, "Electronic Intifada: Pushing the Envelope with Ali Abunimah; a *Tikkun* Interview," p. 51.

Washington Report on Middle East Affairs, January, 2001, "At Princeton, Activist Ali Abunimah Critiques U.S. Media Coverage of Al-Aqsa Intifada," p. 63.

ONLINE

Ali Abunimah Home Page, http://www.abunimah.org (May 2, 2007).

Electronic Intifada, http://electronicintifada.net/ (May 2, 2007).

Electronic Iraq, http://electroniciraq.net/ (May 2, 2007).

Institute for Middle East Understanding, http://imeu.net/ (November 9, 2006), "Ali Abunimah: Proposing Bold Solutions."

Madison Times Online, http://www.themadisontimes.com/ (May 2, 2007), A. David Dahmer, "Interview with Ali Abunimah: Author Points to a Different Plan for Mid East Peace."*

* * *

ADAMSON, Allen P.

PERSONAL: *Education:* Syracuse University, B.S.; New York University, M.B.A.

ADDRESSES: *Office*—Landor New York, 230 Park Ave. S., New York, NY 10003.

CAREER: Business marketing executive and industry commentator. Ogilvy and Mather, beginning 1979; Lever Brothers (manufacturing company), group product manager; Ammirati & Puris, senior vice president, beginning 1990; Landor Associates (branding development firm), New York, NY, managing director.

MEMBER: American Management Association.

WRITINGS:

BrandSimple: How the Best Brands Keep It Simple and Succeed, Palgrave Macmillan (New York, NY), 2006.

Contributor to periodicals, including *Wall Street Journal, Advertising Age, New York Times, New York Post, Orlando Sentinel, USA Today, Washington Post* and *Forbes.*

BIOGRAPHICAL AND CRITICAL SOURCES:

PERIODICALS

Brand Strategy, March 12, 2007, "Simple Strategy: Best to Keep It Simple," p. 34.

Publishers Weekly, July 31, 2006, review of *Brand-Simple: How the Best Brands Keep It Simple and Succeed,* p. 69.

ONLINE

BrandSimple Web site, http://www.brandsimple.com (May 18, 2007).*

* * *

ALLEN, Arthur 1959-

PERSONAL: Born 1959. *Education:* Graduate of University of California, Berkeley.

ADDRESSES: Home—Washington, DC. *E-mail*—artnews@earthlink.net; arthurallenw@aol.com.

CAREER: Journalist; served as a foreign correspondent in El Salvador, Mexico, France, and Germany.

WRITINGS:

Vaccine: The Controversial Story of Medicine's Greatest Lifesaver, W.W. Norton (New York, NY), 2007.

Contributor to periodicals and Web sites, including the *New York Times, Washington Post, New Republic, Mother Jones, Atlantic Monthly, Salon.com,* and *Slate.* Editor of two book-length collections of investigative journalism on water privatization and Latin American military affairs.

SIDELIGHTS: Arthur Allen is an investigative journalist whose studies of biology led to his science writing. Allen's *Vaccine: The Controversial Story of Medicine's Greatest Lifesaver* is a history of vaccination, beginning with its first use by Edward Jenner, who initiated the eradication of smallpox in the eighteenth century, as well as an investigation of issues related to vaccine production and use. In particular, Allen studies how low profit margins threaten the development of future vaccines, the effectiveness of vaccines, and their sometimes negative side effects. The latter includes a suspected link between the preservative thimerosal, used in childhood vaccines, and autism. Also noted are how the dangers of the whooping cough vaccine undermined public confidence in vaccines, the cases of the neurological disorder Guillain-Barre syndrome reported in patients who received the swine flu vaccine during the 1970s outbreak, and how the rubella vaccine became a factor in the abortion debate.

Scientists who devoted their lives to the development of preventative vaccines include rivals Jonas Salk and Albert Sabin, both of whom spent years fighting polio using individual methods. Allen credits them and describes government programs that provided vaccinations to protect children from diphtheria, typhoid fever,

yellow fever, and polio. Allen comments on the contemporary debate over the vaccination of young girls to combat the sexually transmitted human papillomavirus (HPV) that causes cervical cancer. Because of past problems with various vaccines, many parents have come to suspect vaccination programs and are choosing not to submit their children to them. This has resulted in more children becoming susceptible to diseases, some of which, like measles, are on the rise.

Library Journal contributor Kathy Arsenault described the book as a "compelling narrative of the vaccine's undoubted triumphs and troubling challenges."

BIOGRAPHICAL AND CRITICAL SOURCES:

PERIODICALS

Booklist, November 15, 2006, Donna Chavez, review of *Vaccine: The Controversial Story of Medicine's Greatest Lifesaver,* p. 12.
Columbia Journalism Review, January-February, 2007, Rebecca Skloot, review of *Vaccine,* p. 59.
Kirkus Reviews, October 1, 2006, review of *Vaccine,* p. 997.
Library Journal, November 15, 2006, Kathy Arsenault, review of *Vaccine,* p. 87.
Publishers Weekly, October 9, 2006, review of *Vaccine,* p. 46.
Science News, February 3, 2007, review of *Vaccine,* p. 79.
SciTech Book News, March, 2007, review of *Vaccine.*
Washington Post Book World, February 11, 2007, Laurie Garrett, review of *Vaccine,* p. 6.

ONLINE

Arthur Allen Home Page, http://www.vaccinecontroversy.com (April 10, 2007).
Post & Courier Online (Charleston, SC), http://www.charleston.net/ (March 4, 2007), Victoria Hood, review of *Vaccine.*

*   *   *

AMES, Joye
See LAVENE, Jim

AMES, Joye
  See LAVENE, Joyce

*   *   *

ANDERSON, David Brian
  See ANDERSON, D. Brian

*   *   *

ANDERSON, D. Brian 1969-
  (David Brian Anderson)

PERSONAL: Born January 3, 1969, in NJ. *Ethnicity:* "Caucasian." *Education:* University of Texas at Austin, B.J., 1991; University of Houston—Clear Lake, M.A., 1996.

ADDRESSES: Home—Seabrook, TX. *E-mail*—banderson369@hotmail.com.

CAREER: University of Texas at Austin, reporter, entertainment and arts writer, and copy editor of *Daily Texan,* 1989-91; University of Texas Medical Branch, Galveston, managing editor of *Medical Humanities Review* and production editor of *Literature and Medicine* at Institute for the Medical Humanities, 1993; Tryco Enterprises, Houston, TX, copy editor of *Houston Chronicle,* 1994-96; Texas A & M University at Galveston, English teacher, 1996-97; Lunar and Planetary Institute, Houston, technical editor and editor of *Lunar and Planetary Information Bulletin,* 1997-2002; San Jacinto College Central, Pasadena, TX, English teacher, 1999-2004; Texas Southern University, Houston, instructor in developmental English, 2002-04; College of the Mainland, Texas City, TX, assistant professor of English, 2004—. Also taught at San Jacinto College North, 1996-97, and University of Houston—Clear Lake, 1998.

MEMBER: Titanic Historical Society, Two-Year College English Association-Southwest, Texas Community College Teachers Association, Phi Kappa Phi, Sigma Tau Delta.

WRITINGS:

The Titanic in Print and on Screen: An Annotated Guide to Books, Films, and Other Media, McFarland (Jefferson, NC), 2005.

The Titanic Joke Book, Lulu.com (Morrisville, NC), 2006.

Contributor to books, including *Texas Garden Almanac,* edited by Mike Peters, Gulf Publishing, 1997, 1998. Contributor of articles, essays, and reviews to periodicals, including *Houston Review, Marrow, Houston Chronicle Texas, Journal of Scholarly Publishing,* and *Bayousphere.*

SIDELIGHTS: D. Brian Anderson told *CA:* "I write nonfiction primarily out of an almost irrational need to share my obsessions with readers while organizing information in new ways. My first lengthy article was about the first monorail line in the United States. I spent many months researching and writing this article for a small historical journal, and I earned no money from it. I have been writing short fiction lately and am interested to see where that goes. I do not want to write any more books about *Titanic.*"

*   *   *

ANKERSMIT, F.R.
  See ANKERSMIT, Frank

*   *   *

ANKERSMIT, Frank 1945-
  (F.R. Ankersmit)

PERSONAL: Born March 20, 1945, in Deventer, Netherlands; son of Rudolf (a director of a textile factory) and Catharine Ankersmit. *Education:* Attended University of Leiden; University of Groningen, M.A. (history), 1978, M.A. (philosophy), 1977, Ph.D., 1981. *Politics:* Liberal.

ADDRESSES: Home—Glimmen, Netherlands. *Office*—Department of History, University of Groningen, P.O. Box 716, 9700 AS Groningen, Netherlands. *E-mail*—f.r.ankersmit@rug.nl.

CAREER: University of Groningen, Groningen, Netherlands, faculty member, 1973—, professor of intellectual history and philosophy, 1993—. Telders Foundation, member of curatorium. *Military service:* Served in Dutch armed forces.

MEMBER: Dutch Royal Academy of the Sciences, Wissenschaftliche Beirat van het Kulturwissenschaftliches Institute de Essen.

AWARDS, HONORS: Scholar in the United States, Netherlands Organization for the Advancement of Pure Scientific Research (now Netherlands Organization for Scientific Research), 1985.

WRITINGS:

IN ENGLISH

Narrative Logic: A Semantic Analysis of the Historian's Language, Nijhoff (The Hague, Netherlands), 1983.
(Editor) *Knowing and Telling History: History and Theory,* 1986.
(With J.A.A. Mooij) *Knowledge and Language,* Volume 3: *Metaphor and Knowledge,* Reidel (Dordrecht, Netherlands), 1993.
History and Tropology: The Rise and Fall of Metaphor, University of California Press (Berkeley, CA), 1994.
(Editor, with H. Kellner) *A New Philosophy of History,* Reaktion Books (London, England), 1995.
Aesthetic Politics: Political Philosophy beyond Fact and Value, Stanford University Press (Stanford, CA), 1997.
Historical Representation, Stanford University Press (Stanford, CA), 2001.
Political Representation, Stanford University Press (Stanford, CA), 2001.
(Editor, with Henk Te Velde) *Trust: Cement of Democracy?,* Peeters (Dudley, MA), 2004.
Sublime Historical Experience, Stanford University Press (Stanford, CA), 2005.

Shorter works include *The Reality Effect in the Writing of History: The Dynamics of Historiographical Topology,* North-Holland Publishing (Amsterdam, Netherlands), 1990. Editor, *Journal of the Philosophy of History,* 2007—.

OTHER

Denken over geschiedenis. Een overzicht van moderne geschiedfilosofische opvattingen, Wolters/Noordhoff (Groningen, Netherlands), 1983.

De navel van de geschiedenis. Over interpretatie, representatie en historische realiteit, Department of History, University of Groningen (Groningen, Netherlands), 1990.
(With A. Kibedi Varga and M.C. Doeser) *Op verhaal komen. Over narrativiteit in de mensen cultuurwetenschappen,* Kok Agora (Kampen, Netherlands), 1990.
(With G. Nuchelmans, E. Steinmetz, and others) *Tekstinterpretatie,* North-Holland Publishing (Amsterdam, Netherlands), 1990.
De historische ervaring, Department of History, University of Groningen (Groningen, Netherlands), 1993.
(With A. Kibedi Varga) *Akademische beschouwingen over het postmodernisme,* North-Holland Publishing (Amsterdam, Netherlands), 1993.
(Editor, with M. van Nierop and H. Pott) *Hermeneutiek en cultuur. Interpretatie in de kunsten de cultuurwetenschappen,* Boom (Amsterdam, Netherlands), 1995.
(With J. Tollebeek and W. Krul) *Romantiek en historische cultuur,* Department of History, University of Groningen (Groningen, Netherlands), 1996.
De spiegel van het verleden. Explorations deel I: Geschieftheorie, Kok Agora (Kampen, Netherlands), 1996.
De macht van representatie. Explorations deel II: cultuurfilosofie en esthetica, Kok Agora (Kampen, Netherlands), 1996.
Macht door representatie. Explorations deel III: politieke filosofie, Kok Agora (Kampen, Netherlands), 1997.
Tegen de waarheid in de politiek, Rudolf von Laun Instituut (Leeuwarden, Netherlands), 2002.
(With W.E. Krul and E.H. Kossmann) *Geschiedenis is als een olifant. Een keuze uit het werk,* [Amsterdam, Netherlands], 2005.
(With G. Dales, N. Albayrak, and others) *Om de Vrijheid Liberaal Manifest,* [The Hague, Netherlands], 2005.
(Coauthor) *Hart voor de publieke zaak. Rapport van de Nationale Conventie,* [The Hague, Netherlands], 2006.

Contributor of more than 150 articles to scholarly journals. Member of editorial board of the book series "Transformation in Arts and Culture" and of the periodicals *History and Theory, Rethinking History, Clio, Historiography East and West, Journal of the Interdisciplinary Crossroads,* and *Feit en Fictie.*

Ankersmit's writings have been translated into German, Spanish, Italian, Russian, Polish, Finnish, Hungarian, Portuguese, Indonesian, and Chinese.

SIDELIGHTS: Frank Ankersmit told *CA:* "My primary motivation for writing is to understand the social and political world. My main topics of interest are history and politics, mainly the history of political ideas. The instrument I use for this study is the philosophy of language.

"My work is influenced by the idea of representation. Historical writing is a representation of the past, and representative democracy is at the heart of all democratic politics. Both historical writing and democratic politics have their ground in the aesthetic notion of representation.

"Recently I have been interested in how representation and experience are related. I want to discover how representation and experience may explain the social and political world in which we live."

*   *   *

ANSARI, Ali M. 1967-
(Ali Massoud Ansari)

PERSONAL: Born November 24, 1967, in Rome, Italy; son of Mohammad Ali Massoud Ansari and Mariam Dariabegi. *Education:* University College, B.A., 1989; King's College, M.A., 1990; School of Oriental and African Studies, University of London, Ph.D., 1998.

ADDRESSES: Home—Fife, Scotland. *Office*—School of History, University of St. Andrews, Fife KY16 9AL, Scotland; fax: +44 (0) 1334 462927. *E-mail*—aa51@st-andrews.ac.uk.

CAREER: University of Durham, Durham, England, lecturer; University of St. Andrews, Fife, Scotland, began as reader, became professor of Iranian history, director of the Institute for Iranian Studies, director of communications.

MEMBER: Royal Institute for International Affairs (fellow).

WRITINGS:

Iran, Islam, and Democracy: The Politics of Managing Change, Royal Institute of International Affairs (London, England), 2000, revised edition, 2006.
Modern Iran since 1921: The Pahlavis and After, Pearson Education (New York, NY), 2003.
Confronting Iran: The Failure of American Foreign Policy and the Next Great Crisis in the Middle East, Basic Books (New York, NY), 2006, published as *Confronting Iran: The Failure of American Foreign Policy and the Roots of Mistrust,* C. Hurst (London, England), 2006.

Contributor to works by others, including *Iran and Eurasia,* edited by A. Ehteshami and A. Mohammadi, Ithaca Press, 2000; and *Companion to the History of the Middle East,* edited by Youssef Choueri, Blackwell, 2005. Contributor to periodicals, including *Washington Quarterly, Middle Eastern Studies, Soundings, Financial Times,* and London *Independent.*

SIDELIGHTS: Ali M. Ansari is an Iranian studies scholar and the author of several books that examine Iranian history and the country's traditions, as well as changes brought about by Western influence.

Iran, Islam, and Democracy: The Politics of Managing Change, dissects the reform movement in Iran from 1997 to 2005. *Modern Iran since 1921: The Pahlavis and After* is a narrative that details Iranian history from 1921 to the present. Among the events discussed are two that add to Western understanding of the country: the revolution of 1921 to 1925, which resulted in the creation of the Pahlavi dynasty, and the 1979 revolution that ended it and led to the rule of the Ayatollah.

Confronting Iran: The Failure of American Foreign Policy and the Next Great Crisis in the Middle East traces the historical relationship between the United States and Iran back to 1856, when the two countries entered into a mutual trade agreement. The twentieth century found that partnership deteriorating, particularly during the 1950s, and the countries became adversaries, including during the 1979 Iran hostage crisis and U.S. involvement in the Middle East. Ansari contends that the United States and Europe have failed to try to understand Iranian policy, which has exacerbated relations between the West and this volatile country.

BIOGRAPHICAL AND CRITICAL SOURCES:

PERIODICALS

America's Intelligence Wire, July 16, 2006, Julie Banderas, "Conversation with Ali Ansari," interview with author.
Contemporary Review, June, 2004, review of *Modern Iran since 1921: The Pahlavis and After,* p. 381.
Library Journal, July 1, 2006, Michael La Magna, review of *Confronting Iran: The Failure of American Foreign Policy and the Next Great Conflict in the Middle East,* p. 91.
Tikkun, July-August, 2006, review of *Confronting Iran,* p. 81.

ONLINE

St. Andrews Web site, http://www.st-andrews.ac.uk/ (April 10, 2007), brief biography of author.

*　　　*　　　*

ANSARI, Ali Massoud
　　See ANSARI, Ali M.

*　　　*　　　*

ANTHONY, Laura
　　See WILDE, Lori

*　　　*　　　*

APPEL, Gerald 1933-

PERSONAL: Born June 2, 1933, in New York, NY; son of Samuel and Vivian Appel; married Judith Kane, May 26, 1956; children: Marvin Laurence, Marion Fran. *Education:* Brooklyn College, B.A., 1954; New York University, M.S.W., 1956. *Hobbies and other interests:* Photography, tennis, music, sailing.

ADDRESSES: Home—Great Neck, NY. *Office*—Appel Financial Group, 150 Great Neck Rd., Great Neck, NY 11021; fax: 516-466-4676. *E-mail*—gappel@signalert.com.

CAREER: Jewish Family Services, Brooklyn, NY, administrator, 1958-73; psychoanalyst in private practice, Great Neck, NY, 1963-95; Appel Financial Group (Signalert Corporation and Appel Asset Management Corporation), Great Neck, president, 1973—. Served on the boards of directors of the Keystone Center of Music and Arts, 1998-2000, Mountain Laurel Center for the Performing Arts, 2000-04, and Great Neck Center for the Performing Arts, 2000.

MEMBER: American Association of Media Photographers, National Psychological Association for Psychoanalysis (board of directors, vice president).

WRITINGS:

Double Your Money Every Three Years, Windsor Books (Brightwaters, NY), 1974.
99 Ways to Make Money in a Depression, Arlington House (New Rochelle, NY), 1976, revised edition, 1981.
(With Martin E. Zweig Appel) *New Directions in Technical Analysis,* Signalert Corporation (Great Neck, NY), 1976.
The Stock Option and No-Load Switch Fund Scalper's Manual, Windsor Books (Brightwaters, NY), 1979.
Winning Stock Selection Systems: 83 Ways to Beat the Market, Traders Press (Greenville, SC), 1979.
(With W. Frederick Hitschler) *Stock Market Trading Systems,* Dow Jones-Irwin (Homewood, IL), 1980.
The Big Move! How to Trade for the Really Big Market Swings Using the Big Move Composite Trading Index, Scientific Investment Systems (Toronto, Ontario, Canada), 1982.
Time-Trend II: The Advanced Time-Trend Momentum Intermediate Term Trading System, Scientific Investment Systems (Toronto, Ontario, Canada), 1982.

The Moving Average Convergence-Divergence Trading Method, Traders Press (Greenville, SC), 1985.

Time-Trend III, 1988.

Day Trading (video), 1990.

Portraits of Nature, Signalert Corporation (Great Neck, NY), 1992.

(With H. Donald Kroitzsch) *American Photographers at the Turn of the Century: Travel and Trekking,* Diane Publishing (Darby, PA), 1994.

(With others) *The Art of the Human Form: Contemporary Photographic Interpretations,* Five Corners Publications (Plymouth, VT), 1995.

Far Away Faces: A Guide to Better Travel Portraits (video), 1998.

Technical Analysis: Power Tools for Active Investors, Financial Times/Prentice Hall (Upper Saddle River, NJ), 2005.

Opportunity Investing: How to Profit When Stocks Advance, Stocks Decline, Inflation Runs Rampant, Prices Fall, Oil Prices Hit the Roof, and Every Time in Between, Financial Times Press (Upper Saddle River, NJ), 2007.

Contributor to periodicals, including *Smart Money, Barron's,* and *Stocks and Commodities.* Editor, with son, Marvin Appel, of *Systems and Forecasts* (financial newsletter).

SIDELIGHTS: Gerald Appel's long career as a financial advisor began in 1973, and he has made his recommendations to readers of his newsletter, *Systems and Forecasts,* since that time. Appel is also a trained psychoanalyst, but as Peter Brimelow noted in his *Forbes* profile: Appel "shrugs . . . when he's asked about efforts to apply psychology to the markets. Appel's own approach is relentlessly quantitative and systematic. He is a technician who tries to predict the market's direction from patterns of price and volume movements."

In *Technical Analysis: Power Tools for Active Investors,* Appel studies how to determine when markets are most friendly to investors, using historical evidence. "At its best," wrote Art Collins in *Futures,* "this book presents its arguments with similar logic and clarity to the extent that even widely known ideas gain a fresh perspective."

Many of Appel's books offer advice to aggressive day traders, but *Opportunity Investing: How to Profit When Stocks Advance, Stocks Decline, Inflation Runs Rampant, Prices Fall, Oil Prices Hit the Roof, and Every Time in Between* is written for more conservative investors. It does, however, propose that the reader time the markets rather than follow a buy-and-hold strategy.

BIOGRAPHICAL AND CRITICAL SOURCES:

PERIODICALS

Forbes, October 26, 1992, Peter Brimelow, "A Secular Bear," p. 146.

Futures, June, 2005, Art Collins, review of *Technical Analysis: Power Tools for Active Investors,* p. 71.

Publishers Weekly, July 31, 2006, review of *Opportunity Investing: How to Profit When Stocks Advance, Stocks Decline, Inflation Runs Rampant, Prices Fall, Oil Prices Hit the Roof, and Every Time in Between,* p. 72.

Reference & Research Book News, February, 2007, review of *Opportunity Investing.*

ONLINE

Appel Asset Management Web site, http://www.appelasset.com (April 10, 2007).

Appel Financial Group Web site, http://www.appelfinancial.com (April 10, 2007).

Technical Analysis Web site, http://www.technicalanalysisbygeraldappel.com (April 10, 2007).*

*   *   *

APPEL, Jennifer

PERSONAL: Female.

ADDRESSES: Office—Buttercup Franchising, Inc., 973 2nd Ave., New York, NY 10022. *E-mail*—franchise@buttercupbakeshop.com.

CAREER: Writer, business owner, clinical psychologist. Magnolia Bakery, New York, NY, co-owner, 1996-99; Buttercup Bake shop, New York, owner, 1999—.

WRITINGS:

(With Allysa Torey) *The Magnolia Bakery Cookbook: Old-Fashioned Recipes from New York's Sweetest Bakery,* photographs by Rita Maas, Simon & Schuster (New York, NY), 1999.

The Buttercup Bake Shop Cookbook: More Than 80 Recipes for Irresistible, Old-Fashioned Treats, photographs by Sang An, Simon & Schuster (New York, NY), 2001.

Buttercup Bakes at Home: More Than 75 New Recipes from Manhattan's Premier Bake Shop for Tempting Homemade Sweets, photographs by Ann Stratton, Simon & Schuster (New York, NY), 2006.

Author of the blog *Cupcakes Take the Cake.*

SIDELIGHTS: Jennifer Appel was a clinical psychologist who loved to cook, especially desserts, and who changed careers when she and partner Allysa Torey opened Magnolia Bakery in the Greenwich Village section of New York City. In creating their cakes, the bakers often had leftover batter, which they used to make cupcakes. These became such a hit that they were featured in an episode of the television series *Sex and the City,* which is set in New York, further increasing the bakery's exposure. They offered the sort of baked goods that appealed to customers seeking cookies, pies, and other treats that were reminiscent of their childhoods. In 1999 the partnership ended, and Appel opened the Buttercup Bake Shop in midtown Manhattan. Employees of both bakeries also branched out with other shops, including Billy's, Sugar Sweet Sunshine, and Little Cupcake. Many of these shops have also become successful, and Appel went on to franchise Buttercup.

Appel's first cookbook, *The Magnolia Bakery Cookbook: Old-Fashioned Recipes from New York's Sweetest Bakery,* was written with Torey. It contains retro desserts with a contemporary touch, including an icebox cake using Nabisco wafers, and a variety of cheesecakes. Many are variations of recipes that have been published in women's magazines. A *Publishers Weekly* reviewer called the recipes "good, if ordinary."

In *The Buttercup Bake Shop Cookbook: More Than 80 Recipes for Irresistible, Old-Fashioned Treats,* Appel offers recipes for classics that include cakes, cobblers, pies, cookies, and puddings. She also has a section on frostings and fillings and another on seasonal recipes.

BIOGRAPHICAL AND CRITICAL SOURCES:

PERIODICALS

Library Journal, September 15, 2006, Judith Sutton, review of *Buttercup Bakes at Home: More Than 75 New Recipes from Manhattan's Premier Bake Shop for Tempting Homemade Sweets,* p. 82.

New York Times, November 5, 2003, Julia Moskin, "Once Just a Cupcake, These Days a Swell," p. F1.

Publishers Weekly, October 18, 1999, review of *The Magnolia Bakery Cookbook: Old-Fashioned Recipes from New York's Sweetest Bakery,* p. 76.

ONLINE

Bookreporter.com, http://www.bookreporter.com/ (May 3, 2007), review of *The Buttercup Bake Shop Cookbook: More Than 80 Recipes for Irresistible, Old-Fashioned Treats.*

Buttercup Bake Shop Web site, http://www.buttercupbakeshop.com (May 3, 2007).

New York Online, http://nymag.com/ (May 3, 2007), Adam Sternbergh, "Sweet and Vicious."*

*   *   *

ARDALAN, Davar 1964-
(Iran Davar Ardalan)

PERSONAL: Born 1964, in San Francisco, CA; daughter of Nader (an architect) and Mary (a writer and translator) Ardalan; children: Saied, Samira, Aman, Amir. *Education:* University of New Mexico, B.A.

ADDRESSES: Home and office—Annapolis, MD. *Office*—National Public Radio, 635 Massachusetts Ave. N.W., Washington, DC 20001. *E-mail*—davar@mynameisiran.com; dardalan@npr.org.

CAREER: Worked as a model; news anchor in Tehran, Iran; KOAT-TV, Albuquerque, NM, staff member; KUNM-FM, Albuquerque, radio reporter; National

Public Radio (NPR), Washington, DC, temporary production assistant, 1993-94, field producer for *Weekend Sunday Edition,* 1994-2005, producer of *Morning Edition,* 2005—.

AWARDS, HONORS: Associated Press award for health and environmental reporting; Gracie Award (with Jackie Lyden), American Women in Radio and Television, 2002, for *Loss and Its Aftermath* (NPR documentary).

WRITINGS:

My Name Is Iran: A Memoir, Henry Holt (New York, NY), 2007.

SIDELIGHTS: Davar Ardalan was born Iran Davar Ardalan in San Francisco, California, and has lived and worked in Iran and the United States. After twelve years with National Public Radio, she became producer of the long-running *Morning Edition* for which she has produced segments that featured a range of celebrities, from actor and philanthropist Paul Newman to chef Alton Brown. In 2002 she received a Gracie Award with Jackie Lyden for a series about Israeli and Palestinian parents who lost children during the Middle East conflict.

Ardalan was featured in a three-part radio documentary for the NPR *American Radioworks* series, which she produced with Rasool Nafisi. Her similarly titled *My Name Is Iran: A Memoir* documents her multilayered life and those of other generations of women in her family, both American and Iranian. Ardalan is the granddaughter of an Iranian doctor, Abol Ghassem, and Helen, a young American nurse. He learned English in an Iranian mission school at the age of forty alongside children, studied in the United States through a scholarship, worked in a carnival to pay for medical school, and graduated from the University of Syracuse while in his fifties. The couple moved to Iran, where they had seven children and lived in the private hospital they established.

Ardalan's mother and Harvard-educated father moved to Iran when she was an infant. She grew up in Tehran and returned to the United States after her parents'

divorce, relocating to Brookline, Massachusetts, with her father. After the taking of hostages in 1979, which resulted in anti-Iranian sentiment in the United States, she dropped her first name. After finishing high school Ardalan returned to revolutionary Iran, donned the veil, and entered into an arranged marriage. She returned to the United States and was divorced, remarried, and again divorced.

A *Publishers Weekly* contributor wrote: "Ardalan's testimony to the feminist spirit of the pioneering women in her family . . . is a supreme achievement." "What keeps the reader reading *My Name Is Iran,* wrote Michiko Kakutani in the *New York Times,* "is the remarkable trajectory traced by members of three generations of Ms. Ardalan's family, as they moved back and forth between the East and West, Iran and America, trying to balance a personal equation of tradition and modernity, religious faith and individualistic freedom."

BIOGRAPHICAL AND CRITICAL SOURCES:

BOOKS

Ardalan, Davar, *My Name Is Iran: A Memoir,* Henry Holt (New York, NY), 2007.

PERIODICALS

Booklist, November 15, 2006, Deborah Donovan, review of *My Name Is Iran,* p. 18.
Kirkus Reviews, October 15, 2006, review of *My Name Is Iran,* p. 1051.
New York Times, January 5, 2007, Michiko Kakutani, review of *My Name Is Iran,* p. E43.
PR Newswire, January 31, 2007, "From Modeling in Suburban America to an Arranged Marriage in Iran: NPR Producer's Personal Journey between Iran and America."
Publishers Weekly, November 13, 2006, review of *My Name Is Iran,* p. 46.

ONLINE

National Public Radio Web site, http://www.npr.org/ (May 4, 2007), biography of Ardalan.

Davar Ardalan Home Page, http://www.mynameisiran. com (May 4, 2007).

Persian Mirror, http://persianmirror.com/ (May 4, 2007), Shabnam Rezaei, "Talking to Iran Davar Ardalan" (interview).

OTHER

My Name Is Iran, NPR/American Radioworks, 2004.*

*   *   *

ARDALAN, Iran Davar
    See ARDALAN, Davar

*   *   *

ARDITTI, Michael

PERSONAL: Born in Cheshire, England. *Education:* Attended Jesus College, Cambridge.

ADDRESSES: Home—London, England. *Agent*—David Higham Associates, 5-8 Lower John St., Golden Sq., London W1F 9HA, England. *E-mail*—michaelarditti@aol.com.

CAREER: Author and playwright; theater critic for British newspapers, including the *Evening Standard, Times, Sunday Times, Daily Mail,* and *Sunday Express.*

AWARDS, HONORS: Mardi Gras Award, for *Easter;* Harold Hyam Wingate scholar, 2000; Royal Literary Fund fellow, 2001; Hawthornden fellow, 2005; Oppenheim-John Downes Memorial Award, 2003; Arts Council award, 2004.

WRITINGS:

NOVELS, UNLESS OTHERWISE NOTED

The Celibate, Sinclair-Stevenson (London, England), 1993, Soho Press (New York, NY), 1997.

Pagan's Father, Soho Press (New York, NY), 1996, published as *Pagan and Her Parents,* Sinclair-Stevenson (London, England), 1996.

Easter, Arcadia (London, England), 2000.

Good Clean Fun (stories), Maia Press (London, England), 2004.

Unity: Reflections on the Personalities and Politics behind Wolfram Meier's Legendary Lost Film, Maia Press (London, England), 2005.

A Sea Change, Maia Press (London, England), 2006.

PLAYS

The Volunteer, produced in London, England, 1980.

The Freshman, produced at the Edinburgh Festival, Scotland, 1984.

The Ceremony of Innocence, produced in Liverpool, England, 1989.

Author of a play adaptation of *The Factory Lad;* also author of four radio plays, *Something to Scare Off the Birds, The Morning Room, The Chatelaine,* and *The Family Hotel,* produced between 1985 and 1991. Work represented in anthologies, including *The Gay Times Book of Short Stories: The Next Wave,* Gay Times Books, 2001. Contributor to the *Dictionary of National Biography.*

SIDELIGHTS: Michael Arditti began his career by writing plays and theater reviews before concentrating on fiction. His first novel, *The Celibate,* is the story of an unnamed gay novice priest who suffers a breakdown during mass and leaves the Church to enter psychoanalysis and take a job as a walking guide in two historic neighborhoods. One is the site of severe devastation during the Great Plague in 1656, and the other is the district where Jack the Ripper killed his female victims in 1888. The young man actualizes his homosexuality with a prostitute named Jack, and loses friends to AIDS, causing him to fear penetration and negotiate for safe sex.

New Statesman & Society contributor Richard Canning wrote: "We quickly learn of the narrator's Jewish ancestry: perhaps now he can understand the guilt of Holocaust survivors; it is rather like Aids. On regaining his faith, he comes to know Christ's suffering: it is like Aids. Working as a guide to Jack the Ripper's London, he realizes that the tawdry sensationalism of his commentary resembles, well, today's media on Aids."

Pagan's Father was published in England as *Pagan and Her Parents,* and is a story that incorporates the themes of gay parenting, child abuse, adoptive families, and gender reassignment. Leo Young is the gay host of a BBC radio talk show whose roommate, former stripper Candida Mulligan, has died, leaving her five-year-old daughter, Pagan. The novel is narrated by Leo, who is guardian of the child. The identity of her true father is revealed as the story progresses, and in his monologue Leo reveals the nature of his own mother's parenting, which parallels that of Candida's parents, who go to court to gain custody of Pagan. The three-year custody battle is harshest on Pagan, who wants to remain with the gentle and loving Leo, who, although not related by blood, represents the only caring family she has ever known.

A *Publishers Weekly* reviewer felt that Arditti "traces the ever-evolving relationship between Leo and Pagan with skill and genuine feeling." *New Statesman & Society* reviewer Victoria Radin wrote: "Somewhere in all these frolics of a delayed adolescent Family Romance straight out of Freud and Bettelheim are many authentically moving passages between Leo and young Pagan, and some original writing on asexual friendships between men and women."

Unity: Reflections on the Personalities and Politics behind Wolfram Meier's Legendary Lost Film takes a documentary approach to the film based on the life of Hitler consort Unity Mitford and a fictional approach to the life of Felicity Benthall, the actress who played her, and who dies before the completion of the film when she is blown up by a bomb during a commemoration of the Israeli athletes murdered during the Munich Olympics.

An *Economist* reviewer wrote that *A Sea Change,* Arditti's next novel, "is a fine example of how resonant fiction based on real events can be." The fictional memoir of Karl Frankel-Hirsch begins as the fifteen-year-old son of a wealthy German family travels from Hamburg to Cuba as part of a cargo of nine hundred Jews fleeing Nazi persecution. The pas-

sengers are denied entry to Cuba, and the United States declines their access, as well, forcing the ship to turn around and head back to Europe, resulting in the deaths of many. Through Karl the reader learns of adolescent love amidst chaos, but also of the fear of the passengers and barbarism of the Nazi persecutors. The *Economist* reviewer called *A Sea Change* "a powerful novel of courage in the face of betrayal."

BIOGRAPHICAL AND CRITICAL SOURCES:

PERIODICALS

Booklist, September 15, 1996, Whitney Scott, review of *Pagan's Father,* p. 218.

Economist, October 7, 2006, review of *A Sea Change,* p. 91.

Entertainment Weekly, September 13, 1996, Vanessa Friedman, review of *Pagan's Father,* p. 126.

Financial Times, July 16, 2005, Neil Norman, review of *Unity: Reflections on the Personalities and Politics behind Wolfram Meier's Legendary Lost Film,* p. 32.

Lambda Book Report, November, 1997, Tom Musbach, review of *The Celibate,* p. 28; July, 2000, review of *Pagan's Father,* p. 30.

Library Journal, June 15, 1997, Paul Hutchison, review of *The Celibate,* p. 94.

New Statesman, November 20, 2006, Amanda Craig, review of *A Sea Change,* p. 65.

New Statesman & Society, February 5, 1993, Richard Canning, review of *The Celibate;* March 22, 1996, Victoria Radin, review of *Pagan and Her Parents,* p. 37.

New York Times Book Review, October 19, 1997, Philip Gambone, review of *The Celibate.*

Publishers Weekly, July 29, 1996, review of *Pagan's Father,* p. 70; May 5, 1997, review of *The Celibate,* p. 200.

ONLINE

Guardian Online, http://books.guardian.co.uk/ (June 11, 2005), Melissa Benn, review of *Unity.*

Michael Arditti Home Page, http://www.michaelarditti. com (April 11, 2007).

Times Online, http://entertainment.timesonline.co.uk/ (June 4, 2005), Jane Shilling, review of *Unity;* (June 19, 2005), Adam Lively, review of *Unity.*

AUBRAC, Lucie 1912-2007

OBITUARY NOTICE— See index for *CA* sketch: Born June 29, 1912, in Mâcon, Burgundy, France; died March 14, 2007, in Paris, France. Educator and author. Aubrac was best known for her autobiographical book *Outwitting the Gestapo,* which was based on her adventures with the French Resistance during World War II. A teacher who had graduated from the Sorbonne in 1938, she met her future husband, Raymond Samuel, in France after his return from studies at the Massachusetts Institute of Technology. They soon fell in love and married the next year. By then, the war had started, and after France's fall to the Nazis her husband changed his name to Aubrac to disguise his Jewish ancestry. Husband and wife both joined the Resistance in 1940, and her husband was arrested for his activities. Aubrac herself helped with propaganda and the delivery of messages for the Resistance while still working as a teacher publicly. In her *Ils partiront dans l'ivresse: Lyon, mai 43, Londres, febrier 44* (1984), which was translated in 1993 as *Outwitting the Gestapo,* she describes her complicated yet successful attempt to rescue her husband from the hands of Klaus Barbie, the Gestapo officer known as the Butcher of Lyon. Aubrac's romance with her husband and dangerous missions against the Gestapo would later inspire the movies *Army of Shadows* (1969) and *Boulevard of Swallows* (1991); her book was adapted in 1997 as the film *Lucie Aubrac.* That year historian Gérard Chauvy published a book accusing the Aubracs of being double agents who actually helped get French Resistance leader Jean Moulin captured and killed. The Aubracs successfully sued Chauvy and were thus vindicated. Awarded the Legion of Honor by the French government for her brave service, Aubrac spent her later years as a public speaker and political activist, protesting especially against French actions in Algeria. More recently, she was the author of *The Resistance Explained to My Granchildren* (2000).

OBITUARIES AND OTHER SOURCES:

BOOKS

Aubrac, Lucie, *Outwitting the Gestapo,* University of Nebraska Press, 1993.

PERIODICALS

Chicago Tribune, March 16, 2007, Section 3, p. 6.
Los Angeles Times, March 16, 2007, p. B9.

New York Times, March 18, 2007, p. A27.
Washington Post, March 16, 2007, p. B7.

*   *   *

AULT, Sandi

PERSONAL: Married Tracy A. Kerns.

*ADDRESSES: Home—*Pinewood Springs, CO; DuPont, WA. *E-mail—*contact@sandiault.com.

CAREER: Writer, musician, composer, journalist. University of New Mexico, Taos, creative writing instructor; fire information officer and firefighter.

WRITINGS:

Wild Indigo (novel), Berkley Prime Crime (New York, NY), 2006.

SIDELIGHTS: A former journalist, musician, composer, and bandleader, Sandi Ault now writes fiction and teaches writing workshops across the country. She is also a wild land firefighter and fire information officer working in Colorado and nationally on wildfires. Her household has included two wolves: Mountain, on whom the character of the wolf in her novel is based, and Tiwa. She is a woman of the West who created a fictional woman who lives in a similar environment in her debut mystery novel *Wild Indigo.*

Jamaica Wild is a female agent with the Bureau of Land Management whose jurisdiction includes the Tanoah Pueblo. She lives in a remote cabin with her young wolf, Mountain. Her boyfriend is forest ranger Kerry Reed. When Jamaica witnesses the death of a man killed in a buffalo stampede, she tests her relationship with the Tanoah Tribe, suspecting that the man, Jerome Santana was drugged. Although she promises Santana's mother, her mentor, that she will discover the truth, tribal customs prevents an autopsy, and the pueblo closes in honor of a sacred holiday. When tribe accuses Jamaica of having caused the stampede, Jamaica's boss is forced to suspended by her, pending an investigation.

"Ault's portrait of Pueblo life and the conflict of cultures she dramatizes are integral to her rousing debut," wrote a *Kirkus Reviews* contributor. *Booklist* reviewer Sue O'Brien commented: "An enjoyable series debut for fans of Nevada Barr and Tony Hillerman."

BIOGRAPHICAL AND CRITICAL SOURCES:

PERIODICALS

Booklist, December 1, 2006, Sue O'Brien, review of *Wild Indigo,* p. 24.

Kirkus Reviews, October 15, 2006, review of *Wild Indigo,* p. 1046.

Library Journal, December 1, 2006, Jo Ann Vicarel, review of *Wild Indigo,* p. 96.

Mystery Scene, December, 2007, Mary Elizabeth Devine, review of *Wild Indigo.*

New York Times Book Review, January 28, 2007, Marilyn Stasio, review of *Wild Indigo,* p. 23.

Publishers Weekly, November 13, 2006, review of *Wild Indigo,* p. 36.

ONLINE

Denver Post Online, http://www.denverpost.com/ (February 8, 2007), Sybil Downing, review of *Wild Indigo.*

Mystery Reader, http://www.themysteryreader.com/ (May 7, 2007), Lesley Dunlap, review of *Wild Indigo.*

Romantic Times, http://www.romantictimes.com/ (May 7, 2007), Sheri Melnick, review of *Wild Indigo.*

Sandi Ault Home Page, http://www.sandiault.com (May 7, 2007).

Wow! Women on Writing, http://wow-womenon writing.com/ (May 6, 2007), Beryl Hall Bray, interview.

*　　*　　*

AVERY, Ellis

PERSONAL: Partner of Sharon Marcus (a literature professor and writer). *Education:* Bryn Mawr College, graduated 1993; graduate studies at Goddard College.

ADDRESSES: Home and office—New York, NY. *E-mail*—contact@ellisavery.com.

CAREER: Writer. Interned at the *Village Voice,* New York, NY; taught English as a second language (ESL); Columbia University, New York, NY, creative writing instructor.

AWARDS, HONORS: Urasenke Foundation grant.

WRITINGS:

The Smoke Week: September 11-21, 2001, Gival Press (Arlington, VA), 2003.

The Teahouse Fire (novel), Riverhead Books (New York, NY), 2006.

Author of a blog.

ADAPTATIONS: The Teahouse Fire was adapted for audio (unabridged; fourteen CDs), read by Barbara Caruso, HighBridge, 2006.

SIDELIGHTS: Ellis Avery first attended a tea ceremony in Kyoto, Japan, and began a three-year study of this ancient ritual at the Urasenke Chanoyu Center in New York City. She also spent two years learning Japanese and returned to Kyoto for a course on tea ceremony funded by the Urasenke Foundation. She learned that the ceremony had originally been celebrated by powerful men and warriors and that women were either excluded or rarely admitted. *The Teahouse Fire* reflects what she has learned from her study. "Readers who enjoy historical fiction will be dazzled by Avery's attention to detail," wrote Leigh Anne Vrabel in *Library Journal.*

The story features two protagonists. One is Aurelia Bernard, a nine-year-old American orphan who is taken to Kyoto by an abusive uncle who is a Catholic priest and a missionary. When he dies in a fire, she is adopted as a servant and companion to Yukako Shin, the teen daughter of a prominent family that includes generations of tea masters, and her name is changed to Urako. The Shin family is attempting to preserve the ceremony at a time when Westernization is occurring.

Yukako is based on a historical figure who, like her fictional counterpart, introduces the tea ceremony into the curriculum of girls' schools during the 1880s.

Aurelia narrates the story as an elderly woman, and she tells of her relationship with Yukako and their lives as adults. A *Publishers Weekly* contributor wrote: "Avery, making her debut, has crafted a magisterial novel that is equal parts love story, imaginative history and bildungsroman, a story as alluring as it is powerful."

BIOGRAPHICAL AND CRITICAL SOURCES:

PERIODICALS

America's Intelligence Wire, March 15, 2007, "U. Pittsburgh: Author Discusses Cultural Differences in New Novel at U. Pittsburgh."

Booklist, November 15, 2006, Deborah Donovan, review of *The Teahouse Fire,* p. 23.

Kirkus Reviews, November 1, 2006, review of *The Teahouse Fire,* p. 1087.

Library Journal, November 15, 2006, Leigh Anne Vrabel, review of *The Teahouse Fire,* p. 54.

Publishers Weekly, October 30, 2006, "*PW* Talks to Ellis Avery: Tea for Two: Set in Late 19th-century Japan, *The Teahouse Fire,* Follows Aurelia, an American Orphan Who Is Taken In—as Both Servant and Sister—by Yukako, the Daughter of Japan's Most Important Teacher of the Ancient Art of Tea Ceremony," p. 32, and review of *Teahouse Fire,* p. 36.

ONLINE

Brooklyn Rail, http://www.brooklynrail.org/ (May 7, 2007), Cassandra Neyenesch, "Ellis Avery and Sharon Marcus with Cassandra Neyenesch" (interview).

Bryn Mawr College Web site, http://www.brynmawr.edu/ (January 18, 2007), "Bryn Mawr Now: Ellis Avery '93 to Read from *The Teahouse Fire.*"

Contra Costa Times Online, http://www.contracostatimes.com/ (February 4, 2007), Kate Lavin, review of *The Teahouse Fire.*

Ellis Avery Home Page, http://www.ellisavery.com (May 7, 2007).

Powell's Books Original Essays, http://www.powells.com/ (May 7, 2007), Ellis Avery, "Tea and the Writing of *The Teahouse Fire.*"*

B

BAGSHAWE, Louise

PERSONAL: Married Anthony LoCicero; children: one son, one daughter. *Education:* Graduate of Oxford University.

ADDRESSES: Home—East Sussex, England. *Agent*—Michael Sissons, PFD, Drury House, 34-43 Russell St., London WC2B 5HA, England.

CAREER: Writer; worked in the record business.

AWARDS, HONORS: Young Poet of the Year, 1989.

WRITINGS:

NOVELS

Career Girls, Orion (London, England), 1995.
The Movie, Orion (London, England), 1996, published as *Triple Feature,* Simon & Schuster (New York, NY), 1997.
Tall Poppies, Orion (London, England), 1997.
Venus Envy, Orion (London, England), 1998.
When She Was Bad . . . , Orion (London, England), 2001.
A Kept Woman, Orion (London, England), 2001.
For All the Wrong Reasons, St. Martin's Press (New York, NY), 2002.
Three Great Novels: Career Girls, The Movie, Tall Poppies, Orion (London, England), 2002.

The Devil You Know, St. Martin's Press (New York, NY), 2003.
Two Great Novels: Career Girls; The Movie, Orion (London, England), 2004.
Monday's Child, Headline (London, England), 2004, published as *The Go-To Girl,* St. Martin's Griffin (New York, NY), 2005.
Tuesday's Child, Headline (London, England), 2005.
Three Great Novels: Venus Envy; A Kept Woman; When She Was Bad . . . , Orion (London, England), 2005.
Sparkles, Headline Review (London, England), 2006, Plume (New York, NY), 2007.
Glamour, Headline (London, England), 2007.

Contributor to anthologies.

SIDELIGHTS: Louise Bagshawe became a full-time writer in her early twenties. The second of her erotic chick lit novels, *The Movie,* was published in the United States as *Triple Feature.* Megan Silver, the book's protagonist, is a waitress who has written a script for a promising film, and agent Sam Kendrick and his associate, David Tauber, sign Megan, as well as director Fred Florescu, rocker Zach Mason, and temperamental supermodel Roxana Felix for the film that is picked up by Eleanor Marshall, president of Artemis Studios. Eleanor needs a hit and signs on to the production hoping to save her professional career. In her personal life Eleanor is involved with two men and also longing for a child. The film is shot in the Seychelles against a backdrop of drug use, sex, and designer clothing. *Library Journal* contributor Susan Clifford described the novel as being "raunchy, racy and pure commercial fiction."

In reviewing another of Bagshawe's titles, *For All the Wrong Reasons,* in *Booklist,* Kathleen Hughes wrote: "Bagshawe packs her novel with lurid sexual details, and it comes complete with a fairy-tale ending." Diana Verity marries Ernie Foxton, whose new publishing position takes them to New York. When she discovers him with his favorite dominatrix, she walks out on him and the upscale lifestyle she has enjoyed. Diana takes a clerical job and falls for her Bronx-native, blue-collar boss, publisher of children's books Michael Cicero, and her new independence enables her to become successful in her own right. A *Publishers Weekly* contributor wrote: "Bagshawe doesn't try to sugarcoat her characters' ruthless, selfish or venal behavior, giving her story a witty edge."

The Devil You Know is the story of three women who ultimately discover they have something in common. The beautiful Rose Fiorella plans revenge against Rothstein Realty—which destroyed her family's business—through a relationship with heir Jake Rothstein. Dowdy Daisy Markham, who dreams of the glamorous life, finds that she has a talent for writing about it; and Poppy Allen, who is beautiful enough to be a star, is more interested in using her business acumen to create stars of other people.

The protagonist of *Monday's Child,* published in the United States as *The Go-To Girl,* is script reader Anna Brown, a homely young woman whose roommates are gorgeous models. Anna has a script of her own, but when she has the opportunity to pitch it to film director Mark Swan, she bungles the chances for both her script and a possible romance. A *Publishers Weekly* reviewer wrote that "the inevitable makeover scene is good fun."

Sparkles is the story of a jewelry empire. Pierre Massot, the husband of British-born Sophie Roberts, disappears, leaving her to care for their son. After seven years she has him declared legally dead and throws herself into running the business, but she doesn't quite have the business sense to deal with new CEO Gregoire Lazard. Sophie also experiences tension in her relationship with Judy Dean, an American who found a home at House Massot, and a place in Pierre's bed. A *Publishers Weekly* critic compared *Sparkles* to the 1970s best seller *Scruples* and described it as being an "internationally flavored fantasia on love, lies and shopping."

BIOGRAPHICAL AND CRITICAL SOURCES:

PERIODICALS

Booklist, April 15, 1997, Jennifer Henderson, review of *Triple Feature,* p. 1385; February 1, 2002, Kathleen Hughes, review of *For All the Wrong Reasons;* January 1, 2005, Kaite Mediatore, review of *The Go-To Girl,* p. 811.
Kirkus Reviews, December 15, 2001, review of *For All the Wrong Reasons,* p. 1699; September 1, 2003, review of *The Devil You Know,* p. 1085; October 1, 2006, review of *Sparkles,* p. 975.
Library Journal, April 1, 1997, Susan Clifford, review of *Triple Feature,* p. 120.
Publishers Weekly, March 10, 1997, review of *Triple Feature,* p. 50; January 14, 2002, review of *For All the Wrong Reasons,* p. 36; December 13, 2004, review of *The Go-To Girl,* p. 43; January 1, 2007, review of *Sparkles,* p. 30.

ONLINE

Conservative Home.com, http://www.conservative home.blogs.com/ (April 12, 2007), interview with author.
Louise Bagshawe Home Page, http://www.louise-bagshawe.com (May 7, 2007).*

*   *   *

BARILLAS, William

PERSONAL: *Education:* University of Michigan, B.A.; Michigan State University, M.A., Ph.D. *Hobbies and other interests:* Piano, guitar, searching for classic soul on vinyl, hiking, bicycling, gardening, travel.

ADDRESSES: *Office*—University of Wisconsin—La Crosse, 425 Wimberly Hall, La Crosse, WI 54601 *E-mail*—barillas.will@uwlax.edu

CAREER: University of Wisconsin at La Crosse, assistant professor of English.

AWARDS, HONORS: Midwestern Studies Book Award, 2006, for *The Midwestern Pastoral: Place and Landscape in Literature of the American Heartland.*

WRITINGS:

The Midwestern Pastoral: Place and Landscape in Literature of the American Heartland, Ohio University Press (Athens, OH), 2006.

BIOGRAPHICAL AND CRITICAL SOURCES:

ONLINE

University of Wisconsin at La Crosse Department of English Web site, http://www.uwlax.edu/english/ (May 18, 2007), short biography of Barillas.*

*   *   *

BARRON, Francine Stephanie
    See BARRON, Stephanie

*   *   *

BARRON, Stephanie 1963-
    (Francine Stephanie Barron, Francine Mathews)

PERSONAL: Born 1963, in Binghamton, NY; daughter of a general in the U.S. Air Force; children: Sam, one other son. *Education:* Princeton University, B.A., 1985; Stanford University, M.A. *Hobbies and other interests:* Gardening, skiing, needlepoint, shopping for art.

CAREER: Part-time journalist for the *Miami Herald* and *San Jose Mercury News,* late 1980s; Central Intelligence Agency, intelligence analyst, 1988-92; full-time freelance writer, 1992—.

AWARDS, HONORS: Arthur W. Mellon Foundation fellowship in the humanities, Princeton University, c. 1984.

WRITINGS:

"JANE AUSTEN" SERIES; MYSTERY NOVELS

Jane and the Unpleasantness at Scargrave Manor, Bantam Books (New York, NY), 1996.

Jane and the Man of the Cloth, Bantam Books (New York, NY), 1997.
Jane and the Wandering Eye, Bantam Books (New York, NY), 1998.
Jane and the Genius of the Place, Bantam Books (New York, NY), 1999.
Jane and the Stillroom Maid, Bantam Books (New York, NY), 2000.
Jane and the Prisoner of Wool House, Bantam Books (New York, NY), 2001.
Jane and the Ghosts of Netley, Bantam Books (New York, NY), 2003.
Jane and His Lordship's Legacy, Bantam Books (New York, NY), 2005.
Jane and the Barque of Frailty, Bantam Books (New York, NY), 2006.

"MERRY FOLGER" SERIES; MYSTERY NOVELS; UNDER PSEUDONYM FRANCINE MATHEWS

Death in the Off-Season, William Morrow (New York, NY), 1994.
Death in Rough Water, William Morrow (New York, NY), 1995.
Death in a Mood Indigo, Bantam Books (New York, NY), 1997.
Death in a Cold Hard Light, Bantam Books (New York, NY), 1998.

OTHER FICTION; UNDER PSEUDONYM FRANCINE MATHEWS

The Cutout, Bantam Books (New York, NY), 2001.
The Secret Agent, Bantam Books (New York, NY), 2002.
Blown (sequel to *The Cutout*), Bantam Books (New York, NY), 2005.
The Alibi Club, Bantam Books (New York, NY), 2006.

Contributor to *The Sunken Sailor,* 2004.

ADAPTATIONS: Several of the "Jane Austen" mystery series books have been adapted to cassette tape, including *Jane and the Stillroom Maid,* Books on Tape, 2000, and *Jane and the Prisoner of Wool House,* Books on Tape, 2001.

SIDELIGHTS: Stephanie Barron, who also writes under the pen name Francine Mathews, has earned a large fan-following for her historical mysteries as well as for modern crime and thriller novels. As Barron, she is the author of the "Jane Austen" mysteries that fictionalize the famous nineteenth-century author as an amateur crime sleuth. Under her pseudonym, Barron uses her background as a former intelligence analyst with the Central Intelligence Agency to create modern thrillers about neo-Nazi terrorists in her "Merry Folger" series about a Nantucket police detective. Many of Barron's novels have been praised for their historical accuracy, strong characters, and page-turning pace.

After quitting the Central Intelligence Agency (CIA) in 1992, Barron pursued a life as a mother and freelance author. She decided to embark on her new career by selecting crime fiction as her genre of choice and writing under the pseudonym Francine Mathews. Setting her first stories in Nantucket, Barron created police detective Merry Folger, the daughter of the city's police chief. Folger solves a variety of murders in a four-book series that was lauded for its strong sense of place and realistic heroine. For example, reviewing *Death in Rough Water,* a *Publishers Weekly* critic noted that the author "skillfully incorporates close-knit relationships, small-town gossip and a salty Nantucket flavor." Alice DiNizo, critiquing *Death in a Cold Hard Light* for the *Library Journal,* reported that the author "writes appealingly, making her characters human, fallible, and thoughtful and her story line always believable." A *Publishers Weekly* writer, assessing the same novel, felt that "distinctive characterization and deft plotting . . . mark this series."

While still finishing up her Merry Folger stories, Barron began a new series, published under her own name, that featured Jane Austen, the author of such classics as *Pride and Prejudice* and *Emma.* When asked by *Publishers Weekly* interviewer Monica Whitbread why she chose to fictionalize the famous writer and turn her into a sleuth, Barron replied: "I've always been an Austen reader and studied European history and Napoleonic France in my undergraduate days. The mystery format seemed appropriate for a modern reader, rather than a novel of manners. Since Austen is less well known than her characters, I thought it would be interesting to do something with Austen's life itself." Using the fictional premise that she discovered a collection of Austen's papers in a Baltimore, Maryland, home, Barron took advantage of the fact that Austen's sister Cassandra once destroyed many of the author's letters. This left a gap of many years in Austen's biography about which little was known. Barron fills the gap by creating adventures for the bright, young Austen in the early 1800s. "Barron's basic conceit is surprisingly persuasive: the same qualities that made Austen a brilliant writer make her an ace detective, namely, her quick wit and her psychological acuity," reported *Time* contributor Lev Grossman. Beginning with *Jane and the Unpleasantness at Scargrave Manor,* Barron has continued to write about her heroine since 1996.

Initial critical reception to the "Jane Austen" series was somewhat tepid. The debut novel, *Jane and the Unpleasantness at Scargrave Manor,* was called "an appealing idea, but inadequately served here," by a *Publishers Weekly* reviewer, for example. About later installments, however, critics were more enthusiastic. "Barron has masterfully imitated Austen's voice" in *Jane and His Lordship's Legacy,* another *Publishers Weekly* contributor attested. Another critic from this periodical, reviewing *Jane and the Prisoner of Wool House,* similarly praised the way Barron accurately captured the original author's tone of voice, adding that the "novel's real achievement, though, is the portrayal of the minor characters." Historical accuracy in the series was also praised by critics. "Details of early 19th-century country life of all classes ring true," said one *Publishers Weekly* contributor about *Jane and the Stillroom Maid.* Joanne Wilkinson pointed out in a *Booklist* review of *Jane and the Unpleasantness at Scargrave Manor* that the author adopts the formal tone of the era, yet "this is an Austen for the 1990s, complete with a blunt and ardent feminism, and it's all a great deal of fun." Overall, critics echoed the opinion of Jane Davis in the *Decatur Daily,* who concluded in a review of *Jane and His Lordship's Legacy* that "this series is a delight for Jane Austen fans, as Barron presents the same comedy of manners that Austen so aptly extolled."

Beginning with 2001's *The Cutout,* Barron began writing novels, as Francine Mathews, that drew on her days in the CIA. She related to an interviewer for *Bookreporter.com* some details of her former career: "I was trained for a year in operations—which means paramilitary training, tradecraft training, etc.—but worked for three as an intelligence analyst, which essentially means I wrote predictive pieces for the White House and other policymakers on key foreign policy issues. I worked for a small unit that compiled psychological assessments of world leaders—a job I gave my heroine [in *The Cutout* and *Blown*], Caroline Carmichael, who is the expert on a particularly dangerous terrorist's mind. I also spent some time on the Pan Am 103 Task Force, which supported the FBI's investigation into the bombing of that plane over Lockerbie, Scotland, in 1988. The task force lived in the CIA's Counterterrorism Center, and my work there was my introduction to the whole CTC world, which I loved. I respect the people who staff it more than anybody else I know in intelligence. And so I modeled many of my characters in both *The Cutout* and *Blown* on friends or mentors who work counterterrorism issues."

Both *The Cutout* and *Blown* pit Carmichael against a neo-Nazi terrorist group called 30 April (they are named after the date when Adolf Hitler shot himself). In *The Cutout,* 30 April kidnaps the U.S. vice president, and Carmichael's husband, who is also an agent, is suspected of being a traitor. In *Blown,* Carmichael becomes involved in pursuing a 30 April killer who slaughtered hundreds of people using poisoned drinks at a marathon race. A *Publishers Weekly* contributor reviewing *The Cutout* felt that Barron "keeps the action moving at a sprightly pace, and her presentation of espionage and CIA tactics is impeccable." "Because of the author's expertise she is able to personalize the CIA far beyond what any current author has been able to do," remarked Thea Davis in her *Mystery Reader* review. Praising the fast-paced action in *Blown, Bookreporter.com* critic Joe Hartlaub concluded: "Mathews creates the sense that the reader should be holding *Blown* in one hand and a ticking stopwatch in the other." "Though the author . . . executes gripping tension with aplomb," commented Jane Jorgenson in the *Library Journal,* "her characterizations are what hold the reader."

Barron is also the author of the thrillers *The Secret Agent* and *The Alibi Club.* The former is based on a true story in which a U.S. agent named Jim Thompson disappeared in Thailand. The author uses so many authentic details that she had to submit her manuscript to the CIA for approval before she could publish it. Wayne E. Yang, writing for the *Asian Review of Books,* found that "the prose is mostly very good, at times excellent enough to suggest that we need to keep an eye on where Mathews will take her next literary thriller." *The Alibi Club* is a thriller set in 1940 Paris in which an American journalist is killed for knowing too much about France's atomic weapons program.

The novel was favorably compared to "Alan Furst's novels about Paris" by a *Publishers Weekly* critic.

On her Web site, Barron related that her desire to write goes back to her childhood: "When I was young, I put words on paper because I was a solitary child, because my father died when I was a teenager, and the world I could make in the pages of lined notebooks helped keep my loneliness at bay. I wrote to escape, to conceive a more exotic life. I wrote myself out of despair and into adulthood, and words, for me, will always possess a transformative power. But ultimately I wrote because I had no choice. Words are the way I understand existence. Maybe this comes from voracious reading, or maybe from the particles of DNA in my body. I know that I am incapable of drawing more than a stick-figure, incapable of singing an unwavering note; but words are the gift of my particular brain. When I write, I live out my destiny as much as an elk does, bugling in the autumn, or a salmon swimming upstream."

BIOGRAPHICAL AND CRITICAL SOURCES:

PERIODICALS

Booklist, April 1, 1996, Joanne Wilkinson, review of *Jane and the Unpleasantness at Scargrave Manor,* p. 1345; January 1, 1997, Joanne Wilkinson, review of *Jane and the Man of the Cloth,* p. 823; June 1, 1997, Emily Melton, review of *Death in a Mood Indigo,* p. 1667; December 1, 1997, Joanne Wilkinson, review of *Jane and the Wandering Eye,* p. 610; April 15, 1998, John Rowen, review of *Death in a Cold Hard Light,* p. 1389; May 1, 2000, Barbara Bibel, review of *Jane and the Stillroom Maid,* p. 1610; October 15, 2001, Kristine Huntley, review of *Jane and the Prisoner of Wool House,* p. 384; May 1, 2003, Kristine Huntley, review of *Jane and the Ghosts of Netley,* p. 1531; February 15, 2005, Kristine Huntley, review of *Jane and His Lordship's Legacy,* p. 1063; May 15, 2005, Whitney Scott, review of *Jane and His Lordship's Legacy,* p. 1680; October 1, 2006, Allison Block, review of *Jane and the Barque of Frailty,* p. 39.
Kirkus Reviews, October 1, 2001, review of *Jane and the Prisoner of Wool House,* p. 1393; May 1, 2002, review of *The Secret Agent,* p. 603; April 15, 2003, review of *Jane and the Ghosts of Net-*

ley, p. 572; January 15, 2005, review of *Jane and His Lordship's Legacy*, p. 83; March 15, 2005, review of *Blown*, p. 309; October 1, 2006, review of *Jane and the Barque of Frailty*, p. 988.

Library Journal, June 1, 1997, Rex E. Klett, review of *Death in a Mood Indigo*, p. 156; December 1, 1997, Rex E. Klett, review of *Jane and the Wandering Eye*, p. 159; June 1, 1998, Alice Di-Nizo, review of *Death in a Cold Hard Light*, p. 167; March 1, 2000, review of *Jane and the Stillroom Maid*, p. 7; June 1, 2000, Rex E. Klett, review of *Jane and the Stillroom Maid*, p. 210; November 1, 2001, Rex E. Klett, review of *Jane and the Prisoner of Wool House*, p. 136; June 15, 2002, Jane Jorgenson, review of *The Secret Agent*, p. 95; May 1, 2003, Rex E. Klett, review of *Jane and the Ghosts of Netley*, p. 159; February 1, 2005, Rex E. Klett, review of *Jane and His Lordship's Legacy*, p. 57; May 1, 2005, Jane Jorgenson, review of *Blown*, p. 75; April 15, 2006, Sarah Nagle, review of *Jane and the Unpleasantness at Scargrave Manner*, p. 128.

Mystery News, February-March, 2007, Virginia R. Knight, "Francine Mathews: Past, Present, Fact, Fiction," interview with Francine Mathews.

New York Times Book Review, June 22, 2003, review of *Jane and the Ghosts of Netley*, p. 17.

Publishers Weekly, August 14, 1995, review of *Death in Rough Water*, p. 74; March 4, 1996, review of *Jane and the Unpleasantness at Scargrave Manor*, p. 56; November 11, 1996, review of *Jane and the Man of the Cloth*, p. 59; April 21, 1997, review of *Death in a Mood Indigo*, p. 63; November 24, 1997, review of *Jane and the Wandering Eye*, p. 55; March 30, 1998, review of *Death in a Cold Hard Light*, p. 72; January 4, 1999, review of *Jane and the Genius of the Place*, p. 77; July 17, 2000, review of *Jane and the Stillroom Maid*, p. 178; November 27, 2000, review of *The Cutout*, p. 53; November 5, 2001, review of *Jane and the Prisoner of Wool House*, p. 45; November 5, 2001, Monica Whitbread, "PW Talks with Stephanie Barron," p. 44; May 20, 2002, review of *The Secret Agent*, p. 47; February 14, 2005, review of *Jane and His Lordship's Legacy*, p. 57; April 11, 2005, review of *Blown*, p. 33; June 12, 2006, review of *The Alibi Club*, p. 31; October 16, 2006, review of *Jane and the Barque of Frailty*, p. 38.

School Library Journal, March 1, 2001, Linda A. Vretos, review of *Jane and the Stillroom Maid*, p. 281; October 1, 2003, Jane Halsall, review of *Jane and the Ghosts of Netley*, p. 207.

Time, August 11, 2003, Lev Grossman, review of *Jane and the Ghosts of Netley*, p. 58.

ONLINE

Asian Review of Books, http://www.asianreviewofbooks.com/ (September 27, 2002), Wayne E. Yang, review of *The Secret Agent*.

BookLoons, http://www.bookloons.com/ (April 13, 2007), Anise Hollingshead, review of *Jane and the Stillroom Maid*.

Bookreporter.com, http://www.bookreporter.com/ (April 13, 2007), interview with Francine Mathews, and Joe Hartlaub, review of *Blown*.

Decatur Daily Online, http://www.decaturdaily.com/ (April 3, 2005), Jane Davis, "Another 'Just Right' Jane Austen Tale," review of *Jane and His Lordship's Legacy*.

Francine Mathews Home Page, http://www.francinemathews.com (April 13, 2007).

Mystery Reader, http://www.themysteryreader.com/ (April 13, 2007), Jessica Plonka, review of *Jane and the Ghosts of Netley*, Jennifer Monahan Winberry, review of *Jane and the Prisoner of Wool House*, and Thea Davis, reviews of *Blown* and *The Cutout*.

Stephanie Barron Home Page, http://www.stephaniebarron.com (April 13, 2007).*

* * *

BARSKY, Allan E. 1961-
(Allan Edward Barsky)

PERSONAL: Born April 18, 1961, in Regina, Saskatchewan, Canada; married Greg Moore (an accountant); children: Adelle. *Ethnicity:* "Canadian." *Education:* University of Toronto, J.D., 1984, Ph.D., 1995; Yeshiva University, M.S.W., 1988. *Religion:* Jewish.

ADDRESSES: Home—Fort Lauderdale, FL. *Office*—School of Social Work, Florida Atlantic University, Boca Raton, FL 33421-0991; fax: 954-958-9762. *E-mail*—barsky@barsky.org; abarsky@fau.edu.

CAREER: Ryerson University, Toronto, Ontario, Canada, part-time teacher, 1989-91, sessional instructor in social work, 1991-94; University of Calgary,

Calgary, Alberta, Canada, assistant professor, 1994-97, associate professor or social work, 1997-2000, director of research, 1999-2000; Florida Atlantic University, Boca Raton, professor of social work, 2001—.

WRITINGS:

Counsellors as Witnesses, Canadian Law Book (Aurora, Ontario, Canada), 1997.

Conflict Resolution for the Helping Professions, Brooks/Cole-Wadsworth (Belmont, CA), 2000, 2nd edition, 2007.

(Editor, with E. Geva and F. Westernoff, and contributor) *Interprofessional Practice with Diverse Populations: Cases in Point,* Greenwood Press (Westport, CT), 2000.

(With J. Gould) *Clinicians in Court: A Guide to Subpoenas, Depositions, Testifying, and Everything Else You Need to Know,* Guilford Publications (New York, NY), 2002.

Alcohol, Other Drugs, and Addictions: A Professional Development Manual for Social Work and the Human Services, Brooks/Cole-Wadsworth (Belmont, CA), 2006.

Successful Social Work Education: A Student's Guide, Brooks/Cole-Wadsworth (Belmont, CA), 2006.

Contributor to books, including *Family Mediation: Contemporary Issues,* edited by H. Irving and M. Benjamin, Sage Publications (Thousand Oaks, CA), 1995; *Mediation and Conflict Resolution in Social Work and the Human Services,* edited by E. Kruk, Nelson-Hall (Chicago, IL), 1997; *Divorce and Family Mediation: Models, Techniques, and Applications,* edited by J. Folberg, A. Milne, and P. Salem, Guilford Publications (New York, NY), 2004; and *Strengths-Based Generalist Practice: A Collaborative Approach,* edited by J. Poulin, Brooks/Cole-Wadsworth (Belmont, CA), 2005. Contributor to professional journals, including *Child Welfare, Jewish Political Studies Review, Journal of Drug Education, Canadian Social Work Review, Conflict Resolution Quarterly, Arete, Higher Education Research and Development,* and *Journal of Research on Computing in Education.*

SIDELIGHTS: Allan E. Barsky told *CA:* "My primary motivations for writing include improving my teaching, making better learning materials for my students, and promoting excellence in practice for social work-

ers and related professionals. Writers such as Gerald and Marianne Corey have influenced my writing and approach to teaching. Before I write, I fully immerse myself in a field—through practice, teaching, observing, interviewing, and consulting. The peer review process is a critical component of my writing process. My inspirations for writing have generally come from courses I have taught, and from noticing gaps in the existing educational literature."

*   *   *

BARSKY, Allan Edward
   See BARSKY, Allan E.

*   *   *

BAUDRILLARD, Jean 1929-2007

OBITUARY NOTICE— See index for *CA* sketch: Born July 29, 1929, in Reims, France; died of cancer, March 6, 2007, in Paris, France. Philosopher, educator, and author. A postmodernist social theorist, Baudrillard was a regular commentator on the increasingly blurred line between reality and imagination in the modern, media-dominated world. During his early career, he was a translator of German works and a high school teacher. He then attended the University of Paris's Nanterre campus during the 1960s. Here, he was influenced by the radical leftist movement at the time and completed his doctorate in 1966. While a professor at the University of Paris, where he taught until 1987, Baudrillard published books that revealed his early socialist beliefs. Among these are *Le systeme des objets* (1968; translated as *The System of Objects* in 1996) and *La societé des consommation: ses mythes, ses structures* (1969; translated as *The Consumer Society: Myths and Structures* in 1998). In these works, Baudrillard criticized the hollowness of the consumer society that places the acquisition of things above finding a genuinely satisfying life. Rejecting Marxism as no longer relevant in *Le miroir de la production; ou, L'illusion critique du materialisme historique* (1973; translated as *The Mirror of Production* in 1975), the author later drew outrage from his fellow Frenchmen for criticising philosopher Michel Foucault in 1977's *Oublier Foucault.* Though he continued to teach in Paris, Baudrillard was increasingly drawn to the United States, where his works were becoming popular. Fascinated by American culture, he criticized it, as well, but it was his writings about imagination versus reality that really gained him a following in the United States. He constantly questioned what was real and what was not, challenging people to distinguish the two and even making remarkable assertions such as his denial that the 1991 Gulf War actually occurred; he insisted it was simply a media event. Many were outraged, too, when after the September 11, 2001, terrorist attacks Baudrillard declared that they were, in essence, conceived by the American "terrorist imagination." Television, of course, became a common topic for him, with its "reality" shows that do not portray reality; he was also fascinated by films and such other fantasy retreats as the Disney amusement parks. Baudrillard coined the term "hyperreality," which essentially means a conceived reality that makes people believe the "real world" is actually real; he also used the word simulacrum to indicate a duplicate that is actually better than the original. To say his arguments were confusing is an understatement, and Baudrillard's critics maintained that his complex writings, in the end, make no sense and thus mean nothing. Baudrillard, on the other hand, felt that his critics were too preoccupied with the past and that their writings were not relevant to contemporary society. After leaving teaching at the University of Paris, Baudrillard spent his time traveling and lecturing. He drew an increasingly large following, which expanded even more when his philosophy helped inspire the popular *Matrix* science fiction movies. Among his other writings available in English are *Simulations* (1983), *The Illusion of the End* (1994), *The Vital Illusion* (2000), and *The Spirit of Terrorism; and, Requiem for the Twin Towers* (2002).

OBITUARIES AND OTHER SOURCES:

PERIODICALS

Chicago Tribune, March 8, 2007, Section 3, p. 7.
Los Angeles Times, March 11, 2007, p. B15.
Times (London, England), March 8, 2007, p. 60.
Washington Post, March 9, 2007, p. B7.

* * *

BECKER, Cynthia J.

PERSONAL: Married. *Education:* University of New Orleans, B.A., 1987; University of Wisconsin at Madison, M.A., 1991, Ph.D., 2000.

ADDRESSES: Office—Department of Art History, Boston University, 725 Commonwealth Ave., Rm. 305B, Boston, MA 02215. *E-mail*—cjbecker@bu.edu

CAREER: University of Wisconsin at Madison, research assistant, 1993, teaching assistant, 1997-99, lecturer, 1999-2000; University of St. Thomas, St. Paul, MN, assistant professor of art history, 2000-05; Boston University, Boston, MA, assistant professor of art history, 2005—. Faculty director, University of St. Thomas study-abroad course in Morocco, 2002, 2003, and 2005, and in Paris, 2004.

MEMBER: African Studies Association, American Institute of Maghreb Studies, Arts Council of the African Studies Association, Wet African Research Association, College Art Association, Midle Eastern Studies Association, Saharan Studies Association.

AWARDS, HONORS: Fellow, University of Wisconsin—Madison, 1999-2000, and Boston University, 2007; grants from State University of New York, 1995, American Institute for Maghreb Studies, 1995, 1999, 2006, Fulbright grant, 1996, University of St. Thomas, 2001, 2002, 2004, and Humanities Foundation, 2006.

WRITINGS:

Amazigh Arts in Morocco: Women Shaping Berber Identity, University of Texas Press (Austin, TX), 2006.

Contributor to numerous scholarly journals.

BIOGRAPHICAL AND CRITICAL SOURCES:

ONLINE

Boston University Art History Department Web site, http://www.bu.edu/ah/ (May 18, 2007), short biography of Becker.*

* * *

BELMOND, C.A.

PERSONAL: Female.

ADDRESSES: E-mail—cabelmond@cabelmond.com.

CAREER: Novelist, lyricist, poet, and screenwriter. Has taught writing at New York University, New York, NY. Writer, producer, and director of television dramas, documentaries, and children's series.

MEMBER: Writers Guild of America, Authors Guild.

AWARDS, HONORS: Pushcart Press Editors's Book Award finalist; Edward Albee Foundation fellowship; Silver Apple Award for television writing; Karolyi Foundation, France, writer-in-residence.

WRITINGS:

A Rather Lovely Inheritance (novel), New American Library (New York, NY), 2007.

Also author of screenplays. Contributor to the book *Minutes of the Lead Pencil Club,* edited by Bill Henderson, Pushcart, 1996. Contributor to periodicals, including *Blue Light Red Light.*

SIDELIGHTS: The protagonist of C.A. Belmond's debut novel, *A Rather Lovely Inheritance,* is Penelope Nichols, called Penny, who is a New York freelance researcher working on set-design for movies about great women in history. Penny is summoned to London for the reading of the will of a great aunt who, upon her death, leaves her namesake an inheritance that includes a London apartment and the contents of the garage that adjoins a villa on the French Riviera. The prize in the garage is a valuable antique automobile. The villa is left to Penny's handsome but reserved cousin, Jeremy, a lawyer whose blood relationship to the family is questioned by greedy cousin Rollo. Penny and Jeremy team up to prove the validity of his inheritance, and in so doing, Penny finds that she must now put her professional research skills to work to uncover her family history as they travel to the most exciting of European destinations.

Shannon Bigham reviewed *A Rather Lovely Inheritance* for the *Curled Up with a Good Book* Web site, writing that it "is an interesting blend of mystery with a touch of romance and may appeal to mystery and romance readers alike." *Booklist* contributor Kristine Huntley called the book "an entertaining yarn with family drama and intrigue aplenty."

When asked who or what influences her writing, Belmond told *CA:* "My mentor [and author] Margaret Atwood, as well as [authors] Jean and Walter Kerr, Malachi Martin, Nora Johnson, and [writer, actor, and director] Woody Allen."

BIOGRAPHICAL AND CRITICAL SOURCES:

PERIODICALS

Booklist, November 15, 2006, Kristine Huntley, review of *A Rather Lovely Inheritance,* p. 23.
Kirkus Reviews, October 1, 2006, review of *A Rather Lovely Inheritance,* p. 975.
Publishers Weekly, October 23, 2006, review of *A Rather Lovely Inheritance,* p. 34.
Romantic Times, January, 2007, Sheri Melnick, review of *A Rather Lovely Inheritance,* p. 58.

ONLINE

Best Reviews, http://www.thebestreviews.com/ (June 22, 2007), Harriet Klausner, review of *A Rather Lovely Inheritance.*
Blogcritics, http://blogcritics.org/ (April 5, 2007), Katie McNeill, review of *A Rather Lovely Inheritance.*
C.A. Belmond Home Page, http://www.cabelmond.com (December 26, 2006)
Curled Up with a Good Book, http://www.curledup. com/ (April 15, 2007), Shannon Bigham, review of *A Rather Lovely Inheritance.*
Romance Reviews Today, http://www.romrevtoday. com/ (January 2, 2007), Jane Bowers, review of *A Rather Lovely Inheritance.*

*   *   *

BENHAM, Angela 1951-

PERSONAL: Born 1951, in London, England. Married. *Education:* Attended Manchester University.

ADDRESSES: Home—Evington, Leicester, England.

CAREER: Teacher. Voluntary Service Overseas, Thailand; Beaumont Lodge Primary School, Leicester, England; various special schools.

MEMBER: Red Rope Socialist Walking and Climbing Club.

WRITINGS:

Lucky to Be Alive: A First Expedition to the Himalayas, Northern Liberties Press (Philadelphia, PA), 2003.

BIOGRAPHICAL AND CRITICAL SOURCES:

PERIODICALS

Europe Intelligence Wire, May 27, 2003, "Fall Survivor Tells of Mountain Terror.*"

*   *   *

BERMAN, Ilan
   (Ilan I. Berman)

PERSONAL: Education: American University, M.A.; Washington College of Law, J.D.

ADDRESSES: E-mail—berman@afpc.org.

CAREER: American University, School of International Service, Washington, DC, adjunct professor; American Foreign Policy Council, Washington, DC, vice president for policy. Consultant, including to the U.S. Central Intelligence Agency (CIA) and U.S. Department of Defense.

WRITINGS:

Tehran Rising: Iran's Challenge to the United States, Rowman & Littlefield (Lanham, MD), 2005.
(Editor, with J. Michael Waller) *Dismantling Tyranny: Transitioning beyond Totalitarian Regimes,* Rowman & Littlefield (Lanham, MD), 2006.
(Editor) *Taking on Tehran: Strategies for Confronting the Islamic Republic,* Lexington Books (Lanham, MD), 2007.

Contributor to periodicals, including *Financial Times, Asian Wall Street Journal, Wall Street Journal Europe, Middle East Quarterly, Washington Times, Jerusalem Post, Strategic Review, International Herald Tribune,* and *National Interest.*

SIDELIGHTS: Ilan Berman is an expert on security in the regions of the Middle East, Central Asia, and the Russian Federation. In his collection of articles and new writings titled *Tehran Rising: Iran's Challenge to the United States,* he contends that with the revolution led by Iyatolah Khomeini, Iran initiated an Islamist war against the United States decades before the events of 9/11. Berman writes of an "informal accord" between Iran and al Qaeda and of Iran's nuclear weapons program, which he says includes many sites and the capability to produce enriched uranium sufficient to manufacture fifteen to twenty weapons a year. Berman suggests steps that should be taken to diffuse Iran's nuclear threat, including the multinational Proliferation Security Initiative (PSI) and closer ties with Russia. He also suggests that regime change could be accomplished based on the fact that most Iranians are young, poor, and pro-American.

Berman points out that we have limited military options because bombing of Iranian nuclear positions would result in retaliation against both the United States and Israel. Syria is protected because it signed a pact with Iran in 2004, in which Iran agreed to defend it against the United States and Israel. Carlin Romano noted in the *Philadelphia Inquirer:* "To a certain extent, *Tehran Rising* thus mandates the blurb, 'Read this book and weep.'"

BIOGRAPHICAL AND CRITICAL SOURCES:

PERIODICALS

America's Intelligence Wire, August 21, 2006, "Interview with Ilan Berman."
California Bookwatch, May, 2006, review of *Tehran Rising: Iran's Challenge to the United States.*
National Interest, fall, 2005, Richard Weitz, review of *Tehran Rising,* p. 138.
Philadelphia Inquirer, February 1, 2006, Carlin Romano, review of *Tehran Rising.*

Reference & Research Book News, May, 2006, review of *Dismantling Tyranny: Transitioning Beyond Totalitarian Regimes.*

Weekly Standard, January 16, 2006, Peter Hannaford, review of *Tehran Rising.*

ONLINE

Frontpagemag.com, http://www.frontpagemag.com/ (September 13, 2005), Jamie Glazov, *"Tehran Rising"* (interview).*

*   *   *

BERMAN, Ilan I.
   See BERMAN, Ilan

*   *   *

BERNIER-GRAND, Carmen T. 1947-

PERSONAL: Born November 22, 1947, in Coamo, Puerto Rico; daughter of Segundo (an accountant) and Julia (a store manager) Bernier; married Jeremy H. Grand (a system specialist), May 10, 1975; children: William, Juliana Grand Kelly. *Ethnicity:* "Latina." *Education:* Catholic University of Puerto Rico, B.S., 1968; University of Puerto Rico, Mayaguez, M.S., 1972; doctoral study at University of Connecticut, Storrs, 1973-75.

ADDRESSES: Home—Portland, OR. *E-mail*—grand@hevanet.com.

CAREER: University of Puerto Rico, Cayey, instructor in mathematics, 1971-78; ADP Dealer Services, Portland, OR, computer programmer, 1978-81; children's author, 1994—. Springfield Technical Community College, Springfield, MA, instructor, 1975-76; Community of Writers, Portland, speaker, 1999—; also speaker at various schools and conferences.

MEMBER: Authors Guild, Authors League of America, Society of Children's Book Writers and Illustrators, Willamette Writers.

AWARDS, HONORS: Blue ribbon, *Bulletin of the Center for Children's Books,* for *Juan Bobo: Four Folktales from Puerto Rico;* book of the year citation, *El Nuevo Día,* for *Poet and Politician of Puerto Rico: Don Luis Muñoz Marín;* Smithsonian notable book citation, for *In the Shade of the Níspero Tree;* notable book citation, American Library Association, Pura Belpré Honor Award, and citations for notable social studies trade book and book for a global society, all for *César: ¡Sí, se puede!/Yes, We Can!*

WRITINGS:

FOR CHILDREN

Juan Bobo: Four Folktales from Puerto Rico, illustrated by Ernesto Ramos Nieves, HarperCollins (New York, NY), 1994.
Poet and Politician of Puerto Rico: Don Luis Muñoz Marín, Orchard Books (New York, NY), 1995.
Who Helped Ox?, illustrated by Vivi Escrivá, Scholastic Phonics Readers (New York, NY), 1997.
In the Shade of the Níspero Tree, Orchard Books (New York, NY), 1999.
Shake It, Morena: Folklore from Puerto Rico, illustrated by Lulu Delacre, Millbrook Press (Brookfield, CT), 2002.
César: ¡Sí, se puede!/Yes, We Can!, illustrated by David Diaz, Marshall Cavendish (New York, NY), 2004.
Frida: ¡Viva la Vida!/Long Live Life!, Marshall Cavendish (New York, NY), 2007.

Work represented in anthologies, including *Writers in the Kitchen,* compiled by Tricia Gardella, Boyd's Mill, 1998; *Period Pieces: Stories for Girls,* selected by Erzi Deak and Kristin Embry Litchman, HarperCollins (New York, NY), 2003; *Once upon a Cuento,* edited by Lyn Miller-Lachman, Curbstone Press, 2003; and *Translations: New Poems Inspired by Art from Around the World,* edited by Jan Greenberg, Harry N. Abrams (New York, NY), 2007. Contributor to periodicals, including *Faces* and *Spider.*

SIDELIGHTS: Carmen T. Bernier-Grand told *CA:* "Today I am celebrating public libraries. Everybody is rich in the United States. We are rich even when we are poor, because we can read books for free.

"Today I am celebrating bookstores. When I was growing up on Ponce, Puerto Rico, our tiny bookstore had no children's books, but it sold comics.

"Today I am celebrating Little Lulu, Archie, and Donald Duck. I looked at the pictures and made up my own stories.

"Today I am celebrating my sister who told me that I was liar because I was always making up stories. I had to prove to her that I wasn't.

"Today I am celebrating authors and books and the monkeys in *Caps for Sale,* the first story I remember reading in English in a school anthology.

"Today I am celebrating my mother who recited 'Margarita está linda la mar' and sat by me every night so I could read out loud to her in English, my weakest subject. It wasn't until years later I realized that she didn't know English. But her warmth stayed with me.

"Today I am celebrating my father who told me I could be whatever I wanted to be. I could even be a mathematician. That I became. And I learned to research and use logic to plot my stories.

"Today I am celebrating the cute Oregonian who sat by me at a math party at the University of Connecticut. We married and moved to Oregon, where I began to write.

"Today I am celebrating my now grownup children who heard my stories again and again.

"Today I am celebrating the encouragement and help from the members of my writing groups.

"Today I am celebrating the educators who told the publishers that we needed books that reflected diversity in the classrooms.

"Today I am celebrating the publishers who opened the doors to diversity.

"Today I am celebrating my readers, because they are the best awards."

BIOGRAPHICAL AND CRITICAL SOURCES:

ONLINE

Carmen "T" Bernier Grand: Author & Speaker, http://www.carmen-t.com (April 1, 2007).

* * *

BILLE, Matt
  See BILLE, Matthew A.

* * *

BILLE, Matthew A. 1959-
  (Matt Bille)

PERSONAL: Born October 6, 1959; married; children: two. *Education:* Webster University, M.S., 1996.

ADDRESSES: Home—Colorado Springs, CO. *E-mail*—mattwriter@earthlink.net.

CAREER: U.S. Air Force, 1982-94, leaving service as captain; Booz Allen Hamilton (consulting firm), Colorado Springs, CO, associate, 2001—.

MEMBER: American Astronautical Society, American Institute of Aeronautics and Astronautics, National Association of Science Writers.

WRITINGS:

Rumors of Existence: Newly Discovered, Supposedly Extinct, and Unconfirmed Inhabitants of the Animal Kingdom, Hancock House (Blaine, WA), 1995.
(Under name Matt Bille; with Erika Lishock) *The First Space Race: Launching the World's First Satellites,* Texas A&M University Press (College Station, TX), 2004.
Shadows of Existence: Discoveries and Speculations in Zoology, Hancock House (Blaine, WA), 2006.

BIOGRAPHICAL AND CRITICAL SOURCES:

ONLINE

Matt Bille, Author and Researcher: Science, History, Fiction, http://www.mattwriter.com (April 1, 2007).

*   *   *

BLUME, Lesley M.M. 1975-

PERSONAL: Born 1975, in New York, NY; mother a concert pianist. *Education:* Attended Williams College and Oxford University; Cambridge University, M.A. *Hobbies and other interests:* Travel.

ADDRESSES: Home and office—New York, NY. *Agent*—Christine Earle, International Creative Management, 825 8th Ave., New York, NY 10019.

CAREER: Journalist and novelist. ABC News, New York, NY, researcher and reporter for *Nightline* based in Washington, DC.

WRITINGS:

Cornelia and the Audacious Escapades of the Somerset Sisters, Knopf (New York, NY), 2006.
The Rising Star of Rusty Nail, Knopf (New York, NY), 2007.

BIOGRAPHICAL AND CRITICAL SOURCES:

PERIODICALS

Booklist, July 1, 2006, Francisca Goldsmith, review of *Cornelia and the Audacious Escapades of the Somerset Sisters,* p. 55.
Bulletin of the Center for Children's Books, October, 2006, Karen Coats, review of *Cornelia and the Audacious Escapades of the Somerset Sisters,* p. 58.

Kirkus Reviews, June 15, 2006, review of *Cornelia and the Audacious Escapades of the Somerset Sisters,* p. 631.
Publishers Weekly, September 4, 2006, review of *Cornelia and the Audacious Escapades of the Somerset Sisters,* p. 68.
School Library Journal, September, 2006, Tracy Karbel, review of *Cornelia and the Audacious Escapades of the Somerset Sisters,* p. 200.

ONLINE

Lesley Blume Home Page, http www.lesleymmblume. com (April 28, 2007).*

*   *   *

BODMAN, Karna Small
(Karna Small)

PERSONAL: Married Dick Bodman. *Education:* University of Michigan, B.A.

ADDRESSES: Home—Naples, FL; Washington, DC; Jackson, WY. *E-mail*—karna@karnabodman.com.

CAREER: KRON-TV, San Francisco, CA, reporter; KGO-TV, San Francisco, news anchor; WTTG-TV, Washington, DC, news anchor; WRC, Washington, DC, radio host; the White House, Washington, DC, deputy press secretary to President Ronald Reagan; National Security Council, senior director and spokesperson; senior vice president of a public affairs firm.

MEMBER: International Thriller Writers, Mystery Writers of America, Sisters in Crime.

WRITINGS:

Checkmate (novel), Forge (New York, NY), 2007.

SIDELIGHTS: Karna Small Bodman began her career as a radio reporter in San Francisco, and when Ronald Reagan was elected president, she was appointed deputy press secretary under James Brady. In this position Bodman traveled and spoke on behalf of the president, in addition to writing speeches and press releases. She later became senior director of the National Security Council, representing the United States at arms control talks.

Bodman is well qualified to write about international affairs, which she does in her debut thriller *Checkmate,* the plot of which is built on the assumption that the codes that guide a cruise missile can be determined while it is in the air. The protagonist, Cameron "Cammy" Talbot, is leading the antimissile project team at Bandaq, a cutting-edge defense contractor with high standards. Their backing is in danger as Congress threatens to stop their funding and instead support rival Sterling Industries, an unethical firm that is determined to destroy Bandaq. The suspense builds when three stolen cruise missiles must be stopped before an international confrontation is provoked. Meanwhile, Cammy is being stalked by an unknown person intent on killing her. *Armchair Interviews* reviewer Laura Langer described *Checkmate* as "a fast-paced thriller."

When asked what influences her work, Bodman told *CA:* "My experiences serving in President Reagan's White House for six years. I saw firsthand how unplanned events can influence foreign as well as domestic policies. While any morning newspaper offers an author a veritable petri dish of possible plot points for a novel, I know that 'being there' is even more important in being able to convey a real sense of government decision making to the reader.

"When people read *Checkmate* or other novels that I am currently researching, I hope they will come away with a better understanding of how the White House operates, what issues are important, but have a good time reading a 'political thriller' in the process."

BIOGRAPHICAL AND CRITICAL SOURCES:

PERIODICALS

Kirkus Reviews, October 15, 2006, review of *Checkmate,* p. 1031.
Publishers Weekly, October 9, 2006, review of *Checkmate,* p. 37.

ONLINE

Armchair Interviews, http://www.armchairinterviews. com/ (April 15, 2007), Laura Langer, review of *Checkmate..*

Karna Small Bodman Home Page, http://www. karnabodman.com (April 15, 2007).
University of Michigan Web site, http://alumni.umich. edu/ (April 15, 2007), biography.

*　　*　　*

BONHAM-CARTER, Victor 1913-2007

OBITUARY NOTICE— See index for *CA* sketch: Born December 13, 1913, in Bearstead, Kent, England; died March 13, 2007. Journalist, farmer, and author. Bonham-Carter was a former secretary of the Society of Authors and the Royal Literary Fund. The son of a general who was governor of Malta, he studied at Magdalene College, Cambridge, where he earned a master's degree in 1935. After a failed attempt to be hired as a British Broadcasting Corporation announcer, he found work as headmaster of Shrewsbury in 1936. The appointment was short-lived, however, but Bonham-Carter managed to work for the magazine *Countryman.* He left after a year and a half, unable to stand the tyrannical editor Robertson Scott, and joined the *Country Scene and Topic* magazine staff, which ended its run after only three issues. He then worked in the photo reproduction business until the onset of World War II. Joining the British Army, he earned the Belgian Order of Leopold and several war service medals. Afterwards, he found some stability as a farmer, but also tried again to enter broadcasting. He made a radio documentary for the BBC that led to his being hired by the Elmhirst family to write a history of Dartington Hall. This work was unpublished, but he drew on it to write *Dartington Hall: The History of an Experiment* (1958), which was a collaborative effort with William Burnless Curry. Bonham-Carter had developed an interest in writing about English farming and life in the countryside, composing such titles as *The Village Has a Future* (1948), *Farming the Land* (1959), and *The Survival of the English Countryside* (1971). He was hired, initially as a part-time staffer, by the Society of Authors in 1963, and from 1971 until 1978 served as joint secretary. The author wrote about the society in the two-volume *Authors by Profession* (1978, 1984). From 1966 until 1982, he was also secretary for the Royal Literary Fund. Bonham-Carter penned the biography *Soldier True: The Life and Times of Field-Marshall Sir William Robertson, 1860-1933* (1963), which was released in the United States as *The Strategy of Victory: The Life* and Times of the Master Strategist of World War I: Field-Marshal Sir William Robertson* (1964), which led to his being hired as a researcher for the BBC series *The Great War.* More recently he released his autobiography, *What Countryman, Sir?* (1996), as well as the titles *The Essence of Exmoor* (1991) and *A Filthy Barren Ground* (1998).

OBITUARIES AND OTHER SOURCES:

BOOKS

Bonham-Carter, Victor, *What Countryman, Sir?*, privately printed, 1996.

PERIODICALS

Times (London, England), March 21, 2007, p. 64.

* * *

BOOMHOWER, Ray E. 1959-

PERSONAL: Born 1959.

ADDRESSES: Office—Indiana Historical Society, 450 W. Ohio St., Indianapolis, IN 46202. *E-mail*—rboomhower@indianahistory.org; reboomer@yahoo.com.

CAREER: Historian. Indiana Historical Society, managing editor of *Traces of Indiana and Midwestern History,* 1999—. Serves on the board of directors of the Indiana Journalism Hall of Fame.

MEMBER: Society of Children's Book Writers and Illustrators.

WRITINGS:

NONFICTION

Jacob Piatt Dunn, Jr.: A Life in History and Politics, 1855-1924, Indiana Historical Society (Indianapolis, IN), 1997.

The Country Contributor: The Life and Times of Juliet V. Strauss, Guild Press of Indiana (Carmel, IN), 1998.

Destination Indiana: Travels through Hoosier History, photographs by Darryl Jones, Indiana Historical Society (Indianapolis, IN), 2000.

But I Do Clamor: May Wright Sewall, a Life, 1844-1920, Guild Press of Indiana (Zionsville, IN), 2001.

One Shot: The World War II Photography of John A. Bushemi, Indiana Historical Society Press (Indianapolis, IN), 2004.

(Editor, with others) *Gus Grissom: The Lost Astronaut,* Indiana Historical Society Press (Indianapolis, IN), 2004.

(Editor) *Indiana Sporting Life: Selections from "Traces of Indiana and Midwestern History,"* Indiana Historical Society Press (Indianapolis, IN), 2005.

The Sword and the Pen: A Life of Lew Wallace (young adult), Indiana Historical Society Press (Indianapolis, IN), 2005.

The Soldier's Friend: A Life of Ernie Pyle (young adult), Indiana Historical Society Press (Indianapolis, IN), 2006.

Fighting for Equality: A Life of May Wright Sewall, Indiana Historical Society Press (Indianapolis, IN), 2007.

Contributor to periodicals, including *Indiana Magazine of History, Traces,* and *Michigan History.*

SIDELIGHTS: Ray E. Boomhower is a historian whose primary interest is the State of Indiana and those people from the Hoosier State who have gone on to become well known to the rest of the world. His biography *One Shot: The World War II Photography of John A. Bushemi* profiles the talented photojournalist who was hired by *Yank,* a magazine for enlisted men, during World War II. Bushemi covered the combat in the Solomon Islands and Marshall Islands where he died, a casualty of war. The book contains many of Bushemi's photographs.

Gus Grissom: The Lost Astronaut, for which Boomhower is coeditor, is the biography of one of the original Mercury astronauts, a man born in a small Indiana town and who went on to serve as a pilot during the Korean conflict before becoming a pioneer in the space program. Grissom died while participating in the 1967 Apollo mission training, in the fire that destroyed the defective craft. *Booklist* contributor Roland Green described this volume as a "solid biography."

The Soldier's Friend: A Life of Ernie Pyle is Boomhower's biography for younger readers of the newsman who was awarded a Pulitzer Prize in 1944 for his outstanding reportage of World War II. Pyle, who died while covering the conflict, was a talented journalist who was able to convey the drama of war as it was experienced by the combat soldiers who fought it, but he was also a man with personal demons, including both alcohol and depression. The book contains both Pyle's own words and vintage black-and-white photographs. A *Children's Bookwatch* contributor called the biography an "absorbing life story."

BIOGRAPHICAL AND CRITICAL SOURCES:

PERIODICALS

Booklist, May 15, 2004, Ray Olson, review of *One Shot: The World War II Photography of John A. Bushemi,* p. 1593; September 15, 2004, Roland Green, review of *Gus Grissom: The Lost Astronaut,* p. 187.
Children's Bookwatch, February, 2007, review of *The Soldier's Friend: A Life of Ernie Pyle.*
Kirkus Reviews, October 1, 2006, review of *The Soldier's Friend,* p. 1010.

ONLINE

Indiana Historical Society Web site, http://www.indianahistory.org/ (April 15, 2007).
Ray E. Boomhower Home Page, http://rayboomhower.com (April 15, 2007).*

*   *   *

BOWLING, Drew C. 1985-

PERSONAL: Born September 25, 1985.

ADDRESSES: Home—MD. *Agent*—Robin Rue, Writers House, 21 W. 26th St., New York, NY 10010. *E-mail*—drew@drewbowling.com.

CAREER: Writer.

WRITINGS:

The Tower of Shadows (science fiction novel), Del Rey/Ballantine Books (New York, NY), 2006.

SIDELIGHTS: Drew C. Bowling notes on his Web site that he knew he was destined to write fantasy and science fiction after reading *The Lord of the Rings,* given to him by his father when Bowling was in third grade. He was a high school senior when he began writing his debut novel, *The Tower of Shadows,* and when it was accepted for publication, he continued working on it as a college freshman.

The protagonists, like the author, are young. Cade Starcross watched his parents die in a fire set by the Coven, monsters created by fallen angels. Cade was saved by wizard Dale and mercenary Wren Tident and now seeks revenge against the most evil of all demons, Apollyon. In order to summon Apollyon, Cade must find a magic dagger and use it to spill the blood of his brother, Corin. When the two meet, the course of events changes.

"The world of Ellynrie has some wonderful elements and leaves much more to be explored with future works," wrote reviewer Stephen Hubbard for *Bookreporter.com.* "It also provides a glimpse into what Bowling may be able to do in the years to come as he further defines his voice." A *Publishers Weekly* contributor wrote that Bowling "brings an exciting pace and his own exuberant style to a novel suitable for all ages."

BIOGRAPHICAL AND CRITICAL SOURCES:

PERIODICALS

Kirkus Reviews, October 1, 2006, review of *The Tower of Shadows,* p. 994.
Library Journal, December 1, 2006, Jackie Cassada, review of *The Tower of Shadows,* p. 114.
Publishers Weekly, October 9, 2006, review of *The Tower of Shadows,* p. 40.

ONLINE

Bookreporter.com,   http://www.bookreporter.com/ (April 16, 2007), Stephen Hubbard, review of *The Tower of Shadows.*

Drew C. Bowling Home Page, http://www.drew
bowling.com (April 16, 2007).

SciFi.com, http://www.scifi.com/ (April 16, 2007),
Joseph Adams, review of *The Tower of Shadows.**

* * *

BRAITHWAITE, Rodric 1932-
(Rodric Quentin Braithwaite)

PERSONAL: Born May 17, 1932; son of Henry War-
wick and Lorna Constance Braithwaite; married,
April, 1961; wife's name Gillian Mary; children:
Richard, Katharine, Julian and Mark (twins), David.
Education: Christ's College, Cambridge, B.A.

ADDRESSES: Home—London, England.

CAREER: British National Service, 1950-52; British
Diplomatic Service, beginning 1955, ambassador to
Moscow, 1988-92; foreign policy advisor to Prime
Minister John Major, 1992-93; Deutsche Bank AG,
senior advisor, 1994-2002. All Souls College, Oxford,
visiting fellow, 1972-73; member of the supervisory
board of Deutsch Bank Moscow; chairman of the
board of UralMarsh Zovody; chairman of the Britain
Russia Centre and Moscow School of Political
Studies.

AWARDS, HONORS: Grand Cross of St. Michael and
St. George, 1994; honorary degrees from Christ's College and University of Birmingham.

WRITINGS:

(With Robert D. Blackwill and Akihiko Tanaka)
*Engaging Russia: A Report to the Trilateral Com-
mission,* Trilateral Commission (New York, NY),
1995.
*Across the Moscow River: The World Turned Upside
Down,* Yale University Press (New Haven, CT),
2002.
Moscow 1941: A City and Its People at War, Alfred A.
Knopf (New York, NY), 2006.

SIDELIGHTS: Rodric Braithwaite was a career
diplomat and served as the British ambassador to
Moscow during the fall of the Soviet Union. His

experience has enabled him to write of this period in
history, including the book *Across the Moscow River:
The World Turned Upside Down.*

Moscow 1941: A City and Its People at War is Braithwaite's study of the German invasion of Stalin's
Moscow, an event he considers a turning point in
World War II. He draws on memoirs, diaries, letters,
and interviews in forming his portrait of the steps
taken by the Russians to prepare for and defeat the assault on Moscow. He provides a chronological account
of events leading to the invasion, including Stalin's
failure to heed the warnings that it was about to come.
Braithwaite also blames the reluctance of the Russian
people to defend their country, which extorted their
earnings and crops, causing the deaths of millions, and
sent resistors to Siberia to die.

An *Economist* reviewer commented: "Soviet wartime
conditions are painted in all their gruesome inef-
ficiency and brutality," and wrote that the book
provides "a vivid picture of the stark and bloody
struggle for national survival with which Russia's war
began." *Commentary* contributor Edward N. Luttwak
wrote: "Braithwaite is obviously a talented historian,
and one who knows how to write. He also knows Russian, not as a foreigner who has studied the language
but as a highly cultured Russian might. . . . "For the
first time, one feels that one understands every stage
of this story."

BIOGRAPHICAL AND CRITICAL SOURCES:

PERIODICALS

Booklist, September 1, 2006, Gilbert Taylor, review of
Moscow 1941: A City and Its People at War,
p. 39.
Commentary, January, 2007, Edward N. Luttwak,
review of *Moscow 1941,* p. 61.
Economist, September 23, 2006, review of *Moscow
1941,* p. 95.
Publishers Weekly, July 31, 2006, review of *Moscow
1941,* p. 70.
Russian Life, September-October, 2006, Paul E. Rich-
ardson, review of *Moscow 1941,* p. 61.
Spectator, May 27, 2006, M.R.D. Foot, review of
Moscow 1941.

ONLINE

Bookslut, http://www.bookslut.com/ (April 16, 2007), Elizabeth Kiem, review of *Moscow 1941.*

California Literary Review, http://www.calitreview. com/ (December 18, 2006), Peter Bridges, review of *Moscow 1941.*

Center for European Reform Web site, http://www.cer. org.uk/ (April 16, 2007), brief biography.

London Times Online, http://www.timesonline.co.uk/ (March 12, 2006), review of *Moscow 1941.*

Observer Online, http://books.guardian.co.uk/ (April 9, 2006), Viv Groskop, review of *Moscow 1941.**

*   *   *

BRAITHWAITE, Rodric Quentin
See BRAITHWAITE, Rodric

*   *   *

BRUNNER, Theodore F. 1934-2007
(Theodore Friederich Brunner)

OBITUARY NOTICE— See index for *CA* sketch: Born July 3, 1934, in Nuremberg, Germany; died of lung cancer, March 7, 2007, in Laguna Beach, CA. Educator, police officer, and author. A retired professor of classics, Brunner was best known for his leadership role in creating the world's largest electronic database of the Greek language. Along with his family, he left Germany just after World War II, making his way to the United States in 1953 via the Netherlands. That same year, he enlisted in the U.S. Marines, serving in Japan until 1956. Returning to America, he graduated from the University of Wisconsin—Milwaukee in 1960. For his graduate work, he attended Stanford University, completing a master's in 1963 and a doctorate in 1965. His first faculty position was with Ohio State University, before the University of California hired him in 1966 to set up the classics department at the new Irvine campus. In 1972, a generous grant to the university allowed Brunner to begin the Thesaurus Linguae Graecae project. As director, Brunner organized scholars to collect the most authoritative manuscripts by such writers and philosophers as Sophocles, Homer, and Thucydides. Using a computer system called IBYCUS developed by David W. Packard, Brunner and his team had digitized the works of over three thousand authors by 1985. Today, it includes over twelve thousand works from the eighth century B.C.E. through 1453 C.E., the year the Byzantine Empire fell. The collection, available on CD-ROM and on the Internet, has been a windfall to researchers across the globe, who no longer have to travel to university libraries to access this information. Brunner remained at Irvine for the rest of his academic career, serving as department chair from 1968 to 1972 and as associate dean of humanities from 1969 to 1972; he retired in 1998. Interestingly, Brunner took up an entirely new career after this. He attended the Orange County Sheriff's Academy, graduating in 2001 as the oldest officer in his class. He served with the Laguna Beach police as a reserve officer until illness forced him to retire in 2005. Brunner was coauthor of *The Elements of Scientific and Specialized Terminology* (1967) and two indexes, and also cotranslated and coedited a critical edition of Sophocles's *Oedipus Tyrannus* (1970).

OBITUARIES AND OTHER SOURCES:

PERIODICALS

Los Angeles Times, March 11, 2007, p. B17.
Washington Post, March 14, 2007, p. B7.

*   *   *

BRUNNER, Theodore Friederich
See BRUNNER, Theodore F.

*   *   *

BRYANT, Amy 1970-

PERSONAL: Born 1970, in VA; married Bruno Blumenfeld (a musician).

ADDRESSES: Home—New York, NY.

CAREER: Writer.

WRITINGS:

Polly (novel), Harper Perennial (New York, NY), 2007.

SIDELIGHTS: Amy Bryant's debut novel, *Polly,* is the story of a young woman growing up in the Washington suburb of Reston, Virginia, during the 1980s. Uncomfortable with her peer group, Polly Clark finds friends in the hardcore music scene. Bryant told interviewer Susan Henderson of the *Litpark* Web site that the book is an adaptation of stories she wrote about individual young women and the young men they dated. In the novel Polly dates these young men, all of whom fill various needs in her life beginning in sixth grade, as well as some who abuse her. Bryant drew on her own experiences in writing this novel that *Library Journal* contributor Amy Watts noted, contains "enough sex, drugs, and rock'n'roll to make this a risky choice" for younger readers.

"The darker, more interesting subtext is that Polly's perfect suburban family is anything but," wrote a *Kirkus Reviews* contributor. Polly lives with her mother and cold stepfather, and her father lives in North Carolina, where he spends what should be her child support on alcohol. Polly goes on to attend college at Virginia Tech, where she pursues her interest in art and her independence. "She discovers that she does not need to have all the answers right away and that it is OK to explore what you're not familiar with," concluded Marilyn Perez, who reviewed the novel for the *Venuszine.com* Web site.

BIOGRAPHICAL AND CRITICAL SOURCES:

PERIODICALS

Kirkus Reviews, October 1, 2006, review of *Polly,* p. 976.
Library Journal, January 1, 2007, Amy Watts, review of *Polly,* p. 87.
Publishers Weekly, October 9, 2006, review of *Polly,* p. 36.

ONLINE

Litpark, http://litpark.com/ (January 31, 2007), Susan Henderson, interview with Bryant.
Teenwire.com, http://www.teenwire.com/ (January 29, 2007), Kate Rounds, "Teenwire.com Talks to *Polly* Author Amy Bryant."

Venuszine.com, http://venuszine.com/ (April 16, 2007), Marilyn Perez, review of *Polly.**

* * *

BRYANT, Hallman Bell 1936-

PERSONAL: Born August 17, 1936, in Royston, GA; son of William (a cattleman) and Lucile (a homemaker) Bryant; children: Matthew, Beth, Victoria. *Education:* Emory University, B.A., 1959; University of North Carolina Chapel Hill, M.A., 1962; Vanderbilt University, Ph.D., 1968. *Politics:* "Once a Southern Democrat—now without a party to call my own." *Religion:* "Hopeful Agnostic."

ADDRESSES: Home—Clemson, SC. *Office*— Department of English, College of Liberal Arts, Clemson University, Strode Towers, Clemson, SC 29634.

CAREER: Clemson University, Clemson, SC, professor of English, 1967-2004; writer. *Military service:* U.S. Army Military Intelligence Corps, 1962-64.

MEMBER: Modern Language Association.

AWARDS, HONORS: Senior American Scholar Fulbright appointment, 1993.

WRITINGS:

Robert Graves: An Annotated Bibliography, Garland Press (New York, NY), 1986.
A Separate Peace: The War Within, Twayne Publishers (Boston, MA), 1990.
Understanding "A Separate Peace": A Student Casebook to Issues, Sources, and Historical Documents, Greenwood Press (Westport, CT), 2002.

BIOGRAPHICAL AND CRITICAL SOURCES:

PERIODICALS

School Library Journal, April, 2002, Lynn Evarts, review of *Understanding "A Separate Peace": A Student Casebook to Issues, Sources, and Historical Documents,* p. 166.

ONLINE

Greenwood Publishing Group Web site, http://www.
greenwood.com/ (March 19, 2005).*

*   *   *

BURKE, Tina

PERSONAL: Born in Sydney, New South Wales,
Australia; daughter of Ronald V. and Janet F. Burke.
Education: Technical and Further Education, New
South Wales, associate diploma (business); KVB College of Visual Communication, associate diploma
(graphic design). *Hobbies and other interests:* Art,
wildlife art, birds, travel, dance.

ADDRESSES: Home—Coogee, New South Wales,
Australia. *E-mail*—tina@tinaburke.com.au.

CAREER: Children's author. Walt Disney Animation
Australia, Sydney, New South Wales, worked as
animator for six years; Willow Tree Press, Avalon,
New South Wales, worked as desktop publisher for
two years.

MEMBER: Society of Children's Book Writers and Illustrators, Children's Book Council of Australia.

WRITINGS:

Fly, Little Bird (juvenile), Kane/Miller Book Publish-
    ers (La Jolla, CA), 2006.
It's Christmas (juvenile), Penguin Books (Camber-
    well, Victoria, Australia), 2006, Kane/Miller Book
    Publishers (La Jolla, CA), 2007.
Sophie's Big Bed (juvenile), Puffin Baby Books (Cam-
    berwell, Victoria, Australia), 2007.
(Illustrator) Meredith Costain, *Rosie to the Rescue,*
    Penguin Books (Camberwell, Victoria, Australia),
    2007.
Are You Hungry? (juvenile), Penguin Books (Camber-
    well, Victoria, Australia), 2007.

Contributor to periodicals, including *Newswrite.*

SIDELIGHTS: Tina Burke told *CA:* "I've loved reading and drawing since childhood and always wanted
to write and illustrate children's books. That dream
has never left me, so I'm thrilled to be doing it now. It
feels right, and it brings me a lot of joy.

"Prior to my first book being published, I had worked
in desktop publishing for a couple of years. Following
this I trained and worked as an animator for the Walt
Disney Animation Studio in Sydney, where I spent six
years developing my skills while working with some
exceptionally talented and passionate artists.

"After my time at Disney I wrote *Fly, Little Bird* while
thinking about a small bird and some little rounded
children that I had doodled in a sketchbook. I was
thrilled when the book was picked up and published
by Penguin Books in Australia and subsequently
released in the United States.

"Aside from working on my books, I continually strive
to develop as an artist by attending workshops,
seminars, and classes in a variety of creative outlets of
interest to me. These range from writing to dance, to
fine art. They are typically a lot of fun and a great way
to meet people, and they often inspire me in my own
work.

"I try to write and illustrate stories from my heart. My
goal is to create appealing characters that people will
warm to and care about, and to tell satisfying stories
that people will enjoy reading.

"My advice to aspiring writer-illustrators: continually
try to improve your skills as an artist by devoting as
much time as you possibly can to practice. You can
learn a lot from others, but you can only improve by
spending a lot of time on your own work as well.
Don't try to force a style in the beginning. The
combination of your own knowledge, skills, experiences, and inspirations will eventually combine and
help you find your own voice."

BIOGRAPHICAL AND CRITICAL SOURCES:

ONLINE

Tina Burke Home Page, http://www.tinaburke.com.au
    (May 31, 2007).

C

CALLAN, Jim 1951-

PERSONAL: Born January 16, 1951, in Nyack, NY; son of John (a builder) and Viola (a homemaker) Callan; married Polly Corman (a psychotherapist), June 26, 1999. *Ethnicity:* "White." *Education:* Fordham University, B.A., 1973; New York University, M.A., 1975. *Politics:* Democrat.

ADDRESSES: Home—Nyack, NY. *E-mail*—jim callan@optonline.net.

CAREER: Writer.

WRITINGS:

Amazing Scientists, Wiley (New York, NY), 2001.
America in the 1900s and 1910s, Facts on File (New York, NY), 2005.
America in the 1930s, Facts on File (New York, NY), 2005.
America in the 1960s, Facts on File (New York, NY), 2005.

*   *   *

CANOBBIO, Andrea 1962-

PERSONAL: Born 1962, in Turin, Italy.

ADDRESSES: Home—Turin, Italy. *E-mail*—canobbio@einaudi.it.

CAREER: Einaudi (publisher), Turin, Italy, editor.

WRITINGS:

NOVELS

Vasi Cinesi, Einaudi (Turin, Italy), 1989.
Traslochi, Einaudi (Turin, Italy), 1992.
Padri di padri, Einaudi (Turin, Italy), 1997.
Indivisibili, Rizzoli (Milan, Italy), 2000.
Il Naturale disordine delle cose, Einaudi (Turin, Italy), 2004, translation by Abigail Asher published as *The Natural Disorder of Things,* Farrar, Straus & Giroux (New York, NY), 2006.

SIDELIGHTS: Andrea Canobbio is an Italian writer and an editor with the publishing house Einaudi. His fifth novel, *Il Naturale disordine delle cose,* is the first to be translated into English, as *The Natural Disorder of Things.* A *Kirkus Reviews* contributor called the plot "reminiscent of Raymond Chandler."

The narrator, Claudio Fratta, is a garden designer in his thirties. Two events from his past overshadow all else—the bankrupting of his father by loan sharks and his brother's death from a drug overdose. *New York Times Book Review* contributor Vendela Vida wrote: "Canobbio is skilled at conjuring a very real and sympathetic Fabio—the scenes describing his death and Claudio's memories of him are some of the most powerful in the book."

Claudio is haunted by the image of a woman he took to a hospital emergency room after they both witnessed a man killed by a hit-and-run driver in a parking lot.

When Elisabetta Renal contacts Claudio by telephone to ask for his help with her garden, he recognizes her voice. It is the same woman, and the beautiful wife of the wealthy, wheelchair-bound Rossi soon becomes his lover, but Elisabetta has another motive for hiring Claudio.

Library Journal critic Lisa Rohrbaugh commented: "A mystery, a romance, and more, this suspenseful novel builds to a climax that will thoroughly engross the reader." Vida concluded by noting: "A writer this talented deserves to have all his work in translation, so we can see not only his less successful experiments but also witness him at his meditative best."

BIOGRAPHICAL AND CRITICAL SOURCES:

PERIODICALS

Entertainment Weekly, July 21, 2006, Karen Karbo, review of *The Natural Disorder of Things,* p. 74.

Kirkus Reviews, June 1, 2006, review of *The Natural Disorder of Things,* p. 532.

Library Journal, May 1, 2006, Lisa Rohrbaugh, review of *The Natural Disorder of Things,* p. 76.

New York Times Book Review, September 10, 2006, Vendela Vida, review of *The Natural Disorder of Things,* p. 25.*

*   *   *

CANTON, James

PERSONAL: Male.

ADDRESSES: Office—Institute for Global Futures, 2084 Union St., San Francisco, CA 94123.

CAREER: Institute for Global Futures, San Francisco, CA, founder, CEO, and chairman, 1990—. Northwestern University, Kellogg School of Management, Center for Research in Innovation, senior fellow; serves on Motorola's Visionary Advisory Board; consultant and advisor. Commentator for CNN.

WRITINGS:

Technofutures: How Leading-Edge Technology Will Transform Business in the 21st Century, Hay House (Carlsbad, CA), 1999.

The Extreme Future: The Top Trends That Will Reshape the World for the Next 5, 10, and 20 Years, Dutton (New York, NY), 2006.

Author of the *James Canton* blog.

SIDELIGHTS: James Canton, who studied under futurist Alvin Toffler during the 1970s and has advised several administrations, shares his knowledge with clients and others interested in trends in technology and business that will impact the future. He does this through his blog, speaking engagements, and books, which include *Technofutures: How Leading-Edge Technology Will Transform Business in the 21st Century.* Canton describes the volume as "a book of ideas, scenarios, and forecasts sparked by technology" and "a strategic overview of the future shaped by emerging technology." Written at the very end of the twentieth century, the book advises businesses to draw on the power of the Internet and develop marketing techniques to reach its users.

In *The Extreme Future: The Top Trends That Will Reshape the World for the Next 5, 10, and 20 Years,* Canton foresees the future of energy, as well as technology, and bases many of his assessments on the assumptions of climate change and scarcity of natural resources. He suggests jobs that will match our increasingly science-based lives, and will include those related to longevity medicine, security, and globalization. Canton projects that women and Hispanics will make up a more significant percentage of the workforce. A *Publishers Weekly* contributor felt that Canton's "lively scenarios are designed to spark debates, and they surely will." *Booklist* reviewer Mary Whaley called Canton's perspective "important and fascinating."

BIOGRAPHICAL AND CRITICAL SOURCES:

PERIODICALS

Booklist, August 1, 2006, Mary Whaley, review of *The Extreme Future: The Top Trends That Will Reshape the World for the Next 5, 10, and 20 Years,* p. 20.

Business Journal Serving Charlotte and the Metropolitan Area, April 6, 2001, "'Techno phobia' Is Doom for Business," p. 29.

Fort Worth Star-Telegram, November 16, 2006, Cecil Johnson, review of *The Extreme Future.*

Futurist, January-February, 2007, review of *The Extreme Future,* p. 48.

Publishers Weekly, July 31, 2006, review of *The Extreme Future,* p. 72.

Reference & Research Book News, November, 2006, review of *The Extreme Future.*

Research-Technology Management, July-August, 2003, review of *Technofutures: How Leading-Edge Technology Will Transform Business in the 21st Century,* p. 62.

ONLINE

Institute for Global Futures Web site, http://www.futureguru.com (April 19, 2007).*

*   *   *

CAREY, Vincent

PERSONAL: Education: National University of Ireland, Maynooth, B.A. (with honors), 1982, diploma in education, 1983, M.A., 1985; State University of New York, Stony Brook, Ph.D., 1991.

ADDRESSES: Office—History Department, State University of New York, Plattsburgh, Champlain Valley Hall, Plattsburgh, NY 12901. *E-mail*—careyvp@plattsburgh.edu.

CAREER: State University of New York, Plattsburgh, professor of history.

WRITINGS:

EDITOR

(With Clare Carroll) Richard Beacon, *Solon His Follie, or, A Politique Discourse Touching the Reformation of Common-weales Conquered, Declined or Corrupted* (annotated edition), Medieval & Renaissance Texts & Studies (Binghamton, NY), 1996.

(With Ute Lotz-Heumann) *Taking Sides? Colonial and Confessional Mentalites in Early Modern Ireland: Essays in Honour of Karl S. Bottigheimer,* Four Courts Press (Portland, OR), 2003.

(With Ronald Bogdan and Elizabeth A. Walsh) *Voices for Tolerance in an Age of Persecution,* Folger Shakespeare Library (Washington, DC), 2004.

NONFICTION

Surviving the Tudors: The "Wizard" Earl of Kildare and English Rule in Ireland, 1537-1586, Four Courts Press (Portland, OR), 2002.

Contributor to journals, including *Irish Historical Studies.*

SIDELIGHTS: Irish studies scholar Vincent Carey is the editor of a number of volumes, including, with Clare Carroll, an annotated edition of Richard Beacon's *Solon His Follie, or, A Politique Discourse Touching the Reformation of Common-weales Conquered, Declined or Corrupted.* The original was published four centuries earlier in 1594, and is an allegory set in ancient Greece that Beacon dedicated to Queen Elizabeth I.

Markku Peltonen reviewed the volume in the *Renaissance Quarterly,* writing: "The edition contains much of value. The text is meticulously edited; the editors have traced down Beacon's numerous references to classical and Renaissance sources and have written a substantial introduction, which firmly places Beacon's work both in its contemporary political context and in its intellectual context of Renaissance political theory."

Surviving the Tudors: The "Wizard" Earl of Kildare and English Rule in Ireland, 1537-1586 is Carey's study of Gerald Fitzgerald, eleventh earl of Kildare, who escaped the destruction of the house of Kildare in 1537 by Henry VIII, who retaliated for the Kildare family's revolt against him. An aunt fled with the baby to Europe, but the "wizard" earl returned as a young man to claim the family titles and estates and to go on to become a powerful political figure. *English Historical Review* contributor Ciaran Brady wrote that "survival is the organizing theme of Vincent Carey's valuable, expertly researched and eminently balanced study of the earl, the first full-scale biography ever published."

With Ute Lotz-Heumann, Carey is editor of *Taking Sides? Colonial and Confessional Mentalites in Early Modern Ireland: Essays in Honour of Karl S. Bottigheimer.* Contributors comment on Irish history during the period from the late medieval to the eighteenth century, with two essays having as their subjects modern historians. *Irish Literary Supplement* contributor Sandra Hynes described the editors' introduction as "excellent" and noted that they allow individual contributors "to address the question of taking sides in Irish history while also approaching individual and group identities and mentalites."

BIOGRAPHICAL AND CRITICAL SOURCES:

PERIODICALS

Albion, summer, 2003, William Palmer, review of *Surviving the Tudors: The "Wizard" Earl of Kildare and English Rule in Ireland, 1537-1586,* p. 278.

English Historical Review, November, 2002, Ciaran Brady, review of *Surviving the Tudors,* p. 1261.

Irish Literary Supplement, fall, 2006, Sandra Hynes, review of *Taking Sides? Colonial and Confessional Mentalites in Early Modern Ireland: Essays in Honour of Karl S. Bottigheimer,* p. 4.

Journal of Ecclesiastical History, January, 2005, S.J. Connolly, review of *Taking Sides?,* p. 171.

Renaissance Quarterly, autumn, 1998, Markku Peltonen, review of *Solon His Follie, or, A Politique Discourse Touching the Reformation of Commonweales Conquered, Declined or Corrupted,* p. 1027; summer, 2003, Nicholas Canny, review of *Surviving the Tudors,* p. 528; winter, 2004, Mary Ann Lyons, review of *Taking Sides?,* p. 1545.

Utopian Studies, spring, 1998, Toby Barnard, review of *Solon His Follie, or, A Politique Discourse Touching the Reformation of Common-weales Conquered, Declined or Corrupted,* p. 231.

ONLINE

State University of New York Plattsburgh Web site, http://faculty.plattsburgh.edu/ (April 21, 2007), brief biography of Carey.*

CARLYLE, John 1931-2003

PERSONAL: Born January 5, 1931, in Baltimore, MD; died of lung cancer, May 27, 2003, in West Hollywood, CA.

CAREER: Actor in stage productions and in films, including *Dangerous Mission,* 1954; (uncredited) *Untamed,* 1955; (uncredited) *Daddy Long Legs,* 1955; (uncredited) *The Rack,* 1956; (uncredited) *The Monster That Challenged the World,* 1957; and *Whore,* 1991. Actor in numerous television movies and series, 1955-89.

WRITINGS:

Under the Rainbow: An Intimate Memoir of Judy Garland, Rock Hudson and My Life in Old Hollywood, foreword by Robert Osborne, afterword by Taylor Negron, edited by Chris Freeman, Carroll & Graf (New York, NY), 2006.

SIDELIGHTS: John Carlyle's edited memoir, *Under the Rainbow: An Intimate Memoir of Judy Garland, Rock Hudson and My Life in Old Hollywood,* was published several years after his death. It is in part a history of the film industry during the 1950s, 1960s, and 1970s, and the stars who became more successful than Carlyle himself, although he did appear, often uncredited, in many movies. Carlyle was gay during a time when that fact had to be hidden or the consequences of homophobia faced. He experienced intimacy with women, including Garland, and reportedly had encounters with well-known actors, but the focus of the book is on his relationship with Garland, with whom he overindulged in alcohol and drugs.

In reviewing the book for the *Gay & Lesbian Review Worldwide,* Stuart Timmons described these previously untold stories about Garland as being "China White heroin" for her fans. "But one also recognizes a central truth Carlyle appears unable to face: he drowned his frustrations as an actor and an emotionally fragile gay man with a dependence on booze and Dexamyl, as well as obsessive social conquests of legendary film divas." Timmons added: "It is a shame that Mr. Carlyle didn't act less and write more. His sense of story and character is a constant pleasure, as are his arch phrases." Among these is his description of the fictional love affair between closeted gay Rock Hudson and lesbian Phyllis Gates, which Carlyle calls a "Louella Parsons orgasm."

Carlyle found parts in popular television series, working for several decades in that medium before succumbing to lung cancer.

BIOGRAPHICAL AND CRITICAL SOURCES:

BOOKS

Carlyle, John, *Under the Rainbow: An Intimate Memoir of Judy Garland, Rock Hudson and My Life in Old Hollywood,* foreword by Robert Osborne, afterword by Taylor Negron, edited by Chris Freeman, Carroll & Graf (New York, NY), 2006.

PERIODICALS

Booklist, September 15, 2006, Kathleen Hughes, review of *Under the Rainbow,* p. 14.
Gay & Lesbian Review Worldwide, January-February, 2007, Stuart Timmons, review of *Under the Rainbow,* p. 40.
Publishers Weekly, August 28, 2006, review of *Under the Rainbow,* p. 47.

OBITUARIES

PERIODICALS

Hollywood Reporter, June 4, 2003, p. 16.*

*   *   *

CARNEY, Jeff 1962-

PERSONAL: Born 1962, in KY. *Education:* Vassar College, A.B.; University of Illinois, Chicago, M.A.

ADDRESSES: Office—Department of English, Snow College, 150 E. College Ave., Ephraim, UT 84627. *Agent*—Liz Darhansoff, Darhansoff, Verrill, Feldman, 236 W. 26th St., New York, NY 10001. *E-mail*—jeff@ jeffcarney.net; jeff.carney@snow.edu.

CAREER: Snow College, Ephraim, UT, associate professor of English. Previously worked at a Renaissance fair in WI, and as a clerk in a clothing store.

WRITINGS:

The Adventures of Michael MacInnes (young adult novel), Farrar, Straus & Giroux (New York, NY), 2006.

SIDELIGHTS: Jeff Carney notes on his home page that although he did well academically while attending boarding school, he was expelled for making some "bad choices." He was admitted to, and graduated from, Vassar College, but he knew that his first novel would be set in a boarding school.

Carney's debut young adult novel, *The Adventures of Michael MacInnes,* is set in 1924 at a Maryland prep school. "There's lots of swashbuckling fun to be had in this period piece," wrote Paula Rohrlick in *Kliatt.* Michael MacInnes is an orphan and "madman poet" who is attending on scholarship. His independent thinking causes a stir, particularly when he publishes controversial articles and embarks on other adventures with his best friend, Roger Legrande, who is hiding his homosexuality. In one of their adventures, they destroy a bootlegging operation (the story is set during Prohibition), to save the other students from a tainted product.

School Library Journal reviewer Sharon Morrison compared *The Adventures of Michael MacInnes* with Robert Cormier's *The Chocolate War,* "without the excessive violence and with touches of humor."

Carney told *CA:* "I attended a private elementary school that encouraged creativity in many forms. For me this meant writing and theater. The first thing I remember writing was a rehash of some Beverly Cleary stuff. Another was cribbed from the cave section of *Tom Sawyer.*

"I suppose I'm influenced the most by writers who stand out from the crowd. J.D. Salinger, Kurt Vonnegut, Walker Percy, Tim Powers. Writers who have something rebellious to say or a really unique vision to offer.

"These days most of the intensely imagined parts of my stuff come during the outlining stage, which is very quick, loose, and freely-associative. My outlines run to thousands of words. Then comes the more business-like stage of drafting. I hate it. But it must get done. Revising text that exists is always a pleasure. I can turn off the business man and let the juices run again. And again and again, as needed.

"I'd like my readers to look at the world with fresh eyes and challenge the status quo. Things are as they are only because we collectively agree that they must be so. But if enough people are inspired (by others as well as me), then maybe we can work to make things a bit better. I am especially skeptical of the rigidly corporate society that today's young people are growing up to take for granted. Maybe it's naive, but I'd like everyone to spend a summer or even a year living in a hut by Walden Pond. Not the original (it would get crowded and smelly) but everyone's own private version of Thoreau's great laboratory of the mind. We need a better sense of what matters. (Hint: money isn't it.)"

Asked the most surprising thing he has learned as a writer, Carney said: "That after a published book (and a few unpublished ones) I'm still the same me. I think that's a good thing."

BIOGRAPHICAL AND CRITICAL SOURCES:

PERIODICALS

Kirkus Reviews, October 1, 2006, review of *The Adventures of Michael MacInnes,* p. 1011.
Kliatt, January, 2007, review of *The Adventures of Michael MacInnes,* p. 10.
School Library Journal, November, 2006, Sharon Morrison, review of *The Adventures of Michael MacInnes,* p. 130.

ONLINE

Jeff Carney Home Page, http://www.jeffcarney.net (April 21, 2007).

CARR, Jimmy 1972-

PERSONAL: Born September 15, 1972, in London, England; son of Nora May Carr; partner of Karoline Copping. *Education:* Graduate of Gonville and Caius College, Cambridge University. *Hobbies and other interests:* Tennis, parties, premieres.

ADDRESSES: Agent—Hannah Chambers, 23 Long Ln., London EC1A 9HL, England.

CAREER: Comedian, writer. Appearances include the *Royal Variety Show,* 2002; *Late Night with Conan O'Brien,* 2003; *Tonight Show with Jay Leno,* 2003-04; *Comedy Central Special,* 2004; *Your Face or Mine,* 2003; *Distraction,* 2003-04; *Friday Night Project,* 2005; *8 Out of 10 Cats,* 2005-06; national tour, 2007; and guest appearances on numerous other television programs in England and the United States. Has presented radio shows and performed stand-up comedy at festivals, including Edinburgh Fringe Festival, Kilkenny Comedy Festival, Montreal Comedy Festival, and Aspen Comedy Festival.

MEMBER: Groucho.

AWARDS, HONORS: Nominee, Perrier Award, 2002; Billy Marsh Award, 2003; Best Stand Up Time Out Comedy Award, 2003; Best On Screen Newcomer, Royal Television Society Award, 2003; Best Game-show Silver Rose, for *Your Face or Mine,* 2003; nominee, Best Presenter Golden Rose of Montreux, for *Distraction,* 2004; Lafta Award, Best Stand Up, 2005, Funniest Man, 2005.

WRITINGS:

•

(With Lucy Greeves) *Only Joking: What's So Funny about Making People Laugh?,* Gotham Books (New York, NY), 2006, published as *The Naked Jape: Uncovering the Hidden World of Jokes,* Michael Joseph (London, England), 2006.

Also wrote and produced *Jimmy Carr: Stand Up,* 2005, and *Jimmy Carr Live,* 2004, DVDs of his comedy routines. Writer for television comedy shows, including *Meet Ricky Gervais.*

SIDELIGHTS: Jimmy Carr is a British comedian well known on both sides of the Atlantic for his biting wit and deadpan delivery. The host of numerous game shows and comedy series, Carr has achieved a high degree of celebrity in a very short time. As a writer for the *Europe Intelligence Wire* noted: "He's on the box so much it would drive you mad, if he wasn't so good."

Collaborating with writer Lucy Greeves, Carr turned to writing books with the 2006 *Only Joking: What's So Funny about Making People Laugh?* (published in England as *The Naked Jape: Uncovering the Hidden World of Jokes*), a serious look at what makes people laugh. In the book, Carr and Greeves analyze jokes to discover what makes them funny, examining aspects such as timing, surprise, and internal logic. Writing in London's *Financial Times,* Ludovic Hunter-Tilney called the work "an informative tour of the art and science of joking." Jessica Heasley, writing in *Psychology Today,* likewise found *Only Joking* to be a "revealing look" at the mechanism of humor. Heasley also praised the lighthearted and humorous approach the authors take to the subject, commenting that the book is "full of sharp one-liners and dry-as-bone wit." Similar praise came from a *Publishers Weekly* contributor who called the same work an "entertaining and educational book about the history and practice of humor," and from *Booklist* contributor Jack Helbig, who termed *Only Joking* a "lively, intelligent, highly readable, often hilarious coverage of all aspects of what makes people laugh."

BIOGRAPHICAL AND CRITICAL SOURCES:

PERIODICALS

Booklist, September 1, 2006, Jack Helbig, review of *Only Joking: What's So Funny about Making People Laugh?,* p. 36.

Europe Intelligence Wire, February 8, 2007, "Jimmy's Gagging for a Laugh"; February 16, 2007, "Deadpan Delivery with a Hint of Danger"; February 23, 2007, "Comedian Who Does Not Pull Punches."

Financial Times (London, England), November 25, 2006, Ludovic Hunter-Tilney, review of *The Naked Jape: Uncovering the Hidden World of Jokes,* p. 41.

Music Week, May 29, 2004, "Comedian and Xfm DJ Jimmy Carr Is to Host the New Incarnation of Music Week's Creative and Design Awards," p. 2.

Psychology Today, September-October, 2006, Jessica Heasley, review of *Only Joking,* p. 36.

Publishers Weekly, July 24, 2006, review of *Only Joking,* p. 51.

ONLINE

Celebrity Speakers, http://www.speakers.co.uk/ (April 9, 2007), profile of author.

Comedy Central Web site, http://www.comedycentral.com/ (April 9, 2007), profile of author.

Comedy CV, http://www.comedycv.co.uk/ (April 9, 2007), profile of author.

Internet Movie Database, http://www.imdb.com/ (April 9, 2007), profile of author.

Jimmy Carr Home Page, http://www.jimmycarr.com (April 9, 2007).*

*   *   *

CARTER, Steven 1961-

PERSONAL: Born 1961. *Education:* Hiwassee Junior College, A.A.; Tusculum College, B.A.; University of Southern Mississippi, M.A., Ph.D.

ADDRESSES: Home—Georgetown, KY. *Office*—English Department, Georgetown College, 400 E. College St., Georgetown, KY 40324. *E-mail*—scarter@georgetowncollege.edu.

CAREER: Writer, educator. Georgetown College, Georgetown, KY, assistant professor of English.

WRITINGS:

I Was Howard Hughes: A Novel, Bloomsbury (New York, NY), 2003.

Famous Writers School: A Novel, Counterpoint (New York, NY), 2006.

Also author of short stories. Contributor to periodicals, including *Antioch Review, Tin House, Northwest Review, South Dakota Review, American Literary Review, Crescent Review, Mississippi Review,* and *South Carolina Review.* Former editor, *Georgetown Review.*

SIDELIGHTS: An assistant professor of English, Steven Carter is also the author of numerous short stories, as well as longer works of fiction, including *I Was Howard Hughes: A Novel* and *Famous Writers School: A Novel.* Carter's 2003 debut novel, *I Was Howard Hughes,* is a faux biography of the famous entrepreneur, written by the fictional biographer, Alton Reece. Something of a bookstore celebrity because of a *Rolling Stone* piece on Madonna and a biography of Herman Melville, Reece puts together journals, interviews, and letters to form a portrait of the life of the enigmatic Hughes. Carter/Reece serves up anecdotes—some true and some not—involving lovers, such as Jean Harlow and Ava Gardner, and examines Hughes's failed scheme to build Nevada as a pillar of morality. Writing in *Library Journal,* David A. Berona felt that while "this is a clever if terse account of the Hughes legend," the biographer as well as his subject are not "developed adequately to elicit sympathy." A *Publishers Weekly* reviewer had higher praise for this first novel, calling it a "cheeky look at the relationship between biographer and subject." The same reviewer went on to note that Carter's novel builds "a dizzying hall-of-mirrors effect with its double portrait." Similarly, a *Kirkus Reviews* critic lauded *I Was Howard Hughes* as a "madly inventive mock bio," calling it "a darkly diverting, slightly cautionary tale about a barmy billionaire and his batty biographer."

Carter's second novel, the 2006 *Famous Writers School,* features self-styled writing guru Wendell Newton, who parleys a stint as an agricultural journalist and a self-published novel into the status of writing expert and coach. His Famous Writers School has a steady flow of mediocre students, and the novel focuses on his relationship with three of those, developing story and character through letters exchanged and fiction critiqued. Dan is a tractor salesman who has written a hard-edged piece of crime fiction that Newton secretly covets; Rio is a singer from Pittsburgh with whom Newton is trying to carry on a flirtation; and Linda is a homemaker with little visible talent but a grudge against her writing teacher. Newton is free with trite advice and eager to purloin the ideas of his students. A critic for *Kirkus Reviews,* noting the difficulties posed in an epistolary novel developed through four different points of view, called the novel "a smartly conceived send-up of writerly ambition, imperfectly executed." Likewise, a *Publishers Weekly* reviewer thought that while Newton comes across as a full-drawn character, the three students as

characters are "lightly sketched." The same reviewer did, however, praise Carter's "terrific ear for the rumblings of the human ego," as well as his "intuitive sense of how fiction is often substituted for truth." Karen Kleckner, writing in *Library Journal,* had a higher assessment of *Famous Writers School,* calling it a "laugh-out-loud celebration of good storytelling and a satire of scribblers who wear their *New Yorker* rejection letters on their sleeves."

BIOGRAPHICAL AND CRITICAL SOURCES:

PERIODICALS

Kirkus Reviews, July 15, 2003, review of *I Was Howard Hughes: A Novel,* p. 923; August 15, 2006, review of *Famous Writers School: A Novel,* p. 803.
Library Journal, October 15, 2003, David A. Berona, review of *I Was Howard Hughes,* p. 96; October 1, 2006, Karen Kleckner, review of *Famous Writers School,* p. 56.
Publishers Weekly, July 7, 2003, review of *I Was Howard Hughes,* p. 49; July 31, 2006, review of *Famous Writers School,* p. 46.

ONLINE

Georgetown College Department of English Web site, http://spider.georgetowncollege.edu/ (April 9, 2007), faculty profile of author.

*   *   *

CARTON, Evan 1953-

PERSONAL: Born August 2, 1953, in Bellefonte, PA; son of Edwin Beck and Lonnie Frances Carton; married Janis Bergman, December 28, 1974; children: Jacqueline, Rebecca. *Education:* Columbia College, B.A., 1974; Johns Hopkins University, M.A., 1976, Ph.D., 1979. *Politics:* Democrat. *Religion:* Jewish. *Hobbies and other interests:* Travel, tennis, movies, music.

ADDRESSES: Office—Department of English, University of Texas at Austin, 1 University Station, B5000 Austin, TX 78712. *E-mail*—e.carton@mail.utexas.edu.

CAREER: Writer, educator. University of Texas, Austin, instructor, 1978-79, assistant professor, 1979-85, associate professor, 1985-91. professor, 1991—, Joan Negley Kelleher Centennial Professorship in Rhetoric and Composition. University of Lancaster, Lancaster, England, Fulbright lecturer, 1980-81; University of Utah, Salt Lake City, visiting associate professor, 1986; Austin Independent School District, curriculum developer, 1991-92; University of Texas, Brownsville, program developer, 1993. University of Texas Humanities Institute, founder, director, 2001—. American-Israeli Council for Israeli-Palestinian Peace, Washington, DC, member of advisory board, 1982-93; Austin Society for Humanistic Judaism, educational and religious director, 1989.

MEMBER: Modern Language Association, American Association of University Professors, American Literature Association.

AWARDS, HONORS: Fulbright fellow, 1980-81; Guggenheim fellow, 1991-92; Best Books of 2006 list, *Kirkus Reviews,* Robert W. Hamilton Book Award for best book of the year by a University of Texas faculty member, University Cooperative Society, 2007, both for *Patriotic Treason: John Brown and the Soul of America.*

WRITINGS:

The Rhetoric of American Romance: Dialectic and Identity in Emerson, and Dickinson, Poe, and Hawthorne, John Hopkins University Press (Baltimore, MD), 1985.
The Marble Faun: Hawthorne's Transformations, Twayne Publishers (New York, NY), 1992.
(Editor, with Alan W. Friedman) *Situating College English: Lessons from an American University,* Bergin & Garvey (Westport, CT), 1996.
(With Gerald Graff and Robert von Hallberg) *The Cambridge History of American Literature,* Volume 8: *Poetry and Criticism, 1940-1995,* Cambridge University Press (New York, NY), 1996.
(Editor, with Sylvia Gale) *Writing Austin's Lives: A Community Portrait,* Waterloo Press, 2004.
Patriotic Treason: John Brown and the Soul of America, Free Press (New York, NY), 2006.

Contributor of chapters to scholarly books, including *When Boys Cry: Revisiting American Masculinity,* edited by Milette Shamir and Jennifer Travis, Colum-

bia University Press (New York, NY), 2002; and *Historicizing Theory,* edited by Peter Herman, State University of New York Press (New York, NY), 2004. Contributor of articles to journals, including *American Literature, Raritan, Tikkun, American Literary History,* and *ESQ.*

SIDELIGHTS: Evan Carton is an English professor who specializes in nineteenth-and twentieth-century American literature and literary history. The author of numerous books of criticism, Carton published a biography of the famous American abolitionist, John Brown, in 2006. In *Patriotic Treason: John Brown and the Soul of America,* Carton explores several long-term interests, including race relations in the United States, transcendentalism, and the abolitionist movement.

In October of 1859, Brown staged a raid on the U.S. arsenal at Harper's Ferry, Virginia, an attack meant to cause slaves to rise against their masters en masse. He was hanged for treason several months later. Though the attack itself failed, Brown did manage to put slavery at the forefront of a long overdue national discussion. During the Civil War, "John Brown's Body" became something of an iconic hymn and marching song for the Northern army, and Brown himself became a symbol, over time, of resistance to slavery and the abolitionist movement. Writing in the Tacoma, Washington, *News Tribune,* Pat McCoid found Carton's work an "engrossing and thorough narrative history," detailing the background and the repercussions to Brown's raid. McCoid further wrote, "What makes Brown's story compelling is his unwavering dedication to an ideal." Carton makes abundant use of letters by Brown, his family, and friends in *Patriotic Treason* to provide a portrait of Brown both as a failed family man and a devoted activist. "I wanted to write a human story, not just a stereotype," Carton explained to *America's Intelligence Wire* contributor Jamie Mayes. Michael O'Donnell, writing in the *San Francisco Chronicle,* noted: "Throughout the book, Carton emphasizes Brown's deep Calvinist faith as well as his status as something of a deadbeat dad (antislavery work took him away from his family for months at a time)." A contributor for *Publishers Weekly* felt *Patriotic Treason* is "an absorbing and inspiring, though not wholly innovative, biography." Higher praise came from *Booklist* contributor Margaret Flanagan, who termed the biography an "intriguing portrait," and from a *Kirkus Reviews* critic who praised the work as a "bold account," as well as a "rare humanizing of an icon."

BIOGRAPHICAL AND CRITICAL SOURCES:

PERIODICALS

America's Intelligence Wire, June 11, 2003, "U. Texas-Austin: English Professor Records Austin's Oral Narratives"; September 13, 2006, Jamie Mayes, review of *Patriotic Treason: John Brown and the Soul of America.*
Booklist, August 1, 2006, Margaret Flanagan, review of *Patriotic Treason*, p. 31.
Kirkus Reviews, June 15, 2006, review of *Patriotic Treason*, p. 610.
Library Journal, July 1, 2006, Theresa McDevitt, review of *Patriotic Treason*, p. 87.
News Tribune (Tacoma, WA), November 19, 2006, Pat McCoid, review of *Patriotic Treason*.
Publishers Weekly, June 5, 2006, review of *Patriotic Treason*, p. 48.
San Francisco Chronicle, October 23, 2006, Michael O'Donnell, review of *Patriotic Treason*.

ONLINE

Austin Chronicle, http://www.austinchronicle.com/ (October 27, 2006), Spencer Parsons, "The War at Home."
BookPage, http://www.bookpage.com/ (April 9, 2007), Roger Bishop, review of *Patriotic Treason*.
Curled Up with a Good Book, http://www.curledup.com/ (April 9, 2007), Barbara Bamberger Scott, review of *Patriotic Treason*.
University of Texas at Austin Department of English Web site, http://www.utexas.edu/ (April 9, 2007), faculty profile of author.

*   *   *

CARVER, Maryann
See CARVER, Maryann Burk

*   *   *

CARVER, Maryann Burk 1941(?)-
(Maryann Carver)

PERSONAL: Born c. 1941.

CAREER: Writer.

WRITINGS:

(Edited by Sam Halpert) *When We Talk about Raymond Carver: Conversations With Maryann Carver*, G. Smith (Layton, UT), 1991.
What It Used to Be Like: A Portrait of My Marriage to Raymond Carver, St. Martin's Press (New York, NY), 2006.

SIDELIGHTS: The widow of writer Raymond Carver, Maryann Burk Carver wrote a 2006 reminiscence of her turbulent life with the innovative poet and short-story writer. *What It Used to Be Like: A Portrait of My Marriage to Raymond Carver* is an "exacting memoir [that] also presents an unsparing chronicle of entrenched sexism, as well as the boundless joys and demands of marriage and parenthood," according to Donna Seaman in her *Booklist* review of the book. Married to Carver while still in high school, Maryann soon had two children, and a husband driven by his need to write. Other demons pursued him as well; his troubles with alcohol and women have been well documented, and somehow, throughout it all, Maryann stayed with him, always hoping for a fresh start. Money was always scarce until belated fame came Carver's way, and the family lived a peripatetic life, moving from city to city, college to college. Physical abuse was also part of the marriage, and finally, after twenty-seven years of marriage, the couple divorced in 1982, and Carver went on to marry the poet Tess Gallagher before dying at the age of fifty in 1988. Meanwhile, Maryann had long before given up on her youthful plans for law school.

Reviewers largely praised the frankness with which Maryann Carver portrayed her years with her husband. Writing in *Library Journal*, Valeda Dent noted that the author "artfully documents their 27-year marriage with clarity and insight." Similarly, a critic for *Kirkus Reviews* termed the memoir "a bittersweet account of the author's hardscrabble life with her husband." A *Publishers Weekly* reviewer, however, was less impressed with *What It Used to Be Like,* noting that "while [Carver's] story offers some biographical insights . . . it's essentially a cliche-filled tale of the artist's suffering wife." Jonathan Yardley, writing in the *Washington Post Book World,* also commented on the author's "perky, gee-whiz tone to her prose that is ill-suited to what is a cautionary tale if not a downright sad one." Yet Yardley also found the memoir "interesting and instructive and in some ways quite moving." Higher praise came from *Seattle Post-Intelligencer* critic Scott Driscoll, who called the book "a heartbreaking, but bravely told, love story."

BIOGRAPHICAL AND CRITICAL SOURCES:

BOOKS

Carver, Maryann Burk, *What It Used to Be Like: A Portrait of My Marriage to Raymond Carver,* St. Martin's Press (New York, NY), 2006.

PERIODICALS

Booklist, June 1, 2006, Donna Seaman, review of *What It Used to Be Like,* p. 25.
Boston Globe, August 6, 2006, Barbara Fisher, review of *What It Used to Be Like.*
Kirkus Reviews, May 15, 2006, review of *What It Used to Be Like,* p. 503.
Library Journal, August 1, 2006, Valeda Dent, review of *What It Used to Be Like,* p. 87.
New York Times Book Review, September 24, 2006, Joyce Johnson, review of *What It Used to Be Like.*
Publishers Weekly, May 15, 2006, review of *What It Used to Be Like,* p. 64.
Seattle Post-Intelligencer, July 21, 2006, Scott Driscoll, review of *What It Used to Be Like.*
Washington Post Book World, July 16, 2006, Jonathan Yardley, review of *What It Used to Be Like,* p. 2.*

*   *   *

CHAYES, Sarah 1962-

PERSONAL: Born 1962, in Washington, DC; daughter of Abram (a law professor) and Antonia (former undersecretary of the Air Force) Chayes. *Education:* Harvard University, B.A., M.A.

CAREER: Writer, journalist. Monitor Radio, Boston, MA, reporter, 1991-1995; National Public Radio, correspondent, 1996-2002. Afghans for Civil Society, aid worker; Arghand Cooperative, director and founder. Served in the Peace Corps.

AWARDS, HONORS: Radcliffe College History Prize, for the best thesis written by a woman, 1984; Foreign Press Club and Sigma Delta Chi awards, 1999; Best Books of 2006 list, *Kirkus Reviews,* for *The Punishment of Virtue: Inside Afghanistan after the Taliban.*

WRITINGS:

The Punishment of Virtue: Inside Afghanistan after the Taliban, Penguin Press (New York, NY), 2006.

Contributor to the *Christian Science Monitor.*

SIDELIGHTS: Sarah Chayes was a National Public Radio correspondent covering the 2002 war in Afghanistan and its aftermath when she decided to take a break from journalism and attempt to do her own part in rebuilding the country. Commenting in an interview for *Frontline/World,* Chayes discussed her motivation for turning from journalism to humanitarian activist: "Afghanistan is a compelling place. . . . As for me, though I've been called a war reporter, I'm not drawn to conflict; I am drawn to what happens afterward, to the chaos and promise of societies recovering from war. . . . I'm also rather spartan in my habits and tastes, and I think it's the ruggedness of this land and its people, their tenaciousness, their refusal to bend—sometimes to a fault—that draws me. And in contrast to other places I'd been, notably the Balkans, I felt strongly there were a few people acting in the true interests of their country. I felt I just had to throw my lot in with them."

In 2006 Chayes, who has continued to live and work in Afghanistan, published *The Punishment of Virtue: Inside Afghanistan after the Taliban,* an examination of what went wrong after American and other international forces occupied the country. In the work, Chayes criticizes the United States government for allowing war lords to resume their brutal grip on power in various regions of Afghanistan and for allowing the Taliban to infiltrate the country once again. Chayes blames the Bush administration's "war on terror" for distracting the United States from its real mission in Afghanistan. The author also faults neighboring Pakistan for aiding the escalation of violence in Afghanistan. Reviewing *The Punishment of Virtue* in *Booklist,* Jay Freeman felt it is not "a balanced account," but "given her knowledge and experience, [Chayes] merits attention." Higher praise came from *Weekly Standard* contributor Vance Serchuk, who called *The Punishment of Virtue* "arguably the best book yet about politics and power in Afghanistan after the Taliban." Serchuk went on to note that the book is not intended as objective journalism, but rather "an impressionistic, and intensely personal, account of one intrepid explorer there." Similarly, a *Kirkus Reviews* critic called it "absorbing reading," while a *Publishers Weekly* contributor felt that Chayes's "hands-on experience as a deeply immersed reporter and activist gives her lucid analysis and prescriptions a practical scope and persuasive authority." Further praise came from *Time International* writer Aryn Baker, who found the book "haunting and passionate," as well as a "disturbing read." And for David Rohde, writing in the *New York Times Book Review*, *The Punishment of Virtue* is an "engrossing account."

BIOGRAPHICAL AND CRITICAL SOURCES:

PERIODICALS

American Prospect, January-February, 2007, review of *The Punishment of Virtue: Inside Afghanistan after the Taliban,* p. 37.

Booklist, July 1, 2006, Jay Freeman, review of *The Punishment of Virtue,* p. 23.

Boston Globe, May 9, 2006, Declan Walsh, "American Activist Finds Her Calling in Afghan Hot Spot."

Kirkus Reviews, June 15, 2006, review of *The Punishment of Virtue,* p. 611.

Newsday, August 20, 2006, Roy Gutman, review of *The Punishment of Virtue.*

New York Times Book Review, September 17, 2006, David Rohde, review of *The Punishment of Virtue,* p. 33.

Publishers Weekly, June 5, 2006, review of *The Punishment of Virtue,* p. 53.

Time International, January 15, 2007, Aryn Baker, review of *The Punishment of Virtue,* p. F4.

Weekly Standard, January 1, 2007, Vance Serchuk, "The Other War; One Afghan City and American Foreign Policy."

ONLINE

Democracy Now!, http://www.democracynow.org/ (October 10, 2006), "Sarah Chayes on Life in Afghanistan after the Taliban and Why She Left NPR."

Frontline/World, http://www.pbs.org/frontlineworld/ (April 9, 2007), "Interview with Sarah Chayes: Danger, Determination and Destiny."

Transom, http://www.transom.org/ (April 9, 2007), "Sarah Chayes."

OTHER

A House for Haji Baba (video), PBS/Frontline/World, 2003.*

*   *   *

CHESS, Stella 1914-2007

OBITUARY NOTICE— See index for *CA* sketch: Born March 1, 1914, in New York, NY; died of pneumonia, March 14, 2007, in New York, NY. Psychiatrist, educator, and author. Chess was a child psychologist who is best remembered for her theories about childhood temperament and the effects of conflicting child-parent temperaments. Completing undergraduate work at Smith College in 1935, she earned her M.D. from New York University in 1939. After her internship and residency, she set up a private practice in New York City in 1942. She quickly began to focus on child psychiatry, serving as a resident at the Riverdale Children's Association and as a psychiatrist at the Northside Center for Child Development, becoming chief coordinating psychiatrist at the latter through most of the 1950s. She directed the child psychiatry clinic at Metropolitan Hospital during the early 1960s. By the 1950s, she and her psychiatrist husband, Alexander Thomas, were conducting research on human development that would lead to their theories about childhood temperaments. They came to believe that temperament was inherent, and that children typically fell into one of three categories: difficult, easy, or slow to warm up. Furthermore, if a child's temperament was not compatible with its parents—especially the mother—this could lead to psychological distress in the infant. Their early findings were published in 1960; later research indicated that temperaments could evolve over time and were not necessarily fixed, however. In addition to her active practice, Chess taught at the New York Medical College from 1949 until 1966. She then joined the New York University faculty in 1966, becoming a full professor in 1970 and directing child and adolescent psychiatric services.

Chess continued to teach there even after she turned ninety. In addition to her *An Introduction to Child Psychiatry* (1959; 2nd edition, 1969), she was coauthor of such books as *Your Child Is a Person: A Psychological Approach to Parenthood without Guilt* (1965), *Temperament and Development* (1977), *Know Your Child: An Authoritative Guide for Today's Parents* (1987), and *Goodness of Fit: Clinical Applications from Infancy through Adult Life* (1999).

OBITUARIES AND OTHER SOURCES:

PERIODICALS

New York Times, March 22, 2007, p. A23.

*   *   *

CLARE, Horatio 1973-

PERSONAL: Born 1973, in London, England. *Education:* Attended Atlantic College and York University.

ADDRESSES: Home—London, England; Breconshire, South Wales. *Agent*—Tina Bennett, Janklow & Nesbit, 445 Park Ave., New York, NY 10022; Tif Loehnis, Janklow & Nesbit UK, 33 Drayson Mews, Kensington, London, England.

CAREER: Journalist, radio producer, writer. British Broadcasting Corportaion (BBC) Radio Art Department, researcher and producer for *Front Row Nightwaves,* and *The Verb,* 1998-2005.

AWARDS, HONORS: Guardian First Book Award long list, 2006, and Young Writer of the Year Award nominee, *Sunday Times,* 2007, for *Running for the Hills: A Memoir;* Somerset Maugham Award, 2007; Glen Dimplex/Irish Writers Centre New Writing Prize short list.

WRITINGS:

Running for the Hills: Growing Up on My Mother's Sheep Farm in Wales, Scribner (New York, NY), 2006, published as *Running for the Hills: A Memoir,* John Murray (London, England), 2006.

Sicily through Writers' Eyes, Eland Books (London, England), 2006.
Truant: Tales from the Road of Excess, John Murray (London, England), 2006.

Contributor to books, including *Red City: Marrakech through Writers' Eyes,* Sicklemoon Books, 2004; and *Meetings with Remarkable Muslims,* Eland Books (London, England), 2005. Contributor of articles and essays to periodicals, including the *Spectator, New Statesman, Guardian, Financial Times, Sunday Times, Daily Telegraph,* and *Vogue.*

SIDELIGHTS: A former radio producer at BBC Radio in London, Horatio Clare plumbed his experiences growing up on a remote farm in Wales in his 2006 memoir, *Running for the Hills: Growing Up on My Mother's Sheep Farm in Wales.* Clare is the son of London journalists who, in the late 1960s fell in love with and bought the farm, hoping to live out a rural idyll life. However, the harsh life of sheep farming proved divisive to the parents. Separated and then divorced, the father returned to his London career, and young Clare, along with his brother, stayed on the farm with their mother, trying to make a go of it. Finally, however, after several years, they were forced to sell and move on. Speaking with *Bookseller* contributor Benedicte Page, Clare explained part of the inspiration for writing this memoir: "I wanted to write a biography of my parents' divorce for my own reasons. If you think about the time just before you were born, how your parents were then—that was a sort of golden summer, a myth for me. I wanted to find out how true that was and what had happened to it."

Reviewers on both sides of the Atlantic responded positively to this debut work. A contributor for the London *Times* termed *Running for the Hills* a "beautifully observed memoir," while Page found it a "deeply personal story related in graceful and sensitive prose." A reviewer for the *Economist* felt the book was "lifted by its sense of joy and spiritual freedom," and was furthermore "a forgiving tribute to parents who paid a price for following their hearts." Similar praise greeted the American publication of the memoir. A *Kirkus Reviews* critic commended the "remarkably even-handed portraits of [Clare's] parents [that] present their flaws and foibles with generosity and sensitivity." And a *Publishers Weekly* contributor concluded: "Beautifully written, with enormous affection, this is a memoir of an unusual childhood, but also a careful analysis of a 'perfectly, heroically mismatched' marriage."

Clare told *CA:* "I have wanted to write for as long as I can remember. We grew up without television (there was a mountain in the way of the signal), so books were a central part of my childhood. The thrill of storytelling and a love of language were implanted in my brother and me at an early age. Our father loved reading to us and our mother filled the long motorway drive from London to South Wales with retellings of Shakespeare's plays, and dramatic stories from British history. I have been influenced by a great range of writers, from Percy Bysshe Shelley to Alastair Maclean, Samuel Taylor Coleridge to James Baldwin, Dylan Thomas, and Kurt Vonnegut. I read indiscriminately across different forms, genres, and nationalities. When I sit down to do it I know very clearly what the job is—to pursue truth, through clarity and honesty. While still quite young my brother and I were given a volume of George Orwell's essays by my father. 'If you want to write well,' he said, 'write like this.' I tend to do it late at night, with cigarettes (which I am hoping to quit) and coffee (which I am not). Though my books are sold as memoirs they are more like biographies of the (too few) lives and times I have so far seen. I have a feeling that fiction—the techniques of fiction—may be the best way to chase truth. Fiction seems to come closer to clarity than nonfiction, which leads into the clouds of fact. The most surprising thing I have learned through writing is that I am much more honest, in many ways a better person, on paper than I am in life."

BIOGRAPHICAL AND CRITICAL SOURCES:

BOOKS

Clare, Horatio, *Running for the Hills: Growing Up on My Mother's Sheep Farm in Wales,* Scribner (New York, NY), 2006.
Clare, Horatio *Truant: Tales from the Road of Excess,* John Murray (London, England), 2006.

PERIODICALS

Bookseller, November 11, 2005, Benedicte Page, "Biography of a Divorce," p. 23.

Economist, March 18, 2006, review of *Running for the Hills,* p. 81.
Financial Times (London, England), April 1, 2006, Horatio Clare, "Unhappy Endings," p. 7.
Kirkus Reviews, June 15, 2006, review of *Running for the Hills,* p. 612.
Publishers Weekly, May 1, 2006, review of *Running for the Hills,* p. 45.
Times (London, England), March 11, 2007, "And the Shortlist Is . . . . "

ONLINE

Calgary Sun Online, http://www.calgarysun.canoe.ca/ (July 30, 2006), Yvonne Crittenden, review of *Running for the Hills.*
Guardian Online, http://books.guardian.co.uk/ (March 25, 2006), Daniel Butler, review of *Running for the Hills.*
London Daily Mail Online, http://www.dailymail.co.uk/ (February 8, 2007), Nigel Jones, review of *Running for the Hills.*

*   *   *

CLAVIN, Tom 1954-

PERSONAL: Born July 25, 1954, in New York, NY; son of Joseph Francis and Gertrude Anne Clavin; married Nancy Claire Hamma, August 8, 1976; children: Kathryn, Brendan. *Education:* University of Southern California, B.A., 1976; State University of New York, Stonybrook, M.A., 1994.

ADDRESSES: Home—Sag Harbor, NY.

CAREER: Writer, journalist, editor. Suffolk Community College, adjunct professor of journalism, 1987-95; *Independent* (newspaper), East Hampton, NY, editor-in-chief, 1993-2003; *Independent* (newspaper), Southampton, NY, editor-in-chief, 1996-2003; *New York Times,* contributing writer.

AWARDS, HONORS: Six-time recipient, best magazine article of the year award, Society of Professional Journalists.

WRITINGS:

NONFICTION

(With Darlene Powell Hopson and Derek S. Hopson) *Raising the Rainbow Generation: Teaching Your Children to Be Successful in a Multicultural Society,* Simon & Schuster (New York, NY), 1993.

(With Darlene Powell Hopson and Derek S. Hopson) *Juba This and Juba That: 100 African-American Games for Children,* Simon & Schuster (New York, NY), 1996.

(With Martin Obler) *Fatal Analysis: A True Story of Professional Privilege and Murder,* New Horizon Press (Far Hills, NJ), 1997.

(With Bob Bubka) *The Ryder Cup: Golf's Greatest Event,* Crown Publishers (New York, NY), 1999.

Dark Noon: The Final Voyage of the Fishing Boat Pelican, International Marine/McGraw-Hill (Camden, ME), 2005.

Sir Walter: Walter Hagen and the Invention of Professional Golf, Simon & Schuster (New York, NY), 2005.

(With Bob Drury) *Halsey's Typhoon: The True Story of a Fighting Admiral, an Epic Storm, and an Untold Rescue,* Atlantic Monthly Press (New York, NY), 2007.

Contributor to numerous magazines and newspapers, including *Reader's Digest, Golf Magazine, Men's Journal, Woman's Day, Parade,* and *Family Circle.*

SIDELIGHTS: Tom Clavin is a newspaper editor and journalist who has written on topics from sports to the environment. He has also authored numerous book-length nonfiction works, both collaborating with others and writing on his own. His 1993 book *Raising the Rainbow Generation: Teaching Your Children to Be Successful in a Multicultural Society,* written with Darlene Powell Hopson and Derek S. Hopson, is an examination of the origins of racial and ethnic stereotyping, and serves as a guide for parents to raise children without such preconceptions. A reviewer for *Publishers Weekly* found this a "needed" work, with advice that was "realistic, not Pollyannaish, and well-focused, not preachy." In *Fatal Analysis: A True Story of Professional Privilege and Murder,* written with the psychologist Martin Obler, Clavin tells the purportedly real story of a client of Obler's—named Devon Car-

don in the book—whom the psychologist comes to realize is a serial killer. Obler is subsequently torn between professional ethics and a moral need to report the man to the police. For Brian McCombie, writing in *Booklist, Fatal Analysis* presents a "disturbing examination of professional ethics at odds with one's responsibility as a human being." A *Publishers Weekly* reviewer had a more mixed opinion of the book, observing: "Despite wooden descriptions and stilted dialogue, the authors produce a brisk read."

Clavin turned to sports for other titles. *The Ryder Cup: Golf's Greatest Event* provides a historical background to this rivalry between golfers from the United States and Europe. Writing with fellow golf journalist Bob Bubka, Clavin also offered a preview of the 1999 competition with an in-depth description of the 1997 meeting. Writing in *Booklist,* Ilene Cooper noted: "Even those who thought they knew the ins and outs of the Ryder Cup will be caught up in the drama." A reviewer for *Publishers Weekly* concluded that *The Ryder Cup* was "for the true golf fan, the one that shoots 36 holes in subarctic temperatures and is unhappy when darkness falls." Clavin's 2005 title, *Sir Walter: Walter Hagen and the Invention of Professional Golf,* provides a biographical portrait of the man who changed the way golf was perceived by the American public. Growing up poor, Hagen worked as a caddie as a youth. He learned the game from the men whose bags he carried and went on to win five PGA tournaments as well as championships abroad, earning an impressive living from the sport, and becoming a flashy showcase for golf in his personal life. A reviewer for *Publishers Weekly* commented that Clavin "deftly shows how Hagen's success . . . and his showman's personality inspired the 1920s boom in American golf." This led to increased participation, new courses being built, and to the creation of the PGA itself. The same reviewer also felt that the author "infuses his narrative with impressive facts" and also "captivatingly portrays Hagen's personal life." Richard J. Moss, writing in the *Historian,* felt that *Sir Walter* was a "breezy, full account" of the golfer's life and rise to prominence, but that it "does not ask interesting questions about Hagen and his place in modern sport history." However, Moss went on to conclude that the book "will take its place on a growing list of biographies that collectively have enriched golf history." *Booklist* contributor Bill Ott had higher praise, calling *Sir Walter* "a fascinating slice of golf history."

Halsey's Typhoon: The True Story of a Fighting Admiral, an Epic Storm, and an Untold Rescue, written with Bob Drury, uses newly declassified material to describe one of the major maritime events of World War II, one which had gone largely unreported for decades. The famed Admiral William Halsey was partly responsible for losing three destroyers and eight hundred men when he put his fleet in the path of a 1944 typhoon. The authors recount the pressured decision-making that led to this maritime disaster, as well as the heroic efforts to save fellow sailors in the aftermath. A *Publishers Weekly* reviewer wrote that the book is "a vivid tale of tragedy and gallantry at sea." A *Kirkus Reviews* critic faulted the work for weak characterization, but concluded: "The inherent drama of the events compensates for the sometimes lackluster storytelling." However, Roland Green, writing in *Booklist,* had no such critical reservations, terming *Halsey's Typhoon* "an entirely gripping account and a guaranteed hit with maritime buffs."

BIOGRAPHICAL AND CRITICAL SOURCES:

PERIODICALS

Booklist, February 1, 1997, Brian McCombie, review of *Fatal Analysis: A True Story of Professional Privilege and Murder,* p. 912; April 15, 1999, Ilene Cooper, review of *The Ryder Cup: Golf's Greatest Event,* p. 1500; February 15, 2005, Bill Ott, review of *Sir Walter: Walter Hagen and the Invention of Professional Golf,* p. 1049; November 15, 2006, Roland Green, review of *Halsey's Typhoon: The True Story of a Fighting Admiral, an Epic Storm, and an Untold Rescue,* p. 20.
Historian, fall, 2006, Richard J. Moss, review of *Sir Walter,* p. 571.
Internet Bookwatch, March, 2007, review of *Halsey's Typhoon.*
Kirkus Reviews, October 1, 2006, review of *Halsey's Typhoon,* p. 998.
Library Journal, January 1, 2005, Steven Silkunas, review of *Sir Walter,* p. 119.
Publishers Weekly, November 29, 1993, review of *Raising the Rainbow Generation: Teaching Your Children to Be Successful in a Multicultural Society,* p. 61; November 18, 1996, review of *Fatal Analysis,* p. 52; April 26, 1999, review of *The Ryder Cup,* p. 69; December 13, 2004, review of *Sir Walter,* p. 56; October 9, 2006, review of *Halsey's Typhoon,* p. 47.

ONLINE

Halsey's Typhoon Web site, http://www.halseys typhoon.com (April 9, 2007).*

CLUNE, Jackie 1965(?)-

PERSONAL: Born, c. 1965; partner of Richard Hannant (an actor); children: Saoirse, Thady, Frank, Orla. *Education:* Attended Kent University.

ADDRESSES: Home—London, England.

CAREER: Writer, playwright, singer, comedian, actor, radio broadcaster. Royal Holloway College, former lecturer. Red Rag Women's Theatre Company, cofounder and former troop member; performed at Hackney Empire, Hackney, England. Television performer, including *Comedy Nation, Smack the Pony, Eastenders,* and *Staying in Show.* Performer in *Julie Burchill Is Away,* one-woman show, 2002, and *Sing-a-Long-A Sound of Music,* touring show.

WRITINGS:

Extreme Motherhood: The Triplet Diaries, Macmillan (London, England), 2006.
Man of the Month Club (novel), Putnam (New York, NY), 2006.

Also author of stand-up comedy shows, including *Showstopper, Chicks with Flicks, It's Jackie,* and *Follow the Star!*

SIDELIGHTS: British stand-up comedian Jackie Clune lived a lesbian life for a dozen years, performing one-woman shows throughout the United Kingdom and acting on popular British television shows such as the *Eastenders.* Her lesbianism was grist for her stand-up routines; it also formed the basis for most of her relationships. As she wrote on the *Guardian Online:* "In February 1988, I decided to become a lesbian. For the next 12 years I had relationships with women exclusively. Then, in October 2000, I decided to 'go back in' and went straight. The reasons for both these decisions have by turns appalled, fascinated and challenged almost everyone in my life, from my parents, friends and enemies to the loyal lesbian fan base I had built up during my career as a cabaret artist and comedian." Clune's decision to form a heterosexual relationship led to a romance with an actor, and then to the birth of a daughter and quickly thereafter to the birth of triplets. Clune recounts the joys as well as the tribulations of her new maternal state in the 2006 *Extreme Motherhood: The Triplet Diaries.*

Clune also became a novelist with her 2006 publication, *Man of the Month Club,* the tale of a thirty-nine-year-old woman and her attempts to start a family before her biological clock runs out. Amy Stokes operates a fashionable baby boutique in London and wonders if she will ever find the time or maturity to plunge into motherhood, especially in the absence of any father on the horizon. When circumstances convince her to take the plunge, she decides initially to meet with a different handsome man each month at her time of ovulation. Her plans do not always go smoothly, but finally she meets not only the right father, but also the right partner. A *Kirkus Reviews* critic was not overwhelmed with this chick-lit novel, terming it a "sarcastic, forced debut," as well as "a mildly entertaining read, with a dollop of British appeal." However, Stephanie Schneider, writing on the *Romantic Times Online,* had a higher assessment of *Man of the Month Club,* finding it a "witty and bold tale [that] cuts deep into the hilarity of what the dating world can be like."

BIOGRAPHICAL AND CRITICAL SOURCES:

BOOKS

Clune, Jackie, *Extreme Motherhood: The Triplet Diaries,* Macmillan (London, England), 2006.

PERIODICALS

Bookseller, November 18, 2005, "Quercus Buys Clune Novel," p. 15.
Kirkus Reviews, June 15, 2006, review of *Man of the Month Club,* p. 590.

ONLINE

Comedy CV, http://www.comedycv.co.uk/ (April 9, 2007), "Jackie Clune."
Guardian Online, http://www.guardian.co.uk/ (June 14, 2003), Jackie Clune, "My Crime against the Lesbian State."

Internet Movie Database, http://www.imdb.com/ (April 9, 2007), "Jackie Clune."
Romantic Times, http://www.romantictimes.com/ (April 9, 2007), Stephanie Schneider, review of *Man of the Month Club.*
Scotsman.com, http://living.scotsman.com/ (July 31, 2004), Jackie McGlone, "Send in the Clune."
Trashionista, http://www.trashionista.com/ (April 9, 2007), review of *Man of the Month Club.**

*   *   *

COBB, Matthew
  (Matthew J. Cobb)

PERSONAL: Male.

ADDRESSES: Office—Faculty of Life Sciences, University of Manchester, Michael Smith Bldg., Oxford Rd., Manchester M13 9PT, England. *E-mail*—Matthew.J.Cobb@manchester.ac.uk.

CAREER: Writer, educator. Manchester University, Manchester, England, lecturer.

WRITINGS:

Generation: The 17th-Century Scientists Who Unravelled the Secrets of Sex, Life and Growth, Bloomsbury (New York, NY), 2006, published as *The Egg and Sperm Race: The Seventeenth-Century Scientists Who Unravelled the Secrets of Sex, Life and Growth,* Simon & Schuster (London, England), 2006.

Contributor of articles to professional journals. Contributor of reviews to the *Times Literary Supplement.* Has translated several books.

SIDELIGHTS: A lecturer on animal behavior at England's Manchester University, Matthew Cobb has also researched the history of biology and published numerous articles about seventeenth-century biology. Such research led to the writing of the 2006 title, *Generation: The 17th-Century Scientists Who Unravelled the Secrets of Sex, Life and Growth* (published in England as *The Egg and Sperm Race: The*

Seventeenth-Century Scientists Who Unravelled the Secrets of Sex, Life and Growth). In this work Cobb demonstrates that the understanding that babies are the result of the joining of a sperm and an egg came from a small group of scientists at work in the 1600s. These included the British anatomist William Harvey as well as Dutch researchers of the day, including Jan Swammerdam, Nils Stensen, Reinier de Graaf, and Anton Leeuwenhoek. The book was well received by critics and reviewers. *Booklist* contributor Gilbert Taylor felt *Generation* is "an accessible account of a turning point in the history of physiology." Gilbert also noted that the work is "flavored with tales of rivalry among the scientists." Similarly, a *Kirkus Reviews* critic termed the same work "instructive and pleasing history," while a *Publishers Weekly* reviewer praised the "wealth of historical details" Cobb uses in the narrative. Further praise came from *Natural History* contributor Laurence A. Marschall, who noted, "Cobb's scholarship is as meticulous as the work of his protagonists, and it crackles with lively anecdotes from their scientific reports."

BIOGRAPHICAL AND CRITICAL SOURCES:

PERIODICALS

Booklist, August 1, 2006, Gilbert Taylor, review of *Generation: The 17th-Century Scientists Who Unravelled the Secrets of Sex, Life and Growth,* p. 22.
Kirkus Reviews, June 15, 2006, review of *Generation,* p. 612.
Lancet, December 23, 2006, Roger Cooter, review of *Generation,* p. 60.
Natural History, November, 2006, Laurence A. Marschall, review of *Generation,* p. 62.
Publishers Weekly, June 12, 2006, review of *Generation,* p. 44.
SciTech Book News, December, 2006, review of *Generation.*

ONLINE

Egg-and-Sperm.com, http://www.egg-and-sperm.com (April 9, 2007).
University of Manchester, Faculty of Life Sciences Web site, http://www.ls.manchester.ac.uk/ (April 9, 2007), "Dr. Matthew Cobb."*

COBB, Matthew J.
See COBB, Matthew

*   *   *

COBB, William J. 1957-
(William James Cobb)

PERSONAL: Born 1957. *Education:* Texas State University, San Marcos, B.A.; University of Texas, M.A.; University of Houston, Ph.D.

ADDRESSES: Home—PA; CO. *Office*—Department of English, Pennsylvania State University, 117 Burrowes Bldg., University Park, PA 16802. *E-mail*—wjcobb@gmail.com; wjc7@psu.edu.

CAREER: Writer, educator. Pennsylvania State University, University Park, associate professor.

AWARDS, HONORS: National Endowment for the Arts grant for fiction, 1992; Sandstone Prize, Ohio State University Press, 2002, for *The White Tattoo;* Frank O'Connor Award, 2002, for "What Happens to Rain?"; Jesse Jones Award, Dobie-Paisano Fellowship, 2004.

WRITINGS:

The Fire Eaters (novel), W.W. Norton (New York, NY), 1994.
The White Tattoo (short-story collection), Ohio State University Press (Columbus, OH), 2002.
Goodnight, Texas (novel), Unbridled Books (Denver, CO), 2006.

Contributor of short stories to magazines and journals, including the *New Yorker, Mississippi Review, Antioch Review, New Letters,* and *Puerto del Sol.* Contributor to the *Houston Chronicle* and the *New York Times.*

SIDELIGHTS: William J. Cobb is a novelist and short-story writer whose work is typified by the interaction between characters rather than the necessities of plot. In his short-story collection *The White Tattoo,* he presents a "gallery of losers," according to

New York Times Book Review contributor Patricia Kean. Cobb's characters commit all sorts of violence, but in the title story, the unfortunate protagonist must bear only the pain of a broken heart. Kean found these tales "not for the squeamish," but also noted that Cobb's "quirky, mordant prose survives his penchant for the perverse."

"Quirky" is also the way *Texas Monthly* reviewer Mike Shea described Cobb's 2006 novel, *Goodnight, Texas.* Shea, however, also added "likable" to that description. The novel takes place in the coastal town of Goodnight, Texas, where the local shrimp fishermen are having a hard time because of over-fishing and climate change. When an enormous prehistoric zebra fish washes up on the shore, its belly filled with a small horse, local café owner Gusef wants to put it on top of his establishment to attract the tourist trade and save his endangered business. Other characters try to eke out a living and a life in the small town, including the high school dropout Falk, who is Gusef's cook and longs for Una, the waitress at Gusef's diner, and Gabriel, Una's former beau who has lost his job on a shrimp boat and now flirts and more with the students on the school bus he drives. As a hurricane approaches the small town, the characters seek rescue and redemption. Reviewing the novel in *Booklist,* Ian Chipman noted that Cobb "focuses more on atmospherics than plotting" in this novel that is "vivid yet gracefully understated at times." A *Publishers Weekly* reviewer had higher praise for Cobb's writing, noting that he "expertly exploits the claustrophobic and incestuous atmosphere of smalltown Texas." And for *Library Journal* contributor Joy Humphrey, the same novel was "superbly written, dark and amusing."

BIOGRAPHICAL AND CRITICAL SOURCES:

PERIODICALS

Booklist, September 15, 2006, Ian Chipman, review of *Goodnight, Texas,* p. 26.
Library Journal, September 1, 2006, Joy Humphrey, review of *Goodnight, Texas,* p. 134.
New York Times Book Review, July 14, 2002, Patricia Kean, review of *The White Tattoo,* p. 20.
Publishers Weekly, July 17, 2006, review of *Goodnight, Texas,* p. 133.
Texas Monthly, October, 2006, Mike Shea, review of *Goodnight, Texas,* p. 60.

ONLINE

Curled Up with a Good Book, http://www.curledup. com/ (April 9, 2007), Douglass R. Cobb, review of *Goodnight, Texas.*
Pennsylvania State University Web site, http://english. la.psu.edu/ (April 9, 2007), "William J. Cobb, Associate Professor of English."
William J. Cobb Home Page, http://www.williamj cobb.com (April 9, 2007).*

*   *   *

COBB, William James
    See COBB, William J.

*   *   *

COLLINS, James Michael
    See COLLINS, Jim

*   *   *

COLLINS, Jim 1953-
    (James Michael Collins)

PERSONAL: Born 1953. *Education:* University of Iowa, B.A., Ph.D.

ADDRESSES: Office—Department of Film, Television, and Theater, University of Notre Dame, Notre Dame, IN 46556. *E-mail*—james.m.collins.3@nd.edu.

CAREER: University of Notre Dame, Notre Dame, IN, associate professor of film, television, and popular culture.

WRITINGS:

Uncommon Cultures: Popular Culture and Post-Modernism, Routledge (New York, NY), 1989.
(Editor, with Hilary Radner and Ava Preacher Collins) *Film Theory Goes to the Movies,* Routledge (New York, NY), 1993.

Architectures of Excess: Cultural Life in the Information Age, Routledge (New York, NY), 1995.

(Editor) *High-Pop: Making Culture into Popular Entertainment,* Blackwell Publishers (Malden, MA), 2001.

Contributor to books, including *The Film Cultures Reader,* edited by Graeme Turner, Routledge (New York, NY), 2001.

BIOGRAPHICAL AND CRITICAL SOURCES:

PERIODICALS

Choice, September, 1993, D. Toth, review of *Film Theory Goes to the Movies,* p. 132; September, 2002, J.L. Culross, review of *High-Pop: Making Culture into Popular Entertainment,* p. 82.

Contemporary Literature, spring, 1993, John R. Leo, review of *Uncommon Cultures: Popular Culture and Post-Modernism,* p. 123.

Current Sociology, January, 2004, Maria Gornostaeva, review of *High-Pop,* pp. 91-102.

Film Quarterly, spring, 1994, Wheeler Winston Dixon, review of *Film Theory Goes to the Movies,* p. 54.

JQ: Journalism Quarterly, autumn, 1991, review of *Uncommon Cultures,* p. 577.

Media, Culture, and Society, October, 1990, Mike Cormack, review of *Uncommon Cultures,* p. 547.

Quarterly Journal of Speech, May, 1997, Brian L. Ott, review of *Architectures of Excess: Cultural Life in the Information Age,* pp. 259-260.

Times Literary Supplement, April 6, 1990, Brian Rotman, review of *Uncommon Cultures,* p. 379; April 22, 1994, Robert Potts, review of *Film Theory Goes to the Movies,* pp. 18-19; April 19, 2002, Sandy Starr, review of *High-Pop,* p. 30.*

*   *   *

COLLINS, Suzanne

PERSONAL: Born in NJ; father in the Air Force; married; husband's name Cap.

ADDRESSES: Home and office—CT.

CAREER: Novelist and television scriptwriter. Television writer, beginning 1991. Worked previously as a clinical director of services for adults with learning disabilities, Cambridge Health Authority.

MEMBER: Authors Guild.

AWARDS, HONORS: New York Public Library 100 Books for Reading and Sharing selection, 2003, for *Gregor the Overlander.*

WRITINGS:

"UNDERLAND CHRONICLES"; MIDDLE-GRADE NOVELS

Gregor the Overlander, Scholastic (New York, NY), 2003.

Gregor and the Prophecy of Bane, Scholastic (New York, NY), 2004.

Gregor and the Curse of the Warmbloods, Scholastic (New York, NY), 2005.

Gregor and the Marks of Secret, Scholastic (New York, NY), 2006.

Gregor and the Code of Claw, Scholastic (New York, NY), 2007.

OTHER

When Charlie McButton Lost Power (picture book), illustrated by Mike Lester, Putnam (New York, NY), 2005.

Also author of numerous television scripts, including for programs *Clarissa Explains It All, The Mystery Files of Shelby Woo, Little Bear, Oswald, Santa, Baby!, Clifford's Puppy Days,* and *Generation O!*

ADAPTATIONS: Dan Yaccarino's picture book, *Oswald's Camping Trip,* was based on Collins's script for the *Oswald* television program. The "Underland Chronicles" were adapted as audiobooks.

SIDELIGHTS: Suzanne Collins, who has worked as a writer on such television programs as *Clarissa Explains It All, Little Bear,* and *Oswald,* did not plan to write a novel for children. After a conversation with children's book author and illustrator Joe Proimos, however, she was convinced to give it a try. The resulting novel, *Gregor the Overlander,* became the first installment in Collins's "Underland Chronicles," a series of *Alice in Wonderland*-esque tales that find Gregor traversing an urban environment. Collins, who lived in New York City for sixteen years, wanted to gear her fantasy toward cosmopolitan young readers who are more familiar with city streets that sunlit meadows. As a contributor to the Scholastic Web site noted of Collins's inspiration, "in New York City, you're much more likely to fall down a manhole than a rabbit hole and, if you do, you're not going to find a tea party."

Gregor's adventures begin in *Gregor the Overlander* when he follows his two-year-old sister, Boots, through an air duct and into the world below. What he finds in the Underland is not only a hidden human society, but also giant-sized rats, cockroaches, and spiders that are able to communicate in the humans' language. When Gregor arrives, the Underland is on the brink of war—a war that threatens to spread into the Overland, first to Manhattan and then throughout the world. Gregor's first thought is to get home—until he overhears that his father, who has gone missing, may now be in the Underland and need his son's help. Gregor makes new friends in the giant rat Ripred, Temp the cockroach, and Luxa, a mysterious human girl, and together they search for the missing man and put Gregor on track to his destiny.

As Collins told Jen Rees in an interview posted on Collins's home page, she selected the Underland setting because "I liked the fact that this world was teeming under New York City and nobody was aware of it. That you could be going along preoccupied with your own problems and then whoosh! You take a wrong turn in your laundry room and suddenly a giant cockroach is right in your face. No magic, no space or time travel, there's just a ticket to another world behind your clothes dryer." She "creates a fascinating, vivid, highly original world and a superb story to go along with it," wrote Ed Sullivan in a *Booklist* review of *Gregor the Overlander,* while a *Kirkus Reviews* contributor described Collins's story line as a "luminous, supremely absorbing quest." Steven Engelfried, writing in *School Library Journal,* wrote that the story's "plot threads unwind smoothly, and the pace of the book is just right."

As the "Underland Chronicles" series continues, Gregor fulfils a prophecy and becomes a leader in the Un-

derland. Together with his companions Ripred, Temp, and Luxa, in *Gregor and the Prophecy of Bane,* Gregor continues his adventures, undertaking to rescue a kidnap victim named Boots. In her sequel, Collins once again showcases her "careful attention to detail, pacing, and character development," in the opinion of *Horn Book* reviewer Kitty Flynn, and Sullivan dubbed the novel's protagonist "courageous, selfless, and ultimately triumphant." In the third book in the series, *Gregor and the Curse of the Warmbloods,* Gregor's enemy is not an army, but a plague, one that his mother contracts. "Collins maintains the momentum, charm, and vivid settings of the original title," wrote Tasha Saecker her *School Library Journal* review of this title. *Gregor and the Curse of the Warmbloods* "delivers the breakneck adventure and strong characters readers have come to expect," wrote a contributor to *Kirkus Reviews,* and Flynn concluded that, with this third series installment, "character development, plotting, pacing, and description all shine."

Gregor returns in *Gregor and the Marks of Secret,* which finds some of the humans' allies in trouble. Together with Gregor, Luxa and Temp attempt to save the day, and "the breathless pace, intense drama, and extraordinary challenges" of their quest "will leave fans clamoring" for more, according to *School Library Journal* reviewer Mara Alpert. In *Horn Book,* Flynn commented that "vivid description, expert pacing, and subtle character development all enhance" Collins's fourth "gripping fantasy adventure."

Along with her "Underland Chronicles," Collins has produced a picture-book text featuring illustrations by Mike Lester. In the rhyming text of *When Charlie McButton Lost Power,* Charlie spends most of his time playing video games, but must find a new way to entertain himself when his home's power goes out. A contributor to *Children's Bookwatch* called Collins's tale "refreshingly original and moving."

BIOGRAPHICAL AND CRITICAL SOURCES:

PERIODICALS

Booklist, November 15, 2003, Ed Sullivan, review of *Gregor the Overlander,* p. 608; September 1, 2004, Ed Sullivan, review of *Gregor and the Prophecy of Bane,* p. 120; July, 2005, Ed Sullivan, review of *Gregor and the Curse of the Warmbloods,* p. 1924.

Bulletin of the Center for Children's Books, January, 2004, Janice Del Negro, review of *Gregor the Overlander,* p. 185; October, 2004, Timnah Card, review of *Gregor and the Prophecy of Bane,* p. 65; September, 2005, Timnah Card, review of *Gregor and the Curse of the Warmbloods,* p. 11.

Children's Bookwatch, June, 2005, review of *When Charlie McButton Lost Power.*

Horn Book, September-October, 2003, Kitty Flynn, review of *Gregor the Overlander,* p. 609; September-October, 2004, Kitty Flynn, review of *Gregor and the Prophecy of Bane,* p. 578; July-August, 2005, Kitty Flynn, review of *Gregor and the Curse of the Warmbloods,* p. 467; July-August, 2006, Kitty Flynn, review of *Gregor and the Marks of Secret,* p. 437.

Kirkus Reviews, August 1, 2003, review of *Gregor the Overlander,* p. 1014; December 1, 2003, review of *Gregor the Overlander,* p. 1402; August 1, 2004, review of *Gregor and the Prophecy of Bane,* p. 739; May 1, 2005, review of *When Charlie McButton Lost Power,* p. 536; June 15, 2005, review of *Gregor and the Curse of the Warmbloods,* p. 680; May 15, 2006, review of *Gregor and the Marks of Secret,* p. 515.

Publishers Weekly, September 8, 2003, review of *Gregor the Overlander,* p. 77.

School Library Journal, November, 2003, Steven Engelfried, review of *Gregor the Overlander,* p. 134; October, 2004, Beth Meister, review of *Gregor and the Prophecy of Bane,* p. 160; July, 2005, Tasha Saecker, review of *Gregor and the Curse of the Warmbloods,* p. 100; July, 2005, Barbara Auerbach, review of *When Charlie McButton Lost Power,* p. 71; September, 2006, Mara Alpert, review of *Gregor and the Marks of Secret,* p. 202.

Voice of Youth Advocates, April, 2004, review of *Gregor and the Prophecy of Bane,* p. 21; December, 2004, review of *Gregor and the Prophecy of Bane,* p. 402.

ONLINE

Scholastic Web site, http://www.scholastic.com/ (April 28, 2007), "Suzanne Collins."

Suzanne Collins Home Page, http://suzannecollins books.com (April 28, 2007).*

COOK, James F. 1940-

PERSONAL: Born December 3, 1940, in Balboa, Panama Canal Zone; son of James F., Sr. (in U.S. Navy) and Alma (a homemaker) Jenkins; married April 16, 1964; wife's name Ida B. (a nurse); children: Sean H., James F. *Education:* Young Harris College, A.A.; Emory University, B.A.; Georgia State University, M.A.; University of Georgia, Ph.D. *Politics:* Republican. *Religion:* Presbyterian. *Hobbies and other interests:* Playing guitar, gardening, travel.

ADDRESSES: Home—Cedartown, GA. *E-mail*—jcook@highlands.edu.

CAREER: Floyd Junior College (now Georgia Highlands College), Rome, GA, professor of history, 1970-2000.

MEMBER: Georgia Historical Society, Georgia Association of Historians (life member; president, 1983-84), Polk County Historical Society (president, 1989-91), Optimist Club of Cedartown (life member; president, 1976-77, 1995-96).

AWARDS, HONORS: Alex Bealer Award, Atlanta Historical Society.

WRITINGS:

The Governors of Georgia, Strode (Huntsville, AL), 1979, 3rd edition, Mercer University Press (Macon, GA), 2005.

Carl Sanders: Spokesman of the New South, Mercer University Press (Macon, GA), 1993.

Carl Vinson: Patriarch of the Armed Forces, Mercer University Press (Macon, GA), 2004.

We Fly by Night: The History of Floyd College, McNaughton & Gunn (Saline, MI), 2007.

*   *   *

CORERA, Gordon

PERSONAL: Born in London, England. *Education:* Graduated from St. Peter's College, Oxford University; attended Harvard University graduate school.

CAREER: Journalist, writer. BBC news, reporter, U.S. State Department correspondent, foreign affairs reporter, security correspondent. Previously foreign affairs reporter for BBC Radio 4.

WRITINGS:

Shopping for Bombs: Nuclear Proliferation, Global Insecurity, and the Rise and Fall of the A.Q. Khan Network, Oxford University Press (Oxford, NY), 2006.

SIDELIGHTS: Gordon Corera is a BBC correspondent who specializes in security matters. In his 2006 work of nonfiction, *Shopping for Bombs: Nuclear Proliferation, Global Insecurity, and the Rise and Fall of the A.Q. Khan Network,* he examines one of the worst cases of nuclear proliferation on record. Khan, known as the father of the Pakistani bomb, was a young metallurgist in 1971 when Pakistan lost the 1971 war to India. That defeat convinced him he must help his country get an atomic bomb. To that end, as a research scientist in Holland, he stole secrets that enabled Pakistan to build such a weapon. Thereafter, Khan made a profitable living for himself selling nuclear secrets to such rogue states as Libya and North Korea. Though other governments, including that of the United States, long suspected this nuclear black market, other concerns, including the Cold War, diverted attention. It was only in 2004 that the CIA finally presented the Pakistani government with the proof of his behavior; Khan was subsequently subjected to house arrest.

Corera tells this story like a "page-turner," according to a reviewer for the *Economist.* Likewise, a contributor for *California Bookwatch* called *Shopping for Bombs* an "eye-opening analysis." A *Publishers Weekly* critic commented that Corera presents a "measured account." Similarly, Bruce Harding, writing in the *New Zealand International Review,* found the work a "careful descriptive account," as well as "scary." Harding concluded: "Corera's stunning research and detective work have generated in *Shopping for Bombs* a most important book that must be read, and read widely." Bret Stephens, writing in *Commentary,* also had praise for the author, observing: "It is to Corera's great credit that he tells his story straight, without much by way of editorial interpolation or obvious ideological bias."

BIOGRAPHICAL AND CRITICAL SOURCES:

PERIODICALS

Arms Control Today, October, 2006, review of *Shopping for Bombs: Nuclear Proliferation, Global Insecurity, and the Rise and Fall of the A.Q. Khan Network,* p. 51.
BBC Monitoring International Reports, September 27, 2006, "UK Arab Paper Reports BBC Correspondent's Lecture on Nuclear Proliferation."
California Bookwatch, February, 2007, review of *Shopping for Bombs.*
Commentary, November, 2006, Bret Stephens, review of *Shopping for Bombs,* p. 68.
Economist, July 29, 2006, review of *Shopping for Bombs,* p. 75.
New Zealand International Review, November-December, 2006, Bruce Harding, review of *Shopping for Bombs,* p. 28.
Publishers Weekly, July 31, 2006, review of *Shopping for Bombs,* p. 71.

ONLINE

Asia Times Online, http://www.atimes.com/ (December 2, 2006), Sreeram Chaulia, review of *Shopping for Bombs.*
BBC Online, http://www.bbc.co.uk/ (April 9, 2007), "Gordon Corera, Security Correspondent."*

* * *

CRAIG, Kit
See REED, Kit

* * *

CREESE, Mary Rose Stewart Weir
See CREESE, Mary R.S.

* * *

CREESE, Mary R.S. 1935-
(Mary Rose Stewart Weir Creese)

PERSONAL: Born December 22, 1935, in Orkney, Scotland; daughter of Walter George (a minister) and Annie (an elementary schoolteacher) Weir; married

Thomas Creese (a professor of mathematics), July 5, 1964; children: Anna E.S., Catherine S.K. *Ethnicity:* "Native Scottish." *Education:* University of Glasgow, B.Sc. (with first-class honors), 1967; University of California, Berkeley, Ph.D., 1961. *Hobbies and other interests:* Gardening.

ADDRESSES: Home—Lawrence, KS. *E-mail*—creese@math.ku.edu.

CAREER: University of British Columbia, Vancouver, British Columbia, Canada, research associate in chemistry, 1961-62; University of Alberta, Calgary, Alberta, Canada, assistant professor of chemistry, 1962-64; Kansas State University, Manhattan, research associate in chemistry, 1964-65; University of Kansas, Lawrence, research assistant in medicinal chemistry, 1966-89, research assistant in history of science, 1989-91; writer, 1991—.

AWARDS, HONORS: Cited for outstanding academic book in the history of science and technology, *Choice,* 1998, for *Ladies in the Laboratory? American and British Women in Science, 1800-1900: A Survey of Their Contributions to Research.*

WRITINGS:

(With husband, Thomas M. Creese) *Ladies in the Laboratory? American and British Women in Science, 1800-1900: A Survey of Their Contributions to Research,* Scarecrow Press (Lanham, MD), 1998.
(With Thomas M. Creese) *Ladies in the Laboratory II: West European Women in Science, 1800-1900; A Survey of Their Contributions to Research,* Scarecrow Press (Lanham, MD), 2004.

Contributor to reference books. Contributor of articles and reviews to periodicals, including *Endeavour.*

SIDELIGHTS: Mary R.S. Creese told *CA:* "In the late 1980s, when I first became interested in the contributions of nineteenth-century women to scientific research, the field, now a recognized subdivision of the history of science, was still in its infancy. A tremendous amount of material lay waiting to be examined, interpreted, and brought to light. My initial systematic reading of major catalogues of nineteenth-century literature very quickly produced names of now-forgotten women scientists; I was eager to find out as much as I could about them. Since then I have become more and more immersed in this field that is a combination of research and biographical writing—research into a largely forgotten part of the past that offers a glimpse into the lives of some fascinating, at times very colorful, women who pioneered women's entry into modern scientific research two or three generations ago. Over the last decade or so I have been invited to contribute to more and more projects, such as essay collections and national biographical dictionaries.

"In recent years both social historians and women's history specialists have made many contributions to the history of women in science, bringing their own distinctive approaches to the field. However, more input from writers with extensive scientific background is also needed before a realistic and balanced picture can be achieved. (For example, it is difficult to evaluate the research output of a productive past marine biologist without knowing something about her specialty—no small matter.) Coming from a science research background, I hope to help overcome such difficulties."

BIOGRAPHICAL AND CRITICAL SOURCES:

PERIODICALS

Choice, October, 1998, M.H. Chaplin, review of *Ladies in the Laboratory? American and British Women in Science, 1800-1900: A Survey of Their Contributions to Research;* November, 2004, M.H. Chaplin, review of *Ladies in the Laboratory II: West European Women in Science, 1800-1900; A Survey of Their Contributions to Research.*
Reference and User Services Quarterly, Volume 38, number 2, 1998, Laurel E. Duda, review of *Ladies in the Laboratory? American and British Women in Science, 1800-1900,* p. 201.

*   *   *

CROFT, Janet Brennan 1961-

PERSONAL: Born May 5, 1961, in Pittsburgh, PA; daughter of Earl (a chemical engineer) and Marian (a library clerk) Brennan; married Duane Croft (a lawyer), August 11, 1984; children: Sarah. *Ethnicity:*

"White." *Education:* Indiana University, B.A., 1982, M.L.S., 1983. *Hobbies and other interests:* Quilting, costuming, making jewelry.

ADDRESSES: Home—Norman, OK. *Office*—Bizzell Memorial Library, University of Oklahoma, 401 W. Brooks St., Norman, OK 73019. *E-mail*—jbcroft@ou. edu.

CAREER: Jenner & Block (law firm), Chicago, IL, reference librarian, 1983-84; Sewickley Public Library, Sewickley, PA, volunteer, 1984-85, adult services librarian, 1985-88; Carnegie Library of Pittsburgh, Pittsburgh, PA, reference librarian, 1985; Moon Township Public Library, Coraopolis, PA, cataloger and librarian, 1988-89, substitute cataloger, 1990; Wheeler Basin Regional Library, Decatur, AL, acquisitions clerk, 1993; Martin Methodist College, Pulaski, TN, associate professor, 1993-2000, assistant library director, 1993, library director, 1993-2000; University of Oklahoma, Norman, assistant professor, 2001-07, associate professor, 2007—, librarian and head of access services at university library, 2001—. Conference participant and public speaker.

MEMBER: Mythopoeic Society (member of council of stewards, 2006—), Tolkien Society, Popular Culture Association, American Library Association, Mountain Plains Library Association, Oklahoma Library Association, Southwest/Texas Popular Culture Association, New York C.S. Lewis Society.

AWARDS, HONORS: Outstanding article award, *Interlending and Document Supply,* 2001, for an article on licensing and interlibrary loan issues; Mythopoeic Scholarship Award in Inklings Studies, Mythopoeic Society, 2005, for *War and the Works of J.R.R. Tolkien.*

WRITINGS:

War and the Works of J.R.R. Tolkien, Praeger (Westport, CT), 2004.

Legal Solutions in Electronic Reserves and Electronic Delivery of Interlibrary Loan, Haworth (Binghamton, NY), 2004.

(Editor) *Tolkien on Film: Essays on Peter Jackson's "The Lord of the Rings,"* Mythopoeic Press (Altadena, CA), 2004.

(Annotator) Dorothy L. Sayers, *The Travelling Rug,* Mythopoeic Press (Altadena, CA), 2005.

(Editor) *Tolkien and Shakespeare: Essays on Shared Themes and Language,* McFarland (Jefferson, NC), 2007.

Contributor of articles and reviews to periodicals, including *Seven: Anglo-American Literary Review, Mallorn, World Literature Today, Journal of Access Services, College and Undergraduate Libraries, Archival Products News,* and *Journal of Library Administration.* Editor, *Mythlore: Journal of J.R.R. Tolkien, C.S. Lewis, Charles Williams, and Mythopoeic Literature,* 2006—, and *Oklahoma Librarian,* 2006—.

SIDELIGHTS: Janet Brennan Croft told *CA:* "My research has been divided into two fairly distinct areas: librarianship, focusing particularly on legal issues involving copyright of electronic media, and literature and popular culture, specializing in the writings of J.R.R. Tolkien and related authors.

"While the majority of my research has been in Tolkien studies, I feel strongly that it is also important to contribute to my profession. When I was asked to investigate how the interlibrary loan department should deal with our various electronic database licenses, I researched the problem, came up with a solution (which we have adopted), communicated this solution to other libraries through articles and presentations, and broadened my research into closely related areas of copyright law and libraries.

"Although a longtime reader of Tolkien, I had never considered his works as a research topic until I read Paul Fussell's *The Great War and Modern Memory.* Though Fussell does not discuss Tolkien, I found many of his observations on post-World War I literature applicable to Tolkien's novels and stories. After presenting a paper on Tolkien and World War I, I was encouraged to expand on the topic, and eventually I wrote several articles on different aspects of war in Tolkien's works and fleshed them out into a book: *War and the Works of J.R.R. Tolkien.*

"Another area of Tolkien studies that I have explored is various film adaptations of his works. As a result of this research, I edited *Tolkien on Film: Essays on Peter Jackson's "The Lord of the Rings."* As a member of the press's advisory board I was involved in every aspect of producing this book, from the initial call for papers through layout, typography, indexing, and publicity. This led to the invitation to run for editor of the scholarly peer-reviewed journal *Mythlore,* which I began editing in 2006.

"Several of my projects deal with how Tolkien used elements from Shakespeare's plays in his works. This research led to another editing project: *Tolkien and Shakespeare: Shared Language and Themes.* I've also written several articles for the new Tolkien encyclopedia.

"Beyond Tolkien, I was also involved in the production of Dorothy L. Sayers's *The Travelling Rug.* I provided the annotations for this previously unpublished short story by an author who was a close friend of C.S. Lewis and shared many concerns and themes with the Inklings. As with *Tolkien on Film,* I was involved with all aspects of the production of this book. I am also assisting with the editing of *Past Watchful Dragons,* a collection of conference papers on C.S. Lewis. Another project that brings my Tolkien research back to my library roots is an index to over thirty years of the journal *Mythlore.*

"If there is one theme that can tie together these various strands of research, I believe it is an interest in how people and organizations respond to change, particularly moral and legal change. In both librarianship and literature, studying situations in which formerly clear-cut guidelines suddenly become ambiguous, and understanding the most effective ways to handle change while maintaining ethical and legal balance, can be very rewarding. Understanding the implications of copyright laws in flux due to new forms of media and distribution patterns, and how our basic services may be affected, is essential to providing our patrons the best service possible. Seeking an understanding of how war, technology, access to power, and societal pressures of all kinds (including trends and fashions in entertainment) create change can underscore basic human truths and help us find the moral center of these works and in ourselves."

BIOGRAPHICAL AND CRITICAL SOURCES:

ONLINE

University of Oklahoma Faculty-Staff Web site, http://faculty-staff.ou.edu/ (April 2, 2007), faculty profile of author.

CROSSMAN, Phil

PERSONAL: Married; wife's name Elaine (an artist); children: two daughters.

ADDRESSES: Home—Vinalhaven, ME. *Office*—Working Waterfront, Island Institute, P.O. Box 648, Rockland, ME 04841.

CAREER: Builder, writer, and humorist. Tidewater Motel, Vinalhaven, ME, owner. *Military service:* Served in Vietnam.

WRITINGS:

Away Happens, University Press of New England (Hanover, NH), 2005.

Author of regular column in *Working Waterfront* (Rockland, ME). Contributor to *Downeast* and *Yankee.*

BIOGRAPHICAL AND CRITICAL SOURCES:

ONLINE

Phil Crossman Home Page, http://www.philcrossman.com (May 18, 2007), short biography of the author.*

*   *   *

CROWTHER, Yasmin

PERSONAL: Born in England. *Education:* Oxford University, B.A.; University of Kent, Canterbury, M.A.

ADDRESSES: Home—London, England. *Office*—SustainAbility, 20-22 Bedford Row, London WC1R 4EB, England.

CAREER: Writer, consultant. SustainAbility (risk management consulting firm), London, England, director. Has consulted for companies, including Shell,

Novo Nordisk, Microsoft, Coca-Cola, Penguin Ketchum, and Toyota, in sustainable development and corporate responsibility. Worked for the Iraqi Opposition, 1990s. Previously worked for Ketchum, as CSR Director, and for the consultant firm URS/Dames & Moore.

WRITINGS:

The Saffron Kitchen (novel), Viking (New York, NY), 2007.

SIDELIGHTS: A consultant in sustainable development and corporate responsibility, British-born Yasmin Crowther debuted as a novelist with her 2006 *The Saffron Kitchen.* Crowther, whose mother is Iranian and father British, portrays the life of Maryam, the daughter of an Iranian general. Maryam grew up in a life of privilege until a mild indiscretion with her tutor, Ali—with whom she was infatuated—shamed the family. Disowned, she became a nurse and moved to England as a young woman where she married Edward. This past history returns to haunt Maryam when her deceased sister's son, Saeed, comes to stay with Maryam, Edward, and their daughter, Sara, in London. Filled with despair, Saeed at one point tries to kill himself by jumping from the Thames Bridge. Attempting to save him, Sara receives a kick in the stomach that kills her unborn baby. This cruel cycle of events sends Maryam back to the small Iranian town where she once spent comfortable summers; she is devastated at the thought that her own actions years ago set all these events in motion.

Critics on both sides of the Atlantic had high praise for Crowther's first novel. A reviewer for London's *Telegraph* called *The Saffron Kitchen* an "impressive debut," and one that "marks Yasmin Crowther out as a novelist of exceptional honesty and grace." Similarly, Ludovic Hunter-Tilney, reviewing the novel in the *Financial Times,* felt that Crowther "tells this cross-cultural drama with skill." Reviewing the title in *Booklist,* Donna Seaman found it "spellbinding," and further praised Crowther's "illuminating and affecting" examination of a life in two cultures. Likewise, a *Publishers Weekly* contributor thought the author "powerfully depicts Maryam's wrenching romantic and nationalistic longings." Further praise came from *En-tertainment Weekly* critic Jessica Shaw, who termed this first novel "beautiful" and a "heartfelt story." Carlo Wolff, writing in the *Pittsburgh Post-Gazette Online,* also lauded *The Saffron Kitchen,* noting that this "rich debut is a modest, careful fiction that celebrates family and shows, in telling detail, how difficult keeping a family together can be." In a *BookBrowse.com* interview, Crowther revealed part of the inspiration for her novel: "I've always been acutely aware of how privileged my life has been compared to my [Iranian] grandmothers. . . . It seems amazing to me that I have all that choice and freedom, when my grandmothers had so little. I suppose my book is a gift back to them in a way, although I scarcely knew them."

BIOGRAPHICAL AND CRITICAL SOURCES:

PERIODICALS

Booklist, November 15, 2006, Donna Seaman, review of *The Saffron Kitchen,* p. 23.
Entertainment Weekly, January 12, 2007, Jessica Shaw, review of *The Saffron Kitchen,* p. 83.
Financial Times, May 13, 2006, Ludovic Hunter-Tilney, review of *The Saffron Kitchen,* p. 33.
Kirkus Reviews, October 1, 2006, review of *The Saffron Kitchen,* p. 977.
PR Newswire, January 19, 2004, "Sustainability Experts John Elkington and Yasmin Crowther to Keynote Specialty Coffee Conference and Exhibition."
Publishers Weekly, October 2, 2006, review of *The Saffron Kitchen,* p. 38; October 23, 2006, Richard Labonte, "PW Talks to Yasmin Crowther," p. 29.
Vogue, January, 2007, Megan O'Grady, "Vogue 25: The Cultural Highlights of 2007," p. 115.
Telegraph (London, England), April 30, 2006, review of *The Saffron Kitchen.*

ONLINE

BookBrowse.com, http://www.bookbrowse.com/ (January 24, 2007), "A Conversation with Yasmin Crowther."
Curled Up with a Good Book, http://www.curledup.com/ (April 9, 2007), Janelle Martin, review of *The Saffron Kitchen.*

Iranian.com, http://www.iranian.com/ (February 9, 2007), Zohreh Khazai Ghahremani, review of *The Saffron Kitchen.*

Pittsburgh Post-Gazette Online, http://www.post-gazette.com/ (January 14, 2007), Carlo Wolff, review of *The Saffron Kitchen.*

SustainAbility, http://www.sustainability.com/ (April 9, 2007), "Yasmin Crowther."*

*   *   *

CUA, Antonio S. 1932-2007

OBITUARY NOTICE— See index for *CA* sketch: Born July 23, 1932, in Manila, Philippines; died of cancer, March 27, 2007, in Washington, DC. Educator and author. A retired professor of philosophy, Cua was a leading authority on Chinese philosophy and its history. He earned his B.A. from Far Eastern University in Manila before immigrating to the United States for his graduate studies at the University of California at Berkeley. Here he completed an M.A. in 1954 and a Ph.D. in 1958. After completing his doctorate, Cua taught at Ohio University. From 1962 to 1969 he was professor of philosophy and chair of his department at the State University of New York at Oswego. Cua joined the Catholic University of America faculty in 1969, teaching there until his 1996 retirement. In addition to Western philosophy, Cua was interested in Confucian ethics, about which he wrote in such books as *Ethical Argumentation* (1985), *Moral Vision and Tradition: Essays in Chinese Ethics* (1998), and his last book, *Human Nature, Ritual and History: Studies in Xunzi and Chinese Philosophy* (2005). The chief editor of the *Encyclopedia of Chinese Philosophy* (2002), Cua was the president of such organizations as the International Society for Chinese Philosophy, the Society for Asian and Comparative Philosophy, and the Association for Asian Studies.

OBITUARIES AND OTHER SOURCES:

PERIODICALS

Washington Post, May 1, 2007, p. B7.

CUMMINGS, Louise 1970-

PERSONAL: Born August 6, 1970, in Lurgan, Northern Ireland; daughter of Robert Andrew (an assistant director of social services) and Heather Ann Cummings. *Ethnicity:* "White." *Education:* University of Ulster, B.Sc. (hons.), 1993, D.Phil., 2000.

ADDRESSES: Home—Nottingham, England. *Office*—School of Arts and Humanities, Clifton Campus, Nottingham Trent University, Clifton Ln., Nottingham NG11 8NS, England. *E-mail*—louise.cummings@ntu.ac.uk.

CAREER: Queen's University of Belfast, Belfast, Northern Ireland, English language tutor, 1995-2001; Nottingham Trent University, Nottingham, England, faculty member, 2001—, currently reader in linguistics. Harvard University, visiting fellow, 1996-97; Cambridge University, visiting fellow at Centre for Research in the Arts, Social Sciences, and Humanities, 2006. Member of Higher Education Academy, Royal College of Speech and Language Therapists, and Health Professions Council.

AWARDS, HONORS: Eila Campbell Memorial Scholarship, British Federation of Women Graduates, 1999-2000.

WRITINGS:

Pragmatics: A Multidisciplinary Perspective, Edinburgh University Press (Edinburgh, Scotland), 2005.

Contributor to periodicals, including *Language & Communication, Informal Logic, Theoria, Argumentation, Philosophy and Rhetoric, Journal of Speculative Philosophy, Social Epistemology, Metaphilosophy,* and *Journal of Pragmatics.* Issue editor, *Philosophica,* 2002, and *Seminars in Speech and Language,* 2007.

SIDELIGHTS: Louise Cummings told *CA:* "My research and writing have always had a strong multidisciplinary bent. After pursuing an undergraduate degree in speech and language therapy at the University of Ulster, I wanted to take a more theoretical direction in my postgraduate studies. My undergraduate dissertation on inferencing in aphasia sparked an interest in the topic of reasoning. Early in my reading for my doctoral studies I came upon the work of the American philosopher Hilary Putnam. Putnam's work was to become the focus of my doctoral thesis. In 1996 and 1997 I had the opportunity to discuss my work with Putnam while I was a visiting fellow in the Graduate School of Arts and Sciences at Harvard University. I applied a number of Putnam's ideas, particularly his dialectical method in philosophy, to theories and issues in pragmatics, fallacy theory, argumentation, and rhetoric. Much of this work has since been published in international journals.

"Putnam's work has also had a deep influence on my recently published monograph *Pragmatics: A Multidisciplinary Perspective.* This book examines the multidisciplinary character of pragmatics and particularly the interaction between pragmatics and the fields of philosophy, psychology, language pathology, and artificial intelligence.

"I have no desire to work within a single academic discipline. Even at school, my interests spanned science and languages. This is also true today of my academic writing. For example, I am as interested in how we proceed to use and understand language in a range of medical disorders as I am in how philosophers believe language can be about states of affairs in the external world. The opportunity to work between disciplines is one which I deeply value and has a large influence on everything I write.

"I strive in my writing to express complex ideas in as transparent a manner as possible. To achieve clarity of expression, I prefer to write slowly with attention being paid to how each individual sentence contributes to the overall argumentative structure of my text. I believe that a well-written book or journal article should lead the reader by the hand rather than force him or her to engage in logical leaps in order to compensate for deficits on the part of the writer. I want the reader to know that his or her level of understanding is of paramount significance to how I write."

BIOGRAPHICAL AND CRITICAL SOURCES:

PERIODICALS

Cognitive Systems Research, March, 2007, James A. Mason, review of *Pragmatics: A Multidisciplinary Perspective,* pp. 48-52.

Discourse Studies, August, 2006, Aleksander Carapic, review of *Pragmatics,* pp. 591-592.

Modern Language Journal, spring, 2007, Sarah Jourdain, review of *Pragmatics,* p. 125.

Times Higher Education Supplement, December 2, 2005, Raphael Salkie, review of *Pragmatics,* p. 14.

ONLINE

Nottingham Trent University Web site: Louise Cummings Home Page, http://www.ntu.ac.uk/research/school_research/hum/staff/35514.html (April 2, 2007).

D

DALLY, Ann 1926-2007
(Ann Gwendolen Dally, Ann Mullins)

OBITUARY NOTICE— See index for *CA* sketch: Born March 29, 1926, in London, England; died March 24, 2007. Physician and author. Dally was best known for her controversial ideas about rehabilitating drug addicts with serious, long-term drug abuse histories. An obstetrician by training, she did her undergraduate work at Somerville College, where she also completed an M.A. in 1950. She earned her M.B. and B.S. in 1953 at St. Thomas's Medical School, also obtaining a D.Obst. degree there in 1955. Her M.D. from the Welleve Institute came much later, in 1993. During the mid-1950s, she was a surgeon in obstetrics and gynecology at St. James's Hospital, then a research fellow for the Wandsworth Hospital Group. She became interested in psychiatry because of her first husband, who was a psychiatrist. Together, they opened their own clinic and became increasingly involved in treating people who had longstanding addictions to opiates. The philosophy among medical practitioners at the time was to treat addicts by quickly reducing the number of drugs they were taking. This was a viable treatment for those who had not been addicted very long, but more hardcore users usually relapsed and were abandoned by drug dependency units who considered them hopeless. Dally's idea was to wean such addicts off drugs much more slowly, but this got her into trouble with colleagues, who saw her as supplying her patients with illicit drugs for far too long. She also came under scrutiny for treating her patients' psychological problems when she did not herself have a degree in psychiatry. For many years, however, Dally made her mark in the field, and she was even drugs treatment adviser to British Prime Minister Margaret Thatcher. In 1984, furthermore, she was on a committee that wrote the government's Guidelines on Treatment of Drug Misuse. Increasingly frustrated by the status quo in the medical community and its ineffective treatment of the drug crisis, Dally eventually ran afoul of Britain's General Medical Council, which revoked her license to prescribe drugs. She wrote about her professional battles in the autobiography *A Doctor's Story* (1990). Named a fellow of the Royal Society of Medicine, Dally was also the author of several other titles, including *A-Z of Babies* (1961), *Mothers: Their Power and Influence* (1976), *Women under the Knife: A History of Surgery* (1991), and *Fantasy Surgery* (1996).

OBITUARIES AND OTHER SOURCES:

BOOKS

Dally, Ann, *A Doctor's Story,* Macmillan, 1990.

PERIODICALS

Times (London, England), April 4, 2007, p. 64.

*   *   *

DALLY, Ann Gwendolen
See DALLY, Ann

DANFORD, Natalie 1968(?)-

PERSONAL: Born c. 1968; married. *Education:* Yale University, B.A.; New York University, M.F.A.

ADDRESSES: Home—New York, NY. *Agent*—Lisa Bankoff, International Creative Management, 40 W. 57 St., New York, NY 10019. *E-mail*—Natalie@ nataliedanford.com.

CAREER: Writer, editor, translator of Italian.

WRITINGS:

The Complete Idiot's Guide to Cooking Pasta, Alpha Books (New York, NY), 1999.
Inheritance (novel), St. Martin's Press (New York, NY), 2007.

Contributor of articles and reviews to periodicals, including *People, Health, Pages, Paste, Eating Well, Salon, Chicago Sun-Times,* and the *Los Angeles Times.* Series editor, with John Kulka, "Best New American Voices," Harcourt (San Diego, CA), an annual publication, 2000—.

SIDELIGHTS: Natalie Danford is a novelist, food writer, and editor. Her first book, *The Complete Idiot's Guide to Cooking Pasta,* displays her love for things Italian—especially the food. As a college student in Urbino, Danford was introduced to Italian culture and dining; Urbino has continued to figure in her life. From 2000, she has also edited, with John Kulka, the annual series, "Best New American Voices." The stories for the anthology are submitted by instructors from prestigious writing programs, such as the Iowa Writers' Workshop, the writing program at Stanford University, and New York University's graduate program in creative writing, where Danford studied. In an interview for the *Square Table* Web site, Danford noted: "One of the best things about editing the anthology is watching writers we've published develop and grow." Young writers whose work has been published in the anthology have gone on to careers as novelists; one, Kiran Desai, even won the prestigious Man Booker Prize in 2006. "I think the fact that that list is so long is a testament to our process and to the concept of the anthology," Danford

further commented. Each year a new guest editor helps Danford and Kulka pick the top fifteen to seventeen stories for inclusion in the anthology. Reviewing *Best New American Voices 2001* for *Bookreporter.com,* Rob Cline found it a "fine collection of short stories." Similarly, Janice Bees, reviewing the same collection in *Kliatt,* thought the "breadth of subject matter found in these stories is amazing." In a review of *Best New American Voices 2003,* a *Publishers Weekly* contributor concluded: "Overall, there are good reasons to expect promising futures from many of these writers." *School Library Journal* contributor Kim Dare felt that *New American Voices 2005* "include[s] some of the finest fiction coming out of universities and writing workshops today."

Danford turned novelist with her 2006 work, *Inheritance,* about a young Italian American woman, Olivia Bonocchio, who discovers after the death of her immigrant father, Luigi, that she is now the owner of his house in Urbino, Italy. Urbino is also where Danford herself studied while in college and where she lived for several years thereafter. Traveling to Italy to see if the deed to the property is intact, Olivia learns uncomfortable truths about her father's history during World War II. Danford's novel goes back and forth in time and space, charting Luigi's life in Italy, and then in the United States, where he immigrates and marries the daughter of a store owner. A reviewer for *Publishers Weekly* felt "the perspectives of Luigi and Olivia provide intriguing takes on each other's hometown." Similarly, a *Kirkus Reviews* critic noted: "Danford skillfully interweaves Luigi's story with Olivia's to reveal a complex truth." The same reviewer went on to note that the novel is an "engaging debut," Further praise for this first novel came from *Library Journal* contributor Shalini Miskelly, who felt *Inheritance* is "an overall achievement in storytelling," and from *Booklist* writer Donna Seaman, who wrote: "Danford creates involving characters and choreographs intriguing predicaments."

BIOGRAPHICAL AND CRITICAL SOURCES:

PERIODICALS

Booklist, November 15, 2006, Donna Seaman, review of *Inheritance,* p. 24.
Kansas City Star, December 28, 2000, Andy Nelson, review of *Best New American Voices 2000.*

Kirkus Reviews, October 15, 2006, review of *Inheritance,* p. 1032.

Kliatt, May, 2002, Janice Bees, review of *Best New American Voices 2001,* p. 31.

Library Journal, December 1, 2006, Shalini Miskelly, review of *Inheritance,* p. 107.

Publishers Weekly, September 30, 2002, review of *Best New American Voices 2003,* p. 51; August 14, 2006, Michelle Wildgen, review of *Inheritance,* p. 87; October 9, 2006, review of *Inheritance,* p. 36.

School Library Journal, April, 2005, Kim Dare, review of *Best New American Voices 2005,* p. 161.

ONLINE

Bookreporter.com, http://www.bookreporter.com/ (April 9, 2007), Rob Cline, review of *Best New American Voices 2001.*

Curled Up with a Good Book, http://www.curledup. com/ (April 9, 2007), Michael Leonard, review of *Inheritance.*

Natalie Danford Home Page, http://www. nataliedanford.com (April 9, 2007).

Paste Magazine Online, http://www.pastemagazine. com/ (April 9, 2007), Ellen Lindquist, review of *Inheritance.*

Square Table, http://www.thesquaretable.com/ (April 9, 2007), "Interview with Natalie Danford."*

*   *   *

DAVIDSON, Bruce 1933-

PERSONAL: Born September 5, 1933, in Chicago, IL; married Emily Haas, 1967; children: Jenny, Anna. *Education:* Studied at Rochester Institute of Technology, 1951-54, and Yale University, 1955.

ADDRESSES: Home—New York, NY. *Office*—Magnum Photos, 251 Park Ave. S., New York, NY 10010. *E-mail*—davidm@art-dept.com.

CAREER: Photographer. Al Cox Photography, Oak Park, IL, photographer apprentice, 1947; Eastman Kodak, Rochester, NY, dark-room technician, 1954-55; freelance photographer, 1958—; Magnum Photos Co-operative Agency, New York, NY, and Paris, France, photographer, 1958—. Also conducts private photography workshops; *Life* magazine program for young photographers, New York, NY, photographer, 1958; School of Visual Arts, New York, NY, iInstructor in photography, 1964; director of short films, including *Living off the Land* and *Isaac Singer's Nightmare and Mrs. Pupko's Beard,* both 1972.

Exhibitions: "12 Photographers of the American Social Landscape: Bruce Davidson," Rose Art Museum, Brandeis University, Waltham, MA, January 9-February 12, 1967; "Three Views of the North American Landscape: Bruce Davidson, Photographs 1958-1976, Jerry N. Uelsmann, Recent Photographs, National Aeronautics and Space Administration, Photographs from Apollo, E.R.T.S., Landsat and Skylab Missions," Addison Gallery of American Art, Phillips Academy, Andover, MA, October 8-November 21, 1976. Solo exhibitions include Art Institute of Chicago, Chicago, IL, 1965; Moderna Museet, Stockholm, 1966; Museum of Modern Art, New York, 1970; San Francisco Museum of Art, 1971; Galerie Delpire, Paris, 1979; Douglas Kenyon Gallery, 1982. Work exhibited at Museum of Modern Art, New York, NY; International Museum of Photography, George Eastman House, Rochester, NY; Visual Studies Workshop, Rochester, NY; Yale University, New Haven, CT; Addison Gallery of American Art, Andover, MA; Carpenter Center and Fogg Art Museum, Harvard University, Cambridge, MA; Art Institute of Chicago, Chicago, IL; University of Nebraska, Lincoln, NE; Norton Simon Museum, Pasadena, CA; National Gallery of Canada, Ottawa, Ontario, Canada; Museum Ludwig Köln, Köln, Germany; and the Smithsonian, Washington, DC. *Military service:* U.S. Army, 1955-57, served in Georgia, Arizona, and France.

AWARDS, HONORS: Guggenheim Fellowship, 1962; National Endowment for the Arts grant, 1967, 1970; American Film Institute grant, 1970, 1972; and American Film Institute, Critics Prize, 1971, for *Living off the Land;* American Film Institute, First Prize in Fiction, 1973, for *Isaac Singer's Nightmare and Mrs. Pupko's Beard;* Open Society Institute Individual Fellowship, 1998; Lucie Award, 2004, for outstanding achievement in documentary photography; National Arts Club, Gold Medal Visual Arts Award, 2007.

WRITINGS:

PHOTOGRAPHY

(Illustrator) Talcot Parsons, *The Negro American,* Houghton Mifflin (Boston, MA), 1966.

(Photographer) *Toward a Social Landscape by Bruce Davidson,* edited by Nathan Lyons, Horizon Press (New York, NY), 1967.

East 100th Street, Harvard University Press (Cambridge, MA), 1970, St. Ann's Press, 2003.

(Photographer) Carol Hill, *Subsistence U.S.A.,* Holt, Rinehart & Winston (New York, NY), 1973.

Bruce Davidson Photographs, introduction by Henry Geldzahler, Agrinde (New York, NY), 1978.

Welsh Miners, Douglas Kenyon (Chicago, IL), 1982.

Bruce Davidson, Centre National de la Photographie (Paris, France), 1984, Pantheon Books (New York, NY), 1986.

(And author of text) *Subway,* afterword by Henry Geldzahler, Aperture (New York, NY), 1986, St. Ann's Press, 2004.

Central Park, preface by Elizabeth Barlow Rogers, commentary by Marie Winn, Aperture (New York, NY), 1995.

(With Emily Haas) *Brooklyn Gang,* Twin Palms (Santa Fe, NM), 1998.

Bruce Davidson: Portraits, Aperture (New York, NY), 1999.

Time of Change: Civil Rights Photographs, 1961-1965, foreword by John Lewis, essay by Deborah Willis, St. Ann's Press, 2002.

(Photographer) Gay Talese, *The Bridge: The Building of the Verrazano-Narrows Bridge,* Walker 2003.

(Photographer) Isaac Bashevis Singer, *Isaac Bashevis Singer and the Lower East Side,* University of Wisconsin Press (Madison, WI), 2004.

Bruce Davidson: England and Scotland, 1960, introduction by Alan Sillitoe, Harry N. Abrams (New York, NY), 2004.

(Photographer) Peter Boyer, *Bruce Davidson: Circus,* Steidl The Masters, 2007.

Contributor to periodicals, including *Life, Réalités, Du, Esquire, Queen, Look,* and *Vogue.* Contributor to books, including *Popular Photography,* 1962.

SIDELIGHTS: Bruce Davidson is an award-winning photographer who is best known for his depictions of poverty and adversity in American life. Davidson got his start in photography at the age of ten as the apprentice of Oak Park, IL, photographer Al Cox. By the age of sixteen, he had already received national recognition for his work. This was enough to get him into the Rochester Institute of Technology and Yale University. In 1955 he was drafted into the U.S. Army and served a stint in France, where he met Henri Cartier-Bresson. This meeting ultimately led to his joining the exclusive Magnum Photos agency. In addition to his work at Magnum, he freelanced his photographic skills and was published in a variety of periodicals, including *Life, Réalités, Du, Esquire, Queen, Look,* and *Vogue.* Since the 1960s Davidson's photographs have appeared in numerous periodicals, exhibitions, and books of his own design. His skill in doing so was rewarded with a Lucie Award for outstanding achievement in documentary photography in 2004 and a National Arts Club Gold Medal Visual Arts Award in 2007.

One of Davidson's groundbreaking collections of photographs is *Brooklyn Gang,* published in 1998. The photographs were put on display in a solo exhibit at the International Center of Photography in New York and the Rose Gallery in California. Taken in 1959, the images depict lives of a teenage street gang in Brooklyn, NY. While the teenage subjects are living tough lives, their tattoos and hairstyles make wordless statements that show they are not too different from the average teenager of the late 1950s. William V. Ganis, writing in *Art in America,* found that "Davidson masterfully captures pregnant moments within pleasing, formally perfect compositions." Writing in *Booklist,* Raul Nino called the collection "a fine jewel for the eyes," adding: "Davidson's camera seems to have captured something essential that time has not diminished."

Davidson captured one of the most gripping periods in U.S. history in his 2002 publication, *Time of Change: Civil Rights Photographs, 1961-1965.* From 1961 onward, Davidson recorded the history of the Civil Rights Movement through his camera lens, including images of the marches and freedom rides, voter registration campaigns, police brutality, and social aspects of life throughout these times. The images are caption free, letting the photographs speak for themselves. This means that the pictures' "historical importance," noted Ray Olson in a *Booklist* review, "is never upstaged by their artfulness, which is as it should be." A contributor to the *Black Issues Book Review* found that the "engaging images strike a chord somewhere deep beneath the surface of the skin." Matt Claus, writing in *Esquire,* commented that *Time of Change* is "flat-out the best photography book about the civil-rights movement."

BIOGRAPHICAL AND CRITICAL SOURCES:

BOOKS

Contemporary Photographers, 3rd edition, St. James Press (Detroit, MI), 1996.

PERIODICALS

Art in America, July 1, 1999, William V. Ganis, review of *Brooklyn Gang,* p. 94.

Black Issues Book Review, November-December, 2002, review of *Time of Change: Civil Rights Photographs, 1961-1965,* p. 14.

Booklist, February 1, 1996, Brad Hooper, review of *Central Park,* p. 910; April 15, 1999, Raul Nino, review of *Brooklyn Gang,* p. 1499; December 15, 1999, Ray Olson, review of *Bruce Davidson: Portraits,* p. 747; October 15, 2002, Ray Olson, review of *Time of Change,* p. 372.

Esquire, October 1, 2002, Matt Claus, review of *Time of Change,* p. 40.

Guardian (London, England), January 4, 2007, "Bruce Davidson's Best Shot."

Library Journal, April 1, 1999, David Bryant, review of *Brooklyn Gang,* p. 90; April 1, 2006, Raymond Bial, review of *Bruce Davidson: England and Scotland, 1960,* p. 90.

Life, April 15, 2000, "Portrait," p. 68.

New York Times Book Review, December 8, 2002, Andy Grundberg, review of *Time of Change,* p. 29.

People, January 26, 1987, Eric Levin, review of *Subway,* p. 18.

Smithsonian, June 1, 2004, Paul Maliszewski, "Off the Beaten Track: During a Civil Rights March in 1965," p. 25.

Washington Post, Frank Van Riper, "Bruce Davidson's Powerful 'Time of Change.'"

ONLINE

Art Department Web site, http://www.art-dept.com/ (May 9, 2007), author profile.

Magnum Photos Web site, http://www.magnumphotos. com/ (May 9, 2007), author profile.

NNDB, http://www.nndb.com/ (May 9, 2007), author profile.

Soulcatcher Studio Web site, http://www.soulcatcher studio.com/ (May 9, 2007), author profile.*

*   *   *

DEEN, Paula 1947-
(Paula Ann Hiers Deen, Paula H. Deen)

PERSONAL: Born January 19, 1947, in Albany, GA; married Jimmy Deen (a car dealer), 1965 (divorced, 1989); married Michael Anthony Groover, March, 2004; children: Bobby, Jamie, two stepchildren.

ADDRESSES: Office—The Lady and Sons, 102 W. Congress St., Savannah, GA 31401; Uncle Bubba's Oyster House, 104 Bryan Woods Rd., Savannah, GA 31410.

CAREER: Worked as a bank teller, c. 1986; The Bag Lady (catering business), Savannah, GA, owner, 1989-91; The Lady (restaurant), owner, c. 1991-95; Lady and Sons (restaurant), Savannah, owner and chef, 1996—; *Paula's Home Cooking* (television series), Food Network, host, 2002—; also host of *Paula's Party,* Food Network; Uncle Bubba's Oyster House, Savannah, co-owner, c. 2003—; president of Lady Enterprises, Inc.; publisher, with Hoffman Media, LLC, of magazine *Cooking with Paula Deen;* also owner of a gift shop in Savannah; celebrity promoter for Smithfield Foods, Inc. Appeared in film *Elizabeth-town,* 2005.

AWARDS, HONORS: Most Memorable Meal of the Year, *USA Today,* 1999, for food prepared at Lady and Sons restaurant; Small Business Person of the Year, U.S. Small Business Administration, 2003; Georgia Women Entrepreneurs award, Georgia Small Business Development Center, 2003.

WRITINGS:

The Lady & Sons Just Desserts: More Than 120 Sweet Temptations from Savannah's Favorite Restaurant, Simon & Schuster (New York, NY), 2002.

Paula Deen & Friends: Living It Up, Southern Style, photographs by Alan Richardson, Simon & Schuster (New York, NY), 2005.

(With Martha Nesbit) *Paula Deen Celebrates! Best Dishes and Best Wishes for the Best Times of Your Life,* Simon & Schuster (New York, NY), 2006.

(With Sherry Suib Cohen) *Paula Deen: It Ain't All about the Cookin'* (autobiography), Simon & Schuster (New York, NY), 2007.

AS PAULA H. DEEN

The Lady & Sons Savannah Country Cookbook, introduction by John Berendt, Random House (New York, NY), 1998.

The Lady & Sons, Too! A Whole New Batch of Recipes from Savannah, Random House (New York, NY), 2000.

Paula Deen's Kitchen Classics: The Lady & Sons Savannah Country Cookbook and the Lady & Sons, Too!, introduction by John Berendt, Random House (New York, NY), 2005.

Paula Deen's 2008 Calendar, Random House Trade Paperbacks (New York, NY), 2007.

SIDELIGHTS: The host of two popular cable cooking shows, author of books, and owner of two restaurants, Paula Deen is a celebrity chef who promotes down-home Southern cooking. How she achieved this success is a long story, however. Her life began conventionally enough: she married her high school sweetheart when she was still a teenager and soon gave birth to two sons. Her life took a turn for the worse, however, when her father died a year after her marriage. A few years later, her mother died as well, and Deen had to assume the responsibility of raising her younger brother. These pressures took their toll, and the young mother began to experience the symptoms of agoraphobia, the fear of venturing outside one's home. Struggling against the disease, she began to feel more like herself by the mid 1980s and decided to take a job as a bank teller. When she was robbed at gunpoint while at her bank, the symptoms of agoraphobia returned with a vengeance. The problem caused such a strain on her marriage that she and her husband divorced in 1989. Suddenly finding herself in need of an income, Deen gathered up her courage and opened a catering business, The Bag Lady. She did the cooking while her two boys made deliveries. Within a couple of years, the business became a full-fledged restaurant she opened at a Best Western hotel. In 1995 she expanded it as Lady and Sons restaurant. Deen's big break came when her

business was featured on the *Oprah Winfrey Show,* and this was followed by an award for best meal from *USA Today.*

Deen also began writing cookbooks. Her first work was published by Random House in 1998 as *The Lady & Sons Savannah Country Cookbook.* Some cooking purists decried Deen's frequent use of boxed and canned ingredients in her recipes, while others appreciated the convenience and tasty results. "Home cooks will find the recipes easy to follow, and most dishes translate to other regions," remarked *Booklist* critic Mark Knoblauch. A *Publishers Weekly* writer considered the cookbook appropriate for "those looking for some distinctively American comfort food—and in a mood for some decidedly anti-nouvelle regression."

In 2002, Deen began hosting her first cooking show, *Paula's Home Cooking,* later adding another series, *Paula's Party.* Gradually, she has turned her restaurant endeavor into a food, broadcasting, and publishing empire now known as Lady Enterprises, Inc. It includes a magazine, *Cooking with Paula Deen,* and merchandise sold in a gift shop she opened next to her restaurant. Deen also helped her brother open another restaurant, Uncle Bubba's Oyster House, and has even experimented with acting, appearing in the 2005 movie *Elizabethtown* as the distinctly Southern Aunt Dora. She writes frankly about her colorful life story in her memoir, *Paula Deen: It Ain't All about the Cookin',* which *Library Journal* reviewer John Charles described as a "richly emotional culinary memoir" that is "warm, comfortable, and occasionally salty."

BIOGRAPHICAL AND CRITICAL SOURCES:

BOOKS

Deen, Paula, and Sherry Suib Cohen, *Paula Deen: It Ain't All about the Cookin',* Simon & Schuster (New York, NY), 2007.

PERIODICALS

Booklist, May 15, 1998, Mark Knoblauch, review of *The Lady & Sons Savannah Country Cookbook,* p. 1580.

Business Wire, November 8, 2005, "Paula Deen Magazine Launches"; December 5, 2005, "Paula Deen Magazine Sells Out"; September 12, 2006, "Back to Basics Signs Exclusive Endorsement Agreement with Food Network Celebrity Paula Deen."

Daily Press (Newport News, VA), October 21, 2006, "Queen of Cuisine Brings Home the Bacon: The Food Network's Belle of Southern Cooking Will Be the Face of Smithfield Foods"; December 20, 2006, "Down-Home Diva"; January 23, 2007, "Smithfield Partnering with Paula Deen to Sell Non-meat Products"; February 19, 2007, "Paula Deen Raises $200,000 for Local Cause"; February 20, 2007, "Paula Deen Helps Foodbank of Va. Peninsula Raise Dough: The Celebrity Cook Helped the Group Raise More Than $200,000 When She Appeared at a Feb. 10 Fundraiser."

Good Housekeeping, October 1, 2005, Joanne Kaufman, "Southern-Fried Charm: Paula Deen Has a Hit Cooking Show, and Now She's in a Movie. But, Says This Down-Home Chef, Her Life Hasn't Always Been Such a Slice of Sweet Potato Pie," p. 163.

Gourmet Retailer, September 1, 2006, Michelle Moran, "What's Hot This Quarter?," p. 109; November 1, 2006, "Back to Basics Signs Endorsement with Food Network's Paula Deen," p. 14.

Hollywood Reporter, April 4, 2006, Kimberly Nordyke, "Food Net Cooks New Series," p. 57.

Kirkus Reviews, September 15, 2006, "Cooking in Front of the Camera: Best of the Culinary Stars," p. 9.

Library Journal, April 15, 1998, Judith C. Sutton, review of *The Lady & Sons Savannah Country Cookbook,* p. 109; May 15, 2002, Judith Sutton, review of *The Lady & Sons Just Desserts: More Than 120 Sweet Temptations from Savannah's Favorite Restaurant,* p. 122; September 15, 2006, Judith Sutton, review of *Paula Deen Celebrates! Best Dishes and Best Wishes for the Best Times of Your Life,* p. 82; March 15, 2007, John Charles, review of *Paula Deen: It Ain't All about the Cookin',* p. 88.

Miami Herald, February 25, 2007, Lydia Martin, "Culinary Personalities Charm, Dish at Food Festival."

Mississippi Magazine, July 1, 2006, Kyle Brantley, "Dishing with Deen," p. 13.

National Provisioner's Meat & Deli Retailer, September 1, 2006, Richard Mitchell, "Partnering for Pork: Smithfield Foods Inc. Is Teaming with Television Personality Paula Deen to Strengthen Its Brand and Promote Family Dining," p. 44.

Newsweek, April 6, 2007, Jac Chebatoris, "20-Year Bout with Agoraphobia."

New York Times, October 6, 2006, Susan Stewart, "Another Helping of Paula Deen, Cooking and Flirting," p. 25.

Omaha World-Herald, January 17, 2007, "Bluffs' Pancake Man Flips for Paula Deen."

Orlando Sentinel, November 5, 2006, "At the Midnight Hour: Paula Deen and Rachael Ray Offer Their Ideas for a Homey New Year Celebration."

PR Newswire, July 7, 2006, "Flagstaff House Restaurant Featured on New Food Network Show Hosted by Paula Deen's Sons, Jamie and Bobby Deen"; September 19, 2006, "Smithfield Foods, Paula Deen Join Forces to Encourage Families to Eat Meals Together"; September 21, 2006, "Paula Deen Promotes Family Meals at Home as Part of National Eat Dinner Together Week"; October 27, 2006, "Private Cooking Lesson with Celebrity Cook Paula Deen Is Auctioned for Record $210,000"; January 21, 2007, "Smithfield Specialty Foods Group to Offer New Paula Deen Products through Peanut Shop of Williamsburg"; February 2, 2007, "First-Ever 'Food Network Awards,' February 23rd"; March 15, 2007, "The Deen Family Business Expands in Savannah."

People, August 22, 2005, Mike Lipton, "Recipe for Living: Suffering from Acute Agoraphobia, TV Chef Paula Deen Cooked Up Her Own Cure," p. 113.

Publishers Weekly, April 6, 1998, review of *The Lady & Sons Savannah Country Cookbook,* p. 73; February 28, 2005, review of *Paula Deen & Friends: Living It Up, Southern Style,* p. 58.

Savannah Morning News, September 8, 2006, "Paula Deen to Open Gift Shop in Space Now Occupied by Finnegan's Wake."

Supermarket News, October 23, 2006, Lynne Miller, "Smithfield Teams Up with Paula Deen," p. 50.

TelevisionWeek, February 7, 2005, Daisy Whitney, "Food Network Is Serving Up Chefs; Series, Specials Will Spotlight Signature Personalities," p. 3.

ONLINE

Food Network Web site, http://www.foodnetwork.com/ (May 18, 2007), brief biography of Paula Deen.

Lady & Sons Web site, http://www.ladyandsons.com (May 18, 2007).

Paula Deen Home Page, http://pauladeen.com (May 18, 2007).

Paula Deen Magazine Web site, http://www.pauladeenmagazine.com (May 18, 2007).

USA Today Pop Candy, http://blogs.usatoday.com/popcandy/ (December 1, 2005), "A Q&A with . . . Paula Deen."*

* * *

DEEN, Paula Ann Hiers
    See DEEN, Paula

* * *

DEEN, Paula H.
    See DEEN, Paula

* * *

dé ISHTAR, Zohl 1953-

PERSONAL: Born 1953, in Adelaide, South Australia, Australia. *Education:* Macquarie University, Australia, M.A.; University of Sydney, Australia, M.Phil.; Deakin University, Geelong, Australia, Ph.D., 2003.

ADDRESSES: Office—Australian Centre for Peace and Conflict Studies, University of Queensland, Brisbane, Queensland 4072, Australia; fax: +61-7-3346-8796. *E-mail*—z.deishtar@uq.edu.au.

CAREER: Writer, researcher, activist, administrator. Kapululangu Women's Law and Culture Centre, founder, director, 1999-2001; University of Queensland, Australian Centre for Peace and Conflict Studies, Brisbane, Queensland, Australia, researcher. Peace activist and creator of cross-cultural collaborations with Indigenous Australian and Pacific women.

MEMBER: Australian Sociological Association, International Sociological Association, Australian Women's Studies Association, International Association of Community Development.

AWARDS, HONORS: Isi Liebler Prize, 2003; nominee, Nobel Peace Prize, 2005; postdoctoral fellow, Australian Centre for Peace and Conflict Studies, University of Queensland.

WRITINGS:

NONFICTION

Daughters of the Pacific, Spinifex Press (North Melbourne, Victoria, Australia), 1994.

(Editor) *Pacific Women Speak Out for Independence and Denuclearisation,* Pacific Connections (Christchurch, New Zealand), 1998.

Holding Yawulyu: White Culture and Black Women's Law, Spinifex Press (North Melbourne, Victoria, Australia), 2005.

Contributor of chapters to numerous books, including *Feminist Voices, Women Studies Texts for Aotearoa/New Zealand,* Oxford University Press (Auckland, New Zealand), 1992; *Gender and Catastrophe,* Zed Books (London, England), 1998; *Horse Dreams: The Meaning of Horses in Women's Lives,* Spinifex Press (North Melbourne, Victoria, Australia), 2004. Contributor of articles to numerous journals.

SIDELIGHTS: Zohl dé Ishtar is an Irish-Australian lesbian writer and cultural activist, who has focused on promoting the rights of Indigenous Australian and Pacific women, as well as on antinuclear campaigns, environmental concerns, and eradicating colonialism and sexual discrimination. Dé Ishtar's first book, *Daughters of the Pacific,* appeared in 1994, and includes stories collected from indigenous women across the Pacific. However, the stories in the volume are not ones conjuring unspoiled beauty; rather they provide "an engaging account of the issues concerning nuclear colonization and more," according to Lynn B. Wilson, writing in the *Women's Review of Books.* Dé Ishtar traveled extensively in the Pacific for a year interviewing women about how they have been affected by colonialism and militarism. Wilson went on to note that *Daughters of the Pacific* "works holistically, positioning women within their cultural traditions, new political structures and resistance efforts."

While completing her doctoral thesis, dé Ishtar spent two years living with female Aboriginal elders in Western Australia. The resulting thesis was later adapted for publication as *Holding Yawulyu: White Culture and Black Women's Law,* "a challenging new book," according to *Traffic* contributor Robyn Hillman-Harrigan. Dé Ishtar was not a passive observer during her time living with the indigenous women of the community of Wirrimanu; instead she took part in their daily activities and rituals while investigating the ways in which white culture had encroached upon the culture of Wirrimanu. The resulting book "offers valuable insight into the perseverance-through-struggle of the amazing Kapululangu women elders of Wirrimanu," as Hillman-Harrigan concluded.

BIOGRAPHICAL AND CRITICAL SOURCES:

PERIODICALS

Traffic, January, 2006, Robin Hillman-Harrigan, review of *Holding Yawulyu: White Culture and Black Women's Law,* p. 214.

Women's Review of Books, February, 1996, Lynn B. Wilson, review of *Daughters of the Pacific,* p. 16; July-August, 2006, Batya Weinbaum, review of *Holding Yawulyu,* p. 29.

ONLINE

ABC Queensland Online, http://www.abc.net.au/ (August 9, 2005), Steve Austin and Ross Daniels, "Dr. Zohl dé Ishtar."

Deakin University Web site, http://www.deakin.edu.au/ (April 9, 2007), "Alumni in Profile: Dr. Zohl dé Ishtar, Doctor of Philosophy 2003."

University of Queensland, Australian Centre for Peace and Conflict Studies Web site, http://www.uq.edu.au/ (April 9, 2007), "Dr. Zohl dé Ishtar."

*   *   *

DELANEY, Joseph 1945-

PERSONAL: Born 1945, in Preston, England; married; wife's name Marie; children: three. *Education:* Lancaster University, graduated.

ADDRESSES: Home—Lancashire, England.

CAREER: Novelist and educator. Blackpool Sixth Form College, Blackpool, England, professor of English, film, and media studies for twenty years, then head of media and film studies department.

AWARDS, HONORS: Manchester Book Award finalist, 2005, for *The Spook's Apprentice.*

WRITINGS:

"WARDSTONE CHRONICLES"/"THE LAST APPRENTICE" NOVEL SERIES

The Spook's Apprentice, illustrated by Patrick Arrasmith, Bodley Head (London, England), 2004, published as *Revenge of the Witch,* Greenwillow Books (New York, NY), 2005.

The Spook's Curse, illustrated by Patrick Arrasmith, Bodley Head (London, England), 2005, published as *Curse of the Bane,* Greenwillow Books (New York, NY), 2006.

The Spook's Secret, illustrated by David Wyatt, Bodley Head (London, England), 2006, published as *Night of the Soul-Stealer,* Greenwillow Books (New York, NY), 2007.

ADAPTATIONS: Revenge of the Witch was adapted as an audiobook, read by Christopher Evan Welch, HarperChildren's Audio, 2005.

SIDELIGHTS: Joseph Delaney wrote his first novel for children over many months, getting up early to write before going to work. With the success of *The Spook's Apprentice*—published in the United States as *Revenge of the Witch*—Delaney was eventually able to leave his job as head of the media and film studies department at England's Blackpool Sixth Form College. The first volume in Delaney's "Wardstone Chronicles"—known to U.S. readers as the "Last Apprentice" series—*The Spook's Apprentice* has been followed by several more novels that combine history, ghosts, witches, and a generous dose of horror in a compelling saga that has won the author legions of fans.

The "Wardstone Chronicles" introduce thirteen-year-old Thomas Ward who, as the seventh son of a seventh son, is gifted with supernatural powers. Channeling his gift, Tom is apprenticed to Old Gregory, a "Spook" who works to rid the county of evil wherever it may appear. For Tom, the role of apprentice is challenging; twenty-nine young men have already tried and failed at the task of aiding the grim, black-cloaked Gregory, some losing their life in the process. In *Revenge of the Witch,* readers follow Tom's experiences as he learns the signs of evil, overcomes the challenges that help prove him worthy and confronts assorted boggarts. He also meets up with a powerful witch named Mother Malkin who tricks him into setting her free from the underground prison, where she is held by iron and salt. All the while, he is able to see vestiges of past deaths—as well as the terrors others cannot.

In *The Spook's Curse*—published in the United States as *Curse of the Bane*—Tom and Old Gregory travel to the cathedral of Priestown, where the Spook's arch enemy, the Bane, dwells in the catacombs. Soon the powers of evil are arrayed against the Spook and his apprentice, while a being known as the Quisitor also seeks to stop their work fighting creatures from the dark side. The saga continues in *The Spook's Secret,* as Tom follows the Spook to Anglezarke, a dark home on the moors where more challenges await. There the Spook has confined his true love, a witch named Meg, through the use of drugs, while Meg's crazed sister is imprisoned in the home's dark cellar. When one of Tom's predecessor apprentices threatens harm to Tom's father's soul in order to acquire the book of spells that will allow the evil man to send Earth into perpetual winter, Tom confronts his ultimate challenge.

Delaney's medievalesque "Wardstone Chronicles" were widely praised by reviewers and readers alike. Horror fans who enjoy "up-close encounters with the unquiet dead . . . need look no further," noted a *Kirkus Reviews* contributor in an appraisal of *Revenge of the Witch,* while in *Booklist* Ilene Cooper maintained that the talented author "grabs readers by the throat and gives them a good shake." The novel's many grue-some scenes are "amply buffered by an exquisitely normal young hero," Cooper added, while Lesley Farmer noted in *Kliatt* that "Thomas is a likely and resourceful fellow."

While noting that the author "plumb[s] familiar subjects," a *Publishers Weekly* critic added that "expert storytelling and genuinely scary illustrations" by Patrick Arrasmith make for a "fresh" story line. In fact, Delaney's portrait of evil is more complex than that in

many books for young readers, and this fact has at-tracted adult readers to his novels. Calling the "Ward-stone Chronicles" "seriously scary," Amanda Craig noted in London's *Times Online* that the series "show us how close evil is to good, and how even witches can change for the better." "Beautifully produced and consistently surprising, the weird and wonderful 'Wardstone Chronicles' are an annual treat," Craig concluded.

Delaney discussed the evolution of the "Wardstone Chronicles" with interviewer Nikki Gamble for *Write Away!* online. "I have the Bram Stoker approach to writing," the novelist noted, referencing the author of the classic nineteenth-century horror novel *Dracula.* "He created Dracula by writing down his dreams, which took him seven years. It didn't take me quite as long. Before I started writing there were events that I knew were going to happen, but the bits in between came from dreams. Some people plan in great detail and flesh out the bones but I couldn't work like that. For me, writing is very much like reading. I have to write in order to discover what's going to happen next."

BIOGRAPHICAL AND CRITICAL SOURCES:

PERIODICALS

Booklist, August, 2005, Ilene Cooper, review of *Revenge of the Witch,* p. 2022.
Horn Book, November-December, 2005, Anita L. Burkham, review of *Revenge of the Witch,* p. 715.
Kirkus Reviews, August 1, 2005, review of *Revenge of the Witch,* p. 846.
Kliatt, September, 2005, Lesley Farmer, review of *Revenge of the Witch,* p. 7.
Magpies, March, 2006, Kevin Steinberger, review of *The Spook's Curse,* p. 34.
Publishers Weekly, October 10, 2005, review of *Revenge of the Witch,* p. 62.
School Librarian, winter, 2005, Sarah Merrett, review of *The Spook's Curse,* p. 192.
School Library Journal, November, 2005, Beth L. Meister, review of *Revenge of the Witch,* p. 132.
Times Educational Supplement, July 9, 2004, Jan L. Mark, review of *The Spook's Apprentice,* p. 37.

ONLINE

Times Online (London, England), http://www.times online.co.uk/ (July 29, 2006), Amanda Craig, review of *The Spook's Secret.*

Write Away! Web site, http://improbability.ultralab.net/ writeaway/ (August 8, 2004), Nikki Gamble, interview with Delaney.*

* * *

DE MARI, Silvana 1953-

PERSONAL: Born 1953, in Caserta, Italy.

ADDRESSES: Home—Turin, Italy.

CAREER: Writer, novelist, psychotherapist, and physician. Psychotherapist in private practice. Worked as a surgeon in Italy and Ethiopia.

AWARDS, HONORS: Best Children's Books of 2006, *Kirkus Reviews,* for *The Last Dragon.*

WRITINGS:

NOVELS

L'ultima stella a destra della luna, Salani, 2000.
The Last Dragon (published in Italian as *L'Ultimo Orco*), translated by Shaun Whiteside, Miramax Books/Hyperion Books for Children (New York, NY), 2004.
La Bestia y La Bella, Grupo Editorial Norma, 2005.
El Ultimo Elfo (title means "The Last Elf"), Grupo Editorial Norma, 2005.

Contributor of short stories to periodicals and magazines.

SIDELIGHTS: Silvana De Mari is a physician, psychotherapist, and surgeon who has worked in both Europe and Africa. De Mari is also the author of several novels, most with a lighthearted and heroic fantasy element. In *The Last Dragon,* kindhearted and gentle Yorsh is the last elf surviving in a harsh, cold, always rainy world where humans hate him simply because he is an elf. An encounter with a hot-tempered human woman, Sajra, turns out to be beneficial, however, as the woman's sympathy is aroused by the little elf's plight. The two decide to search for drier, more comfortable environment in which to live, and during their travels they meet a third companion, Monser, a hunter who joins their search. When they enter the human city of Daligar, they are captured and imprisoned. Facing death by hanging, they manage to escape, but not before Yorsh divines his destiny from some words on the wall, which state that when the land's last dragon and last elf come together, the world will be saved. Inspired by this message to begin a search for the last dragon, Yorsh and his companions take up the perilous quest. Meanwhile, in a concurrent story, the destiny of a young orphaned human girl develops and soon becomes intertwined in Yorsh's prophecy. Tragedy befalls the group of comrades, and Yorsh discovers that "prophecies are for people who don't want to control their own destiny," in the words of a *Publishers Weekly* reviewer.

De Mari "takes common fantasy elements and combines them in a unique way in this stirring, subtly post-apocalyptic fantasy," observed Anita L. Burkham in the *Horn Book Magazine.* "At times hilarious, at times poignant, and always entertaining," the story of Yorsh's determined quest "will grip young fantasy fans," commented *Booklist* reviewer Sally Estes. A contributor to *Kirkus Reviews* called the book a "wise, warmhearted fairytale." The story's "satisfying, poignant ending does not disappoint," remarked a *Kliatt* contributor. *School Library Journal* critic Sarah Couri concluded that "young fantasy fans will appreciate the many humorous touches and get caught up in this tale of strength and sacrifice."

BIOGRAPHICAL AND CRITICAL SOURCES:

PERIODICALS

Booklist, November 1, 2006, Sally Estes, review of *The Last Dragon,* p. 53.
Horn Book Magazine, November-December, 2006, Anita L. Burkam, review of *The Last Dragon,* p. 707; January-February, 2007, review of *The Last Dragon,* p. 12.
Kirkus Reviews, October 1, 2006, review of *The Last Dragon,* p. 1012.
Kliatt, November, 2006, review of *The Last Dragon,* p. 8.
Publishers Weekly, December 18, 2006, review of *The Last Dragon,* p. 64.

School Library Journal, January 1, 2007, Sarah Couri, review of *The Last Dragon,* p. 126.

ONLINE

Festivaletteratura Web site, http://www. festivaletteratura.it/ (April 24, 2007), biography of Silvana De Mari.*

* * *

DEMATTEIS, J.M. 1953-
(John Marc DeMatteis)

PERSONAL: Born December 15, 1953, in Brooklyn, NY; married; children: one son, one daughter. *Religion:* Hindu. *Hobbies and other interests:* Travel, playing guitar and piano, spending time with family.

ADDRESSES: Home—Upstate New York.

CAREER: Comic-book writer and musician. Formerly worked as a music critic; DC Comics, New York, NY, writer, c. 1970s, late 1980s-91; Marvel Comics, New York, NY, writer for *The Defenders* and *Captain America* series, 1980s, c. 1991—. Musician, performing on *How Many Lifetimes?,* produced 1997.

AWARDS, HONORS: American Library Association Ten Best Graphic Novels designation, for *Brooklyn Dreams;* Eisner Award for Best Humor Publication (with others), 2004, for *Formerly Known as the Justice League.*

WRITINGS:

GRAPHIC NOVELS

Greenberg the Vampire, illustrated by Mark Badger, Marvel Comics (New York, NY), 1986.
Stan Lee Presents Spider Man: Fearful Symmetry—Kraven's Last Hunt (originally published in comic-book format), illustrated by Mike Zeck and others, Marvel (New York, NY), 1989.

Moonshadow (originally published in comic-book format), illustrated by Jon J. Muth and others, Marvel/Epic Comics (New York, NY), 1989, published as *The Compleat Moonshadow,* DC Comics (New York, NY), 1998.
Blood (originally published in comic-book format), illustrated by Kent Williams, Marvel/Epic Comics (New York, NY), 1989, reprinted, 2004.
(With Keith Giffen) *Justice League International: The Secret Gospel of Maxwell Lord,* illustrated by Bill Willingham and others, DC Comics (New York, NY), 1992.
Mercy, illustrated by Paul Johnson, DC Comics (New York, NY), 1993.
Brooklyn Dreams (originally published in comic-book format by Paradox, 1994–95), illustrated by Glenn Barr, Vertigo/DC Comics (New York, NY), 2003.
(With Sherilyn Van Valkenburgh) *Wings,* DC Comics (New York, NY), 2001.
Green Lantern: Willworld, illustrated by Seth Fisher, DC Comics (New York, NY), 2001.
Batman: Absolution, illustrated by Brian Ashmore, DC Comics (New York, NY), 2002.
(With Phil Jimenez and Joe Kelly) *Wonder Woman: Paradise Lost* (originally published in comic-book format), illustrated by Jimenez and others, DC Comics (New York, NY), 2002.
(With others) *Superman: President Lex,* DC Comics (New York, NY), 2003.
(With Keith Giffen) *Formerly Known as the Justice League* (originally published in comic-book format), DC Comics (New York, NY), 2004.
(With Keith Giffen) *I Can't Believe It's Not the Justice League* (originally published in comic-book format), DC Comics (New York, NY), 2005.

"ABADAZAD" GRAPHIC-NOVEL SERIES; FOR CHILDREN

The Road to Inconceivable (originally published in comic-book form by CrossGen), illustrated by Mike Ploog, Hyperion Books for Children (New York, NY), 2006.
The Dream Thief (originally published in comic-book form by CrossGen), illustrated by Mike Ploog, Hyperion Books for Children (New York, NY), 2006.
The Puppet, the Professor, and the Prophet (originally published in comic-book form by CrossGen), illustrated by Mike Ploog, Hyperion Books for Children (New York, NY), 2007.

Author of original comic-book series *Abadazad*, illustrated by Mike Ploog, CrossGen, 2004; and *Stardust Kid*, illustrated by Ploog, Boom! Studios, 2005. Author, with Keith Giffen, of comic-book series *Hero Squared*, for Atomeka Press, and *Planetary Brigade* for Boom! Studios, 2006. Author of graphic miniseries *Into Shambhala*, 1986; *Farewell, The Last One,* and *Seekers into the Mystery.* Writer for ongoing comic-book series, including *The Amazing Spider-Man, The Defenders, Superman, Captain America, Justice League, Doctor Strange, Daredevil, Man-Thing, The Silver Surfer, Wonder Woman, Doctor Fate, Spectre,* and *Batman.*

Also author of episodes for television series, including *The Twilight Zone, The Adventures of Superboy, Earth: Final Conflict, The Real Ghostbusters, Justice League Unlimited,* and *Legion of Super-Heroes.* Also author of unproduced screenplays and of installments in *Justice League* (animated television program), for Cartoon Network. Contributor of reviews to periodicals, including *Rolling Stone.*

SIDELIGHTS: Considered among the most versatile writers working in contemporary comics, J.M. DeMatteis is noted for creating compelling characters and plots involving complex themes. Starting as a music critic, the Brooklyn-born DeMatteis moved into writing for comic books in the late 1970s, and in the years since has contributed to numerous well-known comic-book series as well as creating acclaimed original stories that have been published in graphic-novel format. In his work for well-known publishers DC Comics and Marvel Comics, he has made his creative mark on such series as *The Defenders, Spider-Man, Superman, Batman,* and the superhero spoof *Justice League International,* while in *Brooklyn Dreams, Moonshadow,* and *Abadazad* he presents original stories that appeal to both teens and adult fans of the graphic-novel medium. He has also worked for indie comics publishers such as Boom! Studios, which began publishing DeMatteis's children's comic *Stardust Kid* in 2005.

DeMatteis played a significant role in founding DC's Vertigo imprint, which began publishing horror comics during the 1970s. He then went on to collaborate with artist Mike Zeck on Marvel's *Captain America* series, as well as on "Kraven's Last Hunt," a story arc that ran in the *Spider-Man* series before appearing in graphic-novel format as 1989's *Stan Lee Presents Spider Man: Fearful Symmetry—Kraven's Last Hunt.* DeMatteis also worked with artist Jon J. Muth to produce *Moonshadow,* a work published in book form by Marvel that was noted for being the first fully painted comic series.

Remaining with Marvel throughout much of the 1980s, DeMatteis followed *Moonshadow* with *Blood: A Tale,* a vampire story with mythic undertones that features art by Kent Williams. Returning to DC by the time *Blood* hit bookstores, he took over the reins of the long-running *Justice League of America* superhero saga. When characters from that series, such as G'nort, Mr. Nebula, and Mister Miracle, were recast in the more-humorous *Justice League International,* he worked with coauthor Keith Giffen on developing the series and its various spin-offs. In 2003 DeMatteis joined with Giffen to receive an Eisner award recognizing the story arc published in book form as *Formerly Known as the Justice League.* After five years, he returned to Marvel and shepherded the *Spider-Man* series down a darker path in story arcs such as "The Child Within," working with artist Sal Buscema.

In DeMatteis's autobiographical miniseries *Brooklyn Dreams,* a collaboration with artist Glenn Barr that was issued by DC Comics in 1994, forty-something narrator Carl Santini looks back on his high-school years in the late 1960s. Issues in the teen's tumultuous multi-cultural family, his questions of faith, his friendships, experimental drug use, and romantic entanglements highlight his memoir, bubbling to the story's surface in the form of what *Booklist* contributor Ray Olson described as "richly detailed" and humorous "digressions." Against Santini's teen reality is the narrator's memory of meeting with his guardian angel, a scruffy, stray hound, and this memory also resonates throughout DeMatteis's story. Praising *Brooklyn Dreams* as "a classic of the [comic-book] form," Olson deemed the work "as graphically distinguished and creatively novelistic a graphic novel as has ever been." In *Publishers Weekly,* a critic called DeMatteis's tale "hypnotic," adding that Barr's illustrations follow "the plot's twists, . . . captur[ing] . . . the wild enthusiasms and fears of Carl's world." First published by DC Comics' Paradox Press imprint, *Brooklyn Dreams* was reissued in one volume by Vertigo in 2003.

In 2004 DeMatteis teamed with veteran British artist Mike Ploog to create *Abadazad,* a fantasy comic published by Florida-based publisher CrossGen. Two installments appeared in soft-cover editions before CrossGen went bankrupt, leaving both author and illustrator in a quandary. Fortunately, the series was acquired by Walt Disney Corporation, and the media giant allowed DeMatteis and Ploog to return to the proverbial drawing table and reconfigure their story as a hybrid melding picture book and comic book. The *Abadazad* series resurfaced in 2006 as the illustrated novels *The Road to Inconceivable, The Dream Thief,* and *The Puppet, the Professor, and the Prophet.* The saga is an amalgam of *The Wizard of Oz, Alice in Wonderland,* and the Arabian Nights, with nine-year-old Katie Jameson its Shaharazad. In the story, Katie is a fan of the book series "Martha in Abadazad," and she shares the books with her younger brother Matt. The two have a close relationship until Matt mysteriously vanishes while on a ride at a local carnival. Guilt over Matt's fate transforms Katie's nature, and by her early teens she has become glum and taciturn. A meeting with a quirky neighbor who claims that Martha's Abadazadian adventures were, in fact, real rekindles Katie's fascination with the fantasy world. When the woman provides the teen with the means by which she can enter Abadazad, fourteen-year-old Katie willingly takes a chance, propelled by the belief that there she will discover Matt's fate. Discussing the initial comic-book version of the saga in a *Magazine of Fantasy and Science Fiction* review, Charles De Lint noted that *Abadazad* is engaging due to DeMatteis's "inventiveness" and "attention to real world detail and problems [which] . . . slightly subvert everything in the magical land." Calling the series "kid-friendly," De Lint also noted that DeMatteis's story contains "enough meat and sly asides and bits of humor that adults will enjoy it as well."

The *Abadazad* saga's first book-length installment, *The Road to Inconceivable,* follows Katie into the fantasy world, where the Brooklyn teen confirms that Matt is being held hostage there. DeMatteis's text is multilevel; it alternates between Katie's diary entries and the overarching story line and is cemented by Ploog's anime-style art. Although her search proves fruitless, by the end of the book Katie has started down the path that she will follow in *The Dream Thief.* Helped by the benevolent Little Martha in the saga's second installment, the teen learns that her little brother is being held captive by the sinister Lanky Man. While Sharon R. Pearce wrote in *School Library Journal* that the format of the *Abadazad* books might be "too confusing" for some readers, a *Publishers Weekly*

reviewer maintained that the series "expertly blends art and text" and "Katie's emotionally messy but honest diary" is enhanced by Ploog's "deft brushwork." Writing that the book's "black-and-white art is an appealing mix of realism and exaggeration," Jesse Karp added in *Booklist* that DeMatteis's heroine "makes the story shine" in a "thoughtful read with surprising psychological nuance."

Discussing his *Abadazad* series with Mike Jozic in an online interview for Silver Bullet Comics, DeMatteis noted: "When I look at fantasy books I've enjoyed—from *Alice in Wonderland* to *Oz,* from [J.R.R.] Tolkien to Ray Bradbury—I think it comes down to one essential ingredient: the sense of wonder. Whether you're seven years old or a jaded adult, if your sense of wonder is blown open, if you're drawn into a world that intrigues and excites you and if you believe in that world, then the story is going to appeal. Which is why the best fantasy seems to work on so many levels, for so many age groups." Noting the growing popularity of the fantasy genre in the wake of J.K. Rowling's "Harry Potter" books, DeMatteis told *Comicon.com* interviewer Jennifer M. Contino that when an idea for a story comes to mind, "I have to trust it . . . let it lead me on a journey . . . and reveal the events, and the characters, to me as we go along." According to DeMatteis, "writing is ultimately an act of channeling: it's as if you're opening yourself up to—and transcribing the events in—a world that ALREADY EXISTS. A writer's job . . . is to honor that world and represent it as faithfully as possible. I think if you can do that, your story . . . and your characters . . . will have uniqueness and life."

BIOGRAPHICAL AND CRITICAL SOURCES:

PERIODICALS

Booklist, July, 2003, Ray Olson, review of *Brooklyn Dreams,* p. 1855; July 1, 2006, Jesse Karp, review of *The Road to Inconceivable,* p. 55.

Kirkus Reviews, May 15, 2006, review of *The Road to Inconceivable,* p. 516.

Magazine of Fantasy and Science Fiction, September, 2004, Charles De Lint, review of *Abadazad,* p. 32.

Publishers Weekly, September 29, 2003, review of *Superman: President Lex,* p. 45; August 11, 2003, review of *Brooklyn Dreams,* p. 259; June 12, 2005, review of *The Road to Inconceivable,* p. 53.

School Library Journal, November, 2006, Sharon R. Pearce, review of *The Road to Inconceivable* and *The Dream Thief,* p. 166.

ONLINE

ComicFanatic.com, http://www.comicfanatic.com/ (December 9, 2004), interview with DeMatteis.

Comicon.com, http://www.comicon.com/ (May 5, 2005), Jennifer M. Contino, interview with DeMatteis.

Silver Bullet Comics Web site, http://www.silverbullet comicbooks.com/ (January 14, 2004), Mike Jozic, interview with DeMatteis.*

*   *   *

DeMATTEIS, John Marc
See DeMATTEIS, J.M.

*   *   *

DE WIRE, Elinor 1953-
(Aline Matthews, Jessica Scott)

PERSONAL: Born August 3, 1953, in Frederick, MD; married Jonathan De Wire (a retired Navy officer), December 30, 1972; children: Jessica, Scott. *Education:* University of Connecticut, B.G.S., M.A.

ADDRESSES: Home—Seabeck, WA. *E-mail*—light housekitty@msn.com.

CAREER: Educator, historian, author, and editor, beginning 1980. Workshop presenter and speaker; has appeared on television documentary programs; historical preservationist and consultant.

MEMBER: U.S. Lighthouse Society, American Lighthouse Foundation, Washington Lightkeepers Association (founder and president, 2005—).

AWARDS, HONORS: National League of American Pen Women award for short fiction, 1992; Coast Guard Book Award, 2003, for *Lighthouses of the Mid-* Atlantic Coast, and 2004, for *Lighthouses of the Southern Coast*; Ben Franklin Book Award, 2005, for *Lighthouses of the Southern Coast.*

WRITINGS:

The Guide to Florida Lighthouses, Pineapple Press (Englewood, FL), 1987, 2nd edition, 2001.

Journey through the Universe, Mystic Seaport Museum (Mystic, CT), 1987.

Activities for Young Astronomers, Mystic Seaport Museum (Mystic, CT), 1990.

Reach for the Sky, Mystic Seaport Museum (Mystic, CT), 1994.

Guardians of the Lights: The Men and Women of the U.S. Lighthouse Service, Pineapple Press (Englewood, FL), 1995, 2nd edition, 2007.

The Lighthouse Activity Book, Sentinel Publications, 1995.

Lighthouse Victuals and Verse, Sentinel Publications, 1996.

Sentries along the Shore, Sentinel Publications, 1997.

The Lighthouse Almanac, Sentinel Publications, 2000.

The Florida Night Sky: A Guide to Observing from Dusk till Dawn, Pineapple Press (Sarasota, FL), 2002.

Lighthouses of the Mid-Atlantic Coast: Your Guide to the Lighthouses of New York, New Jersey, Maryland, Delaware, and Virginia, Voyageur Press (Stillwater, MN), 2002.

Lighthouses: Sentinels of the American Coast, photographs by Laurence Parent, Graphic Arts Center Publishing (Portland, OR), 2003.

Lighthouses of the Southern Coast: Your Guide to the Lighthouses of Virginia, North Carolina, South Carolina, Georgia, and Florida, photographs by Daniel E. Dempster, Voyageur Press (Stillwater, MN), 2004.

Florida Lighthouses for Kids, Pineapple Press (Sarasota, FL), 2004.

The Field Guide to Lighthouses of the Pacific Coast: California, Oregon, Washington, Alaska, and Hawai'i, Voyageur Press (Stillwater, MN), 2006.

The Field Guide to Lighthouses of New England, MBI Publishing (St. Paul, MN), 2007.

The Lightkeeper's Menagerie: Stories of Animals at Lighthouses, Pineapple Press (Sarasota, FL), 2007.

Contributor of articles and columns to periodicals, sometimes under pseudonyms Jessica Scott and Aline Matthews, including *Aloha, American History Il-*

lustrated, Beachcomber, Birder's World, Cat Fancy, Compass, Cricket, Dog Fancy, Florida Keys, Heading Out, Horseman, Lighthouse Digest, Mariners Weather Log, Navy Times, Offshore, Sacramento, Sea Frontiers, Soundings, Trailer Boats, Ventura County Coast Reporter, Weatherwise, Western Boatman, and *Yachtsman.* Editor of *Focal Point,* quarterly newsletter of Washington Lightkeepers Association, 2005—.

SIDELIGHTS: Elinor De Wire has been researching, photographing, and writing about lighthouses since 1972, and she shares her interest in books such as *Sentries along the Shore, Field Guide to Pacific Coast Lighthouses,* and *Florida Lighthouses for Kids.* Through her lectures, workshops, articles, and books, De Wire has been an instrumental force in turning public attention toward the importance of preserving the many lighthouses that dot both U.S. coastlines: the "Sentinels along the shore," to quote from the title of one of De Wire's many books.

While many of her books are written for a general audience, De Wire has also focused on a younger audience with *The Lighthouse Activity Book, The Lightkeepers' Menagerie: Stories of Animals at Lighthouses,* and *Florida Lighthouses for Kids,* as well as her kid-oriented column in the periodical *Lighthouse Digest.* In *Children's Bookwatch,* a reviewer praised De Wire's "informed and informative text" in *Florida Lighthouses for Kids* and added that the "form and format" of the book is "ideal for young readers."

BIOGRAPHICAL AND CRITICAL SOURCES:

PERIODICALS

Children's Bookwatch, August, 2005, review of *Florida Lighthouses for Kids.*
Tampa Tribune, June 14, 2004, Steve Kornacki, "Anclote Lighthouse Has Special Place in Author's Heart," p. 2.
Yachting, October, 1995, Tyler Lifton, review of *Guardians of the Lights: The Men and Women of the U.S. Lighthouse Service,* p. 36.

*   *   *

DIBB, Andrew Malcolm Thomas
    See DIBB, Andrew M.T.

DIBB, Andrew M.T. 1956-
    (Andrew Malcolm Thomas Dibb)

PERSONAL: Born April 21, 1956, in Durban, South Africa; son of Cyril Malcolm (a land surveyor) and Rona Melville (a homemaker) Dibb; married Cara Glenn (a teacher), August 20, 1983; children: Malcolm, Meghan, Laird. *Education:* Bryn Athyn College of New Church, B.A.; Academy of the New Church Theological School, M.Div.; University of South Africa, B.Th. (with honors), M.Th., and D.Th. *Religion:* New Church (Swedenborgian). *Hobbies and other interests:* Symphonies, cycling.

ADDRESSES: Home—Abington, PA. *Office*—Academy of the New Church Theological School, P.O. Box 717, Bryn Athyn, PA 19009.

CAREER: Assistant pastor of General Church of the New Jerusalem in Canada, 1984-87; pastor of New Church, Buccleuch, Johannesburg, South Africa, 1988-2002; Academy of the New Church Theological School, Bryn Athyn, PA, professor of theology and history.

MEMBER: Servetus International Society, Society for Biblical Literature.

WRITINGS:

Servetus, Swedenborg, and the Nature of God, University Press of America (Lanham, MD), 2005.

Contributor of articles to the Web site *New Church History.*

SIDELIGHTS: Andrew M.T. Dibb told *CA:* "Writing is a wonderfully creative process, and history and theology provide an endless series of subjects to view creatively. I am primarily a theologian and then a historian—or is it the other way around? History takes on a different meaning when seen in the light of theology, and theology has its context in history. I see my goal as a writer in exploring and examining these two disciplines, juxtaposing them onto each other to get a new understanding of both. The primary influence in my thinking comes from Emanuel Swedenborg, whose theology challenges the long-held belief structures and philosophies of the world.

"When writing history I am less concerned with how Swedenborg came up with his insights than I am with how those insights relate to other people's experiences. The similarity between Michael Servetus (1509-1553) and Emanuel Swedenborg (1688-1772) is fascinating, and I plan to study the subject further. They both made cogent observations about the history of Christian thought that are as interesting and important today as they were in their own times.

"As a professor of theology and history I try to enhance my students' interest in the connections between religion and history. A large part of my curriculum focuses on the process of writing, including research, organization of ideas, and final presentation. My hope is that they too will catch the creativity bug and enjoy it."

*   *   *

DIBDIN, Michael 1947-2007
(Michael John Dibdin)

OBITUARY NOTICE— See index for *CA* sketch: Born March 21, 1947, in Wolverhampton, Staffordshire, England; died March 30, 2007, in Seattle, WA. Author. Dibdin was the creator of Italian police detective Aurelio Zen, who appeared in eleven mystery novels. After earning a B.A. from the University of Sussex in 1968, he traveled to Canada and finished an M.A. at the University of Alberta in 1969. Dibdin then worked as a house painter in Canada before returning to London. Next, he traveled to Italy and taught English for four years in Perugia before finally returning home and settling in Oxford. Dibdin had begun his literary career while still in Canada. He tried to write literary fiction without much luck. He finally was published with 1978's *The Last Sherlock Holmes Story,* which borrowed from the Arthur Conan Doyle stories. This was followed several years later with *A Rich Full Death* (1986), a mystery novel that featured poet Robert Browning as its hero. Dibdin hit his stride in 1988 with his first Aurelio Zen mystery novel, *Ratking* (1988). It would be followed by ten more installments about the Italian detective, including *Cabal* (1992), *Blood Rain* (1999), and *End Games,* which had not yet been published at the time of his death.

OBITUARIES AND OTHER SOURCES:

PERIODICALS

Los Angeles Times, April 13, 2007, p. B8.
New York Times, April 6, 2007, p. C10.
Times (London, England), April 5, 2007, p. 82.

*   *   *

DIBDIN, Michael John
See DIBDIN, Michael

*   *   *

DOBOZY, Tamas 1969-

PERSONAL: Born 1969, in Nanaimo, British Columbia, Canada. *Education:* Victoria University, B.A.; Concordia University, M.A.; University of British Columbia, Ph.D.

*ADDRESSES: Home—*Ontario, Canada. *Office—* Department of English, Wilfrid Laurier University, Leupols 2-123, 75 University Ave. W., Warterloo, Ontario N2L 3C5, Canada. *E-mail—*tdobozy@wlu.ca.

CAREER: Writer, novelist, short-story writer, and educator. Wilfred Laurier University, Waterloo, Ontario, Canada, assistant professor of English and film studies, 2004—; New York University, Fulbright Research Chair in Creative Writing, 2007—. Has taught at Memorial University.

AWARDS, HONORS: subTerrain short fiction contest winner, 1995; Danuta Gleed Award shortlist, for *When X Equals Marylou.*

WRITINGS:

Doggone (novel), Gutter Press (Toronto, Ontario, Canada), 1998.
When X Equals Marylou (novel), Arsenal Pulp Press (Vancouver, British Columbia, Canada), 2002.

Last Notes, and Other Stories, HarperCollins (Toronto, Ontario, Canada), 2005, Arcade Publishing (New York, NY), 2006.

Contributor to books, including *Essays on Canadian Writing,* 2001; *Genre: Forms of Discourse and Culture,* 2004; and *Culture and the State 3: Nationalism,* CRC Humanities Studio, 2004. Contributor to journals and periodicals, including *Modern Fiction Studies* and *Canadian Literature.*

SIDELIGHTS: Tamas Dobozy, a Canadian novelist and short-story writer of Hungarian descent, is a professor of English and film studies at Wilfred Laurier University in Waterloo, Ontario, Canada. His research interests include jazz, American literature, the connection between religion and literature, poststructuralism, and creative writing, according to a biographer for the Wilfred Laurier University Web site.

Dobozy is the author of the short-story collection, *Last Notes, and Other Stories.* "At once deeply sad and deeply funny, Dobozy's stories reference mental illness, family power struggles, and the dubiousness of history, which, according to this author, cannot be trusted," remarked reviewer Tiffany Lee-Youngren, writing in the *San Diego Union-Tribune.* "Given the difficulty of getting at any historical or personal truth," Dobozy infuses his stories with dissenting voices that question given interpretations of events within the story, noted Robert Murray Davis in *World Literature Today.* "This willingness to confront alternatives and not finally to condemn pervades the collection's stories with Hungarian themes," Davis continued, identifying a consistent ethnic tone in Dobozy's tales.

The ten stories in the collection, all narrated in the first person, consider complex emotional issues demonstrated by characters who often interact with their world in unusual ways. In "Into the Ring," Dobozy tells of a married couple who work out their differences through boxing. "Philip's Killer Hat" revolves around two brothers, one of whom is convinced that jazz musician Thelonious Monk's mental troubles were caused by wearing hats that were too tight. Throughout the course of the story, the narrator tries to convince his brother not to send letters to Monk's estate informing the musician's executors of the theory. The narrator of "Four Uncles" tells of his dangerous escape from

Hungary in 1958 and how he reconnects with important relatives through the community of Hungarian exiles living in Canada. Though each man is not without sin, and some are at best rather unpleasant, all have suffered from the loss of their Hungarian homeland. "The Laughing Cat" concerns a group of friends whose two-decade-long association begins to erode after they realize they can no longer hear or tell each other's stories. "The Inert Landscapes of Gyorgy Ferenc" recounts how an exiled Hungarian artist reacts poorly to his new homeland of Canada, finding it to be a country that cannot be reproduced or represented in his paintings. "Dobozy's prose is an artistic and intellectual boon," remarked a *Publishers Weekly* reviewer. The author's "eloquence and piercing intelligence, like Stendhal's, does not allow us to forget but rather to face the harsh and disquieting world he creates," commented Davis.

BIOGRAPHICAL AND CRITICAL SOURCES:

PERIODICALS

Portland Mercury, July 3-July 9, 2003, Marjorie Skinner, review of *When X Equals Marylou.*
Publishers Weekly, July 31, 2006, review of *Last Notes and Other Stories,* p. 50.
San Diego Union-Tribune, November 5, 2006, Tiffany Lee-Youngren, "Taking 'Notes' on the Historical Record," review of *Last Notes and Other Stories.*
World Literature Today, November-December, 2006, Robert Murray Davis, "Diaspora's Children," review of *When X Equals Marylou,* p. 55, and Robert Murray Davis, review of *Last Notes and Other Stories,* p. 65.

ONLINE

Wilfred Laurier University Web site, http://www.wlu.ca/ (April 24, 2007), biography of Tamas Dobozy.
Concordia University Faculty of Arts and Science Web site, http://artsandscience1.concordia.ca/ (April 24, 2007), biography of Tamas Dobozy.

*   *   *

DOHANEY, Rainy
  See FRENCH, Renée

DORFMAN, Joaquín 1979-
(Joaquin Emiliano Dorfman)

PERSONAL: Born February, 1979, in Amsterdam, Netherlands; immigrated to United States, 1980; son of Ariel Dorfman (a playwright). *Education:* Attended New York University.

ADDRESSES: Home and office—NC.

CAREER: Novelist, playwright, and script writer.

WRITINGS:

(With father, Ariel Dorfman) *Burning City,* Random House (New York, NY), 2003.
Playing It Cool, Random House (New York, NY), 2006.

Also author of plays and screenplays, some with Ariel Dorfman.

SIDELIGHTS: Joaquín Dorfman and his father, playwright and activist Ariel Dorfman, have shared many experiences, ranging from being arrested and deported during a visit to Chile when Dorfman was age six to writing the collaborative novel *Burning City.* "Ariel is a lot busier than I am, so I did most of the work," the younger Dorfman quipped to Nadine O'Reagan in an interview for Ireland's *Sunday Business Post* regarding the joint work of fiction. "I took care of the consonants, he took care of the vowels." Even before cowriting his first novel, Dorfman was no stranger to the world of literature. His first play opened at the Edinburgh Festival when he was nineteen years old, and he also wrote two screenplays with his father.

Burning City recounts the events of a single summer in the life of teenage bicycle messenger Heller. While dreaming of becoming the youngest winner of the Tour de France, Heller rides through New York City on various assignments, often delivering bad news to his company's customers. Heller's ability to empathize with his clients allows him to familiarize himself with a wide variety of people, thereby gaining a different sense of his city environment. "Taut writing matches the fast, sweaty pace of Heller's extreme cycling through a sizzling New York summer," wrote Lauren Adams in her *Horn Book* review, and *School Library Journal* contributor Sarah Couri commented that the coauthors' "descriptions of summer in Manhattan are flawless; the city seethes as Heller surges through its streets like an electron, connecting people and lives in complicated ways."

"The pattern was togetherness and separateness," Dorfman told O'Reagan in describing the father-son writing process. "I would go to my apartment in New York at around midnight . . . and sit down and write until morning. Then I would walk to my father's house and show him what I had written. He would say, 'Change this, change that.' Usually I wouldn't listen because I'm very strong-willed." Holly Koelling, reviewing the resulting novel in *Booklist* praised the Dorfmans as "deft writers, smoothly intertwining characters and events in a highly imaginative, intriguing, and almost dreamlike story."

Dorfman moves to solo fiction in *Playing It Cool,* where readers meet master problem-solver Sebastian. Sebastian can fix things, locate people, and help make tough decision. Despite the fact that so many people confide in him, however, no one really knows Sebastian. However, when he takes on the task of tracking down Jeremy's father, the over-competent sleuth must face some of his own personal struggles—including his need for a father that he never knew. Dorfman "writes with a compassion and an energy that will propel readers along," Krista Hutley concluded in her *Booklist* review of *Playing It Cool,* while *School Library Journal* reviewer Susan Oliver considered the book "a sophisticated, mystery/romance/coming-of-age story full of red herrings and elaborate schemes." While some critics, including Hutley and a writer for *Kirkus Reviews,* found Dorfman's use of fragmentary sentences and lack of pronouns somewhat daunting, Claire E. Gross wrote in *Horn Book* that "Dorfman's restless, pointed prose perfectly defines his narrator's fragmented perspective."

BIOGRAPHICAL AND CRITICAL SOURCES:

PERIODICALS

Booklist, April 15, 2005, Holly Koelling, review of *Burning City,* p. 1448; May 1, 2006, Krista Hutley, review of *Playing It Cool,* p. 80.

Bulletin of the Center for Children's Books, September, 2005, Karen Coats, review of *Burning City,* p. 14; September, 2006, Karen Coats, review of *Playing It Cool,* p. 11.

Horn Book, May-June, 2005, Lauren Adams, review of *Burning City,* p. 323; May-June, 2006, Claire E. Gross, review of *Playing It Cool,* p. 312.

Kirkus Reviews, May 1, 2005, review of *Burning City,* p. 537; May 15, 2006, review of *Playing It Cool,* p. 517.

Kliatt, May, 2005, Paula Rohrlick, review of *Burning City,* p. 10; May, 2006, Claire Rosser, review of *Playing It Cool,* p. 8.

Publishers Weekly, June 6, 2005, review of *Burning City,* p. 66; June 19, 2006, review of *Playing It Cool,* p. 64.

School Library Journal, January, 2006, review of *Burning City,* p. 130; June, 2006, Susan Oliver, review of *Playing It Cool,* p. 152.

Voice of Youth Advocates, June, 2005, Liza M. David, review of *Burning City,* p. 128.

ONLINE

Joaquín Dorfman Home Page, http://www.joaquin dorfman.com (April 28, 2007).

Random House Web site, http://www.randomhouse. com/ (April 28, 2007), "Joaquín Dorfman."

Sunday Business Post Online (Ireland), http://archives. tcm.ie/businesspost/ (May 11, 2003), Nadine O'Reagan, "Escaping Pinochet's Shadow."*

*   *   *

DORFMAN, Joaquin Emiliano
    See DORFMAN, Joaquín

*   *   *

DOWNIE, Ruth 1955-

PERSONAL: Born 1955; married; children: two sons.

ADDRESSES: Home—Milton Keynes, England.

CAREER: Writer and novelist.

AWARDS, HONORS: End of Story competition, Fay Weldon section winner, British Broadcasting Corporation (BBC) 3, 2004.

WRITINGS:

Medicus: A Novel of the Roman Empire, Bloomsbury USA (New York, NY), 2006.

SIDELIGHTS: Ruth Downie is the author of *Medicus: A Novel of the Roman Empire.* The book's protagonist, Gaius Petreius Ruso, is a Roman army physician assigned to a legion headquartered in Deva. Ruso is recently divorced; his father has died, leaving his family in financial hardship; his medical duties are many and overwhelming; and he is constantly in conflict with his military superiors. He is also suffering under increased financial strain as he struggles to respond to his brother's requests for resources to help the cash-strapped family. Things become more grim when one slave girl is found murdered and another named Tilla appears with a broken arm and evidence of having been severely beaten. To help Tilla, Ruso "buys" her from her owner, but the uncommunicative young woman will not give him any background information. Worse, she turns out to have few useful skills and costs more to maintain than he can afford. After she works in Ruso's kitchen for a time, she begins to open up, and the doctor discovers that a clandestine slave ring is kidnapping freeborn girls and then selling them into slavery. As he reluctantly begins to look into the case, more young women turn up dead, his plans to supplement his income with a written first-aid guide become derailed, and dangerous involvements threaten to turn deadly.

"Downie's auspicious debut sparkles with beguiling characters and a vividly imagined evocation of a hazy frontier," commented a *Publishers Weekly* reviewer. A *Kirkus Reviews* commentator concluded that "the real achievement here is the lavishly, often hilariously detailed portrayal of the world that absorbs Ruso's exhausted wits and energies," and called the book "a charming novel." The book's story line is "suspenseful and fluidly told, but the evolving bond between master and servant is at the heart of this excellent first work," commented *Library Journal* reviewer Barbara Hoffert.

BIOGRAPHICAL AND CRITICAL SOURCES:

PERIODICALS

Booklist, November 1, 2006, Allison Block, review of *Medicus: A Novel of the Roman Empire,* p. 33.

Kirkus Reviews, October 1, 2006, review of *Medicus,* p. 977.

Library Journal, November 1, 2006, Barbara Hoffert, review of *Medicus,* p. 67.

Publishers Weekly, October 2, 2006, review of *Medicus,* p. 35.

ONLINE

BookLoons, http://www.bookloons.com/ (April 24, 2007), Hilary Williamson, review of *Medicus.**

* * *

DOYLE, Brian 1956-

PERSONAL: Born 1956, in New York, NY; son of James A. (a journalist) and Ethem Clancey Doyle (a teacher); married Mary Miller: children: Lily, Joseph, Liam (twins). *Education:* University of Notre Dame, graduated 1978. *Religion:* Catholic.

ADDRESSES: Office—Portland Magazine, University of Portland, Waldschmidt Hall, 5000 N. Willamette Blvd., Portland, OR 97203-5798. *E-mail*—bdoyle@up.edu.

CAREER: U.S. Catholic (magazine), Chicago, IL, assistant editor; *Boston College Magazine,* Boston, MA, senior writer; *Portland: The University of Oregon Magazine,* Portland, editor.

AWARDS, HONORS: Various national medals for excellence, 1996-2007, for *Portland;* Best Essay Award, *American Scholar,* 2000, for essay on Plutarch; Christopher Award and Catholic Press Association Book Award, both for *Two Voices: A Father and Son Discuss Family and Faith;* Sibley Award for best university magazine in America, 2005, for *Portland;* Pushcart Prize, 2006, for

WRITINGS:

(With father, Jim Doyle) *Two Voices: A Father and Son Discuss Family and Faith,* Liguori Publications (Liguori, MO), 1996.

Credo: Essays on Grace, Altar Boys, Bees, Kneeling, Saints, the Mass, Priests, Strong Women, Epiphanies, a Wake, and the Haunting Thin Energetic Dusty Figure of Jesus the Christ, Saint Mary's Press (Winona, MN), 1999.

Leaping: Revelations and Epiphanies, Loyola Press (Chicago, IL), 2003.

(Editor) *God Is Love: Essays from Portland Magazine,* Augsburg Books (Minneapolis, MN), 2003.

Spirited Men: Story, Soul & Substance, Cowley Publications (Cambridge, MA), 2004.

The Wet Engine: Exploring the Mad Wild Miracle of the Heart, Paraclete Press (Brewster, MA), 2005.

Epiphanies and Elegies: Very Short Stories, Rowman & Littlefield Publishers (Lanham, MD), 2006.

The Grail: A Year Ambling and Shambling through an Oregon Vineyard in Pursuit of the Best Pinot Noir Wine in the Whole Wild World, drawings by Mary Miller Doyle, Oregon State University Press (Corvallis, OR), 2006.

Contributor to anthologies, including *The Best Spiritual Writing,* HarperSanFrancisco (San Francisco, CA), 1999, 2001, 2002; *The Best American Essays,* Houghton Mifflin (Boston, MA), 1998, 1999, 2003, 2005; *In Brief: Short Takes on the Personal,* edited by Judith Kitchen and Mary Paumier Jones, W.W. Norton, (New York, NY) 1999; and *Resurrecting Grace: Remembering Catholic Childhoods,* Beacon Press (Boston, MA), 2002. Editor of *"Best Catholic Writing"* series, Loyola Press, 2004-06. Contributor to periodicals, including *Atlantic Monthly, American Scholar, Harper's, Gourmet, Sydney Morning Herald, Orion,* and the London *Times.* Essayist for *Eureka Street* and the *Age.*

SIDELIGHTS: Brian Doyle is an award-winning author and essayist, and is the editor of *Portland,* a magazine noted for publishing the work of fine writers. Doyle's father, James A. Doyle, was head of the Catholic Press Association for thirty years, and Brian Doyle's work also expresses a deep faith and interest in Catholicism. He offers his reflections on various aspects of Catholicism in the collection *Credo: Essays on Grace, Altar Boys, Bees, Kneeling, Saints, the Mass, Priests, Strong Women, Epiphanies, a Wake, and the Haunting Thin Energetic Dusty Figure of Jesus the Christ.* The selections, all previously published in various periodicals, range from humorous to pious, and all feature "Doyle's enviable skill as a wordsmith," stated a *Publishers Weekly* reviewer. Another of Doyle's essay collections, *Leaping: Revelations and Epiphanies,* is recommended as an engaging read that will "inspire and entertain," wrote John-Leonard Berg in *Library Journal. Spirited Men: Story, Soul & Substance* features Doyle's essays on various influential men, from Plutarch to Van Morrison.

Doyle's experiences as the parent of a child with a serious heart condition are the basis for his book *The Wet Engine: Exploring the Mad, Wild Miracle of the Heart.* Doyle's son Liam, a twin, was born with a heart defect that required risky surgery, and even if he survived the operation, he would still require a heart transplant in adulthood. "Despite the book's emotionally weighty subject, it is completely unsentimental," advised Kris Berggren in the *National Catholic Reporter.* Though the author is emotionally honest in relating how he felt about possibly losing his child, his book is also full of scientific facts and details about surgeries and experiments related to the heart. Berggren felt that Doyle's book offers readers "universal truths." *The Wet Engine* was also recommended by a writer for *Publishers Weekly,* who characterized it as an involving "meditation on the fragile mysteries of human life."

The Grail: A Year Ambling and Shambling through an Oregon Vineyard in Pursuit of the Best Pinot Noir Wine in the Whole Wild World is something of a departure for Doyle, as it focuses on the intricacies of making pinot noir wine. During the course of a year, the writer observed a father-and-son team of vintners, Don and Jesse Lange, as they worked at their vineyard in Dundee, Oregon. In sixty-nine short chapters, Doyle reflects on various aspects of that year and what he learned. He discusses the winemaking process, as well as the people he came to know and the reflections their works stirs in him. "Those who love wine, [and] enjoy short juicy tidbits rather than long explanations . . . will find Doyle's far-ranging essays and adjective-rich prose delightful and easily assimilated," wrote LiDoña Wagner for *Etude Online.* A *Publishers Weekly* writer also praised *The Grail* as a "full-bodied, ebullient account."

Doyle, in response to the question "What first got you interested in writing?", told *CA:* "My dad was and is a wonderful writer—he was a newspaper editor and a man of remarkable blunt grace. He taught me more than anyone or anything that stories swim by the mil-

lions and most of being a writer is listening and seeing and then madly scribbling. Also I grew up in an Irish Catholic American family with lots of siblings so we were addicted to sagas and tall tales and storytelling as a means of making sure you got a place at the table."

When asked who and what influence his work, Doyle said "Twain, Stevenson, Orwell, Flannery O'Connor, the King James Bible, my children's wild joys and chants. Van Morrison, Bruce Springsteen, Pete Townshend, Bono. Hawks and osprey. Sunlight and coffee. Beaches. My lithe and mysterious wife. Chess. Excellent ale."

When questioned about the effects he hopes his books will have, Doyle said, "Hope, joy, laughter, snarling, laughter, that cool moment of contemplation when you stop reading and think Hey. . . and in the end I hope to have prompted readers to a step closer to Blake's dictum: if the doors of perception were cleansed we would see everything as it is, infinite. . . . "

BIOGRAPHICAL AND CRITICAL SOURCES:

PERIODICALS

Christian Century, May 3, 2005, Lawrence Wood, review of *Spirited Men: Story, Soul & Substance,* p. 38.

Christianity Today, August, 2005, Cindy Crosby, review of *The Wet Engine: Exploring the Mad Wild Miracle of the Heart,* p. 70.

Library Journal, March 1, 2003, Graham Christian, review of *God Is Love: Essays from Portland Magazine,* p. 96; August, 2003, John-Leonard Berg, review of *Leaping: Revelations and Epiphanies,* p. 90.

National Catholic Reporter, June 3, 2005, Kris Berggren, review of *The Wet Engine,* p. 18.

Publishers Weekly, October 25, 1999, review of *Credo: Essays on Grace, Altar Boys, Bees, Kneeling, Saints, the Mass, Priests, Strong Women, Epiphanies, a Wake, and the Haunting Thin Energetic Dusty Figure of Jesus the Christ,* p. 70; November 11, 2002, review of *God Is Love,* p. 60; April 11, 2005, review of *The Wet Engine,* p. 50; March 20, 2006, review of *The Grail: A Year*

Ambling and Shambling through an Oregon Vineyard in Pursuit of the Best Pinot Noir Wine in the Whole Wild World, p. 51.

Reviewer's Bookwatch, January, 2005, John Taylor, review of *Spirited Men.*

ONLINE

Etude Online, http://etude.uoregon.edu/ (June 4, 2007), LiDoña Wagner, review of *The Grail.*

Nimble Spirit, http://www.nimblespirit.com/ (May 21, 2007), review of *The Grail.*

Notre Dame Magazine Online, http://www.nd.edu/~ndmag/ (May 21, 2007), review of *The Grail.*

Oregon State University Web site, http://oregonstate.edu/ (April 13, 2006), information about *The Grail.*

*   *   *

DREGNI, Eric 1968-

PERSONAL: Born 1968.

ADDRESSES: Home—Minneapolis, MN.

CAREER: Writer, researcher, journalist, translator, musician, and curator. El Dorado Conquistador Museum, Minneapolis, MN, curator; Vinnie and the Stardusters, guitarist.

AWARDS, HONORS: Fulbright fellow, Norwegian University of Science and Technology, 2004.

WRITINGS:

NONFICTION; WITH BROTHER, MICHAEL DREGNI

Illustrated Motorscooter Buyer's Guide, Motorbooks International (Osceola, WI), 1993.

Scooters!, foreword by Robert H. Ammon, Motorbooks International (Osceola, WI), 1995.

The Scooter Bible: From Cushman to Vespa, the Ultimate History and Buyer's Guide, Whitehorse Press (Center Conway, NH), 2005.

NONFICTION

(With Karl Hagstrom Miller) *Ads That Put America on Wheels,* Motorbooks International (Osceola, WI), 1996.

Scooter Mania!, MBI Publishing (Osceola, WI), 1998.

Minnesota Marvels: Roadside Attractions in the Land of Lakes, University of Minnesota Press (Minneapolis, MN), 2001.

Let's Go Bowling, MBI Publishing (St. Paul, MN), 2005.

Scooters: Everything You Need to Know, photography by Pixel Pete, Motorbooks (St. Paul, MN), 2005.

(With brother, Jonathan Dregni) *Follies of Science: Twentieth Century Visions of Our Fantastic Future,* Speck Press (Denver, CO), 2006.

Midwest Marvels: Roadside Attractions across Iowa, Minnesota, the Dakotas, and Wisconsin, University of Minnesota Press (Minneapolis, MN), 2006.

Zamboni: The Coolest Machines on Ice, MBI Publishing and Voyageur Press (St Paul, MI), 2006.

SIDELIGHTS: Eric Dregni is a researcher, museum curator, and journalist who is also a self-confessed fanatic for motor scooters. The author of several books on scooters, some with his brother Michael, Dregni "demonstrates why the vehicles can seem both nerdy and cool" at the same time, commented Laura Yenn in the *St. Paul Pioneer Press.* Dregni applies this whimsical approach to topics in his other books as well. In *Follies of Science: Twentieth Century Visions of Our Fantastic Future,* written with his other brother, Jonathan Dregni, he muses on past predictions of what the technological world of tomorrow would look like in the year 2006. The Dregnis consider and comment upon numerous inventions and advancements that were anticipated by writers of yesterday in science publications, such as *Popular Mechanics,* and science-fiction magazines, including *Amazing Stories.* They note that items such as antimatter-powered batteries, flying cities, skis with tank treads, and mechanical secretaries did not come into being. Some inventions that did come to pass "probably shouldn't have. But the book shouldn't be read as a cautionary tale," noted Derek Hansell in another *St. Paul Pioneer Press* review. Scientific extrapolation involves both utopian and dystopian outlooks, the Dregnis believe, and consideration must be given to how technology affects the social, political, and human elements of the world. The outlandish and the practical often coexist in the development of technology, and even some of the stranger suggestions of past writers show an appreciation for how technology can enhance and elevate the way humans live and interact. A reviewer in the *Futurist* observed that the Dregnis' book is for the "futurist with a sense of humor."

Dregni's quirky outlook pans across the breadth of Midwestern America in *Midwest Marvels: Roadside Attractions across Iowa, Minnesota, the Dakotas, and Wisconsin.* He describes the unusual, sometimes bizarre, often funny displays, monuments, structures, statues, and other attractions that can make a trip through the Midwest a surrealistic delight. He describes the many examples of taxidermy, including sparring squirrels, at the Moccasin Bar in Haywood, Wisconsin. He visits the Mustard Museum in Mount Horeb, Wisconsin, and the Effigy Mounds of Marquett, Iowa. He documents giant roadside statues of cows, lumberjacks, fish, gorillas, and more. Among the stranger entries are more subdued attractions such as Mount Rushmore and Frank Lloyd Wright's architectural wonder, Taliesin. The book serves as a detailed travel guide with directions, plus "useful information about attractive features, history, locations, hours, prices of admission, and local color stories," noted an *Internet Bookwatch* reviewer. *Library Journal* contributor Susan Belsky commended Dregni's "in-depth coverage of the local wonders."

BIOGRAPHICAL AND CRITICAL SOURCES:

PERIODICALS

ColoradoBiz, December, 2006, Eric Peterson, review of *Follies of Science: Twentieth Century Visions of Our Fantastic Future,* p. 59.

Europe Intelligence Wire, February 16, 2006, review of *Scooters: Everything You Need to Know.*

Futurist, January-February, 2007, review of *Follies of Science,* p. 48.

Internet Bookwatch, August, 2006, review of *Midwest Marvels: Roadside Attractions across Iowa, Minnesota, the Dakotas, and Wisconsin.*

Library Journal, June 15, 2006, Susan Belsky, review of *Midwest Marvels,* p. 91.

Reference & Research Book News, August, 2006, review of *Midwest Marvels.*

Saint Paul Pioneer Press, September 17, 2006, Laura Yuen, "High Priests of Scooter World Deliver the Word," interview with Michael and Eric Dregni; November 14, 2006, Derek Hansell, "Minnesotans' Book Offers a Look Back at the Future," review of *Follies of Science,*

Skeptical Inquirer, January-February, 2007, Kendrick Frazier, review of *Follies of Science,* p. 61.*

*   *   *

DRURY, Bob

PERSONAL: Male.

CAREER: Writer, journalist, and foreign correspondent. *Men's Health,* contributing editor and foreign correspondent; Fox television network, reporter; *New York Newsday,* former staff reporter.

AWARDS, HONORS: Pulitzer Prize nomination; recipient of several national journalism awards.

WRITINGS:

(With Ryne Duren) *The Comeback,* Lorenz Press (Dayton, OH), 1978.

(With Arthur J. Donovan) *Fatso: Football When Men Were Really Men,* William Morrow (New York, NY), 1987.

(With Charles J. Hynes) *Incident at Howard Beach: The Case for Murder,* Putnam (New York, NY), 1990.

(With Lou Eppolito) *Mafia Cop,* Simon & Schuster (New York, NY), 1992.

(Editor, with Carolyn Beauchamp) Joseph "Jo Dogs" Iannuzzi, *The Mafia Cookbook,* Simon & Schuster (New York, NY), 1993.

The Rescue Season: The Heroic Story of Parajumpers on the Edge of the World, Simon & Schuster (New York, NY), 2001.

(With Tom Clavin) *Halsey's Typhoon: The True Story of a Fighting Admiral, an Epic Storm, and an Untold Rescue,* Atlantic Monthly Press (New York, NY), 2007.

Contributor to periodicals, including *Men's Journal, Gentleman's Quarterly, Vanity Fair, New York Times, New York Post,* and *Sports Illustrated.*

ADAPTATIONS: The Rescue Season was made into a documentary film and broadcast on the History Channel.

SIDELIGHTS: As a magazine journalist and foreign correspondent for *Men's Health* magazine, Bob Drury has reported from overseas locations such as Iraq, Afghanistan, Belfast, Haiti, Sarajevo, and Liberia. A Pulitzer Prize nominee, Drury has contributed to all four major New York newspapers, and is a regular contributor to national periodicals and magazines.

In *Incident at Howard Beach: The Case for Murder,* Drury and coauthor Charles J. Hynes report on a notorious modern-day incident of deadly racial violence. In 1986, in the middle-class neighborhood of Howard Beach, Queens, a group of twelve white teenagers brutally attacked three black men who had entered the area, leaving one dead, killed by a car while fleeing his attackers, and the other two severely beaten. Hynes and Drury's account of the attacks and their aftermath "is the story of that ignoble episode and of how Howard Beach became a part of our language of racial despair," commented Linda Wolfe in the *New York Times.* The authors relate the shameful behavior of the authorities in the wake of the attack, during which police treated the victims as though they were criminals themselves. They detail how coauthor Hynes, now the District Attorney for Brooklyn, was appointed special prosecutor in the case, and how he struggled to build an effective case against the attackers. The authors offer behind-the-scenes details of the legal maneuvering, political machinations, trial techniques, and investigative procedures that offered the victims justice, with Hynes eventually winning manslaughter convictions against three of the twelve attackers. Hynes and Drury do not spare criticism of those they found to be at fault, including Mayor Edward Koch, Queens District Attorney John Santucci, and Al Sharpton, who they believe used the attacks to further his own political cause. Genevieve Stuttaford, writing in *Publishers Weekly,* called the book a "brisk, evenhanded, modestly told procedural."

The Rescue Season: The Heroic Story of Parajumpers on the Edge of the World chronicles the time Drury spent with the 210th Alaska Pararescue Squadron during the 1999 rescue season. A unit of the U.S. Air Force, the 210th is one of only three parajumper units in the United States authorized to conduct rescue operations for both civilians and military personnel. Drury provides a detailed account of the daily lives of the rescuers, including their rigorous training and dedication to the mission. In the harsh environment of mountaintops and deep valleys, the members of the 210th regularly pit their wits and strength against natural forces, risking their lives willingly and bravely to save those who should perhaps have known better than to challenge nature's power. Drury avoids excessively romanticizing the parajumpers in his account; instead, "he shows us that they are real people who just happen to do an incredibly difficult job," remarked *Booklist* reviewer David Pitt. Drury "displays a good tactical understanding of alpine rescue methods and convincingly relates the thoughts and motivations of the individual parajumpers," stated a *Publishers Weekly* contributor. "Truly lovely passages emerge from his accounts of the unit's most memorable rescues," as the parajumpers traverse breathtakingly beautiful but deceptive lethal terrain to help those who have been injured, abandoned, or otherwise hard pressed by the unyielding force of nature, noted Louise Jarvis in the *New York Times Book Review. Library Journal* reviewer Jo-Anne Mary Benson called the book a "revealing examination of a remarkable profession."

Halsey's Typhoon: The True Story of a Fighting Admiral, an Epic Storm, and an Untold Rescue, written with Tom Clavin, uses newly declassified material to describe one of the major maritime events of World War II, one which had gone largely unreported for decades. The famed Admiral William Halsey was partly responsible for losing three destroyers and eight hundred men when he put his fleet in the path of a 1944 typhoon. The authors recount the pressured decision-making that led to this maritime disaster, as well as the heroic efforts to save fellow sailors in the aftermath. A *Publishers Weekly* reviewer wrote that the book is "a vivid tale of tragedy and gallantry at sea." A *Kirkus Reviews* critic faulted the work for weak characterization, but concluded: "The inherent drama of the events compensates for the sometimes lackluster storytelling." However, Roland Green, writing in *Booklist,* had no such critical reservations, terming *Halsey's Typhoon* "an entirely gripping account and a guaranteed hit with maritime buffs."

BIOGRAPHICAL AND CRITICAL SOURCES:

PERIODICALS

Booklist, December 15, 2000, David Pitt, review of *The Rescue Season: The Heroic Story of Para-*

jumpers on the Edge of the World, p. 765; November 15, 2006, Roland Green, review of *Halsey's Typhoon: The True Story of a Fighting Admiral, an Epic Storm, and an Untold Rescue,* p. 20.

Internet Bookwatch, March 1, 2007, review of *Halsey's Typhoon.*

Kirkus Reviews, October 1, 2006, review of *Halsey's Typhoon,* p. 998.

Library Journal, December, 2000, Jo-Anne Mary Benson, review of *The Rescue Season,* p. 168.

Men's Health, September 1, 2006, Erin Hobday, biography of Bob Drury, p. 24.

New York Times, February 11, 1990, Linda Wolfe, "One Night in Queens," review of *Incident at Howard Beach: The Case for Murder.*

New York Times Book Review, February 18, 2001, Louise Jarvis, "Saving Fools Gladly: Air Force Parajumpers in Alaska Often Come to the Rescue of Weekend Warriors," review of *The Rescue Season,* p. 13.

Publishers Weekly, January 5, 1990, Genevieve Stuttaford, review of *Incident at Howard Beach,* p. 58; April 20, 1992, review of *Mafia Cop,* p. 44; November 20, 2000, review of *The Rescue Season,* p. 54; October 9, 2006, review of *Halsey's Typhoon,* p. 47.

Washington Monthly, February 1, 1990, Patricia Cohen, review of *Incident at Howard Beach,* p. 60.

ONLINE

Halsey's Typhoon Web site, http://www.halseys typhoon.com (April 24, 2007).*

*   *   *

DUBLIN, D.H.

[A pseudonym]

(Jonathan McGoran)

PERSONAL: Married; children: one. *Education:* Attended college.

ADDRESSES: Home—Elkins Park, PA. *Agent*—Kim Lionetti, BookEnds, LLC, 136 Long Hill Rd., Gillette, NJ 07933. *E-mail*—jonmcgoran@jmcgoran.com.

CAREER: Writer and editor. Has worked as a freelance copywriter.

WRITINGS:

Body Trace, Berkley (New York, NY), 2006.
Blood Poison: A C.S.U. Investigation, Berkley (New York, NY), 2007.

Editor of the *Weavers Way Shuttle.*

SIDELIGHTS: D.H. Dublin is a pseudonym for Jonathan McGoran. His debut novel, *Body Trace,* is the first in his forensic crime series based in Philadelphia and featuring Madison Cross, a former star medical student who leaves medicine behind and joins the Philadelphia Police Department Crime Scenes Unit. *Body Trace* finds the rookie Madison, whose deceased father was a cop, teamed with Melissa Rourke on a case involving the drug deaths of two university sorority sisters. Under pressure from her uncle, David Cross, who oversees the unit, Madison and her partner set out to resolve the case as accidental deaths but quickly end up alienating local politicians and the university president when Madison insists that the evidence just does not add up to accidental overdoses. Instead, she believes that the girls were murdered, and her suspicions are leaked to the newspaper. Eventually, Madison's investigation leads her to the local crime underworld in some of the worst sections of Philadelphia. A *Publishers Weekly* contributor noted that the author's "detailed approach and lively characters make an immersive read." In a review on the *Who-Dunnit.com* Web site, Alan Paul Curtis wrote that the author "provides a slightly new twist on a very well-worn theme, and does it with flair and panache."

BIOGRAPHICAL AND CRITICAL SOURCES:

PERIODICALS

Publishers Weekly, July 24, 2006, review of *Body Trace,* p. 42.

ONLINE

Book Ends Blog, http://bookendslitagency.blogspot. com/ (September 14, 2006), author interview.

Jonathan McGoran My Space Web site, http://www.myspace.com/jonmcgoran (April 21, 2007).

Jonathan McGoran Web site, http://www.jmcgoran.com (September 21, 2007).

Who Dunnit, http://who-dunnit.com/ August 23, 2006), Alan Paul Curtis, review of *Body Trace.*

*   *   *

DULMUS, Catherine N. 1956-

PERSONAL: Born October 31, 1956, in Westfield, NY; children: Joshua B., Katie E., Abigail V. *Ethnicity:* "Caucasian." *Education:* Buffalo State College, B.S.W., 1989; University at Buffalo, M.S.W., 1991, Ph.D., 1999.

ADDRESSES: Home—Williamsville, NY. *Office*—Buffalo Center for Social Research, University at Buffalo, 221 Parker Hall, Buffalo, NY 14214-8004; fax: 716-829-3992. *E-mail*—cdulmus@buffalo.edu.

CAREER: Salvation Army, Jamestown, NY, community outreach director, 1989-91; Olean General Hospital, Olean, NY, medical-psychiatric social worker, 1991-93; Buffalo Psychiatric Center, Olean, social worker and mental health therapist, 1992-93; Olean City School District, Olean, director of Even Start Literacy Program, 1993-95; Cattaraugus County Mental Health, Olean, director of Continuing Day TX Program, 1995; Olean City School District, director of Even Start Literacy Program, 1996-98; East Carolina University, Greenville, NC, assistant professor of social work, 1998-99; University of Tennessee, Knoxville, assistant professor, 1999-2004, associate professor of social work, 2004-05; University at Buffalo, Buffalo, NY, associate professor of social work, associate dean for research, and director of Buffalo Center for Social Research, 2005—. State of New York, certified school social worker and licensed clinical social worker; American Board of Mental Health Specialists, member of clinical board of directors, 2005—; member of Council on Social Work Education, 1998—, and International Consortium for Social Development, 2001—; conference presenter. Program evaluator for health providers; consultant to nursing homes; also mental health consultant.

MEMBER: International Association of School of Social Work, International Federation of Social Workers, Academy of Certified Social Workers, National Association of Social Workers, Society for Social Work and Research, Baccalaureate Social Work Program Directors, Society for Prevention Research, Society for International Cooperation in Social Work.

AWARDS, HONORS: Award from National Association of Black Social Workers, 2004, for work toward diversity in admissions at University of Tennessee; Provost's Excellence in Teaching Award, University of Tennessee.

WRITINGS:

(With J.S. Wodarski, L.A. Rapp-Paglicci, and A.E. Jongsma) *Social Work and Human Service Planner,* John Wiley (New York, NY), 2001.

(With J.S. Wodarski and L.A. Wodarski) *Adolescent Depression and Suicide: A Comprehensive Empirical Intervention for Prevention and Treatment,* Charles C. Thomas Publishers (Springfield, IL), 2003.

(With R. Ellis and J.S. Wodarski) *Essentials of Child Welfare,* John Wiley (New York, NY), 2003.

(Editor, with L.A. Rapp-Paglicci and J.S. Wodarski, and contributor) *Handbook of Preventive Interventions for Children and Adolescents,* John Wiley (New York, NY), 2004.

(Editor, with K.M. Sowers) *How Institutions Are Shaping the Future of Our Children,* Haworth Press (Binghamton, NY), 2004.

(Editor, with K.M. Sowers, and contributor) *Kids and Violence: The Invisible School Experience,* Haworth Press (Binghamton, NY), 2004.

(Editor, with L.A. Rapp-Paglicci, and contributor) *Handbook of Preventive Interventions for Adults,* John Wiley (New York, NY), 2005.

(Editor, with J.A. Blackburn) *Handbook of Gerontology: Evidence-Based Approaches to Theory, Practice, and Policy,* John Wiley (New York, NY), 2007.

Contributor to books, including *Handbook of Empirical Social Work Practice,* edited by B.A. Thyer and J.S. Wodarski, John Wiley (New York, NY), 1998; *Human Behavior and the Social Environment: Integrating Theory and Evidence-Based Practice,* edited by J.S. Wodarski and S. Dziegielewski, Springer (New York, NY), 2002; *Handbook of Violence,* edited by L.A. Rapp-Paglicci, A.R. Roberts, and J.S. Wodarski,

John Wiley (New York, NY), 2002; *Women and Girls in the Social Environment: Behavioral Perspectives,* edited by N.J. Smyth, Haworth Press (Binghamton, NY), 2003; and *Comprehensive Mental Health Practice with Sex Offenders and Their Families,* edited by C. Hilarski and J.S. Wodarski, Haworth Press (Binghamton, NY), 2006. Contributor to professional journals, including *School Social Work Journal, Families in Society, Victims and Offenders, Research on Social Work Practice, Children and Youth Services Review, Brief Treatment and Crisis Intervention,* and *Health and Social Work.* Founding coeditor, *Journal of Evidence-Based Social Work: Advances in Practice, Programming, Research, and Policy,* 2002—, and *Best Practices in Mental Health: An International Journal,* 2004—; founding associate editor, *Stress, Trauma, and Crisis: An International Journal,* 2003—; guest editor, *Journal of Evidence-Based Social Work,* 2004, and *Journal of Human Behavior in the Social Environment,* 2004, 2007.

BIOGRAPHICAL AND CRITICAL SOURCES:

ONLINE

Catherine N. Dulmus Home Page, http://myprofile. cos.com/dulmus1 (April 2, 2007).

* * *

DUMAS, Margaret

PERSONAL: Education: Holds a master's degree.

ADDRESSES: Home—San Francisco, CA. *E-mail*—margaret@margaretdumas.com.

CAREER: Writer, novelist, and technical writer. Former executive at a major software company in San Francisco, CA.

MEMBER: Crime Writers' Association.

AWARDS, HONORS: Debut Dagger Award shortlist, Crime Writers' Association, 2003, for *Speak Now.*

WRITINGS:

NOVELS

Speak Now, Poisoned Pen Press (Scottsdale, AZ), 2004.
How to Succeed in Murder, Poisoned Pen Press (Scottsdale, AZ), 2006.
The Balance Thing, Harper (New York, NY), 2006.

SIDELIGHTS: Margaret Dumas is a technical writer and novelist who once served as an executive in a software company. In her debut mystery novel, *Speak Now,* Dumas introduces Charley Fairfax, nee Van Leeuwen, a wealthy woman in her mid-thirties who runs an independent repertory theater company in San Francisco. During the previous year, Charley sold her apartment and went to England to learn as much as she could about running a theater company. While there, she married a handsome and dashing military meteorologist, Jack Fairfax, after a whirlwind romance that lasted only six weeks. Charley realizes there are some things about Jack she does not really know or understand, such as why he was stationed in the desert, but she passes it all off as secrets she will learn when and if necessary. When the two return to America, they take up temporary residence in a luxury hotel, but their stay is ruined when a dead body is discovered in the bathtub. Soon after, Charley's life begins to get more and more complicated, as she deals with the repercussions of the murder, struggles to keep her theater company together while staging a new show, reacts to friends and family who are curious about her sudden marriage, and begins to realize that Jack conceals many more secrets that even she had suspected. Charley recognizes that the mystery surrounding the murder somehow involves Jack, and soon it becomes apparent that someone from his past has definite intentions to ruin their future. Christine E. Menefee, writing in the *School Library Journal,* observed: "This humorous if unlikely tale will entertain readers who like a light mystery with an urban attitude." A *Publishers Weekly* reviewer concluded that "Dumas's sparkling debut should appeal to both cozy and chick-lit fans."

Charley returns in *How to Succeed in Murder,* Dumas's second mystery. Long-delayed honeymoon plans for Charley and husband, Jack, are once again put on hold when software company CEO Morgan Stokes approaches Jack to seek his help. Stokes is searching for a corporate spy and saboteur who has planted a fatal flaw in the company's flagship product. If the bug is activated, Stokes fears that the repercussions could wipe him out. The danger of the case is intensified by the death of Stokes's fiancee, who died late at night in a health club steam room. Charley undertakes an investigation into the murder and looks for additional assistance from her friends in the theater, while Jack calls on his computer geek colleagues to assist in the investigation of the software bug. To get at the saboteur more easily, Jack and Charley assume the identities of high-powered corporate consultants, nosing around Stokes's company during business hours. While Charley laments the need for her to dress, act, and rise in the morning like her workaday friends, Jack turns up as much information as he can while his assistants corroborate findings. A *Publishers Weekly* reviewer commented favorably on the novel's "charming setting, not-so-serious tension," and "cozy clique of appealing characters."

With *The Balance Thing,* Dumas steps away from the mystery genre and into chick lit. Rebecca "Becks" Mansfield is a career-driven woman in San Francisco whose fortunes have taken a downward turn with the dot-com bust. Unemployed and growing ever more frantic about her situation, Becks finds it difficult to locate an appropriate job to match the one she lost in software marketing. She does work as the voice of an animated character, a female vampire named Vladima who is beloved by tech geeks everywhere. However, voicing Vladima is not what she wants to do. As she seeks other opportunities, Becks realizes that there is a definite attraction between her and Josh, Vladima's creator, who is a bit nerdy but cute. *Library Journal* reviewer Andrea Y. Griffith noted that "both fans of her earlier novels and general chick-lit readers will be more than satisfied" with Becks's adventures.

BIOGRAPHICAL AND CRITICAL SOURCES:

PERIODICALS

Booklist, September 1, 2004, Barbara Bibel, review of *Speak Now,* p. 68; September 1, 2006, Aleksandra Kostovski, review of *The Balance Thing,* p. 54.
Bookwatch, December 1, 2004, review of *Speak Now.*
California Bookwatch, August 1, 2006, review of *How to Succeed in Murder.*

Library Journal, June 1, 2004, Ann Kim, review of *Speak Now,* p. 109; September 1, 2006, Andrea Y. Griffith, review of *The Balance Thing,* p. 135.
Publishers Weekly, September 6, 2004, review of *Speak Now,* p. 50; March 20, 2006, review of *How to Succeed in Murder,* p. 40; July 31, 2006, review of *The Balance Thing,* p. 50.
School Library Journal, January 1, 2005, Christine C. Menefee, review of *Speak Now,* p. 159.

ONLINE

Armchair Interviews, http://www.armchairinterviews. com/ (April 24, 2007), Carrie Padgett, review of *Speak Now.*
BookLoons, http://www.bookloons.com/ (April 24, 2007), Mary Ann Smyth, review of *Speak Now;* Mary Ann Smyth, review of *How to Succeed in Murder.*
Margaret Dumas Home Page, http://www.margaret dumas.com (April 24, 2007).
MyShelf.com, http://www.myshelf.com/ (April 27, 2007), Sheila Griffin, review of *Speak Now.*
Romantic Times, http://www.romantictimes.com/ (April 24, 2007), Cindy Harrison, review of *Speak Now,* and Lauren Spielberg, review of *The Balance Thing.**

*   *   *

DUNNAVANT, Keith 1965(?)-

PERSONAL: Born c. 1965; son of Bob, Sr. (a radio broadcaster) and Marjorie Dunnavant. *Education:* University of Alabama, graduated, 1988.

ADDRESSES: Agent—David Black Literary Agency, 156 5th Ave., New York, NY 10010. *E-mail*—Akd2006@allmail.net.

CAREER: Former sports editor for the *Journal of Athens,* Athens, AL, and a sports correspondent for the *Decatur Daily* and *Huntsville News;* sports writer for newspapers, including the *Birmingham Post-Herald, Dallas Times Herald, Los Angeles Times,* and the *National Sports Daily;* also wrote for *Sports, Inc.* (magazine); Solovox Publishing, Atlanta, GA, founder and president; founder of *Dunnavant's Paydirt Illustrated* magazine, 1993.

AWARDS, HONORS: Recipient of awards for writing and editing from various organizations, including the Football Writer's Association of America, the Society of Professional Journalists, the William Randolph Hearst Foundation, the Magazine Association of the Southeast, the Florida Magazine Association, and the Alabama Sportswriters' Association.

WRITINGS:

Coach: The Life of Paul "Bear" Bryant, Simon & Schuster (New York, NY), 1996, revised edition, Thomas Dunne Books (New York, NY), 2005.
(With Edgar Welden) *Time Out! A Sports Fan's Dream Year,* Will Publishing (Birmingham, AL), 1999.
The Fifty-Year Seduction: How Television Manipulated College Football, from the Birth of the Modern NCAA to the Creation of the BCS, Thomas Dunne Books (New York, NY), 2004.
The Missing Ring: How Bear Bryant and the 1966 Alabama Crimson Tide Were Denied College Football's Most Elusive Prize, Thomas Dunne Books (New York, NY), 2006.

Editor, *Adweek Magazine's Special Report;* executive editor, *Atlanta;* managing editor, *Mediaweek.*

SIDELIGHTS: A former sports journalist who now heads his own publishing business, Keith Dunnavant is well known for his sports books. In two books, he writes about the late college coach Paul Bryant, who led the football team at Dunnavant's alma mater, the University of Alabama. Known as the Crimson Tide, the team is legendary in college football circles. Dunnavant began his sports journalism career at the young age of fourteen, when he convinced the editor of his local paper, the *Journal of Athens,* to create a sports section, which it lacked at the time. While still a high school student, he wrote for other newspapers, as well, and also was a sports announcer on cable television. While at the University of Alabama, he naturally reported on his college's teams and became a big admirer of Bryant, though the coach had retired and passed away some years earlier. Bryant would be the subject of Dunnavant's first book, *Coach: The Life of Paul "Bear" Bryant.*

With 523 wins under his belt when he retired in 1982, Bryant has been called the winningest coach in college football history. Dunnavant, while showing some

bias, strives to portray the coach objectively, including his faults. For example, Bryant had a reputation for being brutally strict with his players, and was considered by many to be more skilled as a motivator than as a strategist. Yet Dunnavant admires Bryant as "the embodiment of the coach as father figure," as Wes Lukowsky noted in a *Booklist* review of this "thought-provoking" portrait. *Sporting News* contributor Steve Gietschier praised the author because he "does not shy from the view that Bryant was always the toughest man in the room and, in some ways, a brutal coach," while still doing the coach "both honor and justice" in the biography.

Dunnavant returns to the story of Bryant in *The Missing Ring: How Bear Bryant and the 1966 Alabama Crimson Tide Were Denied College Football's Most Elusive Prize.* While ostensibly about events that led up to the notorious game against Notre Dame in which the Crimson Tide's opponents deliberately let the clock run out with the game tied, thus denying Alabama a win and a chance at the championship, the book actually is a "broader portrait of the celebrated but flawed University of Alabama football teams coached by Bear Bryant," according to Alan Moores in *Booklist.* Calling the work a "solid if somewhat overlong study," a *Publishers Weekly* reviewer observed that Dunnavant addresses a wide spectrum of influences on the team. While offering "insightful profiles" of the football players, the author also delves into the racial climate of 1960s Alabama.

In addition to his books about the University of Alabama football team, Dunnavant has written on other subjects as well. For example, he helped Edgar Welden write *Time Out! A Sports Fan's Dream Year,* which is about the year Welden took a year away from work to travel the country, watching all kinds of sports and talking to players whenever he could. Also noted as an expert on the business of college sports, Dunnavant wrote *The Fifty-Year Seduction: How Television Manipulated College Football, from the Birth of the Modern NCAA to the Creation of the BCS,* a critique of the negative influence of the media on sports in America. While describing the research as "impressive," *Sports Illustrated* writer Charles Hirshberg regrettably called the result "not very entertaining because, alas, it's mostly about lawsuits and meetings."

On a completely different topic, Dunnavant also worked on a book about rocket scientist Werner von

Braun. He had to drop the project, however, when coworkers accidentally threw out three years of his research. Continuing to work on nonfiction book projects, Dunnavant has made a name for himself in publishing, notably founding *Dunnavant's Paydirt Illustrated* in 1993, a college football magazine with over one hundred thousand subscribers.

BIOGRAPHICAL AND CRITICAL SOURCES:

PERIODICALS

Booklist, September 15, 1996, Wes Lukowsky, review of *Coach: The Life of Paul "Bear" Bryant,* p. 202; September 1, 2006, Alan Moores, review of *The Missing Ring: How Bear Bryant and the 1966 Alabama Crimson Tide Were Denied College Football's Most Elusive Prize,* p. 46.

Decatur Daily, September 19, 2006, review of "South toward Home": *The Missing Ring* Brings Athens High Graduate Back to His Roots in Alabama," profile of Keith Dunnavant.

Insight on the News, May 31, 1999, Dick Heller, "The Ultimate Sports Fan," review of *Time Out! A Sports Fan's Dream Year,* p. 43.

Publishers Weekly, August 12, 1996, review of *Coach,* p. 74; July 31, 2006, review of *The Missing Ring,* p. 73.

Sporting News, March 17, 1997, Steve Gietschier, review of *Coach,* p. 9.

Sports Illustrated, November 1, 2004, Charles Hirshberg, "Shark Tales: Lawsuits, Boardroom Jukes, Negotiating Jive: Who Knew There Was So Much Predatory Behavior behind College Football Telecasts?," review of *The Fifty-Year Seduction: How Television Manipulated College Football, from the Birth of the Modern NCAA to the Creation of the BCS,* p. 12.

ONLINE

Keith Dunnavant Home Page, http://keithdunnavant. com (May 16, 2007).

Missing Ring Web site, http://www.missingring.com (May 16, 2007).*

E

EAGLETON, Thomas F. 1929-2007
(Thomas Francis Eagleton)

OBITUARY NOTICE— See index for *CA* sketch: Born September 4, 1929, in St. Louis, MO; died March 4, 2007, in Richmond Heights, MO. Politician, attorney, and author. A U.S. senator from Missouri, Eagleton is often remembered for his brief candidacy for U.S. vice president in 1972. After graduating from Amherst College in 1950, he completed his law degree at Harvard in 1953 and went into private practice. Eagleton was assistant general counsel to the Anheuser-Busch company and then was elected circuit attorney in St. Louis in 1956. Elected attorney general of Missouri in 1961, he then served as lieutenant governor of his state from 1965 to 1968. Eagleton won the U.S. Senate race in 1968 on the Democratic ticket and was serving in Washington when presidential hopeful George McGovern asked him to be his running mate. Eagleton was not actually McGovern's first choice, but Senator Edward Kennedy had turned down the invitation. The honor would be short-lived for Eagleton, however, who came under media scrutiny. It was discovered that he had undergone psychological treatment for clinical depression on more than one occasion. McGovern initially stood behind his choice of running mate, but only eighteen days after tapping Eagleton he asked the senator to step aside and replaced him with R. Sargent Shriver. In spite of that decision, Eagleton was easily reelected to office in 1974 and remained in the Senate until he decided to retire from office in 1986. During these years, he worked to pass legislation against racial discrimination and in support of abortion rights. His proudest achievement, he would later say, was getting legislation passed in 1973 that stopped the U.S. bombing in Cambodia. After leaving office, Eagleton was on the board of the Chicago Mercantile Exchange for two years and then returned to a private law practice in St. Louis. He taught law at Washington University from 1987 to 1999 and was on the president's foreign intelligence advisory board from 1993 to 1998. One of his happiest achievements in later years was his involvement in convincing the Los Angeles Rams football team to relocate to St. Louis. Eagleton was the author of *War and Presidential Power: A Chronicle of Congressional Surrender* (1974) and, more recently, *Issues in Business and Government* (1991). He was writing a memoir about his years in the Senate at the time of his death.

OBITUARIES AND OTHER SOURCES:

PERIODICALS

Chicago Tribune, March 5, 2007.
Los Angeles Times, March 5, 2007, p. B9.
New York Times, March 5, 2007, p. A21; March 6, 2007, p. A2.
Times (London, England), March 15, 2007, p. 66.

*   *   *

EAGLETON, Thomas Francis
See EAGLETON, Thomas F.

EATON, Susan E.

PERSONAL: Education: Attended University of Massachusetts—Amherst; Harvard University, Ed.D.

ADDRESSES: Home—MA.

CAREER: Harvard University, Cambridge, MA, former assistant director of Project on School Desegregation, former consulting researcher for Civil Rights Project, research director at Charles Hamilton Houston Institute for Race and Justice at the Harvard Law School. Has also worked as a journalist.

AWARDS, HONORS: Awards from the Massachusetts Teachers Association and the National Association of Black Journalists.

WRITINGS:

(With Gary Orfield) *Dismantling Desegregation: The Quiet Reversal of Brown v. Board of Education,* New Press (New York, NY), 1996.
The Other Boston Busing Story: What's Won and Lost across the Boundary Line, Yale University Press (New Haven, CT), 2001.
The Children in Room E4: American Education on Trial, Algonquin Books of Chapel Hill (Chapel Hill, NC), 2007.

Contributor to periodicals, including *New York Times, Nation, Boston Globe Sunday Magazine, Virginia Quarterly Review, Education Week,* and the *Hartford Courant.*

SIDELIGHTS: Susan E. Eaton has written several books about the unfinished school desegregation movement that, she argues, have left American students in poor sections of the country behind their affluent peers. She argues that U.S. courts are reversing early attempts at desegregation and she recounts the effects these judgments are having on school children. In *Dismantling Desegregation: The Quiet Reversal of Brown v. Board of Education,* written with Gary Orfield, Eaton describes how court rulings since *Brown v. the Board of Education* in 1954 have eroded progress in several cases in the 1990s. The authors provide examples of school systems in such places as

Detroit, Michigan, Charlotte, North Carolina, and Little Rock, Arkansas, where there have been both advances and gains. They conclude that busing students does not work all that well, but that the solution lies in greater efforts to desegregate residential communities, an answer that a *Publishers Weekly* contributor considered "possibly good, if not yet politically feasible, advice."

In *The Other Boston Busing Story: What's Won and Lost across the Boundary Line,* Eaton focuses on the case of Boston's Metropolitan Council for Educational Opportunity program (METCO), a voluntary school desegregation program founded in 1965. Interviewing dozens of adults who attended schools through the program, the author found that many felt they had received a better education but that the program also left them feeling alienated from their neighborhoods. Some interviewees, interestingly, also commented that what seemed to matter was not that they actually got a better education but that the perception was that they did. While Eaton does not offer alternatives in this book, "her research, she feels, may help in the designing of future programs to ease racial tensions in education," according to Terry Christner in the *Library Journal. American Enterprise* reviewer Naomi Schaefer felt that "it's unfortunate that Eaton gives short shrift to other options that are now, or might soon become, available to children similar to those who participated in Metco," but a *Publishers Weekly* writer concluded that "general readers who are seriously interested in race relations or education reform will want to read this book."

A lawsuit that lingered in the courts for eighteen years, *Sheff v. O'Neill,* is at the center of Eaton's *The Children in Room E4: American Education on Trial.* The case concerned the way school districts were drawn in Hartford, Connecticut, in such a way that the poorest section of the city was effectively cut off from the surrounding affluent districts. *Sheff v. O'Neill* was an attempt to counteract the earlier *Milliken v. Bradley* case, which allowed for busing without actually having poor students sent to the richer white suburbs. Eaton, in particular, describes the students in one classroom at Simpson-Waverly Elementary led by teacher Lois Luddy. Although Eaton portrays Luddy as a remarkably talented and dedicated teacher, all her efforts cannot adequately compensate for the racial and economic segregation and concentrated disadvantage of the school the children attend and the neighborhood where they live. *American Prospect* contributor Richard D. Kahlenberg commented that the book contains "the subtext that we could make segregated schools work if we only had more truly dedicated teachers. But Eaton turns this familiar script on its head" in this "well-crafted book." Calling Eaton a "graceful and fluent writer," a *Publishers Weekly* critic stated that by "bringing this situation to light, [Eaton] has significantly articulated the problems that challenge politicians, school boards and concerned citizens."

BIOGRAPHICAL AND CRITICAL SOURCES:

PERIODICALS

Adolescence, winter, 1996, review of *Dismantling Desegregation: The Quiet Reversal of Brown v. Board of Education.*

American Enterprise, October 1, 2001, Naomi Schaefer, review of *The Other Boston Busing Story: What's Won and Lost across the Boundary Line,* p. 55.

American Prospect, January 1, 2007, Richard D. Kahlenberg, "Back to Class," review of *The Children in Room E4: American Education on Trial,* p. 41.

Booklist, August 1, 1996, Mary Carroll, review of *Dismantling Desegregation,* p. 1864; March 15, 2001, Vanessa Bush, review of *The Other Boston Busing Story,* p. 1336; February 1, 2007, Vanessa Bush, review of *The Children in Room E4,* p. 21.

Education, summer, 2001, review of *The Other Busing Story.*

Entertainment Weekly, January 19, 2007, Gilbert Cruz, review of *The Children in Room E4,* p. 85.

Kirkus Reviews, October 15, 2006, review of *The Children in Room E4,* p. 1053.

Library Journal, April 1, 2001, Terry Christner, review of *The Other Boston Busing Story,* p. 112; December 1, 2006, Jean Caspers, review of *The Children in Room E4,* p. 137.

Michigan Law Review, May 1, 1997, Davison M. Douglas, review of *Dismantling Desegregation,* p. 1715.

Publishers Weekly, June 3, 1996, review of *Dismantling Desegregation,* p. 68; February 12, 2001, review of *The Other Boston Busing Story,* p. 193; November 13, 2006, review of *The Children in Room E4,* p. 45.*

EDELMAN, Hope

PERSONAL: Married Uzi Eliahou; children: Maya, Eden. *Education:* Northwestern University, B.S.; University of Iowa, M.A. *Hobbies and other interests:* Playing guitar.

ADDRESSES: Home—Topanga, CA. *E-mail*—hope@ hopeedelman.com.

CAREER: Whittle Communications, Knoxville, TN, editor, three years, c. 1980s; Antioch University—Los Angeles, CA, writing instructor, 2001-06. Visiting lecturer, University of Iowa, Provincetown Fine Arts Work Center, Iowa Summer Writing Festival, UCLA Extension; cofounder, West Coast Writers Workshops. Board member, Motherless Daughters of Orange County and PEN West; advisory board member, Mommy's Light Lives On.

MEMBER: PEN West, Authors Guild.

AWARDS, HONORS: Pushcart Prize, for creative nonfiction; *New York Times* notable book award.

WRITINGS:

Motherless Daughters: The Legacy of Loss, Addison-Wesley (Reading, MA), 1994, 2nd edition, Da Capo Press (Cambridge, MA), 2006.

(Editor and author of introduction) *Letters from Motherless Daughters: Words of Courage, Grief, and Healing,* Addison-Wesley (Reading, MA), 1995.

Mother of My Mother: The Intricate Bond between Generations, Dial Press (New York, NY), 1999.

Motherless Mothers: How Mother Loss Shapes the Parents We Become, HarperCollins (New York, NY), 2006.

Contributor to anthologies, including *The Bitch in the House, Toddler,* and *Blindsided by a Diaper.* Contributor to periodicals, including *Glamour, Seventeen, Child, Self, Real Simple, Iowa Review, San Francisco Chronicle, Washington Post, Los Angeles Times,* and the *New York Times. Motherless Daughters* has been translated into seven languages.

SIDELIGHTS: Hope Edelman originally intended to be a journalist. While studying at Northwestern University, however, she came to the conclusion that becoming a reporter was not for her. She considered going into magazine writing; then, while she was studying at the Iowa Writer's Workshop, one of her teachers suggested she write about her mother's death from breast cancer when Edelman was seventeen. Edelman took this advice, and the result was *Motherless Daughters: The Legacy of Loss.* In this work, the author not only talks about her own emotions and thoughts but she also interviews some two hundred and fifty other women who have experienced similar losses in their lives. Edelman notes that how a mother's death affects a daughter depends on several factors, including how old the child was at the time and the circumstances of the death. For example, a daughter whose mother died when she was younger than twelve years old will likely have a more idealized picture of the parent; losing a mother when one is a teenager or older will leave a much more realistic memory of the mother, including both her flaws and more positive attributes. Daughters who lose their mother suddenly, especially to suicide or in an accident will be more traumatized.

Edelman emphasizes that the support of family and others in a child's life is extremely important after a mother's death. "A child should have a stable caregiver who can provide a supportive environment that makes children feel comfortable about expressing their feelings," she explained in a *People* article. "If the family can't provide that, support groups are essential. If everyone around you tells you not to talk about something that has affected you profoundly, you develop a sense of shame. Families should be encouraged to talk about Mom that first Christmas, birthday or holiday without her and to keep her as a part of them. They should let the children know she was important to them and can remain so. A daughter's longing for her mother never disappears, but you don't have to shut the door on the past." *Reviewer's Bookwatch* contributor Mary Cowper called *Motherless Daughters* "an informative and expertly contributive documentation of the psychological and spiritual effects" on a child after a mother has died.

Building on the theme of her first book, Edelman wrote *Mother of My Mother: The Intricate Bond between Generations* and *Motherless Mothers: How Mother Loss Shapes the Parents We Become.* The first book is about grandmothers and their granddaughters. In a style that "is much like reading a diary," as Sheila Devaney commented in the *Library Journal,* the author talks about the influence both her mother and her mother's mother had on her. This makes for "insightful reading," according to Devaney. The author also interviewed seventy other women and surveyed nearly two hundred others about their relationships with their grandmothers. "Edelman is at her best illuminating the complexity of girls' and women's feelings toward their mothers and grandmothers," observed a *Publishers Weekly* writer, who felt that the nature of the research resulted in a "slightly choppy" narrative that is nevertheless a "worthwhile read."

Motherless Mothers draws on Edelman's own emotions after giving birth to her second child. She struggled with balancing a newborn infant along with raising a toddler and taking care of a home. While trying to manage all this work, she longed for her mother's help. Wondering how other women in her situation felt, she surveyed about one thousand people for their insights. "I found that the motherless mothers had a lot of the same thoughts and concerns and fears as other mothers, but they were 'amped up' a little bit," she explained to an interviewer on the *Literary Mama* Web site. Observing that the work is not so much about grief and mourning as it is "a supportive guide for mothers who may feel overwhelmed and alone," a *Publishers Weekly* critic asserted that Edelman "presents emotionally charged concepts in clear, memorable terms."

BIOGRAPHICAL AND CRITICAL SOURCES:

PERIODICALS

Library Journal, May 1, 1999, Sheila Devaney, review of *Mother of My Mother: The Intricate Bond between Generations,* p. 97; February 1, 2006, Lynne Maxwell, review of *Motherless Mothers: How Mother Loss Shapes the Parents We Become,* p. 95.

People, August 8, 1994, "The Loss That Lingers," interview with Hope Edelman, p. 61; April 17, 2006, "When Mom Is Gone," p. 138.

Publishers Weekly, April 11, 1994, review of *Motherless Daughters: The Legacy of Loss,* p. 50; March 8, 1999, review of *Mother of My Mother,* p. 55; January 23, 2006, review of *Motherless Mothers,* p. 194.

Reference & Research Book News, August 1, 2006, review of *Motherless Mothers.*

Reviewer's Bookwatch, May 1, 2006, Mary Cowper, review of *Motherless Daughters.*

ONLINE

Antioch University—Los Angeles Web site, http://www.antiochla.edu/ (May 17, 2007), faculty profile of Hope Edelman.

Hope Edelman Home Page, http://www.hopeedelman.com (May 17, 2007).

Literary Mama, http://www.literarymama.com/ (May 17, 2007), "An Interview with Hope Edelman."

*   *   *

EHRENREICH, Ben

PERSONAL: Male.

ADDRESSES: Home—Los Angeles, CA.

CAREER: Writer.

WRITINGS:

The Suitors (novel), Counterpoint Press (New York, NY), 2006.

Contributor to periodicals, including *L.A. Weekly, New York Times, Village Voice, Topic,* and *Believer.*

SIDELIGHTS: Ben Ehrenreich's novel *The Suitors* is the author's re-imagining of Homer's *Odyssey.* Ehrenreich's version is "richly imagined" and "inspirited by a dazzling display of verbal gifts," wrote Carl Hays in *Booklist.* In the novel, the Odysseus character is called Payne. Payne has built a fortress around his wife, Penny, and then left her as he goes to fight a war in a far-off land. Penny finds herself surrounded by men eager to take Payne's place, but she remains loyal to her absent husband, until a mysterious stranger arrives. Hays felt that while any similarity to the original *Odyssey* is slight, *The Suitors* is worth reading

on the merits of the author's "prodigious, Joycean prose." He also made note of the book's dark humor, fast-paced action, and psychological insight.

The novel's multiple levels of meaning were remarked upon by Victor Or in his *Library Journal* review of *The Suitors.* Or commented that the book's "excessive depiction of sex" might not be to some readers' liking, but he advised: "ultimately readers should look beneath the surface of this fable for its deeper connotations." The novel struck *New York Times Book Review* contributor Michael J. Agovino as somewhat "pretentious and smarter-than-thou," but he also found the book worthwhile despite that flaw, because the author "writes with an ease and pure line-by-line skill that's rare."

BIOGRAPHICAL AND CRITICAL SOURCES:

PERIODICALS

Booklist, February 15, 2006, Carl Hays, review of *The Suitors,* p. 43.

Library Journal, April 1, 2006, Victor Or, review of *The Suitors,* p. 82.

Los Angeles Magazine, April 1, 2006, Robert Ito, review of *The Suitors,* p. 128.

New York Times Book Review, May 14, 2006, Michael J. Agovino, review of *The Suitors,* p. 14.

Publishers Weekly, December 5, 2005, review of *The Suitors,* p. 27.

ONLINE

Agony Magazine, http://trashotron.com/agony/ (May 8, 2006), review of *The Suitors.*

Seattle Weekly, http://www.seattleweekly.com/ (July 5, 2006), Patrick Enright, review of *The Suitors.**

*   *   *

EINSTEIN, Charles 1926-2007

OBITUARY NOTICE— See index for *CA* sketch: Born August 2, 1926, in Boston, MA; died March 7, 2007, in Michigan City, IN. Journalist and author. Einstein regularly wrote about major league baseball and was the author of an authoritative biography of Willie

Mays and a four-volume anthology on baseball. Graduating from the University of Chicago in 1945, he was hired by the International News Service. He worked in Chicago from 1945 to 1953, and then was a freelancer, before joining the *San Francisco Examiner* staff in 1958. It was while covering the Giants that he really became an avid baseball fan, and the *Chronicle* made him its baseball columnist in 1965. He wrote "The Einstein Theory" column for the next five years, and from 1968 to 1970 was also a columnist for *Sport* magazine. Leaving journalism behind in 1970, Einstein went to work for the New York City public relations firm Manning, Selvage & Lee, becoming its senior vice president and editorial director in 1981. He quit in 1986 to return to journalism and wrote an entertainment column for the Newark *Star-Ledger*. Over the years, Einstein published nonfiction—mostly on baseball—as well as several novels and screenplays. Willie Mays was a favorite topic, about whom he wrote three books and two screenplays. The biography *Willie's Time: A Memoir* (1979) was the best received. Among his many other titles are *Willie Mays: Coast to Coast Giant* (1963), *How to Win at Blackjack* (1968), *Captivity: How I Survived 44 Months as a Prisoner of the Red Chinese* (1973), written with Mary Ann Harbert, the novels *The Bloody Spur* (1953), *The Last Laugh* (1956), and *The Blackjack Hijack* (1976), and the movies *Naked City* (1958), *A Man Named Mays* (1963), and *A New Ball Game for Willie Mays* (1974), among others. Several of his novels were adapted by others as movie screenplays. He also edited *The Fireside Book of Baseball,* a four-volume anthology published between 1956 and 1987.

OBITUARIES AND OTHER SOURCES:

PERIODICALS

Los Angeles Times, March 16, 2007, p. B9.
New York Times, March 19, 2007, p. 15.
Washington Post, March 19, 2007, p. B6.

*　　*　　*

ELY, Leanne

PERSONAL: Children: two.

ADDRESSES: Home—NC. *Office*—Saving Dinner, P.O. Box 118, Waxhaw, NC 28173. *E-mail*—leanneely@aol.com.

CAREER: Writer, columnist, journalist, broadcaster, public speaker, entrepreneur, caterer, and certified nutritional consultant. *Daily Courier,* Rutherford County, NC, feature writer. National Frozen and Refrigerated Foods Association (NFRFA), nutrition expert and consultant. Host of radio show, *The Heart of a Woman* and cohost, the *Fly Show.* Guest on television shows and networks, including QVC, HGTV, ABC, CBS, and Ivanhoe Broadcasting.

WRITINGS:

Healthy Foods: An Irreverent Guide to Understanding Nutrition and Feeding Your Family Well, Champion Press (Fox Point, WI), 2001.

Healthy Foods Unit Study: For Grades 6-9, edited by Brook Noel, Champion Press (Vancouver, WA), 2001.

Healthy Foods Unit Study Guide: For Grades K-5, edited by Brook Noel, Champion Press (Vancouver, WA), 2001.

The Frantic Family Cookbook: (Mostly) Healthy Recipes in Minutes, Champion Press (Milwaukee, WI), 2002.

Saving Dinner: The Menus, Recipes, and Shopping Lists to Bring Your Family Back to the Table, Ballantine Books (New York, NY), 2003.

(With Marla Cilley) *Body Clutter: Love Your Body, Love Yourself,* FlyLady (Brevard, NC), 2005.

Saving Dinner for the Holidays: Menus, Recipes, Shopping Lists, and Timelines for Spectacular, Stress-Free Holidays and Family Celebrations, illustrated by Sandy Strunk, Ballantine Books (New York, NY), 2005.

Saving Dinner the Low-carb Way: Healthy Menus, Recipes, and the Shopping Lists That Will Keep the Whole Family at the Dinner Table, Ballantine Books (New York, NY), 2005.

Saving Dinner Basics: How to Cook Even If You Don't Know How, Ballantine Books (New York, NY), 2006.

Saving Dinner the Vegetarian Way: Healthy Menus, Recipes, and Shopping Lists to Keep Everyone Happy at the Table, Ballantine Books (New York, NY), 2007.

Author and editor of weekly newsletter, *Healthy-Foods;* author and editor of subscription nutrition newsletter, "Menu-Mailer"; author of column for *eDiets.com;* author of syndicated newspaper column, "The Dinner Diva"; author of weekly column, "Food for Thought," *Flylady.net;* author of column, "The Manic Housewife," *Daily Courier* (Rutherford County, NC).

SIDELIGHTS: Food expert, cookbook author, and broadcaster Leanne Ely is a certified nutritional consultant whose work often involves techniques for creating nutritious yet appealing family meals. She concentrates particularly on nutrition for children, and her works include hands-on study guides for children in kindergarten through ninth grade. In other books, Ely offers guidance for preparing vegetarian and low-carb meals, and provides instruction for inexperienced cooks who want to learn how to prepare flavorful but nutritional basic meals.

In *Saving Dinner Basics: How to Cook Even If You Don't Know How,* for example, "the fundamentals of cooking are covered in an easy, colloquial style," noted Courtney Greene in the *Library Journal.* Ely offers advice that covers all aspects of food selection, storage, and preparation, including choosing the proper utensils and cookware, stocking a kitchen with dry and frozen foods, choosing meats and fish, and setting a table. She also includes numerous recipes that cover the preparation of uncomplicated meals with salads, soups, desserts, meat dishes, and easy-to-fix main courses. *Kliatt* reviewer Shirley Reis observed that "experienced cooks will find it reassuring that they are 'doing things right,'" whereas newcomers to the kitchen "will find a wealth of essential information" to make cooking easy and enjoyable.

Ely strives to make her food suggestions healthful as well as delicious, and in *Healthy Foods: An Irreverent Guide to Understanding Nutrition and Feeding Your Family Well,* she provides a nutritionally conscious cooking guide that is also sprinkled with a generous helping of humor. She encourages the use of ingredients such as whole-wheat flours, yogurt, buttermilk, and safflower oil, noted *Booklist* reviewer Mark Knoblauch. Though Ely's approach is humorous and irreverent, the ingredients she recommends "are all healthful ones," Knoblauch observed.

BIOGRAPHICAL AND CRITICAL SOURCES:

PERIODICALS

Booklist, February 15, 2001, Mark Knoblauch, review of *Healthy Foods: An Irreverent Guide to Understanding Nutrition and Feeding Your Family Well,* p. 1106.
Kliatt, January 1, 2007, Shirley Reis, review of *Saving Dinner Basics: How to Cook Even If You Don't Know How,* p. 41.
Library Journal, October 1, 2006, Courtney Greene, review of *Saving Dinner Basics,* p. 100.

ONLINE

Fabulous Foods, http://www.fabulousfoods.com/ (May 24, 2007), biography of Leanne Ely.
Flylady.net, http://www.flylady.net/ (May 24, 2007), biography of Leanne Ely.
Saving Dinner Web site, http://www.savingdinner.com/ (May 24, 2007), biography of Leanne Ely.*

*　　*　　*

ENSOR, Barbara

PERSONAL: Children: two. *Education:* Attended Brown University.

ADDRESSES: Home and office—Brooklyn, NY. *E-mail*—info@barbaraensor.com.

CAREER: Illustrator and writer. Worked previously as a puppeteer.

WRITINGS:

Paul Trapido, *Don't Even Think of Parking Here!: The New York City Guide to Parking and Driving,* Simon & Schuster (New York, NY), 1986.
Cinderella: (As If You Didn't Already Know the Story), Schwartz & Wade Books (New York, NY), 2006.

SIDELIGHTS: Barbara Ensor was raised in London, England, is a graduate of Brown University, and also has a distinctive career history as a former puppeteer. As an author and illustrator, she established a unique career start by writing children's titles that spin traditional fairy tales and re-weave them into a story with a contemporary spin. *Cinderella: (As If You*

Didn't Already Know the Story), for instance, retells the classic fairy tale from a third-person point of view by revealing Cinderella's diary letters to her deceased mother. Cinderella's letters detail her daily struggles and express the distress Cinderella experiences with her new stepmother and stepsisters. Ensor's version of *Cinderella* does not end in the traditional happy-ever-after fashion either; she adds to the story by describing Cinderella's life after marriage to the prince. By story's end, she remains happily wedded and has transformed from a helpless damsel in distress into a powerful politician working to reshape her kingdom.

Ensor's text is accompanied by her original cut silhouettes, which Amy Krouse Rosenthal described in the *New York Times Book Review* as "the perfect visual solution." The black-and-white silhouettes are peppered throughout the story and separate Ensor's text "into manageable chunks, making this tale suitable for reluctant readers" as noted by a *Kirkus Reviews* critic. Susan Riley, reviewing the book in *School Library Journal,* described Ensor's version of *Cinderella* as a tale that will "please girls who like undemanding and familiar stories with a twist," while Rosenthal dubbed it "light and playful yet fairy-tale-ish."

BIOGRAPHICAL AND CRITICAL SOURCES:

PERIODICALS

Bulletin of the Center for Children's Books, July-August 2006, Deborah Stevenson, review of *Cinderella: (As If You Didn't Already Know the Story),* p. 495.
Kirkus Reviews, May 1, 2006, review of *Cinderella,* p. 456.
New York Times Book Review, September 10, 2006, Amy Krouse Rosenthal, review of *Cinderella,* p. 18L.
School Library Journal, July, 2006, Susan Riley, review of *Cinderella,* p. 100.

ONLINE

Barbara Ensor Home Page, http://www.barbaraensor. com (April 28, 2007).*

* * *

ERVIN, Clark
See ERVIN, Clark Kent

ERVIN, Clark Kent 1959-
  (Clark Ervin)

PERSONAL: Born April 1, 1959; married Carolyn A. Harris (an educational consultant). *Education:* Harvard University, B.A., 1980, LL.D, 1985; Oxford University, M.A., 1982.

ADDRESSES: Home—Washington, DC. *E-mail*—clark.ervin@aspeninstitute.org.

CAREER: Writer, attorney, broadcaster, security analyst, and U.S. government official. Vison & Elkins, attorney, 1985-89; Office of National Service, associate director of policy, 1989-91; Locke, Liddell, & Sapp, attorney, 1993-95; State of Texas, assistant secretary of state, 1995-99; Texas Attorney General's Office, deputy attorney general, general counsel, and director of administration, 1999-2001; U.S. Department of State, inspector general, 2001-03; U.S. Department of Homeland Security, acting inspector general, 2003, inspector general, 2003-04; Aspen Institute, Paul H. Nitze Fellow and director of Homeland Security Initiative, 2005—. Serves as on-air analyst and contributor for CNN. Guest on television shows, including *The Daily Show with Jon Stewart* and *Nightline.*

MEMBER: Council on Foreign Relations.

AWARDS, HONORS: Rhodes Scholar.

WRITINGS:

Open Target: Where America Is Vulnerable to Attack, Palgrave Macmillan (New York, NY), 2006.

Contributor to periodicals, including the *Wall Street Journal* and the *New York Times.*

SIDELIGHTS: Clark Kent Ervin is a writer, attorney, and security expert whose work often focuses on methods for making U.S. borders, ports, and other areas safer against terrorist attack. He received his superheroic name when his brother, eleven years his senior, encouraged his parents to name the newborn Ervin after the alter-ego of his favorite comic book character, Superman. Ervin has served as the assistant Texas secretary of state and deputy attorney general, and as inspector general of the U.S. Department of State.

Ervin's desire to uncover the truth, however, placed him at odds with many in the government, including President George W. Bush himself. Appointed by the president as inspector general of the U.S. Department of Homeland Security, Ervin quickly delved into the workings of the department. There, he uncovered tremendous waste of resources, ineffective management, stifling bureaucracy, and failed security procedures. Worst of all, he found that the Department of Homeland Security was accomplishing little that would actually make the homeland more secure. These findings caused great conflict between Ervin and his superiors and colleagues. In 2004, he was essentially fired from the job when the president did not act to reappoint him.

In *Open Target: Where America Is Vulnerable to Attack,* Ervin recounts his months on the job with Homeland Security, explains the troubles he uncovered and the controversies he endured, and sounds a warning that the United States is still highly vulnerable to attack from outside sources. In the book, he "details our vulnerabilities in several categories: borders, aviation, ports, mass transit, infrastructure, intelligence and even our capacity to respond after the fact to an attack," commented Lee H. Hamilton, a former congressman from Indiana, in a review in the *Washington Post Book World.* "A common thread is the government's difficulty in setting and acting upon priorities—what targets do you protect, what threats do you protect against, and what vulnerabilities do you tolerate?," Hamilton continued. Ervin did not see himself as an enemy of the department; instead, he was an ally of the government and the American people. "Nothing would please me more than those relatively rare occasions when I could say something good about the department," he stated in an interview with Patience Wait in *Government Computer News.* Above all, Ervin states, he was dedicated to finding and examining the truth, and in making the United States safer and more secure. "I don't take any joy in saying what I am saying—but you have to tell the truth when you are in a job like this," Ervin commented to Michael Scherer in an interview in *Mother Jones.*

Since leaving DHS, Ervin has become the director of the Homeland Security Initiative at the Aspen Institute, a Washington, DC, think tank, where he works to organize seminars and conferences and issue papers on security issues. His goal is to engage with prominent American leaders "to debate the issues and to make recommendations for constructive change" in security policy and procedures, noted a biographer on the Aspen Institute Web site. Though Ervin is no longer directly connected to the government, he continues, stated a *Publishers Weekly* reviewer, to warn that "America remains frighteningly vulnerable to terrorism."

BIOGRAPHICAL AND CRITICAL SOURCES:

PERIODICALS

Government Computer News, January 20, 2005, "Homeland Security Department," p. 8; May 16, 2005, Patience Wait, "DHS' Track Record Invites Continued Scrutiny," interview with Clark Kent Ervin, p. 19.

Government Security, May 4, 2006, "DHS Has Made America Only 'Marginally Safer,' New Book Says," review of *Open Target: Where America Is Vulnerable to Attack.*

Insight on the News, March 4, 2003, Martin Edwin Andersen, "Ervin Nominated for New IG Office at Homeland Security," p. 10.

Jet, August 19, 2002, "Clark Ervin Is State Dept. Inspector General," p. 37; April 5, 2004, Simeon Booker, "Inspector General of the Homeland Security Agency Is Clark Kent Ervin," p. 16.

Mother Jones, March-April, 2005, Michael Scherer, "Not Mild-Mannered Enough: Clark Kent Ervin Was Hired by His Friend President Bush to Expose Flaws in Homeland Security. Trouble Was, He Did," p. 22.

National Defense, August, 2006, Stew Magnuson, "The Gadfly: Former Staffer Becomes Leading DHS Critic," profile of Clark Kent Ervin, p. 10.

Publishers Weekly, March 27, 2006, review of *Open Target,* p. 75.

Texas Lawyer, March 14, 2005, Miriam Rozen, "Staying in the Spotlight," profile of Clark Kent Ervin.

Texas Monthly, April, 2005, Robert Draper, "Truth, Justice, and the (UN)American Way," profile of Clark Kent Ervin, p. 140.

USA Today, December 27, 2004, Mimi Hall, "Clark Kent Ervin, Homeland Security Official Who Exposed Waste and Incompetence, Rewarded with Termination by Bush."

U.S. News & World Report, June 28, 2004, Samantha Levine, "A Job for Superman," biography of Clark Kent Ervin, p. 20.

Washington Post Book World, May 14, 2006, Lee H. Hamilton, "America the Unprepared," review of *Open Target,* p. 4.

ONLINE

Aspen Institute Web site, http://www.aspensinstitute. org/ (May 24, 2007).

Clark Kent Ervin Web lot, http://opentarget.blogspot. com (May 24, 2007).

Government Community News, http://www.gcn.com/ (December 10, 2004), Patience Wait, "Clark Kent Ervin Out as DHS IG."

Leigh Bureau Web site, http://leighbureau.com/ (May 24, 2007), biography of Clark Kent Ervin.

U.S. Department of State Web site, http://www.state. gov/ (May 24, 2007), biography of Clark Kent Ervin.*

*   *   *

ESPINASSE, Kristin 1967-

PERSONAL: Born 1967, in AZ; immigrated to France, 1992; married; children: two. *Education:* Attended college.

ADDRESSES: Home—France.

CAREER: Author and publisher, *French Word-a-Day* (Web log).

WRITINGS:

Words in a French Life: Lessons in Love and Language from the South of France, Touchstone (New York, NY), 2006.

SIDELIGHTS: Kristin Espinasse had been a Francophile for many years, studying French in college and marrying a Frenchman. She moved with her husband to a new home in Provence, where she became the mother of two children. Despite studying the French language and living in that country, she has said she still feels like a foreigner; her children speak the language better than she does, often teasing their mother about her faux pas. Not above making fun of herself, Espinasse began to write and publish an online newsletter called *French Word-a-Day* that attempts to explain the subtler nuances of the language. Her first book, *Words in a French Life: Lessons in Love and Language from the South of France,* is a collection of her favorite pieces from her newsletter. *Library Journal* contributor Linda M. Kaufmann described the book as a collection of "charming short essays on French life." Mark Knoblauch, writing in *Booklist,* praised the author's explanations, which "go far to demystify French idioms for anyone wishing to speak and write more fluent French."

BIOGRAPHICAL AND CRITICAL SOURCES:

PERIODICALS

Booklist, April 15, 2006, Mark Knoblauch, review of *Words in a French Life: Lessons in Love and Language from the South of France,* p. 12.

California Bookwatch, August 1, 2006, review of *Words in a French Life.*

Library Journal, April 15, 2006, Linda M. Kaufmann, review of *Words in a French Life,* p. 97.*

*   *   *

ESTILL, Katie

PERSONAL: Married Daniel Woodrell (an author). *Education:* Kenyon College, B.A.; Iowa Writer's Workshop, M.F.A.

ADDRESSES: Home—West Plains, MO.

CAREER: Author. Has worked as an English tutor in Greece and taught at the collegiate level in the United States.

WRITINGS:

Evening Would Find Me (novel), Ontario Review Press (Princeton, NJ), 2000.

Dahlia's Gone (novel), St. Martin's Press (New York, NY), 2007.

Author's works have been translated into Norwegian and Swedish.

Also author of short stories.

SIDELIGHTS: A graduate of the Iowa Writer's Workshop, Katie Estill is a novelist and short-story writer. Her first novel, *Evening Would Find Me,* was inspired by her years of living in Greece as an English tutor. While she was there, the mentally unbalanced wife of a painter committed suicide by jumping out a window; the author was there to witness the aftermath. In *Evening Would Find Me,* she writes of an American living in Greece who has an affair with a painter whose wife is similarly mentally ill. The three form a complex relationship in which Sylvia's affair with Aristedes is known to his wife, Althea, yet Sylvia also plays a role as confidant to Althea. Calling the work "somewhat uneven," a *Publishers Weekly* critic added that "all the right elements are in place to produce an engrossing story—a seductive setting, attractive characters and dramatic love affair." Vanessa Bush praised the author in *Booklist* for the way she "evokes Greek culture, customs, and landscapes in this story of passion and madness."

Estill's next novel, *Dahlia's Gone,* is set in the Ozark mountains, where the author herself has settled down. On the surface, the book is a murder mystery in which the young girl of the title is killed in her home. The heart of the story, though, concerns how the death affects three female characters: Norah, who is Dahlia's stepmother and was away on vacation at the time; Sand, who was supposed to be watching the girl and her brother, Timothy, at the time; and Patti, a deputy in charge of investigating the crime. Calling the book an "accomplished" and "fast-paced character study," a *Kirkus Reviews* contributor praised the novel as a "perceptive meditation on the bonds of faith and family." "More than an intriguing mystery," Peg Brantley similarly remarked in *Armchair Interviews,* "Katie Estill pulls us into the lives of these women who each must find her own way of coping with tragedy."

BIOGRAPHICAL AND CRITICAL SOURCES:

PERIODICALS

Arkansas Democrat Gazette, April 29, 2007, Sarah E. White, "Grieving Stepmother Readers Love to Hate."

Booklist, April 15, 2000, Vanessa Bush, review of *Evening Would Find Me,* p. 1522.

417, February, 2007, Gregory Holman, "What Women Want," review of *Dahlia's Gone* and interview with Katie Estill.

Kansas City Star, June 30, 2007, Nancy Mays, review of *Dahlia's Gone.*

Kirkus Reviews, November 1, 2006, review of *Dahlia's Gone,* p. 1091.

Midwest Book Review, September 13, 2000, review of *Evening Would Find Me.*

Publishers Weekly, April 17, 2000, review of *Evening Would Find Me,* p. 50; November 6, 2006, review of *Dahlia's Gone,* p. 38.

ONLINE

Armchair Interviews, http://www.armchairinterviews. com/ (May 16, 2007), Peg Brantley, review of *Dahlia's Gone.*

Emerging Writers Forum, http://www.breaktech.net/ emergingwritersforum/ (September 13, 2002), Dan Wickett, "Interview with Katie Estill"; (April 7, 2007), review of *Dahlia's Gone.*

Fresh Fiction, http://freshfiction.com/ (May 16, 2007), review of *Dahlia's Gone.*

Ozarks Magazine Online, http://www.ozarksmagazine. com/ (May 16, 2007), Lin Waterhouse, review of *Dahlia's Gone.*

F

FEENER, R. Michael 1969-

PERSONAL: Born July 19, 1969, in Salem, MA. *Education:* University of Colorado, Boulder, B.A., 1991; Boston University, M.A., 1995, Ph.D., 1999.

ADDRESSES: Office—Asia Research Institute, National University of Singapore, AS7, 4th Fl., Singapore 117570. *E-mail*—arifm@nus.edu.sg.

CAREER: Reed College, Portland, OR, assistant professor, 1999-2002; University of California, Riverside, assistant professor, 2000-06; National University of Singapore, Singapore, associate professor, 2006—.

WRITINGS:

(Editor) *Islam in World Cultures: Contemporary Perspectives,* American Bibliographical Center-Clio Press (Santa Barbara, CA), 2004.

Contributor to reference works, especially books related to Islamic culture and religion. Contributor to journals, including *Archipel, Asian Journal of Social Science, Islamic Law and Society, Journal for Islamic Studies,* and *Studia Islamika.*

*   *   *

FERNÁNDEZ L'HOESTE, Hectór D. 1962-

PERSONAL: Born December 8, 1962, in Barranquilla, Colombia; naturalized U.S. citizen; son of Héctor Fernández Angulo (a medical doctor) and Itala R. L'Hoeste de Fernández (a homemaker); married Lauri McKain (a school principal), May 13, 1995; children: Sebastián. *Ethnicity:* "Latino." *Education:* Universidad de los Andes, B.S., 1987; State University of New York at Stony Brook, M.A., 1993, Ph.D., 1996. *Politics:* "None."

ADDRESSES: Home—Avondale Estates, GA. *Office*—General Classroom Bldg., Georgia State University, Atlanta, GA 30302-2970. *E-mail*—fernandez@gsu.edu.

CAREER: Castleton State College, Castleton, VT, instructor, 1994-96; University of Montevallo, Montevallo, AL, assistant professor, 1996-98; Georgia State University, Atlanta, associate professor, 1998—.

MEMBER: Latin American Studies Association, Southeastern Council of Latin American Studies, Asociación de Colombianistas.

WRITINGS:

Narrativas de representación urbana: un estudio de expresiones culturales de la modernidad latinoamericana, Peter Lang (New York, NY), 1998.
(Editor, with Deborah Pacini Hernández and Eric Zolov) *Rockin' Las Americas: The Global Politics of Rock in Latin America,* University of Pittsburgh Press (Pittsburgh, PA), 2004.

Contributor to books published in English and Spanish, including *Imagination beyond Nation,* edited by Eva Bueno and Terry Caesar, University of Pittsburgh

Press (Pittsburgh, PA), 1999; and *Science, Literature, and Film in the Hispanic World,* edited by Jerry Hoeg and Kevin S. Larsen, Palgrave Macmillan (New York, NY), 2006. Contributor to periodicals, including *Revista Latinoamericana de Estudios sobre la Historieta, National Identities, Hispania, Chasqui, JAISA: Journal of the Association for the Interdisciplinary Study of the Arts,* and *International Journal of Comic Art.*

*   *   *

FIELD, Taylor

PERSONAL: Married. *Education:* Princeton University, M.Div.; Golden Gate Baptist Theological Seminary, Ph.D.

ADDRESSES: Home—New York, NY.

CAREER: Writer, pastor, and novelist. East Seventh Baptist Church, New York, NY, pastor, 1986—; Graffiti on East Seventh Street, pastor, 1991—.

AWARDS, HONORS: Best Outreach Resource Award, Testimony/Biography category, *Outreach* magazine, 2003, for *Mercy Streets.*

WRITINGS:

(With Susan Field) *Peace in a Violent World: A Look into the Garden from the City,* Woman's Missionary Union (Birmingham, AL), 1998.
(With Jo Kadlecek) *A Church Called Graffiti: Finding Grace on the Lower East Side,* Broadman & Holman (Nashville, TN), 2001.
Mercy Streets: Seeing Grace on the Streets of New York, Broadman & Holman (Nashville, TN), 2003.
Squat (novel), Broadman & Holman (Nashville, TN), 2006.

SIDELIGHTS: Taylor Field is a writer and a pastor who has served congregations in some of the bleakest, most violent areas of New York City. In *A Church Called Graffiti: Finding Grace on the Lower East Side,* Field describes how he was called to leave his home in Oklahoma for more challenging surroundings. Field found himself and his family living and working

in the drug-ravaged, dangerous streets of Manhattan's Lower East Side. At first unsure of why he was there, Field eventually settled into a productive routine and spent more than fifteen years in the city. He ministered to a diverse congregation, including a woman whose apartment was filled with a quarter-century's accumulation of trash; a local drug lord; and a homeless man wracked with grief over the death of his dog. Field's adventures in the inner city inspire "important questions for Christians about the meaning of the gospel," commented John Green in *Booklist.* Field speaks honestly and clearly about his "struggles with success, his family's safety, and his season of burnout," noted David E. Carlson in *Leadership.*

In the essay collection *Mercy Streets: Seeing Grace on the Streets of New York,* Field "shows how God can salvage hope amid the wreckage of lives in New York City," commented Cindy Crosby in *Christianity Today.* Field's work with people who are at the lowest point in their lives, including drug addicts and the desperately poor, provide inspiring stories of redemption and the reclamation of lost dignity. For example, an addict watches a small tree fight for survival among the cracks in the concrete and uses the example of its tenacious struggle as a metaphor to help him toward recovery and wholeness. Field also recounts stories of the everyday running of the ministry, and finds additional inspiration in the story of planned events such as "Dog Day Afternoon," in which homeless people are encouraged to bring their pets for veterinary care. Field's proximity to the Twin Towers on September 11, 2001, also provides him with stories of hope, including one about a young couple who held their marriage ceremony in the midst of the cleanup. Crosby called Field's insight into the humanity of his flock "inspiring."

Squat, Field's debut novel, follows protagonist Squid as he traverses twenty-four hours in his life. The young man, suffering from obsessive-compulsive disorder, fears for his life after being involved in a drug deal gone bad. The reader catches a glimpse of the ways in which desperate and impoverished city dwellers survive on the street as Squid begs for money, wanders the streets, and visits a mission to pray for assistance. With this book, Field "paints believably . . . an almost inescapable universe worlds away from the lives of middle-class New Yorkers," commented a *Publishers Weekly* reviewer.

BIOGRAPHICAL AND CRITICAL SOURCES:

PERIODICALS

Booklist, September 15, 2001, John Green, review of *A Church Called Graffiti: Finding Grace on the Lower East Side,* p. 167.
Christianity Today, February 1, 2004, Cindy Crosby, review of *Mercy Streets: Seeing Grace on the Streets of New York,* p. 84.
Leadership, winter, 2002, David E. Carlson, review of *A Church Called Graffiti,* p. 113.
Publishers Weekly, July 31, 2006, review of *Squat,* p. 53.

ONLINE

Bedford Review, http://jimfictionreview.blogspot.com/ (September 14, 2006), interview with Taylor Field, part one; (September 15, 2006), interview with Taylor Field, part two.
Taylor Field Web Log, http://www.taylorfield. wordpress.com (April 24, 2007).*

* * *

FINGER, Anne 1951(?)-

PERSONAL: Born c. 1951. *Education:* Harvard University, B.A. (cum laude), 1976; Stanford University, M.A., 1980.

ADDRESSES: Home—Oakland, CA. *E-mail*—annefinger@earthlink.net; AnnieDigit@mindspring. com.

CAREER: San Francisco Independent Living Resource Center, San Francisco, CA, writer in residence, 1984-85; Woman's Building, Los Angeles, CA, writer in residence, 1987-89; Wayne State University, Detroit, MI, lecturer, 1989-97. Visiting professor, University of Texas, Austin, 1996. Has also taught at community workshops; activist for disability rights; former assistant at an abortion clinic. Resident, Hedgebrook Farm, 1993, Centrum, 1995, and Yaddo, 1995.

MEMBER: Society for Disability Studies (board member, 2001—; president, 2002—).

AWARDS, HONORS: Joseph Henry Jackson Award, San Francisco Foundation, 1984; Barbara Deming Memorial Fund grant, 1986; Ludwig Vogelstein Foundation grant, 1987; Associated Writing Program Award for Short Fiction, 1987; *Southern Review/* Louisiana State University short fiction award for best first collection, 1988, for *Basic Skills;* Literature Fellowship, Brody Arts Fund, 1988; D.H. Lawrence Fellowship, 1991; Diversity Project grant, Wayne State University, 1994; Teaching and Mentoring Award, Journalism Institute for Minorities at Wayne State University, 1994; Arts Foundation of Michigan Literature Grant, 1994-95; summer faculty research fellowship, Wayne State University, 1995; Josephine Nevins Keal Faculty Fellowship, Wayne State University, 1995, 1997; summer faculty research fellowship, College of Urban, Labor and Metropolitan Affairs at Wayne State University, 1996.

WRITINGS:

Basic Skills (short stories), University of Missouri Press (Columbia, SC), 1988.
Past Due: A Story of Disability, Pregnancy, and Birth (autobiography), Seal Press (Seattle, WA), 1990.
Bone Truth (novel), Coffee House Press (Minneapolis, MN), 1994.
Elegy for a Disease: A Personal and Cultural History of Polio (autobiography), St. Martin's Press (New York, NY), 2006.

Also author of *Eulogy for a Virus,* St. Martin's Press. Contributor of short stories and articles to *Southern Review, Ploughshares, Discourse, Kenyon Review, Feminist Studies, Socialist Review, Antioch Review, Thirteenth Moon,* and *Third Coast.*

SIDELIGHTS: A polio survivor, Anne Finger is an activist for the disabled and author who has written about her disability in two autobiographical works. Finger's memoirs *Past Due: A Story of Disability, Pregnancy, and Birth* and *Elegy for a Disease: A Personal and Cultural History of Polio* touch on aspects of polio that are sometimes overlooked. In the former, she talks about her complications with pregnancy, and in the latter the author discusses the neurological and psychological affects of polio on patients. In *Past Due,* Finger recalls her weakened bones, which resulted in several breaks, and the traumatic birth of her son, Max, who had only a fifty percent chance of survival. The "uncompromising frankness" of the narrative makes for "painful but compulsive reading," according to Peggy Kaganoff in *Publishers Weekly.*

Elegy for a Disease covers a longer period in her life, from the time Finger contracted polio when she was three, through the many humiliating and painful treatments she received, her embarrassment at being discriminated against, and finally the depression and suicide attempts she made when she was older. Finger combines her personal experiences with a history of the disease, including some of the abusive nostrums that were inflicted on patients. Remarking that the author is "at her best when vividly delineating the Fifties and Sixties," *Library Journal* contributor James Swanton called the book an "unsentimental, grippingly told story." A *Publishers Weekly* writer similarly complimented the "skillful prose" in the book.

Finger draws on some aspects of her life, including pregnancy and her battle with polio, to create her character Elizabeth Etters in her debut novel, *Bone Truth.* The daughter of communist activists who later become alcoholics, Elizabeth has known a life of abuse complicated further by the pain of a body disabled by polio. Feeling unworthy compared to her parents' past accomplishments in politics and her mother's ability to raise four children while her husband was in prison, the heroine finds herself humiliated by her treatment as a polio patient. Photos of her naked, twisted body are used in medical studies, but she oddly turns this embarrassment around to become a famous photographer whose main subject is nude photos of the disabled. She struggles, furthermore, with trying to make a decision between aborting or keeping an unwanted baby. While Eleanor J. Bader, writing in *Belles Lettres,* called *Bone Truth* an "engrossing and real" novel containing passages that are "beautifully, if painfully, written."

BIOGRAPHICAL AND CRITICAL SOURCES:

BOOKS

Finger, Anne, *Past Due: A Story of Disability, Pregnancy, and Birth,* Seal Press (Seattle, WA), 1990.

Finger, Anne, *Elegy for a Disease: A Personal and Cultural History of Polio,* St. Martin's Press (New York, NY), 2006.

PERIODICALS

Belles Lettres, spring, 1995, Eleanor J. Bader, review of *Bone Truth.*
Booklist, October 15, 1994, Whitney Scott, review of *Bone Truth,* p. 400.
Kirkus Reviews, September 1, 2006, review of *Elegy for a Disease,* p. 886.
Library Journal, September 15, 2006, James Swanton, review of *Elegy for a Disease,* p. 79.
Publishers Weekly, March 16, 1990, Penny Kaganoff, review of *Past Due,* p. 64; August 28, 2006, review of *Elegy for a Disease,* p. 41.

ONLINE

Anne Finger Home Page, http://www.annefinger.com (May 16, 2007).*

*   *   *

FINTUSHEL, Eliot 1947(?)-

PERSONAL: Born c. 1947, in Rochester, NY.

ADDRESSES: Home—Santa Rosa, CA. *E-mail*—fintushel@netzero.net.

CAREER: Novelist and short-story writer. Has worked as performance artist, mime, teacher, and musician.

AWARDS, HONORS: Has twice received Solo Performer Award, National Endowment for the Arts.

WRITINGS:

Breakfast with the Ones You Love (novel), Bantam Books (New York, NY), 2007.

Also author of short stories. Work included in anthologies, including *The Year's Best Science Fiction* and *Jewish Detective Stories for Kids.*

SIDELIGHTS: Eliot Fintushel's first novel, *Breakfast with the Ones You Love,* according to *Nextbook* Web site writer Willa Paskin, is "one weird novel." It follows the adventures of Lea Tillim, a hostile sixteen-year-old who can kill things telepathically. Lea befriends Jack, a pot dealer who believes that God wants him to build a spaceship that will eventually link to another ship in a parallel universe, taking him and several other "Chosen Ones" to the Promised Land. As Jack's activities propel him toward a classic showdown with the forces of evil, Lea learns, through Jack, to deal with her own demons in constructive ways. The novel, Fintushel told Paskin, is at heart a classic coming-of-age story. Yet it also incorporates many disparate elements, including science fiction themes, religion, and comedy, resulting in what Paskin described as "a blunt, trippy, strangely sweet concoction." Noting that "parts of the book have an inherent preposterousness that would lend themselves to being played for laughs," David Hebblethwaite, writing on the *SF site* Web site, added that Fintushel grounds the novel "in a gritty urban reality which ensures that, however weird or daft things get, one thinks twice about chuckling." *Breakfast with the Ones You Love,* Hebblethwaite concluded, "is a fine example of what the maturing field of fantasy can produce in the early 21st century: a work which is not dazzled by the mere presence of the fantastic, but uses it as one element in the wider fabric of its story."

BIOGRAPHICAL AND CRITICAL SOURCES:

PERIODICALS

Booklist, February 15, 2007, Regina Schroeder, review of *Breakfast with the Ones You Love,* p. 45.
Publishers Weekly, February 5, 2007, review of *Breakfast with the Ones You Love,* p. 45.

ONLINE

Nextbook, http://www.nextbook.org/ (April 25, 2007), Willa Paskin, "Strange Trip."
SciFi.com, http://www.scifi.com/ (April 25, 2007), A.M. Dellamonica, review of *Breakfast with the Ones You Love.*
SF site, http://www.sfsite.com/ (April 25, 2007), David Hebblethwaite, review of *Breakfast with the Ones You Love.**

FISHER, Barbara M. 1931-
(Barbara Milberg Fisher)

PERSONAL: Born 1931; daughter of a dentist; married; children: three. *Education:* Holds bachelor's, master's, and doctoral degrees.

CAREER: Writer, dancer, memoirist, and educator. City University of New York, New York, NY, professor emerita of English. Ballet Society and New York City Ballet, soloist, 1947-58; Ballets: USA, principal dancer.

WRITINGS:

Wallace Stevens: The Intensest Rendezvous, University Press of Virginia (Charlottesville, VA), 1990.
Noble Numbers, Subtle Words: The Art of Mathematics in the Science of Storytelling, Fairleigh Dickinson University Press (Madison, NJ), 1997.
In Balanchine's Company: A Dancer's Memoir, Wesleyan University Press (Middletown, CT), 2006.

SIDELIGHTS: Teacher and writer Barbara M. Fisher, who is professor emerita of English at the City University of New York, also enjoyed a long career as a ballet dancer with the prestigious New York City Ballet. The daughter of immigrant Ukrainian Jews, Fisher spent her early years in Brooklyn, growing up during the Depression. An indefatigable and constant reader, Fisher was an energetic child who gravitated naturally to music and physical performance. Dance lessons at age six were intended to help her regain strength after bouts with dysentery and pneumonia, related interviewer Rebecca Milzoff in an article posted at *Nextbook.* At eleven years of age, she was accepted at the School of American Ballet in Manhattan. At age fifteen, she was a professional dancer and working with famed choreographer George Balanchine in his early organization, Ballet Society. Fisher spent more than twelve years dancing with Balanchine's companies, and she relates her experiences with the great choreographer in her book *In Balanchine's Company: A Dancer's Memoir.* Fisher discusses a pivotal collaboration, the 1957 production of *Agon* by Balanchine and Igor Stravinsky. Fisher relates stories that illuminate Balanchine's personality and his genuine affection for his dancers. She notes his fascination for motor scooters and his occasional ribaldry. Fisher "warmly and consistently animates the choreographer as a human being and a creative force, and she does so in the context of a profound love for his imagination and a sense of great privilege for having known him," noted Mindy Aloff in the *Moscow Times.* Fisher's "recollections are exact, vivid, well written, and illustrated by a fine selection of photos," noted a reviewer in *Commentary.* "To this day, the influence of her mentor Balanchine is omnipresent, and her appreciation of a remarkable association is evident in every page in this delightful book," commented Leland Windreich in *Ballet-Dance Magazine.* *Booklist* critic Whitney Scott concluded: "Graced with archival photos, Fisher's elegant memoir is a must for dance lovers." Fisher's "observations as both dancer and literary critic are unparalleled," stated a reviewer in *Publishers Weekly,* who concluded: "This book is indispensable for lovers of ballet and theater."

BIOGRAPHICAL AND CRITICAL SOURCES:

BOOKS

Fisher, Barbara M., *In Balanchine's Company: A Dancer's Memoir,* Wesleyan University Press (Middletown, CT), 2006.

PERIODICALS

Booklist, September 15, 2006, Whitney Scott, review of *In Balanchine's Company,* p. 14.
Dance Magazine, October, 2006, review of *In Balanchine's Company,* p. 80.
Moscow Times (St. Petersburg, Russia), March 9, 2007, Mindy Aloff, review of *In Balanchine's Company.*
Publishers Weekly, July 10, 2006, review of *In Balanchine's Company,* p. 64.

ONLINE

Ballet-Dance Magazine, http://www.ballet-dance.com/ (April 24, 2007), Leland Windreich, review of *In Balanchine's Company.*
Commentary, http://www.commentarymagazine.com/ (April 24, 2007), biography of Barbara M. Fisher.

ForeWord, http://www.forewordmagazine.net/ (April 24, 2007), Peter Skinner, "*ForeWord*'s Ninth Annual Look at the Big Ten/Outstanding Books from University Presses," review of *In Balanchine's Company.*
Nextbook, http://www.nextbook.org/ (November 15, 2006), Rebecca Milzoff, "Turning Point," interview with Barbara M. Fisher.

*   *   *

FISHER, Barbara Milberg
    See FISHER, Barbara M.

*   *   *

FITZGERALD, Laura 1967-

PERSONAL: Born 1967, in Milwaukee, WI; married; children: two. *Education:* University of Wisconsin at Madison, B.A., 1990.

ADDRESSES: Home—Tucson, AZ. *E-mail*—2006@laurafitzgerald.com.

CAREER: Writer.

WRITINGS:

Veil of Roses, Bantam Books (New York, NY), 2007.

SIDELIGHTS: Laura Fitzgerald was inspired to write a novel about another culture after viewing a series of well-received films that showed how two cultures can both clash and meld in modern society, including *My Big Fat Greek Wedding, Bend It Like Beckham,* and *Spanglish.* Fitzgerald, whose husband was born in Iran, decided to write a story about an Iranian woman that showed the lighter, everyday side of modern Persian culture. The result was *Veil of Roses,* a novel about twenty-seven-year-old Tamila "Tami" Soroush, who lives a relatively restricted lifestyle in Iran. When her parents send her to spend three months in Tucson, Arizona, in hopes that she will find a husband there and remain in America, Tami has a chance to see the larger world. She suddenly finds herself able to walk down the streets freely, take English classes at a nearby library, and flirt with Ike, the cute man she meets at Starbucks. Commenting on Ike's story-book charms in a review for the *Romance Reader Web site,* Susan Scribner opined: "If only Fitzgerald had given him a little bit of an edge, a few flaws or some attribute that made him seem more realistic. Tami is such a strong and admirable heroine that she could have managed a soul mate with a few idiosyncrasies." Scribner went on to conclude, however, that the book is "a delightful yet thought-provoking novel." A writer for *Publishers Weekly* called the book "pat but sweet," and Deborah Donovan, in a review for *Booklist,* remarked that it was "a fun, romantic, and thought-provoking debut novel from a promising author."

BIOGRAPHICAL AND CRITICAL SOURCES:

PERIODICALS

Booklist, November 15, 2006, Deborah Donovan, review of *Veil of Roses,* p. 27.

Kirkus Reviews, October 15, 2006, review of *Veil of Roses,* p. 1033.

Publishers Weekly, November 13, 2006, review of *Veil of Roses,* p. 35.

ONLINE

Laura Fitzgerald Home Page, http://www.laura fitzgerald.com (April 22, 2007).

Laura Fitzgerald MySpace Page, http://www.myspace. com/laura_fitzerald (April 22, 2007).

Romance Reader Web site, http://www.theromance reader.com/ (April 22, 2007), Susan Scribner, review of *Veil of Roses.**

*   *   *

FLANAGAN, John 1944-
(John Anthony Flanagan)

PERSONAL: Born 1944, in Sydney, New South Wales, Australia; married; wife's name Leonie; children: Michael.

ADDRESSES: Home and office—Sydney, New South Wales, Australia.

CAREER: Writer. Formerly worked in advertising in Sydney, New South Wales, Australia, London, England, and Singapore; Seven Network, Sydney, head writer for television series *Hey Dad!,* 1987-94; freelance writer, beginning 1970s.

WRITINGS:

(With Gary Reilly) *The Betty Wilson Secretarial Companion* (based on the television series *Hey Dad!*), Penguin (Ringwood, Victoria, Australia), 1990.

"RANGER'S APPRENTICE" FANTASY NOVELS

The Ruins of Gorlan (also see below), Random House Australia (Milsons Point, New South Wales, Australia), 2004, Philomel (New York, NY), 2005.

The Burning Bridge (also see below), Random House Australia (Milsons Point, New South Wales, Australia), 2005, Philomel (New York, NY), 2006.

The Icebound Land, Random House Australia (Milsons Point, New South Wales, Australia), 2005, Philomel (New York, NY), 2007.

Oakleaf Bearers, Random House Australia (Milsons Point, New South Wales, Australia), 2006.

Ranger's Apprentice: One & Two (contains *The Ruins of Gorland* and *The Burning Bridge*), Random House Australia (Milsons Point, New South Wales, Australia), 2006.

The Sorcerer in the North, Random House Australia (Milsons Point, New South Wales, Australia), 2006.

The Siege of Macindaw, Random House Australia (Milsons Point, New South Wales, Australia), 2007.

Author's books have been translated into over a dozen languages.

ADAPTATIONS: The "Ranger's Apprentice" novels have been adapted as audiobooks.

SIDELIGHTS: Beginning his career in advertising, Australian novelist John Flanagan eventually moved in to writing for television, spending eight years as head writer for the popular Australian sitcom *Hey Dad!* In his spare time, Flanagan also wrote for fun, developing short stories for his growing son. "He didn't like reading, and so I based the character on him and did the kinds of things Mike did," Flanagan explained to Ron Charles in an interviewer for the *Washington Post Book World*. Several years later, Flanagan decided that it might be fun to rework these stories into book form; he showed them to his agent, and the "Ranger's Apprentice" series was born. "The book grew and grew and I decided it had better be two books," he later recalled on the Christ Church, New Zealand Libraries Web site. "It kept growing and growing and ended up being four."

The first volume of the "Ranger's Apprentice" is *The Ruins of Gorlan;* first published in Australia in 2004, it has since been released in fourteen countries. The novel introduces Will, a teen who anxiously desires to be accepted into Battleschool as an apprentice, but is denied because of his short stature. Instead, he is apprenticed to a mysterious Ranger and taught skills of speed and stealth. In the larger world, the evil Lord Morgorath sends assassins to murder leaders from Will's society. Now Will and his sometime rival/ sometime friend Horace must hone their skills quickly, because their country is becoming a more dangerous place. Reviewing *The Ruins of Gorlan* for *Booklist,* Carolyn Phelan wrote that the novel's appeal comes from Flanagan's skill at building a convincing fantasy world. "It's the details of everyday living and the true-to-life emotions of the people that are memorable," Phelan noted. Steven Engelfried, writing in *School Library Journal,* commented that the author's "descriptions of Ranger craft are fascinating."

As *The Burning Bridge* opens, Lord Morgorath's army of monstrous wargals gathers. Meanwhile, Will and Horace discover a nearly completed bridge, built by Morgorath's forces as a way to sneak into their kingdom. Aided by disguised noblewoman Evanlyn, the two apprentices must now journey into enemy territory to discover the true extent of Morgorath's plans. "Will's vivid world will entice fantasy readers who are drawn by the lure of high adventure," wrote Phelan, while a *Kirkus Reviews* contributor concluded of *The Burning Bridge* that "it all adds up to a winning formula that should prove out to a long, steady run."

On the Christ Church, New Zealand Libraries Web site, Flanagan talked about the satisfaction he gains from writing fantasy fiction. The best part of his job?

"Planning the story, watching the meat grow on the bones of the framework, realising that your characters are taking on a life of their own and beginning to determine their own actions and how the story develops. Letting it mull round in your head for days or weeks. Putting it aside for a week and them coming back to find it's grown more detail in your subconscious while you weren't thinking about it. Great stuff. Great fun."

BIOGRAPHICAL AND CRITICAL SOURCES:

PERIODICALS

Booklist, June 1, 2005, Carolyn Phelan, review of *The Ruins of Gorlan,* p. 1796; May 15, 2006, Carolyn Phelan, review of *The Burning Bridge,* p. 58.

Kirkus Reviews, May 15, 2005, review of *The Ruins of Gorlan,* p. 588; May 1, 2006, review of *The Burning Bridge,* p. 458.

School Library Journal, June, 2005, Steven Engelfried, review of *The Ruins of Gorlan,* p. 158; August, 2006, Beth L. Meister, review of *The Burning Bridge,* p. 120.

Washington Post Book World, July 23, 2006, Ron Charles, interview with Flanagan, p. 9.

ONLINE

Christ Church, New Zealand Libraries Web site, http://library.christchurch.org.nz/ (April 28, 2007), interview with Flanagan.*

*   *   *

FLANAGAN, John Anthony
See FLANAGAN, John

*   *   *

FLEMING, James 1944-

PERSONAL: Born 1944, in London, England; son of Richard Fleming (a banker); married (divorced); children. *Education:* Oxford University, graduated.

ADDRESSES: Home—Scotland. *Agent*—Felicity Bryan, Felicity Bryan Literary Agency, 2a N. Parade Ave., Oxford OX2 6LX, England; Irene Skolnick, 22 W. 23rd St., 5th Fl., New York, NY 10010. *E-mail*—author@jamesfleming.co.uk.

CAREER: Writer. Has worked as an accountant, farmer, forester, bookseller, and publisher.

WRITINGS:

FICTION

The Temple of Optimism, Hyperion (New York, NY), 2000.
Thomas Gage, Jonathan Cape (London, England), 2003.
White Blood, Jonathan Cape (London, England), 2006, Atria Books (New York, NY), 2007.

SIDELIGHTS: James Fleming comes from a family of writers, including his uncles Peter and Ian Fleming, the latter being the famous creator of the James Bond spy novels. In his own right, Fleming has become a noted author of historical novels. On his Web site, the author lists several reasons why he writes historical fiction, including his idea that "to imagine how one would behave oneself if caught at a great turning point in history, such as the Russian Revolution, is irresistibly frightening."

In his first novel, *The Temple of Optimism,* Fleming sets his story in eighteenth-century rural England. The novel revolves around Edward Home, who grew up in the countryside but has found a new and more exciting life in London. He returns to the family's old country estate with plans of selling it. When he falls in love with Daisy Apreece, the wife of his neighbor Sir Anthony Apreece, Edward soon finds himself in a dangerous affair while trying to protect his land from being taken over by Sir Anthony. "Fleming's style is so befitting to the period . . . that the story . . . becomes completely absorbing," according to Grace Fill in *Booklist.* A *Publishers Weekly* contributor commented that the author's "prose pushes the melodrama in startlingly unconventional directions . . . gentility devolves into near-violent hostility, exposing the greed and solipsism that lay beneath the 18th-century class system."

Fleming tells the story of an 1850s English country landowner in his novel *Thomas Gage.* Married to a wealthy heiress and with two loving children, Thomas spends his time painting and hunting and believing that his life is safe and secure. However, the railroad soon threatens to run tracks across Thomas's land, and his beloved son is killed in a horrific train accident. The pressure sends Thomas into depression and a misguided attempt to run from his grief by living a life of debauchery in London. "James Fleming writes lyrically about the countryside and almost as well about the Victorian town," reported Eric Anderson in the *Spectator.* Anderson also appreciated the author's ability to create a variety of interesting characters, and added: "Fleming is best of all, though, at the moments of stress and elation."

White Blood takes place in Russia in 1917 and features naturalist and womanizer Charlie Doig, who returns to his family home in Russia from scouring primitive jungles for plant and animal life. He has come back to take a job for the Tsarist government but soon finds that this whole aristocratic way of life is threatened. Charlie is eventually trapped in all the horrors of the Bolshevik revolution. "The action sequences virtually sing with energy, and the novel's blistering pace never lets up for a moment," observed a *Kirkus Reviews* contributor. In her *Library Journal* review, Barbara Conaty further remarked: "Charlie Doig, a Nabokovian figure of Russian heritage . . . is an unforgettable character."

When asked what kind of effect he hopes his books will have, Fleming told *CA:* "It's the most important piece of self-examination for any writer of fiction. In order to keep a well-balanced temper and digestion, a writer's default position must be *none*. There can be no exceptions to this rule.

"However, in moments of elation, he or she must also be able to reach the absolute conviction that their skills are second to none, that when justice is done, their genius will be acclaimed universally, and that this will be entirely correct.

"I subscribe wholeheartedly to both these positions."

BIOGRAPHICAL AND CRITICAL SOURCES:

PERIODICALS

Booklist, October 1, 2000, Grace Fill, review of *The Temple of Optimism,* p. 322; December 1, 2006, review of *White Blood,* p. 20.

Guardian (London, England), May 6, 2006, Sam Thompson, review of *White Blood.*

Kirkus Reviews, October 15, 2006, review of *White Blood,* p. 1033.

Library Journal, October15, 2000, Kathy Piehl, review of *The Temple of Optimism,* p. 101; December 1, 2006, Barbara Conaty, review of *White Blood,* p. 109.

Publishers Weekly, October 16, 2006, review of *White Blood,* p. 32; September 25, 2000, review of *The Temple of Optimism,* p. 84.

Spectator, October 11, 2003, Eric Anderson, review of *Thomas Gage,* p. 42; April 8, 2006, Honor Clerk, review of *White Blood,* p. 47.

ONLINE

James Fleming Home Page, http://www.jamesfleming. co.uk (April 17, 2007).

*   *   *

FLORENCE, Tyler 1971-

PERSONAL: Born March 3, 1971, in Greenville, SC; married; wife's name Christie Leer (divorced); children: one son, Miles. *Education:* Graduated from Johnson and Wales University, College of Culinary Arts (with honors), 1991.

ADDRESSES: Home—New York, NY.

CAREER: Served in various positions in the kitchens of New York City restaurants Aureole, Mad 61, and River Café, 1992-95; Cibo, New York, NY, executive chef, 1995-98; Cafeteria, New York, NY, executive chef and creator, 1998; Food Network, host of various cooking shows, including *Food 911, Tyler's Ultimate, Planet Food, All American Festivals* and *My Country, My Kitchen,* 1999—.

WRITINGS:

(With JoAnn Cianciulli) *Tyler Florence's Real Kitchen,* Clarkson Potter (New York, NY), 2003.

Eat This Book: Cooking with Global Fresh Flavors, Clarkson Potter (New York, NY), 2005.

(Author of introduction) Sandra Lee, *Semi-homemade Cooking 2: Sandra Lee,* Meredith Books (Des Moines, IA), 2005.

Tyler's Ultimate: Brilliant Simple Food to Make Any Time, Clarkson Potter (New York, NY), 2006.

SIDELIGHTS: Tyler Florence trained as a chef at the College of Culinary Arts at Johnson and Wales University in South Carolina. After graduating, he moved to New York where he began working at a number of renowned restaurants, including Aureole, where he trained under chef Charlie Palmer; Mad 61, where he worked for Marta Pulini; and The River Café, working for Rick Laakkonen. He eventually became the executive chef of Cibo, also in New York, where he focused the menu on modern American cuisine, and in 1998 opened his own restaurant, Cafeteria. Florence rose to national fame when he began hosting cooking programs for the Food Network, first as a guest, then on the popular show, "Food 911," and then eventually as the star of several cooking series. *Tyler Florence's Real Kitchen,* Florence's first cookbook, written with JoAnn Cianciulli, maintains the same casual attitude toward cooking that Florence projects on television. Categories range from food suitable for a dinner for two to easy items for a backyard barbecue. A *Publishers Weekly* reviewer noted of the book: "This is a decent, if unfocused collection of recipes." Florence followed up with *Eat This Book: Cooking with Global Fresh Flavors,* which focuses on regional cooking from different parts of the world and demonstrates easy methods of achieving varied tastes in the kitchen. Of this effort, a reviewer for *Publishers Weekly* remarked: "Florence's vast culinary knowledge translates well to the page." In *Tyler's Ultimate: Brilliant Simple Food to Make Any Time,* Florence links his recipes directly to his Food Network television show of the same title. In a review for *Publishers Weekly,* one contributor noted that "instructions are clear, and each recipe helpfully comes with an estimated cooking time."

BIOGRAPHICAL AND CRITICAL SOURCES:

PERIODICALS

Business Wire, August 25, 2006, "Applebee's Brings Renowned Chef and Food Network Personality

Tyler Florence to the Neighborhood; Florence and Applebee's Step Up to the Table with One-of-a-Kind Partnership for Innovative Menu Items."

Kirkus Reviews, September 15, 2006, "Cooking in Front of the Camera: Best of the Culinary Stars," p. 9.

Library Journal, February 15, 2003, Judith Sutton, review of *Tyler Florence's Real Kitchen,* p. 164; September 15, 2006, Judith Sutton, review of *Tyler's Ultimate: Brilliant Simple Food to Make Anytime,* p. 84.

Nation's Restaurant News, September 11, 2006, "TV Chef Florence Creates Slate of Applebee's Dishes," p. 32; October 16, 2006, Sarah E. Lockyer, "Tyler Florence: TV Host Teams Up with Chain, Heads Back to Kitchen," p. 48.

New York, May 8, 2006, Robin Raisfeld and Rob Patronite, "Tyler Florence: The Food Network Star and *People Magazine*'s Onetime Sexiest Chef Talks about His New Show, His Mysterious New York Restaurant Project, and How Not to Treat a Cocoa Puff," p. 59.

Orange CountyRegister (Orange County, CA), May 23, 2005, Cathy Thomas, "Chef Tyler Florence's Book Offers Honest Flavors in Perfect Balance."

PR Newswire, April 12, 2005, "Celebrity Chef Tyler Florence to Host Southern Living Cook-Off 2005"; July 28, 2005, "Eat This Blog: Chef Tyler Florence to Help You Savor Flavor."

Publishers Weekly, March 17, 2003, review of *Tyler Florence's Real Kitchen,* p. 68; December 6, 2004, review of *Eat This Book: Cooking with Global Fresh Flavors,* p. 56; July 24, 2006, review of *Tyler's Ultimate,* p. 54.

Seattle Times, March 4, 2007, Nicole Tsong, "It's Not Julia Child Anymore."

Snack Food & Wholesale Bakery, September 1, 2006, "Food for the People," p. 40.

ONLINE

Food Network Home Page, http://www.foodnetwork. com/ (April 22, 2007), Tyler Florence biography.

Internet Movie Database, http://www.imdb.com/ (April 22, 2007), Tyler Florence biography.

NNDB, http://www.nndb.com/ (April 22, 2007), Tyler Florence biography.

Tyler Florence Home Page, http://www.tylerflorence. com (April 22, 2007).*

FRANK, Benis M. 1925-2007
(Benis Morton Frank)

OBITUARY NOTICE— See index for *CA* sketch: Born February 21, 1925, in Amsterdam, NY; died of congestive heart failure, March 10, 2007, in Cheverly, MD. Frank was a former U.S. Marine who later served as a civilian historian for the corps' history and museums division. He was in the Marines during World War II, seeing action at Okinawa and Peleliu, and then continued to serve in the Reserves. Frank returned to active duty for the Korean War, where he was a battalion intelligence officer; he attained the rank of captain before resigning in 1960. Meanwhile, he studied history at the University of Connecticut, where he earned an A.B. in 1949, and attended graduate school at Clark University. Frank worked for various companies during the 1950s, including as a department store assistant buyer, an assistant manager for Franklin Simon in Connecticut, and as a salesman for the Central States Paper & Bag Company in New York City. After teaching history for a year at King School in Stamford, Connecticut, he found satisfying work as historian for the U.S. Marine Corps in Washington, DC. Frank worked here from 1961 to 1997, heading the history section and founding the Marines' oral history program. He was named chief historian in 1991. An active researcher and writer, he contributed to encyclopedias and dictionaries on military history and was managing editor of *Military Collector & Historian,* the journal of the Company of Military Historians for which he also served as governor. Frank was the author of several books, including *A Brief History of the 3d Marines* (1962; revised edition, 1970), *Halsey* (1973), and *U.S. Marines in Lebanon, 1982-1984* (1987). He was awarded the Meritorious Civilian Service Award for his contributions to the Marines, also receiving the Forrest C. Pogue award for excellence in oral history mid-Atlantic region in 1981.

OBITUARIES AND OTHER SOURCES:

PERIODICALS

Los Angeles Times, March 19, 2007, p. B7.
Washington Post, March 15, 2007, p. B8.

*   *   *

FRANK, Benis Morton
  See FRANK, Benis M.

FRENCH, Renée 1963-
(Rainy Dohaney)

PERSONAL: Born 1963; father an auto industry worker; married; husband's name Rob. *Education:* Studied art at Kutztown University. *Hobbies and other interests:* Photography.

ADDRESSES: Home—CA. *E-mail*—Renéefrench@ gmail.com; cornelia@world.std.com.

CAREER: Author and illustrator.

WRITINGS:

ADULT COMICS AND GRAPHIC NOVELS

(And illustrator) *Grit Bath* (comic book), Fantagraphics Books, Issue 1, 1993, Issues 2-3, 1994.
(And illustrator) *The Ninth Gland* (comic book), Dark Horse Comics, 1997.
(And illustrator) *Corny's Fetish* (comic book), Dark Horse Comics, 1998.
(Illustrator) Penn Jillette, *The Adventures of Rheumy Peepers and Chunky Highlights* (comic book), Oni Press, 1999.
(And illustrator) *The Soap Lady,* Top Shelf Productions, 2001.
(And illustrator) *Marbles in My Underpants,* Oni Press, 2001.
The Ticking, Top Shelf Productions, 2006.
Micrographica (from French's Web comic of the same title), Top Shelf Productions, 2007.

Author of *Micrographica,* an Internet comic book. Contributor of illustrations to comic book anthologies, including *Real Stuff #10,* Fantagraphics Books, 1992; *Real Stuff #17,* Fantagraphics Books, 1994; *A Vast Knowledge of General Subjects,* Book One, Fantagraphics Books, 1994; *The Big Book of Death,* Paradox Press, 1995; *The Big Book of Freaks,* Paradox Press, 1996; *Dark Horse Presents Annual 1997,* Dark Horse Comics, 1997; *Free Speeches,* Oni Press, 1998; *The Big Book of Bad,* Paradox Press, 1998; *Comix 2000,* L'Association, 1999; *XX,* Jochen Enterprises, 2000; *Zero Final Issue,* Fantagraphics, 2000; *Tokion,* Japan, 2000; and *Legal Action Comics,* Danny Hellman, 2000.

Contributor to periodicals, including *Village Voice, Comics Journal, Strapazin Magazine, World Art,* and *Utne Reader. Grit Bath* has been translated into German.

PICTURE BOOKS; AND ILLUSTRATOR; UNDER PSEUDONYM RAINY DOHANEY

Tinka, Simon & Schuster (New York, NY), 2003.
My Best Sweet Potato, Simon & Schuster (New York, NY), 2006.

SIDELIGHTS: Renée French is best known for her edgy adult comics and graphic novels that somehow manage to combine horror with sweet and cutesy moments in disturbing ways. An "inimitable and masterful stylist," according to one *Publishers Weekly* critic, French is "a kind of Edward Gorey who draws out the whimsical side of body horror." A characteristic tale by French, an illustrator who writes many of her own tales, is "Mitch and the Mole" from the *Marbles in My Underpants* collection. In this story, a boy has a pet mole he loves. One day, the animal dies, and Mitch tries to bring it back to life by cutting off its paw and putting it in a glass of water to grow. The author's "ability to merge the worlds of terror and innocence allows her to effectively lure readers into her nightmarish world," commented a *Publishers Weekly* reviewer.

Among French's other creations is *The Ticking,* about a horribly deformed boy named Edison who refuses the plastic surgery his father wants him to have. His father then strangely gives him a chimpanzee outfitted in a dress and tells the boy this is his new sister. When he is old enough, Edison ventures out on his own, becoming an artist and drawing for a fly-fishing catalog. Much of the graphic novel is told in pictures only, and French conveys her story increasingly through illustrations that capture life's creepy minutiae. The writer "fashions a gem that means more with every reading," asserted Ray Olson in a *Booklist* review.

French has recently branched out into children's picture books. *Tinka* is an enchanting story about a sheep so small she can ride on the back of a bird, while *My Best Sweet Potato* features a talking toy that begins to say unusual things after coming out of a washing machine.

BIOGRAPHICAL AND CRITICAL SOURCES:

PERIODICALS

Booklist, February 15, 2006, Ray Olson, review of *The Ticking,* p. 56.

Publishers Weekly, October 22, 2001, review of *Marbles in My Underpants,* p. 56; January 23, 2006, review of *The Ticking,* p. 193.

ONLINE

Comicon.com, http://www.comicon.com/ (May 18, 2007), Jennifer M. Contino, "Interview."

Comics Reporter, http://www.comicsreporter.com/ (April 16, 2006), Tom Spurgeon, "An Interview with Renée French."

Silver Bullet Comic Books Web site, http://www. silverbulletcomicbooks.com/ (May 18, 2007), Tim O'Shea, "Renée French: Works of Catharsis and Laughter," interview with Renée French.

Newsarama.com, http://www.newsarama.com/ (May 18, 2007), Alan David Doane, "Five Questions for Renée French."*

*   *   *

FRIED, Daisy 1967-
   (Margaret Fried)

PERSONAL: Born 1967, in Ithaca, NY; married Jim Quinn. *Education:* Swarthmore College, B.A., 1989.

ADDRESSES: *Home*—Northampton,   MA; Philadelphia, PA.

CAREER: Writer, poet, and journalist. Former writing instructor at Warren Wilson College low-residency M.F.A. program, Haverford College, University of Pennsylvania, and Rutgers University at New Brunswick; Smith College, Northampton, MA, Grace Hazard Conkling writer-in-residence.

AWARDS, HONORS: William A. Schnader Print Media Award, the Pennsylvania Bar Association, for the article "Legal Freeze," 1997; Pew fellow in poetry, 1998; Agnes Lynch Starrett Prize for *She Didn't Mean to Do It;* Leeway Award for excellence in poetry, 2001; Bread Loaf fellow, 2002; Hodder fellow, Princeton University, 2004-05.

WRITINGS:

POETRY

She Didn't Mean to Do It, University of Pittsburgh Press (Pittsburgh, PA), 2000.

My Brother Is Getting Arrested Again, University of Pittsburgh Press (Pittsburgh, PA), 2006.

Contributor of poetry to periodicals, including *American Poetry Review, Antioch Review, Colorado Review, Indiana Review, Ploughshares, Prairie Schooner,* and *Threepenny Review;* contributor of nonfiction to publications, including *Philadelphia, Philadelphia Inquirer, Newsday, City Paper,* and *Philadelphia Weekly.*

SIDELIGHTS: Daisy Fried is a poet who has worked at various institutions as a writing teacher, including Warren Wilson College, Haverford College, the University of Pennsylvania, Rutgers University at New Brunswick, and Smith College, where she serves as writer-in-residence. Writing itself, however, is her first love. Her poetry has won numerous accolades, including the Agnes Lynch Starrett Prize for *She Didn't Mean to Do It,* and the Leeway Award for excellence in poetry in 2001. Fried also works as a journalist for various Philadelphia-based publications, a side of her career she credits with making her pay attention to details and encouraging her interest in political and social welfare, all of which carries over into her poetry. In an interview with Tracy Parker for the Philadelphia Arts Writers Web site, Fried remarked: "I listened to the way people talked [in interviews] and I put that in my poems."

She Didn't Mean to Do It, Fried's first collection of poems, met with both critical and popular acclaim in the world of poetry. The volume gathers a series of her early lyrical poems, many of them set in Philadelphia. Her follow-up effort, *My Brother Is Getting Arrested Again,* while still lyrical in nature, delves into more serious subject matter than her first book. A reviewer for *Publishers Weekly* wrote: "Winningly personal, the poems are nevertheless artful, with a light touch to balance their heavy subjects." Sandra M. Gilbert, reviewing for *Poetry,* remarked of the poems that "Fried's avoidance of the obvious is provocative—and subtle."

BIOGRAPHICAL AND CRITICAL SOURCES:

PERIODICALS

Library Journal, March 15, 2006, Rochelle Ratner, review of *My Brother Is Getting Arrested Again,* p. 75.

Philadelphia Inquirer, December 18, 2000, Thomas J. Brady, "The Author: Daisy Fried," review of *She Didn't Mean to Do It.*

Poetry, February 1, 2007, Sandra M. Gilbert, "Eight Takes," review of *My Brother Is Getting Arrested Again,* p. 404.

Publishers Weekly, February 20, 2006, review of *My Brother Is Getting Arrested Again,* p. 138.

Writer, September 1, 2006, Judith Rosen, "Small-Press Success: Authors Tell Why They Went with an Independent Publisher—and Why You Should, Too," p. 50.

ONLINE

American Poems, http://www.americanpoems.com/ (April 22, 2007), author biography.

Cold Front Magazine, http://reviews.coldfrontmag.com/ (April 22, 2007), David Sewell, review of *My Brother Is Getting Arrested Again.*

Famous Poets and Poems, http://famouspoetsandpoems.com/ (April 22, 2007), author biography.

Philadelphia Arts Writers Web site, http://www.philadelphiawriters.com/ (April 22, 2007), Tracy Parker, "After She Did It: Catching Up with Daisy Fried."

Poetry Daily, http://www.poems.com/ (April 22, 2007), author biography.

Whyy.org, http://www.whyy.org/ (April 22, 2007), author biography.*

* * *

FRIED, Margaret
See FRIED, Daisy

FRIEDMAN, D. Dina 1957-

PERSONAL: Born June 13, 1957, in Takoma Park, MD; daughter of Stanley (a writer and television producer) and Susan (a professor of mathematics) Friedman; married Shel Horowitz (a writer and marketing consultant), October 9, 1983; children: Alana, Rafael. *Education:* Cornell University, A.B., 1978; University of Connecticut, M.S.W., 1985. *Religion:* Jewish. *Hobbies and other interests:* Reading, political activism, hiking, gardening, cross-country skiing, music, performing arts events.

ADDRESSES: Home and office—Northampton, MA. *Office*—Isenberg School of Management, University of Massachusetts, Amherst, MA 01003. *E-mail*—dina@ddinafriedman.com.

CAREER: Educator and author. Accurate Writing and More, Hadley, MA, writing coach and marketing consultant. Mount Holyoke College, South Hadley, MA, workshop coordinator in speaking, arguing, and writing program, 1997-2002; University of Massachusetts—Amherst, lecturer in School of Management, 2000—.

AWARDS, HONORS: Voice of Youth Advocates Top Shelf Fiction selection, 2006, and New York Public Library Best Books for the Teen Age selection, Association of Jewish Libraries Notable Book for Older Readers citation, American Library Association Best Books for Young Adults nominee, and Children's Book Council/National Council for the Social Studies Best Trade Book designation, all 2007, all for *Escaping into the Night*; Best Children's Book of the Year designation, Bank Street College of Education, 2007, for *Playing Dad's Song.*

WRITINGS:

Escaping into the Night (young-adult novel), Simon & Schuster (New York, NY), 2006.

Playing Dad's Song (middle-grade novel), Farrar, Straus (New York, NY), 2006.

SIDELIGHTS: D. Dina Friedman always knew that writing was her calling. "I've wanted to be a writer since I was eight, and before writing my novels, I wrote many poems and short stories," Friedman wrote on her home page. Her novels for young readers—*Escaping into the Night* is a work of historical fiction for young adults while *Playing Dad's Song* is geared for middle-grade readers—feature teens discovering their own identity, and learning what their Jewish heritage means to them.

Escaping into the Night is based on the actual historical events around a little-known Holocaust story. Fleeing the Warsaw ghetto, Halina travels to hidden *ziemlankas*—underground caves where a community of Jews are hiding. "Friedman realistically captures the terror of the situation, but, refreshingly, also depicts Halina experiencing her first kiss," noted a *Publishers Weekly* contributor. According to Hazel Rochman in *Booklist*, "Friedman never idealizes the refugees or their rescuers," instead presenting the moral dilemmas Halina and her friends go through in order to survive. "In Halina, Friedman has created a reluctant heroine who is also a believable adolescent," wrote Renee Steinberg in her *School Library Journal* review of *Escaping into the Night*, while a *Kirkus Reviews* contributor concluded that "Halina's experience demonstrates maturity and a resignation that life is worth living at any price."

Friedman grew up in New York City, the setting of *Playing Dad's Song*. Gus Moskowitz wishes he could change the past: make September 11th never happen, which means that his dad would still be alive. Missing his father and jealous of his talented older sister, Gus struggles, until he begins taking oboe lessons from a Holocaust survivor. Their relationship inspires Gus with the means by which he can honor his father in his own way. As a *Kirkus Reviews* contributor noted of the conclusion, "As Gus looks at the empty skyline, it's no longer a hole but a new beginning." "The honest personal drama brings the grief and loss of the terrorist attack home to the reader," wrote Rochman.

Along with her writing work, Friedman is involved in antipoverty work, land-protection issues, and antiwar campaigns. "While writing is one of the central things in my life, equally important is working for a better world," she wrote on her home page. She also offered the following advice to young writers: "In my experience, the hardest thing about writing is to keep going and believe in yourself."

BIOGRAPHICAL AND CRITICAL SOURCES:

PERIODICALS

Booklist, January 1, 2006, Hazel Rochman, review of *Escaping into the Night,* p. 83; November 15, 2006, Hazel Rochman, review of *Playing Dad's Song,* p. 47.
Bulletin of the Center for Children's Books, February, 2006, Loretta Gaffney, review of *Escaping into the Night,* p. 263.
Kirkus Reviews, January 15, 2006, review of *Escaping into the Night,* p. 84; August 15, 2006, review of *Playing Dad's Song,* p. 840.
Publishers Weekly, February 13, 2006, review of *Escaping into the Night,* p. 90.
School Library Journal, March, 2006, Renee Steinberg, review of *Escaping into the Night,* p. 222; September, 2006, Miriam Lang Budin, review of *Playing Dad's Song,* p. 204.
Voice of Youth Advocates, April, 2006, Eileen Kuhl, review of *Escaping into the Night,* p. 42.

ONLINE

Children's Literature Network Web site, http://www.childrensliteraturenetwork.org/ (April 28, 2007), "D. Dina Friedman."
D. Dina Friedman Home Page, http://www.ddinafriedman.com (April 28, 2007).

*   *   *

FRIEND, Catherine 1957(?)-

PERSONAL: Born c. 1957. *Education:* University of Wisconsin—Eau Claire, B.A., 1979; University of Minnesota, M.S. *Hobbies and other interests:* Working on her farm, volunteering on her local library board.

ADDRESSES: Home—Zumbrota, MN. *E-mail*—catherine@catherinefriend.com.

CAREER: Author. Has worked as a freelance editor, technical writer, and as a writing workshop instructor for the Institute of Children's Literature; has also worked at an organic vegetable farm, at a cheese and sausage packing business, at book stores, and as a Christmas decorations assembly-line packager.

WRITINGS:

Hit by a Farm: How I Learned to Stop Worrying and Love the Barn (autobiography), Marlowe (New York, NY), 2006.

FOR CHILDREN

My Head Is Full of Colors, illustrated by Kiki, Hyperion Books for Children (New York, NY), 1994.
The Sawfin Stickleback: A Very Fishy Story, illustrated by Dan Yaccarino, Hyperion Books for Children (New York, NY), 1994.
Funny Ruby, illustrated by Rachel Merriman, Candlewick Press (Cambridge, MA), 2000.
Silly Ruby, illustrated by Rachel Merriman, Candlewick Press (Cambridge, MA), 2000.
Eddie the Raccoon, illustrated by Wong Herbert Yee, Candlewick Press (Cambridge, MA), 2004.
The Perfect Nest, illustrated by John Manders, Candlewick Press (Cambridge, MA), 2007.

SIDELIGHTS: Catherine Friend is a children's book author who writes primarily for pre-and grade-school readers. Her stories are typically simple tales that many critics have found charming. Her *Eddie the Raccoon,* for example, is a beginning reader story about the misadventures of a young raccoon; *Silly Ruby* contains four stories featuring such characters as a sheep, a dinosaur, and a worm; and *The Perfect Nest* has a cat trying to lure a chicken by building a nest, only to have his plans thwarted unexpectedly when the eggs quickly hatch and the chicks think the cat is their father. After having worked in a number of careers, ranging from editing and technical writing to teaching and working on an assembly line, Friend was establishing a career as a successful children's book writer when her life partner, Melissa, inherited a small Wisconsin farm. Insisting that they both move to the country, Melissa and Friend moved to rural Wisconsin. Friend was under the impression that Melissa, who loved the countryside, would occupy herself with the farm animals and crops while she would be allowed to continue writing. Friend quickly found herself drafted into helping out with many of the tasks on the farm,

however. In her memoir, *Hit by a Farm: How I Learned to Stop Worrying and Love the Barn,* Friend relates her aggravation, consternation, and eventual adaptation to farm life.

Hit by a Farm includes many anecdotes about the surprising jobs Friend found herself doing, including some rather embarrassing tasks involving animal husbandry. Many of the moments are designed to convey the humor of a city slicker trying to adapt to the farm, but there are also more poignant, emotional moments, such as when some of their animals die from disease and from coyote attacks. Because of the amount of work needed to maintain the farm, Friend found it more and more difficult to write, and this led to such frustration that it threatened her relationship with Melissa. "This honest look at collaboration and compromise, the pain and the joy of partnership, and the hands-on of farming will find a ready audience," predicted Nancy Bent in *Booklist. New York Times Book Review* contributor Katherine Lanpher found this "chronicle of her transformation from Minneapolis city slicker to rural Minnesota shepherd" to be a "charming memoir," and *Armchair Interviews* writer Connie Anderson declared it "funny, poignant, sad—and educational."

BIOGRAPHICAL AND CRITICAL SOURCES:

BOOKS

Friend, Catherine, *Hit by a Farm: How I Learned to Stop Worrying and Love the Barn,* Marlowe (New York, NY), 2006.

PERIODICALS

Booklist, March 15, 1994, Ilene Cooper, review of *My Head Is Full of Colors,* p. 1372; July 1, 2004, Stephanie Zvirin, review of *Eddie the Raccoon,* p. 1850; April 15, 2006, Nancy Bent, review of *Hit by a Farm,* p. 14.
Eau Claire Leader-Telegram (Eau Claire, WI), June 8, 2006, Ann Barsness, review of *Hit by a Farm.*
Kirkus Reviews, January 15, 2007, review of *The Perfect Nest,* p. 72.
Lambda Book Report, summer, 2006, Warren Keith Wright, review of *Hit by a Farm.*

Library Journal, April 1, 2006, Ilse Heidmann, review of *Hit by a Farm,* p. 114.

New York Times Book Review, July 9, 2006, Katherine Lanpher, "A Nation of Sheep," review of *Hit by a Farm,* p. 19.

Pittsburgh Tribune, March 18, 2007, Nicholas A. Basbanes, "Animals Take the Spotlight in this Month's Offerings," review of *The Perfect Nest.*

Publishers Weekly, April 25, 1994, review of *My Head Is Full of Colors,* p. 77; October 3, 1994, review of *The Sawfin Stickleback: A Very Fishy Story,* p. 68.

Saint Paul Pioneer Press, July 9, 2006, "Life among the Lambs: A Decade of Life on the Farm Provided the Inspiration for a Minnesota Woman's Funny and Touching New Memoir."

School Library Journal, February 1, 2001, Adele Greenlee, review of *Funny Ruby,* p. 100; March 1, 2001, Christina F. Renaud, review of *Silly Ruby,* p. 194; January 1, 2005, Marilyn Taniguchi, review of *Eddie the Raccoon,* p. 92.

ONLINE

Armchair Interviews, http://www.armchairinterviews.com/ (May 18, 2007), Connie Anderson, review of *Hit by a Farm.*

Catherine Friend Home Page, http://www.catherinefriend.com (May 18, 2007).

Hit by a Farm Web site, http://www.hitbyafarm.com (May 18, 2007).*

G

GADDY, L.L. 1949-

PERSONAL: Born June 22, 1949, in Florence, SC; son of L.L., Sr., and B.E. Gaddy; children: L.L. III. *Ethnicity:* "Caucasian." *Education:* University of Georgia, Ph.D., 1985. *Hobbies and other interests:* Tennis, travel, poetry.

ADDRESSES: Home—Columbia, SC. *E-mail*—llgaddy@bellsouth.net.

CAREER: Self-employed consultant, 1979—; Terra Incognita (environmental consultants), president, 1998—.

WRITINGS:

(With J.C. Morse) *Common Spiders of South Carolina,* Clemson University (Clemson, SC), 1985.
A Naturalist's Guide to the Southern Blue Ridge: Linville Gorge, North Carolina, to Tallulah Gorge, Georgia, University of South Carolina Press (Columbia, SC), 2000.
Biodiversity: Przewalski's Horse, Edna's Trillium, the Giant Squid, and Over 1.5 Million Other Species, University Press of America (Lanham, MD), 2005.
Take the Lively Air: An Anthology of Verse, privately printed, 2007.

* * *

GALICHIAN, Rouben 1938-

PERSONAL: Born November 30, 1938, in Iran; son of Aram (a radio engineer) and Cosette (a French teacher) Galichian; married Mariette Arzoumanian (a counselor), 1963; children: Shahen. *Ethnicity:* "Armenian." *Education:* Aston University, B.Sc. (with first-class honors), 1964. *Religion:* Christian. *Hobbies and other interests:* Cartography, photography, music.

ADDRESSES: Home—London, England. *E-mail*—rgalichian@onetel.com.

CAREER: Systems designer, 1964-74; project director and project manager for the oil and gas industry in Tehran, Iran, and Paris, France, 1975-2000; business consultant. Also director of Armenian charities.

MEMBER: International Map Collectors' Society, Institute of Electrical and Electronics Engineers.

WRITINGS:

Historic Maps of Armenia: The Cartographic Heritage, I.B. Tauris (London, England), 2004.
Armenia in International Cartography, Printinfo Publishing House (Yerevan, Armenia), 2005.
Armenia in Medieval Maps, Printinfo Publishing House (Yerevan, Armenia), 2007.

* * *

GARTEN, Ina 1948-

PERSONAL: Born February 2, 1948, in New York, NY; father a physician, surname Rosenberg; married Jeffrey Garten, December 22, 1968. *Education:* Syracuse University, graduate.

ADDRESSES: Office—Barefoot Contessa, 46 New-town Ln., East Hampton, NY 11937.

CAREER: Chef, television host, and author. White House Office of Management and Budget, Washington, DC, budget analyst, 1974-78; Barefoot Contessa (specialty food store), East Hampton, NY, co-owner, 1978-96; *The Barefoot Contessa* (cooking show), Food Network, host, 2002—.

WRITINGS:

The Barefoot Contessa Cookbook: Secrets from the Legendary Specialty Food Store for Simple Food and Party Platters You Can Make at Home, photographs by Melanie Acevedo, Clarkson Potter (New York, NY), 1999.

Barefoot Contessa Parties! Ideas and Recipes for Easy Parties That Are Really Fun, photographs by James Merrell, Clarkson Potter (New York, NY), 2001.

Barefoot Contessa Family Style: Easy Ideas and Recipes That Make Everyone Feel Like Family, photographs by Maura McEvoy, Clarkson Potter (New York, NY), 2002.

Barefoot in Paris: Easy French Food You Can Make at Home, photographs by Quentin Bacon, Clarkson Potter (New York, NY), 2004.

Barefoot Contessa at Home: Everyday Recipes You'll Make Over and Over Again, photographs by Quentin Bacon, Clarkson Potter (New York, NY), 2006.

Author of foreword, *Stonewall Kitchen Favorites: Delicious Recipes to Share with Family and Friends Every Day,* by Jonathan King, Jim Stott, and Kathy Gunst, Clarkson Potter, 2006. Contributor to periodicals, including *O, the Oprah Magazine.* Author of column "Entertaining Is Fun," *Martha Stewart Living Magazine.*

SIDELIGHTS: The popular television host of the cooking show *The Barefoot Contessa,* Ina Garten is also known for her cookbooks which stress easy yet delicious recipes that are perfect for small parties with friends. Interestingly, she began her career as a budget analyst for the White House, where she helped prepare budgets concerning the nation's nuclear energy policies. Her love of food, however, led her to buy a specialty food store in East Hampton, New York, in 1978. She kept the original name of the place, which

was a nickname given to the previous owner by her Italian family after watching a Humphrey Bogart film. Garten turned the venture into a hugely popular store. She sold it to two of her employees in 1996, and the store later closed in 2003. Garten, however, retained the business name for her Food Network cable show and for a series of best-selling cookbooks.

The Barefoot Contessa Cookbook: Secrets from the Legendary Specialty Food Store for Simple Food and Party Platters You Can Make at Home was released in 1999, stunning its publisher by quickly selling nearly two hundred thousand copies. In keeping with her philosophy, Garten includes simple recipes that include ingredients that are easy to find in any grocery store. Each chapter has a recipe for a platter that can be taken to a party, too.

Garten focused on the party aspect of cooking for her follow-up, *Barefoot Contessa Parties! Ideas and Recipes for Easy Parties That Are Really Fun.* "Simplicity is the key," she reiterated to Alex Witchel in a *New York Times* article about the book. "The simpler it is, the more elegant—like a great couturier dress. Eli Zabar was really my mentor in this: all you have to do is cook to enhance the ingredients. With the first book, I was concerned that 'too simple' would be the criticism, but women have full lives, careers, families, houses to take care of. When they give a dinner party they're doing all those other things at the same time. I think people feel empowered by these books. It's all about 'I can do this.'"

Other "Barefoot Contessa" books include *Barefoot Contessa Family Style: Easy Ideas and Recipes That Make Everyone Feel Like Family, Barefoot in Paris: Easy French Food You Can Make at Home,* and *Barefoot Contessa at Home: Everyday Recipes You'll Make Over and Over Again.* A *Publishers Weekly* critic enjoyed the author's style in *Barefoot in Paris,* where Garten "writes personally in a way that feels genuine." In an interview with Peter Smith for *O, the Oprah Magazine* after the release of *Barefoot Contessa at Home,* Garten again talked about her basic philosophy of cooking, saying: "I take familiar things and traditional flavors—and turn the volume up."

BIOGRAPHICAL AND CRITICAL SOURCES:

PERIODICALS

Booklist, April 15, 1999, Mark Knoblauch, review of *The Barefoot Contessa Cookbook: Secrets from the Legendary Specialty Food Store for Simple*

Food and Party Platters You Can Make at Home,
p. 1497; March 15, 2001, Mark Knoblauch,
review of *Barefoot Contessa Parties! Ideas and
Recipes for Easy Parties That Are Really Fun,*
p. 1342; October 15, 2002, Mark Knoblauch,
"Cuisine Du Jour," p. 373.

Good Housekeeping, November 1, 1999, Catherine
Lo, review of *The Barefoot Contessa Cookbook..*

Library Journal, February 15, 2001, Judith Sutton,
review of *Barefoot Contessa Parties!,* p. 194;
September 15, 2002, Judith Sutton, review of
*Barefoot Contessa Family Style: Easy Ideas and
Recipes That Make Everyone Feel Like Family,*
p. 86; October 15, 2004, Judith Sutton, review of
*Barefoot in Paris: Easy French Food You Can
Make at Home,* p. 82; October 15, 2006, Judith
Sutton, review of *Barefoot Contessa at Home:
Everyday Recipes You'll Make Over and Over
Again,* p. 82.

O, the Oprah Magazine, October 1, 2006, Peter Smith,
"Dinner at Home: Ina Garten's Idea of Home
Cooking: Familiar Recipes Zinged by a Small,
Simple Twist That Makes Them Unforgettable,"
p. 330.

Publishers Weekly, January 15, 2001, review of
Barefoot Contessa Parties!, p. 71; September 16,
2002, review of *Barefoot Contessa Family Style,*
p. 65; October 11, 2004, review of *Barefoot in
Paris,* p. 70; October 11, 2004, Lynn Adriani,
"Walking the Streets of Paris, sans Shoes,"
interview with Ina Garten, p. 71; August 21, 2006,
review of *Barefoot Contessa at Home,* p. 64.

Toronto Star, March 31, 2007, Marion Kane, "Love-In
for Contessa."

ONLINE

Barefoot Contessa Web site, http://www.barefoot
contessa.com (May 17, 2007).

*   *   *

GATRELL, V.A.C. 1941-
(Vic Gatrell)

PERSONAL: Born 1941, in South Africa. *Education:*
Rhodes University, B.A.; Cambridge University, B.A.,
Ph.D.

ADDRESSES: Home—Cambridge, England. *Office*—
University of Essex, Wivenhoe Park, Colchester CO4
3SQ, England. *E-mail*—vag1000@cam.ac.uk.

CAREER: Writer, educator. Gonville and Caius College, Cambridge University, fellow, life fellow,
1967—; lecturer, reader, Cambridge Faculty;
University of Essex, professor, 2003—. Visiting fellow, Yale University and Australian National
University.

AWARDS, HONORS: Whitfield Prize, Royal Historical
Society, 1994, for *The Hanging Tree: Execution and
the English People, 1770-1868;* Wolfson Prize and
PEN Hessell-Tiltman Prize, both 2006, both for *City
of Laughter: Sex and Satire in Eighteenth-century
London.*

WRITINGS:

(Editor and author of introduction) *Robert Owen: A
New View of Society and Report to the County of
Lanark,* Penguin (London, England), 1971

(Editor, with Bruce Lenman, and Geoffrey Parker)
*Crime and the Law: The Social History of Crime
in Western Europe since 1500,* Europa Publications (London, England), 1980.

*The Hanging Tree: Execution and the English People,
1770-1868,* Oxford University Press (New York,
NY), 1994.

(As Vic Gatrell) *City of Laughter: Sex and Satire in
Eighteenth-century London,* Atlantic (London,
England), 2006.

Contributor of articles to numerous professional
journals. Contributor of chapters to numerous scholarly
books.

SIDELIGHTS: A professor of history in England,
V.A.C. Gatrell has written books dealing with the history of crime and punishment, sexual politics, and
changing social and cultural manners. With *The Hanging Tree: Execution and the English People, 1770-
1868,* he provides a cultural study of the experiences,
meanings of, and attitudes toward public execution.
With his 2006 work, *City of Laughter: Sex and Satire
in Eighteenth-Century London,* he offers a panoramic

history of late eighteenth-and early nineteenth-century manners and cultural change through a critical study of satirical prints of the age.

Writing in *History Today,* Clive Emsley noted that *The Hanging Tree* "takes the reader on a journey through the mentalities of the judges who sentenced, the politicians who decided on penal reform and the appeals for those sentenced to die, and the different social groups who gathered, sometimes in their thousands, to watch executions." Such executions were public until 1868 and afforded occasions of public entertainment as well as warning. Gatrell was inspired to write his study by the case of one falsely accused man, sentenced to hanging for the supposed rape of his neighbor. Gatrell demonstrates in his book that finally the fearsome example of public execution was no longer necessary as new methods of social control were instituted. Through a wide variety of examples, the author demonstrates the cruelty of public hangings. Writing in the *Journal of Interdisciplinary History,* Roger Lane observed that the work was "important, often maddening, but always compelling." Allen Horstman, writing in the *Historian,* felt that "readers, especially undergraduates, will be frustrated by the lack of clear themes." Horstman further complained that the author's "strong feelings about hanging and death itself certainly raise suspicions that the historian's objectivity has been compromised." However, other reviewers had a higher assessment of *The Hanging Tree.* I.G. Doolittle, writing in the *English Historical Review,* found it a "tour de force," and Peter Roy, reviewing the work in the *New Statesman & Society,* termed it "a mammoth study, penetrating and poignant." Carolyn A. Conley, writing in the *Journal of Social History,* thought it was a "remarkable book, brimming with the enthusiasm of the newly converted."

In *City of Laughter,* Gatrell, as a *Kirkus Reviews* critic noted, "explores exhaustively, albeit most pleasantly, the golden age of graphic satire that flourished in licentious London from 1770 to 1830." In doing so, he also examines the society and culture of the time. Gatrell used for this investigation a wealth of bawdy and satirical prints stored in the British Library, focusing on the prints and professional lives of James Gillray, Thomas Rowlandson and George Cruikshank. The resulting work demonstrates that what was considered humorous in the day was very distant from urbane, subtly witty, and sophisticated humor. On the contrary, it was rather a blend of what could be termed toilet humor along with political satire of the broadest variety. A *Publishers Weekly* contributor noted that Gatrell's book "vividly demonstrates the maliciousness and ribaldry of Georgian London." Similarly, *New Statesman* reviewer John Mullan noted: "Certainly the caricatures show us a disconcerting version of a refined culture's self-images. The London of literary and intellectual clubs was also a city where male sociability was founded on huge alcohol consumption." Further, Gatrell goes on to show that such humor was supplanted by more tasteful (and perhaps less funny) forms as the growing middle classes searched for respectability. A reviewer for *Internet Bookwatch* felt the book was a "key to any in-depth, college-level understanding of 18th century London." Similarly, Gilbert Taylor, writing in *Booklist,* concluded, "Capitalizing marvelously on an era's body of illustrations, Gatrell will captivate students of social history." The *Kirkus Reviews* critic also praised the work as "a lively, erudite study." For Mullan, *City of Laughter* was a "fact-filled, anecdote-rich book," and for Claire Tomalin of the *Spectator* the same work was "valuable and entertaining."

BIOGRAPHICAL AND CRITICAL SOURCES:

PERIODICALS

Booklist, January 1, 2007, Gilbert Taylor, review of *City of Laughter: Sex and Satire in Eighteenth-Century London,* p. 30.

English Historical Review, November 1, 1995, I.G. Doolittle, review of *The Hanging Tree: Execution and the English People, 1770-1868,* p. 1221.

Historian, January 1, 1996, Allen Horstman, review of *The Hanging Tree,* p. 430.

History Today, January 1, 1997, Clive Emsley, review of *The Hanging Tree,* p. 57; June 1, 1997, Barry Godrey, review of *The Hanging Tree,* p. 58; November 1, 2006, Steven Parissien, review of *City of Laughter,* p. 65.

Internet Bookwatch, March 1, 2007, review of *City of Laughter.*

Journal of Interdisciplinary History, fall, 1996, Roger Lane, review of *The Hanging Tree.*

Journal of Social History, spring, 1996, Carolyn A. Conley, review of *The Hanging Tree.*

Journal of Urban History, November 1, 1997, Simon Renton, review of *The Hanging Tree,* p. 130.

Kirkus Reviews, October 15, 2006, review of *City of Laughter,* p. 1054.

Library Journal, February 15, 2007, Scott H. Silverman, review of *City of Laughter,* p. 131.

Michigan Law Review, May 1, 1996, Sara Sun Beale, review of *The Hanging Tree,* p. 1622.

New Statesman, November 6, 2006, John Mullan, "Life Drawing: Our National Obsession with Political Sleaze and Celebrity Misbehaviour Is Nothing New. John Mullan on the Scurrilous Ancestors of Scarfe, Steadman and Spitting Image," p. 54.

New Statesman & Society, September 16, 1994, Roy Porter, review of *The Hanging Tree,* p. 36.

Publishers Weekly, October 23, 2006, review of *City of Laughter,* p. 44.

Spectator, December 16, 2006, Claire Tomalin, "Before We Became Respectable."

Victorian Studies, January 1, 1996, J.S. Cockburn, review of *The Hanging Tree,* p. 286.

ONLINE

Breaking the Seal, http://www.open2.net/breaking theseal/ (May 7, 2007), "Dr. Vic Gatrell."

University of Essex, Department of History Web site, http://www.essex.ac.uk/history/ (May 7, 2007), "Vic (V.A.C.) Gatrell."

*   *   *

GATRELL, Vic
    See GATRELL, V.A.C.

*   *   *

GILLESPIE, Spike 1964-

PERSONAL: Born 1964; children: Henry. *Hobbies and other interests:* Knitting, putting on Teen Rock events.

ADDRESSES: Home—Austin, TX. *E-mail*—spike@ spikeg.com; spikegillespie@gmail.com.

CAREER: Writer, journalist, teacher, documentary filmmaker, and wedding officiant. *Dallas Morning News,* former reporter and columnist. Alkali Marketing, copywriter. Austin Children of Musicians, Artists and Writers Fund, founder.

WRITINGS:

All the Wrong Men and One Perfect Boy: A Memoir, Simon & Schuster (New York, NY), 1999.

Surrender (But Don't Give Yourself Away): Old Cars, Found Hope, and Other Cheap Tricks, University of Texas Press (Austin, TX), 2003.

Pissed Off: On Women and Anger: Finding Forgiveness on the Other Side of the Finger, Seal Press (Emeryville, CA), 2006.

Quilty as Charged: Undercover in a Material World, University of Texas Press (Austin, TX), 2007.

Contributor of articles to magazines and newspapers, including the *New York Times, New York Times Magazine, Smithsonian Magazine, National Geographic Traveler, Real Simple, Washington Post, Playboy, GQ, Elle, Cosmo, Texas Monthly, Salon.com,* and *Nerve.*

SIDELIGHTS: A pioneer in the art of the online confessional and an early cyber celebrity, Texas writer Spike Gillespie parlayed her soul-searching/soul-baring personal columns into her first book, the 1999 title *All the Wrong Men and One Perfect Boy: A Memoir.* Speaking of her online writing, *New Statesman* reviewer Andrew Brown noted: "Parts of it are simply brilliant, shocking in the way that only careful and perceptive writing can be." Online she related her problems with alcohol, cancer, and men, and in her memoir she follows a similar self-revealing style. *Salon.com* contributor Katie Allison Granju commented that in the book, Gillespie "recounts her personal history in an unflinching straight line." Born in New Jersey to working-class parents, Gillespie spent summers at the Atlantic shore and later became a single mother in the artistic setting of Austin, Texas. Along the way she suffered disappointments and depression, much of it brought on by her miserable relationships with men. However, love for her young son helped turn her life around. Reviewing the memoir in the *Library Journal,* Shana C. Fair felt that "women struggling to end destructive relationships and start new lives will find inspiration here." A *Publishers Weekly* reviewer, however, found that "Gillespie's lack of personal responsibility and 'poor me' attitude is wearying." A higher assessment came from Granju, who noted: "Despite the bleak specifics of Gillespie's story, at its heart it is both uplifting and inspiring." Brit Fedorev, writing in *Feminista,* observed: "Gillespie recounts with humor and fearless honesty the most profound events of her life, a journey that has taken her across the country and to hell and back, writing it as she remembers it—without apologies."

Speaking with Fedorev, Gillespie explained her motivation for writing *All the Wrong Men and One Perfect Boy:* "My book is sort of a hard drive for all my memories. My memories haunt me. People tell me to forget stuff, don't dwell on it. . . . Now that so many stories are in the book, I've put them somewhere where I can retrieve them and so I don't dwell as much on, say, what happened between me and my dad. It frees my mind to move on, break bad patterns, come out to a better place."

Gillespie is also the author of *Pissed Off: On Women and Anger: Finding Forgiveness on the Other Side of the Finger,* an "engaging memoir-cure-self-help-book," as Deborah Bigelow described it in a *Library Journal* review. Here Gillespie relates how she came to integrate a sense of forgiveness into her life as an antidote to the rage she had long felt. A reviewer for *Publishers Weekly* found the book a "curious hybrid": part first-person memoir, and part self-help. The same contributor felt that by the end of the book readers would be "rooting for her." Similarly, *Herizons* writer Jennifer O'Connor termed *Pissed Off* an "unflinching look at anger and forgiveness," as well as a "a self-help book for people who hate self-help books."

BIOGRAPHICAL AND CRITICAL SOURCES:

BOOKS

Gillespie, Spike, *All the Wrong Men and One Perfect Boy: A Memoir,* Simon & Schuster (New York, NY), 1999.
Gillespie, Spike, *Pissed Off: On Women and Anger: Finding Forgiveness on the Other Side of the Finger,* Seal Press (Emeryville, CA), 2006.

PERIODICALS

Herizons, spring, 2007, Jennifer O'Connor, review of *Pissed Off,* p. 46.

Library Journal, August 1, 1999, Shana C. Fair, review of *All the Wrong Men and One Perfect Boy,* p. 106; July 1, 2006, Deborah Bigelow, review of *Pissed Off,* p. 93.
New Statesman, August 23, 1999, Andrew Brown, "Strictly Personal," p. 36.
Publishers Weekly, June 28, 1999, review of *All the Wrong Men and One Perfect Boy,* p. 64; March 20, 2006, review of *Pissed Off,* p. 53.

ONLINE

Alkali Marketing Web site, http://www.alkali marketing.com/ (April 15, 2007), "Spike Gillespie."
Austin Mama, http://www.austinmama.com/ (April 15, 2007), Robin Bradford, "Neil Diamond, Cheesecake and a Pack of Dogs: A Movable Chat with Author Spike Gillespie."
Bell Jar Web site, http://www.thebelljar.net/ (April 15, 2007), unpublished novel.
Feminista, http://www.feminista.com/ (April 15, 2007), Brit Fedorev, review of *All the Wrong Men and One Perfect Boy.*
Salon.com, http://www.salon.com/ (August 11, 1998), Katie Allison Granju, review of *All the Wrong Men and One Perfect Boy.**

*   *   *

GILLILAND, Judith Heide

PERSONAL: Daughter of Florence Parry Heide (a writer); married; husband's name Kim; children: Win, Donny. *Education:* University of Wisconsin, B.A., 1970; University of Washington, M.A., 1973.

ADDRESSES: Home and office—Amherst, NH.

CAREER: Children's book author.

AWARDS, HONORS: Children's Picture Book Award, Council of Wisconsin Writers, 1995, for *The Day of Ahmed's Secret*; Outstanding Children's Book Award, New Hampshire Writers and Publishers Project, 1995, for *Sami and the Time of Troubles*; Middle East Book Award, 2000, for *The House of Wisdom.*

WRITINGS:

(With mother, Florence Parry Heide) *The Day of Ahmed's Secret,* illustrated by Ted Lewin, Lothrop (New York, NY), 1990.

(With Florence Parry Heide) *Sami and the Time of the Troubles,* illustrated by Ted Lewin, Clarion (New York, NY), 1992.

River, illustrated by Joyce Powzyk, Clarion (New York, NY), 1993.

Not in the House, Newton!, illustrated by Elizabeth Sayles, Clarion (New York, NY), 1995.

(With Florence Parry Heide) *The House of Wisdom,* illustrated by Mary GrandPré, Dorling Kindersley (New York, NY), 1999.

(With Florence Parry Heide and Roxanne Heide Pierce) *It's about Time! Poems,* illustrated by Cathryn Falwell, Clarion (New York, NY), 1999.

Steamboat! The Story of Captain Blanche Leathers, illustrated by Holly Meade, Dorling Kindersley (New York, NY), 2000.

Strange Birds (novel), Farrar, Straus (New York, NY), 2006.

SIDELIGHTS: Judith Heide Gilliland had a good role model when she decided to become a children's book writer: her mother, Florence Parry Heide, has written more than one hundred books for children. Collaborating with Heide, Gilliland put her master's degree in Near-Eastern languages and her experiences living in the Middle East to good use in her first book. Titled *The Day of Ahmed's Secret,* it was one of two books to be ranked as a notable title about Arabs by the American Library Association. Other books by Gilliland include the story-hour favorite *Not in the House, Newton!* as well as *House of Wisdom,* the novel *Strange Birds,* and the picture-book biography *Steamboat: The Story of Captain Blanche Leathers.*

The Day of Ahmed's Secret follows a young Egyptian as he completes his delivery work in the streets of Cairo. The boy hints at a secret readers eventually discover: the young boy has learned how to write his name in Arabic. The text and pictures create "a sense of place so vivid that readers can almost hear the cry of vendors," according to a *Publishers Weekly* contributor. Another collaboration between mother and daughter, *The House of Wisdom,* is a picture book set in ninth-century Baghdad about Ishaq, a young would-be scholar who lives in the library—called the

House of Wisdom. Although he wants to be a scholar like his father, Ishaq longs for adventure, a desire the Caliph channels by sending the young man across the known world, his mission to gather knowledge. The trip so inspires him that he eventually becomes one of the world's greatest translators of Aristotle. *The House of Wisdom* "is historically informative, [and] written in lyrical prose," according to Judith Gabriel in her review for *Al Jadid* online. According to *Booklist* contributor Ilene Cooper, the coauthors "breathe new life into an event from an often neglected time and place." A note at the back of the book distinguishes the story's fiction from the facts about the real-life Ishaq.

Gilliland once again travels to the Middle East in her coauthored work *Sami and the Time of the Troubles,* a book about war in Lebanon, and spins an environmental tale about the Amazon in *River.* A *Publishers Weekly* contributor deemed *Sami and the Time of the Troubles* "valuable for its portrait of children caught in modern-day conflicts," while another reviewer in the same periodical noted that *River* "exemplifies the best sort of educational writing." The book's "narrative only implies its lessons," the critic added, explaining that the coauthors focus instead on giving readers a sensory experience of the Amazon basin region.

A solo book, Gilliland's *Steamboat! The Story of Captain Blanche Leathers* is a picture-book biography about the Mississippi's first female steamboat captain. Starting her story in the late 1860s, Gilliland details Leathers's growing-up years and her dream of becoming a captain. "This beautifully written picture-book biography is filled with drama," wrote Michael Cart in his *Booklist* review of the work. Citing the illustrations by Holly Meade, a *Publishers Weekly* critic noted that author and illustrator "convincingly expose the mysteries of the Mississippi," while a *Horn Book* writer concluded of *Steamboat!* that "this lively book offers a ship-shape model of the best in picture-book biography."

Along with her picture books, Gilliland has also written the middle-grade novel *Strange Birds.* In this story, eleven-year-old Anna, whose parents have disappeared at sea and whose guardian aunt is neglectful, discovers a nest of miniature winged horses in the branches of a large tree. After discovering a diary, Anna is able to link the existence of the horses to her parents' mysterious disappearance. "Readers will be easily captured by the family secrets, whimsical magic, warm friendship, and brave, intrepid Anna," wrote Gillian Engberg in her *Booklist* review of the novel. Deirdre Root, writing in *Kliatt,* praised *Strange Birds* as "charming and timeless, inspiring without being overly moralistic."

BIOGRAPHICAL AND CRITICAL SOURCES:

PERIODICALS

Booklist, April 1, 1992, Hazel Rochman, review of *Sami and the Time of the Troubles,* p. 1449; November 1, 1993, Julie Corsaro, review of *River,* p. 525; December 15, 1995, Susan Dove Lempke, review of *Not in the House, Newton!,* p. 708; September 15, 1999, review of *The House of Wisdom,* p. 261; March 15, 2000, Michael Cart, review of *Steamboat! The Story of Captain Blanche Leathers,* p. 1374; March 1, 2001, Stephanie Avirin, review of *Steamboat!,* p. 1280; March 1, 2002, Ilene Cooper, review of *Steamboat!,* p. 1147; May 15, 2006, Gillian Engberg, review of *Strange Birds,* p. 58.
Bulletin of the Center for Children's Books, March, 2000, review of *Steamboat!,* p. 243; September, 2006, Karen Coats, review of *Strange Birds,* p. 14.
Horn Book, November-December, 1990, Ethel R. Twichell, review of *The Day of Ahmed's Secret,* p. 739; July-August, 1992, Ellen Fader, review of *Sami and the Time of the Troubles,* p. 445; March, 2000, review of *Steamboat!,* p. 211.
Kirkus Reviews, May 1, 2006, review of *Strange Birds,* p. 458.
Kliatt, May, 2006, Deirdre Root, review of *Strange Birds,* p. 9.
Publishers Weekly, August 10, 1990, review of *The Day of Ahmed's Secret,* p. 444; May 4, 1992, review of *Sami and the Time of the Troubles,* p. 56; October 4, 1993, review of *River,* p. 79; August 23, 1999, review of *The House of Wisdom,* p. 58; April 3, 2000, review of *Steamboat!,* p. 80.
School Library Journal, August, 1990, Luann Toth, review of *The Day of Ahmed's Secret,* p. 130; December, 1990, Trevelyn Jones and Luann Toth, review of *The Day of Ahmed's Secret,* p. 22; May, 1992, Ellen D. Warwick, review of *Sami and the Time of the Troubles,* p. 112; December, 1993, Ruth S. Vose, review of *River,* p. 104; January, 1996, review of *Not in the House, Newton!,* p. 83;

January, 2000, Miriam Lang Budin, review of *The House of Wisdom,* p. 132; March, 2000, Susan Hepler, review of *Steamboat!,* p. 224; January, 2003, Alicia Eames, review of *The House of Wisdom,* p. 83; May, 2006, Carol Schene, review of *Strange Birds,* p. 124.

ONLINE

Al Jadid Online, http://leb.net/~aljadid/ (April 28, 2007), "Judith Heide Gilliland."

*   *   *

GOLDSHER, Alan 1966-

PERSONAL: Born 1966.

ADDRESSES: Home—Chicago, IL. *E-mail*—alanwrites@cs.com.

CAREER: Freelance writer and musician. Served as bass guitarist on recordings by Janet Jackson, Cypress Hill, and Naughty by Nature; toured with Digable Planets; performed at the Grammy Awards, 1994.

WRITINGS:

Hard Bop Academy: The Sidemen of Art Blakey and the Jazz Messengers, Hal Leonard (Milwaukee, WI), 2002.
Jam (novel), Permanent Press (Sag Harbor, NY), 2002.
Modest Mouse: A Pretty Good Read, Thomas Dunne Books (New York, NY), 2006.

Contributor of articles on music to periodicals, including *Bass Player* and *Drum!,* and articles on sports to the Web sites *ESPN.com* and *NBA.com.* Also author of the blog, *Alan Goldsher News/Blog.*

SIDELIGHTS: Musician and journalist Alan Goldsher writes about music and the music scene. *Hard Bop Academy: The Sidemen of Art Blakey and the Jazz Messengers,* Goldsher's first book, is a history of Blakey's jazz group. Goldsher compiled the book from more than thirty interviews with jazz musicians and aficionados, providing the fan's point of view of the music legend. Ronald S. Rush, in a review for the *Library Journal,* remarked on the book's insights, but noted that "though the writing is fairly lucid and engaging, ultimately, more could have been said." In *Modest Mouse: A Pretty Good Read,* Goldsher turns to a more modern-day musical group, providing an unauthorized biography of the titular rock band. The honest account includes details of lead singer Isaac Brock's less-than-pleasant reputation and personality. A *Kirkus Reviews* critic opined that the book was "well-written and researched."

Goldsher's book *Jam* is a novel with a musical theme. The book tells the story of two young jazz fans who would do anything to grow up to be cool jazz musicians, and how success eventually ruins their friendship. A critic for *Kirkus Reviews* noted that Goldsher's strength lies in his musical knowledge and description, rather than characterizations, stating: "With a sharp feel for the music and the sharks that feed on it, all this first novel lacks are characters that transcend caricature." In a review for *Publishers Weekly,* one writer called Goldsher an "engaging if somewhat mawkish storyteller who knows the music business and the details of life as a jazz musician, and he creates a lively and interesting band of characters."

BIOGRAPHICAL AND CRITICAL SOURCES:

PERIODICALS

Kirkus Reviews, November 1, 2001, review of *Jam,* p. 1504; October 1, 2006, review of *Modest Mouse: A Pretty Good Read,* p. 999.
Library Journal, December 1, 2002, Ronald S. Russ, review of *Hard Bop Academy: The Sidemen of Art Blakey and the Jazz Messengers,* p. 130.
Publishers Weekly, November 5, 2001, review of *Jam,* p. 39; October 23, 2006, review of *Modest Mouse,* p. 46.

ONLINE

Alan Goldsher Home Page, http://www.alangoldsher. com (April 22, 2007).

Modest Mouse: A Pretty Good Read Web site, http:// www.myspace.com/aprettygoodread (April 22, 2007).
Paste Magazine Online, http://www.pastemagazine. com/ (April 22, 2007), review of *Modest Mouse.**

*   *   *

**GOSS, Sandra Schweighart
See GOSS LUCAS, Sandra**

*   *   *

**GOSS LUCAS, Sandra 1949-
(Sandra Schweighart Goss)**

PERSONAL: Born May 18, 1949, in Urbana, IL; daughter of Donald Michael (a plumber) and Lois (a homemaker) Schweighart; married Steven A. Goss, August 10, 1974 (died January 19, 1998); married David J. Lucas (a flight instructor), July 16, 2000; children: (first marriage) Stephanie Renee Goss Pittman, Matthew Michael; (second marriage; stepchildren) Kathryn Beth, Daniel James. *Ethnicity:* "Caucasian." *Education:* University of Illinois at Urbana-Champaign, B.A. (with high honors), 1971, M.A., 1972; Indiana University—Bloomington, Ph.D., 1984.

ADDRESSES: Home—Champaign, IL. *Office*—633 Psychology Bldg., University of Illinois at Urbana-Champaign, 603 E. Daniel, Champaign, IL 61820. *E-mail*—gossluca@uiuc.edu.

CAREER: Danville Area Community College, Danville, IL, instructor in social sciences, 1972-74; Parkland Community College, Champaign, IL, instructor in social sciences, 1974-78; Indiana University-Purdue University at Indianapolis, instructor, 1981-1983; University of Illinois at Urbana-Champaign, Champaign, visiting assistant professor, 1984-86, associate course director, 1986-98, adjunct associate professor and director of introductory psychology, 1998—. National Institute on Teaching of Psychology, member of steering committee, 1985—; conference presenter.

MEMBER: American Psychological Association, American Psychological Society.

WRITINGS:

(With Douglas Bernstein) *Teaching Psychology: A Step by Step Guide,* Lawrence Erlbaum Associates (Mahwah, NJ), 2005.

Author of instructor's manuals and other curriculum materials. Contributor to books, including *The Teaching Assistant Handbook: How to Prepare TAs for Their Responsibilities,* edited by L. Prieto and S. Meyers, New Forum Press (Stillwater, OK), 2001; *The Compleat Academic: A Career Guide,* 2nd edition, edited by J. Darley, M. Zanna, and P. Roediger, American Psychological Association (Washington, DC), 2004; and *The Handbook of the Teaching of Psychology,* edited by W. Buskist and S.F. Davis, Blackwell (Malden, MA), 2006. Contributor to periodicals, including *APS Observer.* Writings prior to 2000 appeared under name Sandra Schweighart Goss.

*   *   *

GREEVES, Lucy

PERSONAL: Education: Graduated from Cambridge University.

ADDRESSES: Agent—Simon Trewin, PFD, Drury House, 34-43 Russell St., London WC2B 5HA, England.

CAREER: Comedy venue manager and copywriter.

WRITINGS:

(With Jimmy Carr) *Only Joking: What's So Funny about Making People Laugh?,* Gotham Books (New York, NY), 2006.

SIDELIGHTS: Lucy Greeves has worked as an advertising copywriter and a comedy venue manager, two jobs not commonly paired together. While studying at Cambridge University, Greeves met her best friend and fellow comic, Jimmy Carr, host of Comedy Central's *Distraction* game show. The pair collaborated to create *Only Joking: What's So Funny*

about Making People Laugh? in 2006. The book analyzes the concept of joking and covers a number of related topics punctuated with jokes and dry humor along the way. The opening discusses the importance of laughter, and the development of a sense of humor in children. The middle section hypothesizes on what type of people become comedians, why it is still a male-dominated field, and the use of language to convey your joke. The last section of the book covers the use of potentially problematic topics, such as race and politics. Jack Helbig, writing in *Booklist,* called the book "lively, intelligent, highly readable, often hilarious." In the London *Times,* a reviewer admitted that the book "makes you laugh." A critic in *Publishers Weekly* stated that Greeves and Carr "deserve a round of applause for this entertaining and educational book."

BIOGRAPHICAL AND CRITICAL SOURCES:

PERIODICALS

Booklist, September 1, 2006, Jack Helbig, review of *Only Joking: What's So Funny about Making People Laugh?,* p. 36.
Psychology Today, September-October, 2006, Jessica Heasley, review of *Only Joking,* p. 36.
Publishers Weekly, July 24, 2006, review of *Only Joking,* p. 51.
Times (London, England), November 26, 2006, Roland White, review of *Only Joking.*

ONLINE

Chortle.co.uk Web site, http://www.chortle.co.uk/ (January 24, 2007), Steve Bennett, review of *Only Joking.**

*   *   *

GREY, Stephen 1968-

PERSONAL: Born 1968, in Rotterdam, Netherlands. *Education:* Attended Oxford University.

ADDRESSES: Home—London, England. *Agent*—Robert Kirby, PFD, Drury House, 34-43 Russell St., London WC2B 5HA, England. *E-mail*—stephen@ stephengrey.com.

CAREER: Freelance journalist. *Sunday Times,* London, England, former editor of the investigations unit.

AWARDS, HONORS: Member of British Press Awards' "Team of the Year," for the *Sunday Times'* coverage of the war in Kosovo; Story of the Year runner-up, Foreign Press Association, 2004, for article "American Gulag"; Amnesty International Media Award, for best periodical article, for "America's Gulag," 2005.

WRITINGS:

Ghost Plane: The True Story of the CIA Torture Program, St. Martin's Press (New York, NY), 2006.

Contributor to publications, including the *New York Times, Guardian, Independent, Newsweek,* and the *Atlantic Monthly,* as well as to news programs, including *BBC Newsnight, BBC Radio 4,* and *World Service.*

SIDELIGHTS: Stephen Grey is a London-based journalist who has spent a number of years covering the conflicts in the Middle East. Grey's 2004 article "American Gulag" exposed a secret network of American prisons, and in 2005 the article was awarded the Amnesty International Media Award for best article in a periodical. Grey is also known for breaking the story of the secret CIA planes exporting prisoners to Middle Eastern countries where it would be possible to torture them as part of the interrogation process. This story served as the foundation for his book, *Ghost Plane: The True Story of the CIA Torture Program,* in which Grey takes an in-depth look at CIA practices. He includes detailed accountings of seventy-five individual flights, and the types of torture performed in the destination countries, including Syria, Egypt, and Afghanistan. A contributor to *Kirkus Reviews* called Grey's effort "disturbing in the depth and detail of its evidence that outsourcing interrogation evaded legal issues and led to systematic brutality." Samir el-Youssef, writing for the *New Statesman,* remarked that Grey's book "is not only a brilliant piece of journalistic investigation into the shocking facts of the rendition program, it's also a history of the practice and an argument against it."

BIOGRAPHICAL AND CRITICAL SOURCES:

PERIODICALS

Kirkus Reviews, October 1, 2006, review of *Ghost Plane: The True Story of the CIA Torture Program,* p. 999.
Library Journal, December 1, 2006, Daniel K. Blewett, "The Central Intelligence Agency: Security under Scrutiny," p. 141.
Mother Jones, November 1, 2006, Michael Scherer, review of *Ghost Plane,* p. 95.
New Statesman, December 4, 2006, Samir el-Youssef, "Beyond the Rule of Law," review of *Ghost Plane,* p. 57.
News & Observer (Raleigh, NC), October 24, 2006, "Book Ties Johnston Firm to CIA Activity," review of *Ghost Plane.*
UPI NewsTrack, October 26, 2006, "Book Details Alleged Torture Flights," review of *Ghost Plane.*

ONLINE

Centre for Investigative Journalism Web site, http://www.investigativereporting.org.uk/ (April 23, 2007), author biography.
Ghost Plane Web site, http://www.ghostplane.net (April 23, 2007).
PFD Web site, http://www.pfd.co.uk/ (April 23, 2007), author biography.
Stephen Grey Home Page, http://www.stephengrey.com (April 23, 2007).

*   *   *

GRIFFITHS, Jay

PERSONAL: Education: Graduate of Oxford University.

ADDRESSES: Home—Wales.

CAREER: Writer, journalist.

AWARDS, HONORS: Discover Award for Nonfiction, Barnes & Noble, 2003, for *A Sideways Look at Time.*

WRITINGS:

Pip Pip: A Sideways Look at Time, Flamingo (London, England), 1999, published as *A Sideways Look at Time,* Jeremy P. Tarcher/Putnam (New York, NY), 2002.

Wild: An Elemental Journey, Jeremy P. Tarcher/Penguin (New York, NY), 2006.

Contributor to periodicals, including *London Review of Books, Guardian, Observer, Ecologist, New Internationalist, Utne,* and *Artists Newsletter.*

SIDELIGHTS: British journalist and author Jay Griffiths is the author of works which explore a variety of topics. In *Pip Pip: A Sideways Look at Time* (published in the United States as *A Sideways Look at Time*), she presents a philosophical discussion on how different cultures and different eras dealt with the concept of time. She questions the modern concept of a clock-driven society, and explores more natural forms of time's measurement, as in seasonal time, solar, lunar, and even time as measured by a female's menstrual cycle. Peter Forbes, writing in the *Guardian Online,* was not impressed with Griffiths's debut effort as a book author, complaining that her "one-track attitude and prose blindness lead to . . . unintentionally Bonzo Dog Dooda-ish phrases." However, *Ecologist* contributor Hugh Warwick was more positive in his assessment, commenting that *Pip Pip* "manages to be both revolutionary and readable." Similarly, a critic for the *New Internationalist* called the same work a "splendidly quirky book," as well as "provocative, impassioned, often outrageously witty."

Griffiths continued to question assumptions of Western society in her 2006 work, *Wild: An Elemental Journey,* "an exhaustive and at times exhausting book on all things wild," according to *Library Journal* contributor Lee Arnold. Dividing the concept of wild into six categories—earth, ice, water, air, fire, mind—Griffiths explores regions from the rain forests of the Amazon to Mongolia, looking at the role of the wild in history and in society in general, and concluding that the modern world has marginalized the wild both in nature and in the interior lives of modern humans. Thus, even as we destroy the last pieces of the wild in the world, we are also destroying the sense of the wild in ourselves. Seven years in the writing, *Wild* took Grif-

fiths not just on an international journey to the remaining wild areas of the world, but also on a journey of discovery with some of the remaining indigenous people that inhabit such locales as the Canadian Arctic or the outback of Indonesia. Her experiences ranged from ingesting a hallucinogenic drink administered by a shaman to learning an appreciation for the Dreamtime of Australian Aboriginal people. While Arnold felt that the work was "preachy" in tone, and that its author seemed "pompous, self-absorbed, and pretentious," other reviewers had a much higher opinion of the work. A *Kirkus Reviews* critic thought *Wild* was "an exuberant and erudite exploration of the meaning of wilderness and its place in our lives." The same reviewer further termed the book a "fascinating journey." A *Publishers Weekly* contributor, though, feeling the book lacked "nuance," still praised Griffiths for bringing "fierce conviction and impressive scholarship to her work." Similarly, *New York Times Book Review* critic Elizabeth Royte praised Griffiths's "dexterous and lush" writing, yet complained of a lack of cohesion and overview to the assorted essays. A reviewer for *Internet Bookwatch* concluded that *Wild* was "fascinating, dramatic, [and] moving."

BIOGRAPHICAL AND CRITICAL SOURCES:

PERIODICALS

Ecologist, April 1, 2000, Hugh Warwick, review of *Pip Pip: A Sideways Look at Time,* p. 55.

Internet Bookwatch, March 1, 2007, review of *Wild: An Elemental Journey.*

Kirkus Reviews, October 15, 2006, review of *Wild,* p. 1055.

Library Journal, November 15, 2006, Lee Arnold, review of *Wild,* p. 86.

New Internationalist, December 1, 2000, review of *Pip Pip,* p. 32.

New York Times Book Review, February 11, 2007, Elizabeth Royte, review of *Wild,* p. 13.

Publishers Weekly, October 30, 2006, review of *Wild,* p. 49.

ONLINE

Adelaide Festival of Ideas Web site, http://www.adelaidefestivalofideas.com.au/ (April 15, 2007), "Jay Griffiths."

Barnes & Noble.com, http://www.barnesandnoble. com/ (April 15, 2007), "Interview: Jay Griffiths."

Guardian Online, http://books.guardian.co.uk/ (December 11, 1999), Peter Forbes, review of *Pip Pip.*

London Independent Online, http://enjoyment. independent.co.uk/ (March 9, 2004), "Griffiths' Time Arrives as Lit Brits Storm US Awards."*

*   *   *

GROSSMAN, Elizabeth 1957-

PERSONAL: Born 1957.

ADDRESSES: Home—Portland, OR.

CAREER: Author.

WRITINGS:

(Editor, with Susan Ewing) *Shadow Cat: Encountering the American Mountain Lion,* Sasquatch Books (Seattle, WA), 1999.

Watershed: The Undamming of America, Counterpoint (Washington, DC), 2002.

Adventuring along the Lewis and Clark Trail: Missouri, Illinois, Iowa, Nebraska, South Dakota, North Dakota, Montana, Idaho, Oregon, Washington, Sierra Club Books (San Francisco, CA), 2003.

High Tech Trash: Digital Devices, Hidden Toxics, and Human Health, Island Press (Washington, DC), 2006.

Contributor to periodicals, including *Nation, New York Times Book Review, Chicago Tribune, Newsday, California Wild, Audubon, Oregonian, Orion, Newsday, Washington Post, Yes!, Amicus Journal, Cascadia Times,* and the Web sites *Grist* and the *Environmental News Network.*

SIDELIGHTS: Elizabeth Grossman is the author of books about nature and environmental conservation. Her first book, *Shadow Cat: Encountering the American Mountain Lion,* was edited with Susan Ewing and is a collection of twenty essays by various notable wildlife writers. The work concerns such issues as the growth of the mountain lion population in America, which, along with encroaching human populations, has resulted in increasing attacks on people by these predatory felines. In the *Library Journal,* Nancy J. Moeckel called the book a "nicely balanced collection," while a *Publishers Weekly* critic complimented Grossman and Ewing for bringing "fresh material to what the editors call the 'debate over wildness and wilderness.'"

Grossman drew more critical attention for her first solo work, *Watershed: The Undamming of America,* which addresses in detail the environmental issues involving river dams. During the first two centuries of American history, dams were major components of development projects across the country that were used for creating water reservoirs, and later for generating hydroelectric power. The downside is that dams have a big impact on the environment, interrupting fish migration patterns, disrupting natural water flow, eroding soils, and causing water pollution. Today, however, fewer dams are used for electric power and there have been more dams torn down to allow rivers to return to their natural courses. There is still, however, considerable resistance to removing dams in the dry American West, where dams are important for creating reservoirs of drinking water. Grossman takes specific cases of rivers and dams in several U.S. states to detail the important task of restoring the environment by tearing down dams in what *Oregon Historical Quarterly* writer Jeff Crane called "a useful guide to one of the most important developments in contemporary American environmentalism." A *Publishers Weekly* contributor similarly concluded that "Grossman offers a compelling update on a movement that could reshape the face of America."

While *Adventuring along the Lewis and Clark Trail: Missouri, Illinois, Iowa, Nebraska, South Dakota, North Dakota, Montana, Idaho, Oregon, Washington* is essentially a travel guide for those who wish to retrace the route of that famous expedition, Grossman also adds some undertones of environmentalism. The book offers historical background about Lewis and Clark, then informs readers of highlights to see along the way and includes helpful resources for travelers. The author comments, too, on how the landscape has been degraded over the centuries, but she also "reminds us . . . that many areas along the trail are scenic and open to anyone inclined to enjoy a moderate hike, walk, or paddle," related Ken DuBois in another *Oregon Historical Quarterly* article. DuBois concluded that this is a "useful and engaging guide-book."

A fairly new and potentially devastating threat to the environment is the subject of Grossman's *High Tech Trash: Digital Devices, Hidden Toxics, and Human Health.* While researching pollution in the Willamette River near her home in Oregon, she discovered that much of the toxic waste was the result of the high tech industry. Researching the subject, the author found that heavy metals and other toxic materials used in televi-sions, cell phones, computers, and other electronic devices leak into the environment whenever they are improperly disposed. Cadmium, phosphorous, lead, mercury, chlorine, and other chemicals and metals are lethal not only to wildlife but also to people, and there is a very real possibility that they are a cause of increasing cancer rates. Not only this, but tons of valu-able materials, such as gold, copper, platinum, and silver, are being discarded when they could be recycled instead. Grossman points out her concern that the United States, unlike Europe and Japan, does not enforce standards for recycling high tech components; thus, only about ten percent of all computers, televi-sions, and phones are recycled in America. *Booklist* reviewer Donna Seaman declared *High Tech Trash* an "informative, harrowing, and invaluable report." "Her language is quiet, clear, and compelling," wrote Michael D. Cramer in the *Library Journal.* A *Publish-ers Weekly* reviewer observed that Grossman's "call for action is commendable and critical."

BIOGRAPHICAL AND CRITICAL SOURCES:

PERIODICALS

Booklist, July 1, 2002, Donna Seaman, review of *Watershed: The Undamming of America,* p. 1803; May 1, 2003, Brad Hooper, review of *Adventuring along the Lewis and Clark Trail: Missouri, Il-linois, Iowa, Nebraska, South Dakota, North Dakota, Montana, Idaho, Oregon, Washington,* p. 1575; April 15, 2006, Donna Seaman, review of *High Tech Trash: Digital Devices, Hidden Toxins, and Human Health,* p. 9.

Discover, September 1, 2006, Joseph D'Agnese, "Where Technology Goes to Die," review of *High Tech Trash,* p. 69.

E, January 1, 2007, Jim Motavalli, "Talking Computer Trash," review of *High Tech Trash,* p. 59.

Ecos, June 1, 2006, "A Shame about Your Old TV," review of *High Tech Trash,* p. 32.

Library Journal, April 15, 1999, Nancy J. Moeckel, review of *Shadow Cat: Encountering the American Mountain Lion,* p. 141; July 1, 2002, Nancy Moeckel, review of *Watershed,* p. 113; April 15, 2006, Michael D. Cramer, review of *High Tech Trash,* p. 106.

Oregon Historical Quarterly, spring, 2003, Jeff Crane, review of *Watershed.*

Publishers Weekly, February 8, 1999, review of *Shadow Cat,* p. 201; June 10, 2002, review of *Watershed,* p. 54; March 20, 2006, review of *High Tech Trash,* p. 52.

ONLINE

High Tech Trash Web site, http://www.hightechtrash. com (May 18, 2007).

SearchDataCenter.com, http://searchdatacenter.blog spot.com/ (July 20, 2006), "Q&A with Elizabeth Grossman on E-Waste."*

*   *   *

GUNN, Harry E.
    See GUNN, Harry E. "Bud"

*   *   *

GUNN, Harry E. "Bud" 1930-
    (Harry E. Gunn)

PERSONAL: Born January 3, 1930, in Harvey, IL; son of Harry E. (a metal manufacturing manager) and Irma (a homemaker) Gunn; married February 29, 1966; wife's name Violet C. (an advertising agency employee); children: Buddy S., William L. *Ethnicity:* "Caucasian." *Education:* Beloit College, B.A., 1952; Purdue University, M.S., 1955; Loyola University Chicago, Ph.D., 1961. *Politics:* Independent. *Religion:* Unitarian-Universalist. *Hobbies and other interests:* Golf, children's books.

ADDRESSES: Home—Dyer, IN. *Office*—Mid-America, 8300 S. Broadway, Merrillville, IN 46411. *Agent*—Betram Linder, P.O. Box 352, Wantaugh, NY 11793. *E-mail*—gun139@aol.com.

CAREER: Clinical psychologist and forensic psychologist, 1961—. Member of local village appeals board, 1971-79.

MEMBER: Olympia Fields Country Club.

WRITINGS:

How to Play Golf with Your Wife—and Survive, Greatlakes Living Press (Matteson, IL), 1976.

(With Earl Stewart, Jr.) *Left Hander's Golf Book,* Greatlakes Living Press (Matteson, IL), 1976.

(With Earl Stewart, Jr.) *Golf Begins at Forty,* photographs by Patrick K. Snook, Greatlakes Living Press (Matteson, IL), 1977.

Manipulation by Guilt: How to Avoid It, Greatlakes Living Press (Waukegan, IL), 1978.

(Under name Harry E. Gunn; with wife, Violet C. Gunn) *The Test Yourself Book,* Chicago Review Press (Chicago, IL), 1980.

(Under name Harry E. Gunn; Violet C. Gunn) *The Test for Success Book,* Chicago Review Press (Chicago, IL), 1982.

Investment Euphoria and Money Madness: The Inner Workings of the Psychology of Investing—for Financial Advisors and Their Clients, AMACOM (New York, NY), 2000.

(With Jaswinder Singh) *Minority Report: How African Americans and Hispanics Can Increase Their Test Scores,* Scarecrow Press (Lanham, MD), 2004.

Also author of journal articles.

SIDELIGHTS: Harry E. "Bud"Gunn told *CA:* "My writing process occurs in a passive, receptive state as ideas come to me automatically. I try not to search, and I allow my thoughts to come to me and direct me. Ideas influence my work and the pursuit of new experiences. My hobbies and fun activities have helped direct me, as did my work as a clinical psychologist. One can learn a great deal from listening to others.

"Writing facilitates a free exchange of ideas. It provides an opportunity for people to learn from one another and use our imagination. Writing also helps us critique our own ideas, as we see them presented right in front of us."

H

HALL, Albyn Leah 1965-

PERSONAL: Born 1965. *Hobbies and other interests:* Movies, theater, art, smart restaurants, playing the Irish fiddle, London, soccer, train travel.

ADDRESSES: Home—London, England. *Agent*—Mary Ann Naples, The Creative Culture Inc., 72 Spring St., Ste. 304, New York, NY 10012. *E-mail*—albynsroad@ blueyonder.co.uk.

CAREER: Psychotherapist, writer.

WRITINGS:

Deliria, Serpent's Tail (New York, NY), 1993.
The Rhythm of the Road, Thomas Dunne Books (New York, NY), 2007.

SIDELIGHTS: Albyn Leah Hall was raised in New York, Los Angeles, and eventually London, with side trips to Ireland. She credits this eclectic background with providing her work with a wealth of different cultural influences. Despite being the child of Hollywood parents—her father created the nighttime soap opera *Dallas*—Hall feels equally affected by film, music, and literature, all of which have an emotional impact on her that carries over into her writing. In addition, she works as a psychotherapist, a career that makes her highly sensitive to and aware of human behavior, and that provides excellent inspiration for her stories. Her first novel, *Deliria,* tells the dark story of a young American, Claudia, who escapes life in Los Angeles to attend art school in London, where she falls into a relationship with a drug-dealing Irishman. Lisa Orzepowski, in a review for *Booklist,* called Hall's effort an "excellent dark, and ironically addicting first novel." *Review of Contemporary Fiction* contributor Michelle Latiolais praised Hall's work, writing: "Here is a first novel that is beautifully mature, crafted with tremendous skill, and enlivened almost sentence for sentence with perception so finely honed it startles us back into a world we thought we already knew."

In *The Rhythm of the Road,* Hall writes about Jo, a half-American, half-Irish girl riding with her father Bobby in his truck when he picks up a female hitchhiker from Texas. The girl, a budding country singer, rouses memories of Bobby's one-time musical aspirations, and interrupts the father-daughter bonding time. June Sawyers, writing in *Booklist,* found the book to be "full of flesh-and-blood characters and genuine surprises." A reviewer for *Publishers Weekly* called it "both poignant and unsettling."

BIOGRAPHICAL AND CRITICAL SOURCES:

PERIODICALS

Booklist, October 15, 1994, Lisa Orzepowski, review of *Deliria,* p. 400; December 15, 2006, June Sawyers, review of *The Rhythm of the Road,* p. 21.
Kirkus Reviews, October 15, 2006, review of *The Rhythm of the Road,* p. 1034.

Library Journal, November 15, 2006, Faye A. Chadwell, review of *The Rhythm of the Road,* p. 56.

Publishers Weekly, October 30, 2006, review of *The Rhythm of the Road,* p. 38.

Review of Contemporary Fiction, March 22, 1995, Michelle Latiolais, review of *Deliria,* p. 163.

ONLINE

Albyn Leah Hall Home Page, http://www.albynleahhall.co.uk (April 23, 2007).

Bella Online, http://www.bellaonline.com/ (April 23, 2007), M.E. Wood, "Author Q & A with Albyn Leah Hall."

Best Reviews, http://thebestreviews.com/ (January 23, 2007), Viviane Crystal, review of *The Rhythm of the Road.*

BookLoons, http://www.bookloons.com/ (April 23, 2007), Mary Ann Smyth, review of *The Rhythm of the Road.*

Curled Up with a Good Book, http://www.curledup.com/ (April 23, 2007), Michael Leonard, review of *The Rhythm of the Road.*

Pop Matters, http://www.popmatters.com/ (February 19, 2007), Jason B. Jones, review of *The Rhythm of the Road.**

*   *   *

HART, Darryl Glenn
See HART, D.G.

*   *   *

HART, D.G.
(Darryl Glenn Hart)

PERSONAL: Education: Temple University, B.A., 1979; Westminster Theological Seminar, M.A.R., 1981; Harvard University, M.T.S., 1983; Johns Hopkins University, M.A., 1985, Ph.D., 1988.

ADDRESSES: Office—Intercollegiate Studies Institute, 3901 Centerville Rd., P.O. Box 4431, Wilmington, DE 19807-0431. *E-mail*—dhart@isi.org.

CAREER: Johns Hopkins University, Baltimore, MD, teaching assistant, 1985-88; Duke University, Durham, NC, postdoctoral fellow and lecturer in the divinity

school, 1988-89; Wheaton College, Institute for the Study of American Evangelicals, Wheaton, IL, director, 1989-93; Westminster Seminary California, Escondido, CA, from associate professor to professor and dean of academic affairs, 1993-2000, adjunct professor, 2000—; Intercollegiate Studies Institute, Wilmington, DE, director of academic projects and faculty development, 2003—. Has been an elder in the Christian Reformed Church and the Orthodox Presbyterian Church; member of the Orthodox Presbyterian Church's Committee on Christian Education.

MEMBER: Historical Society, American Historical Association, Organization of American Historians, American Society of Church History.

WRITINGS:

Defending the Faith: J. Gresham Machen and the Crisis of Conservative Protestantism in Modern America, Johns Hopkins University Press (Baltimore, MD), 1994.

The University Gets Religion: Religious Studies in American Higher Education, Johns Hopkins University Press (Baltimore, MD), 1999.

The Lost Soul of American Protestantism, Rowman & Littlefield Publishers (Lanham, MD), 2002.

That Old-Time Religion in Modern America: Evangelical Protestantism in the Twentieth Century, Ivan R. Dee (Chicago, IL), 2002.

(With John R. Muether) *With Reverence and Awe: Returning to the Basics of Reformed Worship,* P&R (Phillipsburg, NJ), 2002.

Recovering Mother Kirk: The Case for Liturgy in the Reformed Tradition, Baker Academic (Grand Rapids, MI), 2003.

Deconstructing Evangelicalism: Conservative Protestantism in the Age of Billy Graham, Baker Academic (Grand Rapids, MI), 2004.

John Williamson Nevin: High Church Calvinist, P&R (Phillipsburg, NJ), 2005.

(As Darryl Hart) *A Secular Faith: Why Christianity Favors the Separation of Church and State,* I.R. Dee (Chicago, IL), 2006.

EDITOR

Reckoning with the Past: Historical Essays on American Evangelicalism from the Institute for the Study of American Evangelicals, Baker Books (Grand Rapids, MI), 1995.

(With R. Albert Mohler, Jr.) *Theological Education in the Evangelical Tradition,* Baker Books (Grand Rapids, MI), 1996.

(With Harry S. Stout) *New Directions in American Religious History,* Oxford University Press (New York, NY), 1997.

(With Bruce Kuklick) *Religious Advocacy and American History,* W.B. Eerdmans (Grand Rapids, MI), 1997.

(With David N. Livingstone and Mark A. Noll) *Evangelicals and Science in Historical Perspective,* Oxford University Press (New York, NY), 1999.

(With Sean Michael Lucas and Stephen J. Nichols) *The Legacy of Jonathan Edwards: American Religion and the Evangelical Tradition,* Baker Academic (Grand Rapids, MI), 2003.

J. Gresham Machen, *Selected Shorter Writings,* P&R (Phillipsburg, NJ), 2004.

A Student's Guide to Religious Studies, Intercollegiate Studies Institute (Wilmington, DE), 2005.

Also editor of the revised edition of *Fides et Historia,* 1992-96, and the *Westminster Theological Journal,* 1996—. General editor, with consulting editor Mark A. Noll, of *Dictionary of the Presbyterian and Reformed Tradition in America,* Intervarsity Press (Downers Grove, IL), 1999.

SIDELIGHTS: Theologian D.G. Hart has written extensively about various aspects of the Christian faith, including evangelicalism and the separation of church and state. In *Defending the Faith: J. Gresham Machen and the Crisis of Conservative Protestantism in Modern America,* the author presents a biography of the early twentieth-century conservative Christian theologian. Writing in *Christianity Today,* Allen C. Guelzo commented that the author "sketches a Machen who was a bundle of 'anomalies': a conservative intellectual who opposed modernism for social reasons as much as religious ones; an old-school Presbyterian who treated liberals and fundamentalists alike as innovators; and an unlikely ally of secular modernists such as Walter Lippmann and H.L. Mencken." Guelzo also wrote: "What makes Hart's achievement remarkable is the skill with which he has synthesized . . . interpretive pieces into a readable and compelling narrative."

The University Gets Religion: Religious Studies in American Higher Education is an examination of the study of religion in academia. The author offers his opinion that, in general, academia has failed to produce first-rate scholarship concerning religion; it goes on to present a case for the removal of religion completely from the academic environment. According to Hart, this would benefit both academia, which could pursue studies on a purely secular line, and religion, which would profit from a new and more effective scholarship. "His focus is on the arguments used to justify this discipline, its scholarly methods, and its place in the modern American university," reported Douglas A. Sweeney in *Books & Culture.*

Hart provides an analysis of the modern evangelical movement in his book *Deconstructing Evangelicalism: Conservative Protestantism in the Age of Billy Graham.* Hart begins by taking a look at the scholarly analysis and construction of evangelicalism and then explores evangelicalism as a religious movement following World War II. Hart also presents his theory that evangelicalism is actually dying due to a splintering of various factions. Mark Galli stated in *Books & Culture* that "I find myself resonating with large parts of Hart's second argument." *Journal of Ecclesiastical History* contributor Steven Tuck commented: "This is an impressively thoughtful book that is generous in its treatment of evangelical leaders and scholars of evangelicalism. It is well suited for under-graduates and pastors as well as experts in the field of religious history. Much of the argument rings true, but of course a provocative book provokes questions."

In his 2006 book, *A Secular Faith: Why Christianity Favors the Separation of Church and State,* the author examines the history of the relationship between the church and state and also the question of whether or not Christianity should be used for political purposes in the form of faith-based politics. As the title suggests, Hart is in favor of a strict separation of church and state based on his belief that the basic tenets of Christianity are not suitable for solving political disputes. To support his theory, the author examines nine typical American concepts concerning the relationship between church and state that Protestant doctrine has been unable to resolve, such as the idea that the only real obligation that Christians have concerning political matters is that they do not interfere with religion and religious practices. "Although demanding to read, Hart's argument is blazingly enlightening," according to Ray Olson in *Booklist.*

BIOGRAPHICAL AND CRITICAL SOURCES:

PERIODICALS

Booklist, October 1, 2006, Ray Olson, review of *A Secular Faith: Why Christianity Favors the Separation of Church and State,* p. 28.

Books & Culture, September 1, 2003, Douglas A. Sweeney, review of *The University Gets Religion: Religious Studies in American Higher Education,* p. 34; January 1, 2004, Mark Galli, review of *Deconstructing Evangelicalism: Conservative Protestantism in the Age of Billy Graham,* p. 22.

California Bookwatch, November 1, 2006, review of *A Secular Faith.*

Christian Century, August 2, 2000, Leigh E. Schmidt, review of *The University Gets Religion,* p. 807.

Christianity Today, November 14, 1994, Allen C. Guelzo, review of *Defending the Faith: J. Gresham Machen and the Crisis of Conservative Protestantism in Modern America,* p. 98; December 6, 1999, review of *Dictionary of the Presbyterian and Reformed Tradition in America,* p. 91.

First Things: A Monthly Journal of Religion and Public Life, October 1, 2003, review of *That Old-Time Religion in Modern America: Evangelical Protestantism in the Twentieth Century,* p. 77.

Journal of Ecclesiastical History, October 1, 2004, Bryan D. Spinks, review of *Recovering Mother Kirk: The Case for Liturgy in the Reformed Tradition,* p. 805; July 1, 2005, Stephen Tuck, review of *Deconstructing Evangelicalism,* p. 633.

Journal of Religion, January 1, 2005, Timothy Larsen, review of *Deconstructing Evangelicalism,* p. 120.

Journal-World, November 16, 2006, Sophia Maines, "Historian to Discuss Developments in Evangelical Movement."

Library Journal, September 15, 2006, Carolyn M. Craft, review of *A Secular Faith,* p. 65.

Reference & Research Book News, November 1, 2006, review of *A Secular Faith.*

Weekly Standard, November 6, 2006, Terry Eastland, review of *A Secular Faith.*

ONLINE

Intercollegiate Studies Institute Web site, http://www.isi.org/ (April 17, 2007), faculty profile of D.G. Hart.

Mars Hill Audio, http://www.marshillaudio.org/ (April 17, 2007), brief profile of D.G. Hart.

Reactionary Radicals, http://www.wscal.edu/ (April 17, 2007), profile of D.G. Hart.

Weekly Standard Online, http://www.theweekly standard.com/ (November 6, 2006), Terry Eastland, review of *A Secular Faith.*

Westminster Seminary California Web site, http://www.wscal.edu/ (April 17, 2007), faculty profile of D.G. Hart.

*   *   *

HART, Philip S. 1944-

PERSONAL: Born June 12, 1944, in Denver, CO; son of Judson D. and M. Murlee (a schoolteacher) Hart; married March 22, 1969; wife's name Tanya (in business); children: Ayanna Hart-Beebe. *Ethnicity:* "African American." *Education:* University of Colorado, Boulder, B.A. (cum laude), 1966; Michigan State University, M.A., Ph.D., 1974. *Politics:* Democrat. *Religion:* Pentecostal, Church of God in Christ.

ADDRESSES: Home—Los Angeles, CA, and Edgartown, MA. *Office*—Urban Land Institute—Los Angeles, 444 S. Flower St., 34th Fl., Los Angeles, CA 90071. *E-mail*—hartpshow@aol.com; hart@uli-la.org.

CAREER: University of Massachusetts at Boston, professor of sociology and director of William Monroe Trotter Institute, 1974-2002, and senior fellow of John W. McCormack Institute of Public Affairs; Hart Realty Advisors, Los Angeles, CA, chief executive officer, 2002—. Tanya Hart Communications, vice president, 1995—; American City Coalition, chief executive officer, 1999-2002; Urban Land Institute Los Angeles, executive director of district council, 2006—; real estate developer; active in urban mass transit; construction management consultant. Producer of documentary films, including *Flyers in Search of a Dream* and *Dark Passages,* both presented by Public Broadcasting Service. University of California, Los Angeles, visiting research sociologist at Ralph Bunche Center for African American Studies. AbilityFirst, chair of housing development task force and vice chair of housing governance board; Hollywood Wilshire Young Men's Christian Association, member of board of managers; member of Hollywood Chamber of Commerce and Los Feliz Homeowners Association.

MEMBER: Urban Land Institute, Rotary Club of Los Angeles.

AWARDS, HONORS: Citation for notable children's trade book in the field of social studies, National Council for the Social Studies and Children's Book Council, 1992, for *Flying Free: America's First Black Aviators;* Distinguished Alumni Gallery, University of Colorado, 1995; Martin Luther King, Jr. Human Dignity Award, Young Men's Christian Association of Metropolitan Los Angeles, 2004.

WRITINGS:

(With James E. Blackwell) *Cities, Suburbs, and Blacks: A Study of Concerns, Distrust, and Alienation,* General Hall Books (New York, NY), 1982.
Institutional Effectiveness in the Production of Black Baccalaureates, Southern Education Foundation (Atlanta, GA), 1984.
Flying Free: America's First Black Aviators (juvenile), Lerner Publishing (Minneapolis, MN), 1992.
Up in the Air: The Story of Bessie Coleman (juvenile), Carolrhoda Books (Minneapolis, MN), 1996.
Bessie Coleman: Just the Facts (juvenile), Lerner Publishing (Minneapolis, MN), 2005.
African Americans and the Future of New Orleans: Rebirth, Renewal, and Rebuilding—An American Dilemma, Amber Books (Phoenix, AZ), 2007.

Writer (and producer) of syndicated radio programs *Hart Moments, Hollywood Live with Tanya Hart,* and *Ray Charles: The Music Lives On.* Contributor to books, including *In Pursuit of Inequality in Higher Education,* General Hall Books (New York, NY), 1987; and *In the Vineyards: Churches and Community Development,* 2007. Contributor to periodicals, including *Urban Land.*

SIDELIGHTS: Philip S. Hart told *CA:* "I have always loved writing. I began writing as a teenager. My first article was published when I was twenty-two. I continue to love writing with the new technologies. I like nonfiction writing and biographies, so those writers who do this type of work have always inspired me.

"I have always worked in the academy or in business while writing on an almost full-time basis. I write when I find a block of time that fits. I write about what I know or experience.

"My first book was published in 1982 and was for a general audience. My first book for young readers was published in 1992. Writing a book for young readers made me more aware of being clear and concise, which has helped improve my writing overall.

"I hope my books, whether for young readers or a general audience, can inform and inspire."

BIOGRAPHICAL AND CRITICAL SOURCES:

ONLINE

Hart Realty Advisors, http://www.hartrealtyadvisors. com (April 3, 2007).
Urban Land Institute-Los Angeles Web site, http:// www.uli-la.org (April 3, 2007).

*   *   *

HÄRTEL, Charmine E.J. 1959-
(Charmine E.J. Hartel)

PERSONAL: Born October 9, 1959, in Anchorage, AK; daughter of Charles (a power plant operator) and Jean (a homemaker) Crane; married Gunter Härtel (a biostatistician), June 28, 1980; children: Jameson Brice Gunter, Jasmin Catherine Rose. *Ethnicity:* "Italian-American." *Education:* University of Colorado, B.A., 1986; Colorado State University, M.A., 1988, Ph.D., 1991. *Politics:* "None." *Hobbies and other interests:* Writing poetry, art, music, fishing, nature.

ADDRESSES: Home—Sandringham, Victoria, Australia. *Office*—Department of Management, Monash University, Clayton, Victoria 3800, Australia. *E-mail*—charmine.hartel@buseco.monash.edu.au.

CAREER: University of Tulsa, Tulsa, OK, assistant professor of organizational psychology, 1991-95; University of Queensland, Brisbane, Queensland, Australia, senior lecturer in human resource management, 1995-2000; Monash University, Melbourne, Victoria, Australia, professor or organizational behavior, 2000-03; Deakin University, Melbourne, professor and research professor of strategic management, 2004-05; Monash University, professor of organizational behavior and director of research, 2006—. GE Medical Systems, affiliated with top management team development, 1997; ANZ Bank, senior consultant in employee development, 2000-02.

MEMBER: International Society for Research on Emotion, American Psychological Association, Society of Industrial and Organizational Psychologists, Academy of Management (United States).

AWARDS, HONORS: Martin E.P. Seligman Applied Research Award, 1990; Richard M. Suinn Commendation Award for Excellence in Research and the Advancement of Psychology, 1990; Distinguished Leadership Award, 1994; Jacob E. Hautaluoma Distinguished Alumni Award, Colorado State University, 2003; Vice Chancellor's Award for Postgraduate Supervision Excellence, Monash University, 2003; Janet Chusmir Service Award, Gender and Diversity Division, Academy of Management, 2005; Supervisor of the Year for the Faculty of Business and Law, Deakin University, 2005.

WRITINGS:

(Editor) *Emotions in the Workplace: Research, Theory, and Practice,* Quorum Books (Westport, CT), 2000.

(Editor, with Wilfred J. Zerbe and Neal M. Ashkanasy) *Managing Emotions in the Workplace,* M.E. Sharpe (Armonk, NY), 2002.

(Editor, with Wilfred J. Zerbe and Neal M. Ashkanasy) *Emotions in Organizational Behavior,* Lawrence Erlbaum Associates (Mahwah, NJ), 2004.

(Editor, with Wilfred J. Zerbe and Neal M. Ashkanasy) *Research on Emotion in Organizations,* Elsevier JAI (Amsterdam, Netherlands), Volume 1: *The Effect of Affect in Organizational Settings,* 2005, Volume 2: *Displaying and Managing Emotions in Organizations,* 2006.

(With Y. Fujimoto, V.E. Strybosch, and K. Fitzpatrick) *Human Resource Management: Transforming Theory into Innovative Practice,* Pearson Education Australia (Frenchs Forest, New South Wales, Australia), 2007.

Contributor to books, including *Key Issues in Organisational Communication,* edited by D. Tourish and O. Hargie, Routledge (London, England), 2003; *Strategy and Performance: Achieving Competitive Advantage in the Global Market Place,* edited by A. Ghobadian, N. O'Regan, and others, Centre for Interdisciplinary Strategic Management Research, Middlesex University (London, England), 2004; *Skill Formation and Globalization,* edited by M. Powell, Ashgate Publishing, 2005; *Dimensions of Well-Being: Research and Intervention,* edited by A. Della Fave, Franco Angeli (Milan, Italy), 2006; and *Love@Work,* edited by C. Barker and A. Payne, Wiley Australia, 2006. Contributor of more than sixty articles to professional journals, including *Journal of Applied Psychology, International Journal of Work Organisation and Emotion, Academy of Management Review, Journal of Management, Human Resource Management Review, Leadership Quarterly, Journal of Business and Psychology, Social Science Information, Industrial Marketing Management, Journal of Cross-Cultural Management, Journal of Public Affairs, Australian Journal of Management, Doing Business across Borders Journal, Career Development International, Asia Pacific Journal of Human Resources,* and *Cross-Cultural Management: An International Journal.*

SIDELIGHTS: Charmine E.J. Härtel once told *CA:* "I approach issues of concern to management, employees and other business stakeholders with the aim of identifying work design and management interventions that improve quality of work life, cross-cultural relations, organizational justice, employee and community well being, and achievement of personal and organizational work goals. Currently, I am exploring these issues in the performance of service work, in the management and processes of diverse work groups, in the social and emotional aspect of groups and organisations, and in organizational change."

*   *   *

HARTEL, Charmine E.J.
See HÄRTEL, Charmine E.J.

HASLETT, John 1964(?)-

PERSONAL: Born c. 1964; married Annie Biggs.

ADDRESSES: Home—Los Angeles, CA. *Agent*—James C. Vines, Vines Agency Inc., 648 Broadway, Ste. 901, New York, NY 10012.

CAREER: Freelance writer and explorer.

WRITINGS:

Voyage of the Manteno: The Education of a Modern-Day Expeditioner, St. Martin's Press (New York, NY), 2006.

SIDELIGHTS: John Haslett is a writer and adventurer who has spent the majority of his adult life researching and exploring the ancient cultures of pre-Columbian Ecuador. Haslett has built a number of sailing rafts made of balsa wood and based on the designs of the Mantenos, a pre-Columbian civilization that thrived in northern Ecuador in approximately 500 A.D. He has then sailed these rafts on the Pacific Ocean in an attempt to recreate long-distance voyages that were potentially made by the original designers. Haslett's book, *Voyage of the Manteno: The Education of a Modern-Day Expeditioner,* chronicles his experiences building the rafts, as well as his attempts to sail them, during two separate journeys he made during the 1990s. A *Kirkus Reviews* critic remarked: "His insights are interesting, though sometimes overly dramatic; one gets the sense he's attempting to make his already impressive journeys even more epic." A reviewer for *Publishers Weekly* found the author to be "at his best describing his struggles and the superhuman endurance necessary to mount expeditions of this type." Jesse Berrett, writing for the *San Francisco Chronicle,* commented that "Haslett never opens his tale more widely into any of the areas on which it might touch—ecology, politics, economics; he remains tightly focused on the realities of paying for, staffing and then actually undertaking expeditions."

BIOGRAPHICAL AND CRITICAL SOURCES:

BOOKS

Haslett, John, *Voyage of the Manteno: The Education of a Modern-Day Expeditioner,* St. Martin's Press (New York, NY), 2006.

PERIODICALS

Kirkus Reviews, October 1, 2006, review of *Voyage of the Manteno,* p. 1000.
Publishers Weekly, October 9, 2006, review of *Voyage of the Manteno,* p. 50.

ONLINE

Latin American Studies, http://www.latinamerican studies.org/ (January 6, 1999), "CNN: Adventurers Retrace Ancient Route in Wooden Craft."
San Francisco Chronicle Online, http://www.sfgate. com/ (December 17, 2006), Jesse Berrett, "The Journey Is the Point for Longtime Adventurer."*

*   *   *

HATFIELD, Sharon 1956-

PERSONAL: Born 1956, in VA. *Education:* Graduated from Lincoln Memorial University.

ADDRESSES: Home—OH. *Office*—Department of Arts and Sciences, Hocking College, 3301 Hocking Pkwy., Nelsonville, OH 45764. *E-mail*—hatfield_s@ hocking.edu.

CAREER: Coalfield Progress, Norton, VA, former reporter; Hocking College, Nelsonville, OH, professor of writing; Lincoln Memorial University, Harrogate, TN, teacher with Mountain Heritage Literary Festival, 2007.

AWARDS, HONORS: Weatherford Prize, and the Chaffin Award for Appalachian Literature, both for *Never Seen the Moon: The Trials of Edith Maxwell.*

WRITINGS:

(Editor, with Gurney Norman and Danny Miller) *An American Vein: Critical Readings in Appalachian Literature,* Ohio University Press (Athens, OH), 2005.

Never Seen the Moon: The Trials of Edith Maxwell, University of Illinois Press (Urbana, IL), 2005.

SIDELIGHTS: Sharon Hatfield is a journalist and an educator. She has worked as a reporter for the *Coalfield Progress,* a semiweekly publication in Norton, Virginia. While covering the justice system in Wise County, Virginia, Hatfield spent time in the courtroom where Edith Maxwell was tried for murder. The experience inspired Hatfield to write *Never Seen the Moon: The Trials of Edith Maxwell,* which has garnered a number of awards, including the Chaffin Award for Appalachian Literature and the Weatherford Prize. The Maxwell trial was a major media event in Appalachia, as Edith Maxwell was tried twice for the murder of her father and convicted both times. Maxwell was considered a sensation because she was a young woman, and also because the case became an example of old fashioned ideas clashing with progress. Hatfield uses trial transcripts and original documents to provide a detailed account of the events. Richard F. Hamm, writing for the *Journal of Southern History,* remarked that "Hatfield draws sound conclusions about every aspect of the affair."

BIOGRAPHICAL AND CRITICAL SOURCES:

PERIODICALS

Journal of Southern History, August 1, 2006, Richard F. Hamm, review of *Never Seen the Moon: The Trials of Edith Maxwell,* p. 705.

ONLINE

Bookslut, http://www.bookslut.com/ (April 23, 2007), Sarah Vance, review of *Never Seen the Moon.*
Lincoln Memorial University Web site, http://www.lmunet.edu/ (April 23, 2007), biography of Hatfield.*

*   *   *

HAWKE, Steve 1959-

PERSONAL: Born 1959, in Australia; son of Bob Hawke (a former Australian prime minister).

ADDRESSES: Home—Kimberley, Western Australia, Australia.

CAREER: Writer.

WRITINGS:

Noonkanbah: Whose Land, Whose Law, Fremantle Arts Centre Press (South Fremantle, Western Australia, Australia), 1989.
Polly Farmer: A Biography, Fremantle Arts Centre Press (South Fremantle, Western Australia, Australia), 1994.
Barefoot Kids, Fremantle Arts Centre Press (South Fremantle, Western Australia, Australia), 2007.

BIOGRAPHICAL AND CRITICAL SOURCES:

ONLINE

Notre Dame Australia Web site, http://www.nd.edu.au/ (May 18, 2007), "Former Prime Minister's Son, Steve Hawke, Launches Novel, *Barefoot Kids,* at Notre Dame in Fremantle and Sydney.*"

*   *   *

HAYCAK, Cara 1961-

PERSONAL: Born 1961; married J. Miller Tobin (a television director). *Education:* Attended Reed College, Cornell University, University of California, Los Angeles Extension, and Bennington College; Columbia University, M.F.A. *Hobbies and other interests:* Travel.

ADDRESSES: Home—Los Angeles, CA. *Agent*—Dan Mandel, Sanford J. Greenburger Associates, 55 5th Ave., New York, NY 10003. *E-mail*—redpalms@ earthlink.net.

CAREER: Writer, editor, and Web-site programmer. Formerly worked in films as set decorator, documentary film production, script reader, and story editor.

MEMBER: Society of Children's Book Writers and Illustrators.

AWARDS, HONORS: Society of Children's Book Writers and Illustrators works-in-progress grant, 2000, for *Red Palms.*

WRITINGS:

Red Palms (young-adult novel), Wendy Lamb Books (New York, NY), 2004.

Contributor to periodicals, including *Kliatt* and *First for Women.*

SIDELIGHTS: A former set designer and story editor in the motion-picture industry, Cara Haycak worked in Web and print editing before making her fiction debut with the young-adult novel *Red Palms.* The book draws readers back in time to the early 1930s and introduces fourteen-year-old Benita. Financially ruined by the worldwide economic collapse known as the Great Depression, Benita's bankrupt father is forced to give up the family's lavish city home in Guayaquil, Ecuador. Although the man is determined to do the best he can for his family, his response is to do something drastic: he moves Benita and the rest of the family to the remote tropical island where he intends to start a coconut plantation. A stubborn man, Benita's father refuses to let go of his dream despite his lack of farming knowledge; only with the help of Paita Island's kindhearted residents does the plantation have any chance of success. Unfortunately, Benita's father openly expresses contempt for the unsophisticated natives, and this grows as the situation deteriorates. When Benita falls in love with a handsome, Spanish-speaking islander named Raul, she makes the fateful choice to move from girlhood into womanhood, leaving behind all vestiges of her comfortable, civilized life in the process.

Reviewing *Red Palms* in *Booklist,* Gillian Engberg called Haycak's fiction debut "fascinating," describing the work as a "captivating, insightful" tale with well-drawn protagonists and a "vividly evoked setting." In *Kliatt,* Claire Rosser noted the novelist's "experience working with tribal people in South America," adding that "Benita is a highly intelligent and sensitive young woman, who learns to survive a bad relationship and a difficult family situation." Remarking on the "over-tones of magical realism" that characterize the second part of the novel, *School Library Journal* critic Bruce Anne Shook deemed *Red Palms* "an absorbing tale," while a *Kirkus Reviews* critic praised Haycak's story as "unique and beautiful." In *Publishers Weekly* a critic concluded that the young heroine's "unquenchable thirst for knowledge and ultimate liberation" provides Haycak's coming-of-age tale with "an uplifting" ending.

In an essay for *Kliatt,* Haycak described the genesis of her debut novel. Although *Red Palms* started out with an adult focus when Haycak began writing it as her M.F.A. thesis, she noted that "creative works always take on a life of their own, despite all your intentions and labor to shape them a particular way." "The book I found myself writing was a tale of high adventure," the author soon realized, "with perils, pitfalls and personal triumphs." As Haycak explained, she soon realized that her novel-in-progress "would more thoroughly entertain a younger reader."

Although *Red Palms* was inspired by the wealth of childhood memories Haycak's mother shared with her only daughter, its central story is grounded in a good deal of research. As the author explained in her *Kliatt* essay, "topics as wide-ranging as water systems of medieval monasteries, ancient priestesses and their rituals, the habits of jaguars in the wild, and languages of ancient South American people filled out the story in ways I could not possibly invent all on my own."

BIOGRAPHICAL AND CRITICAL SOURCES:

PERIODICALS

Booklist, November 15, 2004, Gillian Engberg, review of *Red Palms,* p. 595.

Bulletin of the Center for Children's Books, January, 2005, Timnah Card, review of *Red Palms,* p. 210.

Kirkus Reviews, November 1, 2004, review of *Red Palms,* p. 1044.

Kliatt, January, 2005, Cara Haycak, "Writing *Red Palms,*" p. 4; May, 2006, Claire Rosser, review of *Red Palms,* p. 19.

Publishers Weekly, December 6, 2004, review of *Red Palms,* p. 60.

School Library Journal, December, 2004, Bruce Anne Shook, review of *Red Palms,* p. 147.

Voice of Youth Advocates, December, 2004, review of *Red Palms,* p. 404.

ONLINE

Red Palms Web site, http://www.red-palms.com (May 10, 2007).

*   *   *

HENRY, Elyssa
    See LAVENE, Jim

*   *   *

HENRY, Elyssa
    See LAVENE, Joyce

*   *   *

HENRY THE CHEESE MAN
    See TEWKSBURY, Henry

*   *   *

HIGHLAND, Frederick 1945-

PERSONAL: Born February 13, 1945, in Audubon, NJ; son of Frederick William, Sr., and Emily Barbara Highland; children: Sophia Angela. *Education:* Suffolk University, B.A., 1967; University of Wisconsin, M.A, 1971, Ph.D, 1983.

ADDRESSES: E-mail—highland@frederickhighland. com.

CAREER: Peace Corps, volunteer in the South Pacific, 1967-69; University of Wisconsin, Milwaukee, teaching assistant, 1969-75; Upward Bound Program, Milwaukee, instructor, 1970-73; Bir Zeit University, Palestinian Authority, instructor, 1975-76; Chapman College, Orange, CA, PACE professor, 1977-79;

Department of the U.S. Navy, Cubi Point, Philippines, education specialist, 1979-85; Hawaii Pacific University, Honolulu, professor, 1984-95; City Colleges of Chicago, Pearl Harbor, HI, director of PACE Hawaii, 1985-87; Highland Wordsmith (freelance writing and speaking service), Bellingham, WA, owner, 1996—. Also has worked as a sailor in the merchant marine and as a tropical agriculturist; former editor and founder of several periodicals.

MEMBER: Mystery Writers of America, Authors Guild, Authors League of America, American Philatelic Society (Writer's Unit).

WRITINGS:

The Mystery Box (short stories), Ana-Libri Press (Bellingham, WA), 1998.

Ghost Eater, Thomas Dunne Books/St. Martin's Press (New York, NY), 2003.

Night Falls on Damascus, Thomas Dunne Books (New York, NY), 2006.

Contributor of articles and short stories to periodicals.

SIDELIGHTS: In his debut novel, *Ghost Eater,* Frederick Highland tells the story of Ulysses Vanders, a young sea captain who embarks on an adventure into remote jungle rivers in nineteenth-century Sumatra to rescue lost missionaries. Sailing on his riverboat the *Lorelei,* Ulysses is accompanied by the pirate hunter Claridge and escaped convict Rowan Fahey. When two Malayan women come aboard, Ulysses and his companions learn of some strange mystical practices and local voodoo rights. Later, after the adventurers finally arrive at the mission, they find that one of the young women missionaries has gone native and may be leading a violent cult. *Library Journal* critic Fred M. Gervat called *Ghost Eater* "a rousing adventure story." A *Publishers Weekly* contributor similarly commented that "this is a swashbuckling, seafaring novel with mystical overtones." Other critics also praised Highland for his riveting storytelling abilities. Referring to the novel as "an exciting, smoothly written naval adventure," *Booklist* reviewer Joanne Wilkinson called it "exhilarating escapist fare," and *New Mystery Reader* contributor Narayan Radhakrishnan promised that *Ghost Eater* "will enthrall and enchant the lover of mysteries."

Highland's second novel, *Night Falls on Damascus,* takes place in 1933 and features Nikolai Faroun, the chief of police in Damascus. When Vara Tamiri, a female activist in a strict patriarchal society, is murdered, the general public opinion, as well as that of Nikolai's colleagues, is that the woman got what she deserved. Nikolai, however, is determined to bring the killer to justice, making him almost as much of an outcast as the victim. As Nikolai investigates, he finds a wide range of suspects, from embarrassed family members to Vara's numerous lovers. In the end, he begins to suspect that the woman's murder may be due to political intrigue resulting from enemies first made two millennia earlier. Writing in *Booklist,* Keir Graff commented that the author "seems to have done his research," making the novel's "exotic locales and intrigue-laden power struggles" all the more real. Michael Leonard wrote on the *Curled Up with a Good Book* Web site: "Author Frederick Highland beautifully evokes an era where a thousand dark stories inhabit the furtive back streets of this city, a metropolis of memory, of ancient gates and monuments, tombs and catacombs. The novel is indeed a kaleidoscope of images of this ancient capital." Some reviewers also pointed out that the author provides insights into the political and social world of the Middle East. For example, a *Kirkus Reviews* contributor called the novel "the perfect guide to understanding just how wrong-headed the Westerners have been about Levantine politics."

BIOGRAPHICAL AND CRITICAL SOURCES:

PERIODICALS

Booklist, August 1, 2003, Joanne Wilkinson, review of *Ghost Eater,* p. 1953; October 15, 2006, Keir Graff, review of *Night Falls on Damascus,* p. 30.
Kirkus Reviews, October 1, 2006, review of *Night Falls on Damascus,* p. 990.
Library Journal, August 1, 2003, Fred M. Gervat, review of *Ghost Eater,* p. 131.
Publishers Weekly, June 30, 2003, review of *Ghost Eater,* p. 51; October 2, 2006, review of *Night Falls on Damascus,* p. 42.

ONLINE

Curled Up with a Good Book, http://www.curledup. com/ (April 17, 2007), Michael Leonard, review of *Night Falls on Damascus.*

Frederick Highland Home Page, http://www.frederick highland.com (April 17, 2007).
Ghost Eater Web site, http://www.ghosteater.com (April 17, 2007).
Mystery Box Web site, http://www.themysterybox.com (April 17, 2007), brief profile of Frederick Highland.
New Mystery Reader, http://www.newmysteryreader. com/ (April 17, 2007), Narayan Radhakrishnan, review of *Ghost Eater.*

*   *   *

HITCHCOCK, David 1963-

PERSONAL: Born September 22, 1963, in Derby, England; son of Gordon and Christine Hitchcock; married August 8, 1987; wife's name Kerry (a secretary).

ADDRESSES: Home—Derby, England. *Office*—Derby Evening Telegraph, Northcliffe House, Meadow Rd., Derby DE1 2DW, England. *E-mail*—black_boar1@ yahoo.com.

CAREER: Prontaprint, Derby, England, graphic artist, 1980-86; Citiprint, Derby, graphic artist, 1986-87; *Derby Evening Telegraph,* Derby, editorial artist, 1987—. Black Boar Press, artist and publisher

WRITINGS:

The Spirit of the Highwayman (graphic novel), Black Boar Press, 1998.
Whitechapel Freak, Black Boar Press, 2001.
Springheeled Jack, Black Boar Press, 2003.

Creator of the minicomic *The Bridge.* Contributor to the comic book *Meanwhile . . .* and the periodical *Skeleton Crew,* as well as Internet Web journals, including *Comics-International.com* and *Millidge.com.*

SIDELIGHTS: Comic book creator David Hitchcock got his start working on the *Skeleton Crew* comic in the early 1990s. That book, however, was short lived, and Hitchcock continued to work on his portfolio, sharing his efforts with industry professionals in an attempt to garner interest. Famed comic book artist Alex Ross praised Hitchcock's work, and encouraged him to continue his efforts. Hitchcock's break out came with his self-published comic *Whitechapel Freak,* which takes a twisted look at the events surrounding Jack the Ripper, elaborating on the factual account by introducing a traveling freak show. A reviewer for *Ninth Art* remarked that, although this addition makes Hitchcock's book similar to the typical story of the disenfranchised outsider, his effort "distinguishes itself . . . in the unflinching way in which it confronts its characters and their emotions. These are people pushed to the edge of their dignity and restraint." Hitchcock also enjoys experimenting with format, and with this book chose newspaper-quality paper to increase the impact of his artwork and help set the tone. Alasdair Stuart in the *Savant* wrote: "The format is a masterstroke, simultaneously mirroring the papers of the time and drawing instant attention to the comic. It's also indicative of Hitchcock's style, a relentless drive to get him noticed, to do something different from the crowd." Hitchcock has since become known for his books that combine English history and the supernatural. His follow-up effort, *The Spirit of the Highwayman,* was published by Black Boar Press, and also invokes a mysterious facet of English history as its subject matter.

Hitchcock told *CA:* "From a very early age I was entranced by the power of comic books, particularly books which sported art by the king of comics, Jack Kirby. His imagination was second to none, with artistic power to match. Since the very first issue of his "Avengers," I was hooked. From then on, I discovered many more artists working in the comics field, all with their own style. Great art motivated me to pursue a semi-career in comics, creating my own characters. I then followed that with writing my own work, too. Creating a comic book is like directing your own movie. Sadly I'm no relation to *the* great cinematic director Alfred, but I do aim to produce work which stands out from the crowd."

BIOGRAPHICAL AND CRITICAL SOURCES:

ONLINE

Black Boar Press Web site, http://www.blackboar.co. uk/ (April 25, 2007), listing of author's work.

Hold the Front Page Web site, http://www.holdthefront page.co.uk/ (April 25, 2007), "Hitchcock Horror Lives On."

Lambiek.net, http://lambiek.net/ (April 25, 2007), author biography.

Ninth Art, http://www.ninthart.com/ (August 6, 2001), Alasdair Stuart, interview with David Hitchcock; (November 23, 2001), review of *Whitechapel Freak.*

Savant, http://www.savantmag.com/ (April 25, 2007), Alasdair Stuart, review of *Whitechapel Freak.*

Sequential Tart: A Comics Industry Web Zine, http://www.sequentialtart.com/ (April 25, 2007), Marcia Allass, "Springheeled Jack Leaps Again!"

Zum Comics, http://www.zumcomics.info/ (April 25, 2007), review of *Spirit of the Highwayman.*

* * *

HODGE, Brian 1960-
(Brian Keith Hodge)

PERSONAL: Born 1960; companion of Dolly Nickel. *Hobbies and other interests:* Photography, music, and hiking.

ADDRESSES: Home—Boulder, CO. *E-mail*—brian@ brianhodge.net.

CAREER: Author. Has previously worked in the advertising department of a newspaper.

AWARDS, HONORS: Bram Stoker award nomination, 1993, for *Death Grip,* 1995, for novelette *The Alchemy of the Throat,* 1997, for *The Convulsion Factory,* and 1998, for short story "Madame Babylon"; International Horror Guild Award for outstanding short fiction, 2004, for "With Acknowledgments to Sun Tzu."

WRITINGS:

Dark Advent (novel), Pinnacle Books (New York, NY), 1988.
Oasis (novel), Tor (New York, NY), 1989.

Nightlife (horror novel), Dell Publishing (New York, NY), 1991.

Deathgrip (novel), Dell Publishing (New York, NY), 1992.

The Darker Saints (horror novel), Dell Publishing (New York, NY), 1993.

Shrines and Desecrations (stories), TAL Publications (Leesburg, VA), c. 1994.

Prototype (novel), Dell Publishing (New York, NY), 1996.

The Convulsion Factory (stories), Silver Salamander Press (Seattle, WA), 1996.

Falling Idols (stories), limited edition, Silver Salamander Press (Seattle, WA), 1998.

Wild Horses (novel), William Morrow (New York, NY), 1999.

Lies & Ugliness (novel; includes music CD *Inkarnate*), limited edition, Night Shade Books (San Francisco, CA), 2001.

On Earth as It Is in Hell ("Hellboy" series; novel), Pocket (London, England), 2005.

World of Hurt (novel), limited edition, Earthling (Northborough, MA), 2006.

Mad Dogs (novel), Cemetery Dance (Forest Hill, MD), 2006.

Contributor to "Hellboy" series of books. Work represented in anthologies.

SIDELIGHTS: Nominated for several Bram Stoker Awards, Brian Hodge is the author of horror and crime fiction. In his novel *Nightlife,* Hodge tells the story of a green powder called skullflush that can turn its users into human versions of wild beasts who go on killing rampages. When the drug is smuggled from the Venezuelan mountains to the United States, a Yanomamo warrior named Kerebawa comes to America to retrieve the drug, but not before various people find out its effects too late. *Wild Horses* features Allison Willoughby, who, after discovering that her lover has cheated on her, begins a cross-country trip. Allison does not realize, however, that she has left with some of her boyfriend's extremely valuable computer files. The files actually belong to some tough thugs, who set out after her. Noting that Hodge provides "action tough and dirty," Nancy McNicol also wrote in her *Library Journal* review that the author has "an amazingly delicate touch . . . [with] the vulnerable aspects of his characters." A *Publishers Weekly*

contributor commented that Hodge's "well-drawn criminals make a memorable batch of bottom-feeders."

In his short-story collection *Lies & Ugliness,* Hodge presents twenty-one horror stories focusing on the erotic. His tales feature a wide range of well-known horror figures, including Vlad the Impaler, Grendel, and the Green Man. In a review for *Booklist,* Ray Olson felt that since the author "writes bright, sassy prose, suspending disbelief is usually a pleasure." A *Publishers Weekly* contributor commented that "readers will have to look far to find a more thoughtful and thought-provoking collection of dark fantasies."

Hodge writes of fame gone bad in his novel *Mad Dogs.* When a cop mistakenly identifies unknown actor Jamey Sheppard as the criminal Duncan MacGregor, whom Jamey played on *America's Most Wanted,* the cop accidentally dies while trying to arrest the actor. As a result, Jamey finds himself pursued by both the law and Duncan as he tries to clear his name. A *Publishers Weekly* contributor appreciated the author's "acidic commentary on 'reality crime,'" while *Booklist* critic David Pitt called *Mad Dogs* a "big, fast-paced thriller."

In his novel *World of Hurt,* Hodge takes a closer, somewhat skewed look at heaven in a story about a Gnostic avatar who gathers the souls of people who have had near-death experiences. "Hodge manages to combine fragility and sheer terror, to erect tender emotions and then rend them from the flesh of his characters," wrote a contributor to the *Agony Column Book Reviews and Commentary* Web site.

BIOGRAPHICAL AND CRITICAL SOURCES:

PERIODICALS

Booklist, August, 2002, Ray Olson, review of *Lies & Ugliness,* p. 1938; November 15, 2006, David Pitt, review of *Mad Dog,* p. 34.

Kirkus Reviews, February 1, 1999, review of *Wild Horses,* p. 167.

Kliatt, November, 1993, Melinda D. Waugh, review of *The Darker Saints,* pp. 7-8.

Library Journal, February 15, 1999, Nancy McNicol, review of *Wild Horses,* p. 183.

Locus, February, 1991, Faren Miller, review of *Nightlife,* pp. 15, 60; September, 1993, Edward Bryant, review of *The Darker Saints,* pp. 19, 21; June, 1999, Edward Bryant, review of *Wild Horses,* pp. 27-28, 61.

Publishers Weekly, February 1, 1991, Penny Kaganoff, review of *Nightlife,* p. 78; February 8, 1999, review of *Wild Horses,* p. 196; August 5, 2002, review of *Lies & Ugliness,* p. 57; June 19, 2006, review of *World of Hurt,* p. 45; October 2, 2006, review of *Mad Dogs,* p. 41.

Science Fiction Chronicle, June, 1991, D. D'Ammassa, review of *Nightlife,* p. 34; October, 1992, D. D'Ammassa, review of *Deathgrip,* p. 33; October, 1993, D. D'Ammassa, review of *The Darker Saints,* p. 39.

ONLINE

Agony Column Book Reviews and Commentary, http://trashotron.com/agony/ (April 17, 2007), review of *World of Hurt.*

Brian Hodge Home Page, http://www.brianhodge.net (April 17, 2007).*

*   *   *

HODGE, Brian Keith
See HODGE, Brian

*   *   *

HOFFMAN, Lynn 1944-

PERSONAL: Born December 18, 1944; divorced; father. *Hobbies and other interests:* Food, wine, cooking, playing pool, kayaking, fishing, and sailing.

ADDRESSES: Home—Philadelphia, PA.

CAREER: Writer. Drexel University, Scholar in Residence in Food and Culture; Wine School of Philadelphia, teacher.

WRITINGS:

The New Short Course in Wine (nonfiction), Prentice Hall (New York, NY), 2006.
Bang-Bang (novel), Kunati (Largo, FL), 2007.

Also author of a novel, *The Bachelor's Cat,* and a blog on *Amazon.com.* Contributor to various Web sites, including *Gather.com.* Author of weekly wine column for the *Philadelphia Daily News.*

SIDELIGHTS: Lynn Hoffman has a fascination with food and drink—particularly wine—that shines through in his writing. He has written a book on wine, *The New Short Course in Wine,* and enjoys indulging in his favorite beverage in his free time. Hoffman's novel, *Bang-Bang,* includes plenty of details recounting the food and wine choices of his characters. The plot centers on Paula Sherman, a waitress and singer whose close friend is killed in a street shooting. Paula finds herself the poster child for the United Gun Association (UGA), a pro-gun lobby, when she is quoted as blaming the killer for her friend's death rather than the weapon itself. Horrified and unable to separate herself from her new gun-toting image, Paula decides to turn the tables on the UGA by shooting up the windshields of people displaying pro-UGA bumper stickers. Hoffman demonstrates his wit as well as his political leanings in this well-received novel. David Pitt, in a review for *Booklist,* remarked that "brilliant might be too big a word for this novel but not by much." Writing for *Foreword,* Joe Taylor said of Hoffman: "He brings the reader along for a through-the-lens narration, writing in immediate, sensuous, snapshot-style prose." In an article on writing that Hoffman wrote for *Gather.com,* he stated that "the important thing to bear in mind is that while anybody can write, it takes a real writer to keep on rewriting until it comes out right."

BIOGRAPHICAL AND CRITICAL SOURCES:

PERIODICALS

Booklist, January 1, 2007, David Pitt, review of *Bang-Bang,* p. 54.

Kirkus Reviews, October 1, 2006, review of *Bang-Bang,* p. 979.

ONLINE

Foreword, http://www.forewordmagazine.com/ (April 25, 2007), Joe Taylor, review of *Bang-Bang.*
Lynn Hoffman Home Page, http://lynnhoffman. squarespace.com (April 25, 2007).*

* * *

HOLABIRD, Jean 1946-

PERSONAL: Born December 3, 1946, in Boston, MA; daughter of John Augur, Jr., and Donna Katharine Holabird. *Education:* Bennington College, B.A., 1969; has also attended Columbia University and the Arts Students League. *Politics:* Democrat. *Hobbies and other interests:* Environmental issues, literature.

ADDRESSES: Home—New York, NY. *Office*—81 Warren St., New York, NY 10007. *E-mail*—jholabird@ nyc.rr.com.

CAREER: Artist. Guest lecturer at the School of Visual Arts, Parsons School, Cooper Union, and Pratt Institute, New York, NY, 1975-79; Catherine Mosley Studio, New York, NY, assistant printer, 1981-82; *St. Marks Poetry Project Newsletter,* New York, NY, art editor, 1987-90. Has exhibited at group shows in New York, NY, and in Mexico.

WRITINGS:

Out of the Ruins: A New York Record: Lower Manhattan, Autumn 2001, Gingko Press (Corte Madera, CA), 2002.
(Illustrator) Vladimir Nabokov, *Vladimir Nabokov, Alphabet in Color,* Gingko Press (Corte Madera, CA), 2005.

SIDELIGHTS: Jean Holabird is an artist and resident of lower Manhattan and, like many New Yorkers, was profoundly affected by the terrorist attacks of September 11, 2001. Living only a few blocks from the World Trade Center where thousands died, Holabird made daily pilgrimages to the site of Ground Zero following the terrorist attacks, and chronicled the clean-up process through her art. The result was a series of sketches and watercolors that reveal the trauma, pain, and devastation so prevalent in the area. The images range from cranes and other rescue equipment to American flags. Holabird told Maria Puente in an article for *USA Today.com:* "The ruins were so moving and iconic and said everything that needed to be said about the barbarity of bombing." Holabird combined the paintings with bits of poetry and prose after a publisher friend saw one of the sketches and encouraged her to publish them. *Out of the Ruins: A New York Record: Lower Manhattan, Autumn 2001* collects Holabird's visual and emotional chronicle of the recovery process as a memorial of sorts. Wendy Lukehart, in a review for the *School Library Journal,* called the work "sobering, solemn, provocative, probing, hopeful, celebratory," as well as "a quietly paced opportunity for introspection." Holabird combined her art with the writing of Vladimir Nabokov in *Vladimir Nabokov, Alphabet in Color,* consisting of selections from Nabokov's book and Holabird's own illustrations, based on Nabokov's claim that he could "hear" color. A reviewer for *Small Press Bookwatch* called the book a "unique and original study."

BIOGRAPHICAL AND CRITICAL SOURCES:

PERIODICALS

Arts, May, 1988, Robert Mahoney, "Jean Holabird," p. 102.
Publishers Weekly, July 15, 2002, review of *Out of the Ruins: A New York Record: Lower Manhattan, Autumn 2001,* p. 68.
School Library Journal, March, 2003, Wendy Lukehart, review of *Out of the Ruins,* p. 261.
Small Press Bookwatch, January, 2006, review of *Vladimir Nabokov, Alphabet in Color.*

ONLINE

ClassBrain.com, http://www.classbrain.com/ (September 19, 2002), Carolyn Weaver, "Living History."

Gingko Press, http://www.gingkopress.com/ (October 8, 2004), Donna Wiemann, interview with Jean Holabird.

USA Today Online, http://www.usatoday.com/ (September 9, 2004), Maria Puente, "The Powerful Art of Sept. 11 Is Yet to Emerge."

*   *   *

HOPKINSON, Michael
(Michael A. Hopkinson)

PERSONAL: Education: Earned an M.A. and Ph.D. from Cambridge University.

ADDRESSES: Home—Scotland. *Office*—Department of History, University of Stirling, Stirling FK9 4LA, Scotland. *E-mail*—m.a.hopkinson@stir.ac.uk.

CAREER: University of Kent at Canterbury, Canterbury, England, former faculty member; Queen's University, Belfast, Northern Ireland, faculty member, 1971-74; University of Stirling, Stirling, Scotland, lecturer in history, 1974—. Murdoch University, visiting fellow, 1991-92; Queen's University, Belfast, senior visiting research fellow, 1998-99.

WRITINGS:

Green against Green: The Irish Civil War, St. Martin's Press (New York, NY),1988.

(Editor) *Frank Henderson's Easter Rising: Recollections of a Dublin Volunteer,* Cork University Press (Cork, Ireland), 1998.

(Editor and author of introduction) *The Last Days of Dublin Castle: The Mark Sturgis Diaries,* Irish Academic Press (Portland, OR), 1999.

The Irish War of Independence, Gill & Macmillan (Dublin, Ireland),2002.

Contributor to history journals.

SIDELIGHTS: Writer and historian Michael Hopkinson has served on the history faculties of several universities, including the University of Kent at Can-

terbury, the University of Belfast, and the University of Stirling in Scotland. Hopkinson's primary areas of research include Irish and Irish-American history of the twentieth century, and he has written several volumes on the subject, including *Green against Green: The Irish Civil War,* which was a best seller in Ireland. In *The Irish War of Independence,* Hopkinson offers a detailed account of the war, including issues of military, diplomatic, and political importance. He carefully analyzes the effects of the war on each region of the country, noting that violence was far more prevalent in certain areas than in others. In addition, Hopkinson illustrates the British and American involvement and reactions to the war, noting that the United States provided funding for the Irish and that the British were ultimately responsible for the escalation of the war, which started mostly as a skirmish between the IRA and local police. A reviewer for *Publishers Weekly* opined that "the book's strongest point is its exploration of the behind-the-scenes shifts in British policy." Paul A. Townsend, writing for *Albion,* called the book an "informative and well-researched narrative," and "a very useful overview of the conflict in Ireland."

BIOGRAPHICAL AND CRITICAL SOURCES:

PERIODICALS

Albion, spring, 2004, Paul A. Townsend, review of *The Irish War of Independence,* p. 192.

Booklist, December, 1988, Brad Hooper, review of *Green against Green: The Irish Civil War,* p. 614.

Canadian Journal of History, December, 2005, Peter Hart, review of *The Irish War of Independence,* p. 551.

Choice, May, 1989, J.W. Auld, review of *Green against Green,* p. 1576; November, 2003, D.M. Cregier, review of *The Irish War of Independence,* p. 611.

Contemporary Review, July, 2003, John McGruk, review of *The Irish War of Independence,* p. 53.

History: Reviews of New Books, summer, 1989, John Kendle, review of *Green against Green,* p. 175.

History Today, July, 2003, Charles Townshend, review of *The Irish War of Independence,* p. 56.

International History Review, December, 2003, David Harkness, review of *The Irish War of Independence,* p. 931.

Irish Literary Supplement, fall, 1989, Tom Garvin, review of *Green against Green,* p. 41.

New Statesman, January 17, 2000, "Hating the Irish," review of *The Last Days of Dublin Castle: The Mark Sturgis Diaries,* p. 55; January 27, 2003, Maurice Walsh, review of *The Irish War of Independence,* p. 48.

Past and Present, February, 1990, review of *Green against Green,* p. 203.

Publishers Weekly, October 14, 2002, review of *The Irish War of Independence,* p. 74.

Sunday Business Post (Cork, Ireland), January 19, 2003, David O'Donoghue, review of *The Irish War of Independence.*

ONLINE

Socialist Review Online, http://www.socialistreview. org.uk/ (April 25, 2007) Chris Bambery, review of *The Irish War of Independence.*

University of Stirling Web site, http://www.history.stir. ac.uk/ (October 2, 2004), biography of Hopkinson.*

*   *   *

HOPKINSON, Michael A.
   See HOPKINSON, Michael

*   *   *

HOU, Joseph P. 1929-
   (Joseph Puhsier Hou)

PERSONAL: Born October 15, 1929, in China; naturalized U.S. citizen; married; wife's name Helen. *Education:* University of Wisconsin—Madison, Ph.D.

ADDRESSES: Home—Orlando, FL. *Office*—2224 E. Concord St., Orlando, FL 32803.

CAREER: Research scientist and acupuncturist.

WRITINGS:

The Myth and Truth about Ginseng, A.S. Barnes (South Brunswick, NJ), 1978.

(With M.D. Youyu) *Alternative Therapies for Cancer and Common Ailments: A Practical Guide to the Healing Properties of Chinese Herbal Remedies and Health Food,* AuthorHouse (Bloomington, IN), 2001.

The Healing Power of Chinese Herbs and Medicinal Recipes, Haworth Press (Binghamton, NY), 2002.

*   *   *

HOU, Joseph Puhsier
   See HOU, Joseph P.

*   *   *

HOWARD, Donald E. 1933-

PERSONAL: Born August 22, 1933, in Lenoir County, NC; son of Bruce W. (a farmer) and Estelle T. (a homemaker) Howard; married; wife's name Regina H. (divorced January 15, 1989); children: Sharon, Donna, Laura. *Ethnicity:* "English/Irish." *Education:* Barton College, A.B.; North Carolina State University, M.S.; Duke University, Ed.D. *Politics:* Independent. *Religion:* Protestant. *Hobbies and other interests:* Reading, travel, dancing.

ADDRESSES: Home—Radford, VA. *E-mail*—dehvilla@aol.com.

CAREER: High school counselor for public schools of Duplin County, NC, 1962-63; teacher and principal at public schools in Raleigh, NC, between 1963 and 1969; Radford University, Radford, VA, professor and administrator, 1969-96; retired, 1996. *Military service:* U.S. Air Force, 1953-57; became staff sergeant.

WRITINGS:

The Role of Reading in Nine Famous Lives, McFarland (Jefferson, NC), 2005.

Contributor to education journals and to the Internet magazine *WorldandI.com.*

SIDELIGHTS: Donald E. Howard told *CA:* "Sometime during my late teens and early twenties I began to think that writing was something I would like to do. During my years in college and university training I wrote scores of papers and reports. Throughout my career as a professional educator, I published some articles in education periodicals. When I retired I decided I would devote my retirement years to reading and writing. I thoroughly enjoy the reading, research, and creative process that is a part of writing. That process helps me to seek new knowledge and refine what I learn into a cogent product for presentation.

"My interest is principally in education, history, and literature. I have been influenced by many of the major historical and literary writers—people like Leo Tolstoy, H.G. Wells, Douglas Southall Freeman, C.P. Snow, Boris Pasternak, Thomas Wolfe, Konstantin Paustovsky, and hundreds of others. I enjoy learning about people who have lived unusual lives, and through my reading and research I try to find common connections that produce outstanding personalities.

"When I want to write, I begin by reading widely on my subject and collecting notes in composition books. I then group my notes into common topics, arrange them in an orderly sequence, and being writing with an introduction to the written product I hope to produce. I try hard to get the introduction correct. If I succeed with that, the remainder of the product seems to follow much more easily. Reviewing and rewriting is very much a part of my writing process.

"My inspiration to write probably stems from my appreciation of books. The libraries of the world hold such a treasure trove of enriching material that I wanted to be a part of that heritage. I believe that reading widely is the single most important thing a person can do to prepare himself or herself for life. As a writer I want to contribute to that body of literature because I appreciate what reading has meant to my development and my life."

*   *   *

HUANG, Chi

PERSONAL: Married; wife's name Kristin; children: three daughters. *Education:* Texas A & M University, B.S.; Harvard University, Harvard Medical School, M.D. (cum laude), 1998.

ADDRESSES: Home—MA. *Office*—Boston Medical Center, Pediatric Inpatient Pediatric Unit, Menino Pavilion, 840 Harrison Ave., 4th Fl. East, Boston, MA 02118.

CAREER: Boston Medical Center, Boston University School of Medicine, Boston, MA, assistant professor of pediatrics, medical director of inpatient pediatrics, director of the pediatric global health initiative, and internal medicine hospitalist attending. Casa Bernabe children's home, cofounder, 2001.

MEMBER: Bolivian Street Children Project (founder, 2002).

WRITINGS:

(With Irwin Tang) *When Invisible Children Sing,* Salt-River (Carol Stream, IL,), 2006.

SIDELIGHTS: Chi Huang serves as a pediatrician and assistant professor of pediatric medicine at Boston University's Medical Center and School of Medicine. In addition, he is the director of their global pediatric health initiative, a position that ties in with his longtime involvement in improving the lives and health of children in developing nations. Huang first traveled to Bolivia in 1997 as a medical student, in association with Boston's Park Street Church and La Iglesia La Communidad in La Paz. At night, walking the streets of the city, Huang was disturbed by the dangerous conditions and the number of children living on the street. He helped as many as he could, particularly those who were ill and in need of medical assistance. Huang's experiences led him to participate in the founding of a home for Bolivian street children, Casa Bernabe, and later to found the Bolivian Street Children Project, which serves to provide shelter and support to these children. In *When Invisible Children Sing,* Huang chronicles his experiences in Bolivia and his efforts to improve the lives of the children he encountered there. A reviewer for *Publishers Weekly* found Huang's effort "touching and sometimes painful," and remarked that the book "inspires readers to reach out, even to just one child, and make a difference in a life." *Booklist* contributor Donna Chavez concluded that "Huang's powerful testimony sounds a clarion call."

BIOGRAPHICAL AND CRITICAL SOURCES:

BOOKS

Huang, Chi, *When Invisible Children Sing,* SaltRiver (Carol Stream, IL), 2006.

PERIODICALS

Booklist, September 15, 2006, Donna Chavez, review of *When Invisible Children Sing,* p. 13.
Internet Bookwatch, January 1, 2007, review of *When Invisible Children Sing.*
Publishers Weekly, August 28, 2006, review of *When Invisible Children Sing,* p. 50.

ONLINE

Bolivian Street Children Project Web site, http://www.bolivianstreetchildren.org/ (April 25, 2007), author biography.
Boston Medical Center Web site, http://www.bmc.org/ (April 25, 2007), faculty biography.*

*   *   *

HUEBNER, Andrew

PERSONAL: Born in NJ.

ADDRESSES: Home—New York, NY.

WRITINGS:

American by Blood (novel), Simon & Schuster (New York, NY), 2000.
We Pierce (novel), Simon & Schuster (New York, NY), 2003.

SIDELIGHTS: In his debut novel, *American by Blood,* Andrew Huebner writes about three American army scouts who arrived at Little Bighorn the day after the famous battle in which the Indians wiped out General George Custer and his army. Basing his story on many real-life characters, including his own great-great-grandfather, August Huebner, the author describes the scouts' response to the horrifying scene of the massacre. The author then follows the scouts over the next year as they help track down the Sioux and Cheyenne, and how they ultimately destroy the Nez Perce Indian tribe. In the process, they must face questions about their own part in the horrors that result from their hunt. "Punctuated with beautiful descriptive passages of wilderness flora and fauna, the novel graphically details the skirmishes that followed the military disaster," reported a *Publishers Weekly* contributor. Several reviewers commented on the author's pared-down style and generally praised Huebner's first effort. For example, *Booklist* critic Budd Arthur felt the author's "style makes for some of the purist prose ever found in a historical novel."

With his novel *We Pierce,* the author turns his attention to a modern military encounter. This time Huebner writes about the Gulf War of the early 1990s and the conflict between two brothers, Smith and Sam. One brother enlists in the army out of a sense of duty and becomes a tank commander fighting in Iraq; the other is a pacifist who protests the war and is battling a cocaine addiction. The novel follows the brothers as they deal with the problems that arise from the paths they have chosen. Several reviewers perceived autobiographical elements of the novel. For example, the brothers' last names are Huebner and the author's own brother is a Gulf War veteran. As with his first novel, several reviewers praised the author's writing style. Referring to the book as "starkly realistic and timely," a *Publishers Weekly* critic stated that the author's "blunt, unvarnished prose lends impact to the questions he poses about the necessity and morality of the Gulf War." Janet Maslin, writing in the *New York Times,* commented that Huebner has produced "a spare, forceful novel," adding that the author "is often capable of a terse, angry eloquence that unifies the book's divergent threads."

BIOGRAPHICAL AND CRITICAL SOURCES:

PERIODICALS

Booklist, January 1, 2000, Budd Arthur, review of *American by Blood,* p. 877; April 15, 2003, Allen Weakland, review of *We Pierce,* p. 1448.

Boston Review, February-March, 2000, Stewart O'Nan, review of *American by Blood.*

Denver Post, March 12, 2000, Tom Walker, review of *American by Blood.*

Kirkus Reviews, March 1, 2003, review of *We Pierce,* pp. 334-335.

Library Journal, February 1, 2000, Robert Conroy, review of *American by Blood,* p. 117.

New York Times, March 5, 2000, Steven Varni, review of *American by Blood*; May 1, 2003, Janet Maslin, review of *We Pierce,* p. E9.

New York Times Book Review, March 5, 2000, Steven Varni, review of *American by Blood,* p. 24; May 4, 2003, D.T. Max, review of *We Pierce,* p. 30; May 9, 2004, Scott Veale, review of *We Pierce,* p. 24.

Publishers Weekly, January 31, 2000, review of *American by Blood,* p. 80; April 21, 2003, review of *We Pierce,* p. 38.

ONLINE

Bookreporter, http://www.bookreporter.com/ (April 18, 2007), Joe Hartlaub, review of *American by Blood.*

Boston Review, http://bostonreview.net/ (April 18, 2007), Stewart O'Nan, review of *American by Blood.*

City Paper, http://www.citypaper.com/ (April 18, 2007), Patrick Sullivan, review of *We Pierce.**

* * *

HUGHES, Mary-Beth

PERSONAL: Female.

ADDRESSES: Agent—Melanie Jackson, The Melanie Jackson Agency, 41 W. 72nd St., New York, NY 10023.

CAREER: Writer.

WRITINGS:

Wavemaker II, Atlantic Monthly Press (New York, NY), 2002.

Contributor to literary journals, including *Ploughshares, St. Ann's Review, Paris Review,* and the *Georgia Review.*

SIDELIGHTS: Mary-Beth Hughes's novel *Wavemaker II* combines history and fiction to tell an emotional story of loyalty and relationships gone awry. The novel is set in the summer of 1964, and features the Clemens family, struggling due to their associations with Roy Cohn, the former defense attorney for Senator Joseph McCarthy. Will Clemens, the head of the family, is serving time in prison because he refused to testify against Cohn; son Bo has cancer and is bedridden in a New York hospital; daughter Lou-Lou, approaching her teenage years, founders unnoticed as her mother, Kay, struggles to deal with the crumbling family. Hughes chronicles each family member's experiences, rotating points of view to show how each of them is affected by Will's decisions and loyalty to Cohn. A contributor to *Kirkus Reviews* found *Wavemaker II,* "a consistently accomplished debut that's still hard to take because the family's anguish seems too little distinguished from the general social funk to provide much narrative energy." However, a reviewer for *Publishers Weekly* found that "Hughes's slice of mid-20th-century culture is fascinating, and her fictional recreation of the notorious Cohn, though many will find it implausible, is highly original." Beverly Lowry, writing for the *New York Times Book Review,* remarked that "Hughes is a writer of dexterity and imagination, with a great feel for sensory images."

BIOGRAPHICAL AND CRITICAL SOURCES:

PERIODICALS

Booklist, November 15, 2001, Joanne Wilkinson, review of *Wavemaker II,* p. 554.

Kirkus Reviews, October 15, 2001, review of *Wavemaker II,* p. 1445.

Library Journal, February 1, 2002, Christine Perkins, review of *Wavemaker II,* p. 131.

New York Times Book Review, March 31, 2002, Beverly Lowry, review of *Wavemaker II,* p. 6; June 2, 2002, review of *Wavemaker II,* p. 25.

O, The Oprah Magazine, March, 2002, Lisa Shea, "Biblio: From Our Shelf to Yours," p. 132.

Ploughshares, spring, 2002, Fred Leebron, review of *Wavemaker II,* p. 199.

Publishers Weekly, November 26, 2001, review of *Wavemaker II,* p. 36.

ONLINE

BookPage, http://www.bookpage.com/ (September 16, 2004), Sarah Goodrum, review of *Wavemaker II.*

*   *   *

HULL, Richard T. 1939-
(Richard Thompson Hull)

PERSONAL: Born December 29, 1939, in Oklahoma City, OK; son of John Montague (an administrative assistant) and Wilma (a newspaper reporter) Hull; married Barbara Elaine Mangelsdorf (a behavioral neuroscientist); children: Geoffrey Alaric (deceased). *Education:* Austin College, B.A., 1963; Indiana University—Bloomington, Ph.D., 1971. *Politics:* Democrat. *Religion:* Atheist. *Hobbies and other interests:* Classical music.

ADDRESSES: Home—Tallahassee, FL. *Office*—Text and Academic Authors Association, 3241 Heather Hill Ln., Tallahassee, FL 32309. *E-mail*—rthull62@ hotmail.com.

CAREER: State University of New York at Buffalo, professor of philosophy, 1967-97; Texas Council for the Humanities, Austin, executive director, 1997-99; freelance book producer, 1999-2002; Center for Inquiry Transnational, Amherst, NY, director of development, 2002-04; Center for Inquiry Community of Tallahassee, Tallahassee, FL, founder and principal, 2005—. Agricultural Management Systems, Inc., president, 2000—; Text and Academic Authors Association, principal. Headmaster of a preparatory school, 1983-86; Southwest Texas State University, member of philosophy faculty; University of Montana, visiting distinguished professor. *Military service:* U.S. Army Reserve, between 1958 and 1965.

MEMBER: American Philosophical Association, American Society for Value Inquiry (past president).

WRITINGS:

(Editor and author of introduction) *Ethical Issues in the New Reproductive Technologies,* Wadsworth Publishing (Belmont, CA), 1990, 2nd edition, Prometheus Books (Amherst, NY), 2005.

(Editor) *A Quarter Century of Value Inquiry: Presidential Addresses of the American Society for Value Inquiry,* Rodopi (Atlanta, GA), 1994.

William H. Werkmeister, Martin Heidegger on the Way, Rodopi (Atlanta, GA), 1996.

(Editor) *Presidential Addresses of the American Philosophical Association, 1901-1910,* Kluwer Academic (Boston, MA), 1999.

(Editor) *Presidential Addresses of the American Philosophical Association, 1910-1920,* Kluwer Academic (Boston, MA), 1999.

(Editor) *Presidential Addresses of the American Philosophical Association, 1921-1930,* Kluwer Academic (Boston, MA), 1999.

(Editor) *Presidential Addresses of the American Philosophical Association, 1931-1940,* Kluwer Academic (Boston, MA), 2001.

(Editor) *Presidential Addresses of the American Philosophical Association, 1941-1950,* Prometheus Books (Amherst, NY), 2005.

(Editor) *Presidential Addresses of the American Philosophical Association, 1951-1960,* Prometheus Books (Amherst, NY), 2006.

Contributor to books. Author of about one hundred articles.

SIDELIGHTS: Richard T. Hull told *CA:* "My aim in my books has been to preserve the history and traditions of philosophical societies, from large ones like the American Philosophical Association to small ones like the American Society for Value Inquiry. Most professional philosophers present their work publicly before colleagues from their local region or state, and only occasionally at national meetings. An enormous amount of philosophical activity occurs in small venues. Part of my work has been to recover and preserve materials that were in danger of being lost.

"My books began flowing after I had achieved tenure and was well into my years as a professor. I write daily, usually in the early hours of the day, often before six o'clock. I believe that another habit I have cultivated is writing subconsciously, using bits of time to 'download' what my subconscious has written; in effect I serve as the secretary of the subconscious.

"I have also started a new career as a nonprofit organization director, and I am the president of a high-tech agricultural service corporation that is currently developing high-yield, low-input ethanol technology."

BIOGRAPHICAL AND CRITICAL SOURCES:

BOOKS

Boepple, E.D., editor, *Sui Generis: Essays Presented to Richard Thompson Hull on the Occasion of His 65th Birthday,* AuthorHouse (Bloomington, IN), 2005.

Soble, Alan, and Carol Steinberg Gould, *A Mini-Festschrift in Honor of Richard T. Hull,* 2004.

*   *   *

HULL, Richard Thompson
See HULL, Richard T.

*   *   *

HUNTER, Faith

PERSONAL: Born in LA; married. *Hobbies and other interests:* White-water rafting, fishing, crabbing, weight lifting, jewelry making, yoga.

ADDRESSES: Agent—Lucienne Diver, Spectrum Literary Agency, 320 Central Park W., Ste. 1D, New York, NY 10025. *E-mail*—faith@faithhunter.net.

CAREER: Writer.

WRITINGS:

Bloodring, Roc (New York, NY), 2006.
Seraphs, Roc (New York, NY), 2007.

SIDELIGHTS: Faith Hunter's first novel, *Bloodring,* is set in an alternate universe where a series of plagues have decimated the population, and the planet is covered in ice. A war between good and evil continues to ravage Earth, with humans caught in the middle between demons and seraphs. Certain humans have special abilities that classify them as "neomages," and one such human, Thorn St. Croix, struggles to hide her abilities in order to maintain her freedom. Frieda Murray, in a review for *Booklist,* called the book a "very professionally executed, tasty blend of dark fantasy, mystery, and romance." Writing for *Kliatt,* contributor Cara Chancellor praised Hunter's originality, noting that the book "departs from the usual fantasy realm, but Hunter's enchanting narration makes the reader hope she will return to this apocalyptic world again—and soon!" Hunter revisits her original realm in her follow-up effort, *Seraphs.*

BIOGRAPHICAL AND CRITICAL SOURCES:

PERIODICALS

Booklist, November 1, 2006, Frieda Murray, review of *Bloodring,* p. 35.
Kirkus Reviews, October 1, 2006, review of *Bloodring,* p. 994.
Kliatt, March 1, 2007, Cara Chancellor, review of *Bloodring,* p. 26.
Library Journal, October 15, 2006, Jackie Cassada, review of *Bloodring,* p. 54.

ONLINE

Best Reviews.com, http://www.thebestreviews.com/ (November 5, 2006), Harriet Klausner, review of *Bloodring.*
Faith Hunter Home Page, http://www.faithhunter.net (April 26, 2007).
Pop Syndicate Web site, http://www.popsyndicate.com/ (April 26, 2007), review of *Bloodring.*
Spectrum Literary Agency Web site, http://www.spectrumliteraryagency.com/ (April 26, 2007), author biography.*

HURWIN, Davida Wills 1950-

PERSONAL: Born 1950, in San Francisco, CA; married; husband's name Gene; children: Frazier Malone (daughter).

ADDRESSES: Home and office—Southern CA.

CAREER: Dancer, actor, educator, and writer. Crossroads School for Arts and Sciences, Santa Monica, CA, instructor in drama.

AWARDS, HONORS: Iowa Teen Award nomination, 1998-99, for *A Time for Dancing;* New York Public Library Best Book for the Teen Age selection, 2003, for *The Farther You Run.*

WRITINGS:

A Time for Dancing, Little, Brown (Boston, MA), 1995.
The Farther You Run, Viking (New York, NY), 2003.
Circle the Soul Softly, HarperCollins (New York, NY), 2006.

ADAPTATIONS: A Time for Dancing was adapted as a film, released in 2000.

SIDELIGHTS: In her fiction for young adults, Davida Wills Hurwin focuses on young women coming of age. Her debut novel, *A Time for Dancing,* draws on Hurwin's experiences as a dancer, while *Circle the Soul Softly* benefits from Hurwin's insight as a high-school drama instructor.

Hurwin's first novel, *A Time for Dancing,* is a story of grief and loss. Samantha and Juliana are best friends, and have been since childhood. They perform together in the same dance company and attend the same school. However, when Juliana is diagnosed with cancer, their friendship changes, and Samantha has to learn to say goodbye. "Few YA dramas deal with the issue of terminal illness as intimately as this gripping first novel," wrote a *Publishers Weekly* contributor, while Anne O'Malley wrote in *Booklist* that *A Time for Dancing* "will hold fans of this genre glued to the page." Samantha and Juliana "are likable, fully drawn characters who immediately engage the reader," wrote Maeve Visser Knoth in her *Horn Book* review of the novel, which was also adapted as a film.

The Farther You Run begins six months after *A Time for Dancing,* and continues Hurwin's focus on Samantha as she struggles through her grief, refusing to dance. Her new friend, Mona, tries to get close, but Samantha pushes her away, unwilling to accept emotional support. "The emotional intensity and vibrant characters will hook readers from the first page," wrote Anne O'Malley in her *Booklist* review. While feeling that the book would mainly appeal to fans of the first novel, Miranda Doyle noted in *School Library Journal* that "the friendship between the two girls is convincing." A *Kirkus Reviews* contributor found *The Farther You Run* "immensely appealing and slightly unrealistic in the depiction of life on one's own."

In *Circle the Soul Softly,* Kate O'Connor suffers from post-traumatic stress disorder following the death of her father. Following a move to a Los Angeles suburb with her family several years later, Kate is terrified of literally running into things and people. She is also sure she is being stalked by a presence she calls the Monster. As school progresses, she begins to connect to people in her drama group, and when she begins to suspect that one of her new friends is abused, her suspicions help Kate face issues from her own past. "Hurwin's creation is tender, thought-provoking, and emotionally profound, with an inescapable crescendo," wrote J.A. Kaszuba Locke in a review of *Circle the Soul Softly* for *BookLoons* online. Myrna Marler, writing in *Kliatt,* described Kate's narrative voice as "likeable and believable," and *School Library Journal* critic Susan Riley predicted that "teen girls will strongly relate to the protagonist's feelings."

BIOGRAPHICAL AND CRITICAL SOURCES:

PERIODICALS

Booklist, November 1, 1995, Anne O'Malley, review of *A Time for Dancing,* p. 470; August, 2003, Anne O'Malley, review of *The Farther You Run,* p. 1980.

Bulletin of the Center for Children's Books, October, 1995, review of *A Time for Dancing,* p. 58; April, 2006, Loretta Gaffney, review of *Circle the Soul Softly,* p. 357.

Horn Book, January-February, 1996, Maeve Visser Knoth, review of *A Time for Dancing,* p. 78.

Journal of Adolescent and Adult Literacy, November, 1997, review of *A Time for Dancing,* p. 215.

Kirkus Reviews, June 15, 2003, review of *The Farther You Run,* p. 859; February 1, 2006, review of *Circle the Soul Softly,* p. 133.

Kliatt, March, 2006, Myrna Marler, review of *Circle the Soul Softly,* p. 12.

Publishers Weekly, October 9, 1995, review of *A Time for Dancing,* p. 87; December 22, 1997, review of *A Time for Dancing,* p. 61; June 30, 2003, review of *The Farther You Run,* p. 82.

School Library Journal, August, 2003, Miranda Doyle, review of *The Farther You Run,* p. 160; March, 2006, Susan Riley, review of *Circle the Soul Softly,* p. 223.

Voice of Youth Advocates, December, 1995, review of *A Time for Dancing,* p. 302; August, 2003, review of *The Farther You Run,* p. 225; February, 2006, Laura Woodruff, review of *Circle the Soul Softly,* p. 487.

ONLINE

BookLoons, http://www.bookloons.com/ (April 28, 2007), J.A. Kaszuba Locke, review of *Circle the Soul Softly.*

HarperCollins Web site, http://www.harpercollins.com/ (April 28, 2007), "Davida Wills Hurwin.*

*   *   *

HYDE, Shelley
  See REED, Kit

I-J

INGS, Simon 1965-

PERSONAL: Born 1965, in Horndean, England.

ADDRESSES: Home—London, England. *Agent*—Peter Tallack, Conville & Walsh, 2 Ganton St., London W1F 7Ql, England. *E-mail*—simon@fisheye.demon.co.uk.

CAREER: Writer.

WRITINGS:

NOVELS

Hot Head, Grafton Books (London, England), 1992.
City of the Iron Fish, Collins (London, England), 1994.
Hotwire, Collins (London, England), 1995.
Headlong, HarperCollins (London, England), 1999.
Painkillers, Bloomsbury Publishing (London, England), 2000.
The Weight of Numbers, Atlantic Books (London, England), 2006.

NONFICTION

The Eye: A Natural History, Bloomsbury Publishing (London, England), 2007.

Contributor of short stories to magazines.

SIDELIGHTS: Simon Ings has become known for imaginative, well-crafted science fiction tales that are often classified as cyberpunk. Indeed, Ings welcomes this label, observing in *Infinity Plus* that cyberpunk "offers now the chance, not to wed sf to some putative 'real fiction' but—through its very specificity—to convey and interpret the world better than any other popular form." Cyberpunk, he went on to say, has become such a necessary genre in the twenty-first century, "because the world itself has become speculative and fantastical. . . . We live in an environment whose artificiality reaches inside us, poking through the blood-brain barrier with fingers of Prozac and Amitriptyline."

After publishing several cult novels, Ings attracted a wider readership with *The Weight of Numbers.* Often compared to the novels of Paul Auster and David Mitchell, the book follows several disparate narrative strands and includes both fictional and actual characters, moving from Blitz-era London to an Israeli kibbutz in 1950, from the NASA programs of the 1960s to guerilla warfare in 1992 Mozambique, from the fashionable London radicalism of 1968 to the decadence of late 1990s Hollywood. While some critics admired Ings's ability to spin such a complex narrative while revealing the subtle interconnections of its various plot lines, others found the novel frustrating. "Ings gets almost everything right" in this novel, wrote London *Independent* contributor Charles Shaar Murray, "yet it doesn't work." The problem, in Murray's view, is that the novel lacks "real emotional or intellectual pay-off." Erica Wagner, in the *New York Times Book Review,* concluded that "the structure of this book is simply too elaborate, the stories and lives too fragmented, to engage the reader in any meaningful way. If Ings's point is that the center cannot hold, that's a point that's been made before, and more coherently and with more concision, too." A *Publishers Weekly* reviewer, on the other hand, described *The Weight of Numbers* as a "Pynchon-on-speed romp" that is "held together to the very last page by humor, vivid depictions and a deeply compelling emotional core."

Ings's nonfiction book *The Eye: A Natural History* explains the chemistry, biology, physics, and psychology of the eye and eyesight. Doug Johnstone, writing in the London *Times,* praised Ings's meticulous research and clear prose, calling *The Eye* a "thoroughly engaging book [written] with refreshing clarity, enthusiasm and vigour."

BIOGRAPHICAL AND CRITICAL SOURCES:

PERIODICALS

Calgary Herald, August 13, 2006, Aritha van Herk, "Fiction by Numbers."

Independent (London, England), March 24, 2006, Charles Shaar Murray, review of *The Weight of Numbers.*

Kirkus Reviews, November 1, 2006, review of *The Weight of Numbers,* p. 1093.

Library Journal, January 1, 2007, Barbara Love, review of *The Weight of Numbers,* p. 94.

New Scientist, May 12, 2001, Hugh Nissenson, "Superhumantity," p. 52.

New Statesman, March 27, 2006, Alastair Sooke, "Tangled Web," p. 53.

New York Times Book Review, March 11, 2007, Erica Wagner, "Unintended Consequences."

Publishers Weekly, October 23, 2006, review of *The Weight of Numbers,* p. 28.

Times (London, England), March 10, 2007, Doug Johnsone, "Read with a Trembling Eye."

Times Literary Supplement, June 30, 2006, Roz Keveney, "How the Sixties Felt," p. 23.

ONLINE

Infinity Plus, http://www.infinityplus.co.uk/ (May 18, 2007), "Ribbon Development,"

SF Site, http://www.sfsite.com/ (May 18, 2007), David Mathew, "Headlong, Backwards and Forwards: An Interview with Simon Ings."

Simon Ings Home Page, http://www.simonings.net/ homepages/simonings.html (May 18, 2007).

Strange Horizons, http://www.strangehorizons.com/ review/ (May 18, 2007) review of *The Weight of Numbers.**

*   *   *

IRELAND, Lynne M. 1953-

PERSONAL: Born August 31, 1953, in Fremont, NE. *Education:* Nebraska Wesleyan University, B.A., 1974; State University of New York College at Oneonta, M.A., 1981.

ADDRESSES: Home—Lincoln, NE. *Office*—Nebraska State Historical Society, 155 R St., P.O. Box 82554, Lincoln, NE 68501. *E-mail*—lireland@nebraska history.org.

CAREER: Nebraska State Historical Society, Lincoln, chief education and research officer, 1979—.

WRITINGS:

(With Hugh H. Genoways) *Museum Administration: An Introduction,* Alta Mira Press (Walnut Creek, CA), 2003.

Author of "Seasoned to Taste," a weekly food column in *Lincoln Star-Journal,* 1999—.

*   *   *

IZENOUR, George Charles 1912-2007

OBITUARY NOTICE— See index for *CA* sketch: Born July 24, 1912, in New Brighton, PA; died March 24, 2007, in Philadelphia, PA. Designer, educator, and author. An innovator in theater design, Izenour invented automated lighting and mechanical systems that are used in television studios and for live theater. An alumnus of Wittenberg College, he earned a B.A. in 1934 and an M.A. in physics in 1936. His master's thesis work led to his Izenour system of automated lighting. Hired by Yale University as director of the Electromechanical Laboratory for the School of Drama in 1939, he completed his lighting system in 1947. It allowed one stagehand rather than two or three people to control lighting. Initially used in television studios, it was later adapted for use in live theater, as well. The lighting system was followed by an automated winch system, and in the 1950s Izenour developed a way to convert proscenium stages into thrust stages in just fifteen minutes. What this did is turn a traditional stage into a stage that was surrounded on three sides by the audience. Now known as Izenour theaters, this automated stage system is used around the world, with the notable exception of Broadway. Izenour continued to work for Yale through 1977, including as professor of theatre design and technology for the last seventeen years of his tenure. Afterwards, he became a theater design consultant and founded George C. Izenour Associates. He was the author of *Theater Technology* (1988) and *Roofed Theaters of Classical Antiquity* (1992).

OBITUARIES AND OTHER SOURCES:

PERIODICALS

New York Times, March 30, 2007, p. C9.

*   *   *

JAY, Debra 1954-

PERSONAL: Born 1954; married Jeff Jay (a counselor).

ADDRESSES: Home—Grosse Pointe Farms, MI.

CAREER: Hazelden Foundation, Center City, MN, former addiction specialist; certified drug and alcohol intervention counselor in private practice.

WRITINGS:

(With husband, Jeff Jay) *Love First: A New Approach to Intervention for Alcoholism and Drug Addiction,* foreword by George McGovern, Hazelden Information & Educational Services (Center City, MN), 2000.

(With Jeff Jay) *Aging & Addiction: Helping Older Adults Overcome Alcohol or Medication Dependence,* foreword by Barry McCaffrey, Hazelden (Center City, MN), 2002.

No More Letting Go: The Spirituality of Taking Action against Alcoholism and Drug Addiction, Bantam Books (New York, NY), 2006.

Columnist for *Grosse Pointe News.*

SIDELIGHTS: A certified drug and alcohol intervention counselor, Debra Jay has written two books with her husband, fellow counselor Jeff Jay. In *Love First: A New Approach to Intervention for Alcoholism and Drug Addiction* the Jays offers step-by-step guidance for families dealing with addiction. They explain the intervention process in which loved ones meet with the addicted person to urge him or her to seek professional help, and they argue that timely intervention can prevent years of abusive behavior and dysfunction in the family. *Aging & Addiction: Helping Older Adults Overcome Alcohol or Medication Dependence* offers specific suggestions about intervention if the drug or alcohol abuser is over age fifty-five, when such issues as medical conditions, retirement, and social isolation can create particular complications.

In *No More Letting Go: The Spirituality of Taking Action against Alcoholism and Drug Addiction,* Jay writes a solo work that explores the physical, emotional, and spiritual needs of addicts and identifies the struggle against addiction as a spiritual one. A contributor to *Publishers Weekly* found Jay's spiritual focus intriguing, and her summary of current research into the genetics and neurology of addiction "fascinating." In a starred review in *Library Journal,* Melody Ballard called *No More Letting Go* a "landmark" book that is both clear and "poignantly written."

BIOGRAPHICAL AND CRITICAL SOURCES:

PERIODICALS

Library Journal, May 15, 2006, Melody Ballard, review of *No More Letting Go: The Spirituality of Taking Action against Alcoholism and Drug Addiction,* p. 116.
Publishers Weekly, March 27, 2006, review of *No More Letting Go.*

ONLINE

No More Letting Go Web site, http://www.nomore lettinggo.com (May 20, 2007).*

*   *   *

JOBE, Steve 1956-
(Steven H. Jobe)

PERSONAL: Born 1956; married; wife's name Terry; children: Phillip. *Education:* University of the South, B.A., 1978; University of North Carolina at Chapel Hill, M.A., 1981, Ph.D., 1988.

ADDRESSES: Office—Department of English, Hanover College, P.O. Box 108, Hanover, IN 47243. *E-mail*—jobe@hanover.edu.

CAREER: Educator and writer. Hanover College, Hanover, IN, professor of English, 1990—.

WRITINGS:

(Editor, with Susan E. Gunter) *A Calendar of the Letters of Henry James and a Biographical Register of Henry James's Correspondents* (online database), University of Nebraska Press (Lincoln, NE), 1999.
(Editor, with Susan E. Gunter) *Dearly Beloved Friends: Henry James's Letters to Younger Men,* University of Michigan Press (Ann Arbor, MI), 2001.

Contributor to books, including *Henry James and Homo-erotic Desire,* edited by John Bradley, Macmillan (London, England), 1999. Contributor of articles to journals, including *Studies in American Fiction, Henry James Review,* and *American Literary Realism.*

SIDELIGHTS: A professor of English at Hanover College, Steve Jobe specializes in literature from the eighteenth and nineteenth centuries, focusing particularly on Nathaniel Hawthorne and Henry James. Since the early 1990s, Jobe has written

extensively on topics related to the works of Henry James, contributing to various periodicals, books, and online resources. He worked with Susan E. Gunter to create the online *A Calendar of the Letters of Henry James and a Biographical Register of Henry James's Correspondents.* The resource provides access to a database of James's personal letters, biographical details about the letters' recipients, and information on where original copies of the letters are kept.

Jobe collaborated with Gunter once again to compile and annotate a selection of those letters in *Dearly Beloved Friends: Henry James's Letters to Younger Men.* Jobe and Gunter carefully chose 166 letters written by James to four young correspondents, providing insight into the prominent author's passions and torments. A reviewer for *Publishers Weekly* remarked that the book's "elegant introductory remarks and helpful footnotes provide crucial context and background information not necessarily available in letters that focus on physical well-being, travel plans and social news." Jim Marks wrote in a review for the *Lambda Book Report* that "the correspondence is beautifully edited, lavishly footnoted, and abounding in useful information." Writing for *Victorian Studies,* Dennis Denisoff remarked that the "power of the book lies in the selection, editing, and publication of these pieces" and that the editors do "an excellent job of annotating and presenting the letters chosen for inclusion." Denisoff added: "The amount of archival work that this compilation required is impressive and the depth and precision of their research never wanes. The majority of the notes, moreover, are informative, convenient, and succinct, reflecting the editor's familiarity with James's works and life."

BIOGRAPHICAL AND CRITICAL SOURCES:

PERIODICALS

Lambda Book Report, March, 2002, Jim Marks, review of *Dearly Beloved Friends: Henry James's Letters to Younger Men,* p. 19.
Publishers Weekly, December 24, 2001, review of *Dearly Beloved Friends,* p. 53.
Victorian Studies, September 22, 2003, Dennis Denisoff, review of *Dearly Beloved Friends,* p. 122.

ONLINE

Hanover College Web site, http://www.hanover.edu/ (April 24, 2007), faculty profile of Steve Jobe.

JOBE, Steven H.
   See JOBE, Steve

*　　*　　*

JOHNSON, Dennis Loy 1957-

PERSONAL: Born 1957; married Valerie Merians (a poet, visual artist, and publisher). *Education:* University of Iowa Writers' Workshop, M.F.A.

ADDRESSES: Home—Hoboken, NJ. *Office*—Melville House Publishing, 300 Observer Hwy., 3rd Fl., Hoboken, NJ 07030.

CAREER: Melville House Publishing, Hoboken, NJ, cofounder and copublisher, 2002—; Allegheny College, Meadville, PA, professor of English; has also taught at Carnegie-Mellon University, Pittsburgh, PA, University of Iowa, Iowa City, and the University of Pittsburgh.

AWARDS, HONORS: Pushcart Prize; fellow, National Endowment for the Arts.

WRITINGS:

(Editor, with wife, Valerie Merians) *Poetry after 9/11: An Anthology of New York Poets,* Melville House Publishing (Hoboken, NJ), 2002.
The Big Chill: The Great, Unreported Story of the Bush Inauguration Protest, Melville House Publishing (Hoboken, NJ), 2004.
(Editor, with Valerie Merians) *What We Do Now,* Melville House Publishing (Hoboken, NJ), 2004.

Work represented in anthologies, including *New Stories from the South.* Editor and publisher of the weekly column "Moby Lives," originally syndicated to newspapers, then published as an Internet column, beginning 2001. Contributor of short stories, articles, essays, and reviews to periodicals, including *Georgia Review, Idler, New England Review, Ploughshares, Populist, Salon.com, Story, USA Today,* and *Weekly Planet Online.*

SIDELIGHTS: Dennis Loy Johnson has had a varied career as a writer of fiction and as a nonfiction editor and publisher. He founded Melville House Publishing partly as way to get an anthology of poetry published quickly. The anthology, *Poetry after 9/11: An Anthology of New York Poets,* which Johnson edited with Valerie Merians, features a variety of poems focusing on the September 11, 2001, terrorist attacks and the grief associated with the aftermath. Included are poems from award-winning writers such as Jean Valentine, Alicia Ostriker, and Rachel Hadas. The anthology also includes less-famous poets. Commenting on the poems as a whole in a review in the *Library Journal,* Barbara Hoffert observed that "overall the effect is one of meditation and of slowly gathering one's forces to conquer fear." A *Publishers Weekly* contributor wrote that the poets "eloquently" present their thoughts on the tragedy.

Johnson is also author of *The Big Chill: The Great, Unreported Story of the Bush Inauguration Protest.* Here, Johnson provides a first-person account of a large protest on the second inauguration of President George W. Bush, which included a strong police and military presence and bursts of violence that largely went unreported by the national press. Danny Schechter, writing on the *CommonDreams.org* Web site, called *The Big Chill* "a must-read little book."

BIOGRAPHICAL AND CRITICAL SOURCES:

PERIODICALS

Library Journal, September 15, 2002, Barbara Hoffert, review of *Poetry after 9/11: An Anthology of New York Poets,* p. 67.
Village Voice, September 28, 2004, Howard Hampton, review of *The Big Chill: The Great, Unreported Story of the Bush Inauguration Protest.*
Publishers Weekly, August 26, 2002, review of *Poetry after 9/11,* p. 53.

ONLINE

Beatrice, http://www.beatrice.com/ (October 29, 2004), interview with Dennis Loy Johnson.
Bookslut, http://www.bookslut.com/ (Aril 18, 2007), Jessa Crispin, "An Interview with Dennis Loy Johnson."

Brooklyn Rail, http://www.thebrooklynrail.org/ (April 18, 2007), Kate Trainor, "Thar She Blows: Dennis Loy Johnson and Valerie Merians."

CommonDreams.org, http://commondreams.org/ (January 17, 2005), Danny Schechter, "Will the Anti-Inaugural Protests Be Covered?,"includes brief discussion of *The Big Chill.*

MobyLives.com, http://www.mobylives.com/ (May 27, 2003), profile of Dennis Loy Johnson.*

*   *   *

JOLLUCK, Katherine R.

PERSONAL: Children: (with Norman Naimark) a son. *Education:* Harvard University, B.A.; Stanford University, M.A., 1990, Ph.D., 1995.

ADDRESSES: Office—Department of History, Stanford University, 450 Serra Mall, Bldg. 200, Stanford CA 94305-2024. *E-mail*—jolluck@stanford.edu.

CAREER: University of North Carolina—Chapel Hill, affiliated with Curriculum in Women's Studies, 1994-95, assistant professor of history, 1997; Stanford University, Stanford, CA, acting assistant professor, 2000-01, senior lecturer in history, 2003—; has also taught at the Naval Post-Graduate School.

AWARDS, HONORS: Humanities Center graduate fellowship, Stanford University, 1991-92; Kosciuszko Foundation Domestic Scholarship, 1993-94; American Fellowship, American Association of University Women, 1993-1994; MacArthur Foundation Fellowship, Center for International Security and Arms Control, 1994-95; Hoover Institution on War, Revolution and Peace, Postdoctoral Research Fellowship, 1996-97; American Council of Learned Societies/ Social Science Research Council Joint Committee on Eastern Europe Postdoctoral Fellowship, 1997-98; Junior Faculty Development Award, University of North Carolina—Chapel Hill, 1999; Institute for Human Sciences Visiting Fellowship, 2005.

WRITINGS:

Exile and Identity: Polish Women in the Soviet Union during World War II, University of Pittsburgh Press (Pittsburgh, PA), 2002.

Contributor to books, including *Antisemitism and Its Opponents in Modern Poland,* edited by Robert Blobaum, Cornell University Press (Ithaca, NY), 2005. Contributor to academic journals and popular periodicals, including *Contemporary European History, San Jose Mercury News, American Historical Review, Journal of Modern History,* and *Slavic Review.*

SIDELIGHTS: Katherine R. Jolluck is a historian who specializes in areas such as modern Eastern Europe and women in war. In her debut book, *Exile and Identity: Polish Women in the Soviet Union during World War II,* Jolluck relies largely on personal testimonies to provide a look at the deprivations suffered by the thousands of Polish women who were exiled to the Soviet Far North, Siberia, and Central Asia as part of an early 1940-41 agreement between Germany and the Soviet Union to split up Poland. Writing in the *Library Journal,* Harry Willems praised the author for "showing the tensions that resulted when early Polish feminists encountered the Soviet Union's forcible removal of the gender gap." Other critics lauded Jolluck for providing a totally new look at the Polish experience during World War II. "Jolluck's book is pathbreaking not only for presenting an engaging analysis of the experiences of Polish female deportees in the Soviet Union but also for pioneering a more detailed investigation of the gender dimensions of Polish national identity," asserted Nameeta Mathur in *History: Review of New Books.* Helena Goscilo, writing in the *Journal of Modern History,* commented that the author "breaks new ground on three fronts: it is the first gender-driven Anglophone examination of Polish deportees' experience under the Soviets during World War II; it draws on the exiles' subsequent firsthand reports; and its analysis takes into account not only gender but also ethnicity, education, and social background."

BIOGRAPHICAL AND CRITICAL SOURCES:

PERIODICALS

American Historical Review, October, 2003, Irena Grudzinska-Gross, review of *Exile and Identity: Polish Women in the Soviet Union during World War II,* pp. 1247-1248.

Choice, April, 2003, G.E. Snow, review of *Exile and Identity,* p. 1420.

History: Review of New Books, winter, 2003, Nameeta Mathur, review of *Exile and Identity,* p. 79.

Journal of Modern History, September, 2005, Helena Goscilo, review of *Exile and Identity,* p. 874.

Library Journal, September 15, 2002, Harry Willems, review of *Exile and Identity,* p. 75.

Russian Review, October, 2003, review of *Exile and Identity,* pp. 637-668.

Slavic Review, spring, 2004, Piotr Wrobel, review of *Exile and Identity,* pp. 160-161.

Slavonic and East European Review, October, 2003, K. Turton, review of *Exile and Identity,* pp. 764-766.

ONLINE

Stanford University, Department of History Web site, http://www.stanford.edu/dept/history/ (April 18, 2007), faculty profile of Katherine R. Jolluck.*

*   *   *

JUDAH, Sophie 1949-

PERSONAL: Born 1949, in Jabalpur, India; immigrated to Israel, 1973; married March 19, 1972; children: five. *Religion:* Jewish.

ADDRESSES: Home—Hod Hasharom, Israel.

CAREER: Writer

WRITINGS:

Dropped from Heaven: Stories, Schocken Books (New York, NY), 2007.

SIDELIGHTS: The nineteen pieces in Sophie Judah's debut collection, *Dropped from Heaven: Stories,* are inspired by her experiences growing up as a member of the Bene Israel, a tiny Jewish community in central India. Though Jews have been present in India for centuries, their numbers are very small and Judah's family, which moved often because of her father's position as an army officer, was often the only Jewish family in town. This background, according to a reviewer for *Publishers Weekly,* provides Judah with rich material for fiction. Her stories touch on several major themes, including the India-Pakistan partition, the roles of women, and migration to Israel. Ellen Loughran, writing in *Booklist,* admired Judah's "fascinating" depiction of a minority community shaped by religious difference. *Library Journal* reviewer Leora Bersohn also enjoyed *Dropped from Heaven*'s unique perspective, adding that, though its prose is plain and simple, the book is filled with "deep sympathy and humanity." In a starred review, a contributor to *Kirkus Reviews* praised the book's blend of family myth with sociological and psychological observation, deeming the volume a "fascinating mix of the exotic and the familiar." Indeed, it is this very sense of life that inspired Judah to write. As she explained to *Nextbook.org* writer Amy Rosenberg, what little she was able to find when she researched the Bene Israel "was all anthropology. They're looking at you through a microscope: 'Are you Jewish, aren't you Jewish; this tradition, that tradition.' And then the history. But there was no humanity, the human touch was missing."

BIOGRAPHICAL AND CRITICAL SOURCES:

PERIODICALS

Booklist, February 15, 2007, Ellen Loughran, review of *Dropped from Heaven: Stories,* p. 35.

Kirkus Reviews, January 15, 2007, review of *Dropped from Heaven,* p. 44.

Library Journal, January 1, 2007, Leora Bersohn, review of *Dropped from Heaven,* p. 102.

Publishers Weekly, January 1, 2007, review of *Dropped from Heaven,* p. 33.

ONLINE

Nextbook.org, http://www.nextbook.org/ (May 21, 2007), Amy Rosenberg, "Out of India: Sophie Judah's Stories Chronicle a Vanishing Tribe."*

*   *   *

JURGENS, Dan 1959-

PERSONAL: Born 1959, in MN. *Education:* Minneapolis College of Art and Design, B.F.A.

CAREER: Comic book writer and artist. DC Comics, New York, NY, artist and writer for comic books, beginning c. 1982. Also writer and artist for comic books published by other companies, including Marvel Comics, 1995-96; formerly worked as a graphic designer.

WRITINGS:

WITH OTHERS; COMIC BOOK COLLECTIONS

Superman: Panic in the Sky, DC Comics (New York, NY), 1992.

The Death of Superman, DC Comics (New York, NY), 1993.

(And artist) *Zero Hour: Crisis in Time,* DC Comics (New York, NY), 1994.

(And layout artist) *Superman/Doomsday: Hunter/Prey,* DC Comics (New York, NY), 1995.

Superman: Krisis of the Krimson Kryptonite, DC Comics (New York, NY), 1996.

(And layout artist) *Superman: Eradication! The Origin of the Eradicator,* DC Comics (New York, NY), 1996.

Superman: Bizarro's World, DC Comics (New York, NY), 1996.

Superman: The Death of Clark Kent, DC Comics (New York, NY), 1997.

Superman Transformed!, DC Comics (New York, NY), 1997.

Superman: The Wedding and Beyond, DC Comics (New York, NY), 1997.

Superman: Exile, DC Comics (New York, NY), 1998.

OTHER

(With others, and artist) *Superman: Time and Time Again,* DC Comics (New York, NY), 1994.

(And layout artist) *Superman/Aliens,* DC Comics (New York, NY), 1995.

(With Art Thibert and Greg Wright) *Superman, Fantastic Four: The Infinite Destruction,* DC Comics (New York, NY), 1999.

(And layout artist) *Superman: The Doomsday Wars,* DC Comics (New York, NY), 1999.

(And layout artist) *Superman: Day of Doom,* DC Comics (New York, NY), 2003.

Contributor of artwork to collections, including *Superman: Doomsday and Beyond,* by Louise Simonson, Bantam Books (New York, NY), 1993; *DC versus Marvel Comics,* by Ron Marz and Peter David, DC Comics (New York, NY), 1996; and *Heroes: The World's Greatest Super Hero Creators Honor the World's Greatest Heroes 9-11-2001,* Marvel Comics (Washington, DC), 2001. Writer and occasional layout artist for numerous comic magazines, including *Action Comics, Aquaman, Booster Gold, Captain America, Justice League of America, Rising Stars: Bright, Superman, Thor, Top Cow,* and *Warlord.*

SIDELIGHTS: An early exposure to comic books had a significant influence on Dan Jurgens's eventual career choice. In an interview with *Comic Book Resources,* Jurgens explained: "The first time I ever picked up a comic was shortly after the live-action *Batman* TV series started. I was walking home and saw some kids on a porch reading a stack of comics. I had no idea they even existed, and I remember walking over and seeing the 'Robin Dies At Dawn' issue of *Batman* and being immediately floored. What do you mean Robin is dead!? I just saw him on TV last night! That image so hooked me that I went out and started buying comics a few days later." Jurgen went on to study art at the Minneapolis College of Art and Design, and had the chance to show his portfolio to DC Comics artist Mike Grell at a local comic book store. Jurgens work was impressive enough to warrant a job offer, immediately launching his career as a comic book writer and artist.

Since 1982, Jurgens has contributed to many prominent comic book series, including *Superman, Thor, Justice League, Spiderman, G.I. Joe, Tomb Raider,* and *Captain America.* He drew attention in the mid-1990s for creating the much-hyped "Death of Superman" story line, garnering mixed reviews, but overall has earned a reputation as being among the industry's best comic creators.

"My basic goal as a writer," Jurgens told *Silver Bullet Comic Books* contributor Markisan Naso, "is pretty damn simple. When the reader finishes the book, I want him or her to want to buy the next issue. I don't mean that in the commercial sense but the editorial sense. . . . When all of this is said and done, I want them to think the trip was worth their time and money.

I've always thought that the goal of a writer should be that, once their time on a book ends, it should be in better shape than when they started."

BIOGRAPHICAL AND CRITICAL SOURCES:

PERIODICALS

Library Journal, March 1, 2004, Steve Raiteri, review of *Superman: Day of Doom,* p. 61.

ONLINE

B-Independent.com, http://www.b-independent.com/ (July 26, 1998), John Dalton, interview with Dan Jurgens.
Comic Book Resources, http://www.comicbook resources.com/ (April 30, 2006), Robert Taylor, interview with Dan Jurgens.
Silver Bullet Comics, http://www.silverbulletcomic books.com/ (August 19, 2004), Markisan Naso, interview with Dan Jurgens.*

K

KADOW, Jeannine

PERSONAL: Born in Los Angeles, CA. *Education:* University of Columbia, graduated.

ADDRESSES: Home—New York, NY; southern France.

CAREER: Commercial photographer; previously worked as a television news reporter and anchor; former vice president of television sales for Warner Brothers.

WRITINGS:

Shooting Stars, Hodder & Stoughton (London, England), 1997.
Blue Justice, Signet (New York, NY), 1998.
Burnout (novel; "Lacie Wagner" series), Dutton (New York, NY), 1999.
Dead Tide: A Novel of Suspense (novel; "Lacie Wagner" series), New American Library (New York, NY), 2002.

SIDELIGHTS: A former television journalist, Jeannine Kadow is now a commercial photographer and novelist. *Burnout* is the author's third novel and her first in the "Lacie Wagner" thriller series. The reader is introduced to Lacie as a young anchorwoman and the mother of a fourteen-year-old teenager who is kidnapped. After receiving a videotape of her daughter, Skyla, Lacie realizes that the kidnapper has appeared previously in her nightmares. She then goes out to look for him with the help of FBI Special Agent Jack Stein. *Library Journal* critic Jo Ann Vicarel predicted that "this fast-paced thriller is sure to please readers who like strong female characters fighting against the odds." A *Publishers Weekly* contributor had similar praise: "The story is dramatic, and . . . readers will be drawn in by some ingenious twists."

Dead Tide: A Novel of Suspense finds Lacie vacationing on Nantucket when she comes across a horribly burned corpse. Drawn to the case, Lacie discovers an association between the "Jane Doe" and a secret special ops group known only to a few in government. Before long, Lacie has joined forces with retired investigator Nick St. James to help her solve the case, which ends up involving torture and numerous other missing women. A *Kirkus Reviews* contributor referred to *Dead Tide* as a "fleet, unnerving thriller." Another *Publishers Weekly* critic shuddered at the novel's "disturbing physiological effects."

BIOGRAPHICAL AND CRITICAL SOURCES:

PERIODICALS

Kirkus Reviews, January 1, 1999, review of *Burnout,* p. 9; June 15, 2002, review of *Dead Tide: A Novel of Suspense,* p. 842.
Library Journal, November 15, 1999, Jo Ann Vicarel, review of *Burnout,* p. 132.
Publishers Weekly, February 15, 1999, review of *Burnout,* p. 90; July 1, 2002, review of *Dead Tide,* p. 58.

Washington Post Book World, February 27, 1999, Joan Richter, review of *Burnout,* p. 8.

ONLINE

Jeannine Kadow Home Page, http://www.jeannine kadow.com (April 18, 2007).
Les Romantiques, http://www.lesromantiques.com/ (April 18, 2007), biographical information on Jeannine Kadow.
Romantic Times Book Club, http://www.romantic times.com/ (September 16, 2002), Toby Bromberg, review of *Dead Tide.*
Star Tribune Online, http://www.startribune.com/ (August 11, 2002), Ken Wisneski, review of *Dead Tide.**

*   *   *

KAISH, Stanley 1931-

PERSONAL: Born 1931. *Education:* Cornell University, B.A.; University of Pennsylvania, M.B.A.; New York University, Ph.D.

ADDRESSES: *Home*—Springfield, NJ. *E-mail*—stankaish@verizon.net.

CAREER: Rutgers School of Management, Newark, NJ, former associate dean and professor emeritus of finance and economics.

WRITINGS:

Microeconomics: Logic, Tools, and Analysis, Harper & Row (New York, NY), 1976.
(Editor, with Benjamin Gilad) *Handbook of Behavioral Economics,* JAI Press (Greenwich, CT), 1986.
(With Norman Salsitz) *Three Homelands: Memories of a Jewish Life in Poland, Israel, and America,* Syracuse University Press (New York, NY), 2002.

Contributor of articles to periodicals.

SIDELIGHTS: Stanley Kaish is a retired economics professor who has written extensively about a wide range of financial topics. He also assisted Norman Salsitz with the writing of Salsitz's memoir, *Three Homelands: Memories of a Jewish Life in Poland, Israel, and America.* The book recounts Salstiz's early life with his orthodox Jewish family, and then his life following his father's murder by the Nazi's in 1942. Salsitz spent the greater part of World War II hiding from and resisting the Germansin Poland. After the war was over, he pretended to be a Catholic and used a false identity to become part of the Polish Army's national security force, a position he used to help other Jews escape anti-Semitism in Poland. Salsitz eventually spent time in Israel and then immigrated to America, where he still harbored an anger for those who caused his family and many others to suffer so horrendously. The story is told in a series of approximately one hundred short vignettes and includes more than fifty photographs. Salsitz died in 2006. George Cohen, writing in *Booklist,* called *Three Homelands* "a penetrating account of human resilience and courage." A *Publishers Weekly* contributor commended both Salsitz and Kaish for their ability to create a "sense of place" and appreciated "the way the characters seem to spring off the page."

BIOGRAPHICAL AND CRITICAL SOURCES:

PERIODICALS

Booklist, December 15, 2002, George Cohen, review of *Three Homelands: Memories of a Jewish Life in Poland, Israel, and America,* p. 729.
Publishers Weekly, October 28, 2002, review of *Three Homelands,* p. 61.

*   *   *

KAPISZEWSKI, Diana

PERSONAL: *Education:* Dartmouth College, B.A., 1988; Middlebury College, M.A., 1991; Georgetown University, M.A., 1994; University of California at Berkeley, M.A., 2001, currently doctoral program student. *Hobbies and other interests:* Biking, running, hiking, music.

ADDRESSES: *E-mail*—dianakap@berkeley.edu.

CAREER: Political scientist and writer. Georgetown University, director of academic programs for Center for Latin American Studies, 1996-2000.

AWARDS, HONORS: Fulbright U.S. student fellow, 2004-05.

WRITINGS:

(Editor) *Encyclopedia of Latin American Politics,* Oryx Press (Westport, CT), 2002.

SIDELIGHTS: In the *Encyclopedia of Latin American Politics,* Diana Kapiszewski presents chapters by various scholars on the eighteen Spanish-speaking republics of Latin America, as well as Puerto Rico, Brazil (where the language is Portuguese), and Haiti (where the language is French). The authors write within a standardized format that provides a wide range of information on each country with a primary focus on the structure of the government. Also included is a list of the government leaders, a bibliography, and Web resources. Each country description comes with a chart that lists important information concerning economic, political, and social data. Noting that the "entries are concise, [and] well written," a *Booklist* contributor added that "this volume's country-by-country focus on twentieth-century politics makes it unique." Sylvia D. Hall-Ellis commented in the *Library Journal:* "Easy to use, . . . this important volume offers clear explanations of events, individuals, and dynamics."

BIOGRAPHICAL AND CRITICAL SOURCES:

PERIODICALS

Booklist, January 1, 2003, review of *Encyclopedia of Latin American Politics,* p. 936.
Library Journal, September 15, 2002, Sylvia D. Hall-Ellis, review of *Encyclopedia of Latin American Politics,* p. 54.*

*   *   *

KARR, Jillian
     See TINTORI, Karen

KATZ, Joy 1963-

PERSONAL: Born 1963, in Newark, NJ; married Rob Handel (a playwright). *Education:* Ohio State University, B.S.; Washington University, St. Louis, MO, M.F.A.

ADDRESSES: Home—Brooklyn, NY. *Office*—New School University, 66 W. 12th St., New York, NY 10011. *E-mail*—jbkatz@mindspring.com.

CAREER: Poet. New School University, New York, NY, faculty member; has taught writing and literature at Washington University and Stanford University.

AWARDS, HONORS: Crab Orchard Award, 2002, for *Fabulae;* Wallace Stegner fellowship, Stanford University; Nadja Aisenberg fellowship, MacDowell Colony.

WRITINGS:

Fabulae (poetry), Southern Illinois University Press (Carbondale, IL), 2002.
The Garden Room (poetry), Tupelo Press (Dorset, VT), 2006.
(Editor, with Kevin Prufer) *Dark Horses: Poets on Overlooked Poems: An Anthology,* University of Illinois Press (Urbana, IL), 2007.

Contributor to the anthology *The New Young American Poets,* and to periodicals, including *Parnassus, LIT, Margie, Hat, Indiana Review, Southwest Review, Antioch Review, Chelsea, Verse, Barrow Street, Fence, New York Times Book Review, Bomb, Conduit,* and *Village Voice.* Art director for *Parnassus: Poetry in Review;* senior editor for *Pleiades.*

SIDELIGHTS: Joy Katz turned to poetry as a career later in life, initially being trained as an industrial designer but ultimately earning a master of fine arts degree from Washington University. Katz, called a "gifted mythographer" by *Blackbird Online* contributor Susan Settlemyre Williams, is now a senior editor at *Pleiades,* a faculty member at the New School University in New York, and a frequent contributor to literary journals. Two collections of Katz's poetry have been published: *Fabulae,* mythical and spiritual poems about love and loss, and *The Garden Room,* a look at the sometimes magical and sometimes mundane influences of everyday household objects and rooms. *Booklist* reviewer Donna Seaman described *Fabulae* as a "smart, imaginative, and mesmerizing collection." Writing of *The Garden Room,* a contributor to *Publishers Weekly* commented: "Over the course of this subtle collection, Katz builds a quietly moving story about the complexities of love and domesticity."

Katz next collaborated with fellow *Pleiades* editor Keven Prufer on *Dark Horses: Poets on Overlooked Poems: An Anthology.* The collection features poems that are generally little-known or "overlooked," selected by dozens of modern American poets. Each poem is accompanied by a personal essay explaining the selection's impact or draw, a feature described by Janet St. John in a *Booklist* review as a "clever twist" achieving a "nobler outcome."

BIOGRAPHICAL AND CRITICAL SOURCES:

PERIODICALS

American Poet, spring, 2002, review of *Fabulae,* p. 57.
Booklist, March 1, 2002, Donna Seaman, review of *Fabulae,* p. 1086; December 15, 2006, Janet St. John, review of *Dark Horses: Poets on Overlooked Poems: An Anthology,* p. 13.
Publishers Weekly, November 20, 2006, review of *The Garden Room,* p. 40.

ONLINE

Blackbird Online, http://www.blackbird.vcu.edu/ (April 28, 2007), Susan Settlemyre Williams, review of *Fabulae.*
Southern Illinois University Press, http://www.siu.edu/ (October 7, 2004), biography of Joy Katz.*

*   *   *

KATZ, Karen A.
    See TINTORI, Karen

KENNEDY, Brian 1966-
    (Brian Edward Patrick Kennedy)

PERSONAL: Born October 12, 1966, in Belfast, Northern Ireland.

ADDRESSES: Home—Ireland.

CAREER: Singer, songwriter, and novelist. Recordings include *The Great War of Words,* 1990; *A Better Man,* 1996; *Now That I Know What I Want,* 1999; *Get On with Your Short Life,* 2002; *On Song,* 2003; *On Song 2,* 2005; and *Homebird,* 2006.

AWARDS, HONORS: Irish Music Industry Award for best Irish male album and Hot Press/2TV Award for best Irish male artist, both for *A Better Man,* 1996; D.Litt., University of Ulster, 2006.

WRITINGS:

The Arrival of Fergal Flynn, Hodder Headline (London, England), 2006.
Roman Song, Hodder & Stoughton (London, England), 2006.

Contributor of short stories to *Black Mountain Review.*

SIDELIGHTS: Brian Kennedy first rose to prominence in his native Ireland as a singer, releasing his first solo album in 1990, spending six years traveling with Van Morrison's Blues and Soul World Tour, and releasing a number of highly successful solo albums in succession between 1996 and 2006. Gaining a worldwide audience, Kennedy was selected a number of times to perform for former U.S. president Bill Clinton, chosen to perform on Broadway with the show *Riverdance,* and hired to host a television music show. In the early 2000s, Kennedy ventured into a new branch of artistic expression: writing. His short stories were anthologized in a number of Irish collections, and not long after, he was offered a two-book publishing deal.

Kennedy's first novel, *The Arrival of Fergal Flynn,* is based loosely on experiences he had as a child. The protagonist is a young man growing up in 1980s Belfast, amidst the violence of war and the negligence and abuse of a dysfunctional family. A burgeoning friendship with a local priest helps the teen to discover his talent for singing and also to explore his sexual identity. The novel's sequel, *Roman Song,* finds Fergal traveling to Rome to study singing with a famed opera star. The story follows his attempts to adjust to a new city, establish a musical career, and find love. Writing for *RTÉ Online,* Katie Moten remarked that "Kennedy's humour and honesty combine to make him a natural storyteller and his first book a moving and enjoyable read." In *Roman Song,* Moten appreciated the "very heartfelt moments."

BIOGRAPHICAL AND CRITICAL SOURCES:

ONLINE

Brian Kennedy Home Page, http://briankennedy.co.uk (March 26, 2007).
RTÉ, http://www.rte.ie/ (September 10, 2004), Katie Moten, review of *The Arrival of Fergal Flynn;* (January 31, 2006), Katie Moten, review of *Roman Song.**

*   *   *

KENNEDY, Brian Edward Patrick
    See KENNEDY, Brian

*   *   *

KERRIN, Jessica Scott

PERSONAL: Born in Canada; married; husband's name Peter; children: Elliott. *Education:* University of Calgary, B.A.; Nova Scotia College of Art and Design, B.F.A.; Dalhousie University, M.P.A.

ADDRESSES: Home—Halifax, Nova Scotia, Canada. *E-mail*—jessica_kerrin@yahoo.com.

CAREER: Arts administrator (manager of galleries, dance schools, and museums) and children's author. Speaker to children's groups.

MEMBER: Canadian Society of Children's Authors, Illustrators, and Performers, Canadian Children's Book Centre, Writers' Federation of Nova Scotia.

AWARDS, HONORS: Cited among top books of 2005, New York Public Library, best of 2005, *Horn Book,* and notable books, Association for Library Service of Children, 2006, all for *Martin Bridge: Ready for Takeoff!*

WRITINGS:

FOR CHILDREN

Martin Bridge: Ready for Takeoff!, Kids Can Press (Toronto, Ontario, Canada), 2005.
Martin Bridge: On the Lookout!, Kids Can Press (Toronto, Ontario, Canada), 2005.
Martin Bridge: Blazing Ahead!, Kids Can Press (Toronto, Ontario, Canada), 2006.
Martin Bridge: Sound the Alarm!, Kids Can Press (Toronto, Ontario, Canada), 2007.

BIOGRAPHICAL AND CRITICAL SOURCES:

PERIODICALS

Horn Book, June 1, 2005, review of *Martin Bridge: Ready for Takeoff!;* December 1, 2005, review of *Martin Bridge: On the Lookout!;* October, 2006, review of *Martin Bridge: Blazing Ahead!.*
Kirkus Reviews, August 15, 2005, review of *Martin Bridge: On the Lookout!;* July 26, 2006, review of *Martin Bridge: Blazing Ahead!.*
School Library Journal, May 1, 2005, review of *Martin Bridge: Ready for Takeoff!;* June, 2006, review of *Martin Bridge: On the Lookout!.*

ONLINE

Jessica Scott Kerrin Home Page, http://www.writers.ns.ca/Writers/jkerrin.html (April 4, 2007).

*   *   *

KILLGORE, James 1959-

PERSONAL: Born 1959, in New Orleans, LA; married; children: Emily, Max. *Education:* Louisiana State University, B.S.; New York University, M.S.J.; attended Napier University.

ADDRESSES: Home—Glasgow, Scotland.

CAREER: Editor and novelist. Medical and Dental Defence Union, Glasgow, Scotland, publications editor.

WRITINGS:

Buck Falaya, Polygon (Edinburgh, Scotland), 1995.
The Passage, Peachtree (Atlanta, GA), 2006.

SIDELIGHTS: Born and raised in Louisiana, James Killgore first traveled to the United Kingdom as an undergraduate exchange student. He was later drawn back after earning his master's degree in science journalism. He settled in Edinburgh with his Scottish-born wife. Killgore's primary career has been in medical editing, but in the mid-1990s he ventured into novel writing with the publication of his first work of fiction, *Buck Falaya.* The story centers on two young brothers growing up in Louisiana in the 1960s.

With his second novel, written more than ten years later, Killgore tried his hand at writing for young adults and teens. The idea for *The Passage* came out of an already abandoned epic novel about the American Civil War, for which Killgore had done extensive research. The novel is set in Mississippi during the Civil War, and follows a fifteen-year-old boy who forges his grandfather's signature to enlist in the Confederate Navy, convincing his best friend to do the same. The experience is ultimately devastating and results in tragedy, leading the young man back to his home town with a vastly different outlook on life. The story is "well-told," according to a *Kirkus Reviews* contributor. It was described by Claire Rosser in a review for *Kliatt* as "serious Civil War fiction based on Killgore's careful research" that "thoughtfully examines the meaning of bravery and honor."

BIOGRAPHICAL AND CRITICAL SOURCES:

PERIODICALS

Kirkus Reviews, October 1, 2006, review of *The Passage,* p. 1017.
Kliatt, November 1, 2006, Claire Rosser, review of *The Passage,* p. 12.

ONLINE

Books, Reading, and Writing (BRAW) Web site, http://www.braw.org.uk/ (April 25, 2007), profile and interview with James Killgore.*

*   *   *

KINGSLEY, Kaza

PERSONAL: Born in Cleveland, OH. *Hobbies and other interests:* Traveling, movies.

ADDRESSES: Home—Cincinnati, OH. *E-mail*—kazakingsley@fuse.net.

CAREER: Writer, artist, and singer.

WRITINGS:

Erec Rex: The Dragon's Eye (novel), illustrated by Melvyn Grant, Firelight Press (Cincinnati, OH), 2006.

SIDELIGHTS: In her first fantasy novel, *Erec Rex: The Dragon's Eye,* Kaza Kingsley tells the story of young Erec Rex, who finds a secret door in Grand Central Station that leads to a magical world. Erec is out to save his kidnapped mother whom he can see and speak to anytime he wants through a pair of magic eyeglasses. In the process of trying to rescue his mother and discover the real villains, Erec and his friend Bethany find themselves participating in a series of contests that will decide who will be the rulers of three magical kingdoms. "Entertaining magics and magical gear, along with polished vignettes from Grant, animate familiar fantasy tropes in this seriocomic debut," reported a *Kirkus Reviews* contributor. Other reviewers also had praise for the novel. A contributor to the *Watcher* Web site, for instance, called it "an entertaining book" and added: "The characters are riveting." On the *Fantasy Novel Review* Web site, Sherryl King-Wilds referred to *Erec Rex* as "a fun, fascinating book that makes you want to chill out for a while and just read." Like several other critics, King-Wilds also acknowledged the book's debt to the extremely successful "Harry Potter" fantasy series by J.K. Rowling. Nevertheless, King-Wilds pointed out that "the Harry Potter books may have inspired Kaza Kingsley in writing *The Dragon's Eye,* but this book bloody well stands on its own!"

BIOGRAPHICAL AND CRITICAL SOURCES:

PERIODICALS

Kirkus Reviews, October 1, 2006, review of *Erec Rex: The Dragon's Eye,* p. 1017.

ONLINE

Erec Rex Web site, http://www.erecrex.com (April 19, 2007).
Fantasy Novel Review, http://www.fantasynovelreview. com/ (April 19, 2007), Sherryl King-Wilds, review of *Erec Rex.*
Watcher, http://www.readthewatcher.org/ (April 19, 2007), review of *Eric Rex.*

*   *   *

KIRBY, F.E. 1928-2007
(Frank Eugene Kirby, II)

OBITUARY NOTICE— See index for *CA* sketch: Born April 6, 1928, in New York, NY; died March 24, 2007, in Chicago, IL. Musicologist, educator, and author. A retired Lake Forest College music professor, Kirby was a noted scholar of Richard Wagner. He was a 1950 graduate of Colorado College, after which he earned his doctorate in music history from Yale. During his early career, he worked briefly as a music cataloguer for the Peabody Institute Library and as a visiting or guest professor at the Universities of Virginia and Texas. An assistant professor at West Virginia University from 1961 to 1963, Kirby joined the Lake Forest faculty in 1963. He would remain there until his 1993 retirement. Here he developed the college's first course in jazz music history and was chair of the department for ten years. He was the author of such books as *A Short History of Keyboard Music* (1966) and *Music for Piano: A Short History* (1995); his last book, *Wagner's Themes: A Study in*

Musical Expression (2004), was on his favorite subject. Kirby, who spoke fluent German, was fascinated by eighteenth-and nineteenth-century German composers and was interested in how Wagner used certain themes in relation to characters and emotions. In addition to his academic pursuits, he was also a talented amateur magician and enthusiastic outdoorsman who was still ascending mountain peaks at the age of seventy-two.

OBITUARIES AND OTHER SOURCES:

PERIODICALS

Chicago Tribune, April 2, 2007, Section 3, p. 9.

*   *   *

KIRBY, Frank Eugene, II
   See KIRBY, F.E.

*   *   *

KIRINO, Natsuo 1951-

PERSONAL: Born October 7, 1951, in Kanazawa, Ishikawa, Japan; daughter of an architect father; married, 1975; children: one daughter. *Education:* Law degree.

ADDRESSES: *Home*—Tokyo, Japan.

CAREER: Author. Has also worked as a movie theater film scheduler and as a magazine editor and writer.

AWARDS, HONORS: Edogawa Ranpo Award, 1993, for *Kao ni furikakaru ame;* Mystery Writers of Japan Award, 1998, and Edgar Allan Poe Award nomination for best novel, Mystery Writers of America, 2004, both for *Out;* Naoki Award, 1999, for *Soft Cheeks;* Isumi Kyoka Literary Award, 2004, for *Grotesque;* Shibata Renzaburo Award, 2005, for *Zangyakuki;* Fujinkoron Literary Award, for *Tamamoe!*

WRITINGS:

Kao ni furikakaru ame (title means "Rain Falling on My Face"), Kodansha (Tokyo, Japan), 1993.

Zangyakuki, c. 1995.

Out (novel), translated by Stephen Snyder, Kodansha International (New York, NY), 2003.

Gurotesuku, Bungei Shunju (Japan), 2003, translated by Rebecca Copeland as *Grotesque,* Alfred A. Knopf (New York, NY), 2007.

(With Rod Slemmons) *Love Hotels: The Hidden Fantasy Rooms of Japan* (essays), photographs by Misty Keasler, Chronicle Books (San Francisco, CA), 2006.

Also author of *Soft Cheeks, Tenshi ni misuterareta yoru, Yawaraka na hou,* and *Tamamoe!*

ADAPTATIONS: Several of the author's novels or stories have been adapted for film, including *Tenshi ni misuterareta yoru,* 1999; *Yawaraka na hou,* 2001; *Out,* 2002; and *Tamamoe!,* 2007.

SIDELIGHTS: Although Natsuo Kirino did not begin to write seriously until she was in her forties, the short-story writer and novelist went on to develop a reputation in Japan as an author of unconventional crime stories that not only present a mystery but also offer a critique of Japanese society. *Out,* which won a major Japanese fiction award, was the first novel by Kirino to appear in English. The mystery-thriller revolves around four women who work the night shift at a factory and who decide to help one of the women cover up the strangulation of her husband. Led by the middle-aged Masako Katori, the women soon find themselves involved a tense game of deceit with the police. "The novel tackles disturbing themes: the subjugation of women, domestic abuse and a woman's murder of her husband," reported Hideko Takayama in *Newsweek International.*

While it took six years for *Out* to get published in English, critics followed their Japanese counterparts in appreciating the author. "Skillfully crafted, the novel reveals the frustrations and pressures that drive these women to . . . extreme measures," stated Ron Samul in *Library Journal.* Referring to *Out* as having "the force of a juicy tabloid scandal," *New York Times Book Review* contributor Katherine Wolff went on to write that the author "depicts a bleak subculture where women routinely endure taxing physical labor." Joe Hartlaub, writing on *Bookreporter.com,* commented: "Kirino, as is the case with the best of mystery writ-

ers, combines a strong plot with a canny description of contemporary Japanese mores and culture to make this an unforgettable work."

In her thriller *Grotesque,* Kirino tells the story of a complex case dubbed by the Japanese police and press as the Apartment Serial Murders. After two prostitutes are murdered, Chinese immigrant Zhang Zhe-zhong is arrested and admits to the first killing but denies that he committed the identical second murder. The story of the murders and arrest is told from a variety of perspectives by characters such as Zhang's jealous sister. "This mesmerizing tale of betrayal reveals some sobering truths about Japan's social hierarchy," according to a *Publishers Weekly* critic. An *America's Intelligence Wire* contributor noted: "Kirino's book must be read with caution. Its dark twists easily consume the minds of its readers." Several reviewers also observed that the author once again is presenting a commentary on Japanese society as much as a gripping thriller. For example, a *Canberra Times* writer remarked on how the author's presentation of various views of the murdered womens' lives, as well as that of Zhang's sister, results in a comprehensive sociological view of the women. The reviewer explained: "This gradual, merciless exposure has the dual effect of creating emotional involvement with the characters while placing them in the greater context of Japanese society, so that the narrative becomes something other than the mere dismantling of motives behind a crime." Leigh Anne Vrabel, writing in the *Library Journal,* believed that "readers who enjoy psychological horror tales might well relish . . . Kirino's critique of contemporary Japan."

BIOGRAPHICAL AND CRITICAL SOURCES:

PERIODICALS

America's Intelligence Wire, March 23, 2007, review of *Grotesque.*

Asia Africa Intelligence Wire, July 6, 2003, review of *Out;* July 17, 2004, "Kirino Rejects Mystery Writer Label."

Booklist, July 1, 2003, Carrie Bissey, review of *Out,* p. 1870.

Canberra Times (Canberra, Australia), March 3, 2007, review of *Grotesque.*

Entertainment Weekly, Lori L. Tharps, August 22, 2003, review of *Out,* p. 135.

Guardian (London, England), November 27, 2004, Stephen Poole, review of *Out.*

Kirkus Reviews, June 15, 2003, review of *Out,* p. 836.

Library Journal, June 15, 2003, Ron Samul, review of *Out,* p. 101; March 1, 2007, Leigh Anne Vrabel, review of *Grotesque,* p. 74.

M2 Best Books, November 18, 2003, "Natsuo Kirino's Feminist Crime Thriller Translated into English."

Newsweek International, August 18, 2003, Hideko Vrabel, review of *Out,* p. 50.

New York Times, November 17, 2003, Howard W. French, review of *Out,* p. E1.

New York Times Book Review, Katherine Wolff, August 17, 2003, review of *Out,* p. 16.

Observer (London, England), November 14, 2004, Peter Guttridge, review of *Out.*

Publishers Weekly, May 26, 2003, review of *Out,* p. 52; January 22, 2007, review of *Grotesque,* p. 157.

San Francisco Chronicle, August 17, 2003, Eve Kushner, review of *Out.*

Village Voice, September 17, 2003, Greg Tate, review of *Out.*

ONLINE

Bookreporter.com, http://www.bookreporter.com/ (April 19, 2006), Joe Hartlaub, review of *Out.*

Natsuo Kirino Home Page, http://www.kirino-natsuo. com (April 19, 2007).

USA Today Online, http://www.usatoday.com/ (August 18, 2003), Carol Memmott, review of *Out.**

*   *   *

KLAGES, Ellen 1954-

PERSONAL: Born July 9, 1954, in Columbus, OH. *Education:* University of Michigan, B.A.

ADDRESSES: Home—San Francisco, CA. *E-mail*— ellen@ellenklages.com.

CAREER: Writer. Worked variously as a pinball mechanic, photographer, printer, and proofreader for a hands-on science museum.

AWARDS, HONORS: Nebula Award for best novelette, 2005, for "Basement Magic"; Scott O'Dell Award for Historical Fiction, 2007, for *The Green Glass Sea.*

WRITINGS:

FICTION

The Green Glass Sea (novel), Viking (New York, NY), 2006.

Portable Childhoods (short stories), Tachyon Publications (San Francisco, CA), 2007.

Contributor of short fiction to publications such as *Magazine of Fantasy and Science Fiction, Black Gate,* and *Firebirds Rising,* as well as to numerous anthologies.

NONFICTION

Harbin Hot Springs: Healing Waters, Sacred Land, Harbin Springs Publishing (Middletown, CA), 1991.

(With others) *The Science Explorer: Family Experiments from the World's Favorite Hands-on Science Museum,* Henry Holt (New York, NY), 1996.

(With others) *Exploratorium: A Year of Discoveries,* Chronicle Books (San Francisco, CA), 1997.

(With others) *The Science Explorer Out and About: Fantastic Science Experiments Your Family Can Do Anywhere!,* Henry Holt (New York, NY), 1997.

(With others) *The Brain Explorer (Exploratorium at Home),* Owl Books (New York, NY), 1999.

SIDELIGHTS: Ellen Klages first ventured into professional writing when, as a proofreader working for a hands-on science museum in San Francisco, California, she began working on a series of nonfiction activity books aimed at getting children excited about science. One member of her writing team was a published science fiction author who encouraged Klages to try her hand at writing fiction. She began submitting short stories to various literary magazines, and by 2007 had more than a dozen stories published, including one ("Basement Magic") that was a 2005 Nebula Award winner. Many of Klages's published stories are in the collection *Portable Childhoods,* published in 2007. The book's selections were described variously as "haunting," "great frothy fun," "pure joy," and "just plain funny" by *Green Man Review* contributor Faith J. Cormier.

Klages's first novel, *The Green Glass Sea,* began as a short story of the same title. It takes place during the 1940s at Los Alamos, New Mexico, birthplace of the atomic bomb. Two preteen girls—one a geeky outsider fascinated by inventions, the other nicknamed the "Truck" by classmates she is desperate to impress—live at the compound with their scientist parents. The girls are drawn together through personal tragedy, as the once-theoretical weapon of mass destruction becomes a reality. Roger Sutton described the novel in a review for *Horn Book Magazine* as "an intense but accessible page-turner" in which "history and story are drawn together with confidence." *School Library Journal* reviewer Steven Engelfried wrote: "Clear prose brings readers right into the unusual atmosphere of the secretive scientific community." John Green, a *Booklist* contributor, maintained that Klages's "characters are exceptionally well drawn, and the compelling, unusual setting makes a great tie-in for history classes." "You'd never know this was a first novel from reading it," commented *Magazine of Fantasy and Science Fiction* reviewer Charles De Lint. He added: "Klages writes with a simple assurance, vividly bringing to life the world of the forties."

BIOGRAPHICAL AND CRITICAL SOURCES:

PERIODICALS

Booklist, November 15, 2006, John Green, review of *The Green Glass Sea,* p. 61.
Horn Book Magazine, November-December, 2006, Roger Sutton, review of *The Green Glass Sea,* p. 716.
Magazine of Fantasy and Science Fiction, January 1, 2007, Charles De Lint, review of *The Green Glass Sea,* p. 39.
School Library Journal, November, 2006, Steven Engelfried, review of *The Green Glass Sea,* p. 138.

ONLINE

Ellen Klages Home Page, http://www.ellenklages.com (April 19, 2007).

Green Man Review, http://www.greenmanreview.com/ (April 19, 2007), Faith J. Cormier, review of *Portable Childhoods.**

*   *   *

KLIMASEWISKI, Marshall N. 1966-

PERSONAL: Born 1966, in Hartford, CT. *Education:* Carnegie Mellon University, B.A., 1988; Bowling Green State University, M.F.A.; Boston University, M.A.

ADDRESSES: E-mail—mnklimas@artsci.wustl.edu.

CAREER: During early career, worked as a short-order cook, electrical technician, temporary office worker, and special projects coordinator for WGBH, Boston, MA; has taught creative writing at Bowling Green State University, Emory University, and the University of Hartford; Washington University, St. Louis, MO, writer in residence, 1999—.

AWARDS, HONORS: Cohen Award, *Ploughshares,* 1995, for short story "Snowfield."

WRITINGS:

The Cottagers (novel), W.W. Norton (New York, NY), 2006.

Contributor of short fiction to periodicals, including *Ploughshares, Antioch Review, Quarterly West, ONTHEBUS, Tri-Quarterly, Yale Review, Missouri Review,* and the *New Yorker;* contributor to the anthology *Best American Short Stories.*

SIDELIGHTS: Marshall N. Klimasewiski is the author of short stories, and his debut novel, *The Cottagers,* appeared in 2006. The book tells of two couples who are renting a cabin together on Vancouver Island with the idea of leading a simple existence while they write their respective books. Meanwhile, tensions are high between the locals and the tourists, and teenager Cyrus Coddington comes to town and serves as the catalyst that brings things to a head. A contributor for

Kirkus Reviews called the book "a limp first novel, shallow in its characterizations and lacking narrative energy." However, *Ploughshares* critic Fred Leebron found it "an edgy and compelling story." Steven Heighton described it in the *New York Times Book Review* as a "flawed, complex, intelligent novel," and "a novel of grim insights and troubling pronouncements." Heighton added that one of Klimasewiski's strengths is "his willingness to create a cast of characters who are unlikable in very human ways— and who become less sympathetic as their story unfolds."

BIOGRAPHICAL AND CRITICAL SOURCES:

PERIODICALS

Booklist, June 1, 2006, Bill Ott, review of *The Cottagers,* p. 44.
Kirkus Reviews, April 15, 2006, review of *The Cottagers,* p. 372.
Library Journal, May 1, 2006, Debbie Bogenschutz, review of *The Cottagers,* p. 80.
Ploughshares, fall, 2006, Fred Leebron, review of *The Cottagers.*
Publishers Weekly, March 27, 2006, review of *The Cottagers,* p. 53.

ONLINE

New York Times Book Review Online, http://www.nytimes.com/ (July 30, 2006), Steven Heighton, "Vanishing Point," review of *The Cottagers.*
Washington University Web site, http://artsci.wustl.edu/ (May 15, 2007), faculty profile on Marshall N. Klimasewiski.*

*　　*　　*

KNEE, Jonathan A.

PERSONAL: Education: Boston University, B.A., 1981; Trinity College, Dublin, Ireland, M.Sc., 1984; Stanford Graduate School of Business, M.B.A., 1987; Yale Law School, J.D., 1988.

ADDRESSES: Home—New York, NY. *E-mail*—jk2110@columbia.edu.

CAREER: Investment banker, lawyer, educator, and writer. Officer of Governor, Springfield, IL, governor's fellow, 1981-82; State of Illinois, Chicago, youth services coordinator, 1982-83; Yale University, New Haven CT, acting instructor of economics, 1984-85; Powell, Goldstein, Frazer & Murphy, Washington, DC, attorney, 1988-92; United Airlines, Chicago, senior staff executive for international affairs, 1992-94; Northwestern University School of Law, Chicago, adjunct professor, 1992-94; Goldman Sachs, London, England, and New York, NY, vice president of Communications, Media & Technology Group and head of Publishing Sector, 1994-98; Morgan Stanley, New York, NY, principal of Media group, 1998-99, managing director of Media Group, 1999-2003, Co-Head of Media Group, 2001-03; Columbia Graduate School of Business, New York, NY, adjunct professor of finance and economics, 2001—, director of media program, 2004—; Evercore Partners, New York, NY, senior managing director, 2003—. Has also served on nonprofit boards and in various community programs, including Homeless Children's Tutorial Project, Washington DC, steering committee, 1989-92; Commission on Human Rights, Washington, DC, hearing examiner, 1990-92; Chicago Council of Foreign Relations, Chicago, Committee on Foreign Affairs, 1992-94, Chicago United, Chicago, IL, deacon, 1993-94; New York City Investment Fund, New York, NY, Media and Entertainment Sector Group, 1996—. Also serves on the board of directors of Arts Connection, New York, NY, 2002—, Citizens' Committee for Children of New York, New York, NY, 2002—, Fort Valley State University Foundation, Fort Valley, GA, 2002—, New Alternatives for Children, New York, NY, 2002—, National Women's Law Center, Washington, DC, 2002—, and Yale Law School Fund, New Haven, CT, 2003—.

MEMBER: Phi Beta Kappa.

WRITINGS:

The Accidental Investment Banker: Inside the Decade That Transformed Wall Street, Oxford University Press (New York, NY), 2006.

SIDELIGHTS: Jonathan A. Knee has worked in investment banking and is the author of *The Accidental Investment Banker: Inside the Decade That*

Transformed Wall Street. In an interview on the *OUP-blog* site, the author explained his reason for writing the book: "Over the years as an investment banker and a business school teacher, two related phenomena have always struck me. First, how little the general public understands what investment bankers actually do . . . [and] second, how little investment bankers themselves understand about the historical context of the role that they do play." The author continued: "I wanted to find a way to tell the story of investment banking that had some impact on both of these phenomena."

The Accidental Investment Banker focuses on the operation of two major investment banking firms that the author worked for in the 1990s and early into the twenty-first century: Goldman Sachs and Morgan Stanley. The author explores the role of investment bankers and explains the making and completion of business deals requiring investment banking. The author also has some harsh words for the investment banking industry concerning its loss of integrity and how this has negatively impacted both business and individuals. "He weaves a fascinating tale of his employers and a multibillion-dollar industry," wrote Mary Whaley in *Booklist.* Justin McHenry, writing on the *Blogcritics* Web site, noted: "Knee's ability to bring the characters he's met alive on the page—and his willingness to dish the gossip on how they treated others and were treated themselves in the stormy internal politics of these firms—makes the book more of a page-turner than you'd expect."

BIOGRAPHICAL AND CRITICAL SOURCES:

PERIODICALS

Atlantic Monthly, October, 2006, review of *The Accidental Investment Banker: Inside the Decade That Transformed Wall Street,* p. 126.
Booklist, September 1, 2006, Mary Whaley, review of *The Accidental Investment Banker,* p. 30.
Fortune, July 24, 2006, Nadira Hira, "An Adman and an I-Banker Tell All" (includes brief review of *The Accidental Investment Banker*), p. 190.

ONLINE

Blogcritics, http://blogcritics.org/ (September 18, 2006), Justin McHenry, review of *The Accidental Investment Banker.*

Columbia University Web site, http://www0.gsb.columbia.edu/whoswho/getpub.cfm?pub=1027 (May 17, 2007), author's curriculum vitae.
OUPblog (Oxford University Press USA), http://blog.oup.com/ (August 24, 2006), "A Conversation with Jonathan Knee: Author of *The Accidental Investment Banker.*"*

*   *   *

KOSKO, Bart 1960-

PERSONAL: Born 1960. *Education:* University of Southern California, B.A.; University of California at San Diego, M.A.; University of California at Irvine, Ph.D.; Concord Law School, J.D.

ADDRESSES: Office—Los Angeles, CA. *E-mail*—kosko@usc.edu.

CAREER: Admitted to the State Bar of California. University of Southern California, Los Angeles, professor of electrical engineering.

WRITINGS:

(Editor) *Neural Networks for Signal Processing,* Prentice Hall (Englewood Cliffs, NJ), 1992.
Neural Networks and Fuzzy Systems: A Dynamical Systems Approach to Machine Intelligence, Prentice Hall (Englewood Cliffs, NJ), 1992.
Fuzzy Thinking: The New Science of Fuzzy Logic, Hyperion (New York, NY), 1993.
Fuzzy Engineering, Prentice Hall (Upper Saddle River, NJ), 1997.
Nanotime (science fiction novel), Avon Books (New York, NY), 1997.
The Fuzzy Future: From Society and Science to Heaven in a Chip, Harmony Books (New York, NY), 1999.
(Editor, with Simon Haykin) *Intelligent Signal Processing,* IEEE Press (New York, NY), 2001.
Noise, Viking (New York, NY), 2006.

SIDELIGHTS: A professor of electrical engineering, Bart Kosko is known as one of the pioneer theorists behind the intriguing fuzzy logic theory. This revolutionary idea is used in computer programming and recognizes that reality is not as clear-cut as the traditional binary system of yes/no computer responses allows. Fuzzy logic theory allows calculations to be performed that recognize the gray area between absolutes so that responses might be made based on percentages, such as seventy percent of one thing or thirty percent of another, rather than all or nothing. Kosko's work, while still cutting-edge, is already being used in some of today's technology. For example, it permits camcorders with computer chips to more accurately focus lenses and is used in computerized automatic transmissions in cars to allow them to shift gears more smoothly and efficiently; it may also be used in future artificial intelligence technology. The engineer first published his ideas in *Neural Networks and Fuzzy Systems: A Dynamical Systems Approach to Machine Intelligence.* Not meant for the general reader, the textbook includes mathematical exercises on an accompanying computer disk that are aimed at those who understand linear algebra and advanced calculus. The work explains how to integrate fuzzy logic into neural networks.

Kosko followed this work up with books that are more friendly toward the general reader: *Fuzzy Thinking: The New Science of Fuzzy Logic* and *The Fuzzy Future: From Society and Science to Heaven in a Chip.* The title of *Fuzzy Thinking* might lead one to believe it is a book on sloppy logic, but Kosko patiently explains his ideas, which some critics have observed are based on Eastern ways of thinking rather than on the Aristotelian tradition of the West. "Writing with style and risk, Kosko challenges assumptions," remarked a *Publishers Weekly* critic.

The Fuzzy Future is Kosko's look ahead at the possibilities of a fuzzy logic revolution. The engineer sees it as influencing everything from technology and medicine to politics and art. He even speculates that a computer chip might be developed that could be used to download people's personalities, thus making them immortal. The consequences of this type of engineering might not always be positive for humanity, however, and the author makes "the disturbing prediction that cruise missiles guided by fuzzy logic chips will become so cheap and accurate that attacking an enemy will become more cost-effective than defending against him," reported Jeff Minerd in a *Futurist* review. Minerd went on to comment that much of the text is philosophical, not practical, in nature, and that it will

be enjoyed more by readers who like to indulge in speculation than those "looking for detailed descriptions of future technological marvels." "Fairly demanding, but certain to appeal to readers curious about where leading-edge computer types are headed," commented Mary Carroll in *Booklist.*

Indulging in some speculation himself, Kosko imagined a world influenced by fuzzy logic technology in his first novel, *Nanotime.* The story is about a future world where oil is almost depleted and countries are on the verge of World War III. The hero, John Grant, invents a molecule that will allow hydrogen to be used as an efficient and cheap form of fuel, replacing the need for oil. He soon finds himself to be the rope in an international tug-of-war between those who want to kidnap him for their own use and those who wish to kill him so that their oil reserves do not become worthless. While critics found the concept of the book intriguing, many were not impressed by Kosko's fiction-writing skills. "Kosko's abilities to plot and develop characters aren't equal to his skills at the speculative blackboard," as one *Publishers Weekly* contributor put it, adding that the hero "is thoroughly unpleasant." Robert C. Moore, writing in the *Library Journal,* found the plot "tedious" and that it had a "disappointing finish for such a promising story."

Kosko was back in his element with his next nonfiction work, *Noise.* The book is literally about the concept of noise, which is "defined as any unwanted signal," as one *Science News* writer explained. Noise is usually considered an irritant, something that gets in the way of reception, but Kosko points out that noise can be a good thing at times. For example, when skillfully applied, it can actually be used to enhance signal transmissions. Kosko covers all forms of noise and its issues, including environmental impacts (disturbing the communications of whales, for example) and legal issues (Kosko, a licensed attorney as well as scientist, goes into some depth on such topics as public nuisance laws). *Booklist* contributor David Pitt declared *Noise* "an endlessly fascinating book" by "an engaging writer." "Heady reading from a polymath popularizer," concluded a *Kirkus Reviews* writer, "but exhilarating nonetheless."

BIOGRAPHICAL AND CRITICAL SOURCES:

PERIODICALS

AI Expert, March 1, 1992, review of *Neural Networks and Fuzzy Systems: A Dynamical Systems Ap-*

proach to Machine Intelligence, p. 20; December 1, 1993, review of *Fuzzy Thinking: The New Science of Fuzzy Logic,* p. 41.

American Scientist, May 1, 2000, review of *Fuzzy Future: From Society and Science to Heaven in a Chip,* p. 270.

Booklist, June 1, 1993, review of *Fuzzy Thinking,* p. 1737; August 1, 1999, Mary Carroll, review of *Fuzzy Future,* p. 2003; September 1, 2006, David Pitt, review of *Noise,* p. 30.

Byte, October 1, 1993, review of *Fuzzy Thinking,* p. 50.

Choice, December 1, 1993, review of *Fuzzy Thinking,* p. 619; February 1, 2000, R. Bharath, review of *Fuzzy Future,* p. 1133.

Computing, September 30, 1993, review of *Fuzzy Thinking,* p. 39.

Futurist, October 1, 1999, Jeff Minerd, review of "A Sharp Look at Fuzzy Logic," p. 50.

IEEE Transactions on Neural Networks, March 1, 1993, review of *Neural Networks for Signal Processing,* p. 372.

ISR: Intelligent Systems Report, July 1, 1991, review of *Neural Networks and Fuzzy Systems,* p. 16.

Journal of Economic Dynamics & Control, May 1, 1993, review of *Neural Networks and Fuzzy Systems,* p. 523.

Journal of Public Administration Research and Theory, April 1, 1996, review of *Fuzzy Thinking,* p. 315.

Kirkus Reviews, June 15, 2006, review of *Noise,* p. 618.

Library Journal, June 1, 1993, review of *Fuzzy Thinking,* p. 184; March 1, 1994, review of *Fuzzy Thinking,* p. 55; October 15, 1997, review of *Nanotime,* p. 92; July 1, 1999, Joe J. Accardi, review of *Fuzzy Future,* p. 127.

Nature, June 23, 1994, review of *Fuzzy Thinking,* p. 618; October 12, 2006, P.V.E. McClintock, "Background Buzz," p. 635.

New Scientist, December 3, 1994, review of *Fuzzy Thinking,* p. 46; October 25, 1997, review of *Nanotime,* p. 49.

Publishers Weekly, April 19, 1993, review of *Fuzzy Thinking,* p. 42; September 15, 1997, review of *Nanotime,* p. 51; July 12, 1999, review of *Fuzzy Future,* p. 83.

Quarterly Review of Biology, June 1, 1995, review of *Fuzzy Thinking,* p. 210.

Science Books & Films, July 1, 2000, review of *Fuzzy Future,* p. 167; November 1, 2000, review of *Fuzzy Future,* p. 252.

Science News, August 19, 2006, review of *Noise,* p. 127.

SciTech Book News, September 1, 1991, review of *Neural Networks and Fuzzy Systems,* p. 7; August 1, 1992, review of *Neural Networks for Signal Processing,* p. 34.

Times Higher Education Supplement, August 12, 1994, review of *Fuzzy Thinking,* p. 19.

World Futures, March 1, 1995, review of *Fuzzy Thinking,* p. 71.

ONLINE

Bart Kosko Home Page, http://sipi.usc.edu/~kosko (May 11, 2007).*

*　　*　　*

KUHN, Bowie 1926-2007
(Bowie Kent Kuhn)

OBITUARY NOTICE— See index for *CA* sketch: Born October 28, 1926, in Takoma Park, MD; died of complications from pneumonia, March 15, 2007, in Jacksonville, FL. Attorney and author. Kuhn was best remembered for his years as the commissioner of baseball from 1969 to 1984. A 1947 Princeton graduate who earned his law degree from the University of Virginia in 1950, he worked for the law firm of Wilkie Farr & Gallagher in New York City during the 1950s and 1960s. His law firm, where he was made partner in 1961, was the official firm of the National League, and his work on a 1966 antitrust case involving the Braves drew attention to him. He was selected to succeed William D. Eckert as baseball commissioner in 1969. The next fifteen years proved to be a significant time of transition in professional baseball. Many changes involving players' contracts and negotiating rights, the reorganization of the league, and the influence of broadcast television on the sport meant that Eckert's decisions were closely scrutinized by critics. Eckert would maintain that it was always his intention to retain the integrity of the sport, but his detractors would charge him with everything from being too harsh on players and too willing to bow to team owners, to being too lenient on players and too willing to fine owners. During his two seven-year terms, he oversaw the addition of many expansion teams to the league, the introduction of nighttime games, the reorganization of the league into divisions, and the enormous increase in players' salaries along with their right to become free agents. Many of his decisions evoked both positive and negative reactions. For example, when he initiated night games in 1971, many were appalled by the violation of tradition, but at the same time this brought in considerably more revenue because it allowed for more television and radio coverage. Kuhn could anger players and owners alike. In one incident, he offended Oakland Athletics owner Charles O. Finley by preventing him from trading three players to the Yankees for 2.5 million dollars in a move Finley designed to earn money before the players became free agents. Kuhn also upset slugger Hank Aaron by not showing up to the game where Aaron broke Babe Ruth's home-run record. Adamant that baseball should not be associated with gambling, Kuhn barred Hall of Famers Mickey Mantle and Willie Mays from being associated with the league because they had been hired to promote casinos. Mantle and Mays were later reinstated after Kuhn was replaced by Peter Ueberroth. Kuhn was often distraught by the escalating salaries of baseball players, which he felt would eventually ruin the game, but it was one battle he did not win. After failing to be reelected commissioner, he returned to his old law firm in 1984. He left in 1987 to be a partner with Myerson & Kuhn, but the firm went bankrupt a year later. Moving to Florida, he was president of the Kent Group, Inc., and then of the consulting firm Sports Franchises, Inc., in Connecticut. He wrote about his years as commissioner in *Hardball: The Education of a Baseball Commissioner* (1987).

OBITUARIES AND OTHER SOURCES:

BOOKS

Kuhn, Bowie, *Hardball: The Education of a Baseball Commissioner,* Times Books, 1987.

PERIODICALS

Los Angeles Times, March 16, 2007, p. B8.
New York Times, March 16, 2007, p. A25.
Times (London, England), April 2, 2007, p. 50.

*   *   *

KUHN, Bowie Kent
  See KUHN, Bowie

KUMASHIRO, Kevin K.

PERSONAL: Ethnicity: "Asian American." *Education:* University of Wisconsin—Madison, Ph.D.

ADDRESSES: Office—College of Education, University of Illinois at Chicago Circle, 1040 W. Harrison St., Chicago, IL 60607. *E-mail*—kumashiro@ antioppressiveeducation.org.

CAREER: National Education Association, Washington, DC, senior program specialist in human and civil rights, 2004-06; University of Illinois at Chicago Circle, Chicago, associate professor of education, 2006—. Center for Anti-Oppressive Education, director, 2002—.

AWARDS, HONORS: Gustavus Myers Outstanding Book award, Gustavus Myers Center for the Study of Bigotry and Human Rights, 2003, for *Troubling Education: Queer Activism and Anti-Oppressive Education.*

WRITINGS:

(Editor) *Troubling Intersections of Race and Sexuality: Queer Students of Color and Anti-Oppressive Education,* Rowman & Littlefield (Lanham, MD), 2001.
Troubling Education: Queer Activism and Anti-Oppressive Education, Routledge (New York, NY), 2002.
(Editor) *Restored Selves: Autobiographies of Queer Asian/Pacific American Activists,* Harrington Park Press (New York, NY), 2004.
Against Common Sense: Teaching and Learning toward Social Justice, Routledge (New York, NY), 2004.
(Editor, with Bic Ngo) *Six Lenses for Anti-Oppressive Education: Partial Stories, Improbable Conversations,* Peter Lang (New York, NY), 2007.

Coeditor of special issue, *Race, Ethnicity, and Education,* 2006.

*   *   *

KYLE, Aryn

PERSONAL: Education: Graduate of University of Montana.

ADDRESSES: Home—Missoula, MT.

CAREER: Writer.

AWARDS, HONORS: National Magazine Award for Fiction, for the short story "The Foaling Season."

WRITINGS:

The God of Animals (novel), Scribner (New York, NY), 2007.

Short stories have appeared in periodicals, including the *Atlantic, Georgia Review,* and *StoryQuarterly;* contributor to anthologies, including *Best New American Voices 2005.*

SIDELIGHTS: In her first novel, *The God of Animals,* author Aryn Kyle tells the story of twelve-year-old Alice Winston as she deals with a depressed mother who won't leave the bed, her own feelings over her older sister Nona's elopement with a rodeo cowboy, the drowning death of a classmate in a canal, and the potential loss of the family's horse ranch in Colorado. In the meantime, Alice is also conducting a telephone relationship with her male seventh-grade teacher, Mr. Delmar. "Kyle delivers the story in graceful, translucent prose, while the mood of the book is overwhelmingly bleak and steadily focused on the gathering storm," wrote a *Kirkus Reviews* contributor.

Other reviewers also praised Kyle's debut. *Library Journal* reviewer David Doerrer wrote that *The God of Animals* "brims with a confidence and assuredness atypical of a debut." *Booklist* contributor Keir Graff called the novel "a powerful tale, from a writer with real promise." In addition, several reviewers noted the author's ability at characterization. Francine Prose, writing in *People,* commented that the author "has a gift for creating character, for making even the most minor players in Alice's drama come alive." A *Publishers Weekly* contributor wrote that "Kyle imbues her protagonist with a genuine adolescent voice."

BIOGRAPHICAL AND CRITICAL SOURCES:

PERIODICALS

Booklist, November 15, 2006, Keir Graff, review of *The God of Animals,* p. 29.
Kirkus Reviews, November 1, 2006, review of *The God of Animals,* p. 1095.
Library Journal, December 1, 2006, David Doerrer, review of *The God of Animals,* p. 111.
People, March 26, 2007, Francine Prose, review of *The God of Animals,* p. 49.
Publishers Weekly, October 16, 2006, review of *The God of Animals,* p. 27.
Vogue, March, 2007, Megan O'Grady, review of *The God of Animals,* p. 450.

ONLINE

Aryn Kyle Home Page, http://www.arynkyle.com (May 17, 2007).
LockerGnome Reflections blog, http://www.locker gnome.com/nexus/lockergnome/ (March 31, 2007), review of *The God of Animals.*
Simon & Schuster Web site, http://www.simonsays. com/ (May 17, 2007), brief profile of author.*

L

LAKE, Peter G.

PERSONAL: Education: Clare College, Cambridge, B.A., 1973, Ph.D., 1978.

ADDRESSES: Office—Department of History, Princeton University, 216 Dickinson Hall, Princeton, NJ 08544.

CAREER: University of London, London, England, former instructor; Princeton University, Princeton, NJ, professor of history, 1992—.

WRITINGS:

Moderate Puritans and the Elizabethan Church, Cambridge University Press (New York, NY), 1982, reprinted, 2004.

(Editor, with Marie Dowling) *Protestantism and the National Church in Sixteenth-Century England,* Croom Helm (New York, NY), 1987.

Anglicans and Puritans? Presbyterianism and English Conformist Thought from Whitgift to Hooker, Unwin Hyman (Boston, MA), 1988.

(Editor and author of introduction, with Kevin Sharpe) *Culture and Politics in Early Stuart England,* Stanford University Press (Stanford, CA), 1993.

(Editor, with Michael Questier) *Conformity and Orthodoxy in the English Church, c. 1560-1660* ("Studies in Modern British Religious History" series), Boydell Press (Rochester, NY), 2000.

The Boxmaker's Revenge: Orthodoxy, Heterodoxy, and the Politics of the Parish in Early Stuart London, Stanford University Press (Stanford, CA), 2001.

(With Michael Questier) *The Antichrist's Lewd Hat: Protestants, Papists, and Players in Post-Reformation England,* Yale University Press (New Haven, CT), 2002.

(Editor and contributor, with Thomas Cogswell and Richard Cust) *Politics, Religion, and Popularity in Early Stuart Britain: Essays in Honour of Conrad Russell,* Cambridge University Press (New York, NY), 2002.

Contributor to books, including *Puritanism: Transatlantic Perspectives on a Seventeenth-Century Anglo-American Faith,* edited by Francis J. Bremer, Massachusetts Historical Society (Boston, MA), 1993.

SIDELIGHTS: Peter G. Lake is a historian whose special interests are Tudor-and Stuart-era British history and the Church during the reign of the Tudors. In *Culture and Politics in Early Stuart England,* Lake and fellow editor Kevin Sharpe provide a series of essays discussing the relationship between culture and politics in Stuart England. For example, one essay focuses on the writings of Ben Jonson within a cultural and political context while another essay examines the political aspects of architecture at that time. "The editors' introduction in particular is essential reading for historians of early Stuart politics," wrote Richard Cust in the *English Historical Review.* Cust went on to call *Culture and Politics in Early Stuart England* "a very important collection which should do much to define a fresh agenda for the study of early Stuart politics."

Lake also edited, with Michael Questier, *Conformity and Orthodoxy in the English Church, c. 1560-1660.* The volume's various essays focus on how to distinguish the differences between "religious history" as opposed to the more narrowly focused church history. "The strength of this collection is to be found not only in its essays but also in its editorial shaping," wrote Lori Anne Ferrell in *Church History*. Ferrell also noted: "There's not a weak essay in the book." *Journal of Ecclesiastical History* contributor Arnold Hunt commented: "This is the second volume in a promised series, Studies in Modern British Religious History, and if future volumes live up to the high standard of this one, university libraries would be well advised to place a standing order for the whole series."

In *The Boxmaker's Revenge: Orthodoxy, Heterodoxy, and the Politics of the Parish in Early Stuart London*, Lake, according *History: Review of New Books* contributor Alice Tobriner, writes about "the communal contentiousness between a cleric and a layman living out the heterodoxy-orthodoxy conundrum of early Stuart London."The focus of this contention was Stephen Dennison, an orthodox preacher, and John Etherington, an artisan who went to prison for heresy. The author uses the two-decades-long verbal battle that ensued between these two men to illustrate the debate over church reform. Writing in the *Journal of British Studies*, Paul S. Seaver called *The Boxmaker's Revenge* "a vehicle for exploring the nature of early Stuart Puritanism." Critics generally praised the book for its insights. "This substantive investigation of parochial politics is . . . a dynamic narrative about popular opinion in flux," wrote Tobriner. *Journal of Ecclesiastical History* contributor William Lamont concluded: "This is a brilliant book which only Peter Lake could have written."

Lake collaborated with Michael Questier to write *The Antichrist's Lewd Hat: Protestants, Papists, and Players in Post-Reformation England*. The book focuses on how various groups—from Protestants, Catholics, and Puritans to the press and popular stage groups—used for their own ideological and commercial purposes the extremely popular, lurid pamphlets about murders printed in Tudor England at the time. The book includes prints from various woodcuts that were used to illustrate the pamphlets. In a review for *History Today*, David G. Chandler felt that *The Antichrist's Lewd Hat* contains "many insights, revelations and conclusions" and also described the volume as "teeming, energetic and perceptive." Leah S. Marcus, writing in the *Journal of British Studies*, further reflected: "If Peter Lake's book requires an outrageous amount of effort on the part of readers who may struggle to make their way through its densely packed pages, it also provides, at its best, ample rewards in terms of a supple, labile methodology for dealing in a historically responsible way with the complexity of cultural dissonance and ambiguity."

Lake, along with Thomas Cogswell and Richard Cust, also served as editor of and contributor to *Politics, Religion, and Popularity in Early Stuart Britain: Essays in Honour of Conrad Russell*. The book's various essays, according to *Journal of Ecclesiastical History* contributor Michael Questier, focus "on the considerable impact which Conrad Russell's own work has made on the field of early modern and, particularly, civil war historiography." *Albion* contributor Eric Josef Carlson remarked that Russell "certainly deserves, if anyone does, a volume of essays in his honor, and this is a volume worthy of its honoree."

BIOGRAPHICAL AND CRITICAL SOURCES:

PERIODICALS

Albion, fall, 2002, David Cressy, review of *The Boxmaker's Revenge: Orthodoxy, Heterodoxy, and the Politics of the Parish in Early Stuart London*, p. 479; summer, 2003, Susan Wabuda, review of *The Antichrist's Lewd Hat: Protestants, Papists, and Players in Post-Reformation England*, p. 280; spring, 2004, Eric Josef Carlson, review of *Politics, Religion and Popularity in Early Stuart Britain: Essays in Honour of Conrad Russell*, p. 124.

American Historical Review, December, 1989, Marvin A. Breslow, review of *Anglicans and Puritans? Presbyterianism and English Conformist Thought from Whitgift to Hooker*, pp. 1368-1369.

British Book News, November, 1982, James Atkinson, review of *Moderate Puritans and the Elizabethan Church*, p. 670.

Canadian Journal of History, December, 2002, Ian Gentles, review of *The Boxmaker's Revenge*, p. 530.

Catholic Historical Review, April, 2002, Keith Lindley, review of *The Boxmaker's Revenge*, pp. 363-364.

Choice, June, 1988, D.P. King, review of *Protestantism and the National Church in Sixteenth-Century England*, p. 1572; July, 1988, D.P. King, review of *Anglicans and Puritans?*, p. 1711; November, 2002, A. Kugler, review of *The Antichrist's Lewd Hat*, p. 542.

Church History, December, 2002, Lori Anne Ferrell, review of *Conformity and Orthodoxy in the English Church, c. 1560-1660,* p. 899; March, 2004, Cecile Zinberg, review of *The Boxmaker's Revenge,* p. 215.

English Historical Review, April, 1985, Christopher Haigh, review of *Moderate Puritans and the Elizabethan Church,* pp. 348-350; October, 1990, Claire Cross, review of *Protestantism and the National Church in Sixteenth-Century England,* p. 1021; April, 1991, Christopher Haigh, review of *Anglicans and Puritans?,* pp. 456-457; June, 1996, Richard Cust, review of *Culture and Politics in Early Stuart England,* p. 713; February, 2003, Christopher Haigh, review of *The Antichrist's Lewd Hat,* p. 147; September, 2003, Ivan Roots, review of *Politics, Religion, and Popularity in Early Stuart Britain,* p. 997.

Historical Journal, September, 1991, Nichols Tyacke, reviews of *Protestantism and the National Church in Sixteenth-Century England* and *Anglicans and Puritans?,* pp. 743-754.

History: Review of New Books, fall, 2001, Alice Tobriner, review of *The Boxmaker's Revenge,* p. 19.

History Today, December, 2002, David G. Chandler, review of *The Antichrist's Lewd Hat,* p. 54.

Journal of British Studies, April, 1996, John Kenyon, review of *Culture and Politics in Early Stuart England,* pp. 262-269; April, 2004, Paul S. Seaver, review of *The Boxmaker's Revenge,* p. 266; October 2004, Leah S. Marcus, review of *The Antichrist's Lewd Hat,* p. 514.

Journal of Ecclesiastical History, July, 2002, Arnold Hunt, review of *Conformity and Orthodoxy in the English Church, c. 1560-1660,* p. 609; January, 2003, William Lamont, review of *The Boxmaker's Revenge,* p. 174; January, 2004, Michael Questier, review of *Politics, Religion, and Popularity in Early Stuart Britain,* p. 195.

London Review of Books, September, 2002, Patrick Collinson, review of *The Antichrist's Lewd Hat,* pp. 15-16.

Religious Studies Review, October, 1983, Keith L. Sprunger, review of *Moderate Puritans and the Elizabethan Church,* p. 386.

Renaissance Quarterly, autumn, 2002, Stephen L. Collins, review of *Conformity and Orthodoxy in the English Church, c. 1560-1660,* pp. 1102-1106; fall, 2004, Renee Bricker, review of *Politics, Religion and Popularity in Early Stuart Britain,* p. 1124.

Review of English Studies, May, 1996, David Loewenstein, review of *Culture and Politics in Early Stuart England,* p. 244.

Sixteenth Century Journal, summer, 1996, Paul E.J. Hammer, review of *Culture and Politics in Early Stuart England,* pp. 602-604; fall, 2001, Dale Walden Johnson, review of *Conformity and Orthodoxy in the English Church, c. 1560-1660,* pp. 797-798.

Times Literary Supplement, September 3, 1982, Claire Cross, review of *Moderate Puritans and the Elizabethan Church,* p. 954; July 5, 2002, Euan Cameron, review of *The Antichrist's Lewd Hat,* p. 32.

ONLINE

Princeton University History Department Web site, http://his.princeton.edu/ (April 19, 2007), faculty profile of author.*

*   *   *

LAVENE, Jim
(Joye Ames, a joint pseudonym, Elyssa Henry, a joint pseudonym)

PERSONAL: Married Joyce Lavene (an author), c. 1971; children: Christopher, Jennifer, Emily. *Hobbies and other interests:* Music, photography, line drawing, taking road trips.

ADDRESSES: Home—Midland, NC. *E-mail*—jim@joyceandjimlavene.com.

CAREER: Writer. Also teaches writing workshops. Has worked as a computer specialist.

MEMBER: Romance Writers of America, Mystery Writers of America, Carolina's Romance Writers.

AWARDS, HONORS: Master's Choice award (with Joyce Lavene), for best first mystery novel.

WRITINGS:

(Under pseudonym Elyssa Henry; with wife, Joyce Lavene) *A Family for the Sheriff,* Silhouette Romance (Don Mills, Ontario, Canada), 1999.

(With Joyce Lavene) *Paper Roses* (novel), Southern Charm Press (Hampton, GA), 2003.

(With Joyce Lavene) *Kiss the Past Goodbye* (novel), Southern Charm Press (Hampton, GA), 2003.

(With Joyce Lavene) *The Everything Guide to Writing a Novel: From Completing the First Draft to Landing a Book Contract—All You Need to Fulfill Your Dreams* (nonfiction), Adams Media (Avon, MA), 2004.

(With Joyce Lavene) *Swapping Paint: A Stock Car Racing Mystery,* Midnight Ink (Woodbury, MN), 2007.

Also contributor to periodicals and e-zines, including *Writers Weekly.*

"SHERIFF SHARYN HOWARD" MYSTERY SERIES; WITH JOYCE LAVENE

Last Dance, Avalon Books (New York, NY), 1999.

One Last Good-Bye, Avalon Books (New York, NY), 2000.

The Last to Remember, Avalon Books (New York, NY), 2001.

Until Our Last Embrace, Avalon Books (New York, NY), 2001.

Dreams Don't Last, Avalon Books (New York, NY), 2002.

For the Last Time, Avalon Books (New York, NY), 2002.

Last Fires Burning, Avalon Books (New York, NY), 2003.

Glory's Last Victim, Avalon Books (New York, NY), 2004.

Last One Down, Avalon Books (New York, NY), 2004.

Last Rites, Avalon Books (New York, NY), 2004.

Before the Last Lap, Avalon Books (New York, NY), 2005.

The First Shall Be Last, Avalon Books (New York, NY), 2007.

NOVELS; WITH JOYCE LAVENE; UNDER JOINT PSEUDONYM JOYE AMES

If Not for You, Avalon Books (New York, NY), 1999.

Only You, Avalon Books (New York, NY), 1999.

A Time for Love, Avalon Books (New York, NY), 1999.

Save Your Heart for Me, Avalon Books (New York, NY), 2000.

The Dowager Duchess, Avalon Books (New York, NY), 2002.

Madison's Miracles, Avalon Books (New York, NY), 2004.

"PEGGY LEE GARDEN" MYSTERY SERIES; WITH JOYCE LAVENE

Pretty Poison, Berkley Prime Crime (New York, NY), 2005.

Fruit of the Poisoned Tree, Berkley Prime Crime (New York, NY), 2006.

Poisoned Petals, Berkley Prime Crime (New York, NY), 2007.

"E-BOOKS"; WITH JOYCE LAVENE

Flowers in the Night, Awe-Struck E-Books, 1999.

Mask of the Stranger, Awe-Struck E-Books, 2000.

'Till There Was You, Awe-Struck E-Books, 2001.

Still the One, Awe-Struck E-Books, 2001.

Two of Hearts, Awe-Struck E-Books, 2002.

The Singing Trees, Awe-Struck E-Books, 2002.

Alternative Diabetic (nonfiction), Awe-Struck E-Books, 2002.

Chrysalis, Awe-Struck E-Books, 2003.

Treasures of the Heart, Awe-Struck E-Books, 2003.

Constant Craving, Awe-Struck E-Books, 2004.

Amelia Gallant, Awe-Struck E-Books, 2004.

Heart of Shadows, Awe-Struck E-Books, 2005.

Paper Roses, Awe-Struck E-Books, 2005.

SIDELIGHTS: For sidelights on Jim Lavene, see *CA* entry on Joyce Lavene.

BIOGRAPHICAL AND CRITICAL SOURCES:

PERIODICALS

Booklist, February 15, 2005, Sue O'Brien, review of *Last One Down,* p. 1065; August 1, 2005, Sue O'Brien, review of *Before the Last Lap,* p. 2000.

Kirkus Reviews, March 1, 2007, review of *Swapping Paint: A Stock Car Racing Mystery,* p. 197.

Library Journal, August 1, 2002, Rex Klett, review of *For the Last Time,* p. 150.

MBR Bookwatch, April 1, 2005, review of *Pretty Poison.*

Publishers Weekly, November 26, 2001, "December Publications," includes review of *Until Our Last Embrace,* p. 43.

ONLINE

Author Network, http://www.author-network.com/ (April 19, 2007), biography of Jim Lavene.

Avalon Books, http://www.avalonbooks.com/ (October 8, 2004), biographical information on Joyce and Jim Lavene.

Awe-Struck E-Books, http://www.awe-struck.net/ (October 8, 2004), interview with Joyce and Jim Lavene, and descriptions of e-books.

Best Reviews, http://thebestreviews.com/ (April 19, 2007), Harriet Klausner, review of *Pretty Poison,* and Dawn Dowdle, review of *Pretty Poison.*

Carolina Conspiracy, http://www.carolinaconspiracy. com/ (April 19, 2007), brief profile of Jim Lavene.

EscapetoRomance.com, http://www.escapetoromance. com/ (April 19, 2007), Elena Channing, review of *Save Your Heart for Me.*

Fallen Angel Reviews, http://www.fallenangelreviews. com/ (April 19, 2007), review of *Last One Down.*

Ivy Quill, http://www.ivyquill.com/ (April 19, 2007), Randi Bradford, review of *Still the One,* Sally G. Laturi, review of *Mask of the Stranger,* and Cindy Vallar, reviews of *'Till There Was You, Until Our Last Embrace,* and *The Last to Remember.*

Joyce and Jim Lavene Home Page, http://www. joyceandjimlavene.com (April 19, 2007).

Love Romances, http://www.loveromances.com/ (October 8, 2004), "An Interview with Jim and Joyce Lavene."

Nascar Mystery Web site, http://www.nascarmysteries. com (April 19, 2007).

New Mystery Reader.com, http://www. newmysteryreader.com/ (April 19, 2007), Susan Illis, review of *Before the Last Lap.*

Peggy Lee Garden Mystery Web site, http://www. peggyleegardenmysteries.com (April 19, 2007).

Road to Romance, http://www.roadtoromance.ca/ (August 16, 2004), Jennifer Ray, review of *Madison's Miracles.*

Romantic Times, http://www.romantictimes.com/ (April 19, 2007), Pamela B. Cohen, review of *A Family for the Sheriff,* and Deborah Brent, review of *Save Your Heart for Me.*

Roundtable Reviews, http://www.roundtablereviews. com/ (April 19, 2007), Pam Bless, review of *Constant Craving,* Tracy Farnsworth, reviews of *Fruit of the Poisoned Tree* and *Pretty Poison,* Deb Jones, review of *Glory's Last Victim,* and Josie de Dios, review of *Treasures of the Heart.*

Sharyn Howard Mystery Web site, http://www. sharynhowardmysteries.com/ (April 19, 2007).*

*   *   *

LAVENE, Joyce
   (Joye Ames, a joint pseudonym, Elyssa Henry, a joint pseudonym)

PERSONAL: Married Jim Lavene (a computer specialist and author), c. 1971; children: Christopher, Jennifer, Emily. *Hobbies and other interests:* Watercolor painting, sculpting, alternative medicine, gardening, photography, taking road trips.

ADDRESSES: Home—Midland, NC. *E-mail*—joyce@ joyceandjimlavene.com.

CAREER: Writer.

MEMBER: Romance Writers of America, Mystery Writers of America.

AWARDS, HONORS: Master's Choice award (with Jim Lavene), for best first mystery novel.

WRITINGS:

(Under pseudonym Elyssa Henry; with husband, Jim Lavene) *A Family for the Sheriff,* Silhouette Romance (Don Mills, Ontario, Canada), 1999.

(With Jim Lavene) *Paper Roses* (novel), Southern Charm Press (Hampton, GA), 2003.

(With Jim Lavene) *Kiss the Past Goodbye* (novel), Southern Charm Press (Hampton, GA), 2003.

(With Jim Lavene) *The Everything Guide to Writing a Novel: From Completing the First Draft to Landing a Book Contract—All You Need to Fulfill Your Dreams* (nonfiction), Adams Media (Avon, MA), 2004.

(With Jim Lavene) *Swapping Paint: A Stock Car Racing Mystery,* Midnight Ink (Woodbury, MN), 2007.

Also contributor to periodicals and e-zines, including *Writers Weekly.*

"SHERIFF SHARYN HOWARD" MYSTERY SERIES; WITH JIM LAVENE

Last Dance, Avalon Books (New York, NY), 1999.

One Last Good-Bye, Avalon Books (New York, NY), 2000.

The Last to Remember, Avalon Books (New York, NY), 2001.

Until Our Last Embrace, Avalon Books (New York, NY), 2001.

Dreams Don't Last, Avalon Books (New York, NY), 2002.

For the Last Time, Avalon Books (New York, NY), 2002.

Last Fires Burning, Avalon Books (New York, NY), 2003.

Glory's Last Victim, Avalon Books (New York, NY), 2004.

Last One Down, Avalon Books (New York, NY), 2004.

Last Rites, Avalon Books (New York, NY), 2004.

Before the Last Lap, Avalon Books (New York, NY), 2005.

The First Shall Be Last, Avalon Books (New York, NY), 2007.

NOVELS; WITH JIM LAVENE; UNDER JOINT PSEUDONYM JOYE AMES

If Not for You, Avalon Books (New York, NY), 1999.

Only You, Avalon Books (New York, NY), 1999.

A Time for Love, Avalon Books (New York, NY), 1999.

Save Your Heart for Me, Avalon Books (New York, NY), 2000.

The Dowager Duchess, Avalon Books (New York, NY), 2002.

Madison's Miracles, Avalon Books (New York, NY), 2004.

"PEGGY LEE GARDEN" MYSTERY SERIES; WITH JIM LAVENE

Pretty Poison, Berkley Prime Crime (New York, NY), 2005.

Fruit of the Poisoned Tree, Berkley Prime Crime (New York, NY), 2006.

Poisoned Petals, Berkley Prime Crime (New York, NY), 2007.

"E-BOOKS"; WITH JIM LAVENE

Flowers in the Night, Awe-Struck E-Books, 1999.

Mask of the Stranger, Awe-Struck E-Books, 2000.

'Till There Was You, Awe-Struck E-Books, 2001.

Still the One, Awe-Struck E-Books, 2001.

Two of Hearts, Awe-Struck E-Books, 2002.

The Singing Trees, Awe-Struck E-Books, 2002.

Alternative Diabetic (nonfiction), Awe-Struck E-Books, 2002.

Chrysalis, Awe-Struck E-Books, 2003.

Treasures of the Heart, Awe-Struck E-Books, 2003.

Constant Craving, Awe-Struck E-Books, 2004.

Amelia Gallant, Awe-Struck E-Books, 2004.

Heart of Shadows, Awe-Struck E-Books, 2005.

Paper Roses, Awe-Struck E-Books, 2005.

SIDELIGHTS: Husband-and-wife team Joyce and Jim Lavene have collaborated on numerous mystery and romance novels, including the "Peggy Lee Garden" and "Sheriff Sharyn Howard" mystery series. The latter series of books takes place in North Carolina in the Uwharrie Mountains. The novels feature Howard, the female sheriff of the small town of Diamond Springs, as she simultaneously solves a mystery from the past along with a current murder. For example, *The Last to Remember* features the murder of a wealthy citizen who confesses to killing a young boy forty years ago after the body has recently been recovered. Writing on the *Ivy Quill* Web site, Cindy Vallar commented that the authors "have created a wonderful cast of characters that make for a most engaging murder mystery." Vallar added: "The twists and turns . . . will keep readers intrigued, compelling them to turn the page until the puzzle is solved." In *Before the Last Lap,* the Lavenes present Howard trying to clear her assistant Trudy and her husband of the murder of a racecar driver named Duke Beatty. In the meantime, Howard is also trying to discover the truth behind the death of her father years ago. Sue O'Brien, writing in *Booklist,* appreciated the novel's "likable characters, fast pacing, and an intriguing subplot."

The "Peggy Lee Garden" mysteries feature widow and botanist Peggy Lee, a Charlotte, North Carolina, resident who owns and operates the Potting Shed. In the first book in the series, *Pretty Poison*, Peggy finds a man's body in the back of her store. The victim's head has been bashed in with one of her shovels. When a homeless man that Peggy has befriended is arrested for the crime, Peggy sets out to prove him innocent. She is soon faced with the possibility that the dead man was killed by one of her own clerks, Keely Prinz, who had become pregnant after having an affair with the man. Referring to the mystery as a "charming story," an *MBR Bookwatch* contributor added: "This mystery will appeal to men and women of all ages as *Pretty Poison* is a great tale." *Fruit of the Poisoned Tree* finds Peggy looking into the death of a close friend who supposedly committed suicide by driving off a bridge. "The blend of romance, mystery, and botany blend into a fascinating and hard to put down tale," according to Tracy Farnsworth on the *Roundtable Reviews* Web site.

The couple have also started a mystery series that features mysteries taking place at various NASCAR race tracks across the country. The first book in the series, *Swapping Paint: A Stock Car Racing Mystery,* revolves around the murder of the NASCAR racer Ricky Sanders, who was universally disliked. As a result, suspects abound, including an ex-girlfriend who bore his child and another race-car driver, Bobby Furr, with whom Sanders had an accident on the race track. Although Furr is the primary suspect and has something to hide, his brother-in-law, Glad, a retired homicide detective, sets out to find the real killer. "Racing buffs will like this latest from the Lavenes," assured a *Kirkus Reviews* contributor.

BIOGRAPHICAL AND CRITICAL SOURCES:

PERIODICALS

Booklist, February 15, 2005, Sue O'Brien, review of *Last One Down,* p. 1065; August 1, 2005, Sue O'Brien, review of *Before the Last Lap,* p. 2000.

Kirkus Reviews, March 1, 2007, review of *Swapping Paint: A Stock Car Racing Mystery,* p. 197.

Library Journal, August 1, 2002, Rex Klett, review of *For the Last Time,* p. 150.

MBR Bookwatch, April 1, 2005, review of *Pretty Poison.*

Publishers Weekly, November 26, 2001, "December Publications," includes review of *Until Our Last Embrace,* p. 43.

ONLINE

Author Network, http://www.author-network.com/ (April 19, 2007), biography of Jim Lavene.

Avalon Books, http://www.avalonbooks.com/ (October 8, 2004), biographical information on Joyce and Jim Lavene.

Awe-Struck E-Books, http://www.awe-struck.net/ (October 8, 2004), interview with Joyce and Jim Lavene, and descriptions of e-books.

Best Reviews, http://thebestreviews.com/ (April 19, 2007), Harriet Klausner, review of *Pretty Poison,* and Dawn Dowdle, review of *Pretty Poison.*

Carolina Conspiracy, http://www.carolinaconspiracy. com/ (April 19, 2007), brief profile of Jim Lavene.

EscapetoRomance.com, http://www.escapetoromance. com/ (April 19, 2007), Elena Channing, review of *Save Your Heart for Me.*

Fallen Angel Reviews, http://www.fallenangelreviews. com/ (April 19, 2007), review of *Last One Down.*

Ivy Quill, http://www.ivyquill.com/ (April 19, 2007), Randi Bradford, review of *Still the One,* Sally G. Laturi, review of *Mask of the Stranger,* and Cindy Vallar, reviews of *'Till There Was You, Until Our Last Embrace,* and *The Last to Remember.*

Joyce and Jim Lavene Home Page, http://www. joyceandjimlavene.com (April 19, 2007).

Love Romances, http://www.loveromances.com/ (October 8, 2004), "An Interview with Jim and Joyce Lavene."

Nascar Mystery Web site, http://www.nascarmysteries. com (April 19, 2007).

New Mystery Reader.com, http://www.newmystery reader.com/ (April 19, 2007), Susan Illis, review of *Before the Last Lap.*

Peggy Lee Garden Mystery Web site, http://www. peggyleegardenmysteries.com (April 19, 2007).

Road to Romance, http://www.roadtoromance.ca/ (August 16, 2004), Jennifer Ray, review of *Madison's Miracles.*

Romantic Times, http://www.romantictimes.com/ (April 19, 2007), Pamela B. Cohen, review of *A Family for the Sheriff,* and Deborah Brent, review of *Save Your Heart for Me.*

Roundtable Reviews, http://www.roundtablereviews. com/ (April 19, 2007), Pam Bless, review of *Constant Craving,* Tracy Farnsworth, reviews of *Fruit of the Poisoned Tree* and *Pretty Poison,* Deb Jones, review of *Glory's Last Victim,* and Josie de Dios, review of *Treasures of the Heart.*

Sharyn Howard Mystery Web site, http://www. sharynhowardmysteries.com/ (April 19, 2007).*

LEAR, Jonathan

PERSONAL: Education: Yale University, B.A., 1970; University of Cambridge, B.A., 1973, M.A., 1976; Rockefeller University, Ph.D., 1978; graduate of Western New England Institute of Psychoanalysis, 1995.

ADDRESSES: Office—Committee on Social Thought, University of Chicago, 1130 E. 59th St., Chicago, IL 60637. *E-mail*—jlear@midway.uchicago.edu.

CAREER: Philosopher, psychoanalyst, educator, and writer. University of Cambridge, Cambridge, England, Trinity Hall, research fellow, 1977-78, Clare College, fellow, 1979-85, assistant lecturer in philosophy, 1979-82, lecturer in philosophy, 1982-85; Yale University, New Haven, CT, assistant professor, 1978-79, associate professor, 1985-86, professor of philosophy, 1986-95, chair of the department of philosophy, 1988-90, Kingman Brewster Professor of the Humanities, 1995-96; University of Chicago, Chicago, IL, John U. Nef Distinguished Service Professor at the Committee on Social Thought and in the Department of Philosophy, 1996—. Also served as faculty member at the Chicago Institute for Psychoanalysis, Western New England Institute for Psychoanalysis, and New York University Institute for Psychoanalysis.

AWARDS, HONORS: Mellon Fellowship, 1970-72; Robert Greene Cup, Clare College, 1973, for academic distinction; research fellowship, Trinity Hall, 1977-78; National Endowment for the Humanities fellowship, 1984-85; John Simon Guggenheim Memorial Fellowship, 1987-88; Gradiva Award, National Association for Psychoanalysis, 1995, for best article on the subject of psychoanalysis for "The Shrink Is In," 1998, for best psychoanalytic book for *Open Minded,* 2000, for best psychoanalytic book for *Happiness, Death, and the Remainder of Life;* Heinz Hartmann Award, New York Psychoanalytic Institute, 1992, for best psychoanalytic publication for *Love and Its Place in Nature;* Eric T. Carlson Award for Outstanding Contribution to the History of Psychiatry, Department of Psychiatry, Cornell Medical School, 2004.

WRITINGS:

NONFICTION

Aristotle and Logical Theory, Cambridge University Press (New York, NY), 1980.

Aristotle: The Desire to Understand, Cambridge University Press (New York, NY), 1988.

Love and Its Place in Nature: A Philosophical Interpretation of Freudian Psychoanalysis, Farrar, Straus (New York, NY), 1990.

Open Minded: Working Out the Logic of the Soul, Harvard University Press (Cambridge, MA), 1998.

Happiness, Death, and the Remainder of Life, Harvard University Press (Cambridge, MA), 2000.

Therapeutic Action: An Earnest Plea for Irony, Other Press (New York, NY), 2003.

Freud, Routledge (New York, NY), 2005.

Radical Hope: Ethics in the Face of Cultural Devastation, Harvard University Press (Cambridge, MA), 2006.

SIDELIGHTS: Jonathan Lear is a philosophy professor whose primary interest is in the philosophical conceptions of the human psyche from Socrates to the present. He is also the author of several books looking both at philosophy and psychology. The author interprets Freudian psychoanalysis in his book *Love and Its Place in Nature: A Philosophical Interpretation of Freudian Psychoanalysis.* Placing his examination firmly within the realm of philosophy, Lear examines love as a force integral to human nature and the root of Freudian theory. *Publishers Weekly* reviewer Genevieve Stuttaford called *Love and Its Place in Nature* a "heartfelt and scholarly treatise."

In *Open Minded: Working Out the Logic of the Soul,* Lear examines the field of psychology via the thinking of philosophers such as Plato and Wittgenstein, as well as the writings of Freud and others in the field of psychoanalysis. According to the author, psychoanalysis is an inheritor of the ancient Greeks' efforts to examine the mind and that philosophy and psychoanalysis should come together in an effort to be open-minded when it comes to inquiring into the human "soul." "On the whole, the book gives the reader much occasion for thought, reflection, and an appreciation of the open-mindedness that has led its author to the serious consideration of the interminable questions which, for reflective human beings, not merely for members of our 'profession,' are, as Socrates and Freud would doubtless agree, both impossible and necessary," wrote Robert Rethy in the *Review of Metaphysics.*

Happiness, Death, and the Remainder of Life stems from a three-part lecture on human values that Lear gave at Harvard University. In the book, the author explores psychoanalysis and whether or not it really makes a difference in people's lives and in their overall understanding of life. The author touches upon such topics as happiness and death as he explores Freud's theory of the unconscious and the philosophy of Aristotle. "In the end, Lear ties the ideas of these two rather different thinkers together in a cogent . . . way," wrote a *Publishers Weekly* contributor. Richard Rorty, writing in the *New York Times Book Review*, referred to the book as "daring and provocative" and also wrote that "his book will excite the interest of anyone who has ever been bowled over by either of those two men."

In his book *Freud*, Lear looks at the life and career of the father of psychoanalysis, Sigmund Freud, and compares Freud with modern psychoanalysts. According to the author, today's psychoanalysts differ greatly from Freud in that they have little interest in the mysteries of human life or in art, culture, and religion as a part of nature. Lear's 2006 book, *Radical Hope: Ethics in the Face of Cultural Devastation*, looks at the Crow Indian nation's demise in the early twentieth century as Lear ponders the way in which cultures are unable to comprehend their potential devastation, which he calls their "blind spot." The author explores how the disappearance of the buffalo affected the Crows' psychology and played an important role in the attack on their culture. He also considers the writings of philosophers such as Plato and Aristotle in terms of cultural demise. Deborah Donovan, writing in *Booklist*, noted that the book is "relevant to mainstream readers . . . [because of] his application of the blind-spot hypothesis to the present." *Library Journal* contributor Scott Duimstra called the book "engaging" and went on to write that the author "creatively uses philosophical ideas to explain" the changes the Crow had to undergo.

BIOGRAPHICAL AND CRITICAL SOURCES:

PERIODICALS

American Imago, winter, 2003, Elliot L. Jurist, review of *Happiness, Death, and the Remainder of Life*.

American Journal of Psychoanalysis, September, 1999, Mathew Tolchin, review of *Open Minded: Working Out the Logic of the Soul*, p. 291.

American Journal of Psychotherapy, fall, 1999, Carl Goldberg, review of *Love and Its Place in Nature: A Philosophical Interpretation of Freudian Psychoanalysis;* fall, 1999, Richard D. Chessick, review of *Open Minded*.

American Journal of Sociology, July, 2006, Jeffrey Prager, "Beneath the Surface of the Self: Psychoanalysis and the Unseen Known," p. 276.

Ancient Philosophy, spring, 2002, Barbara Hannan, review of *Happiness, Death, and the Remainder of Life*.

Booklist, September 1, 2006, Deborah Donovan, review of *Radical Hope: Ethics in the Face of Cultural Devastation*, p. 23.

Choice, May, 2001, J. Gough, review of *Happiness, Death, and the Remainder of Life*, p. 1640.

Christian Century, November 2, 1988, review of *Aristotle: The Desire to Understand*, p. 994; March 20, 1991, Don Browning, review of *Love and Its Place in Nature*, p. 340.

Christian Science Monitor, April 20, 1988, review of *Aristotle*, p. 21.

Cross Currents, fall, 2001, James E. Giles, review of *Happiness, Death, and the Remainder of Life*.

Ethics, July, 1990, review of *Aristotle*, p. 917; July, 1990, Scott G. Schreiber, review of *Aristotle*, p. 917.

Greece & Rome, April, 1989, Richard Wallace, review of *Aristotle*, p. 122.

Isis, June, 1989, R.J. Hankinson, review of *Aristotle*, p. 306.

Journal of Philosophy, May, 1999, Maria Cavell, review of *Open Minded*, p. 263.

Journal of the History of Philosophy, April 1, 1991, Robert Friedman, review of *Aristotle*, p. 301.

Library Journal, October 1, 1990, Paul Hymowitz, review of *Love and Its Place in Nature*, p. 105; July 1, 2006, Scott Duimstra, review of *Radical Hope*, p. 80.

Mind, October, 2001, Elijah Millgram, review of *Love and Its Place in Nature*, p. 1087; October, 2004, Grant Gillett, review of *Therapeutic Action: An Earnest Plea for Irony*, p. 769.

Mnemosyne, spring, 1992, David T. Runia, review of *Aristotle*.

New Leader, July 15, 1991, Michael Kott, review of *Love and Its Place in Nature*, p. 19.

New York Times, December 13, 1990, Christopher Lehmann-Haupt, review of *Love and Its Place in Nature*, p. 20; August 3, 1998, Christopher Lehmann-Haupt, review of *Open Minded*, p. 6; November 4, 2000, Dinitia Smith, "Returning to Freud for Help with the Riddles of Philosophy; Jonathan Lear Believes Psychology Provides a Way to Rethink Life's Most Profound Issues," p. 13.

New York Times Book Review, October 22, 2000, Richard Rorty, review of *Happiness, Death, and the Remainder of Life,* p. 14.

Philosophical Quarterly, April, 2001, Sebastian Gardner, review of *Open Minded,* p. 254.

Philosophical Review, July, 1991, Richard Kraut, review of *Aristotle,* p. 522.

Philosophy, April, 1989, D.W. Hamlyn, review of *Aristotle,* p. 262.

Philosophy of the Social Sciences, December, 2000, Joseph Agassi, "How Ignoring Repeatability Leads to Magic," p. 528.

Publishers Weekly, August 17, 1990, Genevieve Stuttaford, review of *Love and Its Place in Nature,* p. 59; August 21, 2000, review of *Happiness, Death, and the Remainder of Life,* p. 60.

Quarterly Journal of Speech, August, 1989, Robert W. Smith, review of *Aristotle,* p. 381.

Reference & Research Book News, November, 2003, review of *Therapeutic Action,* p. 8; November, 2005, review of *Freud.*

Review of Metaphysics, December, 2000, Robert Rethy, review of *Open Minded,* p. 449.

Teaching Philosophy, September, 2006, Jeffrey M. Jackson, review of *Freud,* p. 272.

Times Educational Supplement, April 17, 1992, Anthony Clare, review of *Love and Its Place in Nature,* p. 22.

Times Literary Supplement, September 9, 1988, Julia Annas, review of *Aristotle,* p. 998; March 1, 1991, Robert Brown, review of *Love and Its Place in Nature,* p. 22; January 8, 1999, Liam Hudson, review of *Open Minded,* p. 9; December 8, 2000, Andrew Stark, review of *Happiness, Death and the Remainder of Life,* p. 12; June 4, 2004, Sebastian Gardner, review of *Therapeutic Action,* p. 26; January 6, 2006, Andrew Scull, "Disciples of the Couch," p. 25; December 22, 2006, Terry Eagleton, review of *Radical Hope,* p. 32.

Virginia Law Review, March, 2000, Anne C. Dailey, review of *Open Minded,* p. 349.

Wilson Quarterly, spring, 1999, review of *Open Minded.*

ONLINE

University of Chicago Chronicle Web site, http://chronicle.uchicago.edu/ (November 16, 2000), Arthur Fournier, "Q&A with . . . Jonathan Lear."

University of Chicago Department of Philosophy Web site, http://philosophy.uchicago.edu/ (May 17, 2007), faculty profile of author and author's curriculum vitae.*

*　　　*　　　*

LEAVY, Jane

PERSONAL: Married.

ADDRESSES: Home—Washington, DC.

CAREER: New York Daily News, New York, NY, sports reporter, c. 1970s-1980s; *Washington Post,* Washington, DC, sports writer.

WRITINGS:

Squeeze Play (novel), Doubleday (New York, NY), 1990.

Sandy Koufax: A Lefty's Legacy (biography), HarperCollins (New York, NY), 2002.

SIDELIGHTS: Sports and feature writer Jane Leavy is the author of the comic novel *Squeeze Play.* Like Leavy, the novel's heroine, A.B. (Ariadne Bloom) Berkowitz, is a sports journalist, and in the novel she is covering the then-mythical expansion team the Washington Senators. The book is presented in the form of A.B.'s journal, as she writes about the challenges of being a woman sports writer, including ballplayers who try variously to gross her out or seduce her. A.B.'s troubles are compounded by the fact that her editor wants scoops no matter how she gets them, plus her boyfriend is cheating on her. "*Squeeze Play* is loosely inspired by my experiences in the locker room," Leavy told Al Dente in an interview on the *Bronx Banter* Web site. Leavy went on to note: "Now in *Squeeze Play,* the character in question, A.B. Berkowitz, has a different experience than mine. She is much more hassled and much, much more horrified. Her experience is far more difficult than my own was. That's why I say it's loosely autobiographical."

Squeeze Play received praise from many critics. David Hiltbrand, for one, stated in *People* that "this is not just a diamond fantasy but a real novel, with digressions into journalism, politics and religion." Several reviewers warned that the novel contains potentially offensive language and scenes but that they are all presented in a humorous vein. In a review in *Publishers Weekly*, for example, Sybil Steinberg commented that "this tale . . . will delight readers willing to accept a healthy dose of vulgarity with their humor."

Leavy's next book, *Sandy Koufax: A Lefty's Legacy*, is a biography of the famous Los Angeles Dodgers Hall-of-Fame pitcher. Although Koufax has remained largely reclusive since his retirement from baseball in the 1960s when he was thirty due to arm troubles, the pitcher agreed to tangentially cooperate with Leavy for her biography. He did, however, refuse to have any interviews with him personally go "on the record." In her *Bronx Banter* interview with Dente, Leavy explained that "this is a book about him as a ballplayer, and about the time in which he lived and how he dominated it." The author added: "It was never intended to be an exposé."

Once again, Leavy struck a chord with the critics. The "book affords a lucid examination of arguably major league baseball's all-time greatest southpaw pitcher," wrote R.C. Cottrell in the *Library Journal*. Several reviewers also observed that the book is more than a mere baseball biography. For example, Daniel Okrent, writing in *Time*, commented that the author "has hit it out of the park" with her biography, pointing out that the book is "a consideration of how we create our heroes, and how this hero's self-perception distinguishes him from nearly every other great athlete in living memory." Referring to the book as a "marvellous sociocultural biography," *Catholic New Times* contributor Ted Schmidt declared it "fascinating."

BIOGRAPHICAL AND CRITICAL SOURCES:

PERIODICALS

Biography, spring, 2003, Allen Barra, review of *Sandy Koufax: A Lefty's Legacy*, p. 367.
Book, September-October, 2002, Adam Langer, "Pitcher in the Rye," p. 18.
Booklist, September 1, 2002, Wes Lukowsky, review of *Sandy Koufax*, p. 41; September 1, 2003, Bill Ott, "Top 12 Sports Nonfiction," p. 41.

Catholic New Times, May 18, 2003, Ted Schmidt, review of *Sandy Koufax*, p. 18.
Coach and Athletic Director, January, 2003, Herman L. Masin, review of *Sandy Koufax*, p. 10.
Commentary, October, 2002, J. Bottum, "Achilles on the Mound," p. 74.
Economist, October 19, 2002, review of *Sandy Koufax*.
Kirkus Reviews, September 1, 2002, review of *Sandy Koufax*, p. 1284.
Library Journal, September 15, 2002, R.C. Cottrell, a review of *Sandy Koufax*, p. 68; March 15, 2003, Cliff Glaviano, review of *Sandy Koufax*, p. 133; April 15, 2004, Cliff Glaviano, review of *Squeeze Play*, p. 147.
Los Angeles Times Book Review, May 27, 1990, Keith Tuber, "I Don't Care If We Never Get Back," pp. 1, 7.
New York Times Book Review, April 22, 1990, Merrill Perlman, review of *Squeeze Play*, p. 24; October 13, 2002, Allen Barra, "Artful Dodger, Damn Yankee: Sandy Koufax Was a Role Model, Mickey Mantle, an Anti-Role Model," p. 18.
People, May 14, 1990, David Hiltbrand, review of *Squeeze Play*, p. 32.
Publishers Weekly, February 16, 1990, Sybil Steinberg, review of *Squeeze Play*, p. 68; August 19, 2002, review of *Sandy Koufax*, p. 79.
Time, September 30, 2002, Daniel Okrent, "A Prince of a Pitcher," p. 92.
Women's Review of Books, July, 1990, Mariah Burton Nelson, "Striking Out," p. 36.

ONLINE

BookPage, http://www.bookpage.com/ (April 20, 2007), Ron Kaplan, review of *Sandy Koufax*.
Bronx Banter, http://www.all-baseball.com/bronx banter/ (August 20, 2003), Al Dente, "Bronx Banter Interview: Jane Leavy."
Online NewsHour, http://www.pbs.org/newshour/ (October 21, 2002) Terence Smith, "Conversation: Lefty's Legacy."*

*   *   *

LE BRETON-MILLER, Isabelle

PERSONAL: Born in Montreal, Quebec, Canada; married Danny Miller (a research professor). *Education:* University of Montreal, B.B.A., 1986, M.Sc., 1996.

ADDRESSES: Home—Montreal, Quebec, Canada. *Office*—University of Alberta, Edmonton, Alberta, Canada. *E-mail*—lebreton@generation.net.

CAREER: University of Montreal, Montreal, Quebec, Canada, researcher at HEC Montreal (business school), 1987-97, conference administrator, 1995-97; National Bank of Canada, Montreal, assistant to director of personnel for Montreal region, 1997-98; Generation Net, Montreal, director of administration and human resources, 1998-99; McKinsey and Co., Boston, MA, external consultant in organizational design, 2000-01; University of Alberta, Edmonton, Alberta, Canada, senior research associate, 2001—. Guest speaker at business conferences and universities.

WRITINGS:

(With D. Miller) *Managing for the Long Run: Lessons in Competitive Advantage from Great Families Businesses,* Harvard Business School Publishing (Boston, MA), 2005.

Managing for the Long Run has been translated into Japanese, Italian, Spanish, Chinese, and Korean.

Contributor to books, including *The Family Business Research Handbook,* edited by P.Z. Poutziouris, K.X. Smyrnios, and S.B. Klein, Edward Elgar Publishing (Northampton, MA), 2006; *Advances in Strategic Management: Strategy and Ecology,* edited by J. Baum and others, JAI Elsevier (Oxford, England), 2006; and *2005 Kellogg Family Business Conference: Best Practices & New Ideas,* edited by L.E. Shefsky and J.L. Ward, Duff & Phelps (Evanston, IL), 2005. Contributor to periodicals, including *Strategic Organization, Family Business Review, Entrepreneurship Theory and Practice, Leader to Leader, Long Range Planning, Families in Business, Journal of Business Venturing, Journal of Management Studies, Journal of Corporate Finance,* and *Journal of Management Inquiry.* Member of editorial board, *Business Horizons,* 2005—, and *Entrepreneurship Theory and Practice,* 2007—.

*   *   *

LEE, Rebecca Hagan

PERSONAL: Married. *Education:* College graduate.

ADDRESSES: Home—GA. *E-mail*—rhaganlee@yahoo.com.

CAREER: Author. Has also worked in radio and television and as a genealogical library assistant and pet groomer.

AWARDS, HONORS: Waldenbooks award, 1992, for *Golden Chances.*

WRITINGS:

ROMANCE FICTION

Homespun Mother's Day, Berkley/Diamond (New York, NY), 1994.
Taking Chances, Diamond (New York, NY), 1994.
Gossamer, Berkley/Jove (New York, NY), 1999.
Whisper Always, Berkley/Jove (New York, NY), 1999.
A Hint of Heather, Berkley/Jove Seduction (New York, NY), 2000.

Also contributor to the anthology *Talk of the Ton,* Jove (New York, NY), 2005.

"JORDAN-ALEXANDER FAMILY" SERIES; ROMANCE NOVELS

Golden Chances, Berkley/Diamond Homespun (New York, NY), 1992.
Harvest Moon, Berkley/Diamond Homespun (New York, NY), 1993.
Something Borrowed, Berkley/Diamond Homespun (New York, NY), 1995.

"MARQUESS OF TEMPLESTON'S HEIRS" SERIES; ROMANCE NOVELS

Once a Mistress, Berkley/Jove (New York, NY), 2001.
Ever a Princess, Berkley/Jove (New York, NY), 2002.
Always a Lady, Berkley/Jove (New York, NY), 2002.

"FREE FELLOWS LEAGUE" SERIES; ROMANCE NOVELS

Barely a Bride, Berkley Sensation (New York, NY), 2003.

Merely the Groom, Berkley Sensation (New York, NY), 2004.

Hardly a Husband, Berkley Sensation (New York, NY), 2004.

Truly a Wife, Berkley Sensation (New York, NY), 2005.

SIDELIGHTS: Rebecca Hagan Lee writes historical romances in which, as described on the author's Web site, the "heroines get their men and help them become ideal husbands, lovers, friends and fathers." In *Ever a Princess,* the second book in the "Marquess of Templeston's Heirs" series, Lee's Victorian heroine is a princess who flees after her parents are killed in a coup. While hiding in Scotland, she meets and falls in love with American Adam McKendrick, the new owner of the lodge where she is staying. In *Always a Lady,* an American man who inherits an earldom in Ireland falls in love with someone he promised to marry when she was an orphan. The novel is the final book in the "Marquess of Templeston's Heirs" series, which *Booklist* contributor John Charles called "a charmingly clever romance deftly seasoned with wit and graced with some delightfully unforgettable characters." *Truly a Wife* is part of the author's "Free Fellows League" series. The story tells of the love between a French smuggler, who is a member of the Free Fellows League, and the Amazonian-like Miranda. In a review in *MBR Bookwatch,* a contributor commented: "The story line is exciting and is character driven, a trademark of this series."

In addition to another series titled the "Jordan-Alexander Family" series, the author has also written several stand-alone romances. In *Gossamer,* Lee tells the story of Elizabeth Sadler, who develops a hatred for the Chinese after discovering that her brother died in an opium den. When she is hired by James Cameron Craig to be a governess for his adopted daughters, Elizabeth is shocked to find out that they are all of Chinese origin. As the novel progresses, Elizabeth falls in love with both the children and James as she overcomes her own prejudices and James's heartbreaking past. "Warmth, love, tenderness and humanity fill the pages to overflowing in another beautifully rendered romance" by the author, wrote Kathe Robin on the *Romantic Times* Web site. *Romance Reader* contributor Bev Hill called *Gossamer* "delightful" and went on to note: "My hat's off to the mind of this author, for creating a vision I'll be happy to entertain for a good long while."

Whisper Always features Christina Fairfax, who tries to escape from a highest-bidder marriage to the Hapsburg Prince Rudolph and, in the process, falls in love with her London escort, Blake Ashford. Kathe Robin, once again writing for *Romantic Times,* called the novel "a sophisticated, fascinating romance that brings readers into a glittering world and a thrilling romance." In *A Hint of Heather,* Lee features Lady Jessalyn, laird of the Scottish Clan MacInnes, which has come upon hard times because of the war with the British. Looking for a husband for Lady Jessalyn, the clan kidnaps Neil Claremont, English Earl of Dared, a man who finds himself falling for Lady Jessalyn despite his hatred of Scotland. *Romantic Times* critic Robin stated that the author "captures the allure of Scotland through the eyes of her memorable characters."

BIOGRAPHICAL AND CRITICAL SOURCES:

PERIODICALS

Booklist, February 1, 2002, John Charles, review of *Ever a Princess,* p. 928; October 15, 2002, John Charles, review of *Always a Lady,* p. 395; September 15, 2004, John Charles, review of *Hardly a Husband,* p. 220.

MBR Bookwatch, April, 2005, review of *Truly a Wife.*

Publishers Weekly, January 14, 2002, review of *Ever a Princess,* p. 46.

ONLINE

Best Reviews, http://thebestreviews.com/ (August 31, 2001), Harriet Klausner, review of *Once a Mistress;* (January 9, 2002), Janice Bennett, review of *Ever a Princess;* (September 15, 2002), Harriet Klausner, review of *Always a Lady;* (July 14, 2003), Suzanne Tucker, review of *Barely a Bride;* (March 10, 2004), Suzanne Tucker, review of *Merely the Groom;* (September 10, 2004), Harriet Klausner, review of *Hardly a Husband;* (March 25, 2005), Harriet Klausner, review of *Truly a Wife;* (April 29, 2005), Sharon Galligar Chance, review of *Talk of the Ton.*

Rebecca Hagan Lee Home Page, http://www.rhaganlee.com (April 20, 2007).

Romance Reader, http://theromancereader.com/ (April 20, 2007), Bev Hill, review of *Gossamer,* and Nancy J. Silberstein, review of *Whisper Always.**

Romantic Times, http://www.romantictimes.com/ (April 20, 2007), Kathe Robin reviews of *A Hint of Heather, Always a Lady, Barely a Bride, Ever a Princess, Gossamer, Merely the Groom, Truly a Wife,* and *Whisper Always,* and Joan Hammond, review of *Once a Mistress.**

*   *   *

LEIGH, Tamara

PERSONAL: Married; husband's name David; children: Skyler and Maxen. *Education:* Master's degree. *Hobbies and other interests:* Volunteer work, faux painting, and reading.

ADDRESSES: Home—Nashville, TN. *E-mail*—tamaraleigh@comcast.net.

CAREER: Writer. Formerly worked as a speech pathologist.

WRITINGS:

ROMANCE NOVELS

Warrior Bride, Bantam (New York, NY), 1994.
Virgin Bride, Bantam (New York, NY), 1994.
Saxon Bride, Bantam (New York, NY), 1995.
Pagan Bride, Bantam (New York, NY), 1995.
Misbegotten, HarperCollins (New York, NY), 1996.
Unforgotten, HarperCollins (New York, NY), 1997.
Blackheart, Leisure Books (New York, NY), 2001.
Stealing Adda, NavPress (Colorado Springs, CO), 2006.
Perfecting Kate, Multnomahr Publishers (Colorado Springs, CO), 2007.

SIDELIGHTS: Tamara Leigh made a name for herself as a historical romance writer and later began incorporating her strong beliefs concerning the Christian faith into her tales of romance. In one of her earlier novels, *Saxon Bride,* Leigh tells the story of Maxen Pendery, who sets out to seek revenge for the murder of his brother Thomas, supposedly by Rhiannyn, a Saxon girl who was to wed Thomas, albeit unwillingly. However, Rhiannyn declares her in-nocence, and soon the reluctant Maxen comes to believe her. "With a deft pen Tamara Leigh draws you into a passionate tale ablaze with vibrant characters and tumultuous emotions," wrote Lizabelle Cox on the *Romantic Times* Web site. *Pagan Bride* takes place in the fifteenth century harems of the Ottoman Empire and features Alessandra and English captive Lucien De Gautier. Kathe Robin, writing on the *Romantic Times* Web site, commented that the author once again "combines a hot headed pair of lovers with smoldering sexual tension, an enthralling backdrop then adds a dash of adventure."

In *Unforgotten,* Leigh tells a romantic tale based on time travel. Collier Marrow loses his beloved Aryn Viscott but discovers a 500-year-old painting of Catherine Algeron, who supposedly fought and died for the ill-fated Lancaster King Henry. Astounded by the resemblance to his dead lover, Collier inspects the painting closely and is sent plunging into the past to get a second chance at love. "Ms. Leigh makes her characters human and lovable, and her ending utterly satisfying," wrote Cyndie Dennis-Greer on the *Romantic Times* Web site. "This is definitely a 'keeper.'"

Blackheart features the strange tale of Lord Bernart Kinthrope, who sends his wife Julianna to sleep with Gabriel de Vere. Lord Bernart is unable to make his wife pregnant, and Gabriel is the man who made Lord Bernart sterile. In his twisted mind, Lord Bernart believes that his wife becoming pregnant by Gabriel will allow him to seek revenge by taking Gabriel's child. However, complications arise when Julianna is kidnapped by Gabriel and love blooms between the two. Anne Bulin, writing on the *Romantic Reader* Web site, called *Blackheart* "a good read, a definite page turner that was difficult to put down."

Leigh turns from historical romance to a modern tale in *Stealing Adda.* Adda Sinclair is a *New York Times* best-selling author whose husband deserted her. To further complicate matters, Adda is suffering from writer's block. However, when she meets the publisher Nick Farnsworth, she begins to see a way to save her career. Bev Huston, writing on the *Romantic Times* Web site, called *Stealing Adda* "a hilarious, though sometimes scandalous, look at the world of publishing."

Perfecting Kate is a Christian romance fiction featuring Kate Meadows, who narrates her own story of a tough life that she has tried to overcome by various self-improvement methods, including cosmetic procedures. Along the way Kate meets a serious love interest and learns some valuable lessons about what is important in life. A *Publishers Weekly* contributor noted that "Kate's love-hate relationship with a series of cosmetic procedures makes for a fun read."

BIOGRAPHICAL AND CRITICAL SOURCES:

PERIODICALS

Library Journal, April 1, 2006, Tamara Butler, review of *Stealing Adda,* p. 74.
Publishers Weekly, November 20, 2006, review of *Perfecting Kate,* p. 35.

ONLINE

Christianbook.com, http://www.christianbook.com/ (May 18, 2007), brief profile of author.
Romance Reader, http://www.theromancereader.com/ (May 18, 2007), Anne Bulin, review of *Blackheart.*
Romantic Times, http://www.romantictimes.com/ (May 18, 2007), Cyndie Dennis-Greer, reviews of *Unforgotten* and *Perfecting Kate,* Bev Huston, review of *Stealing Adda,* Lizabelle Cox, review of *Saxon Bride,* Kathe Robin, review of *Pagan Bride,* Maria C. Ferrer, review of *Misbegotten,* and Gabrielle Pantera, review of *Blackheart.*
Tamara Leigh Home Page, http://www.tamaraleigh. com (May 18, 2007).*

*   *   *

LOCKFORD, Lesa 1958-

PERSONAL: Born June 1, 1958, in Salt Lake City, UT; daughter of Joyce Lockford (an educator); married Stephen Bond (divorced, 1991). *Ethnicity:* "Anglo-European." *Education:* University of California, Los Angeles, B.A. (magna cum laude), 1980; Royal Academy of Dramatic Art, acting diploma, 1983; California State University, Northridge, M.A. (with distinction), 1993; Southern Illinois University at Carbondale, Ph.D., 1998. *Politics:* Democrat.

ADDRESSES: Home—Toledo, OH. *Office*—Department of Theatre and Film, Bowling Green State University, 228 South Hall, Bowling Green, OH 43403. *E-mail*—lockflo@bgnet.bgsu.edu.

CAREER: Professional actress on stage, film, television, and radio, 1983-90; Centenary College of Louisiana, Shreveport, assistant professor of theater, speech, and dance, 1998-2000, holder of Mattie Allen Broyles chair, 1998-99; Bowling Green State University, associate professor of theater, specializing in acting, voice, and performance studies, 2000—. Moving Target Theatre Company, London, England, cofounder and joint artistic director, 1984-88; British Council, tour officer for drama and dance, 1987-88; also stage director. Performances as an actress include appearances in training programs; producer and performer, *Alone and on Stage: An Evening of Solo Performances,* Kilpatrick Auditorium, Shreveport, 1999, 2000; also conference participant. Antelope Valley College, adjunct instructor, 1993.

MEMBER: National Communication Association, Americas RADA Network, British Actors' Equity Association, Central States Communication Association, International Congress of Qualitative Inquiry.

WRITINGS:

(And producer and director) *Sacred Monster* (play), produced at Studio Theater, California State University (Northridge, CA), 1992.
(And director and performer) *What's a Nice Commodity Like You Doing in a Spectacle Like This* (play), produced at Quigley Auditorium, Southern Illinois University at Carbondale, 1995.
(And director) *Blood/Lust* (play), produced at Marion Kleinau Theater, Southern Illinois University at Carbondale, 1996.
(With others; and performer) *Overexposed* (play), produced at Marion Kleinau Theater, Southern Illinois University at Carbondale, 1996.
(With others; and performer) *Censor* (stage performance), produced at Marion Kleinau Theater, Southern Illinois University at Carbondale, 1997.
Performing Femininity: Rewriting Gender Identity, AltaMira Press (Walnut Creek, CA), 2004.
(And performer) *in/habit/us* (solo show), produced in Returning Artists Program, Southern Illinois University at Carbondale, 2004.

Contributor to books, including *Ethnographically Speaking: Autoethnography, Literature, and Aesthetics,* edited by Carolyn Ellis and Arthur P. Bochner, AltaMira Press (Walnut Creek, CA), 2001. Contributor of articles and reviews to periodicals, including *Theatre Annual, Theatre Topics, Qualitative Inquiry, Text ad Performance Quarterly, On Stage Studies, Women's Studies in Communication,* and *Studies in Symbolic Interaction.* Member of editorial board, *Liminalities: A Journal of Performance Studies;* member of review editorial board, *Text and Performance Quarterly,* 2000—.

BIOGRAPHICAL AND CRITICAL SOURCES:

PERIODICALS

Forum: Qualitative Social Research, March, 2006, Mary Gergen, review of *Performing Femininity: Rewriting Gender Identity.*

*   *   *

LOCKHART, Zelda

PERSONAL: Children: one daughter, one son. *Education:* Graduated from Norfolk State University and Old Dominion University.

ADDRESSES: Home—Hillsborough, NC. *E-mail*—fifthbornnovel@aol.com.

CAREER: Author. Has worked as a director of a cultural center, a human resources trainer, an editor, and a grant writer.

WRITINGS:

Fifth Born (novel), Atria Books (New York, NY), 2002.
Cold Running Creek (novel), LaVenson Press (Hillsborough, NC), 2006.
The Evolution (novella), USAToday.com, 2006.

Contributor of essays, poetry, and fiction to periodicals, including *Sinister Wisdom, Sojourner, Calyx,* and *WordWrights.*

SIDELIGHTS: Zelda Lockhart is a novelist, poet, essayist, and community activist from Hillsborough, North Carolina. Her first novel, *Fifth Born,* tells the story of an African American girl who endures unimaginable abuses at the hands of her parents and finds an unlikely savior in a long-lost relative. It is Lockhart's hope, as shared in an interview with *Lambda Book Report* contributor Riggin Waugh, that the book "speaks to something inside people, makes them hunger for the truth, makes folks think about the women they love, and the amazing acts of heroism that may be unspoken there." Waugh went on to comment: "Lyrical, poignant, and powerful, *Fifth Born* explores how secrets can tear families apart and unravel people's lives." *O: The Oprah Magazine* reviewer Lisa Shea remarked: "Lockhart's mastery of sensory detail—the tastes, smells, sounds, and sights of Odessa's world—roots us moment to moment in the hardscrabble life of this transcendent tale." Lockhart's protagonist, wrote a contributor to *Kirkus Reviews,* is "possessed of a keen perception that brings the hazy memories of childhood into sharp relief," part of what makes the book an "impressively mature piece of work." "The narrative is straightforward and lyrical," wrote a *Publishers Weekly* reviewer, "Odessa's voice is believable and the evolution of her character in the face of overwhelming alienation is as engaging as it is heartbreaking."

Lockhart's second book has roots in her personal family history—she discovered that her maternal great-grandmother was Native American, of Choctaw descent. Extensive research led Lockhart to the realization that relations between African Americans and Native Americans during the nineteenth century were complicated at best and violent at worst; racism was rampant and slavery was not uncommon. *Cold Running Creek* is a fictional work based on facts uncovered during Lockhart's research, and follows three generations of African American and Native American women.

BIOGRAPHICAL AND CRITICAL SOURCES:

PERIODICALS

Kirkus Reviews, June 1, 2002, review of *Fifth Born,* p. 770.
Lambda Book Report, February-March, 2003, Riggin Waugh, "Amazing Acts of Heroism: Riggin Waugh Interviews Zelda Lockhart," p. 6.

O: The Oprah Magazine, August, 2002, Lisa Shea, "Biblio: From Our Shelf to Yours," p. 76.

Publishers Weekly, July 29, 2002, review of *Fifth Born,* p. 53.

ONLINE

Zelda Lockhart Home Page, http://www.zeldalockhart. com (April 25, 2007).

*   *   *

LOWITT, Richard 1922-

PERSONAL: Born February 25, 1922, in New York, NY; son of Eugene and Eleanor Lowitt; married Suzanne Catharine Carson, September, 1953; children: Peter Carson, Pamela Carson Bennett. *Education:* City College of New York, B.S.S.; Columbia University, M.A., 1945, Ph.D., 1950.

ADDRESSES: Home—Norman, OK.

CAREER: Writer and educator. University of Maryland, College Park, instructor, 1948-52; University of Rhode Island, Kingston, assistant professor, 1952-53; Connecticut College, New London, faculty member, 1953-66, professor of history, 1966; Florida State University, Tallahassee, professor of history, 1966-68; University of Kentucky, Lexington, 1968-77; Iowa State University, Ames, professor, 1977-89, chairman of the department of history, 1977-87; University of Oklahoma, Norman, professor, 1990-97; University of Science and Arts of Oklahoma, Chickasha, regents professor, 1998.

MEMBER: Agricultural History Society (president, 1991-92), American Historical Association, Southern Historical Association, Western History Association (board of editors, 1986), Organization of American Historians (board of editors, 1985-87).

AWARDS, HONORS: John Simon Guggenheim Foundation fellow, 1957; National Endowment for the Humanities fellow, 1974; Gaspar Pérez de Villagrá Award, Historical Society of New Mexico, 1993; Muriel H. Wright Award, Oklahoma Historical Society, 1995 and 2006.

WRITINGS:

A Merchant Prince of the Nineteenth Century, William E. Dodge, Columbia University Press (New York, NY), 1952.

George W. Norris: The Making of a Progressive, 1861-1912, Greenwood Press (Westport, CT), 1963.

The Truman-MacArthur Controversy, Rand McNally (Chicago, IL), 1967.

George W. Norris: The Persistence of a Progressive, 1913-1933, University of Illinois Press (Urbana, IL), 1971.

(Editor, with Joseph F. Wall) *Interpreting Twentieth-Century America: A Reader,* Crowell (New York, NY), 1973.

George W. Norris: The Triumph of a Progressive, 1933-1944, University of Illinois Press (Urbana, IL), 1978.

America in Depression and War, Forum Press (St. Louis, MO), 1979.

Journal of a Tamed Bureaucrat: Nils A. Olsen and the BAE, 1925-1935, Iowa State University Press (Ames, IA), 1980.

(Editor, with Maurine Beasley) *One Third of a Nation: Lorena Hickok Reports on the Great Depression,* University of Illinois Press (Urbana, IL), 1981.

(Compiler, with Robert E. Burke) *The New Era and the New Deal, 1920-1940,* Harlan Davidson (Arlington Heights, IL), 1981.

The New Deal and the West, Indiana University Press (Bloomington, IN), 1984.

Letters from an American Farmer: The Eastern European and Russian Correspondence of Roswell Garst, Northern Illinois University Press (Dekalb, IL), 1987.

(Editor, with Judith Fabry) *Henry A. Wallace's Irrigation Frontier: On the Trail of the Corn Belt Farmer, 1909,* University of Oklahoma (Norman, OK), 1991.

Bronson M. Cutting: Progressive Politician, University of New Mexico Press (Albuquerque, NM), 1992.

Politics in the Postwar American West, University of Oklahoma Press (Norman, OK), 1995.

Fred Harris: His Journey from Liberalism to Populism, Rowman & Littlefield Publishers (Lanham, MD), 2002.

(With Valerie Sherer Mathes) *The Standing Bear Controversy: Prelude to Indian Reform,* University of Illinois Press (Urbana, IL), 2003.

American Outback: The Oklahoma Panhandle in the Twentieth Century, Texas Tech University Press (Lubbock, TX), 2006.

(Editor, with Carolyn G. Hanneman) Elmer Thomas, *Forty Years a Legislator,* University of Oklahoma Press (Norman, OK), 2007.

SIDELIGHTS: Richard Lowitt is a prolific writer and editor whose published works have focused on American history, particularly topics related to early twentieth-century politics. Several of his books are biographies of American politicians, including *George W. Norris: The Making of a Progressive, 1861-1912, George W. Norris: The Persistence of a Progressive, 1913-1933, George W. Norris: The Triumph of a Progressive, 1933-1944, Bronson M. Cutting: Progressive Politician,* and *Fred Harris: His Journey from Liberalism to Populism.* Other works have been more subject-oriented, specifically assessing politics and life in post-World War II America, such as *The Truman-MacArthur Controversy, America in Depression and War, The New Deal and the West,* and *Politics in the Postwar American West.*

Many of Lowitt's books have been noted for their depth of research and careful analysis. *Journal of Southern History* contributor Phillip M. Simpson called *Fred Harris* "an important book for citizens, politicians, activists, and scholars, including historians and political scientists" and "a very worthy book about one of Oklahoma's favorite sons and one of the more interesting politicians of recent American politics." *The Standing Bear Controversy: Prelude to Indian Reform,* which Lowitt wrote with Valerie Sherer Mathes, was described as an "insightful and valuable work" by *Library Journal* reviewer John Burch. As coeditor of *One Third of a Nation: Lorena Hickok Reports on the Great Depression,* Lowitt earned this remark by *Journal of Sociology and Social Welfare* contributor John M. Herrick: "The editors' work in compiling Hickok's reports is commendable."

BIOGRAPHICAL AND CRITICAL SOURCES:

PERIODICALS

Journal of Sociology and Social Welfare, March, 2002, John M. Herrick, review of *One Third of a Nation: Lorena Hickok Reports on the Great Depression,* p. 183.

Journal of Southern History, May, 2005, Phillip M. Simpson, review of *Fred Harris: His Journey from Liberalism to Populism,* p. 503.

Library Journal, August, 2003, John Burch, review of *The Standing Bear Controversy: Prelude to Indian Reform,* p. 103.

*   *   *

LUBASCH, Lisa

PERSONAL: Female.

ADDRESSES: Home—New York, NY.

CAREER: Author.

AWARDS, HONORS: Norma Farber First Book Award for *How Many More of Them Are You?*

WRITINGS:

How Many More of Them Are You? (poems), Avec Books (Penngrove, CA), 1999.
Vicinities (poems), Avec Books (Penngrove, CA), 2001.
To Tell the Lamp (poems), Avec Books (Penngrove, CA), 2004.
Twenty-one After Days (poems), Avec Books (Penngrove, CA), 2006.

Translator of *A Moral Lesson,* by Paul Éluard, Green Integer Books; contributor to *The Gertrude Stein Awards 2005-2006,* Green Integer Books, 2006. Also translator of other French works. Selections from *How Many More of Them Are You?* have been translated into French. Contributing editor, *Double Change* (Web journal).

SIDELIGHTS: Lisa Lubasch is an experimental poet who has been inspired by French writers, whose work she has also translated. Her first collection, the award-winning *How Many More of Them Are You?,* uses verse-sentences, lengthy notes, and white space in a series of six philosophical apostrophes. *Chicago Review* critic Geoffrey Treacle found Lubasch's style to be rather academically pretentious, commenting that the "self-consciously 'experimental'" nature of the writing "rings false or flat," though sometimes she "manages to rescue her fragments from being mere floating quotes." On the other hand, a *Publishers Weekly* reviewer appreciated the poet's attempt to express "a poetic identity shaken of its philosophical surety," adding that "one looks forward to what her future . . . holds."

Vicinities, Lubasch's follow-up collection, aims at "finding a way out of the abyss" addressed in her first work, according to another *Publishers Weekly* contributor. Calling the style "daringly spare," the reviewer felt that *Vicinities* shows the poet extricating herself from the influence of other writers in order to achieve "something new and genuine." As an editor for the Franco-American poetry journal *Double Change,* as well as a translator of verse by such French writers as Paul Éluard, Jean-Michel Espitallier, and Fabienne Courtade, Lubasch also "borrows heavily from [French poet Antonin] Artaud," as Treacle observed in his review of *How Many More of Them Are You?* By her third collection, *To Tell the Lamp,* the poet was still being "strongly influenced here by her recent translations of French poetry," as Jonathan Weinert stated in a *Harvard Review* article. As well, the poet continues to dwell in the realm of ideas, rather than concrete subjects. "Whether you find such an enterprise audacious and edgy or exasperating and remote will likely depend on your tolerance for high-concept experimentation," suggested Weinert, adding: "Her boldness and refusal to compromise are exhilarating. On the other hand, her renunciations produce a certain monotony of diction, rhythm, and subject matter."

Lubasch's exploration of the abstract continues with *Twenty-one After Days,* a "very beautiful" collection that "reaches new heights of formal variety," according to a *Publishers Weekly* contributor. Lauren Levin, writing on the blog *CuBank,* explained the essence of the collection this way: "Lubasch orchestrates the changeable relationships of subject, object, and language into a drama of perceptual shifts. The examining consciousness and what it examines interweave kaleidoscopically." Levin continued: "On my first reading of *Twenty-one After Days* I looked for externalized inward states, moods coaxed into impersonating rivers and mountains. Reading further into the book, I discovered it to be much more complex than that first take. Part of the pleasure I found in re-

reading was the lack of easy equivalences. You don't have to look far in poetry to find examples of an inner self that seeks its match in the outer world. The difference in Lubasch's work is that the terms used to organize such comparisons are unstable." Observing that the collection is very aesthetic in nature, Victor Schnickelfritz remarked on the *Great American Pinup* blog that the "beauty that Lubasch evokes is a very private one, one that I presume many others will have difficulty in appreciating. . . . One luxuriates with Lubasch the way one takes a hot bath or throws back a scotch or a beer or a glass of wine at the end of a stressful day."

BIOGRAPHICAL AND CRITICAL SOURCES:

PERIODICALS

Boston Review, February-March, 2000, Geneva Chao, review of *How Many More of Them Are You?*
Chicago Review, March 22, 2000, Geoffrey Treacle, review of *How Many More of Them Are You?,* p. 131.
Harvard Review, June 1, 2005, Jonathan Weinert, review of *To Tell the Lamp,* p. 190.
Jacket Magazine, October, 2005, Chris Pusateri, "To the Laboratory," review of *To Tell the Lamp.*
Publishers Weekly, August 30, 1999, review of *How Many More of Them Are You?,* p. 78; May 24, 2004, review of *To Tell the Lamp,* p. 60; April 3, 2006, review of *Twenty-one after Days,* p. 42; September 3, 2001, review of *Vicinities,* p. 84.

ONLINE

CuBank, http://cutbankpoetry.blogspot.com/ (October 7, 2006), Lauren Levin, review of *Twenty-one After Days.*
Great American Pinup, http://greatamericanpinup. blogspot.com/ (January 7, 2007), Victor Schnickelfritz, review of *Twenty-one After Days.**

*　　*　　*

LYGA, Barry 1971-

PERSONAL: Born September 11, 1971, in Southbridge, MA. *Education:* Yale University, B.A., 1993.

ADDRESSES: Home—Hanover, PA.

CAREER: Writer. Has worked in the marketing department for Diamond Comic Distributors.

AWARDS, HONORS: Winner of Mid-Atlantic Horror Writers' Association Short Story Contest, 2002.

WRITINGS:

(With wife, Allyson A.W. Lyga) *Graphic Novels in Your Media Center: A Definitive Guide,* Libraries Unlimited (Westport, CT), 2004.
The Astonishing Adventures of Fanboy and Goth Girl (novel), Houghton Mifflin (Boston, MA), 2006.
Boy Toy, Houghton Mifflin (Boston, MA), 2007.

Contributor of short fiction and nonfiction to *Glimmer Train, Florida Review, Byline,* and *Into the Blue.*

SIDELIGHTS: Barry Lyga began writing fiction in early childhood, sending his first formal short-story submissions when he was still in middle school and tackling his first novel in high school. An avid comic book reader, Lyga tried his hand at writing fan fiction, becoming a regular contributor to several comic book fan club Web sites. On his home page, Lyga shared why his early fan fiction pieces were valuable learning tools: "For a teenager looking for writing practice, discipline, and feedback, those days of writing fanfic were absolutely invaluable. . . . Since I was using someone else's characters and universe, I didn't have to worry about backstory or exposition—everyone reading the stories had a common frame of reference. I was able to focus almost exclusively on dialogue, structure, plot development, stuff like that. And if I wanted regular feedback, I had to hit regular deadlines." Lyga went on to attend Yale University, studying English literature and exploring the comic book genre from an academic perspective. After graduating, he spent more than ten years working for Diamond Comic Distributors, experimented with comic book writing, contributed to a nonfiction book about graphic novels, and continued to submit fictional works for publication. Lyga's years of persistence paid off when he published two novels: *The Astonishing Adventures of Fanboy and Goth Girl* in 2006 and *Boy Toy* in 2007.

Both novels are set at the same fictional high school but are told from the perspectives of different characters. In *The Astonishing Adventures of Fanboy and Goth Girl,* two young outsiders bond over a mutual love of comic books and a mutual hatred for their schoolmates and dysfunctional families. In *Boy Toy,* a teen who was molested five years prior by a teacher must deal with resurfacing emotions as the abuser is released from prison. Lyga's debut novel was described as "authentic and well-written" by a *Kirkus Reviews* contributor. Stephanie L. Petruso, writing for the *School Library Journal,* commented that Lyga's "love of comics carries over into all three teen characters, breathing animation into a potentially sad but often funny story." "A penetrating and convincing look inside high school life," remarked *Kliatt* reviewer Paula Rohrlick. Gillian Engberg wrote in a review for *Booklist:* "Fanboy's whip-smart, often hilariously sarcastic voice skillfully captures a teenager's growing self-awareness, and adds a fresh, urgent perspective to age-old questions."

BIOGRAPHICAL AND CRITICAL SOURCES:

PERIODICALS

Booklist, September 1, 2006, Gillian Engberg, review of *The Astonishing Adventures of Fanboy and Goth Girl,* p. 113.
Kirkus Reviews, October 1, 2006, review of *The Astonishing Adventures of Fanboy and Goth Girl,* p. 1018.
Kliatt, November, 2006, Paula Rohrlick, review of *The Astonishing Adventures of Fanboy and Goth Girl,* p. 14.
School Library Journal, November, 2006, Stephanie L. Petruso, review of *The Astonishing Adventures of Fanboy and Goth Girl,* p. 141.

ONLINE

Barry Lyga Home Page, http://www.barrylyga.com (April 26, 2007).

*   *   *

LYONS, Andrew

PERSONAL: Born in St. Louis, MO. *Education:* Attended Washington University, St. Louis, MO.

ADDRESSES: Home—Los Angeles, CA.

CAREER: Has worked as a writer for television programs, including *Marilu* and *The Stephanie Miller Show;* film researcher for *Access Hollywood,* until 2000; associate producer for VH-1, 2001—.

WRITINGS:

Darkness in Him (novel), St. Martin's Press (New York, NY), 2003.

SIDELIGHTS: After graduating from Washington University, Andrew Lyons set off for Los Angeles, California, to find work as a writer in the television industry. He spent several years writing for shows that were ultimately cancelled, then became a film researcher for *Access Hollywood.* During this time Lyons began work on a novel in his off-hours, a project that took priority in 2000 when he quit his job to write full-time. The finished product was purchased by St. Martin's Press in the fall of 2001, and published as *Darkness in Him* in 2003.

The novel is told from the perspective of Jake, a do-no-wrong college senior intent on going to Harvard University for law school, joining his father's prestigious law firm after graduation, and marrying his beautiful and popular girlfriend. When the repercussions of a one-night stand threaten to derail Jake's future plans, he ruthlessly commits a series of crimes to cover up his indiscretion. *Booklist* reviewer David Hellman remarked that Lyons does "a persuasive job of creating a creepy and almost charming antihero." "A psychologically chilling picture of a contemporary Raskolnikov," commented Roland Person in a *Library Journal* review. Ava Dianne Day wrote in a review for *Bookreporter.com* that Lyons "has the insight to choose a subject that beats close to the pulse of America's competitive, success-driven heart. If he continues to choose his subjects so unerringly and unflinchingly, his future looks bright."

BIOGRAPHICAL AND CRITICAL SOURCES:

PERIODICALS

Booklist, November 15, 2002, David Hellman, review of *Darkness in Him,* p. 572.
Library Journal, December, 2002, Roland Person, review of *Darkness in Him,* p. 179.

ONLINE

Andrew Lyons Home Page, http://www.andrewlyons. com (April 26, 2007).
Bookreporter.com, http://www.bookreporter.com/ (June 10, 2003), Ava Dianne Day, review of *Darkness in Him.**

M

MADDISON, Lauren

PERSONAL: Education: J.D.

ADDRESSES: Home—CA.

CAREER: Writer. Former district attorney.

WRITINGS:

"CONNOR HAWTHORNE" SERIES; MYSTERY NOVELS

Deceptions, Alyson Books (Los Angeles, CA), 1999.
Witchfire, Alyson Books (Los Angeles, CA), 2001.
Death by Prophecy, Alyson Books (Los Angeles, CA), 2002.
Epitaph for an Angel, Alyson Books (Los Angeles, CA), 2003.
The Eleventh Hour, Alyson Books (Los Angeles, CA), 2004.

SIDELIGHTS: A former district attorney, Lauren Maddison turned to a career as a mystery writer and created the "Connor Hawthorne" series. Like Maddison, Connor is a former district attorney turned mystery writer. The mysteries in each of the novels include supernatural and mystical elements. In the first installment, *Deceptions,* Connor is on the trail of the person who murdered her lover, Ariana. Complications arise when Connor's father, ex-U.S. senator and presidential advisor Benjamin Hawthorne, begins a cover-up to keep the identity of his lesbian daughter a secret. Soon Connor discovers that she is being tracked by a hit man. Along with Laura Nez, a Native American hired by her father to protect her, Connor ends up in a Navaho ceremonial center, where they encounter ancient mystical powers. *Library Journal* contributor Rex E. Klett felt that the novel is "rich in . . . incredible psychological suspense . . . and delicate layers of deceit." *Witchfire* finds Connor heading off to England to investigate why two grave robbers are found murdered and the coffin of her deceased grandmother is filled with rocks and no body. Assisted by her girlfriend Laura Nez, her father, and her policeman friend Malcom, Connor discovers that her grandmother was a good "witch" and the grave robbers were looking for a powerful talisman that is destined to play an important role in a battle between good and evil. Writing in the *Lambda Book Report,* Julia Sarkessian observed: "The author has the English idioms and speech patterns down, and all that talk of scones and jam was enough to make any reasonable reader want a proper English 'tea.'"

Maddison's third book in the series, *Death by Prophecy,* finds Connor and Laura using their spiritual gifts to help them solve the murder of a priest that they recently met. It seems the priest was considered a potential heretic by the Vatican and may have had information on a long-lost artifact that could change the Catholic Church's history. "Maddison creates edgy, moody settings very well," wrote Whitney Scott in *Booklist. Library Journal* critic Klett commented that the author "once again serves up entrancing prose, intricate plotting, and masterly characterizations." *Lambda Book Report* contributor Sandra de Helem noted that the book is not the usual mystery, stating:

"It's long and densely written like a rich tapestry; this is a book to take to bed with you on long winter nights."

Connor investigates three deaths, including her mother's murder, in *Epitaph for an Angel*. Connor traces the mystery of the murders back to Colonial America and also discovers ties with Hitler's Third Reich. *Boston Phoenix* contributor David Valdes Greenwood praised the book and wondered "how Maddison can top this." *The Eleventh Hour* finds Connor and Laura investigating a friend's death and ending up in England, where they encounter a cult led by a woman with supposed healing powers. Connor soon learns that Sister Sonia may be delving into ancient rites and powers that could seriously backfire on her and those around her. A contributor to the *GLBT Fantasy Fiction Resources* Web site called *The Eleventh Hour* a "great thriller."

BIOGRAPHICAL AND CRITICAL SOURCES:

PERIODICALS

Booklist, April 15, 1999, Whitney Scott, review of *Deceptions,* p. 1481; May 15, 2001, Whitney Scott, review of *Witchfire,* p. 1736; November 15, 2002, Whitney Scott, review of *Death by Prophecy,* p. 581.
Lambda Book Report, March, 1999, Lynne Maxwell, review of *Deceptions,* p. 19; November-December, 2002, Sandra de Helem, review of *Death by Prophecy,* p. 31; January, 2002, Juliet Sarkessian, review of *Witchfire,* p. 26; November, 2002, Sandra de Helem, review of *Death by Prophecy,* p. 31.
Library Journal, April 1, 1999, Rex E. Klett, review of *Deceptions,* p. 132; November 1, 2002, Rex E. Klett, review of *Death by Prophecy,* pp. 131-132.
Publishers Weekly, April 26, 1999, review of *Deceptions,* p. 59; May 28, 2001, review of *Witchfire,* p. 54.

ONLINE

Alyson Books Web site, http://www.alyson.com/ (September 16, 2004), Robert Pela, interview with Lauren Maddison.

Boston Phoenix Online, http://thephoenix.com/ (April 20, 2007), David Valdes Greenwood, review of *Epitaph for an Angel.*
GLBT Fantasy Fiction Resource, http://www.glbtfantasy.com/ (April 20, 2007), reviews of *Witchfire* and *The Eleventh Hour.*
Orange County Weekly Online, http://www.ocweekly.com/ (November 22, 2002), Wyn Hilty, review of *Death by Prophecy.**

*   *   *

MAGUEIJO, João C.R.

PERSONAL: Education: Cambridge University, Ph.D.

ADDRESSES: Office—Department of Physics, Imperial College, H/510 Huxley Bldg., South Kensington Campus, London SW7 2AZ, England. *E-mail*—j.magueijo@imperial.ac.uk.

CAREER: Imperial College, London, England, began as lecturer, became professor of theoretical physics, 2006—. Visiting researcher, University of California—Berkeley and Princeton University.

AWARDS, HONORS: Royal Society fellowship.

WRITINGS:

Faster Than the Speed of Light: The Story of a Scientific Speculation, Perseus Publishing (Cambridge, MA), 2003.

Also author of preface to *The Complete Idiot's Guide to Albert Einstein,* Penguin Books, 2004. Contributor to books, including *Vision of the Future: Astronomy and Earth Science,* edited by J.M.T. Thompson, Cambridge University Press, 2001; *Science and Ultimate Reality: Quantum Theory, Cosmology, and Complexity,* Cambridge University Press, 2004; and *Einstein: A Hundred Years of Relativity,* edited by A. Robinson, Palazzo Editions, 2005. Contributor to periodicals, including *Physics Review, Brazilian Journal of Physics, International Journal of Modern Physics, Physics World, Scientific American, Physical*

Review Letters, and the *Times Higher Education Supplement. Faster Than the Speed of Light* has been translated into German.

SIDELIGHTS: In *Faster Than the Speed of Light: The Story of a Scientific Speculation* physicist João C.R. Magueijo proposes a startling theory: the speed of light is not an unalterable constant, as Albert Einstein had asserted. Breaking ranks with accepted theories, Magueijo believes that the speed of light was actually faster soon after the Big Bang—the event that scientists believe created the universe—than it is today. By making this assumption, now called the varying speed of light (VSL) theory, it might become easier to resolve some of the problems with the current Big Bang Theory, as well as theoretical problems that have thus far prevented the discovery of a Grant Unified Theory that will explain how all the forces in nature operate.

Magueijo makes the case for change in the speed of light carefully. "Leaning on several well known, as well as obscure, thinkers," reported *FrontWheelDrive. com* contributor Brandon Pierce, "Magueijo carefully builds the foundations for a discussion of Big Bang cosmology, and then segues into the second half of the book, which is devoted to VSL theory." Labeled an iconoclastic rebel by some scientists, Magueijo has complained that many researchers and academics get bogged down by generally accepted theories, which prevents them from thinking in new ways in order to solve some of science's most puzzling predicaments. This was true even with Einstein, according to Magueijo, who told a *New Scientist* interviewer that Einstein's "view that mathematical beauty is important is responsible for all the string theory crap about 'elegant' theories. Einstein wasn't like that when he was young."

Magueijo's attitude toward the scientific community is apparent in *Faster Than the Speed of Light,* lending the book an aggressive tone about which many reviewers have commented. For example, a *Kirkus Reviews* contributor said that the author's "obvious lack of interest in pretending to be polite to those he has identified as enemies makes this one of the more scathing scientific memoirs of recent years." *Booklist* critic Donna Seaman similarly noted that "Magueijo is exhilaratingly frank in his condemnation of the creativity-killing politics and bureaucracy of science."

More forcefully, Catherine H. Crouch declared in *Books & Culture:* "The second half of *Faster Than the Speed of Light* is filled with griping that ranges from petty complaints to crude, infantile attacks. One of the many objects of his spleen is the process of obtaining grants for scientific research. According to Magueijo, middle-aged scientific bureaucrats, threatened by new ideas, try to frustrate the work of their few genuinely productive colleagues by burdening them with administrative duties." But although Magueijo can be opinionated, a *Publishers Weekly* writer asserted that "his science is lucidly rendered, and even his penchant for *sturm und drang* sheds light on the tensions felt by scientists incubating new ideas."

"And this is exactly how science progresses," Pierce declared. "In reality, it's experimentation and exploration. It's throwing around ideas, destroying old theories, salvaging the useful parts, and rebuilding. It's bouncing ideas off your peers, collaborating, in a process that can be just as painful as productive." "Whatever the final verdict on VSL, where experimental results will act as the ultimate referee," stated *Guardian* contributor Manjit Kumar, "Magueijo and his collaborators have developed a theory that is now being taken seriously, against all the odds. As the young Einstein once remarked: 'Foolish faith in authority is the worst enemy of truth.'"

BIOGRAPHICAL AND CRITICAL SOURCES:

PERIODICALS

Astronomy, June, 2003, Michael S. Turner, "Dethroning Einstein?," p. 94.

Booklist, January 1, 2003, Donna Seaman, review of *Faster Than the Speed of Light: The Story of a Scientific Speculation,* p. 820.

Books & Culture, January-February, 2004, Catherine H. Crouch, "The Curious Case of the Exploding Universe," p. 41.

Guardian (London, England), March 29, 2003, Manjit Kumar, review of *Faster Than the Speed of Light.*

Kirkus Reviews, December 1, 2002, review of *Faster Than the Speed of Light,* p. 1752.

Library Journal, February 15, 2003, Marcia R. Franklin, review of *Faster Than the Speed of Light,* p. 166.

New Scientist, February 8, 2003, "Hero or Heretic?," interview with João Magueijo, pp. 46, 48-49.

Newsweek International, March 10, 2003, Fred Guterl, "Crazy Speed Demon: An Idiosyncratic Cambridge Scientist Says the Fastest Thing in the Universe Was Once Even Faster," p. 44.

New York Times Book Review, February 9, 2003, George Johnson, "E=mc², Except When It Doesn't: A Young Portuguese Scientist Proposes a Theory that Could Shake Up Theoretical Physics," p. 9.

Portland Mercury (Portland, OR), February 6, 2003, review of *Faster Than the Speed of Light.*

Publishers Weekly, December 16, 2002, review of *Faster Than the Speed of Light,* p. 54.

Science News, April 19, 2003, review of *Faster Than the Speed of Light,* p. 255.

U.S. News & World Report, May 26, 2003, Robert Kunzig, "Taking a Shot at Einstein," p. 48.

ONLINE

Bookslut, http://www.bookslut.com/ (April, 2003), review of *Faster Than the Speed of Light.*

FrontWheelDrive.com, http://frontwheeldrive.com/ (October 5, 2004), Brandon Pierce, "Frontier Cosmology."

*   *   *

MAJOR-BALL, Terry 1932-2007

OBITUARY NOTICE— See index for *CA* sketch: Born July 2, 1932, in Old Malden, Surrey, England; died March 13, 2007. Businessperson, electrician, and author. The manager of a garden ornament company, Major-Ball's claim to fame was being the older brother of former British Prime Minister John Major. He was an undistinguished student who attended Stoneleigh East Central before embarking on a series of jobs. After his National Service, he was thrown out of a manager trainee program at Woolworth's department store. He worked in the plastics industry for a year, and then the South Eastern Electricity Board hired him as a maintenance man for eleven years. Here he gained the reputation of a klutz who was subject to tripping down stairs and, in once incident, electrocuting himself. Through all this, he managed his father's business, which produced garden gnomes. Though he kept his ailing father's business afloat, he continued to work other jobs. After leaving South

Eastern, he spent fifteen years with Philips Service, which was part of Philips Electronics, retiring in 1989. When his brother John became prime minister in 1990 the politician's family member was a bit of an embarrassment to the leader of Britain, but Major-Ball did nothing to create a stir for his brother. He was surprised to receive considerable attention, which included chances to travel abroad and dine in fine restaurants. He also wrote columns in British newspapers and frequently appeared on television, yet he refused to reveal any family secrets that might cause the prime minister to blush. After retiring, he began researching his family history, which led to his only book, *Major Major: Memories of an Older Brother* (1994). When his brother left office, Major-Ball retreated into obscurity, though when recognized he never felt ashamed of talking about his years making garden gnomes.

OBITUARIES AND OTHER SOURCES:

PERIODICALS

Times (London, England), April 21, 2007, p. 76.

*   *   *

MALEAR, Julie 1921-

PERSONAL: Born December 12, 1921, in Columbus, OH; daughter of David S. and Lucy E. Benbow; married B.F. Cook; children: Marie, Donna, Bettie Laura, Melody. *Education:* Attended Coyle-Devore School of the Theatre, Central Academy of Commercial Art, and Famous Writers School; Antioch College, received degree. *Religion:* Protestant.

ADDRESSES: Home—Delray Beach, FL. *E-mail*—jmalear@bellsouth.net.

CAREER: Studio Girl, Phoenix, AZ, manager and distributor, 1949; owned a commercial art business, beginning 1950; textbook illustrator in Peru, 1958-59; Field Enterprises Education Corp., Palm Beach County, FL, district manager, 1960-62; feature writer, cartoonist, and editor for *Delray & Boynton News*

Journals, beginning 1969; freelance commercial artist; has also worked as a film script doctor. Has exhibited artworks nationally.

MEMBER: National League of American PEN Women (secretary of Delray, FL, branch), Mensa, Delray Art League.

AWARDS, HONORS: Columbus Art School scholarship; has won several ribbons for her artwork.

WRITINGS:

(With Cindy Band) *Shattered Bonds: A True Story of Suspicious Death, Family Betrayal and a Daughter's Courage,* New Horizon Press (Far Hills, NJ), 2003.
(Editor, with Monika Conroy) *Tales from Below the Frost Line: Stories for Discriminating Readers by South Florida Writers,* Anrald Press (Boynton Beach, FL), 2004.
More Precious Than Rubies, Anrald Press (Delray Beach, FL), 2006.

Also author of true crime books and contributor to *Best True Crime.*

SIDELIGHTS: In *Shattered Bonds: A True Story of Suspicious Death, Family Betrayal and a Daughter's Courage,* crime journalist Julie Malear, along with Cindy Band, tells the story of the murder of Cindy's mother, Florence, at their home on Long Island, New York. Although Cindy's father, Howard, tried to present the death as the result of an accidental fall, evidence collected by a local detective suggested that Howard himself was responsible for Florence's murder. "Her father assaulted Cindy, threatened through [his girlfriend] Liz to kidnap her following his eventual indictment," explained a *Kirkus Reviews* contributor, "and tried to discredit her grand-jury testimony by conniving to have her involuntarily held in a mental hospital for ten days." Despite these efforts, Howard Band was indicted by a grand jury and was eventually convicted of Florence's murder. He died years later, having confessed his guilt to Cindy and her sister Paula. *Shattered Bonds,* stated a reviewer for *Publishers Weekly,* explains how Cindy dealt with "her emotional upheaval, her fears of her father and how her 'privileged childhood' turned tragic and troubled."

"What made me turn from feature writing to true crime?" Julie Malear wrote on her Web page. "Well, to begin with, I'd always enjoyed reading detective stories. I liked learning that the good guys had outsmarted the bad—that right had overcome evil. I enjoyed the puzzle aspect of the crime solving. I was also intrigued by the psychological aspect, that touch of fate that turned some people into criminals." "Life isn't long enough to do all I have in mind," she concluded.

BIOGRAPHICAL AND CRITICAL SOURCES:

PERIODICALS

Kirkus Reviews, July 1, 2002, review of *Shattered Bonds: A True Story of Suspicious Death, Family Betrayal and a Daughter's Courage,* p. 926.
Publishers Weekly, July 8, 2002, review of *Shattered Bonds,* p. 42.*

ONLINE

Julie Malear Home Page, http://www.juliemalear.com (April 25, 2007).*

*   *   *

MAOZ, Zeev 1951-

PERSONAL: Born June 28, 1951, in Bistriza, Romania; brought to Israel, 1958; son of Moshe and Zipora Moses; married Zehava Navo; children: Inbal, Omry. *Education:* Hebrew University, Jerusalem, B.A., 1976, M.A., 1978; University of Michigan, Ph.D., 1981.

ADDRESSES: Office—Department of Political Science, University of California—Davis, 1 Shield Ave., Davis, CA 95616. *E-mail*—zmaoz@ucdavis.edu.

CAREER: University of Haifa, Haifa, Israel, lecturer, 1982-85, senior lecturer, 1985-89, associate professor, 1989-91, professor of political science and chair of department, 1991-94, director of Center for Policy and Security Studies, 1992-94; Tel Aviv University, Tel

Aviv, Israel, professor of political science, 1994-2004, Brian Mulroney Professor of Government, 2004, head of Jaffee Center for Strategic Studies, 1994-97, head of graduate school of government policy, 2000-03; University of California, Davis, professor of political science, 2004—, director of international relations program, 2006—. Visiting fellow, Carnegie-Mellon University, 1981-82; visiting professor, Rice University, 1997-98, and University of Michigan, 2003-04. Academic director, M.A. program in national security for the National Defense College of the Israel Defense Forces, 1990-93. *Military service:* Israel Defense Forces, 1969-73; became captain.

MEMBER: Israeli Political Science Association (member of executive committee, 1983-85, 1991-93), International Studies Association (vice president, 2000-01), Israeli Association of International Studies (acting president, 2001-03), American Political Science Association (chair of the Conflict Processes Section, 2002-05), Peace Science Society (president, 2007-08).

AWARDS, HONORS: Political economy fellowship, Carnegie-Mellon University, 1981-82; Yigal Allon fellowship, Israeli Council of Higher Education, 1983-85; presidential fellowship, New York University, 1987-88; Karl W. Deutsch Outstanding Young Scholar Award, International Studies Association, 1989; Ford Foundation grants, 1990-92, 1994-96; recipient of many other grants and awards; National Science Foundation grant, 2000-02; Israel Defense Forces grant, 2001-02.

WRITINGS:

Paths to Conflict: International Dispute Initiation, 1816-1976, Westview Press (Boulder, CO), 1982.
National Choices and International Processes, Cambridge University Press (New York, NY), 1990.
Paradoxes of War: On the Art of National Self-Entrapment, Unwin Hyman (Boston, MA), 1990.
Domestic Sources of Global Change, University of Michigan Press (Ann Arbor, MI), 1996.
(Editor) *Regional Security in the Middle East: Past, Present, and Future,* Frank Cass (Portland, OR), 1997.
(Editor, with Azar Gat, and contributor) *War in a Changing World,* Jaffee Center for Strategic Studies, University of Michigan Press (Ann Arbor, MI), 2001.

Bound by Struggle: The Strategic Evolution of Enduring International Rivalries, University of Michigan Press (Ann Arbor, MI), 2002.
(Editor, with Emily Landau and Tamar Maltz) *Regional Security Regimes,* Frank Cass (Portland, OR), 2003.
(Editor, with Alex Mintz, Cliff Morgan, Glenn Palmer, and Richard Stoll, and contributor) *Multiple Paths to Knowledge in International Relations: Methodology in the Study of Conflict Management and Conflict Resolution,* Lexington Books (Lanham, MD), 2004.
(Editor, with Emily B. Landau and Tamar Malz) *Building Regional Security in the Middle East: International, Regional and Domestic Influences,* Frank Cass (Portland, OR), 2004.
Defending the Holy Land: A Critical Analysis of Israel's Security and Foreign Policy, University of Michigan Press (Ann Arbor, MI), 2006.

Contributor to books, including *Quantitative Indicators in World Politics: Early Warning and Timely Assurance,* edited by J. David Singer and Richard J. Stroll, Praeger, 1984; *Syria under Asad,* edited by Moshe Maoz and Avner Yaniv, Croom Helm, 1985; *International War: An Anthology and Study Guide,* edited by Melvin Small and J. David Singer, Dorsey Press, 1985; *Dynamic Models of International Conflict,* edited by Urs Luterbacher and Michael D. Ward, Lynne Rienner Publishers, 1985; *Paradoxical Effects of Social Behavior: Essays in Honor of Anatol Papoport,* edited by Peter Mitter and Andreas Diekman, Physica-Verlag, 1986; *Text Analysis Procedures for the Study of Decision Making,* edited by I.N. Gallhofer, W.E. Saris, and Marianne Melman, Sociometric Research Foundation, 1986; *Theory and Decision: Essays in Honor of Werner Liefellner,* edited by Gerald Eberlein and Hal Berghel, D. Riedel, 1987; *Measuring the Correlates of War,* edited by J. David Singer and Paul Diehl, University of Michigan Press, 1990; *Contemporary Laboratory Experiments in Political Economy,* edited by Thomas R. Palfrey, University of Michigan Press, 1991; *Syria and Israel's National Security,* edited by Avner Yaniv, Moshe Maoz, and Avi Kober, Ma'arachot, 1991; *Psychological Contributions to Peace Research,* edited by Knud Larsen, Sage, 1993; *Classics of International Politics,* edited by John A. Vasquez, Prentice Hall, 1995; *Democracy, War, and Peace in the Middle East,* edited by David Garnham and Mark Tessler, Indiana University Press, 1995; *The Middle East Military Balance, 1994-95,* edited by Ephraim Kam, Westview Press, 1996; *Foreign Policy*

Decisionmaking: The Cognitive-Rational Debate, Lynne Rienner Publications, 1997; *The Clausewitzian Dictum and the Future of Western Military Strategy,* edited by Gert de Nooy, Martinus Nijhoff, 1997; *Wars in the Midst of Peace: The International Politics of Ethnic Conflict,* Pittsburgh University Press, 1997; *Conflict in World Politics,* edited by Frank Harvey and Ben D. Mor, Macmillan, 1998; *The Dynamics of Enduring Rivalries,* edited by Paul Diehl, University of Illinois Press, 1998; *What Do We Know about War?,* edited by John A. Vasquez, Rowman & Littlefield, 2000; *Studies in Israeli Diplomacy, Zionism, and International Relations,* edited by Abraham Ben-Zvi and Aharon Klieman, Frank Cass, 2001; *Balancing of Power,* edited by Colin Elman and John A. Vasquez, Rowman & Littlefield, 2002; *Millennium Reflections on International Studies,* edited by Michael Brecher and Frank Harvey, University of Michigan Press, 2002; *The Scourge of War,* edited by Paul F. Diehl, University of Michigan Press, 2004; *New Directions for International Relations,* edited by Alex Mintz and Bruce Russett, Lexington Press, 2005; and *Approaches, Levels, and Methods of Analysis in International Relations: Crossing Boundaries,* edited by Harvey Starr, Palgrave/Macmillan, 2006.

Contributor to periodicals, including *Journal of Politics, International Interactions, Journal of Peace Research, International Studies Review, Journal of Strategic Studies, International Security, International Studies Quarterly, World Politics, Journal of Conflict Resolution, Electoral Studies, Public Choice, Jerusalem Journal of International Relations, Review of International Studies, Conflict Management and Peace Studies, American Political Science Review, Security Studies, British Journal of Political Science, Journal of Theoretical Politics, Behavioral Science, Theory and Decision, Social Behaviour* and *Political Psychology.* Series editor, "Innovations in the Study of World Politics," Lexington Books, 2003—. Member of editorial boards, *Dilemmas in World Politics,* 1986—, *Conflict Management and Peace Science,* 1991—, *International Studies Quarterly,* 1990-2000, and *International Interactions,* 1996—; member of international advisory board, *Journal of Conflict Resolution,* 1989—.

SIDELIGHTS: Political science professor Zeev Maoz specializes in the examination of conflict and resolution in today's troubled Middle East. In works such as *National Choices and International Processes, Regional Security in the Middle East: International,* *Regional and Domestic Influences,* and *Defending the Holy Land: A Critical Analysis of Israel's Security and Foreign Policy,* Maoz examines the ways in which modern states in the region interrelate and suggests how theoretical concepts about relations in general could be changed as a result. *National Choices and International Processes,* for instance, "is ambitious, complex, 'messy' (but not sloppy), and often indeterminate," stated Bruce Russett in *World Politics.* The book "rejects intellectual efforts to ignore the domestic political determinants of foreign policy choice, and it attempts to develop a systematic model of the foreign policy process." "Maoz insists that one must identify the conditions that trigger a particular decision rule," Russett concluded. "Actors may follow particular reasoning principles, such as maximizing their expected utilities, in some political contexts but not in others. By incorporating this refinement, Maoz is able to connect game theory with other aspects of bargaining theory, social psychology, and theories of the international system."

In *Defending the Holy Land,* wrote Raymond G. Helmick in *Tikkun,* "Maoz examines the behavior of the Israel Defense Force in every war or military engagement since the 1950s, focusing on the IDF's security doctrines and their influence on foreign policy and every other part of government decision-making." He comes to the conclusion that the force operates almost independently of civil control, and that its influence on foreign policy has significantly contributed to the wars that have plagued Israel since its founding. "Maoz claims that this book is the product of three decades of thought—and it shows," declared Stuart A. Cohen in the *Middle East Journal.* "The endnotes and bibliography provide ample evidence of the breadth of Maoz's reading and his sensitivity to the research of other scholars."

BIOGRAPHICAL AND CRITICAL SOURCES:

PERIODICALS

Middle East Journal, September 22, 2006, Stuart A. Cohen, review of *Defending the Holy Land: A Critical Analysis of Israel's Security and Foreign Policy,* p. 804.
Orbis, September 22, 1998, review of *Regional Security in the Middle East: International, Regional and Domestic Influences,* p. 619.

Reference & Research Book News, November 1, 2006, review of *Defending the Holy Land.*

Tikkun, November 1, 2006, Raymond G. Helmick, "Breaching the Iron Wall," review of *Defending the Holy Land,* p. 87.

World Politics, January 1, 1995, Bruce Russett, "Processes of Dyadic Choice for War and Peace," review of *National Choices and International Processes,* p. 268.

*　　*　　*

MARKS, Howard 1945-

PERSONAL: Born August 13, 1945, in Kenfig Hill, Wales; married Ilze Kadegis (marriage ended); married Judy Lane (divorced); children: Tina, Myfanwy, Amber, Francesca, Patrick. *Education:* Balliol College, Oxford, received physics degree, 1967, postgraduate work in philosophy.

CAREER: Former drug smuggler, serving jail time in Terre Haute, IN, 1988-95; ran unsuccessfully for office in the British Parliament on the Legalize Cannabis Party ticket. Actor in films and on television, including *The Falconer,* 1998, *Human Traffic,* 1999, *Wish You Were Here,* 2005, *Heartbeat,* 2006, *Get Back,* 2006, and *Ecstasy,* 2007. Also appeared on television, including in *Howard Makes His Mark,* 1999, *Cable TV,* 2002, *The Wright Stuff,* 2003, *Celebrity Poker Club,* 2004, and *This Week,* 2005.

WRITINGS:

Mr. Nice: An Autobiography, Secker & Warburg (London, England), 1996.

The Howard Marks Book of Dope Stories, Vintage (London, England), 2001.

(With Simon Bond) *101 Uses of a Dead Roach,* Arrow (London, England), 2002.

Also author of *Howard Marks: A Video Diary.*

ADAPTATIONS: Mr. Nice and *The Howard Marks Book of Dope Stories* have been adapted as audiobooks by RH Audio in 1999 and 2001, respectively.

SIDELIGHTS: Once one of the world's most notorious marijuana smugglers, Howard Marks has found a different kind of celebrity through his television and film appearances, his one-man stage shows, and his story *Mr. Nice: An Autobiography.* An Oxford graduate, Marks seems on the surface an unlikely person to have become a hugely successful drug smuggler. "With the help of friends and fellow students at Oxford University," explained a *Europe Intelligence Wire* reporter, "Marks built a worldwide smuggling network that allegedly became responsible for the majority of marijuana smoked in the western world throughout the 1970s and most of the 1980s." Over the years, he moved hundreds of tons of marijuana throughout the western world before being arrested and serving seven years in Terre Haute Penitentiary. He also "collected multiple identities, passports, and bank accounts, as well as a handful of legitimate business operations," reported a *Kirkus Reviews* contributor, "although, he reports, 'I enjoyed being a smuggler most of all.'" He has since been an advocate for the legalization of marijuana, speaking out against what he calls "selective enforcement" of antidrug laws by local police. "Howard's theories are sound," wrote Claire Giltrow in her *Urban75* interview, "and as he relates his arguments against the current issues of police selective enforcement towards cannabis users, you wish for once Westminster would stand up and listen." His account of his life has sold more than half a million copies.

BIOGRAPHICAL AND CRITICAL SOURCES:

BOOKS

Marks, Howard, *Mr. Nice: An Autobiography,* Secker & Warburg (London, England), 1996.

PERIODICALS

Bookseller, November 4, 2005, "Author Edits News," p. 44.

Europe Intelligence Wire, November 3, 2002, "A Surprise Love Child for Mr. Nice"; October 31, 2005, "Life Begins at 60 as Mr. Nice Enjoys His Nice Nights In"; September 18, 2006, "No More Mr. Nice over Drug Claims"; October 5, 2006, "For Mr. Nice Fame Is a Kind of Freedom."

Financial Times, May 27, 2006, Catherine Neilan, "In Brief—Mr. Nice and Mrs. Marks," p. 33.

Kirkus Reviews, September 15, 2002, review of *Mr. Nice,* p. 1369.

London Independent, October 14, 2006, Sophie Lam, "Howard Marks: My Life in Travel."

London Review of Books, January 23, 1997, Iain Sinclair, "Narco Polo," pp. 26-28.

Observer (London, England), September 8, 1996, Will Self, "Splendour in the Grass," p. 15.

Times Literary Supplement, October 4, 1996, Peter J.M. Wayne, "Rotten from the Start," p. 30.

ONLINE

Euronet Internet, http://www.euro.net/ (April 25, 2007), brief biography of Howard Marks.

Free Radical Sounds, http://freeradicalsounds.com/ (April 25, 2007), "High on Hope: Howard Marks Talks to Free Radical Sounds."

Howard Marks Home Page, http://www.howardmarks.co.uk (April 25, 2007).

MrNice.net, http://www.mrnice.net (April 25, 2007).

Urban75.com, http://www.urban75.com/ (April 25, 2007), Clare Giltrow, "Howard Marks Interview."*

*   *   *

MARTIN, Andrew 1962(?)-

PERSONAL: Born c. 1962 (one source says 1952), in England.

ADDRESSES: Home—London, England

CAREER: Author and journalist. Journalist for the *Guardian,* the *Daily Telegraph,* the *Independent on Sunday,* and *Granta,* among other publications. Weekly columnist for the *New Statesman.*

AWARDS, HONORS: Young Writer of the Year, *Spectator.*

WRITINGS:

Bilton (novel), Faber & Faber (London, England), 1998.

The Bobby Dazzlers (novel), Faber & Faber (London, England), 2001.

(Editor) *Funny You Should Say That: Amusing Remarks from Cicero to the Simpsons* (nonfiction), Penguin Books (New York, NY), 2005.

"JIM STRINGER MYSTERY" SERIES

The Necropolis Railway: A Novel of Murder, Mystery, and Steam, Faber & Faber (London, England), 2002, Harcourt (Orlando, FL), 2006.

The Blackpool Highflyer, Faber & Faber (London, England), 2004, Harcourt (Orlando, FL), 2006.

The Lost Luggage Porter: A Jim Stringer Mystery, Faber & Faber (London, England), 2006, Harcourt (Orlando, FL), 2008.

Murder at Deviation Junction, Faber & Faber (London, England), 2007.

SIDELIGHTS: In 2002, Andrew Martin followed up his first two novels, *Bilton* and *The Bobby Dazzlers,* with *The Necropolis Railway: A Novel of Murder, Mystery, and Steam,* his debut novel in a mystery series that follows the adventures of Jim Stringer, a railway man and amateur sleuth. Stringer leaves behind a menial job in rural England at the Yorkshire train station to pursue his lifelong dream of driving locomotives in London. Stringer soon discovers that life in London in 1903 is dirty and hard. He is put to work on the Necropolis Railway, a mysterious graveyard line where the men he works with acquire an immediate distaste for him and suspect him of being a company spy. Things get worse for the young hero (who is only nineteen years old) when he finds out that his predecessors have met their respective demises under suspicious circumstances. With his own life in danger, Stringer and his landlady work together to unravel the motives behind the mysterious deaths. *Spectator* contributor Andrew Barrow observed, "This book is, as its publishers rightly claim, 'fabulously rich in atmosphere and period detail.'" *The Necropolis Railway* "creates an authentic ambience of clattering dread," according to *Agony Column* reviewer Rick Kleffel. "Martin weaves the dark menace of London expertly into this tale," remarked *New Statesman* reviewer Matthew Jennings. "Martin's job is not to reflect the present in the past, nor to show off his research skills. Ultimately, that's why *The Necropolis Railway* succeeds; interested in itself and its own, beautifully constructed world, it [proceeds] from A to B, with some excellent scenery along the way," commended Alex Clark in the London *Guardian.*

Jim Stringer returns to the rails and amateur sleuthing in Martin's 2004 novel, *The Blackpool Highflyer*. "Despite his changed circumstances, Jim is much the same—inquisitive but dopey, apt to go off on wild-goose chases and get cracked over the head by members of the criminal classes, who are considerably bigger than he is," observed *New Statesman* reviewer Hugo Barnacle. The book takes place in 1905, and Jim has left London to return to his native Yorkshire as a fireman on the old Lancashire and Yorkshire Railway, which makes routine excursions from Halifax to Blackpool and Scarborough. The plot revolves around an attempted derailment of one of the Blackpool-bound trips. Although the train stops just in time, the one wounded passenger dies while Stringer is attempting to help her. This causes Stringer enough guilt to embark on a mission to discover the saboteur. "One struggles to throw oneself in with Jim's quest," according to a reviewer for the London *Telegraph*. However, Martin is able to successfully create a rich and lively atmosphere through which Stringer conducts his investigation. "Along the way there are several flavourful scenes in the streets, pubs and music halls of Halifax, Blackpool and Scarborough," Barnacle commented. The reviewer went on to note that the story "is another atmospheric experience, a trip to a lost world in amusing company," he later added in his review.

Martin's third novel in the series, *The Lost Luggage Porter: A Jim Stringer Mystery,* is a "heavy, clanking, finely wrought adventure story," said Barrow, again writing in the *Spectator*. The story begins in winter, 1906, and Stringer has returned with a new job as an official railway detective at York station. His new investigation sweeps him off to Paris and then back to York in a story that is "full of memorable images," as Barrow put it. "Unerringly sharp and pioneeringly original, it locks the reader in from start to finish," he commended.

BIOGRAPHICAL AND CRITICAL SOURCES:

PERIODICALS

Guardian (London, England), August 10, 2002, Alex Clark, "Single to Brookwood," review of *The Necropolis Railway: A Novel of Murder, Mystery, and Steam.*

Kirkus Reviews, October 1, 2006, review of *The Necropolis Railway,* p. 992.
Library Journal, December 1, 2006, Jo Ann Vicarel, review of *The Necropolis Railway,* p. 99.
New Statesman, November 25, 2002, Matthew Jennings, "Novel Thoughts," review of *The Necropolis Railway,* p. 53; September 6, 2004, Hugo Barnacle, "Journey to a Lost World," review of *The Blackpool Highflyer,* p. 55.
Spectator, September 21, 2002, Andrew Barrow, "The Way to the Tomb," review of *The Necropolis Railway,* p. 44; May 27, 2006, Andrew Barrow, "Under the Shadow of the Minister," review of *The Lost Luggage Porter: A Jim Stringer Mystery.*
Telegraph (London, England), October 24, 2004, "A Hymn to the Age of Steam," review of *The Blackpool Highflyer.*

ONLINE

Agony Column, http://trashotron.com/ (October 5, 2004), Rick Kleffel, review of *The Necropolis Railway.*
Andrew Martin Home Page, http://www.jimstringer novels.com (May 1, 2007).*

*   *   *

MASTERS, Brooke A.

PERSONAL: Born in New York, NY; daughter of Jon J. (a lawyer and businessman) and Rosemary (a psychoanalyst) Masters; married John L. Farry, July 21, 1996; children: two. *Education:* Harvard University, graduated 1989; London School of Economics, M.S.

ADDRESSES: Home—Mamaroneck, NY.

CAREER: Writer and journalist. *Washington Post,* reporter, 2002-06; *Financial Times,* senior business reporter, 2006—.

WRITINGS:

Spoiling for a Fight: The Rise of Eliot Spitzer, Times Books (New York, NY), 2006.

SIDELIGHTS: Brooke A. Masters is a writer and journalist whose work centers largely on business law. As a reporter for the *Washington Post,* Masters covered a beat that included Wall Street and white-collar crime. She has covered a number of high-profile court cases, including the trials of Martha Stewart and Frank Quattrone, noted a biographer on her home page.

A frequent subject of her work at the *Washington Post* was the many investigations undertaken by former New York attorney general Eliot Spitzer. In *Spoiling for a Fight: The Rise of Eliot Spitzer,* Masters expands her coverage of the pugnacious Spitzer, elected New York's governor in 2006, to a full-scale biography. In creating her biography, Masters was afforded "extraordinary access both to the man himself and to the inner workings of his sprawling operation, and this has enabled her to shed fresh light on his thinking and to contextualize him historically in a way that makes us see him anew," observed Greg Sargent in the *Washington Monthly.* With this level of inside access to draw on, Masters crafts a portrait of Spitzer that hails his triumphs and supports his position as the champion of the powerless, but also his faults, missteps, and occasionally unsavory characteristics. Masters "is studiously even-handed in telling the story, but it is clear where her sympathies lie," remarked a reviewer in the *Economist.* She traces Spitzer's early background, privileged upbringing, prestigious education, and service in the Manhattan District Attorney's office. She examines his early political aspirations and his campaign for the New York Attorney General's position. "Spitzer's rise, as she explains in a cogent introductory chapter, is the tale of an intense, passionately committed politician who helped restore a progressive ideology to the center of Democratic politics," commented Joe Conason in the *New York Times Book Review.*

The majority of Masters's biography centers on Spitzer's numerous battles as attorney general, and the political and legal wrangling behind many of his highly visible cases. She covers his vigorous policing of Wall Street and the investigations conducted there, many of which revealed misbehavior ranging from simple improprieties to outright fraud. She explores how Spitzer skillfully resurrected almost forgotten rules and legislation, such as the 1921 Martin Act, which provides New York attorneys general "broad power to investigate and penalize financial fraud,"

noted Michael Orey in *Business Week.* In this way, Spitzer emerges as a tireless advocate for the small investor and those who have no way to protect themselves and fight back against financial wrongdoings. Conversely, Masters also considers Spitzer's darker side: his quick temper, his tendency toward intimidation and bullying tactics, and his technique of publicly accusing targets without bringing official charges. "In sum, if Spitzer does overreach, if he is occasionally carried away by his own white-knight image, he's still a man who's at bottom fundamentally fair-minded and genuinely committed to effective public service," Sargent concluded.

"Masters's book is a well-reported compendium of the high-profile probes that catapulted Spitzer onto the national stage, and it contains substantial input from allies and adversaries alike. Anyone seeking a balanced and full account of his tenure as AG will find it a worthwhile read," commented Orey in *Business Week.* Rebecca Porter, writing in *Trial,* called Masters's book an "insightful study of a man and his mission." A *Kirkus Reviews* critic named it an "adept blend of legal, political, and business journalism."

BIOGRAPHICAL AND CRITICAL SOURCES:

PERIODICALS

Booklist, August 1, 2006, Vanessa Bush, review of *Spoiling for a Fight: The Rise of Eliot Spitzer,* p. 18.

Books, August 13, 2006, "A Smart, Dramatic Account of Eliot Spitzer's Crusades," review of *Spoiling for a Fight,* p. 10.

Book World, August 6, 2006, Bryan Burrough, "The Contender: New York's Wildly Ambitious Attorney General Took on Wall Street Corruption—and Isn't Done Yet," review of *Spoiling for a Fight,* p. 5.

Business Week, August 21, 2006, Michael Orey, "Lots of Evidence, No Verdict; Invaluable Reformer or Prosecutor Run Amok? The Author Lets the Reader Decide," review of *Spoiling for a Fight,* p. 142.

Corporate Counsel, February 1, 2007, review of *Spoiling for a Fight,* p. 97.

Economist, July 22, 2006, "Hero or Bully? American Law and Politics," review of *Spoiling for a Fight,* p. 81.

Kirkus Reviews, June 1, 2006, review of *Spoiling for a Fight,* p. 561.

New York Law Journal, August 2, 2006, Harry Reynolds, review of *Spoiling for a Fight.*

New York Times Book Review, August 6, 2006, Joe Conason, "The Man Who Would Be Governor," review of *Spoiling for a Fight,* p. 1.

Publishers Weekly, May 15, 2006, review of *Spoiling for a Fight,* p. 62.

Recorder, September 22, 2006, Justin Scheck, "Points & Authorities: The War of Art," review of *Spoiling for a Fight.*

Reference & Research Book News, November 1, 2006, review of *Spoiling for a Fight.*

Trial, January 1, 2007, Rebecca Porter, review of *Spoiling for a Fight,* p. 60.

Washington Monthly, July 21, 1996, "Weddings"; September 1, 2006, Greg Sargent, "Hero or Hack? Eliot Spitzer Pushes the Limits of Prosecutorial Progressivism," review of *Spoiling for a Fight,* p. 46.

ONLINE

Brooke A. Masters Home Page, http://www.brookeamasters.com (May 2, 2007).

International Speakers Bureau Web site, http://www.internationalspeakers.com/ (May 2, 2007), biography of Brooke A. Masters.*

* * *

MASUR, Louis P.

PERSONAL: Education: State University of New York, Buffalo, B.A., 1978; Princeton University, M.A., 1982, Ph.D., 1985.

ADDRESSES: Home—Hartford, CT. *Office*—Department of American Studies, Trinity College, 300 Summit St., Hartford, CT 06016. *E-mail*—Louis.Masur@trincoll.edu.

CAREER: Princeton University, Princeton, NJ, lecturer, 1984-86; University of California, Riverside, assistant professor, 1986-90, associate professor of history, 1990-92; City College of the City University of New York, New York, NY, associate professor, 1992-95, professor of history and professor at the Graduate Center, 1996-2004; Trinity College, Hartford, CT, William R. Kenan, Jr., Professor of American Institutions and Values, 2004—.

AWARDS, HONORS: Princeton University fellowship, 1979-83; Frances Hiatt Fellowship, American Antiquarian Society, 1982; Whiting Fellowship in the Humanities, Princeton University, 1983-84; National Endowment for the Humanities stipend, 1987; University of California Regents' Faculty Fellowship, summer, 1988; Mellon Faculty Fellowship in the humanities, Harvard University, 1989-90; John Clive Prize for Excellence in Teaching, Harvard University, 1992; Professional Staff Congress/City University of New York research award, 1993, 1994; Rifkind Center for the Humanities Fellowship, 1993, 2002; Kate B. and Hall J. Peterson Fellow, American Antiquarian Society, 1998; Andrew Mellon Foundation Fellowship, Library Company of Philadelphia, 1999; elected fellow of the Society of American Historians, 2005.

WRITINGS:

NONFICTION

Rites of Execution: Capital Punishment and the Transformation of American Culture, 1776-1865, Oxford University Press (New York, NY), 1989.

(Editor and author of introduction) *The Autobiography of Benjamin Franklin,* Bedford Books (Boston, MA), 1993.

(Editor) *The Real War Will Never Get in the Books: Selections from Writers during the Civil War,* Oxford University Press (New York, NY), 1993.

(Editor) *The Challenge of American History,* Johns Hopkins University Press (Baltimore, MD), 1999.

1831: Year of Eclipse, Hill & Wang (New York, NY), 2001.

Autumn Glory: Baseball's First World Series, Hill & Wang (New York, NY), 2003.

Contributor to periodicals, including *New England Quarterly, William and Mary Quarterly, Journal of American Studies, Reviews in American History, Massachusetts Review,* and *Criminal Justice History.* Contributor to books, including *Nat Turner: A Slave Rebellion in History and Memory,* edited by Kenneth

Greenberg, Oxford University Press (New York, NY), 2003. *Reviews in American History,* member of editorial board, 1992-97, editor, 1998—.

SIDELIGHTS: Louis P. Masur is a historian who has written books on subjects ranging from public executions to baseball. His first publication was *Rites of Execution: Capital Punishment and the Transformation of American Culture, 1776-1865.* It was published in 1989, at a time when many states were reinstating the death penalty after years of not using it. The book prompted William S. McFeely, in the *Nation,* to comment: "If the past can speak to the present, no recent book about nineteenth-century America speaks more clearly than *Rites of Execution.* McFeely found the book "handsomely written," and appreciated Masur's way of discussing the issues of capital punishment through real stories of executions. Once considered public spectacles, executions began to be staged out of public view during the 1830s, coinciding with a shift in the nation's consciousness.

In his history *1831: Year of Eclipse,* Masur suggests that the course of American history changed significantly and permanently in 1831. He has organized his study of that year into four sections, covering the dynamics between nature and machine, nation and state, religion and politics, and slavery and abolition. His book describes an eclipse of the sun that took place in February, 1831, which was seen by many as an ominous foreshadowing of doom. The fight against slavery intensified that year, and the rights of Native Americans were also being debated, even as President Andrew Jackson prepared to sign the Indian Removal Act, authorizing the forced relocation of the Cherokees from the state of Georgia. Reviewing Masur's book for the *New York Times Book Review,* David Traxel commented that while he didn't believe that 1831 was an absolute turning point, he felt that there were many reasons to write about it "even if it does not mark a major change in the flow of history. A study of 1831, helps us understand events that happened both before and after, gives insight into the character of the United States and, also important, entertains with the stories it provides. This is especially true when the study is as thoroughly researched and well written as this one."

In *Autumn Glory: Baseball's First World Series,* Masur gives a detailed history of the 1903 championship series between the Boston Americans and the Pitts-burgh Pirates. *Autumn Glory* includes all the box scores and statistics a baseball fan would expect, as well as many photographs. Each game in the best-of-nine series, which Boston won in eight games, is given a chapter unto itself. Masur also looked at the human stories of the star players, the owners, and others involved with the series. He discusses the gambling associated with the games, which was widespread, even among the players. Masur's writing on gambling is "stellar," stated David Exum in a *Bookreporter.com* review. Exum also praised Masur's coverage of the two teams' followers, calling *Autumn Glory* "an absolute treasure trove of how passionate fans were about their baseball teams in Boston and Pittsburgh during the early days of the game." According to *Nine,* contributor Richard J. Puerzer, Masur's "fine book provides considerable detail not only on the ball games making up the Series but also on the cultural implications of the Series in the world of baseball as well as in American society."

BIOGRAPHICAL AND CRITICAL SOURCES:

PERIODICALS

American Heritage, July, 2001, review of *1831: Year of Eclipse,* p. 16.

American Historical Review, October, 1990, Myra C. Glenn, review of *Rites of Execution: Capital Punishment and the Transformation of American Culture, 1776-1865,* p. 1273.

American Journal of Legal History, July, 1990, Francis A. Allen, review of *Rites of Execution,* p. 317.

American Studies International, April, 1990, Richard Stott, review of *Rites of Execution,* p. 101.

Annals of the American Academy of Political and Social Science, May, 1990, Paul M. Pruitt, Jr., review of *Rites of Execution,* p. 188.

Booklist, July 1, 1993, Margaret Flanagan, review of *The Real War Will Never Get in the Books: Selections from Writers during the Civil War,* p. 1938; February 1, 2001, Mary Carroll, review of *1831,* p. 1037; March 15, 2003, GraceAnne DeCandido, review of *Autumn Glory: Baseball's First World Series,* p. 1267.

Choice, October, 1989, E. Cassara, review of *Rites of Execution,* p. 378; November 1, 2001, K. Winkle, review of *1831,* p. 579; October 1, 2003, review of *Autumn Glory,* p. 378.

Christian Science Monitor, June 5, 2003, review of *Autumn Glory,* p. 15.

Journal of American History, June, 1990, Blanche Linden-Ward, review of *Rites of Execution,* p. 283; March, 2002, review of *1831,* p. 1521.

Journal of Social History, fall, 1990, Steven Wilf, review of *Rites of Execution,* p. 199.

Journal of Southern History, February, 1995, review of *The Real War Will Never Get in the Books,* p. 159.

Journal of the Early Republic, fall, 1990, review of *Rites of Execution,* p. 415.

Kirkus Reviews, April 15, 2003, review of *Autumn Glory,* p. 590.

Law and History Review, spring, 1992, review of *Rites of Execution,* p. 182.

Law and Social Inquiry, summer, 1989, review of *Rites of Execution,* p. 623.

Library Journal, June 1, 1993, Brooks D. Simpson, review of *The Real War Will Never Get in the Books,* p. 152; January 1, 2001, Jim Doyle, review of *1831,* p. 131; March 15, 2003, R.C. Cottrell, review of *Autumn Glory,* p. 90.

Los Angeles Times, March 12, 2001, review of *1831,* p. E3.

Nation, January 29, 1990, William S. McFeely, review of *Rites of Execution,* p. 140.

New England Quarterly, December, 2003, review of *Autumn Glory,* p. 627.

New York Review of Books, April 7, 1994, C. Vann Woodward, review of *The Real War Will Never Get in the Books,* p. 36.

New York Times Book Review, February 11, 2001, David Traxel, review of *1831,* p. 19; May 26, 2002, review of *1831,* p. 20.

Nine, fall, 2004, review of *Autumn Glory,* p. 135.

Nineteenth-Century Literature, March 1, 1994, review of *The Real War Will Never Get in the Books,* p. 564.

Publishers Weekly, December 11, 2000, review of *1831,* p. 70; March 10, 2003, review of *Autumn Glory,* p. 60.

Reference & Research Book News, November 1, 1999, review of *The Challenge of American History,* p. 46; August 1, 2001, review of *1831,* p. 54.

Tribune Books (Chicago, IL), December 26, 1993, review of *The Real War Will Never Get in the Books,* p. 3; June 15, 2003, review of *Autumn Glory,* p. 1; December 7, 2003, review of *Autumn Glory.* p. 5.

William and Mary Quarterly, January, 1990, review of *Rites of Execution,* p. 161.

ONLINE

BookPage, http://www.bookpage.com/ (April 17, 2007), Roger K. Miller, review of *1831.*

Bookreporter.com, http://www.bookreporter.com/ (April 17, 2007), David Exum, review of *Autumn Glory.*

Mostly Fiction, http://www.mostlyfiction.com/ (April 17, 2007), Chuck Barksdale, review of *Autumn Glory.**

*   *   *

MATHEWS, Francine
    See BARRON, Stephanie

*   *   *

MATTHEWS, Aline
    See De WIRE, Elinor

*   *   *

MATTHEWS, David 1967(?)-
(David Ralph Matthews)

PERSONAL: Born c. 1967; son of Ralph Matthews, Jr. (a journalist and activist).

CAREER: Writer and memoirist. Guest on television programs, including the *Tavis Smiley Show* and the *CBS Sunday Morning Show.*

WRITINGS:

Ace of Spades: A Memoir, Henry Holt (New York, NY), 2007.

SIDELIGHTS: Author and memoirist David Matthews explores timeless issues of race, poverty, and the search for individual identity in *Ace of Spades: A Memoir,* his chronicle of growing up in Baltimore, Maryland, during the 1970s and 1980s. Matthews, the son of an African American father and a Jewish mother, faced his early life without his mother; schizophrenic, she abandoned him and disappeared shortly after his birth. His father, a prominent black journalist and activist who was friends with such prominent black figures as Malcolm X and Miles Davis, worked to raise him, sometimes helped, sometimes hindered by the other women in his life. At least one of his father's girlfriends was kind and nurturing, but others were indifferent at best, and viciously abusive at worst. Within this turbulent atmosphere, Matthews confronted issues of being racially mixed early in his life. He was born light-skinned, and his skin tone and features allowed him to pass as white. When pressed about his racial heritage by curious and menacing classmates at a new school, Matthews declared to them that he was white. After experiencing violence and robberies committed against him by blacks, he denied the African American elements of his background, much to his father's anger. As he grew and matured, the young Matthews increasingly considered himself to be white, both as his individual identity and as a defense against the hostile world around him. Difficulties with school ensued, and Matthews eventually became involved with drugs and petty crime. However, the influence of his kindly grandmother, who helped raise him, helped keep him centered. Through it all, he remained curious about his absent mother, but few answers were forthcoming.

Though he dropped out of high school, Matthews remained a constant reader, intellectually curious despite his surroundings. He finally obtained a GED and attended college. Eventually, he located some of his mother's family members, who told him about her life and history of mental illness. Tragically, they also informed him that she had died. As unanswered questions about his family's past were resolved, Matthews developed a new appreciation for his father and the hardships that the man endured while raising his son. Matthews's own struggles eventually illuminate his concepts of race and help him come to terms with who he is. "In this stylish, astute, often frustrating memoir, Matthews examines the zigzags in his path between black and white identities before finally settling somewhere in between," observed *New York Times Book Review* critic Bliss Broyard.

Booklist reviewer Vernon Ford called the book a "loving portrait of a close relationship between a father and son" that was "slightly delayed by the fog of race."

Coloradoan reviewer Erin Texiera noted that Matthews's memoir "is not a happy read. Yet Matthews' admirable honesty and mostly fluid writing are enticing—and he doesn't bother with blame or self-pity. Instead, the memoir comes off as an important primary source about the tortured byways of racial integration in the 1970s, especially as lived by one lonely, confused child," Texiera concluded. "The journey of *Ace of Spades* is one every high school student ought to read, as it is a discussion of race that's candid, complicated and, most of all, necessary," commented John Stoehr in the *Savannah Morning News*. A *Kirkus Reviews* critic remarked that Matthews "shows remarkable energy and imagination, as well as appealing self-deprecation, in his tale of success erected on a foundation of failure."

BIOGRAPHICAL AND CRITICAL SOURCES:

BOOKS

Matthews, David, *Ace of Spades: A Memoir,* Henry Holt (New York, NY), 2007.

PERIODICALS

Baltimore Sun, March 1, 2007, Philana Patterson, "Hiding in Plain Sight," review of *Ace of Spades.*
Booklist, October 1, 2006, review of *Ace of Spades,* p. 22.
Coloradoan (Ft. Collins, CO), April 2, 2007, Erin Texiera, "Memoir a Haunting Tale of Biracial Angst," review of *Ace of Spades.*
Kirkus Reviews, October 1, 2006, review of *Ace of Spades,* p. 1001.
Library Journal, October 1, 2006, "Prepub Alert," review of *Ace of Spades,* p. 48.
New York Times Book Review, February 11, 2007, Bliss Broyard, "Half and Half," review of *Ace of Spades,* p. 6.
Publishers Weekly, October 23, 2006, review of *Ace of Spades,* p. 41.
Savannah Morning News, January 14, 2007, John Stoehr, "The Passing of David Matthews," review of *Ace of Spades.*

ONLINE

Henry Holt Web site, http://henryholt.com/ (April 2, 2007), biography of David Matthews.

Memoirville, http://www.smithmag.net/memoirville/ (February 7, 2007), Rachel Kramer Bussel, interview with David Matthews.*

*   *   *

MATTHEWS, David Ralph
    See MATTHEWS, David

*   *   *

MAX, Daniel T.
    See MAX, D.T.

*   *   *

MAX, D.T.
    (Daniel T. Max)

PERSONAL: Born in New York, NY; married; children: two. *Education:* Harvard University, graduated 1984.

ADDRESSES: Home—Washington, DC.

CAREER: Writer, journalist, and editor. *New Yorker* and *New York Times Magazine,* reporter, 1999—. Worked as a book editor and a book review editor.

WRITINGS:

The Family That Couldn't Sleep: A Medical Mystery, Random House (New York, NY), 2006.

Contributor to books, including *The Best American Science Writing 2006.* Contributor to periodicals, including the *New York Observer.*

SIDELIGHTS: D.T. Max is a journalist and science writer whose first book, *The Family That Couldn't Sleep: A Medical Mystery,* examines a variety of inexplicable, often fatal medical conditions that have so far defied attempts to cure or even successfully treat them. The book, a "gracefully written medical detective story, explores the mysteries of fatal familial insomnia, their eventual decoding, and the strange history of one family," commented William Grimes in the *New York Times.* Fatal familial insomnia, or FFI, is a neurodegenerative disease that has affected one particular Italian family for well over two centuries. Max has traced the disease to its probable first victim, a doctor in Venice who died in 1765, Grimes noted. Since then, the disease has been misdiagnosed in numerous cases. Little is known about FFI's cause, nor have there been any advances toward a treatment or cure. The effects of the disease, however, are well documented. The disease first manifests itself during middle age. Symptoms include profuse sweating, loss of appetite, impotence, constipation, sudden onset of menopause, and the complete inability to sleep. Under the stress of sleep deprivation, the victim's bodily systems suffer great damage and begin to fail; worse, however, is the fact that the individual remains fully aware of what is happening but unable to do anything about it. Approximately fifteen months after onset, the sufferer falls into a coma-like state and dies. With his work, Max has "crafted a powerfully empathetic account of their efforts to make sense of their suffering and find a cure," remarked a *Publishers Weekly* contributor. In Max's estimation, FFI could very well be the "worst disease in the world," noted Natalie Angier in the *New York Times Book Review.*

With his discussion of FFI as his base, Max branches out into discussion of other mysterious diseases, many of which leave scientists and medical professionals baffled. He covers conditions such as mad cow disease, a neurodegenerative disease of cattle which may be transferable to humans; scrapie, a neurological disorder that afflicts sheep; Creutzfeldt-Jakob disease, a degenerative brain condition that results in memory loss, physical deterioration, and death; the "laughing death," a condition that afflicted New Guinea natives who practiced cannibalism; and more. Max investigates a suspected cause of such diseases: prions, an abnormally folded protein that adheres to other proteins and causes additional folding, resulting in disease. Prions defy traditional theories of infection; since they are not living and contain no genetic material, scientists originally thought they could not infect. Current research, however, suggests that it is the abnormal structure and damaging effects of the prions that cause disease. "Max is the latest of many excellent writers who have reported on prions, but his book is probably the most gripping and sympathetic," commented Laurence A. Marschall in *Natural History.*

Booklist reviewer David Pitt remarked that the book is "too unsettling and scary" to be classified as "entertaining," but concluded that "it's certainly very timely and compellingly written."

BIOGRAPHICAL AND CRITICAL SOURCES:

PERIODICALS

Booklist, September 1, 2006, David Pitt, review of *The Family That Couldn't Sleep: A Medical Mystery,* p. 32.

Natural History, February, 2007, Laurence A. Marschall, review of *The Family That Couldn't Sleep,* p. 48.

New York Times, September 2, 2006, William Grimes, "Books of the Times: Tracing the Strange History of a Family with a Mysterious, Incurable Disease," review of *The Family That Couldn't Sleep,* p. 14.

New York Times Book Review, October 8, 2006, Natalie Angier, "A Sickness unto Death," review of *The Family That Couldn't Sleep,* p. 9.

Publishers Weekly, July 31, 2006, review of *The Family That Couldn't Sleep,* p. 69.

ONLINE

D.T. Max Home Page, http://dtmax.com (April 2, 2007).

*   *   *

McGARRY, Terry

PERSONAL: Born in New York, NY; daughter of an actor. *Education:* Princeton University, B.A., 1984. *Hobbies and other interests:* Traditional Irish music, biking, gardening, martial arts.

ADDRESSES: Home—New York, NY. *E-mail*—robocat@sflit.com; mcgarry@eidenmyr.com.

CAREER: Writer, novelist. Has worked as a bartender, street trader in Ireland, and page proofer for the *New Yorker.*

MEMBER: Science Fiction and Fantasy Writers of America (served as president and vice president), Authors Guild, Waverly Omnivorous Writers' Workshop.

AWARDS, HONORS: Anamnesis Press Chapbook Competition, winner, 1997, for *Imprinting;* three-time Boomerang Award winner, *Aboriginal SF* readers; *Illumination* was listed by *Library Journal* as one of the top five best SF/fantasy titles of 2001.

WRITINGS:

Imprinting (poetry chapbook), Anamnesis Press (Ridgecrest, CA), 1997.

"EIDEN MYR" SERIES

Illumination, Tor (New York, NY), 2001.
The Binder's Road, Tor (New York, NY), 2003.
Triad, Tor (New York, NY), 2005.

Contributor of short fiction to anthologies, including *Blood Muse, Sword and Sorceress 16, The Confidential Casebook of Sherlock Holmes, Horrors! 365 Scary Stories, Outside the Box: The Best Short Fiction from Bookface.com, The Ultimate Halloween, Live without a Net, Women Writing SF as Men, I, Alien,* and *Dead Cats Bouncing.* Contributor to periodicals, including *Amazing Stories, Realms of Fantasy, Space and Time, Fantasy, Elysian Fiction, Quantum SF, Aboriginal Science Fiction, Talebones, Magazine of Speculative Poetry, Star*Line, H.P. Lovecraft Magazine of Horror, Fantastic Stories,* and *Terra Incognita.*

SIDELIGHTS: Author Terry McGarry is a novelist and short-story writer in the science fiction and fantasy genre. When not writing, McGarry is a musician who plays traditional Irish music in pub sessions and other performance venues.

Liath, the young protagonist of McGarry's debut novel *Illumination,* has just passed her mage's examination, validating the years of study she has devoted to becoming an illuminator of magical runes. Her success makes her a member of one of the groups that form the triad, magic users who create spells on the human-shaped island kingdom of Eiden Myr. The triad include wordsmiths, who create and shape the spells; binders, who sign the spells into existence; and illuminators, who decorate and illuminate the written scrolls containing the spells. Magic in Eiden Myr is controlled by the Ennead, a group of nine powerful mages who live in the city. To Liath's dismay, shortly after she gains her status as a mage, she loses her Magelight, the inner source of light that gives her magical powers. Stunned and shamed, she travels to the city to petition the Ennead to help her regain her Magelight and abilities. To secure their help, they assign her the difficult task of capturing the darkmage Torrin, who is threatening the Ennead's position by teaching the realm's children to read and think for themselves. On her quest, Liath encounters numerous difficulties, finds herself falling in love with someone she is supposed to hate, and learns more about the world around her, and whether it can be saved or destroyed. Worse, she has to confront her attitudes about the magic systems that govern Eiden Myr, and whether Torrin's efforts to unseat the Ennead are diabolical or heroic. "McGarry's first novel is a beauty, with an exciting plot and characters that capture the heart," commented Paula Luedtke in *Booklist.* She "demonstrates a powerful skill at storytelling" as well as a "creative approach to the metaphysics of magic," remarked *Library Journal* critic Jackie Cassada.

In McGarry's next book in the "Eiden Myr" series, *The Binder's Road,* the realm is feeling the devastating effects of the loss of magic and the overthrow of the Ennead, including drought, plagues, contamination, earthquakes, and other disasters. Multiple factions are at work to influence the realm: some are searching for a binder who can find a way to bring magic back to the world, others are interested in controlling a binder for their own purposes, and still others seek to prevent magic from ever returning. Pelufer, Elora, and Caille, three young girls with potentially strong magical powers, struggle to protect themselves against forces who wish to do them harm, with the help of warrior Louarn. Elsewhere on the island, Lerissa, a surviving member of the Ennead, has made a pact with a group of seaborne warriors who want to conquer Eiden Myr, and female warrior Verlein finds herself involved in a prophecy that predicts she is fated to slay Lerissa. As war threatens, the many characters must do what they must to survive, while serving their role in keeping the island realm safe and intact. Cassada, in another *Library Journal* review, commented favorably on the novel's "strong characterizations, an intriguing magic

system, and powerful themes of justice, rebellion, and forgiveness." *Booklist* contributor Roland Green observed that McGarry's complex story and multiple viewpoints presents some difficulty for the reader, but concluded "there is no denying the power and fertility of her imagination." Similarly, a *Publishers Weekly* reviewer noted that the story's complexity makes it challenging to read, but observed that McGarry's "talent for world-building and sure use of language will leave fans . . . feeling more satisfied than confused."

Magic has been restored to Eiden Myr in *Triad,* and once again illuminators, wordsmiths, and binders apply their powers and skills. However, the island is still under siege and requires much effort by the protagonists to save the embattled realm. A journey to a haunted land and the use of forbidden magics enlivens a complex narrative of hope and redemption. Readers "will be rewarded by the absorbing metaphysics of this intricate fantasy world," commented a *Publishers Weekly* reviewer.

BIOGRAPHICAL AND CRITICAL SOURCES:

PERIODICALS

Booklist, August, 2001, Paula Luedtke, review of *Illumination,* p. 2101; March 15, 2003, Roland Green, review of *The Binder's Road,* p. 1286; November 15, 2005, Frieda Murray, review of *Triad,* p. 33.

Kirkus Reviews, July, 2001, review of *Illumination,* p. 905; March 1, 2003, review of *The Binder's Road,* p. 352.

Library Journal, August, 2001, Jackie Cassada, review of *Illumination,* p. 170; January, 2002, Rex Klett, Jackie Cassada, and Kristin Ramsdell, review of *Illumination,* p. 51; March 15, 2003, Jackie Cassada, review of *The Binder's Road,* p. 119.

Locus September, 2001, review of *Illumination.*

Publishers Weekly, July 9, 2001, review of *Illumination,* p. 52; February 17, 2003, review of *The Binder's Road,* p. 61; October 3, 2005, review of *Triad,* p. 51.

ONLINE

BookBrowser, http://www.bookbrowser.com/ (May 2, 2007), Harriet Klausner, review of *Illumination.*

Eiden Myr Web site, http://www.eidenmyr.com (May 2, 2007).

Green Man Review, http://www.greenmanreview.com/ (May 2, 2007), Michael M. Jones, review of *Illumination.*

ReaderCon Web site, http://www.readercon.org/ (May 2, 2007), biography of Terry McGarry.

Visions, Eidolons, & Chimeras, http://www.sff.net/people/terry_mcgarry (May 2, 2007), Terry McGarry home page.*

*   *   *

McGORAN, Jonathan
    See DUBLIN, D.H.

*   *   *

McKAY, Ami 1968-

PERSONAL: Born 1968, in IN; married; children: two sons. *Education:* Indiana State University, B.A.; completed some graduate studies.

ADDRESSES: Home—Canning, Nova Scotia, Canada. *Agent*—Helen Heller, The Helen Heller Agency, 892 Avenue Rd., 3rd. Fl., Toronto, Ontario M5P 2K6, Canada. *E-mail*—ami@amimckay.com; amimckay@yahoo.ca.

CAREER: Writer, novelist, journalist, radio writer, documentary producer, and educator. Worked as a music teacher at an inner-city high school in Chicago, IL. Writer and producer of documentaries for Canadian Broadcasting Corporation (CBC) Radio for programs such as *Maritime Magazine, This Morning, OutFront,* and the *Sunday Edition.*

MEMBER: Writers' Federation of Nova Scotia (member of Writers' Council), PEN Canada, PEN Canada Rapid Action Network.

AWARDS, HONORS: Excellence in Journalism Medallion, Atlantic Journalism Awards, 2003, for documentary *Daughter of Family G;* Nova Scotia Department of Tourism, Culture, and Heritage grant; Short Prose Competition finalist, Writers' Union of Canada.

WRITINGS:

The Birth House (novel), William Morrow (New York, NY), 2006.

Antigonish Review, associate editor of fiction.

SIDELIGHTS: Born and raised in rural Indiana, Ami McKay spent years as a music teacher in Chicago while nurturing her desire to write fiction. A single mother of a two-year-old at the time, McKay "kept my words to myself, having decided that a career in writing would have to wait," she commented on her home page. In 2000, she moved to Scots Bay, Nova Scotia, to be with the man who would later become her husband. While waiting for her residency to be approved, and with encouragement from her partner, she began to submit her writing. Her first projects involved writing and sending thank-you notes to people she did not know. Her goodwill efforts landed her an appearance on the Oprah Winfrey show. Galvanized by this success, McKay attended a workshop on writing for radio, which led to freelance work writing and producing documentaries for Canadian radio. An apprenticeship in the Writers' Federation of Nova Scotia mentorship program afforded her the opportunity to work on what would become her debut novel, *The Birth House.*

The Birth House originated in stories McKay heard from local women in Scots Bay while she was pregnant with her second child, she related in an interview on the *Birth House* Web site. At one time, a local midwife named Rebecca Steele had lived in the home where McKay and her family resided. She visited a local woman, now ninety years old and living in a nursing home, who was the daughter of the midwife. The woman, who had been adopted by the midwife after the death of her biological mother, told McKay numerous stories about her adopted mother's skill and compassion. The experience led McKay to seek the assistance of a midwife for the birth of her second child. Additional information on Rebecca Steele's life proved difficult to find, but McKay felt hers was an important story to tell. These events provided the foundation for *The Birth House.*

In the novel, set in the early twentieth century, seventeen-year-old Dora Rare has become the apprentice of midwife Marie Babineau, who has long practiced her healing arts in an isolated rural village in Nova Scotia. Dora quickly learns the skills of midwifery and intends to carry on the tradition. Shortly before Dora's wedding to Archer Bigelow, Marie abruptly disappears, leaving Dora to carry on her practice. Conflict arises when Dr. Gilbert Thomas, a modern medical doctor, arrives in the area with the intention of convincing the local women to abandon their reliance on the area's midwives and instead turn to his modern maternity hospital. The expectant mothers of the area, as well as their husbands, become bitterly split on the issue of midwifery, even as Thomas's attacks against Dora become more vengeful while he continues to portray midwife-assisted births as dangerous. Adding to Dora's troubles are her own difficult marriage, the ongoing pressures of her duties, a newborn unexpectedly left with her to raise, and the outbreak of World War I. "This sensitively written novel . . . will appeal to readers who enjoy gentle humor and plenty of homespun wisdom," commented Sarah Johnson, writing in *Booklist.* Mary Margaret Benson, writing in the *Library Journal,* called McKay a "wonderful storyteller with a strong sense of place and time," while a *Publishers Weekly* contributor noted that "McKay handles the proceedings with winning, unsentimental care."

BIOGRAPHICAL AND CRITICAL SOURCES:

PERIODICALS

Booklist, September 1, 2006, Sarah Johnson, review of *The Birth House,* p. 57.
Books in Canada, May 1, 2006, review of *The Birth House,* p. 38.
Library Journal, September 15, 2006, Mary Margaret Benson, review of *The Birth House,* p. 50.
Publishers Weekly, July 31, 2006, review of *The Birth House,* p. 51.
Special Delivery, June 22, 2006, review of *The Birth House,* p. 31.
United Church Observer, July 1, 2006, review of *The Birth House,* p. 39.

ONLINE

Ami McKay Home Page, http://www.amimckay.com (April 2, 2007).

Ami McKay Web log, http://amimckay.blogspot.com (April 2, 2007).
Birth House Web site, http://www.thebirthhouse.com (April 2, 2007).*

*   *   *

McLARTY, Ron 1947-

PERSONAL: Born April 26, 1947, in Providence, RI; married; wife's name Diane (deceased); married Kate Skinner (an actor), January 1, 2004; children: three sons.

ADDRESSES: Home—New York, NY. *Agent*—Richard Fisher, Abrams Artists, 275 7th Ave., 26th Fl., New York, NY 10001.

CAREER: Writer, novelist, actor, director, audiobook reader, and playwright. Actor in films, including *The Sentinel,* Universal Pictures, 1977; *The Feud,* WETA-TV, 1992; *Daniel,* Paramount Pictures, 1983; *The Flamingo Kid,* 20th Century Fox, 1984; *Heartburn,* Paramount Pictures, 1986; *The Feud,* American Playhouse, 1990; *Two Bits,* 1995; *The Postman,* Warner Bros., 1997; *Batman: Dark Tomorrow,* 2001.

Actor in television movies, including *Johnny, We Hardly Knew Ye,* NBC, 1977; *Bloodbrothers,* 1978; *The Berenstain Bears' Christmas Tree,* 1979; *Nurse,* Viacom, 1980; *King Crab,* ABC, 1980; *The Berenstain Bears Meet Big Paw,* 1980; *The Berenstain Bears' Easter Surprise,* 1981; *The Berenstain Bears' Valentine Special,* 1982; *Berenstain Bears' Littlest Leaguer,* 1983; *Enormous Changes at the Last Minute,* ABC, 1983; *Tiger Town,* 1983; *Finnegan Begin Again,* HBO, 1985; *The Father Clements Story,* NBC, 1987; *A Little Piece of Heaven,* 1991; *Grace & Glorie,* Hallmark Entertainment, 1998; *Mean Streak,* Showtime Networks, 1999; *Trump Unauthorized,* ABC, 2005; and *Into the Fire,* 2005.

Actor in television series, including *Ryan's Hope,* 1975; *Spenser: For Hire,* 1985-88; *Cop Rock,* 1990; *Law & Order,* 1991-2000; *Pointman,* 1995; *Champs,* 1996; *Trinity,* 1998; *Third Watch,* 2000-02; *Sex and the City,* 2000; *Ed,* 2002; *The Practice,* 2003; *Judging Amy,* 2003; *The Jury,* 2004; *Jonny Zero,* 2005; *Law & Order: Trial By Jury,* 2005; and *Law & Order: Special Victims Unit,* 2006.

AWARDS, HONORS: ACE Award for best actor nomination, for *Tiger Town;* Norfolk Southern Festival of New Works Award, 1992, for *The Dropper;* two AudioFile Earphones Awards, one for *The Memory of Running.*

WRITINGS:

The Dropper (play), produced in Norfolk, VA, 1992.
Sandpilot (play), produced in Montclair, NJ, at Luna Stage, 2003.

NOVELS

The Memory of Running (audiobook format), Recorded Books (Prince Frederick, MD), 2000, published in hardcopy, Viking (New York, NY), 2004.
Art in America, Viking (New York, NY), 2006.
Traveler, Viking (New York, NY), 2007.

Also author of the plays *Akela,* produced in Los Angeles, CA, by Road Theater Company; and *The Fulsom Head,* produced in New York, NY, at Currican Theater.

ADAPTATIONS: Screen rights to *The Memory of Running* were sold to Warner Bros.

SIDELIGHTS: Veteran actor Ron McLarty is a playwright, director, and performer. He has appeared in numerous films and stage productions, and is a familiar presence on network television in programs such as *Spenser: For Hire, Sex and the City,* and *Law & Order.* McLarty's work as a narrator of recorded books led to him becoming a successful author as well. Throughout his lengthy acting career, McLarty had consistently been a writer, though publication eluded him. His "more than thirty years of writing longhand five hours a day" resulted in "ten unpublished novels, forty-four unpublished plays, hundreds of unpublished short stories, and 'an encyclopedia's worth' of unpublished poems," reported Gregory Kirschling in *Entertainment Weekly.* "I never expected to make a penny from my writing. It gave me a respite from bad times, and it explained the world to me," he told Kirschling. In 2000, while voicing several novels for the company Recorded

Books, McLarty persuaded the company to let him record one of his own novels as a straight-to-audio project. The company agreed, and McLarty recorded *The Memory of Running.* Sometime later, author Stephen King encountered the audiobook and wrote a highly favorable review of it for *Entertainment Weekly,* in which he called the work "the best book you can't read." King's praise ignited a bidding war between several publishers interested in publishing the novel. A similar flurry erupted in Hollywood, leaving the fifty-six-year-old McLarty involved in a film and publishing deal worth in excess of two million dollars.

The Memory of Running tells the story of Smithson "Smithy" Ide, who works in a toy factory in Rhode Island, and his struggle for personal redemption after losing his entire family in one horrific week. Ide was once a slender runner in excellent physical condition, but his heavy drinking and general lack of concern for himself has caused him to balloon to almost 280 pounds. As a boy, Ide could often be seen riding his Raleigh bicycle, searching for his sister, Bethany, a beautiful young girl who was plagued with mental illness and who would often wander away from the family's home. When Bethany finally disappears and cannot be found, the toll on the family is enormous. Now, Ide's mother and father have been killed in a car wreck. Adding to his trauma, he uncovers an official letter stating that Bethany has been found dead in California and that her body is in a Los Angeles morgue. Drunk, possibly in shock, with no money and little thought for the immediate future, Ide climbs on his trusty old Raleigh bike and pedals off west. Along the way, he falls into many humorous situations, meets a diverse cast of colorful characters, discovers much about the world, and earns a newfound respect for himself. "In the tradition of literary heroes, Smithy Ide rallies as he rides west to rescue his sister one last time," observed Catherine Gilbride in the *School Library Journal,* who also called the book "a great first novel." With his writing, McLarty "unspools passage after passage of devastating grace and melancholy," commented *Entertainment Weekly* reviewer Adam B. Vary. A *Reviewer's Bookwatch* critic remarked that "McLarty combines vibrant and real characters, a gripping plot of personal growth, and awe-inspiring descriptions of his cross-country adventure into an absolute joy of words." A *Publishers Weekly* reviewer concluded that the novel is a "funny, poignant, slightly gawky debut that aims like its protagonist, to please— and usually does."

BIOGRAPHICAL AND CRITICAL SOURCES:

PERIODICALS

Booklist, November 15, 2006, Joanne Wilkinson, review of *Traveler,* p. 32.

Bookseller, November 5, 2004, "A Life Transformed," profile of Ron McLarty, p. 23.

Daily Variety, October 7, 2003, Michael Fleming, "Payday for Hyped Novel," p. 1.

Entertainment Weekly, September 19, 2003, Stephen King, "The Best Book You Can't Read," p. 92; January 14, 2005, Gregory Kirschling, "The Running Man: Unpublished for Thirty Years, Ron McLarty Is Now a Millionaire Debut Novelist, Thanks to Some Help from Stephen King," p. 54; January 14, 2005, Adam B. Vary, review of *The Memory of Running,* p.94; January 26, 2007, Gilbert Cruz, review of *Traveler,* p. 76.

Kirkus Reviews, November 1, 2004, review of *The Memory of Running,* p. 1026; October 15, 2006, review of *Traveler,* p. 1038.

Los Angeles Times Magazine, March, 2004, Amy Wallace, "Act or Fiction? Actor Ron McLarty Wrote Novels for Fun. Then Stephen King Made Him Famous."

New York Post, October 8, 2003, "Stephen King Turns Unknown Scribe into Millionaire," p. 69.

New York Times, June 15, 2003, Neil Genzlinger, "Parallel Stories, across Generations," review of *Sandpilot,* p. 9.

New York Times Book Review, January 23, 2005, Mark Kamine, "And the Loser Is," review of *The Memory of Running,* p. 25; January 29, 2006, Ihsan Taylor, "Paperback Row," review of *The Memory of Running,* p. 24.

People, January 17, 2005, Francine Prose, review of *The Memory of Running,* p. 61.

Publishers Weekly, June 24, 2001, Trudi Rosenblum, "Audio-Only Novel Is Audie Finalist," p. 26; August 9, 2004, Natalie Danford, review of *The Memory of Running,* p. 127; November 1, 2004, review of *The Memory of Running,* p. 41; October 9, 2006, review of *Traveler,* p. 34.

Reviewer's Bookwatch, April, 2005, Catherine Ekbert, review of *The Memory of Running.*

School Library Journal, May, 2005, Catherine Gilbride, review of *The Memory of Running,* p. 169.

Times Literary Supplement, March 4, 2005, Stanley Trachtenberg, review of *The Memory of Running,* p. 21.

Variety, January 31, 2005, "Y tu 'Memory' Tambien," review of *The Memory of Running,* p. 2.

ONLINE

Blogcritics.org, http://www.blogcritics.org/ (March 16, 2005), review of *The Memory of Running.*

BookPage, http://www.bookpage.com/ (May 2, 2007), Jay MacDonald, "A Long, Strange Trip," interview with Ron McLarty.

Bookreporter.com, http://www.bookreporter.com/ (May 2, 2007), biography of Ron McLarty.

Internet Movie Database, http://www.imdb.com/ (May 2, 2007), filmography of Ron McLarty.

Ron McLarty Home Page, http://www.ronmclarty.com (May 2, 2007).*

* * *

McMILLIAN, Elizabeth Jean

PERSONAL: Education: University of Southern California, Ph.D.

ADDRESSES: Agent—Rizzoli Universe International Publications, 300 Park Ave. S., 3rd Fl., New York, NY 10010.

CAREER: Santa Monica, CA, landmarks commissioner; *Architectural Digest,* architecture editor, 1982-92; University of Southern California, instructor.

MEMBER: Society of Architectural Historians, Southern California Chapter.

AWARDS, HONORS: J.P. Getty Memorial Fellowship.

WRITINGS:

Beach Houses: From Malibu to Laguna, photographs by Melba Levick, Rizzoli (New York, NY), 1994.

Casa California: Spanish-Style Houses from Santa Barbara to San Clemente, photographs by Melba Levick, Rizzoli (New York, NY), 1996.

Living on the Water, Rizzoli (New York, NY), 1998.

California Colonial: The Spanish and Rancho Revival Styles, photography by Matt Gainer and Elizabeth McMillian, Schiffer Publications (Atglen, PA), 2002.

Deco & Streamline Architecture in L.A.: A Moderne City Survey, Schiffer Publications (Atglen, PA), 2004.

BIOGRAPHICAL AND CRITICAL SOURCES:

PERIODICALS

Booklist, June 1, 1996, Barbara Jacobs, review of *Casa California: Spanish-Style Houses from Santa Barbara to San Clemente,* pp. 1662-1663.

Library Journal, July, 1994, Glenn Masuchika, review of *Beach Houses: From Malibu to Laguna,* p. 90; September 1, 1996, Russell Clement, review of *Casa California,* p. 175; September 15, 2002, Gayle A. Williamson, review of *California Colonial: The Spanish and Rancho Revival Styles,* p. 61.

Los Angeles Times, April 18, 2002, Kathy Bryant, "Design Notes," review of *California Colonial,* p. E2.

Los Angeles Times Book Review, May 15, 1994, Michael Webb, "Constructing Fantasy," review of *Beach Houses,* p. 10.

Reference & Research Book News, May 1, 2002, review of *California Colonial,* p. 181; August 1, 2004, review of *Deco & Streamline Architecture in L.A.: A Moderne City Survey,* p. 241.*

*   *   *

MEDAWAR, Mardi Oakley

PERSONAL: Born in Olla, LA. *Education:* Attended San Diego State University.

ADDRESSES: Home—Red Cliff Chippewa Reservation, WI.

CAREER: Writer, artist, historian.

MEMBER: Wordcraft Circle of Native Writers and Storytellers, Western Writers, Sisters in Crime.

AWARDS, HONORS: Medicine Pipe Bearer's Award, best first western novel, 1994, for *People of the Whistling Waters;* Prose Fiction Writer of the Year Award, Wordcraft Circle of Native Writers, 1998, for *Death at Rainy Mountain.*

WRITINGS:

NOVELS

People of the Whistling Waters, Affiliated Writers of America (Encampment, WY), 1993.

Remembering the Osage Kid, Bantam (New York, NY), 1997.

Murder on the Red Cliff Rez, St. Martin's Press (New York, NY), 2002.

"TAY-BODAL" MYSTERY SERIES

Death at Rainy Mountain, St. Martin's Press (New York, NY), 1996.

Witch of the Palo Duro, St. Martin's Press (New York, NY), 1997.

Murder at Medicine Lodge, St. Martin's Press (New York, NY), 1999.

The Ft. Larned Incident, St. Martin's Press (New York, NY), 2000.

SIDELIGHTS: Mardi Oakley Medawar's novels are set in various places and historical eras, but all of them give readers some flavor of Native American life. Her first book, *People of the Whistling Waters,* is a multigenerational saga that depicted the Crow tribe during the late 1800s. The central character is Egbert Higgins, born to white settlers in Montana in 1854 but eventually raised among the Crow people. Egbert and his descendants interact with various historical characters, including U.S. General George Custer and Native American leader Crazy Horse. Incorporating some of the oral history of the Crow, the author illustrates the sweeping societal changes that undercut the Native American way of life. Her book is "expansive," according to a *Publishers Weekly* reviewer.

Medawar's next book, *Death at Rainy Mountain,* is a mystery set in the American West during the post-Civil War era. It is narrated by a member of the Kiowa tribe named Tay-bodal. He is something of a loner, interested in healing with herbs, and not much involved with tribal councils or war parties. When a likely candidate for the position of tribal chief is murdered, however, Tay-bodal's knowledge of medicine and the human body draw him into the case. Emily Melton, a contributor to *Booklist,* praised this book as a "beautifully written, life-affirming, heartwarming story full of adventure, humor, and tears."

Tay-bodal is featured in other books, including *Witch of the Palo Duro, Murder at Medicine Lodge,* and *The Ft. Larned Incident.* These stories see Tay-bodal marry and take part in some of the key events in the history of the American West. His scientific interest in the human body is at odds with the traditions of his tribe, but it serves him well as he acts as both detective and healer. In *Murder at the Medicine Lodge,* Tay-bodal must clear the name of Kiowa chief White Bear after a U.S. soldier is murdered during treaty talks. In *The Ft. Larned Incident,* Tay-bodal extracts a confession from a suspected murder, but is troubled by a sense that something about it was not right. Fifty years later, the truth about the crime begins to surface, in a mystery that is infused with "dry, sometimes raucous humor," and which gives readers a "fascinating" look at Native American history, according to John Rowen in *Booklist.*

Medawar moves from historical to contemporary mystery in a new series that begins with *Murder on the Red Cliff Rez.* It is set on the Red Cliffs Chippewa reservation in northern Wisconsin, where Medawar lives. The sleuth in this murder mystery is Karen Charboneau, a woman known both for her work in ceramics and her prowess as a tracker. Very modern yet also deeply rooted in the ancient traditions of her people, Karen investigates the murder of a lawyer who was disliked by many people, for many reasons. Karen, who is romantically involved with the chief of the tribal police force, is depicted as stubborn and independent. A *Publishers Weekly* reviewer called the new series "promising."

BIOGRAPHICAL AND CRITICAL SOURCES:

PERIODICALS

Armchair Detective, fall, 1996, Laurence Coven, review of *Death at Rainy Mountain,* p. 489.

Booklist, July, 1996, Emily Melton, review of *Death at Rainy Mountain,* p. 1810; September 15, 1997, John Rowen, review of *Witch of the Palo Duro,* p. 214; February 1, 1999, John Rowen and Jack Helbig, review of *Murder at Medicine Lodge,* p. 965; August, 2000, John Rowen, review of *The Ft. Larned Incident,* p. 2121.

Drood Review of Mystery, July, 2002, review of *Murder on the Red Cliff Rez,* p. 13.

Kirkus Reviews, June 1, 1996, review of *Death at Rainy Mountain,* p. 785; October 1, 1997, review of *Witch of the Palo Duro,* p. 1489; January 15, 1999, review of *Murder at Medicine Lodge,* p. 108; August 1, 2000, review of *The Ft. Larned Incident,* p. 1079; March 15, 2002, review of *Murder on the Red Cliff Rez,* p. 371.

Kliatt, July, 1997, Elaine S. Patterson, review of *People of the Whistling Waters,* pp. 9-10; January, 1998, Elaine S. Patterson, review of *Remembering the Osage Kid,* pp. 10-11.

Library Journal, November 1, 1997, Rex E. Klett, review of *Witch of the Palo Duro,* p. 119; March 1, 1999, Rex E. Klett, review of *Murder at Medicine Lodge,* p. 113; August 1, 2000, Rex E. Klett, review of *The Ft. Larned Incident,* p. 166; May 1, 2002, Rex E. Klett, review of *Murder on the Red Cliff Rez,* p. 139.

Publishers Weekly, July 5, 1993, review of *People of the Whistling Waters,* p. 63; July 1, 1996, review of *Death at Rainy Mountain,* p. 46; September 22, 1997, review of *Witch of the Palo Duro,* p. 75; February 22, 1999, review of *Murder at Medicine Lodge,* p. 69; June 26, 2000, review of *The Ft. Larned Incident,* p. 54; May 20, 2002, review of *Murder on the Red Cliff Rez,* p. 50.

School Library Journal, April, 1998, Pam Johnson, review of *Witch of the Palo Duro,* pp. 158-159.

ONLINE

Gotta Write Network, http://www.gottawritenetwork. com/ (April 28, 2007), review of *Murder on the Red Cliff Rez.*

Mystery Reader, http://www.themysteryreader.com/ (April 20, 2007), Jeri Wright, reviews of *Witch of the Palo Duro* and *Murder at Medicine Lodge.*

Romance Reader, http://www.theromancereader.com/ (April 20, 2007), Tracy Farnsworth, review of *Murder on the Red Cliff Rez.*

Scribes World, http://www.scribesworld.com/ (April 20, 2007), review of *Murder on the Red Cliff Rez.**

MEHTA, Sunita
(Sunita B. Mehta)

PERSONAL: Partner of Stephan; children: Guatama, Akash (sons). *Education:* Douglass College, Rutgers University, B.A.; SNDT Women's University, Mumbai, India, M.A.

ADDRESSES: Office—The Sister Fund, 116 E. 16th St., 7th Fl., New York, NY 10003. *E-mail*—sunitabmehta@aol.com; smehta@sisterfund.org; sunita@fcaaids.org.

CAREER: Writer, editor, educator, nonprofit executive, and activist. The Sister Fund, New York, NY, director of grants, 1998-2005; Omega, faculty member, 2003—; Funders Concerned about AIDS, executive director, 2005—; Women for Afghan Women, cofounder; Soros Reproductive Health and Rights Fellowship, Columbia University, associate director; member of board, Women in Media and News; former member of board of SAKHI (a South Asian Women's Center for Anti-Violence Education) and the Third Wave Foundation.

WRITINGS:

(Editor) *Women for Afghan Women: Shattering Myths and Claiming the Future,* Palgrave Macmillan (New York, NY), 2002.

SIDELIGHTS: Sunita Mehta is a writer, editor, educator, and activist whose work focuses on women's rights and health in areas throughout the world. Mehta is particularly focused on the plight of women in Afghanistan, and is the founder of the human rights organization Women for Afghan Women, which seeks to improve the conditions of women in Afghanistan, a country long known for misogynistic, often violent treatment of females, especially under the oppressive Taliban regime.

Mehta is the editor of *Women for Afghan Women: Shattering Myths and Claiming the Future,* which collects a series of essays by women who have been active in human rights causes and who have experiences related to Afghanistan. Both Afghan writers, including Sima Wali, Weeda Mansour, and Saira Shah, and American essayists, including Gloria Steinem and Angela King, are represented. Other contributors include Qur'anic scholars, journalists, feminist theologians, and U.S. citizens with ties to Afghanistan. Many of the essays originated in papers presented at a conference inaugurating the organization Women for Afghan Women, conducted in November, 2001.

Among the contributors, Sanaa Nadim presents an overview of women and equality within Islam, and American writer Arline Lederman gives a thirty-five-year perspective on the role of women in Afghanistan. Weeda Mansour describes the struggle of the women's rights group Revolutionary Association of the Women of Afghanistan (RAWA) against Soviet occupiers and the mujahidin factions that became the ruling Taliban. She also cautions against considering the Northern Alliance, which toppled the Taliban, as Afghanistan's liberators, as they also have a long record of human rights violations. Fahima Vorgetts describes her life of activism on behalf of women in Afghanistan. Other authors consider women's roles in Afghan reconstruction, reestablishment of public health policies and facilities, the difficulties faced by Afghan women seeking asylum in the United States, and the twisted interpretations of the Muslim religion that reverse women's once-respected roles within the faith.

"This book is a first-rate compilation of brief but discerning articles on women's status in Afghanistan," stated Carol Riphenburg in the *Middle East Women's Studies Review.* "This particularly well-written, readable work provides timely insights and information" on Afghanistan and Islam, commented *Library Journal* reviewer Deborah Bigelow. "The events of September 11, 2001 provided an auspicious time to highlight the status of Afghan women and provide information to a public hungry for it," Riphenburg noted, concluding: "In this, the book provides a tremendous service."

BIOGRAPHICAL AND CRITICAL SOURCES:

PERIODICALS

Choice, May 1, 2003, review of *Women for Afghan Women: Shattering Myths and Claiming the Future,* p. 1602; September 1, 2003, review of *Women for Afghan Women,* p. 90.
Chronicle of Philanthropy, January 12, 2006, "Funders Concerned about AIDS," p. 45.

Library Journal, October 15, 2002, Deborah Bigelow, review of *Women for Afghan Women,* p. 87.

Middle East Women's Studies Review, spring-summer, 2003, Carol Riphenburg, review of *Women for Afghan Women,* p. 15.

New Statesman, October 6, 2003, Salil Tripathi, "Women's Rights after the Taliban," review of *Women for Afghan Women.*

off our backs, March-April, 2003, Carol Anne Douglas, review of *Women for Afghan Women,* p. 33.

Washington Post Book World, October 13, 2002, Etelka Lehoczky, review of *Women for Afghan Women,* p. 7.

Women's Review of Books, April, 2003, Amy Zalman, review of *Women for Afghan Women.*

ONLINE

Awakened Woman, http://www.awakenedwoman.com/ (November 19, 2002), Diane Schultz, "A Call for Understanding and Action."

Funders Concerned about Aids Web site, http://www.fcaaids.org/ (May 2, 2007), biography of Sunita Mehta.

Madre.org, http://www.madre.org/ (May 2, 2007), biography of Sunita B. Mehta.

Sawnet, http://www.umiacs.umd.edu/users/sawweb/sawnet/ (May 2, 2007), Huma Ahmed-Ghosh, review of *Women for Afghan Women.*

Women for Afghan Women Web site, http://womenforafghanwomen.org (September 29, 2004).

Women in Media and News, http://www.wimnonline.org/ (May 2, 2007), biography of Sunita B. Mehta.*

*   *   *

MEHTA, Sunita B.
    See MEHTA, Sunita

*   *   *

MEIER, Richard L. 1920-2007
    (Richard Louis Meier)

OBITUARY NOTICE— See index for *CA* sketch: Born May 16, 1920, in Kendallville, IN; died of pneumonia and congestive heart failure, February 26, 2007, in Berkeley, CA. Educator, urban planner, chemist, and author. Meier was a pioneer in the field of urban planning, predicting the importance of sustainable development and renewable energy sources before many of his colleagues did. A chemist by training, he earned a B.S. from the University of Illinois in 1940 and an M.A. and Ph.D. from the University of California at Los Angeles over the next four years. He worked as a research chemist for several years and was executive secretary of the Federation of American Scientists in the late 1940s. Meier joined the University of Chicago faculty in 1950. After a term as a visiting professor at Harvard from 1959 to 1960, he taught at the University of Michigan. During the early 1960s, he was an associate professor at the School of Natural Resources there, then professor of resources planning from 1965 to 1967. Meier spent the next thirty-five years at the University of California at Berkeley, where he taught students in the departments of architecture and urban and regional planning. As a researcher and author, Meier was concerned about population growth and the dwindling of natural resources. He was one of the early proponents of solar power and other alternative energies and also sought ways to improve the lives of the poor through better urban planning. Among his many books are *Science and Economic Development* (1956; 2nd edition, 1966), *Planning for an Urban World* (1974), and *Urban Futures Observed in the Asian Third World* (1980).

OBITUARIES AND OTHER SOURCES:

PERIODICALS

Los Angeles Times, April 6, 2007, p. B8.

*   *   *

MEIER, Richard Louis
    See MEIER, Richard L.

*   *   *

MELZER, Patricia 1970-

PERSONAL: Born 1970.

ADDRESSES: Office—Women's Studies, Temple University, 811 Anderson Hall, 1114 W. Berks St., Philadelphia, PA 19122. *E-mail*—pmelzer@temple.edu.

CAREER: Writer, educator, and administrator. Temple University, Philadelphia, PA, assistant professor and director of Women's Studies, 2003—.

AWARDS, HONORS: Carrie Chapman Catt Research Prize, Iowa State University, 2004, for "'Terroristenmadchen:' Women in Radical Left Political Groups in Germany and the U.S. in the 1970s."

WRITINGS:

Alien Constructions: Science Fiction and Feminist Thought, University of Texas Press (Austin, TX), 2006.

SIDELIGHTS: An assistant professor and director of Women's Studies at Temple University, Patricia Melzer is an academic whose work focuses on feminist thought as represented in science fiction and on how transgender theory has influenced feminist theory and politics, noted a biographer on the Temple University Web site.

In *Alien Constructions: Science Fiction and Feminist Thought,* a book based on her "Gender and Technology in Popular Culture" course, Melzer looks at science fiction as a "realm for feminist-informed issues and cultural norms," commented a reviewer in *Reference & Research Book News.* She considers the role of a number of different types of nonhuman constructions, such as cyborgs, and how they represent feminist perspectives on personal and cultural concepts such as otherness, sexuality, power, identity, and science itself. Melzer offers a detailed discussion of how "women's issues, from gender stereotypes to sexuality have been treated through the lens of science fiction, as well as how science fiction writing can be used as a platform from which to experiment with alternative societal organizations," observed reviewer Sheldon Ztvordokov on the *Frustrated Writer* Web site. She explores these issues as represented in works by three primary authors: Octavia Butler (*Survivor, Wild Seed, Dawn,* and *Imago*), Richard Calder (*Dead Girls*), and Melissa Scott (*Shadow Man*), with additional reference to films such as *The Matrix* and the "Alien" series.

BIOGRAPHICAL AND CRITICAL SOURCES:

PERIODICALS

Reference & Research Book News, November, 2006, review of *Alien Constructions: Science Fiction and Feminist Thought.*

ONLINE

Frustrated Writer, http://www.frustratedwriter.com/ (September 15, 2006), Sheldon Ztvordokov, review of *Alien Constructions.*
Temple University Web site, http://www.temple.edu/ (May 2, 2007).
Carrie Chapman Catt Center for Women and Politics Web site, http://www.iastate.edu/~cccatt/ (May 2, 2007).*

*   *   *

MENGESTU, Dinaw 1978-

PERSONAL: Name is pronounced "dih-*now* men-*guess*-too"; born 1978, in Addis Ababa, Ethiopia; immigrated to the United States, 1980. *Education:* Georgetown University, graduated; Columbia University, M.F.A.

ADDRESSES: Home—New York, NY.

CAREER: Writer, novelist, journalist, and educator. Lannan Visiting Writer, Georgetown University, 2007. Worked as a teacher in an after-school program in Harlem and as a teacher of English as a second language at the City University of New York.

AWARDS, HONORS: New York Foundation for the Arts fellowship in fiction, 2006.

WRITINGS:

The Beautiful Things That Heaven Bears (novel), Riverhead Books (New York, NY), 2006.

Contributor to periodicals, including *Harper's, Jane,* and *Rolling Stone.*

SIDELIGHTS: Dinaw Mengestu is a novelist, educator, and journalist. Born in Ethiopia in 1978, Mengestu came to the United States in 1980 with his mother and sister. There, they reunited with his father, who had fled their country two years earlier to avoid the communist revolution occurring there. As an author, Mengestu "belongs to that special group of American voices produced by global upheavals and intentional, if sometimes forced, migrations," remarked Chris Abani in the *Los Angeles Times*. These writers must constantly work to reconcile the life and country they have left behind with the new life they are building for themselves in America, Abani noted. Mengestu's debut novel, *The Beautiful Things That Heaven Bears*, "is the wrenching and important book he has made of this struggle," Abani stated.

The story takes place over eight months in Logan Circle, an impoverished inner-city Washington, DC, neighborhood that is gradually being renovated and gentrified. The main protagonist, Sepha Stephanos, is an immigrant from Ethiopia who for seventeen years has run a small grocery store. Resigned to his situation, Sepha concentrates on his business, which is dwindling in the face of upscale stores moving into the area, while nourishing himself intellectually with books and literature. His two best friends are also African immigrants: Kenneth from Kenya and Joseph from Congo, both of whom went to college in America and took on professional jobs. The three spend much time contemplating the home they left and the new lives they are building in America, but "the book's molten core belongs to Sepha and his witty though elegiac voice," observed Abani. The men, especially Sepha, have reached a level of peace and acceptance of their American lives, but their complacency is threatened by a new arrival in the neighborhood. When an American woman, Judith, a lovely white academic, and her mixed-race daughter, Naomi, move into a run-down house next to Sepha's store and begin renovating it, their efforts and their presence are felt throughout Logan Circle as emblematic of the upscale trends that threaten to change the neighborhood forever. Soon, however, Judith and Sepha have formed a close friendship, and Naomi begins to see him almost as a mentor, spending days in his store reading and discussing literature. As their relationship develops, Sepha begins to see the possibilities of the world beyond the microcosm of Africa he has created with his friends, and entertains a glimmer of hope for something more than friendship with the alluring Judith.

Booklist reviewer Vanessa Bush saw Mengestu's novel as a "deftly drawn portrait of dreams in the face of harsh realities" as told from the immigrant point of view. "It's a poignant story providing food for thought for those concerned with poverty and immigration," commented Debbie Bogenschutz in the *Library Journal*. A *Publishers Weekly* contributor remarked that "Mengestu's assured prose and haunting set pieces . . . are heart-rending and indelible." Mengestu "paints a beautiful portrait of a complex, conflicted man struggling with questions of love and loyalty," observed a *Kirkus Reviews* critic. "With *The Beautiful Things That Heaven Bears*, Mengestu has made, and made well, a novel that is a retelling of the immigrant experience, one in which immigrants must come to terms with the past and find a way to be loyal to two ideas of home: the one they left and the one they've made in America," Abani concluded. *People* reviewer Francine Prose named the book a "tender, thoughtful novel" that considers important themes such as the "meaning of home and family, of nationality and exile, of isolation and connection."

BIOGRAPHICAL AND CRITICAL SOURCES:

PERIODICALS

Booklist, December 1, 2006, review of *The Beautiful Things That Heaven Bears*, p. 22.

Books, February 25, 2007, Laura Ciolkowski, "An Emigre's Search for Permanence in the United States," review of *The Beautiful Things That Heaven Bears*, p. 5.

Entertainment Weekly, March 2, 2007, Jennifer Reese, "Disturbin' Renewal," review of *The Beautiful Things That Heaven Bears*, p. 70.

Kirkus Reviews, November 15, 2006, review of *The Beautiful Things That Heaven Bears*, p. 1150.

Library Journal, November 15, 2006, Debbie Bogenschutz, review of *The Beautiful Things That Heaven Bears*, p. 58.

Los Angeles Times, March 4, 2007, Chris Abani, review of *The Beautiful Things That Heaven Bears*.

People, March 12, 2007, Francine Prose, review of *The Beautiful Things That Heaven Bears*, p. 53.

Publishers Weekly, November 21, 2005, Matthew Thornton, "First Novel to Riverhead," p. 6; August 14, 2006, Liz Hartman, review of *The Beautiful Things That Heaven Bears*, p. 87; November 20, 2006, review of *The Beautiful Things That Heaven Bears*, p. 34.

ONLINE

BookBrowse.com, http://www.bookbrowse.com/ (March 12, 2007), biography of Dinaw Mengestu; (May 2, 2007), interview with Dinaw Mengestu.

DailyCandy.com, http://www.dailycandy.com/ (March 2, 2007), "Just Like Heaven," review of *The Beautiful Things That Heaven Bears.*

Georgetown University Web site, http://www8.georgetown.edu/ (May 2, 2007), biography of Dinaw Mengestu.*

*   *   *

MENOCAL, Maria Rosa 1953-

PERSONAL: Born April 9, 1953, in Havana, Cuba; naturalized U.S. citizen. *Education:* University of Pennsylvania, A.B., 1973, M.A., 1975, Ph.D., 1979.

ADDRESSES: Office—Department of Foreign Languages, Yale University, New Haven, CT 06520.

CAREER: Bryn Mawr College, Bryn Mawr, PA, Mellon fellow in comparative literature, 1979-80; University of Pennsylvania, Philadelphia, assistant professor of Romance languages, 1980-87; Yale University, New Haven, CT, professor of Spanish and Portuguese, Sterling Professor of the Humanities, and director of Whitney Humanities Center, 1988—.

MEMBER: Modern Language Association, Linguistic Society of America, American Association of Teachers of Italian.

WRITINGS:

NONFICTION

(With Helen McFie and Luigi Sera) *Primavera: An Introduction to Italian Language and Culture,* Holt, Rinehart, Winston (New York, NY), 1983.

The Arabic Role in Medieval Literary History: A Forgotten Heritage, University of Pennsylvania Press (Philadelphia, PA), 1987.

Writing in Dante's Cult of Truth: From Borges to Boccaccio, Duke University Press (Durham, NC), 1991.

Shards of Love: Exile and the Origins of the Lyric, Duke University Press (Durham, NC), 1994.

(Editor, with Raymond P. Scheindlin and Michael Sells) *The Literature of Al-Andalus,* Cambridge University Press (New York, NY), 2000.

The Ornament of the World: How Muslims, Jews, and Christians Created a Culture of Tolerance in Medieval Spain, Little, Brown (Boston, MA), 2002.

The Arabic Role in Medieval Literary History: A Forgotten Heritage, University of Pennsylvania Press (Philadelphia, PA), 2004.

Contributor of articles to periodicals.

SIDELIGHTS: Maria Rosa Menocal's book *The Ornament of the World: How Muslims, Jews, and Christians Created a Culture of Tolerance in Medieval Spain* documents the culture and history of the Andalusian kingdom at its high point. The book covers seven centuries, beginning with the Muslim invasion of the Iberian peninsula, and ending with the expulsion from Spain of all Muslims and Jews who refused to convert to Christianity. Between those two turning points, there was a period of about three hundred years when the Muslim, Jewish, and Christian cultures coexisted peacefully and harmoniously. Menocal shows how the three religious groups adapted to each other and coexisted for so long in Spain, creating a unique culture. She does so by telling the stories of sixteen individuals who lived during this era when, although the Muslim culture dominated and influenced the Jewish and Christian subcultures, all three had considerable respect for one another. In an epilog, the author speculates on the lessons this period has to offer the contemporary world, which is marked by tensions between these same religious groups.

"This study of medieval Spain, written for a nonacademic audience, shows that a powerful Islamic society and its committed Christian opponents were once capable of contending in arms, for mastery of a rich territory, without losing their sense of mutual respect," remarked Stephen Schwartz in the *National Review.* "Al-Andalus, the southern Iberian province in which Arab governance was consolidated, produced some of the greatest cultural achievements of Islamic civilization; architecture and philosophy are the best known. The very same region—and its fabled cities, Cordoba, Granada, and Sevilla—also nurtured the Jewish intellect, and provided a prosperous home for Christians."

Menocal's book is "splendid," stated Robert Kuttner, in an *American Prospect* review. Some reviewers, such as Charles E. Butterworth in *Middle East Policy,* regretted that the author did not go into even greater depth with certain aspects of her subject. Yet Butterworth concluded: "Great plaudits are due Maria Rosa Menocal for the fascinating, most appealing, and ever so positive brief history she has provided." A *Publishers Weekly* writer praised the author's "engaging prose and lucid insights," which "provide glimpses into a little-discussed chapter of religious history." Menocal's book calls to mind a novel, according to John Green in *Booklist.* He stated that this "seductively written history" stands as a monument to past achievements and as an inspiration for the future.

In her book *The Arabic Role in Medieval Literary History: A Forgotten Heritage,* Menocal attempts to bring to light the considerable influence that the Arab world has had on Western culture as a whole. Because of anti-Arab feeling, she believes, Arab contributions to European culture have always been downplayed. Menocal shows the many ways that Arab culture has infused the European world, especially during the Renaissance. This book mounts "a spirited challenge to a cultural orthodoxy that has prevailed for rather too long," according to Richard Hitchcock in *Medium Aevum.*

BIOGRAPHICAL AND CRITICAL SOURCES:

PERIODICALS

American Prospect, November, 2004, Robert Kuttner, "What Would Jefferson Do? An Essay on Faith, Terror, and Democracy," p. 31.

Booklist, May 15, 2002, John Green, review of *The Ornament of the World: How Muslims, Jews, and Christians Created a Culture of Tolerance in Medieval Spain,* p. 1572.

Choice, July, 1988, L.L. Bronson, review of *The Arabic Role in Medieval Literary History: A Forgotten Heritage,* p. 1690; February, 2003, review of *The Ornament of the World,* p. 1050.

Christian Science Monitor, July 25, 2002, Jane Lampman, "Religious Tolerance before It Was Hip," section 2, p. 15.

Comparative Literature, winter, 1991, Luce Lopez-Baralt, review of *The Arabic Role in Medieval Literary History,* pp. 99-103; summer, 1996, A.M. Jeannet, review of *Writing in Dante's Cult of Truth: From Borges to Boccaccio,* pp. 307-311; winter, 2002, review of *Ornament of the World,* p. 14.

Comparative Literature Studies, annual, 1996, review of *Writing in Dante's Cult of Truth,* p. 307; summer, 1996, review of *Writing in Dante's Cult of Truth,* p. 307.

Hispanic Review, summer, 1989, Charles S.F. Burnett, review of *The Arabic Role in Medieval Literary History,* pp. 359-361; spring, 1999, John Dagenais, reviews of *Shards of Love: Exile and the Origins of the Lyric* and *Writing in Dante's Cult of Truth,* pp. 250-253; spring, 2003, review of *The Literature of Al-Andalus,* p. 271.

Journal of the American Oriental Society, April-June, 1991, Julie Scott Meisami, review of *The Arabic Role in Medieval Literary History,* pp. 343-352; April-June, 1996, Julie Scott Meisami, review of *Shards of Love,* pp. 313-316.

Kirkus Reviews, March 15, 2002, review of *The Ornament of the World,* p. 388.

Library Journal, September 15, 2002, Clay Williams, review of *The Ornament of the World,* p. 75.

Medium Aevum, spring, 1993, G.H. McWilliam, review of *Writing in Dante's Cult of Truth,* p. 150; spring, 1994, Richard Hitchcock, review of *The Arabic Role in Medieval Literary History,* pp. 177-179; fall, 2003, review of *The Ornament of the World,* p. 378.

Middle East Policy, winter, 2004, Charles E. Butterworth, review of *The Ornament of the World,* p. 148.

Modern Language Notes, March, 1992, Bernhard Teuber, review of *Writing in Dante's Cult of Truth,* pp. 150-152; December, 1996, Stephen G. Nichols, "'Supple Like Water': Lyric and Diaspora," pp. 990-1009.

National Review, June 17, 2002, Stephen Schwartz, review of *The Ornament of the World,* p. 57.

Notes and Queries, December, 1989, Marcella McCarthy, review of *The Arabic Role in Medieval Literary History,* pp. 490-491; June, 1992, Charlotte C. Morse, review of *Writing in Dante's Cult of Truth,* pp. 208-210.

Publishers Weekly, April 29, 2002, review of *The Ornament of the World,* p. 62.

Reference & Research Book News, June, 1994, review of *Shards of Love,* p. 44; May, 2003, review of *The Ornament of the World,* p. 38.

Renaissance Quarterly, winter, 1993, Karla Taylor, review of *Writing in Dante's Cult of Truth,* pp. 819-820.

Romance Philology, February, 1993, L.P. Harvey, review of *The Arabic Role in Medieval Literary History,* pp. 366-367.

Shofar, January, 2003, review of *The Ornament of the World,* p. 196.

Speculum, October, 1988, Dorothee Metlitzki, review of *The Arabic Role in Medieval Literary History,* pp. 957-959; October, 1996, Diana de Armas Wilson, review of *Shards of Love,* pp. 980-983; October, 2002, review of *The Literature of Al-Andalus,* p. 1359; July, 2004, review of *The Ornament of the World,* p. 801.

Times Literary Supplement, June, 2001, Geert Jan Van Gelder, review of *The Literature of Al-Andalus,* p. 7.

U.S. Catholic, August, 2003, Peter Gilmour, review of *The Ornament of the World,* p. 6.

Wall Street Journal, April 26, 2002, Claudia Roden, review of *The Ornament of the World,* p. 12.

ONLINE

BookLoons, http://www.bookloons.com/ (April 30, 2007), Hilary Williamson, review of *The Ornament of the World.*

Jewish Press, http://www.thejewishpress.com/ (August 7, 2002), Michael Skakum, review of *The Ornament of the World.*

Society for Crypto Judaic Studies, http://cryptojews.com/ (April 30, 2007), Arthur Benveniste, review of *The Ornament of the World.*

Time Warner Bookmark, http://www.twbookmark.com/ (April 27, 2007), biographical information about Maria Rosa Menocal.

Yale University Web site, http://www.yale.edu/ (April 22, 2007), biographical information about Maria Rosa Menocal.*

*   *   *

MEYER, Anna 1976-

PERSONAL: Born 1976, in New Zealand; married; husband's name Andrew. *Education:* Holds an undergraduate degree, with honors, from Massey University; Australian National University, Ph.D.

CAREER: Freelance science writer and editor.

WRITINGS:

Hunting the Double Helix: How DNA Is Solving Puzzles of the Past, Allen & Unwin (Crows Nest, New South Wales, Australia), 2005, published as *The DNA Detectives: How the Double Helix Is Solving Puzzles of the Past,* Thunder's Mouth Press (New York, NY), 2006.

SIDELIGHTS: Anna Meyer is a freelance science writer and editor from New Zealand. As a doctoral candidate, Meyer focused her research on the genre of popular science books, the branch of science writing that presents technical and scientific subjects for a sophisticated and intellectually curious but non-specialist reading audience. Her first book, *Hunting the Double Helix: How DNA Is Solving Puzzles of the Past* (published in America as *The DNA Detectives: How the Double Helix Is Solving Puzzles of the Past*), originated in her Ph.D. thesis and is itself a "popular science book about the field of ancient DNA research, which involves the study of any DNA that still exists in the remains of living things that have died," Meyer stated in an interview on the Australian National University Web site.

In the book, Meyer provides a "breezy survey of forensic DNA techniques at work in history and archaeology," noted a *Kirkus Reviews* contributor. Following an explanation of the basics of DNA and its role in genetics and heredity, Meyer addresses the study of ancient DNA and how genetic material can often be extracted from the remains of living organisms up to 100,000 years old. She looks at a number of important questions regarding genetics and the study of ancient DNA, among which are considerations of several long-term mysteries than can be solved through genetic testing. Among the subjects she probes are whether humans are descended from Neanderthals; why the 1918 flu pandemic proved to be so deadly; whether the Black Death and the bubonic plague were the same disease; and the relationship of the enormous New Zealand moa to other flightless birds. She considers the fates of Anastasia, youngest daughter of Czar Nicholas II of Russia, allegedly killed during the Russian Revolution, and the French Dauphin Louis XVII, son of King Louis XVI and Marie Antoinette, who reportedly died in prison during the French Revolution. Meyer also reports that there is little possibility of being able to clone and resurrect ancient extinct creatures such as dinosaurs because of the 100,000-year limit on the survival of viable DNA. Even those experiments that have been tried on more recently extinct species, such as Tasmanian tigers, have been unsuccessful, Meyer notes.

"With a storyteller's flair, Meyer explains in simple terms the science" behind ancient DNA research, commented a *Publishers Weekly* contributor. Gilbert Taylor, writing in *Booklist,* remarked that "Meyer sweetens the science and the history with an amiable sense of curiosity." The *Kirkus Reviews* critic concluded that the book is a "lively exposition of an interesting topic: Meyer is a science writer to watch."

BIOGRAPHICAL AND CRITICAL SOURCES:

PERIODICALS

Booklist, July 1, 2006, Gilbert Taylor, review of *The DNA Detectives: How the Double Helix Is Solving Puzzles of the Past,* p. 17.

Kirkus Reviews, May 15, 2006, review of *The DNA Detectives,* p. 508.

Publishers Weekly, March 20, 2006, review of *The DNA Detectives,* p. 52.

ONLINE

Allen & Unwin Web site, http://www.allenandunwin. com/ (May 2, 2007), biography of Anna Meyer.

Australian National University Web site, http://www. anu.edu.au/ (May 2, 2007), interview with Anna Meyer.

*   *   *

MILLAR, Mark 1969(?)-

PERSONAL: Born December 24, 1969 (some sources say 1970), in Coatbridge, Scotland; married, 1993; wife's name Gillian; children: Emily. *Religion:* Catholic.

ADDRESSES: Home and office—Glasgow, Scotland.

CAREER: Writer. Marvel Comics, senior writer and story consultant, 2001—. Writer for 2000 AD, DC Comics, and for British television. Creator of Millar-world, a creator-owned line of comics.

WRITINGS:

"ULTIMATE X-MEN" SERIES; GRAPHIC NOVELS

The Tomorrow People, illustrated by Andy Kubert and Adam Kubert, Marvel Comics (New York, NY), 2001.

Return to Weapon X, illustrated by Adam Kubert, Tom Raney, and Tom Derenick, Marvel Comics (New York, NY), 2002.

World Tour, illustrated by Adam Kubert and Chris Bachalo, Marvel Comics (New York, NY), 2002.

Hellfire and Brimstone, illustrated by Adam Kubert, Miki Danny, and Andrew Kaare, Marvel Comics (New York, NY), 2003.

Ultimate War, illustrated by Chris Bachalo, Marvel Comics (New York, NY), 2003.

Return of the King, illustrated by Adam Kubert and David Finch, Marvel Comics (New York, NY), 2003.

"THE AUTHORITY" SERIES; GRAPHIC NOVELS

Jenny Sparks: The Secret History of "The Authority," WildStorm Productions (La Jolla, CA), 2001.

(With Tom Peyer) *The Authority: Transfer of Power,* illustrated by Frank Quitely and D. Nguyen, DC Comics (New York, NY), 2002.

The Authority: Earth Inferno and Other Stories, DC Comics (New York, NY), 2002.

Absolute Authority, Volume 2, DC Comics (New York, NY), 2003.

OTHER

(With Grant Morrison) *Vampirella: Ascending Evil,* 1998.

The Ultimates, Volume 1, "Super-Human," illustrated by Brian Hitch, Marvel Comics (New York, NY), 2002.

(With Antony Williams) *The Unfunnies,* four volumes, Avatar Press (Rantoul, IL), 2003.

(With Peter Gross) *Wanted,* Top Cow Productions (Los Angeles, CA), 2003.

(With Ashley Wood) *Run,* Dark Horse Comics (Milwaukie, OR), 2003.

Marvel Knights Spider-Man, Volume 1, "Down among the Dead Men," Marvel Comics (New York, NY), 2004.

Trouble, Marvel Comics (New York, NY), 2004.

Superman: Red Son, illustrated by Dave Johnson and Kilian Plunkett, DC Comics (New York, NY), 2004.

The Chosen, illustrated by Allan Gross, Dark Horse (Milwaukie, OR), 2004.

Superman Adventures, DC Comics (New York, NY), 2004–.

Kick-Ass, illustrated by John Romita, Jr., 2007.

Also author of *Wolverine: Agent of Shield, The Authority: Under New Management, The Ultimates,* Volume 2, "Homeland Security," *The Ultimates: Gods and Monsters, Marvel Knights Spider Man: Venomous, Ultimate Fantastic Four,* Volume 1, "The Fantastic," *Superman Adventures: Last Son of Krypton,* and *Marvel Knights SpiderMan: The Last Stand.* Writer of unreleased television series, *Sikeside.*

ADAPTATIONS: Sikeside, an unreleased television program by Millar, has been optioned for theatrical release.

SIDELIGHTS: Mark Millar is a highly successful writer of English-language comics, known for bringing a somewhat satirical, postmodern sensibility to the genre. Millar's first success was on the already established comic book series "The Authority," published by Wildstorm Productions. He followed this with work on several popular series that updated classic Marvel characters for new audiences. These included "Ultimate X-Men," "Marvel Knights Spider-Man," "Ultimate Fantastic Four," and "Wolverine." He created the best-selling graphic novel *Superman: Red Son,* in which the Superman story is rewritten so that young Superman is raised under Communist rule in the Soviet Union. In 2007, Millar collaborated with John Romita, Jr., with whom he had previously worked on "Wolverine," to create *Kick-Ass,* advertised as the most violent comic ever written.

Millar's early success, "The Authority," features a group of superheroes who cut through the red tape. In a cynical twist, the stories acknowledge that in traditional superhero tales, the real villains usually get away, only to confront the hero again. The Authority makes its own laws and takes on missions that vary from foiling corrupt governments to saving the lives of refugees. But despite their good deeds, the Authority members are more narcissistic than noble, reveling in their power and fame.

In "The Authority," Millar takes classic superhero characters and gives them new quirks. The Hulk is characterized as a mass murderer instead of a misun-

derstood mutant; Giant-Man is guilty of domestic violence; and Thor is dangerous radical. The superheroes battle extraterrestrials and their own inner demons. Millar was also instrumental in creating the groundbreaking Marvel Comics series "Civil War." This unusual saga pits various major Marvel superheroes against each other in an epic struggle. Millar commented in an interview with a *Newsarama.com* contributor: "Above all else, this was a beat-em-up featuring every hero in the Marvel Universe. One of the huge differences between Marvel and DC for me as a wee boy was that Marvel guys would always meet, fight and then realize the error of their ways. It was peculiar, but also very unpredictable and exciting. That was honestly my big intention with the book. Superheroes fighting. Does it get more lowbrow than that? I'm sorry, but that's what excites my inner ten-year-old and I'm heartened to hear retailers and friends tell me how much kids are into it." Asked if "Civil War" was meant to be read as allegory on the political situation in the Middle East, Millar replied: "Who cares what I think of current U.S. foreign policy? People just want to see Hercules braining Thor."

Reviewing a compilation of "The Authority" issues, a *Publishers Weekly* writer stated that it "turns the concept of superheroics on its head in loving, cynical fashion and tells a mean, fast story along the way." Reviewing the same compilation for *Entertainment Weekly,* Jeff Jensen wrote: "Exhilarating yet ruthless, this may be the final word on superheroes."

BIOGRAPHICAL AND CRITICAL SOURCES:

PERIODICALS

Advocate, July 18, 2000, Michael Glitz, "Authority Always Wins," p. 49.

Booklist, March 15, 2002, review of "Ultimate X-Men," p. 1238; November 1, 2005, Ray Olsen, review of *The Chosen,* p. 34; May 15, 2006, review of *Superman Adventures: Last Son of Krypton,* p. 45.

Daily Mail (London, England), January 29, 2001, Iain Fleming, "Marvellous Move for a Superman in the World of Comics," p. 26.

Entertainment Weekly, August 18, 2000, Jeff Jensen, review of "The Authority," p. 122; June 27, 2003, Nisha Gopalan, review of *Trouble,* p. 144.

Evening Times (Glasgow, Scotland), January 27, 2001, "America's Superheroes Get a Trendy Makeover from Lanarkshire Comic Writer," p. 7; April 24, 2004, Maureen Ellis, "Glasgow's Hollywood Heroes," p. 12.

Library Journal, September 1, 2004, Steve Raiteri, review of *The Ultimates,* Volume 2, "Homeland Security," p. 128; March 15, 2005, review of *Ultimate Fantastic Four,* Volume 1, "The Fantastic," p. 64.

Library Media Connection, April, 2003, review of *Ultimate X-Men: The Tomorrow People,* p. 17.

Mirror (London, England), May 13, 2002, Shaun Milne, "Hoops Super Heroes Sign Up X-Men," p. 4.

Observer (London, England), May 9, 2004, David Thompson, review of *Superman: Red Son,* p. 18.

Plain Dealer (Cleveland, OH), August 4, 2001, Michael Sangiacomo, "Marvel Adds a New Twist to Characters," p. E7.

Publishers Weekly, December 8, 2003, review of *The Absolute Authority,* Volume 2, p. 49; July 5, 2004, review of *The Ultimates,* Volume 2, "Homeland Security," p. 41.

School Library Journal, December, 2003, Douglas P. Davey, review of *Ultimate X-Men: The Tomorrow People,* p. 89.

Scotsman (Edinburgh, Scotland), January 29, 2001, Matt Warren, "Millar's Tales of Marvel," p. 4; April 2, 2001, "Mediaphile Mark Millar," p. 4; February 28, 2004, Stephen McGinty, review of *Superman: Red Son,* p. 8.

Star-Ledger (Newark, NJ), October 3, 2004, Drew Sheneman, "This Week's Comic," p. 6.

Sun (London, England), May 13, 2002, Toby Mc-Donald, "X Men to Be Hooped Crusaders," p. 3.

Sunday Herald (Glasgow, Scotland), July 11, 2004, Peter Ross, "Caped Crusader," p. 17.

Sunday Times (London, England), September 13, 1998, Mark Millar, "Mark Millar's Diary," p. 3; May 30, 1999, Emma Cowing, "Superman Loses to Supermac," p. 12; January 28, 2001, Phil Miller, "Super Scot Wins Top Job in Comics," p. 9; February 3, 2002, Phil Miller, "Marvel Superheroes Get Trainspotting Makeover," p. 13; April 27, 2003, Mark Millar, "Is It a Bird?" p. 1, Senay Boztas, "Superman Declares War on America," p. 5.

U.S. News and World Report, December 18, 2000, James M. Pethokoukis, "Breaking the Comic-Book Mold," p. 69.

ONLINE

Blog Critics, http://www.blogcritics.org/ (September 24, 2006), Mel Odom, review of *The Ultimates.*

Comic Book Galaxy, http://www.comicbookgalaxy.com/ (September 25, 2003), Alan David Doane, "Millarworld: An Interview with Mark Millar."

Continuity Pages, http://www.continuitypages.com/ (April 30, 2007), Julian Darius, "Mark Millar's 'The Authority' and the Polemic over Iraq."

MillarWorld, http://www.millarworld.tv (April 24, 2007).

Newsarama.com, http://www.newsarama.com/ (May 12, 2007), interview with Mark Millar.

Sequential Tart, http://www.sequentialart.com/ (May 12, 2007), Barb Lien-Cooper, "Speaking with the Authority: Mark Millar."

Silver Bullet Comic Books, http://www.silverbuttetcomicbooks.com/ (September 25, 2003), Marv Wolfman, interview with Mark Millar.

Superman Homepage, http://www.supermanhomepage.com/ (May 1, 2007), Steven Younic, interview with Mark Millar.*

*   *   *

MILLER, T. Christian 1970(?)-
(Tee Miller)

PERSONAL: Born c. 1970; married; children: two. *Education:* University of California at Berkeley, graduated.

CAREER: Writer, journalist, investigative reporter, and foreign correspondent. *Los Angeles Times,* investigative reporter. Worked as a foreign correspondent in Bogota, Colombia. Guest on television networks, including MSNBC, and on radio programs, including *All Things Considered,* National Public Radio.

AWARDS, HONORS: Livingston Award for international reporting.

WRITINGS:

Blood Money: Wasted Billions, Lost Lives, and Corporate Greed in Iraq, Little, Brown (New York, NY), 2006.

SIDELIGHTS: T. Christian Miller is a multiple award-winning journalist and investigative reporter who works for the *Los Angeles Times*. In his career, he has covered "four wars, a presidential campaign, and reported from more than two dozen countries," noted a biographer on Miller's *Amazon.com* Web log. As part of his duties, Miller has extensively covered the reconstruction effort in Iraq. His work uncovered deep-seated corruption, malfeasance, and misconduct that helped lead to the initiation of several investigations, the cancellation of a flawed arms contract, and the ouster of at least one senior Pentagon official, the biographer stated.

A further result of his in-depth research is his first book, *Blood Money: Wasted Billions, Lost Lives, and Corporate Greed in Iraq.* With this work, Miller offers a "searing account of how the Bush administration has mismanaged the Iraq war and reconstruction," commented Vanessa Bush in *Booklist*. He "presents compelling evidence to support the by-now familiar claim that civilian leaders, military commanders, and planners from the top down gave little thought to the post-combat phase of Operation Iraqi Freedom," observed James E. Verner in the *Military Review.* Miller exposes the "officially sponsored looting, absence of accountability, and shameless profiteering—all ongoing" that has plagued the Iraq effort since the run-up to the war, noted a *Kirkus Reviews* critic. He reports on how American businesses have exploited the nearly endless stream of money flowing from the U.S. government to Iraq, and how companies such as security firm Custer Battles, Bechtel, and Halliburton were enriched through often secret noncompetitive-bid contracts. Though Miller introduces a multitude of villains in his indictment of the Iraq fiasco, he also "uncovers the heroes of the reconstruction, the mid-level bureaucrats and contractors who stood up to Pentagon and Iraqi corruption, risking their careers and lives," commented Michael Scherer in *Mother Jones*. In the end, "Miller makes a compelling point that reconstruction is destined to fail in a country whose environment is as unstable as Iraq's," Verner noted, especially in an environment where the war "has turned into a corporate affair, where companies battle for contracts and life-and-death decisions are based on the bottom line."

BIOGRAPHICAL AND CRITICAL SOURCES:

PERIODICALS

Booklist, June 1, 2006, Vanessa Bush, review of *Blood Money: Wasted Billions, Lost Lives, and Corporate Greed in Iraq,* p. 4.

Book World, September 3, 2006, Michael Hirsh, "The Spoils of War: A Reporter Accuses the Bush Administration of Turning Nation-Building into a Pork Buffet," review of *Blood Money,* p. 6.

Kirkus Reviews, June 1, 2006, review of *Blood Money,* p. 561; December 15, 2006, Jerome Kramer, "*Kirkus Reviews* Best Books of '06: Thirty Outstanding Titles That Deserve Your Attention," review of *Blood Money,* p. 1.

Military Review, November 1, 2006, James E. Varner, review of *Blood Money,* p. 104.

Mother Jones, September-October, 2006, Michael Scherer, review of *Blood Money,* p. 100.

Washington Lawyer, January 1, 2007, Ronald Goldfarb, review of *Blood Money,* p. 42.

ONLINE

Armchair Interviews, http://www.armchairinterviews.com/ (May 2, 2007), Lawrence McMicking, review of *Blood Money.*

T. Christian Miller's Amazon Blog, http://www.amazon.com/ (May 2, 2007).*

*   *   *

MILLER, Tee
See MILLER, T. Christian

*   *   *

MILLER, Wayne 1976-

PERSONAL: Born 1976, in Cincinnati, OH. *Education:* Oberlin College, B.A.; University of Houston, M.F.A.

ADDRESSES: Home—Kansas City, MO. *Office*—Department of English, University of Central Missouri, P.O. Box 800, Warrensburg, MO 64093. *E-mail*—waynemiller5@yahoo.com; wjmiller@ucmo.edu.

CAREER: Writer, poet, translator, editor, and educator. University of Central Missouri, Warrensburg, assistant professor of English. Worked for the Manhattan District Attorney.

AWARDS, HONORS: Bess Hokin Prize, *Poetry* magazine, 2001, for poems in July, 2001 issue; Ruth Lilly fellow, the Poetry Foundation; Lucille Medwick Memorial Award, the Poetry Society of America; George Bogin Memorial Award, the Poetry Society of America.

WRITINGS:

What Night Says to the Empty Boat (Notes for a Film in Verse) (poetry chapbook), Greentower (Maryville, MO), 2005.

Only the Senses Sleep (poetry), New Issues/Western Michigan University (Kalamazoo, MI), 2006.

(Translator, with the author) Moikom Zeqo, *I Don't Believe in Ghosts: Poems from Meduza,* BOA Editions (Rochester, NY), 2007.

(Editor, with Kevin Prufer) *The New European Poetry,* Graywolf Press (St. Paul, MN), 2008.

Contributor to periodicals, including *Epoch, Field, Boulevard, Chelsea, Crazyhorse, Gettysburg Review, Hotel Amerika, LIT, Paris Review, Quarterly West,* and *Sycamore Review.* Editor, *Pleiades: A Journal of New Writing.*

SIDELIGHTS: Poet, editor, and educator Wayne Miller is an assistant professor of English at the University of Central Missouri. He is the author of four books of poetry and translator of the works of Albanian poet, writer, and archaeologist Moikom Zeqo. In *Only the Senses Sleep,* Miller presents a collection of thirty-five free-verse poems concerned with the night and the feelings, sensations, and experiences that humans can find there. "Emptiness haunts Wayne Miller—unfurnished rooms, human absences, each moment's retreat into the past—but from this void he fashions a quiet, [Georg] Trakl-influenced voice that lends feeling to the fragile, sensory world," observed Ned Balbo in the *Antioch Review.* For Miller, even the darkness contains places and objects that inspire the imagination and the pursuit of active thought. In "Empty Warehouse," Miller considers the structure and muses that "Its mere emptiness invites imagination, / which invited, enters." He argues that in darkness or light, the present steadily melds into the past, carried along by the experience of the day, as when he writes in "For the 20th Century" that "Our past hums red / like a blood slide held up to the light," and exhorts the listener: "Why not brush on another layer of red?"

Miller's work "sublimely captures . . . environmental experiences in the dark that pervade the corners of human consciousness," commented an *Internet Bookwatch* reviewer. A reviewer in *Publishers Weekly* remarked that the poet "describes both the visible and the invisible with elegant ease," and commented that "Miller's is a welcome new voice." *Kansas City Star* critic John Mark Eberhart stated that Miller "writes some very fine poetry."

BIOGRAPHICAL AND CRITICAL SOURCES:

PERIODICALS

Antioch Review, winter, 2007, Ned Balbo, review of *Only the Senses Sleep,* p. 197.

Internet Bookwatch, January, 2007, review of *Only the Senses Sleep.*

Kansas City Star, November 19, 2006, John Mark Eberhart, "Ten Dark Highlights," review of *Only the Senses Sleep.*

Poetry, November, 2001, "Announcement of Prizes for 2001," p. 119.

Publishers Weekly, July 31, 2006, review of *Only the Senses Sleep,* p. 54.

ONLINE

University of Central Missouri, http://www.cmsu.edu/index.xml/ (May 15, 2007).

Only the Senses Sleep Web site, http://www.onlythesenses.com (May 2, 2007).

Western Michigan University Web site, http://www.wmich.edu/ (May 2, 2007), biography of Wayne Miller.

*   *   *

MILLER, William 1947-

PERSONAL: Born January 9, 1947, in Philadelphia, PA; son of Julius (a naval purchasing agent) and Norma (a homemaker) Miller; married; wife's name Anne (marriage ended); married May 5, 2006; wife's name Kathleen (a librarian); children: Jessica, Miriam. *Education:* Temple University, B.A. (cum laude), 1968; University of Rochester, M.A., Ph.D., 1974; University of Toronto, M.L.S., 1976.

ADDRESSES: Office—S.E. Wimberly Library, Florida Atlantic University, P.O. Box 3092, Boca Raton, FL 33431. *Agent*— *E-mail*—miller@fau.edu.

CAREER: University of Rochester, Rochester, NY, supervisor in library circulation department, 1971-74; University of Toronto, Toronto, Ontario, Canada, supervisor of medical library, 1975-76; Albion College, Albion, MI, reference librarian, 1976-80, assistant professor of English, 1977-80; Michigan State University, East Lansing, assistant head of reference department, 1980-81, head of reference and government documents departments, 1981-84; Bowling Green State University, Bowling Green, OH, associate dean of libraries and learning resources and associate professor of English, 1984-87; Florida Atlantic University, Boca Raton, director of libraries and member of governing board of Florida Center for Library Automation, both 1987—. University of South Florida, teacher of library courses. Florida State Library Network Council, member, 1995-98; conference speaker; contest judge.

MEMBER: American Library Association (chair of bibliographic instruction section, 1984-85), Association of College and Research Libraries (chapter president, 1981-82; member of executive board, 1995-98; president, 1996-97), Southeast Florida Library Information Network (past president and treasurer), Association of Specialized and Cooperative Library Agencies, English-Speaking Union (president of Boca Raton branch, 1992-94), Boca Raton Literary Society (president, 1996—), Torch Club of Boca Raton (president, 1996-98; member of executive board), Southeastern Library Information Network (governing board member, treasurer, 2007-08).

WRITINGS:

Citation Analysis of Humanities Literature: Implications for Collection Development, Blackwell North America (Beaverton, OR), 1977.

(Editor, with D. Stephen Rockwood) *College Librarianship,* Scarecrow Press (Metuchen, NJ), 1981.

(Editor, with Helen Laurence) *Academic Research on the Internet: Options for Scholars and Libraries,* Haworth Press (Binghamton, NY), 2000.

(Editor, with Rita M. Pellen) *Joint-Use Libraries,* Haworth Information Press (Binghamton, NY), 2001.

(Editor, with Rita M. Pellen) *Cooperative Efforts of Libraries,* Haworth Press (Binghamton, NY), 2002.

(Editor, with Rita M. Pellen) *Improving Internet Reference Services to Distance Learners,* Haworth Information Press (Binghamton, NY), 2004.

(Editor, with Rita M. Pellen) *Innovations in Science and Technology Libraries,* Haworth Information Press (Binghamton, NY), 2004.

(Editor, with Rita M. Pellen) *Internet Reference Support for Distance Learners,* Haworth Information Press (Binghamton, NY), 2004.

(Editor, with Rita M. Pellen) *Libraries and Google,* Haworth Information Press (Binghamton, NY), 2005.

(Editor, with Rita M. Pellen) *Libraries beyond Their Institutions: Partnerships That Work,* Haworth Information Press (Binghamton, NY), 2005.

(Editor, with Rita M. Pellen) *Libraries within Their Institutions: Creative Collaborations,* Haworth Information press (Binghamton, NY), 2005.

(Editor, with Rita M. Pellen) *Evolving Internet Reference Resources,* Haworth Information Press (Binghamton, NY), 2006.

Contributor to books, including *Marketing Instructional Services,* edited by Carolyn Kirkendall, Pierian Press (Ann Arbor, MI), 1986; *The Evolving Educational Mission of the Library,* edited by Betsy Baker and Mary Ellen Litzinger, American Library Association (Chicago, IL), 1992; and *Outsourcing Library Technical Services Operations,* edited by Karen A. Wilson and Marylou Colver, American Library Association (Chicago, IL), 1997. Contributor to professional journals, including *Library Administration and Management, Media Probe, College and Research Libraries, American Libraries,* and *Journal of Academic Librarianship.* Contributing editor, *Library Issues: Briefings for Faculty and Administrators,* 1997—. Editor of academic column in *Michigan Librarian,* 1979-81. *Choice,* member of editorial board, 1979-82, board chair, 1980-82; member of editorial board, *Michigan Librarian,* 1979-82, and *Library Administration and Management,* 1986-90.

SIDELIGHTS: William Miller told *CA:* "My writing has been focused on issues in librarianship, a field that has changed enormously since I entered it thirty years ago, and one that continues to change almost daily. I teach literature and writing also. My influences are George Orwell, E.B. White, and Hemingway—I try to simplify and shorten, and I always tell my writing classes about Mark Twain's remark in a letter to a friend: 'I'm sorry this is so long; I didn't have time to make it short.'"

BIOGRAPHICAL AND CRITICAL SOURCES:

ONLINE

Florida Atlantic University Web site: William Miller Home Page, http://www.library.fau.edu/geninfo/people/miller.htm (April 4, 2007).

*   *   *

MILLIONAIRE, Tony 1956-
(Scott Richardson)

PERSONAL: Born Scott Richardson, 1956, in Gloucester, MA; married Becky Thyre (an actress); children: Phoebe, Pearl. *Education:* Attended Massachusetts College of Art.

ADDRESSES: Home—Pasadena, CA. *E-mail*—millionaire@maakies.com.

CAREER: Cartoonist.

AWARDS, HONORS: Winner of multiple Harvey and Eisner awards.

WRITINGS:

NONFICTION

The Queens Jazz Trail: Homes of Jazz Legends Past and Present, Places of Interest for Jazz Fans, Flushing Town Hall (Flushing, NY), 1998, 2nd edition published as *The Queens Jazz Trail, a Full-color Illustrated Map: Homes of Jazz Legends Past and Present, Places of Interest for Jazz Fans,* 2003.
Lower Manhattan, a History Map, Ephemera Press (Brooklyn, NY), 2003.

Harlem Renaissance, One Hundred Years of History, Art, and Culture, Ephemera Press (Brooklyn, NY), 2003.

WRITER AND ILLUSTRATOR

The Adventures of Sock Monkey, Dark Horse Comics (Milwaukie, OR), 2000.
Maakies, Fantagraphics Books (Seattle, WA), 2001.
Sock Monkey: A Children's Book, Dark Horse Comics (Milwaukie, OR), 2001.
(With Chip Kidd) *The House at Maakies Corner,* Fantagraphics Books (Seattle, WA), 2002.
(With J. Otto Seibold) *Sock Monkey: The Glass Doorknob,* Dark Horse Comics (Milwaukie, OR), 2002.
Mighty Mite: The Earmite, Fantagraphics Books (Seattle, WA), 2003.
When We Were Very Maakies, Fantagraphics Books (Seattle, WA), 2004.
Little and Large, Dark Horse Comics (Milwaukie, OR), 2005.
Der Struwwelmaakies, Fantagraphics Books (Seattle, WA), 2005.
Billy Hazelnuts, Fantagraphics Books (Seattle, WA), 2006.

Also author of *Premillennial Maakies: The First Five Years.* Work appears in numerous newspapers and periodicals, including the *New York Press* and *Village Voice.*

ADAPTATIONS: Maakies has been adapted for television as *The Drinky Crow Show,* produced by Cartoon Network.

SIDELIGHTS: Tony Millionaire is the creator of "Maakies," a popular weekly comic strip featured in the *Village Voice* and other periodicals. "Maakies" is very dark in tone, not intended for children. Set at sea and revolving around a hard-drinking, suicidal crow, the strip is frequently violent and crude. Millionaire also produces a gentler version of "Maakies" called "Sock Monkey." Drawn in a completely different style, but with similar characters, "Sock Monkey" shows the adventures of Drinky Crow and Uncle Gabby, who exist "in a sort of alternate universe to Maakies," according to a writer for the *Adventures Underground* Web site.

Millionaire grew up in an artistic family and studied fine art in college. His Drinky Crow character got his start as a doodle on a bar napkin. The bartender liked it enough to offer Millionaire free beer for more drawings. Eventually, the collection led to a chance to do a comic strip for the weekly *New York Press.*

"Maakies" "often speaks in poetic visions, rendered with subtlety and imagination," according to James Norton on the *flakmagazine* Web site. "Millionaire's nautical illustrations are varied, dynamic and hypnotically detailed. The strip is soaked with ruminations on alcohol, the occasionally crushing emptiness of life and the hilarious pain of romantic relationships." Norton quoted Millionaire as saying that "Maakies" reflects his "writing and drawing about all the things that make me want to jump in the river, laughing at the horror of being alive. People send me letters saying that Maakies helps them cope with the embarrassment and the disgust of everything. It's depressing being a living human, and laughing about it is the only thing you can do after awhile."

Millionaire offers a fable-like tale for children in *Billy Hazelnuts.* It is the story of a band of mice who create a little man out of lard and garbage, hoping he will protect them from the woman who is trying to eradicate them from her kitchen. The lard creature is found by Becky, a young girl who embarks on a series of adventures with him. The story "evokes the anything-goes child-logic found in darker fairy tales and the Oz stories with a pinch of Lewis Carroll thrown in for the sheer bizarreness of it all," according to a *Publishers Weekly* contributor.

Millionaire's style is highly detailed and has both natural and exaggerated components. He cites the newspaper comics of the 1920s and 1930s as a strong influence, as well as the work of Johnny Gruelle, who illustrated the original "Raggedy Ann and Andy" books, and Ernest Shepard, who illustrated A.A. Milne's stories of Winnie the Pooh. In an interview with Bill Smith for *LA Weekly,* Millionaire discussed his desire to make books for children, and stated: "Some philosopher—I don't remember who—his theory was: You've got to give kids really beautiful children's books in order to turn them into revolutionaries. Because if they see these beautiful things when they're young, when they grow up, they'll see the real world and say, 'Why is the world so ugly?! I remember when the world was beautiful.' And then they'll fight, and they'll have a revolution. They'll fight against all of our corruption in the world, they'll fight to try to make the world more beautiful. That's the job of a good children's-book illustrator."

BIOGRAPHICAL AND CRITICAL SOURCES:

PERIODICALS

Booklist, December 1, 2002, Ray Olson, review of *The House at Maakies Corner,* pp. 641-642; August 1, 2004, Ray Olson, review of *When We Were Very Maakies,* p. 1916; August 1, 2005, review of *Der Struwwelmaakies,* p. 2001; February 1, 2006, review of *Billy Hazelnuts,* p. 39.
LA Weekly, November 17, 2005, Bill Smith, interview with Tony Millionaire.
Los Angeles Magazine, May, 2000, Robert Ito, "Who Wants to Be a Millionaire?," p. 32.
Matrix, fall, 2004, reviews of *The House at Maakies Corner* and *When We Were Very Maakies,* p. 59.
New York Press, Volume 15, number 45, John Strausbaugh, "Comics."
Publishers Weekly, January 8, 2001, review of *Maakies,* p. 48; February 10, 2003, review of *The House at Maakies Corner,* p. 165; August 22, 2005, review of *Little and Large,* p. 43; February 20, 2006, review of *Billy Hazelnuts,* p. 142; November 13, 2006, review of *Premillennial Maakies: The First Five Years,* p. 40.
Time, February 16, 2001, Andrew D. Arnold, "A Millionaire's Sock Monkey Offers Strange Comfort."
Voice of Youth Advocates, June, 2001, Kat Kan, review of *The Adventures of Sock Monkey,* pp. 116-117.

ONLINE

Adventures Underground, http://www.advunderground.com/ (April 4, 2006), Logan Kaufman, interview with Tony Millionaire.
Daily Cross Hatch, http://thedailycrosshatch.com/ (May 1, 2007), Brian Heater, interview with Tony Millionaire.
Dark Horse Comics Web site, http://www.darkhorse.com/ (May 1, 2007), James Norton, review of *Maakies;* M. Peg, interview with Tony Millionaire.

Emerald City, http://www.emcit.com/ (May 1, 2007), Peter Wong, review of *Billy Hazelnuts.*

flakmagazine, http://www.flakmag.com/ (May 1, 2007), James Norton, interview with Tony Millionaire.

Maakies Web site, http://www.maakies.com (May 1, 2007).

Tony Millionaire Home Page, http://www.tony millionaire.com (May 1, 2007).*

*   *   *

MILLS, Scott

PERSONAL: Male.

ADDRESSES: Home—Abingdon, MD. *E-mail*—scott@scottmills.net.

CAREER: Writer, cartoonist, and comics writer.

AWARDS, HONORS: Xeric Award, 1999, for *Cells;* Ignatz Award for outstanding story, 2002, for *Trenches;* Ignatz Award nomination, 2003, for *My Own Little Empire.*

WRITINGS:

Big Clay Pot, Top Shelf Productions (Marietta, GA), 2000.

Trenches, Top Shelf Productions (Marietta, GA), 2002.

My Own Little Empire, AdHouse Books (Richmond, VA), 2003.

Zebedia the Hillbilly Zombie Redneck Bites the Dust, OddGod Press (Richmond, VA), 2003.

The Masterplan, Top Shelf Productions (Marietta, GA), 2003.

Seamonsters and Superheroes (collection), Slave Labor Graphics (San Jose, CA), 2003.

Also author of comic book *Cells* and of regular Web comic, *Space Devil.*

SIDELIGHTS: Comics writer and artist Scott Mills is a comic book creator who describes himself as an "alternative cartoonist," he said in an interview with Sébastien Dumesnil on the *Top Two Three Films: Adventures into Digital Comics* Web site. Mills told Dumesnil that he considers creating comics to be "very intimate. Aside from the occasional input from an editor or art director, the process is very personal. From start to finish, from scripting to illustrating, I'm pretty much working on my own." Though he is aware of the financial limitations of the comic book market, and realizes that the audience for comics work seems to be shrinking, he remains optimistic and echoes the sentiments of many creators when he concludes: "We're making comics because we HAVE to. We love them!"

In his graphic novel *Trenches,* Mills tells the story of two British brothers, Lloyd and Davey Allenby, who face the prospect of going to serve in the bloody trenches of World War I. In 1914, the two enlist together and prepare to depart, each in their own way: Lloyd with an emotional farewell from his wife, Davey with a final fling with two sisters. As they enter the service, they meet the story's third main character, Jonathan Hemmingway, who will become their commanding officer in Europe. When the two find themselves on the front lines in France, they have to face their dangerous current situation as well as old sibling rivalries. In between scenes of combat, Mills places flashbacks detailing the two brothers' younger lives, their conflicts, and their connections. Soon, the more impulsive and brash Davey distinguishes himself in combat, and later, so does Lloyd. The bond deepens between Hemmingway and the Allenbys as together they face the horrors of gas attacks, the interminable boredom of trench life, and the ghastly reality of hard-fought warfare. Ultimately, the inevitable tragedy of war strikes the trio, and the remaining two must come to terms with their loss. "Although clichéd in spots, Mills's story is sweet and humane, presenting immensely likable characters trapped in a grim situation," commented a *Publishers Weekly* reviewer. Mills's "simple art . . . gives the book a casual air of understatement unusual for a war story," observed Steve Raiteri in the *Library Journal.*

BIOGRAPHICAL AND CRITICAL SOURCES:

PERIODICALS

Library Journal, January, 2003, Steve Raiteri, review of *Trenches,* p. 84.

Publishers Weekly, November 25, 2002, review of *Trenches,* p. 45.

ONLINE

Scott Mills Home Page, http://www.scottmills.net (May 2, 2007).

Silver Bullet Comics Web site, http://www.silverbullet comicbooks.com/ (May 2, 2007), Tim O'Shea, "Scott Mills: Q&A."

Top Two Three Films: Adventures into Digital Comics, http://www.toptwothreefilms.com/ (October 4, 2004), Sébastien Dumesnil, interview with Scott Mills.*

*   *   *

MILLS, Steven 1959-

PERSONAL: Born 1959, in Ontario, Canada; partner of Christine Leman. *Education:* College graduate; attended the Victoria School of Writing and the Kootenay School of the Arts.

ADDRESSES: Home—Kelowna, British Columbia, Canada. *E-mail*—steven@stevenmills.com.

CAREER: Writer and educator. Paramedic Academy, Justice Institute of British Columbia, Kelowna, British Columbia, Canada, instructor. Has worked as a house painter, park ranger, construction worker, pizza maker, city transit clerk, tow truck dispatcher, Presbyterian Church minister, flagger, farmer, and first-aid attendant.

MEMBER: SF Canada, Federation of British Columbia Writers.

WRITINGS:

Burning Stones (novel), Cosmos Books (Canton, OH), 2006.

Contributor to anthologies, including *Sky Songs II: Spiritual SF.* Contributor to periodicals, including *Interzone, Event 33, subTerrain, On Spec, Windsor Review, TickleAce,* and *New Quarterly.*

SIDELIGHTS: Canadian author and educator Steven Mills is a writer of science fiction. Mills serves as an instructor of paramedics and first responders at the Justice Institute of British Columbia's Paramedic Academy. A frequent contributor of short stories to science fiction periodicals, Mills has also seen success as a mainstream author when his short story, "The Postmodern Man," earned him a spot as delegate to the British Columbia Festival of the Arts in 2002.

Reviewers have taken note of Mills's short stories. In a review on *BestSF.net,* critic Mark Watson commented on Mills's short work "Blue Glass Pebbles," published in the July-August, 2006, issue of *Interzone.* Watson called the tale the "longest and strongest story" in that particular issue of the magazine. Mills posits a future Earth where global warming has made water as precious a commodity as oil is today. Canada has become a major supplier of water to the rest of the world, but constantly faces the possibility of military action by countries without water. The family that provides the main protagonists of the story is headed by a former Canadian prime minister who harbors a lethal plan to inflict a nanovirus on the populace. When her son and his daughter discover the plan, they have to determine what their next move will be, and whether they can defy the family's strong matriarch. "For a newish writer the story bodes well for the future, with strong characterisation, and a no-easy-answers ending," Watson concluded.

Mill's story "Jubilee," published in *Sky Songs II,* an anthology of spiritual science fiction, contains everything that "makes speculative fiction great," commented Eric Joel Bresin on *Tangent Online.* When the barriers between our universe and other dimensions start breaking down, a pastor must deal with the reactions of his flock as the dividing lines between normal and abnormal gradually vanish.

Mills is also the author of the novel *Burning Stones,* in which the residents of a small town near the border of Washington State and British Columbia struggle to deal with the repercussions of a succession of three international disasters. One disaster involves a lethal type of bird flu; another is a virus that turns humans into bestial savages, called "lucies," and the third is the multiple wildfires that erupt when there are few people left to fight them. Protagonist Sage Van Pelt, an ex-librarian, struggles to endure after being incarcerated in a concentration-like camp run by the

Federal Emergency Management Agency. Elsewhere, Alex Gautier, a paramedic, and Ronnie Sapriken, a member of the Royal Canadian Mounted Police, work to fight the out-of-control wildfires and a gang that traps lucies and sells them as slaves. A *Publishers Weekly* critic concluded that "this grim near-future tale showcases the best and worst of humanity" while avoiding the "tyranny of the happy ending."

BIOGRAPHICAL AND CRITICAL SOURCES:

PERIODICALS

Publishers Weekly, July 31, 2006, review of *Burning Stones,* p. 59.

ONLINE

BestSF.net, http://www.bestsf.net/ (July 23, 2006), Mark Watson, review of *Interzone* July-August, 2006, issue.

Federation of British Columbia Writers Web site, http://www.bcwriters.com/ (May 2, 2007), biography of Steven Mills.

Steven Mills Home Page, http://www.stevenmills.com (May 2, 2007).

Tangent Online, http://www.tangentonline.com/ (May 8, 2005), Eric Joel Bresin, review of *Sky Songs II: Spiritual SF.**

*   *   *

MINKOFF, George Robert 1943-

PERSONAL: Born February 9, 1943, in Brooklyn, NY; son of Harry and Ruth Minkoff; married Gail Garrick, October 18, 1968 (divorced, 1980); children: Charles Garrick, Kenan Russell. *Education:* Clark University, B.A., 1965.

ADDRESSES: Home—Great Barrington, MA. *Office*—George Robert Minkoff, Inc., Rare Books, 26 Rowe Rd., Alford, MA 01230. *E-mail*—grm@minkoffbooks.com.

CAREER: Bookseller and writer. George Robert Minkoff, Inc., Rare Books, Alford, MA, owner, 1967—.

MEMBER: Poetry Society of America (member of board of directors, 1986—).

WRITINGS:

A Bibliography of the Black Sun Press, G.R. Minkoff (Great Neck, NY), 1970.

(Editor, with J.D. McClatchy) *The Poetry of Song: Five Tributes to Stephen Sondheim,* Poetry Society of America (New York, NY), 1992.

The Weight of Smoke (novel), McPherson (Kingston, NY), 2006.

SIDELIGHTS: A prominent dealer in rare books, George Robert Minkoff began his own writing career as a playwright in the 1960s. His first book was *A Bibliography of the Black Sun Press,* a survey of works published by the publishing house founded by American poet Harry Crosby. Minkoff later coedited *The Poetry of Song: Five Tributes to Stephen Sondheim,* a series of essays examining the works of the noted Broadway lyricist.

The Weight of Smoke is Minkoff's first novel and written as the first in a proposed trilogy titled "In the Land of Whispers." Described as "epic historical fiction" that is "elegantly expressed in the prose of the seventeenth-century Englishman" by *ForeWord* contributor Nelly Heitman, the novel is set in the early 1600s as the Jamestown colony is first established in what would later become Virginia. Key characters include Jamestown leader John Smith, Native American chief Powhatan and his daughter Pocahontas, and English naval commander Sir Francis Drake. Heitman described the novel as "rich with metaphorical language." A contributor to *Kirkus Reviews* called the book "meticulously researched." An *Internet Bookwatch* reviewer remarked that *The Weight of Smoke* "reads with the flourish of an odyssey, and the dark reality of grim history."

BIOGRAPHICAL AND CRITICAL SOURCES:

PERIODICALS

Internet Bookwatch, March, 2007, review of *The Weight of Smoke.*

Kirkus Reviews, October 1, 2006, review of *The Weight of Smoke,* p. 982.

ONLINE

ForeWord Online, http://www.forewordmagazine.com/ (May/June, 2007), Nelly Heitman, review of *The Weight of Smoke.*

George Robert Minkoff, Inc., Rare Books Web site, http://www.minkoffbooks.com (May 1, 2007).

* * *

MIRALDI, Robert

PERSONAL: Education: State University of New York at Oneonta, B.A., 1972; Boston University, M.S., 1974; New York University, Ph.D., 1985.

ADDRESSES: Home—Stoneridge, NY. *Office*—State University of New York, New Paltz, CSB 48, 75 S. Manheim Blvd., New Paltz, NY 12561. *E-mail*—miraldir@newpaltz.edu.

CAREER: Writer. *Staten Island Advance,* reporter, 1974-80; New York State Assembly, public relations counsel, 1980-82; *Poughkeepsie Journal,* columnist, 1992—; State University of New York, New Paltz, associate professor of journalism, 1983—.

AWARDS, HONORS: Fulbright scholar, Royal University at Utrecht, Netherlands, 1991; John Peter Zenger Award, New York State Bar Association, best commentary on legal issues in New York, 1993 and 1994; Scripps-Howard National Journalism Award, Edward Willis Scripps Award for the First Amendment, runner-up finalist, 1994, 1996; Intellectual Freedom Award, honorable mention, New York State Library Association, 1996; first prize for distinguished column writing, New York Newspaper Publishers Association, 1998, second prize, 1999; Frank Luther Mott Award, Kappa Tau Alpha, 2003, for *The Pen Is Mightier.*

WRITINGS:

Muckraking and Objectivity: Journalism's Colliding Traditions, Greenwood Press (New York, NY), 1990.

The Pen Is Mightier: The Muckraking Life of Charles Edward Russell, Palgrave Macmillan (New York, NY), 2003.

EDITOR

The Muckrakers: Evangelical Crusaders, Praeger (Westport, CT), 2000.

Roger Kahn, *Beyond the Boys of Summer: The Very Best of Roger Kahn,* McGraw-Hill (New York, NY), 2005.

Contributor of articles to newspapers and journals.

SIDELIGHTS: Robert Miraldi is a college professor of journalism, media law, and public relations. His particular passion is the defense of free speech; for eight years he wrote a *Poughkeepsie Journal* column titled "First Freedom" that tackled First Amendment issues. As a novice journalist in the 1970s, Miraldi got a taste for a crusading arm of investigative journalism known as "muckraking." He would go on to study muckraking as a doctoral student and eventual faculty researcher, writing two books on the subject: *Muckraking and Objectivity: Journalism's Colliding Traditions* and *The Pen Is Mightier: The Muckraking Life of Charles Edward Russell.*

The Pen Is Mightier is the result of twelve years of research and a National Endowment for the Humanities grant to study the papers of Charles Russell, a Pulitzer Prize-winning journalist from the turn of the twentieth century. The book, described *Library Journal* reviewer Scott Hightower, "studies Russell's professional achievements at great length, placing them in historical context and shedding light on his subject's largely ignored legacy." Miraldi earned recognition from the national honor society Kappa Tau Alpha by winning the 2003 Frank Luther Mott Award for best research-based book about journalism.

Miraldi also contributed as editor on two projects: *The Muckrakers: Evangelical Crusaders,* and *Beyond the Boys of Summer: The Very Best of Roger Kahn.* His introduction to *The Muckrakers* was lauded by critics such as James Boylan, who wrote for the *Columbia Journal Review* that the book is "much enhanced by the contributions of the editor," adding that Miraldi "offers fresh insights on old-time muckraking." *News-*

paper *Research Journal* contributor Frank Fee described the book as "informative" and "provocative," further commenting that Miraldi's collection "contributes to knowledge and appreciation of the crusading journalists of the Progressive Era" and "offers encouragement for further research as well for, as Miraldi says, 'more is yet to be uncovered and learned.'" *Beyond the Boys of Summer* is a compilation of writings spanning fifty years from noted sports reporter and columnist Roger Kahn.

BIOGRAPHICAL AND CRITICAL SOURCES:

PERIODICALS

Columbia Journalism Review, January, 2001, James Boylan, review of *The Muckrakers: Evangelical Crusaders,* p. 79.

Library Journal, March 1, 2003, Scott Hightower, review of *The Pen Is Mightier: The Muckraking Life of Charles Edward Russell,* p. 98.

Newspaper Research Journal, fall, 2000, Frank Fee, review of *The Muckrakers,* p. 115.

ONLINE

State University of New York at New Paltz Web site, http://www.newpaltz.edu/ (September 20, 2000), "Professor's Book Stresses Journalists' Commitment."*

*   *   *

MOIR, John

PERSONAL: Male.

CAREER: Writer. National Science Teachers Association, staff writer; Elkhorn Slough National Estuarine Research Reserve, Moss Landing, CA, tour leader and assistant researcher.

MEMBER: Authors Guild, National Association of Science Writers, Northern California Science Writers Association, American Birding Association.

AWARDS, HONORS: East of Eden Writing Conference first place for nonfiction, National Steinbeck Center, 2004, for "Bringing Back the Condor,"

WRITINGS:

Just In Case: Everyone's Guide to Disaster Preparedness and Emergency Self-Help, Chronicle Books (San Francisco, CA), 1980.

Return of the Condor: The Race to Save Our Largest Bird from Extinction, Lyons (Guilford, CT), 2006.

Contributor to periodicals, including *Birding.* Contributor to *2006 Writer's Market,* Writer's Digest Books, 2005; and *Best of Novel Advice,* Noveladvice Press, 2002.

SIDELIGHTS: Science writer John Moir first became interested in the California condor while conducting research for a *Birding* magazine piece featuring the endangered species. The award-winning article, titled "Bringing Back the Condor," became the basis for *Return of the Condor: The Race to Save Our Largest Bird from Extinction,* published in 2006. The book chronicles the story of the birds' depletion to near extinction in the 1980s, and the ultimately successful yet controversial captive breeding program that restored populations in the wild. The book was described by a contributor to *California Bookwatch* as a "riveting, readable story" that is "inspiration to any who read about human-influenced extinctions." A *Publishers Weekly* reviewer noted that Moir writes "deftly" and "convincingly," adding that the book "keeps the reader in suspense." Henry T. Armistead detailed in a review for *Library Journal:* "Moir's useful, annotated appendixes detail condor web sites as well as where to see wild and captive condors." Moir's interest in birds goes beyond the investigative: He is a member of the American Birding Association and tour leader for the Elkhorn Slough National Estuarine Research Reserve in Moss Landing, California.

Moir is also writer of the 1980 disaster management text *Just In Case: Everyone's Guide to Disaster Preparedness and Emergency Self-Help* and contributor to two books on writing as a profession: *2006 Writer's Market* and *Best of Novel Advice.*

BIOGRAPHICAL AND CRITICAL SOURCES:

PERIODICALS

California Bookwatch, February, 2007, review of *Return of the Condor: The Race to Save Our Largest Bird from Extinction.*

Library Journal, October 1, 2006, Henry T. Armistead, review of *Return of the Condor,* p. 102.

Publishers Weekly, July 31, 2006, review of *Return of the Condor,* p. 70.

ONLINE

John Moir Home Page, http://returnofthecondor.com (May 2, 2007).*

* * *

MONEY, Nicholas P.

PERSONAL: Education: Attended undergraduate school at Bristol University; University of Exeter, Ph.D., 1986.

ADDRESSES: Office—Department of Botany, Miami University, 344 Pearson Hall, Oxford, OH 45056. *E-mail*—MoneyNP@muohio.edu.

CAREER: Miami University, Oxford, OH, from associate professor to professor.

WRITINGS:

Mr. Bloomfield's Orchard: The Mysterious World of Mushrooms, Molds, and Mycologists (essays), Oxford University Press (New York, NY), 2002.

Carpet Monsters and Killer Spores: A Natural History of Toxic Mold, Oxford University Press (New York, NY), 2004.

The Triumph of the Fungi: A Rotten History, Oxford University Press (New York, NY), 2007.

Contributor of articles to journals.

SIDELIGHTS: As a mycologist, Nicholas P. Money is an internationally recognized expert on mechanisms of fungal growth and development. In an interview with Frank Diller on the *American Scientist* Web site, Money explained that he initially wanted to be a mathematician, but "a series of introductory lectures on fungi left me awestruck." The author continued: "Until then, I had some vague idea that fungi were an unusual type of plant. I had no idea that their cells were constructed in a unique way, nor that fungi grow and reproduce in a decidedly unplantlike fashion. Since then, I have been hooked on mushrooms (so to speak)."

Money has taken his fascination with fungi and turned it into several books designed to be entertaining reading for the general public. In his first work, *Mr. Bloomfield's Orchard: The Mysterious World of Mushrooms, Molds, and Mycologists,* Money presents a series of essays that investigate various molds and fungi, from relatively harmless molds and fungi such as those that cause dandruff and athlete's foot to more dangerous strains that can wreak havoc on people's lungs and nervous systems. "Not for the faint of heart, but definitely for science devotees who appreciate rollicking good humor," according to Alice Joyce in *Booklist. Library Journal* contributor William H. Wiese noted that the author's "practically nonstop humor is irreverent and offbeat, which makes for some lively reading."

Carpet Monsters and Killer Spores: A Natural History of Toxic Mold focuses on the history of molds and especially on a black fungus called stachybotrys, which can plague houses and apartments with poisonous results. Money traces the fungus's origins to damp wallpaper in Prague in the nineteenth century and then follows its spread to North America. The author also discusses the true dangers of stachybotrys, which he sees as minimum, and the health effects of other molds. Frank Diller, writing in the *American Scientist,* remarked that the author "brings some much-needed common sense to . . . concerns about fungal threats to property and peace of mind."

Money presents eight essays about the most notorious fungal diseases in history in *The Triumph of the Fungi: A Rotten History.* In his survey of these diseases, the author writes about the people who studied them and the populations that have been adversely affected, including the Irish who suffered terribly during the potato famine, which was caused by a fungus. Money also writes about the ecological damage these fungi can inflict, including a particular fungus that grows in coastal forests in Australia and can kill more than three-quarters of the plant species. "The book rewards its readers—including those who begin the book with little interest in fungi—by focusing on plants with obvious importance to people," reported Chris Brodie in the *American Scientist.*

BIOGRAPHICAL AND CRITICAL SOURCES:

PERIODICALS

American Scientist, September-October, 2004, Frank Diller, review of *Carpet Monsters and Killer Spores: A Natural History of Toxic Mold,* p. 470; January-February, 2007, Chris Brodie, review of *The Triumph of the Fungi: A Rotten History,* p. 88.

Booklist, October 1, 2002, Alice Joyce, review of *Mr. Bloomfield's Orchard: The Mysterious World of Mushrooms, Molds, and Mycologists,* p. 293.

Choice, February, 2003, S. Hammer, review of *Mr. Bloomfield's Orchard,* p. 1007.

Library Journal, September 15, 2002, William H. Wiese, review of *Mr. Bloomfield's Orchard,* p. 87.

Nature, September 19, 2002, Elio Schaechter, "A Stroll with the Moulds," review of *Mr. Bloomfield's Orchard,* p. 253.

New Yorker, March 10, 2003, Mark Rozzo, "Mycological Positivism," p. 20.

Science Books & Films, November, 2003, review of *Mr. Bloomfield's Orchard,* p. 247.

Science News, November 23, 2002, review of *Mr. Bloomfield's Orchard,* p. 335; July 17, 2004, review of *Carpet Monsters and Killer Spores,* p. 47.

SciTech Book News, December, 2006, review of *The Triumph of the Fungi.*

Seattle Times, October 31, 2002, Irene Wanner, "Welcome to the Beautiful, Yet Bizarre, World of Fungi," p. G6.

ONLINE

American Scientist Online, http://www.american scientist.org/ (April 21, 2007), Frank Diller, "The Bookshelf Talks with Nicholas P. Money."

Miami University Department of Botany Web site, http://www.cas.muohio.edu/botany/bot/ (April 27, 2007), faculty profile of Nicholas P. Money.*

* * *

MOORE, Kevin D. 1964-

PERSONAL: Born October 10, 1964, in Kansas City, MO; son of Jerry (a shipping company manager) and Eloyce Kay (a homemaker) Moore; companion of Jason Siebenmorgen (a landscape architect). *Ethnicity:* "White." *Education:* Attended St. Peter's College, Oxford, 1985-86; William Jewell College, B.A., 1987; University of Missouri—Kansas City, M.A., 1996; Princeton University, M.A., 1997, Ph.D., 2002. *Politics:* Democrat.

ADDRESSES: Home—North Branch, NY. *E-mail*—kdmoore@alumni.princeton.edu.

CAREER: Nelson-Atkins Museum of Art, Kansas City, MO, worked in library acquisitions, 1987-92; Hallmark Photographic Collection, Kansas City, research assistant, 1993-94; Nelson-Atkins Museum of Art, curatorial assistant, 1994-95; Metropolitan Museum of Art, New York, NY, Chester Dale fellow in department of photographs, 1999-2000; Harvard University, Cambridge, MA, curatorial assistant at Fogg Art Museum, 2002, Henry Luce Foundation research associate in American art, 2002-04; Art Advisory Services, New York, NY, senior specialist in photography, 2004-06; private art curator, 2006—. Boston University, visiting professor, 2002; speaker at other institutions, including University of Kansas, University of Toronto, and Williams College; also appeared in British television documentaries about Jacques Henri Lartigue.

MEMBER: College Art Association of America.

AWARDS, HONORS: Grant from Mellon Foundation, 1997; grant for Paris, Institut Français de Washington, 1997; Fulbright grant for Paris, 1998-99; Whiting Foundation grant, 2000-01.

WRITINGS:

Jacques Henri Lartigue: The Invention of an Artist, Princeton University Press (Princeton, NJ), 2004.

Contributor to books, including *Lartigue: The Album of a Century,* Harry N. Abrams (New York, NY), 2003; *Jackie Nickerson: Faith,* 2006; and *New York Rises: Photographs by Eugene de Salignac,* Aperture (New York, NY), 2007. Contributor to periodicals, including *History of Photography.*

*　　*　　*

MORRIS, Jim 1958-

PERSONAL: Born January 25, 1958; son of James R., Jr. (an educator) and Myrtle (an actress and homemaker) Morris; children: Jesse, Jodi Morris Hudson. *Ethnicity:* "Caucasian." *Education:* Attended College of Wooster and Virginia Commonwealth University. *Politics:* Democrat.

ADDRESSES: Home—Pagosa Springs, CO. *Office*—Bristecone Learning Press, 135 Country Center Dr., Ste. B5, PMB 225, Pagosa Springs, CO 81147. *E-mail*—jim@bristleconelearning.com.

CAREER: Virginia Health Center, Richmond, director of Challenge Discovery program, 1981-89; Santa Fe Mountain Center, Santa Fe, NM, associate director, 1989-93; Outward Bound, Rockland, ME, program director, 1993-94; Pecos River Learning Centers, Eden Prairie, MN, director of Adventure Learning Programs, 1994-97; One World Learning, Atlanta, GA, chief operating officer, 1997-2000; Experiential Training and Development Alliance, Portland, OR, chair. Bristlecone Learning Press, senior partner; Outward Bound Discovery, board member; Pagosa Springs Art Alliance, member.

WRITINGS:

(Coauthor) Pat Costello, senior editor, *The A-Z Guide of Experiential Training and Development,* ETD Alliance (Portland, OR), 2006.
The Five Insights of Enduring Leaders, Bristlecone Learning Press (Pagosa Springs, CO), 2007.

Contributor to periodicals.

SIDELIGHTS: Jim Morris told *CA:* "*The Five Insights of Enduring Leaders* is based on my experience teaching executive-level leadership classes through my business. We spent billions of dollars each year sending executives to expensive, pedigreed training programs that are amazing, except for one thing: they (we) are teaching the wrong thing. I wanted to write a book that included relevant examples of twenty-first century leaders, with exercises to help leaders stretch and develop their skills. I tied this around an invitation to senior leaders to build businesses that are socially and environmentally responsible."

*　　*　　*

MULLINS, Ann
See DALLY, Ann

*　　*　　*

MURDOCH, Joyce

PERSONAL: Married Deb Price (an editor and columnist), 2003. *Education:* University of Georgia, graduated (summa cum laude).

ADDRESSES: Home—Tacoma Park, MD. *E-mail*—jmurdoch@nationaljournal.com.

CAREER: Detroit News, Detroit, MI, bureau chief in Washington, DC; *Washington Post,* Washington, DC, editor; *National Journal,* Washington, DC, managing editor for politics; has also worked as a congressional press secretary and as an *Atlanta Journal* reporter; former owner of an independent news service company.

WRITINGS:

(With Deb Price) *And Say Hi to Joyce: America's First Gay Column Comes Out,* Doubleday (New York, NY), 1995.
(With Deb Price) *Courting Justice: Gay Men and Lesbians v. the Supreme Court,* Basic Books (New York, NY), 2001.

SIDELIGHTS: Longtime journalist Joyce Murdoch is also the author of books with her partner, Deb Price. The couple's first book together, *And Say Hi to Joyce:*

America's First Gay Column Comes Out, is a collection of Price's columns for the *Detroit News* covering the period of 1992 to 1994. Murdoch contributes intermittent narrative chapters that focus on how the column was created and details reader response. She also writes about her relationship with Price and the many people the couple have met since they have come out as openly homosexual. Price's columns focus primarily on gay and lesbian issues within various social contexts, such as the military and religion. Ann Northrop, writing in the *Lambda Book Review,* commented: "All in all, this book will work well for the same audience that reads the column. It is not a primer for gay activists. But it does consistently and wholeheartedly urge everyone to come out and be proud, and it does it with some useful historical perspective." Referring to Price's columns as "engaging and spirited," a *Publishers Weekly* contributor also observed that Murdoch's narrative chapters feature "good-humored prose" as she discusses the need for gay journalists.

Murdoch and Price collaborated once again for *Courting Justice: Gay Men and Lesbians v. the Supreme Court.* Here the authors provide an historical perspective of Supreme Court decisions and treatment of gay and lesbian issues dating back to the 1950s. In addition to covering the dozen or so cases the court has reviewed with full briefing and oral arguments, the authors include six cases that obtained summary judgments and the many cases the court has refused to hear. They also profile many of the people involved in these cases, from the plaintiffs to lawyers, judges, and clerks. "The cast of characters involved is fascinating," reported Mary Carroll in *Booklist.* Writing in the *Washington Monthly,* Stephanie Mencimer noted that the authors "scoured the National Archives, interviewed former court clerks, and tracked down many of the original plaintiffs and defendants to hear their tales." Mencimer went on to state that "Murdoch and Price show how much the work for their acceptance, at least by the nation's highest court, is only beginning."

In addition to the book's appeal to general readers, reviewers have felt that *Courting Justice* also has educational value. The work helps to gauge "the extent to which the Supreme Court acknowledges and incorporates evolving societal norms," according to Philip Y. Blue in the *Library Journal.* Referring to the book as a "well-researched, highly informative and chatty history," a *Publishers Weekly* contributor added that *Courting Justice* "fills a gap in lesbian and gay studies and legal studies."

BIOGRAPHICAL AND CRITICAL SOURCES:

PERIODICALS

Advocate, May 30, 1995, Liz Smith, review of *And Say Hi to Joyce: America's First Gay Column Comes Out,* p. 61.

Booklist, June 1, 2001, Mary Carroll, review of *Courting Justice: Gay Men and Lesbians v. the Supreme Court,* p. 1814.

Choice, January, 2002, P.K. Cline, review of *Courting Justice,* p. 972.

Curve, August, 2001, Rachel Pepper, review of *Courting Justice,* p. 45.

DePaul Law Review, summer, 2002, Donald H.J. Hermann, review of *Courting Justice,* pp. 1215-1224.

Gay & Lesbian Review Worldwide, January-February, 2002, Jo Ann Citron, review of *Courting Justice,* p. 30.

Lambda Book Report, July-August, 1995, Ann Northrup, review of *And Say Hi to Joyce,* p. 31.

Law and Social Inquiry, winter, 2002, review of *Courting Justice,* p. 189.

Library Journal, June 15, 2001, Philip Y. Blue, review of *Courting Justice,* p. 89.

New Jersey Law Journal, June 11, 2001, Tony Mauro, review of *Courting Justice,* p. 22.

New York Law Journal, July 27, 2001, William Heinzen, review of *Courting Justice,* p. 2.

New York Times Book Review, October 22, 1995, Carolyn T. Hughes, review of *And Say Hi to Joyce,* p. 36.

Publishers Weekly, June 5, 1995, review of *And Say Hi to Joyce,* p. 46; May 28, 2001, review of *Courting Justice,* p. 72.

Reference & Research Book News, November, 2002, review of *Courting Justice,* p. 113.

Washington Monthly, July, 2001, Stephanie Mencimer, review of *Courting Justice,* p. 56.

Washington Post, June 4, 2001, Charles Lane, "Book Traces Justices' Stance toward Gays," p. A17; June 11, 2001, Hastings Wyman, "Homosexuality and the High Court," review of *Courting Justice,* p. C05.

ONLINE

Advocate Online, http://www.advocate.com/ (July 23, 2003), "*Washington Post* Publishes First Gay Marriage Announcement."

CommonDreams.org, http://www.commondreams.org/ (June 4, 2001), Charles Lane, review of *Courting Justice.*

InsightOut Book Club, http://www.insightoutbooks.com/ (September 17, 2004), review of *Courting Justice.*

National Journal Web site, http://nationaljournal.com/ (April 22, 2007), brief profile of Joyce Murdoch.

Perseus Book Group, http://www.perseusbooksgroup.com/ (April 22, 2007), brief profile of Joyce Murdoch.

Rain Taxi Online, http://www.raintaxi.com/ (April 22, 2007), Jane S. Van Ingen, review of *Courting Justice.**

*   *   *

MURPHY, Rita

PERSONAL: Married; children: one son.

CAREER: Author and educator.

AWARDS, HONORS: Delacorte Press Prize for First Young-Adult Novel, 1999, for *Night Flying.*

WRITINGS:

Night Flying, Delacorte (New York, NY), 2000.
Black Angels, Delacorte (New York, NY), 2001.
Harmony, Delacorte (New York, NY), 2002.
Looking for Lucy Buick, Delacorte (New York, NY), 2005.

ADAPTATIONS: Night Flying was adapted as an audiobook.

SIDELIGHTS: There was a time when author Rita Murphy literally wrote in the closet. Writing was her hobby then, and in order to keep from bothering her husband and son in the family's one-room apartment, "I pulled a lamp and my computer into a closet where I wouldn't disturb them," Murphy explained to *Publishers Weekly* contributor Shannon Maughan. Murphy's writing habits changed after her first novel, *Night Flying,* was selected for the Delecorte Press Prize for First Young-Adult Novel. "Murphy's work station has moved from the closet to a desk near the kitchen, where she now writes for about four hours each morning," Maughan explained.

Night Flying introduces almost-sixteen-year-old Georgia Hansen. Like all of the women in her family, Georgia can fly. Of course, she must obey the rules of her domineering grandmother, the same rules the whole family must obey. Then Georgia meets her Aunt Carmen, who was cast out of the family years before. As Georgia begins to uncover old family secrets and lies, she must ultimately decide whether to honor family tradition or choose her own path. Murphy "infuses Georgia's narrative voice with a naïve lyricism that beautifully captures the human desire to soar," wrote Debbie Carton in a review of *Night Flying* for *Booklist.* A *Publishers Weekly* critic commented that the novelist "seamlessly links the metaphor of flying with Georgia's rite of passage."

In *Black Angels,* Murphy moves from fantasy to real-life Mystic, Georgia. The year is 1961, when Celli, who lives on the white side of town, discovers that her father was half black and passing for white. Confused by the racial tensions erupting in her town, Celli must now chose a side on the racial divide. While Hazel Rochman wrote in *Booklist* that parts of the plot are contrived, "what will hold readers is the young girl's viewpoint of politics coming to town and right into her home."

In *Harmony,* Murphy returns to the fantastic; Harmony is a young girl who came to her parents from the stars. She has incredible powers, and is able to make things happen with only a thought. Fitting into her small mountain community is a challenge for Harmony, however, and she has to learn how to use her gifts for the good of the community. "Once again, Murphy introduces us to strong female characters and adds a touch of the super-natural as well," wrote Paula Rohrlick in *Kliatt.* A *Kirkus Reviews* contributor dubbed the novel "a magical story written with a light, lyrical touch" that is "always rooted in the particulars of the mountain setting," and GraceAnne A. DeCandido wrote in *Booklist* that Murphy uses "sweet, sharp language as clear as the scent of pine."

Looking for Lucy Buick is a contemporary novel about a girl who grows up among a family of surrogate aunts and uncles. The reason? Lucy was discovered, as an infant, in the back seat of a Buick won by an "aunt" in a bet. Lucy grows up determined to find her birth family, whom she refers to as the Buicks, and when she turns eighteen, a fire allows her to fake her own death and make her way from New York to Iowa. There, she finds not her birth family, but a colorful cast of people who become a real family to her. Nicole Marcuccilli, writing in *School Library Journal*, considered the novel "an excellent read about a teen searching for her identity and where she belongs," while a *Kirkus Reviews* contributor dubbed *Looking for Lucy Buick* "sweet and light as a feather but with the substantial charm of music or a summer's day."

BIOGRAPHICAL AND CRITICAL SOURCES:

PERIODICALS

Booklist, December 15, 2000, Debbie Carton, review of *Night Flying,* p. 809; February 15, 2001, Hazel Rochman, review of *Black Angels,* p. 1149; March 15, 2001, review of *Night Flying,* p. 1366; September 15, 2002, GraceAnne A. DeCandido, review of *Harmony,* p. 222; October 15, 2005, Ilene Cooper, review of *Looking for Lucy Buick,* p. 47.

Book Report, May, 2001, Heather Hepler, review of *Night Flying,* p. 61.

Bulletin of the Center for Children's Books, January, 2001, review of *Night Flying,* p. 190; March, 2001, review of *Black Angels,* p. 272; January, 2006, Deborah Stevenson, review of *Looking for Lucy Buick,* p. 243.

Horn Book, September, 2000, Lauren Adams, review of *Night Flying,* p. 577; January-February, 2003, Lauren Adams, review of *Harmony,* p. 81; January-February, 2006, Philip Charles Crawford, review of *Looking for Lucy Buick,* p. 85.

Kirkus Reviews, September 1, 2002, review of *Harmony,* p. 1316.

Kliatt, July, 2002, Paula Rohrlick, review of *Night Flying,* p. 31; November, 2002, Paula Rohrlick, review of *Harmony,* p. 14; November, 2005, Myrna Marler, review of *Looking for Lucy Buick,* p. 9.

Publishers Weekly, November 27, 2000, review of *Night Flying,* p. 77; December 18, 2000, Shannon Maughan, "Rita Murphy," p. 28; February 5, 2001, review of *Black Angels,* p. 89; April 22, 2002, review of *Night Flying,* p. 73; September 23, 2002, review of *Harmony,* p. 73.

School Library Journal, November, 2000, Sharon Grover, review of *Night Flying,* p. 160; July, 2001, Louise L. Sherman, review of *Black Angels,* p. 111; October, 2002, Saleena L. Davidson, review of *Harmony,* p. 169; November, 2005, Nicole Marcuccilli, review of *Looking for Lucy Buick,* p. 143.

Voice of Youth Advocates, October, 2000, review of *Night Flying,* p. 277; December, 2002, review of *Harmony,* p. 400.

ONLINE

Crescent Blues Book Views Online, http://www.crescentblues.com/ (April 28, 2007), Lynne Marie Pisano, review of *Night Flying.*

Random House Web site, http://www.randomhouse.com/ (April 28, 2007), interview with Murphy.

*   *   *

MYERS, B.R. 1963-
(Brian R. Myers, Brian Reynolds Myers)

PERSONAL: Born 1963, in NJ; married Myunghee Ko. *Education:* Ruhr University, Bochum, South Korea, M.A. 1989; University of Tübingen, Ph.D., 1992.

ADDRESSES: Home—South Korea.

CAREER: Korea University, Seoul, South Korea, faculty member, 2001-05; Inje University, Busan, South Korea, assistant professor, 2005-06; Dongseo University, Busan, South Korea, researcher; has also taught German in Japan and worked for an automobile manufacturer in China.

WRITINGS:

Han Sorya and North Korean Literature: The Failure of Socialist Realism in the DPRK, East Asia Program, Cornell University (Ithaca, NY), 1994.

A Reader's Manifesto: An Attack on the Growing Pretentiousness in American Literary Prose, Melville House (Hoboken, NJ), 2002.

Also contributor to periodicals, including the *New York Times, Korea Times,* and *Wall Street Journal.* Contributing editor, *Atlantic Monthly.*

SIDELIGHTS: B.R. Myers was born in America and has lived in the United States and various other countries, including South Korea. He is an academic, and his interests include North Korean history, society, and politics. In the summer of 2001, Myers raised many eyebrows in the literary community when he came out with a scathing analysis in the *Atlantic* of some of America's most noted writers, including Don Delilo and Annie Proulx. The expanded version of his essay was published in 2002 as *A Reader's Manifesto: An Attack on the Growing Pretentiousness in American Literary Prose.* In the book the author discusses what he calls the "bad writing" of Delilo, Proulx, Cormac McCarthy, David Gutterson, and Paul Auster, with a focus on both the authors' style and matters of content. Among the books discussed are *Blood Meridian, The Body Artist, White Noise, Beloved,* and *Snow Falling on Cedars.* Not only does the author provide a more comprehensive criticism of these authors in his book as compared to his article, but he also takes the opportunity to rebut many of those who criticized his original analyses of these American writers.

Critics generally praised *A Reader's Manifesto,* despite the fact that the author's critique also includes many of the critics themselves for their approval of what he considers bad books. "What makes this entertaining book so important isn't the . . . relative correctness of Myers's argument . . . but that . . . someone has dared to say, with energy and insight, what many have privately concluded," wrote a *Publishers Weekly* contributor. A *Complete Review* contributor commented that "*A Reader's Manifesto* is a short book and, despite the many examples of bad writing on offer, a breezy, entertaining read." The reviewer went on to write that "Myers' book will have served its purpose if it helps readers feel more confident in their own judgements—and teaches them that there are few people less reliable than critics of any sort."

Despite several positive reviews, some critics did not agree with all of Myers's judgments. For example, writing on *GoodReports.net,* a contributor commented:

"While I would quarrel over some matters of taste, he is a responsible critic. And his declaration that taste and sensibility are all that any of us need to distinguish good books from bad books has rarely seemed so necessary." James Marcus, writing on the *House of Mirth* blog, noted that he "had to agree with at least some of the thwacking that Myers administered," while adding that Myers "tends to approach English sentences like an efficiency expert." A contributor to *Blogcritics.org* concluded: "Although I don't agree with all of his choices, I agree with the underlying sentiment."

BIOGRAPHICAL AND CRITICAL SOURCES:

PERIODICALS

Books in Canada, January-February, 2003, Harold Hoefle, review of *A Reader's Manifesto: An Attack on the Growing Pretentiousness in American Literary Prose.*
Entertainment Weekly, October 4, 2002, Troy Patterson, review of *A Reader's Manifesto,* p. 148.
Far Eastern Economic Review, March 2, 1995, Ann Lee, "Birth of a Hero: Han Sorya and North Korean Literature," review of *Han Sorya and North Korean Literature: The Failure of Socialist Realism in the DPRK,* p. 39.
Korea Journal, summer, 1994, review of *Han Sorya and North Korean Literature,* p. 122.
New Criterion, December, 2002, Mark Bauerlein, review of *A Reader's Manifesto,* p. 84.
Pacific Affairs, spring, 1995, Kichung Kim, review of *Han Sorya and North Korean Literature,* p. 127.
Publishers Weekly, September 2, 2002, review of *A Reader's Manifesto,* p. 73
World Literature Today, winter, 1995, Yearn Hong Choi, review of *Han Sorya and North Korean Literature,* p. 229.

ONLINE

Blogcritics.org, http://blogcritics.org/ (October 8, 2005), review of *A Reader's Manifesto.*
Complete Review, http://www.complete-review.com/ (April 22, 2007), review of *A Reader's Manifesto.*
GoodReports.net, http://www.goodreports.net/ (April 22, 2007), review of *A Reader's Manifesto.*

House of Mirth Blog, http://housemirth.blogspot.com/ (February 16, 2006), James Marcus, "B.R. & I."

JoongAng Daily Web site, http://joongangdaily.joins. com/ (May 29, 2005), Kim Sun-jung, "The Remarkable B.R. Myers Revealed."

Opinion Journal, http://opinionjournal.com/ (August 30, 2002), Claudia Rosett, review of *A Reader's Manifesto.**

MYERS, Brian R.
   See MYERS, B.R.

*   *   *

MYERS, Brian Reynolds
   See MYERS, B.R.

N-O

NEWTON, Jim 1963-

PERSONAL: Born 1963, in Palo Alto, CA; married Karlene Goller (a lawyer); children: Jack. *Education:* Dartmouth College, graduated, 1985.

ADDRESSES: Home—Pasadena, CA. *Office*—Los Angeles, CA. *E-mail*—Jim.Newton@latimes.com.

CAREER: During early career, worked as a columnist's clerk for the *New York Times* and city desk reporter for the *Atlanta Journal-Constitution; Los Angeles Times,* Los Angeles, CA, reporter, bureau chief, and editor, 1989-2007, editorial page editor, 2007—.

AWARDS, HONORS: Pulitzer Prize (with *Los Angeles Times* staff), 1993, for coverage of the Los Angeles riots, and 1995, for coverage of the Northridge earthquake; IGS John Jacobs fellow, University of California at Berkeley, 2003-04.

WRITINGS:

Justice for All: Earl Warren and the Nation He Made (biography), Riverhead Books (New York, NY), 2006.

SIDELIGHTS: As a journalist with the *Los Angeles Times,* California native Jim Newton has reported on the state's most newsworthy events since 1989. He brought with him several years of experience with the *New York Times,* where he clerked for senior columnist James Reston, and the *Atlanta Journal-Constitution,* where he covered city politics. As a *Los Angeles Times* staff reporter, Newton was a key contributor to coverage of the O.J. Simpson murder trial, the federal prosecution of Los Angeles police officers accused of beating Rodney King, the riots that succeeded the officers' acquittal in state court, and the 1994 Northridge earthquake.

Newton's first book, a biography of former California governor and Supreme Court Justice Earl Warren, was published in 2006. Described by a *Publishers Weekly* reviewer as the "definitive biography" of the historical figure, *Justice for All: Earl Warren and the Nation He Made* covers all aspects of Warren's career, from his start as a county prosecutor, to his governorship, his appointment as chief justice, his landmark decisions such as the 1954 *Brown v. Board of Education* ruling, and his role as chair of the commission investigating the murder of President John F. Kennedy. "Newton's masterful narrative synthesizes Warren in all his contradictory guises," continued the *Publishers Weekly* reviewer. Steven Puro commented in a review for *Library Journal* that the "clear and concise writing results in a thorough and thoughtful view of Warren." *Los Angeles Magazine* contributor Tom Carson remarked: "Newton makes an expert guide. . . . His reconstructions of the dickerings, compromises, and psychological gamesmanship that went into forging each ruling under Warren's guidance are fascinating, exceptionally lucid in laying out the legal issues and political context of every major case, and organized with compelling narrative momentum."

BIOGRAPHICAL AND CRITICAL SOURCES:

PERIODICALS

Library Journal, September 15, 2006, Steven Puro, review of *Justice for All: Earl Warren and the Nation He Made,* p. 74.
Los Angeles Magazine, January, 2007, Tom Carson, "The Chief: In His Biography of Earl Warren, Jim Newton Renders a Politician and a Justice Who Read the Constitution as a User's Manual," p. 60.
Publishers Weekly, September 11, 2006, review of *Justice for All,* p. 47.

ONLINE

University of California Berkeley Center on Politics, http://politics.berkeley.edu/ (May 16, 2007), profile of Jim Newton.

*   *   *

NIEDZVIECKI, Hal 1971-

PERSONAL: Born January 9, 1971, in Brockville, Ontario, Canada; married; wife is a psychologist. *Education:* University of Toronto, B.A.; Bard College, M.F.A.

ADDRESSES: Home—Toronto, Ontario, Canada. *E-mail*—hal@brokenpencil.com.

CAREER: Writer and editor. *Broken Pencil* magazine, cofounder and editor, 1995-2002, then president of the board of directors and special projects coordinator, c. 2002—; Canzine festival of Underground Culture, cofounder and director, 1995-2002. Also correspondent for the Canadian Broadcasting Corporation's (CBC) *Brave New Waves.*

WRITINGS:

FICTION

(Editor) *Concrete Forest: The New Fiction of Urban Canada,* M&S (Toronto, Ontario, Canada), 1998.

Smell It: Stories, Coach House Books (Toronto, Ontario, Canada), 1998.
Lurvy: A Farmer's Almanac, illustrated by Hoge Day and Marc Ngui, Coach House Books (Toronto, Ontario, Canada), 1999.
Ditch (novel), Random House Canada (Toronto, Ontario, Canada), 2001.
The Program (novel), Random House Canada (Toronto, Ontario, Canada), 2005.

NONFICTION

We Want Some Too: Underground Desire and the Reinvention of Mass Culture, Penguin Books (Toronto, Ontario, Canada), 2000.
(With Steve Mann) *Cyborg: Digital Destiny and Human Possibility in the Age of the Wearable Computer,* Random House Doubleday Canada (Toronto, Ontario, Canada), 2001.
(With Darren Wershler-Henry) *The Original Canadian City Dweller's Almanac: Facts, Rants, Anecdotes and Unsupported Assertions for Urban Residents,* illustrations by Marc Ngui, Viking Canada (Toronto, Ontario, Canada), 2002.
Hello, I'm Special: How Individuality Became the New Conformity, City Lights Books (San Francisco, CA), 2006.

Contributor to periodicals, including *Adbusters, Utne Reader, Globe and Mail, National Post, Toronto Life, Geist, Azure,* and *This Magazine.*

SIDELIGHTS: Hal Niedzviecki is a writer whose books range from social criticism to fiction. In *We Want Some Too: Underground Desire and the Reinvention of Mass Culture,* the author focuses on pop culture and how a new kind of artist is evolving from the constant onslaught of mass media and pop culture outlets. A *This Magazine* contributor called the book "a happy response to the rash of ponderous, doom-ridden cultural forecasts." Referring to the book as "both accessible and dynamically complex," Liisa Kelly, in *Canadian Woman Studies,* also wrote: "Every word he writes is a celebration of art by and for the consumption of everyone, projecting his enthusiasm for freedom of expression and mass involvement in the creation of culture."

Niedzviecki collaborated with computer scientist Steve Mann to write *Cyborg: Digital Destiny and Human Possibility in the Age of the Wearable Computer.* The book reports largely on Mann's longtime experiment of making himself a type of cyborg by living with and wearing a camera eye and wireless Internet connection that is constantly on. *Perspectives in Biology and Medicine* contributor Derrick de Kerckhove called *Cyborg* "important for people who want to break new ground in human understanding, who feel the need to explore their own circumstances with greater acuity."

The Program is a novel about brothers Maury and Cal Stern and Maury's son Danny, who leads a reclusive, detached inner life and eventually becomes a cyborg. Maury is the author of a best-selling book titled *Get with the Program* that focuses on the power of slogans. Meanwhile, Cal may have something to do with Danny's withdrawal from life due to an episode one night when Cal was babysitting Danny. Joe Wiebe, writing on *Straight.com,* commented that the author's "potent talents show up in moments of brilliant clarity."

In his 2006 book *Hello, I'm Special: How Individuality Became the New Conformity,* Niedzviecki explores the idea that nonconformity has become the norm, leaving the author to question who is really special and different and whether there is really anyone left to rebel against. Examining various aspects of modern pop, consumer, and counter culture, the author discusses such topics as celebrity culture, marketing's use of individualism to sell people identical products, and political activism that is sometimes committed more to the idea of "specialness" than political goals. "Niedzviecki, who writes with a mainstream nonconformist's informality, seems torn about the despondency that the I'm Special phenomenon can illicit," wrote a contributor to the *Fourth-Rate Reader* Web site. "He is empathetic to people who are broken down by their failure to successfully fit in by standing out. He recognizes that it is almost impossible for a person to escape the zeitgeist of their times."

Hello, I'm Special received several favorable reviews. Zachary Houlem, writing on the *PopMatters* Web site, noted that "what makes Niedzviecki's groundbreaking new book so refreshing . . . [is that] he reminds us that pop culture itself isn't an absolute means to an end; it's the people who exchange it and want to be a part of it all that remain its most fascinating components." A contributor to *Tikkun* wrote that with this book the author "gives us everything that makes his brand of literary genius so . . . special."

BIOGRAPHICAL AND CRITICAL SOURCES:

PERIODICALS

Canadian Book Review Annual, annual, 1999, review of *Concrete Forest: The New Fiction of Urban Canada,* p. 242; annual, 2000, review of *We Want Some Too: Underground Desire and the Reinvention of Mass Culture,* p. 354; annual, 2002, review of *Ditch,* p. 176; annual, 2005, Tami Oliphant, review of *The Program,* p. 184.

Canadian Forum, April, 2000, Derek Chezzi, review of *Lurvy: A Farmer's Almanac,* p. 37.

Canadian Literature, spring, 2004, Charles E. May, "Contemporary Short Stories."

Canadian Woman Studies, winter-spring, 2001, Liisa Kelly, review of *We Want Some Too,* p. 160.

Catholic New Times, June 5, 2005, Susannah Schmidt, "No Dreams: Christian Realism," p. 20.

Library Journal, April 15, 2006, Ellen D. Gilbert, review of *Hello, I'm Special: How Individuality Became the New Conformity,* p. 94.

Maclean's, August 21, 2000, Charles Gordon, "Why Ignore Local Talent?," p. 55.

Perspectives in Biology and Medicine, summer, 2003, Derrick de Kerckhove, review of *Cyborg: Digital Destiny and Human Possibility in the Age of the Wearable Computer.*

Publishers Weekly, March 27, 2006, review of *Hello, I'm Special,* p. 76.

Quill & Quire, April, 1998, review of *Smell It,* p. 26; May, 1998, review of *Concrete Forest,* p. 29; March, 2000, review of *We Want Some Too,* p. 34; April, 2000, review of *We Want Some Too,* p. 43; July, 2001, review of *Ditch,* p. 39.

Reference & Research Book News, May, 2006, review of *Hello, I'm Special.*

This Magazine, May-June, 2000, review of *We Want Some Too,* p. 43; November-December, 2004, Andrew Potter, review of *Hello, I'm Special,* p. 57; January-February, 2005, Pike Wright, "Fightin' Words," p. 8.

Tikkun, May-June, 2006, review of *Hello, I'm Special,* p. 81.

University of Toronto Quarterly, winter, 1999, Neil Besner, "Fiction."

ONLINE

Bookslut, http://www.bookslut.com/ (May 21, 2007), Daniel Nester, "An Interview with Hal Niedzviecki."

Coach House Books Web site, http://www.chbooks. com/ (May 21, 2007), brief profile of author.

Fourth-Rate Reader, http://lit.fictionary.ca/ (April 21, 2006), review of *Hello, I'm Special.*

January Magazine, http://www.januarymagazine.com/ (May 21, 2007), Linda Richards, "Hal Niedzviecki January Interview."

PopMatters, http://www.popmatters.com/ (December 7, 2004), Zachary Houle, review of *Hello, I'm Special.*

Smell It: The Web Site of Hal Niedzviecki, http://www. brokenpencil.com/smellit/bio/index.shtml (May 21, 2007).

Straight.com, http://www.straight.com/ (October 7, 2004), Joe Wiebe, review of *Hello, I'm Special;* (March 24, 2005), Joe Wiebe, review of *The Program.*

*   *   *

OCKERT, Jason

PERSONAL: Born in IN. *Education:* University of Florida, B.A., 1995; Syracuse University, M.F.A., 2000.

ADDRESSES: Home—NY. *Office*—Ithaca College, 126 Administration Annex, Ithaca, NY 14850. *E-mail*—jockert@ithaca.edu.

CAREER: Ithaca College, Ithaca, NY, assistant professor of writing, 2000-07; Coastal Carolina University, Conway, SC, assistant professor, 2007—. Also worked as a fact-checker for *National Geographic.*

AWARDS, HONORS: Atlantic Monthly Fiction Contest winner, 1999; Mary Roberts Rinehart National Fiction Award, 2002.

WRITINGS:

Rabbit Punches (short stories), Low Fidelity Press (Brooklyn, NY), 2004.

Contributor of short fiction to books, including *Virgin Fiction 2,* Rob Weisbach Books, 1999; *New Stories from the South,* 2007; and *The Best American Mystery Stories,* 2007. Contributor of short fiction to periodicals, including *Indiana Review, Panhandler, H_NGM_N, Mid-American Review, Oxford American, Alaska Quarterly Review, Bathhouse, Black Warrior Review, Knight Literary Journal, Highway 14, Oyster Boy Review, CutBank, RiverCity,* and *McSweeney's.* Contributor of short fiction to Web sites, including *Reinventingtheworld.com.*

SIDELIGHTS: Jason Ockert told *CA:* "I first started writing in order to exert some kind of control over the way in which I understood the world. As a child and adolescent, I didn't feel as if I had much say in how my life was run. Writing became a kind of emotional stabilizer.

"My work has most been influenced by the southern grotesque and the Russian gothic genres. Music has also had an impact on the way I write. I've been affected by bands like The Replacements, XTC, Tom Waits, and Pavement, to name a few.

"My process for writing short stories is to begin with some core emotional dilemma or consideration and then wrap sentences around that idea until I get it as close to right as possible. I am most interested in writing pieces that walk the 'improbable line' without getting carried away. I do a lot of revising and restructuring.

"When writing a novel, I write down tons of notes—ideas, impressions, snippets of dialogue, anything that happens to come to mind. At some point, those notes spill over to the narrative and I begin an initial draft.

"The most surprising thing I have learned as a writer is that I am a writer. I grew up appreciating the value of a hard day of work on the job. Writing was something I did on my own time and I coveted it in a way. To be able to answer the question here to you now is the biggest surprise.

"The writing project I've completed most recently is always my favorite.

"I want my work to resist being forgotten by the reader."

BIOGRAPHICAL AND CRITICAL SOURCES:

PERIODICALS

Bloomsbury Review, July-August, 2006, Mark Budham, review of *Rabbit Punches.*

Chicago Reader, March 14, 2006, Jerome Ludwig, review of *Rabbit Punches.*

Publishers Weekly, March 27, 2006, review of *Rabbit Punches.*

Rain Taxi, fall, 2006, review of *Rabbit Punches.*

ONLINE

Ink 19, http://www.ink19.com/ (May 14, 2006), Linda Tate, review of *Rabbit Punches.*

Ithaca College Web site, http://www.ithaca.edu/ (May 14, 2006), faculty profile of author.

Ithacan Online, http://www.theithacan.org/ (April 13, 2006), Brian Kravitz, "Professor Uses Writing Experience to Encourage Student Work."

*   *   *

O'DWYER, Jeffrey Starbuck
See O'DWYER, Starbuck

*   *   *

O'DWYER, Starbuck
(Jeffrey Starbuck O'Dwyer)

PERSONAL: Born in Rochester, NY. *Education:* Graduated from Princeton University, 1989, Oxford University, and Cornell University.

ADDRESSES: Home—Washington, DC. *E-mail*—info@starbuckodwyer.com

CAREER: Lawyer, writer, and radio host. Host of "Starbuck's Supreme Court" segment on WZID-FM Radio, Manchester, NH. Guest appearances on numerous television and radio shows. Admitted to the Bars of New York, Illinois, and District of Columbia.

WRITINGS:

Red Meat Cures Cancer (novel), Midnight Books (Bethesda, MD), 2002.

SIDELIGHTS: Starbuck O'Dwyer is a Washington, DC, lawyer who has made a name for himself with his frequent guest appearances on television and radio shows as a legal commentator and comic, in addition to hosting a regular show on a New Hampshire radio station. O'Dwyer's first novel, *Red Meat Cures Cancer,* was written during his off-hours as a practicing attorney. It tells the story of a fast-food chain executive who comes up with an off-the-wall ad campaign aimed at picking up lagging sales—succumb to temptation and "Torture Your Body" with the restaurant's cholesterol-laden food. Regarding the novel's exaggerated premise, O'Dwyer remarked in an interview with *Princeton Alumni Weekly Online* contributor Rob MacKay: "The main purpose of the book is to entertain and make people laugh. . . . But it's also intended to make people think about the impact of the American consumer culture on their daily lives." A reviewer for *Publishers Weekly* pointed out the novel's "undeniable gutbusters," adding that O'Dwyer "deserves points for sheer chutzpah." Leo Champion described the book as a "very competent first novel" on the *Boston's Weekly Dig* Web site, commenting that "as satire goes, the book is first rate." O'Dwyer, wrote a *Kirkus Reviews* contributor, "paints *Red Meat Cures Cancer* with broad, primary strokes burnished with a healthy dose of ribaldry," the result being "deep-fried comic genius."

BIOGRAPHICAL AND CRITICAL SOURCES:

PERIODICALS

Kirkus Reviews, October 1, 2002, review of *Red Meat Cures Cancer,* p. 1422.

Publishers Weekly, January 13, 2003, review of *Red Meat Cures Cancer,* p. 44.

OTHER

Boston's Weekly Dig, http://www.weeklydig.com/ (May 2, 2007), Leo Champion, review of *Red Meat Cures Cancer.*

Princeton Alumni Weekly Online, http://www. princeton.edu/~paw/ (May 14, 2003), Rob MacKay, "More Fries, Big Trouble," interview with Starbuck O'Dwyer.

Starbuck O'Dwyer Home Page, http://www.starbuck odwyer.com (May 2, 2007).*

OKERLUND, Arlene

PERSONAL: Education: University of California at San Diego, Ph.D.

ADDRESSES: E-mail—okerlund@email.sjsu.edu.

CAREER: San Jose State University, San Jose, CA, former professor of English. Member, Peninsula Banjo Band.

WRITINGS:

Elizabeth Wydeville: The Slandered Queen, Tempus (Stroud, Gloucestershire, England), 2005.

SIDELIGHTS: Arlene Okerlund has researched literature of the Renaissance period, particularly works by authors such as William Shakespeare, Edmund Spenser, and Christopher Marlowe. She took the opportunity after retiring from San Jose State University to focus her research on the historical context of the life of Elizabeth Wydeville, queen consort of King Edward IV and grandmother of Henry VIII. Elizabeth became the center of fifteenth-century controversy by marrying Edward in secret and for arranging lucrative marriages for her relatives. She is also known as the mother of two princes who disappeared, presumably, at the hand of Richard III, when they were declared illegitimate. In *Elizabeth Wydeville: The Slandered Queen,* Okerlund deviates from previous historical accounts that portray Elizabeth as a selfish manipulator, and attempts to prove that the negative light in which she has been portrayed is unwarranted. It is Okerlund's assertion that many historical accounts of Elizabeth's life and actions were slanderous; instead, her character was more objective and complex than historians make her out to be. Writing in the *English Historical Review,* J.L. Laynesmith remarked that "for the general reader, this is an entertaining and accessible book, well-equipped with timelines and genealogical tables, and attractively illustrated."

Okerlund told *CA:* "I started writing in the 1950s as editor of my high school newspaper in Taneytown, Maryland—a rural school with a high school graduating class of forty-four students. Writing is essential to clarifying my understanding of the world, both what I experience and what I read. Shakespeare—the master of style and content—has taught me everything I know about economy of statement and the profound subtleties of vocabulary."

When asked to describe her writing process, she said: "In writing biography, I begin by gathering every fact known about a person's life from original documents. I supplement that information with secondary materials in which subsequent writers have described and analyzed the person. Initially, I am always overwhelmed by too much information, but I slowly sort it out chronologically. A timeline of important events from birth to death provides a starting point for organizing the biography.

"As I begin writing, I organize the material into chapters that focus on a central event, some crucial influence within the individual's life, or a chronological period. Initially, I include everything. As I write, I select, delete, and organize material into coherent chapters, editing and reorganizing constantly as I write. After I complete a first draft, I start from the beginning and rewrite at least twice.

"Most importantly, writing requires discipline. Authors must establish a schedule for writing that is inviolate. That means skipping dates with friends and limiting activities in which normal people indulge. Especially if one has a day job, a firm and undeviating schedule for thinking and writing is crucial.

"*Elizabeth Wydeville* tells the story of an extraordinary woman whose human spirit survived unimaginable and incomprehensible tragedies. I was compelled to write this book when I discovered that the negative reputation of this queen and her family originated in propaganda and slander fomented by political enemies—the same enemies who executed her father, three sons, and two brothers, then declared her nineteen-year marriage to Edward IV to be adulterous and their ten children 'bastards.' The failure of historians to consider the source, perspective, and context of the stories perpetuated about Queen Elizabeth offended my sense of justice and motivated me to set the record straight."

When asked what effect she hopes her books will have, Okerlund said: "I hope a broad audience of general readers will reflect on the human experience—both theirs and others—as they read about the lives of important historical figures."

BIOGRAPHICAL AND CRITICAL SOURCES:

PERIODICALS

English Historical Review, September 1, 2006, J.L. Laynesmith, review of *Elizabeth Wydeville: The Slandered Queen,* p. 1170.

ONLINE

San Jose State University Web Site, http://www.sjsu. edu/ (May 16, 2007), faculty profile of Arlene Okerlund.

*   *   *

OLSZEWSKI, Peter 1948-

PERSONAL: Born 1948 in Australia.

CAREER: Journalist in Australia and Myanmar. University lecturer in journalism. Founder, Australian Marijuana Party. Worked as a columnist for *Truth* newspaper, publicity director for the Australian tour of Hunter S. Thompson, and served as editor for many Australian publications, including the Australian edition of *Playboy.*

WRITINGS:

A Salute to the Humble Yabby, Angus & Robertson (Sydney, New South Wales, Australia), 1980.
Land of a Thousand Eyes: The Subtle Pleasures of Everyday Life in Myanmar, Allen & Unwin (Crows Nest, New South Wales, Australia), 2005.

Contributor to periodicals, including *Australian Men's Health.*

SIDELIGHTS: In *Land of a Thousand Eyes: The Subtle Pleasures of Everyday Life in Myanmar,* Australian journalist Peter Olszewski tells the story of his sojourn in the secluded southeast Asian country formerly known as Burma. Cut off from the rest of the world for years by a repressive military dictatorship,

the people of Myanmar live life at a different pace than the rest of the world. *Land of a Thousand Eyes* records Olszewski's impressions of Myanmar, concentrating on the experiences of ordinary people rather than on its socialist-oriented government. Referring to the author, who was a consultant to an English-language paper in the city of Yangon (the former Rangoon), a *Kirkus Reviews* contributor wrote, "Olszewski led a privileged expatriate existence: attending parties and opening nights of cultural events, . . . [and] eyeing . . . passing women." "Some of Olszewski's revelations will enrage fellow expatriates," declared *Irriwaddy News Magazine* contributor David Scott Mathieson, "with references to cocaine snorting, dubious lady companions, the murky dealings of business people, and scenes of drunken debauchery that only those with money and diplomatic immunity are capable of." "Finally he falls in love with a local woman," concluded Robin Osborne in *Northern Rivers Echo,* "who [im]migrates to Australia to join him—proof that at least something can happily come out of Burma."

BIOGRAPHICAL AND CRITICAL SOURCES:

PERIODICALS

Irrawaddy News Magazine, June, 2006, David Scott Mathieson, "The Year of Living Degenerately."
Kirkus Reviews, October 1, 2006, review of *Land of a Thousand Eyes: The Subtle Pleasures of Everyday Life in Myanmar,* p. 1002.
Sydney Morning Herald (Sydney, New South Wales, Australia), November 16, 2005, Bruce Elder, review of *Land of a Thousand Eyes.*

ONLINE

Chiang Mai Citylife Online, February, 2006, http://www.chiangmainews.com/ (May 1, 2007), "Polecat," review of *Land of a Thousand Eyes.*
Northern Rivers Echo, http://www.echonews.com/ (May 1, 2007), Robin Osborne, review of *Land of a Thousand Eyes.**

*   *   *

OOI, Keat Gin 1959-

PERSONAL: Born October 10, 1959, in George Town, Penang, Malaysia; son of Ewe Boo (a manager of a rubber plantation) and Ai Gek (a homemaker) Ooi; married Beh Swee Im (a cardiac technologist),

October 20, 2002. *Ethnicity:* "Chinese." *Education:* Universiti Sains Malaysia, B.A. (hons.), 1983; National University of Singapore, M.A., 1991; University of Hull, Ph.D., 1995. *Religion:* "Buddhism/Daoism/Confucianism." *Hobbies and other interests:* Travel, cooking, reading, family activities.

ADDRESSES: Home—Penang, Malaysia. *Office*—School of Humanities, Universiti Sains Malaysia, 11800 Penang, Malaysia. *E-mail*—kgooi@hotmail.com.

CAREER: High school history teacher and department head in Sarawak, Malaysia, 1983-88; senior high school teacher in Penang, Malaysia, 1989-90; Universiti Sains Malaysia, Penang, assistant lecturer, 1991-92, senior research fellow, 1992-95, lecturer, 1995-2002, associate professor of history, 2002—. State Museum of Penang, historian, advisor, and member of board of trustees, 1996-2005; Leong San Tong Khoo Kongsi, historian and consultant, 1997-2001; State Art Gallery, committee member, 2004-05.

MEMBER: European Association for Southeast Asian Studies, Malaysian Historical Society (Penang branch), Malaysian Association for the Prevention of Tuberculosis, Royal Historical Society (England; fellow), Royal Asiatic Society (Malaysian branch), Sarawak Association (England; life member), Association of South-East Asian Studies in the United Kingdom, Old Frees' Association (life member), Sabah Society.

AWARDS, HONORS: Pingat Jasa Kebaktian, 2002; citations for best reference work, *Library Journal,* 2004, and outstanding academic title, *Choice,* 2005, both for *Southeast Asia: A Historical Encyclopedia, from Angkor Wat to East Timor.*

WRITINGS:

The History of St. Xavier's Institution, Penang, 1852-1992, La Salle Christian Brothers (Penang, Malaysia), 1992.

World beyond the Rivers: Education in Sarawak from Brooke Rule to Colonial Office Administration, 1841-1963, Department of South-East Asian Studies, University of Hull (Hull, England), 1996.

Of Free Trade and Native Interests: The Brookes and the Economic Development of Sarawak, 1841-1941, Oxford University Press (Kuala Lumpur, Malaysia), 1997.

(Editor and author of introduction) *Japanese Empire in the Tropics: Selected Reports and Documents of the Japanese People in Sarawak, Northwest Borneo, 1941-1945,* two volumes, Ohio University Press (Athens, OH), 1998.

Rising Sun over Borneo: The Japanese Occupation of Sarawak, 1941-1945, St. Martin's Press (New York, NY), 1999.

Malaysia, revised edition, American Bibliographical Canter-Clio Press (Santa Barbara, CA), 1999.

One Hundred Years of Tin Smelting, 1898-1998, Escoy Smelting (Penang, Malaysia), 2001.

From Colonial Outpost to Cosmopolitan Centre: The Growth and Development of George Town, Penang, from Late 19th Century to Late 20th Century, Asia-Pacific Research Program, Academia Sinica (Taipei, Taiwan), 2002.

(Editor, with Laurence Loh Kwong Yu) *Early Views of Penang and Malacca, 1660-1880,* Museum Board (Penang, Malaysia), 2002.

(Editor and contributor) *Southeast Asia: A Historical Encyclopedia, from Angkor Wat to East Timor,* three volumes, American Bibliographical Center-Clio Press (Santa Barbara, CA), 2004.

Traumas and Heroism: The European Community in Sarawak during the Pacific War and Japanese Occupation, 1941-1945, Opus Publications (Kota Kinabalu, Sabah, Malaysia), 2007.

Contributor to books, including *Southeast Asian Minorities in the Wartime Japanese Empire,* edited by Paul H. Kratoska, RoutledgeCurzon (London, England), 2002; and *From Buckfast to Borneo: Essays Presented to Father Robert Nicholl on the 85th Anniversary of His Birth 27 March 1995,* edited by Victor T. King and A.V.M. Horton, Center for South-East Asian Studies, University of Hull (Hull, England), 1995. Contributor to Asian studies journals, including *Journal of Southeast Asian Studies, Journal of the Malaysian Branch of the Royal Asiatic Society, Modern Asian Studies, Indonesia and the Malay World,* and *Sarawak Museum Journal.*

SIDELIGHTS: Keat Gin Ooi told *CA:* "Two motives basically spurred my writing passion. Just the sheer joy of putting my thoughts to paper or computer screen is an encouraging force that makes writing, not a task to get over with, but an enjoyment to savor. The second encouragement lies in the hope that my writings will promote greater understanding of the past that can in turn contribute to planning for the future. History brings forth the good, the bad, and the ugly in human nature, and it is my intention that we should know more about ourselves. Understanding encourages tolerance, while ignorance breeds suspicion. Utilizing historical writings to disseminate knowledge and understanding among people of different background, culture, religion, creed, and ethnicity is an essential step toward peaceful coexistence.

"The greatest influence on my work is the immeasurable contributions of scribes, artisans, scholars, and diarists who wrote of ancient times. Without the written word, ancient wisdom, knowledge, and skills would be unimaginable in the present. I am deeply fascinated and awed at the written word and the system of writing. No particular individual has influenced my work; all scholarly writings with a bias toward history are a great inspiration to me. Of my contemporaries from various corners of Southeast Asia in particular and throughout Asia in general, I wish to see more of their works in indigenous languages made available in English for a wider, global readership.

"As a professional historian, putting ink to paper [or computer equivalent] is the culmination of a long-winded process that starts with putting my thoughts and ideas on paper. After that I follow the paper trail at the archives, libraries, and other repositories. When data collection is concluded, reading and analyzing become the major preoccupation. When all the materials are sorted out, I begin to write. I invest a lot of time in planning the organization of a book. I believe that if I get it right from the layout stage, the rest tends to flow and fall in line as the writing proceeds. I have no set order in writing; the completion of chapter four does not necessarily mean that I begin work on chapter five. Exceeding a prescribed word limit is my norm; cutting down is a struggle and emotionally draining, but sometimes it can be fun as well. I make it a point to complete manuscripts at least a fortnight prior to the deadline. It is a habit to have peace of mind, knowing that the project is finished.

"Here are some comments on the objectives behind some of my writings. In composing *Of Free Trade and Native Interests: The Brookes and the Economic Development of Sarawak, 1841-1941*, my aim was to show the maverick character of James Brooke and of the Brooke White Rajahs in their uniqueness as colonizers of Asian peoples and territories. The Brooke tradition of protecting and promoting the interests of the indigenous inhabitants from foreign (European and Chinese) encroachment and exploitation, corruption, and contamination was singularly admirable in the era of European imperialism throughout Asia and Africa during the second half of the nineteenth century. While *Japanese Empire in the Tropics: Selected Reports and Documents of the Japanese People in Sarawak, Northwest Borneo, 1941-1945* was about the wartime situation in Sarawak from eyewitness accounts of various participants, on the other hand *Rising Sun over Borneo: The Japanese Occupation of Sarawak, 1941-1945* offered a professional historian's interpretation and perspective. I wrote *From Colonial Outpost to Cosmopolitan Centre: The Growth and Development of George Town, Penang, from Late 19th Century to Late 20th Century* to showcase the historical roots of my home city of George Town, Penang. Penang, a little tropical island on the northeast of the northern mouth of the Straits of Melaka is where I was born and educated, and where I live today with my family. Here lie my heart, my home, and my love. My aim in *Southeast Asia: A Historical Encyclopedia, from Angkor Wat to East Timor* was to offer a user-friendly, dictionary-style source for facts and figures and understanding of the historical development of Southeast Asia as a whole region and as a collection of individual nation states, presented in a simple, non-technical format for a non-specialist audience."

BIOGRAPHICAL AND CRITICAL SOURCES:

PERIODICALS

Journal of Asian Studies, August, 2002, Craig A. Lockard, review of *Rising Sun over Borneo: The Japanese Occupation of Sarawak, 1941-1945,* pp. 1121-1123.
Pacific Affairs, spring, 2000, Bill Sewell, review of *Rising Sun over Borneo,* pp. 149-150.

*   *   *

O'REILLEY, Mary Rose

PERSONAL: Born in Pampa, TX. *Education:* College of St. Catherine, Minneapolis, MN, B.A.; University of Wisconsin—Milwaukee, M.A., Ph.D.

ADDRESSES: Home—St. Paul, MN. *E-mail*—mroreilley@stthomas.edu.

CAREER: Educator, writer, and poet. St. Thomas College, St. Paul, MN, faculty member, including professor emerita of English, 1978—.

AWARDS, HONORS: Walt Whitman Award, 2005, for *Half Wild;* also recipient of grants, including a Contemplative Studies Grant from the American Council of Learned Societies, a Bush Artist Grant, and the McKnight Award of Distinction.

WRITINGS:

NONFICTION

The Peaceable Classroom, foreword by Peter Elbow, Boynton/Cook Publishers (Portsmouth, NH), 1993.

Radical Presence: Teaching as Contemplative Practice, Boynton/Cook Publishers (Portsmouth, NH), 1998.

The Barn at the End of the World: The Apprenticeship of a Quaker, Buddhist Shepherd (memoir), Milkweed Editions (Minneapolis, MN), 2000.

The Garden at Night: Burnout and Breakdown in the Teaching Life, Heinemann (Portsmouth, NH), 2005.

The Love of Impermanent Things: A Threshold Ecology, Milkweed Editions (Minneapolis, MN), 2006.

OTHER

Half Wild: Poems, Louisiana State University Press (Baton Rouge, LA), 2006.

SIDELIGHTS: Mary Rose O'Reilley is a longtime English professor whose spiritual life forms the basis for most of her books, which include books on teaching and a memoir. For example, *Radical Presence: Teaching as Contemplative Practice* is a brief, forty-eight-page book that presents O'Reilley's sometimes radical concept of teaching based on her life as a Buddhist, Catholic, and Quaker. The author talks about essential concepts for teachers, such as being able to listen well to students and honoring students' desire to learn. Writing on the *FGConnections* Web site, Jean Marie Barch wrote that the author "draws us into the essence of a whole different way of looking at what can go on in the classroom."

In her spiritual memoir *The Barn at the End of the World: The Apprenticeship of a Quaker, Buddhist Shepherd,* O'Reilley recounts one year in her life as she tries to live "consciously." As a part of this effort, the author recounts working on a sheep farm and spending time in a Buddhist monastery in France. As the author conducts a thorough self-assessment of her life, she reveals to the reader her personal struggles with questions about her own attitudes towards life. Writing in *Booklist,* Patricia Monaghan called *The Barn at the End of the World* "a substantial contribution to spiritual autobiography." Donna Scanlon, writing on *Rambles.net,* noted that the author "will make you laugh and think and perhaps become more conscious of your own direction."

In her book *The Garden at Night: Burnout and Breakdown in the Teaching Life,* O'Reilley returns to writing about teaching and working in general as a contemplative way of life. In the process, the author discusses Buddhism and provides numerous anecdotes about the difficult times she has gone through as a teacher. "Though the book is aimed specifically at teachers, it is applicable to the workplace in general," wrote Antonia Ryan in the *National Catholic Reporter.*

O'Reilley won the prestigious Walt Whitman Award for *Half Wild: Poems.* Many of the poems in the collection focus on the natural world, including the poems "Bees in Autumn" and "Field Guide to North Shore Geology." The author also writes about modern life, culture, the soul, and death. In a review on the *Spirituality & Practice* Web site, Frederic and Mary Ann Brussat wrote: "There is an impressive attentiveness in all these poems." *Library Journal* contributor Louis McKee noted that "curiosity and quest are at the heart of her poetry."

In *The Love of Impermanent Things: A Threshold Ecology,* the author writes about keeping one's own identity of self while taking risks in life. In the process, O'Reilley presents a series of vignettes about nature and about her own life. Referring to *The Love of Impermanent Things* as a "quiet, quirky book," a *Publishers Weekly* contributor also wrote: "Her language is . . . lovely."

BIOGRAPHICAL AND CRITICAL SOURCES:

BOOKS

O'Reilley, Mary Rose, *The Barn at the End of the World: The Apprenticeship of a Quaker, Buddhist Shepherd,* Milkweed Editions (Minneapolis, MN), 2000.

PERIODICALS

Booklist, April 15, 2000, Patricia Monaghan, review of *The Barn at the End of the World,* p. 1503.

Feminist Collections: A Quarterly of Women's Studies Resources, fall, 2003, Alice A. Keefe, review of *The Barn at the End of the World,* p. 12.

Library Journal, April 15, 2000, Leroy Hommerding, review of *The Barn at the End of the World,* p. 97; August 1, 2006, Louis McKee, review of *Half Wild: Poems,* p. 92.

National Catholic Reporter, April 14, 2006, Antonia Ryan, review of *The Garden at Night: Burnout and Breakdown in the Teaching Life,* p. 14.

Publishers Weekly, March 27, 2000, review of *The Barn at the End of the World,* p. 75; January 23, 2006, review of *The Love of Impermanent Things: A Threshold Ecology,* p. 129; April 10, 2006, review of *The Love of Impermanent Things,* p. 68.

Women's Review of Books, February, 2001, review of *The Barn at the End of the World,* p. 21.

ONLINE

Coldfrontmag Blog, http://reviews.coldfrontmag.com/ (May 17, 2006), Melinda Wilson, review of *Half Wild.*

FGConnections, http://www.fgcquaker.org/ (May 22, 2007), Jean Marie Barch, review of *Radical Presence: Teaching as Contemplative Practice.*

New Connexion, http://www.newconnexion.net/ (May 22, 2007), Connie Hill, "An Interview With Mary Rose O'Reilley."

Nimble Spirit, http://www.nimblespirit.com/ (May 22, 2007), Margaret Wurtele, review of *The Barn at the End of the World.*

Poets.org, http://www.poets.org/ (May 22, 2007), brief profile of author.

Rambles.net, http://www.rambles.net/ (May 22, 2007), Donna Scanlon, review of *The Barn at the End of the World.*

Spirituality & Practice, http://www.spiritualityandpractice.com/ (May 22, 2007), Frederic and Mary Ann Brussat, review of *Half Wild.*

University of St. Thomas Web site, http://www.stthomas.edu/ (May 22, 2007), faculty profile of author.*

*   *   *

ORTOLON, Julie

PERSONAL: Married; husband a journalist. *Education:* Attended Schreiner College.

ADDRESSES: E-mail—julie@ortolon.com.

CAREER: Artist and writer. Former art gallery owner.

WRITINGS:

Drive Me Wild, Dell (New York, NY), 2000.
Dear Cupid, St. Martin's Paperbacks (New York, NY), 2001.

"PEARL ISLAND" TRILOGY

Falling for You, St. Martin's Paperbacks (New York, NY), 2002.
Lead Me On, St. Martin's Paperbacks (New York, NY), 2003.
Don't Tempt Me, St. Martin's Paperbacks (New York, NY), 2004.

"PERFECT" TRILOGY

Almost Perfect, New American Library (New York, NY), 2005.
Just Perfect, New American Library (New York, NY), 2005.
Too Perfect, Signet Eclipse (New York, NY), 2005.

SIDELIGHTS: Julie Ortolon wanted to be a writer ever since she was little girl, but, partly because of her severe dyslexia, turned to a career in art instead. However, when the author's husband brought home a computer and Ortolon discovered spell check, she once again thought of writing as a career and eventually became a published romance writer. "It took me ten years of hard work, lots of sacrifices . . . in order to focus on writing, and four manuscripts that didn't sell before I finally sold my fifth manuscript, *Drive Me Wild,*" Ortolon told Claire E. White in an interview on the *Writers Write* Web site. Her first romance novel tells the story of Brent Michaels, a successful television anchor, and Laura Beth Morgan, a woman from his hometown who has led a lackluster life. When Laura invites Brent back to their small Texas town to appear in a local version of *The Dating Game,* Brent purposely picks Laura as his date and a romance ensues. Cathy Sova, writing for *Romance Reader,* commended Ortolon on her debut and added: "Hats off to a bright new voice in the contemporary romance field. *Drive Me Wild* is going to do just that to a lot of romance readers!"

Ortolon has gone on to write several successful romance novels, including her "Pearl Island" and "Perfect" trilogies. *Don't Tempt Me,* the last book in the "Pearl Island" trilogy, completes the story of three sisters. Adrian St. Claire's two sisters fall in love in the first two romances in the trilogy and now it's Adrian's turn. Adrian's man turns out to be Jackie Taylor, an owner of a cruise ship and a treasure hunter who seeks information about a treasure that may be in a saved letter from Adrian's great-grandfather. Maria Hatton, writing in *Booklist,* described the novel as both "humorous and stirring."

Almost Perfect, the first book in the "Perfect" trilogy, features three friends who decide to face their biggest fears after another friend writes a self-help book and uses them as examples of people who let fear control their lives. The first book focuses on the widowed Maddy, who falls for her old flame when she decides to pursue her dream of being an artist and takes the arts-and-crafts director job at a summer camp headed by an old high-school flame. *Booklist* contributor Hatton called the novel a "funny and compelling story of two unforgettable characters." *Too Perfect,* the final book in the trilogy, has Amy facing her fear of traveling alone. However, she soon finds herself stranded on a Caribbean island, where she gets a job supposedly

working for a disfigured man. In reality, however, her new employer is a Hollywood star hiding from the paparazzi. A *Publishers Weekly* contributor noted that "the fanciful plot twists are fun."

BIOGRAPHICAL AND CRITICAL SOURCES:

PERIODICALS

Booklist, June 1, 2001, Maria Hatton, review of *Dear Cupid,* p. 1854; January 1, 2003, Maria Hatton, review of *Lead Me On,* p. 859; February 1, 2004, Maria Hatton, review of *Don't Tempt Me,* p. 955; September 1, 2005, Maria Hatton, review of *Almost Perfect,* p. 73.

Publishers Weekly, May 21, 2001, review of *Dear Cupid,* p. 87; March 18, 2002, review of *Falling for You,* p. 84; December 9, 2002, review of *Lead Me On,* p. 68; January 19, 2004, review of *Don't Tempt Me,* p. 59; October 3, 2005, review of *Too Perfect,* p. 52.

ONLINE

All about Romance, http://www.likesbooks.com/ (October 5, 2004), Andrea Pool, review of *Dear Cupid.*

Best Reviews, http://thebestreviews.com/ (March 2, 2002), Harriet Klausner, review of *Falling for You;* (April 5, 2002), Kathy Boswell, review of *Falling for You;* (December 15, 2002), Harriet Klausner, review of *Lead Me On;* (February 10, 2003), Tanzey Cutter, review of *Lead Me On.*

Crescent Blues Book Views, http://www.crescentblues.com/ (July 10, 2003), Patricia Lucas White, review of *Dear Cupid;* (April 23, 2007), Jen Foote, review of *Lead Me On.*

Curvy Novels, http://curvynovels.com/ (October 5, 2004), review of *Dear Cupid.*

Escape to Romance, http://www.escapetoromance.com/ (October 5, 2004), Marlene Breakfield, review of *Lead Me On.*

Julie Ortolon Home Page, http://www.ortolon.com (April 23, 2007).

Music City Romance Writers, http://www.mcrw.com/ (August, 2002), Trish Milburn, "Author Q & A: Julie Ortolon."

Readers Read, http://www.readersread.com/ (October 5, 2004), reviews of *Dear Cupid* and *Falling for You.*

Romance Reader, http://www.theromancereader.com/ (March 20, 2000), Cathy Sova, review of *Drive Me Wild;* (August 27, 2001), Cathy Sova, review of *Dear Cupid;* (March 25, 2002), Susan Scribner, review of *Falling for You.*

Writers Write, http://www.writerswrite.com/ (September 23, 2007), Claire E. White, "A Conversation with Julie Ortolon."*

*   *   *

OSBORNE, Roger

PERSONAL: Born in England. *Education:* Attended Manchester University.

CAREER: Writer, 1992—. Publisher of scientific, medical, and technical books, 1976-91.

WRITINGS:

(With Peter Freyberg) *Learning in Science: The Implications of Children's Science,* Heinemann (London, England), 1985.

(With Donald Tarling) *The Viking Historical Atlas of the Earth: A Visual Exploration of the Earth's Physical Past,* Viking (London, England), 1995, published as *The Historical Atlas of the Earth: A Visual Exploration of the Earth's Physical Past,* Holt (New York, NY), 1996.

(With Michael Benton) *The Viking Atlas of Evolution,* Viking (London, England), 1996.

The Floating Egg: Episodes in the Making of Geology, Jonathan Cape (London, England), 1998.

The Deprat Affair: Ambition, Revenge, and Deceit in French Indo-China, Jonathan Cape (London, England), 1999.

The Dreamer of the Calle San Salvador, Jonathan Cape (London, England), 2001.

Civilization: A New History of the Western World, Pegasus, 2006.

SIDELIGHTS: Science writer Roger Osborne trained as a geologist at Manchester University in the early 1970s before going into scientific and medical publishing. Becoming a full-time writer in 1992, he has since published several well-received books popularizing the earth sciences.

Osborne's collaborative effort with Donald Tarling, *The Viking Historical Atlas of the Earth: A Visual Exploration of the Earth's Physical Past* (published in the United States as *The Historical Atlas of the Earth: A Visual Exploration of the Earth's Physical Past),* is a blend of text and illustrations detailing the geological history of Earth. Their approach uses paleogeographical maps that show the formation of the continents at various times throughout Earth's history, emphasizing the importance of plate tectonics. Readers are taken on a visual tour through the geological history of the Earth, from the Pennsylvania coal belts to the creation of the chalky downs of southern England in this heavily illustrated atlas. A reviewer for the *New Statesman* commented: "A thousand maps add value to this excellent book." In a review for the *Geographical Journal,* L.E. Craig concluded: "Overall this is a helpful book for the non-specialist as an introduction to the subject of earth sciences." Writing in *Booklist,* Gilbert Taylor asserted that "tyros who will work on furthering the earth science may fondly remember devouring this excellent info-jammed atlas." Osborne, collaborating with Michael Benton, did much the same service for evolution with his *The Viking Atlas of Evolution,* a book which Lorraine Craig, writing in the *Geographical Journal,* thought should be "recommended to school children as a useful text."

In his 1998 work, *The Floating Egg: Episodes in the Making of Geology,* Osborne provides another novel introduction to the world of geology. As Richard Fortey noted in a *New Scientist* review: "If it crossed your mind that geology was dull, Roger Osborne's *The Floating Egg* will disabuse you of that notion." In a series of twenty-five stories dealing with the development of the science of geology from a gentleman's pastime into a true science, Osborne tells of the early discoveries of hyena bones and fossil reptiles in the Yorkshire landscape. In the pages of this book, readers meet men such as geologist William Smith and the explorer Captain James Cook. "Osborne's delightful book weaves intimate details of locality with the life histories of those who sought to understand the deep fabric of our islands," Fortey commented, concluding that "it is all most entertaining: quirky and thoroughly Yorkshire."

In *The Deprat Affair: Ambition, Revenge, and Deceit in French Indo-China,* Osborne tells the story of a French geologist whose career was ruined after being accused of scientific fraud. Jacque Deprat was well on his way to becoming one of France's most renowned geologists, when in 1919 he was drummed out of the French academic world for allegedly having placed European fossils among those he had gathered in China and Indo-China. A possible victim of the old-boy network in Paris, the young Deprat thereafter recreated himself as Herbert Wilde and became a prolific writer and mountaineer. Osborne presents a tale that is part detective story, part social history, part science history, and all human drama. Reviewing the book in the *Times Literary Supplement,* Eugen Weber allowed that the debate about Deprat is still going on in French scientific circles and commented that *The Deprat Affair* "provides an intriguing and knowledgeable account of it." Weber further noted that Osborne, a "trained geologist and experienced science writer . . . , makes the scientific stakes and details mercifully accessible to lay readers."

Something of a departure for Osborne is his 2001 title, *The Dreamer of the Calle San Salvador,* a recreation of the life and dreams of Lucrecia de Leon. This nineteen-year-old girl, living in sixteenth-century Spain, had such vivid and seemingly prophetic dreams that a group of disaffected clerics actually transcribed and published some four hundred of the dreams, considering them to be messages from God. Interpreters found that these dreams foretold political and military events. As some of these prophecies proved true, authorities in Madrid grew disdainful, and Lucrecia was ultimately arrested, a victim of the Inquisition. Osborne produces thirty-five of her dreams in his book, transcriptions of which were uncovered in the archives of the Spanish Inquisition.

In *Civilization: A New History of the Western World,* a *Kirkus Reviews* contributor stated, Osborne "set himself a daunting task—to confine to fewer than 500 pages the sprawl of western history." Moving from the prehistoric creators of Stonehenge to the present day, he examines the ways in which patterns of thought—particularly rationalism—have dominated the West. Western civilization, David Keymer stated in the *Library Journal,* has been responsible for "the ruthless marginalization of non-Western peoples and their cultures, enslavement, genocide, the destruction of native ways and values," and a large percentage of disenfranchised, disillusioned people within its own borders—part of the price we pay for our definition of progress. "This often sinister rationalism works in counterpoint, and sometimes opposition," the *Publish-*

ers Weekly commentator concluded, "to what he sees as the redeeming organicity of Western culture," its ability to adapt to different conditions in different times without abandoning its roots. "Osborne has woven a narrative of extraordinary scope and clarity that ranges from the cave paintings of Altamira 7,000 years ago to today's video artists of urban black America," Tim Gardam wrote in the *Guardian.* "At his best, Osborne is a refreshingly unacademic synthesiser and his is an anthropological, philosophical, technological and social history of the West and its collisions with other cultures." "Mr. Osborne, with great skill," declared *New York Times* reviewer William Grimes, "ties his disparate topics together into a coherent narrative, as absorbing as any novel, with felicitous turns of phrase, and tidy summations, on virtually every page."

BIOGRAPHICAL AND CRITICAL SOURCES:

PERIODICALS

Booklist, April 15, 1996, Gilbert Taylor, review of *The Historical Atlas of the Earth: A Visual Exploration of the Earth's Physical Past,* p. 1403; December 1, 1996, review of *The Historical Atlas of the Earth,* p. 664; December 1, 1999, review of *The Historical Atlas of the Earth,* p. 677; December 15, 2006, Jay Freeman, review of *Civilization: A New History of the Western World,* p. 15.

Choice, July 1, 1996, review of *The Historical Atlas of the Earth,* p. 1824.

Farmers Weekly, May 10, 2002, "Royal-Winner Hangs Up Boots," p. 99.

Geographical Journal, July 1, 1997, L.E. Craig, review of *The Viking Historical Atlas of the Earth: A Visual Exploration of the Earth's Physical Past,* p. 228; July 1, 1998, Lorraine Craig, review of *The Viking Atlas of Evolution,* p. 231.

Geographical Magazine, August 1, 1996, review of *The Viking Atlas of Evolution,* p. 51.

Geography, January 1, 1997, review of *The Viking Historical Atlas of the Earth,* p. 91.

Geotimes, March 1, 1997, review of *The Historical Atlas of the Earth,* p. 32.

Guardian, January 29, 2006, Tim Gardam, "Civilised? On Our Good Days."

History Today, January 1, 2006, Roger Osborne, "Digging Up the Origins of Civilization: Geologist and Historian Roger Osborne Wants to Know Just What People Mean When They Use The 'C' Word," p. 70.

Independent (London, England), February 5, 2006, A.C. Greyling, "Reason: The Villain of the Story."

Kirkus Reviews, October 1, 2006, review of *Civilization,* p. 1002.

Library Journal, November 1, 2006, David Keymer, review of *Civilization,* p. 87.

Nature, April 18, 1996, review of *The Viking Historical Atlas of the Earth,* p. 592; November 12, 1998, review of *The Floating Egg: Episodes in the Making of Geology,* p. 131.

New Scientist, November 25, 1995, review of *The Viking Historical Atlas,* p. 54; October 10, 1998, Richard Fortey, "Set in Stone," p. 45; May 29, 1999, review of *The Floating Egg,* p. 47; December 25, 1999, review of *The Deprat Affair: Ambition, Revenge, and Deceit in French Indo-China,* p. 84.

New York Times, December 7, 2006, William Grimes, "Hurtling through History at the Speed of Enlightenment," p. E9.

Publishers Weekly, October 9, 2006, review of *Civilization,* p. 48.

Times Higher Education Supplement, May 26, 2006, "The Long Look Backwards to Find a Story of Ourselves," p. 24.

Times Literary Supplement, December 24, 1999, Eugen Weber, "Dreyfus of the Fossils?," p. 32; March 10, 2006, "Spirit of Victory," p. 10.*

* * *

OSTASHEVSKY, Eugene 1968-

PERSONAL: Born 1968, in St. Petersburg, Russia. *Education:* Stanford University, Ph.D.

ADDRESSES: E-mail—eo27@nyu.edu.

CAREER: During early career, worked as an instructor at Bilkent University, Turkey, at Università degli Studi di Bergamo, Italy, and at Stanford University; New York University, New York, NY, master teacher of humanities. Founder, 9x9 Industries (writers consortium), San Francisco, CA.

AWARDS, HONORS: Wytter Bynner Poetry Translation Fellowship, 2003, for translations from Russian; Artists' Fellowship for Poetry, New York Foundation for the Arts, 2005.

WRITINGS:

POETRY

Off-Centaur, Germ Folios (Brooklyn, NY), 2002.

Iterature, Ugly Duckling Presse (Brooklyn, NY), 2005.

Infinite Recursor or the Bride of DJ Spinoza, StudioRADIA/Ugly Duckling Presse (Brooklyn, NY), 2006.

DJ Spinoza's Dozen, Octopus Books (Ottawa, Ontario, Canada), 2007.

OTHER

(Editor and cotranslator) *OBERIU: An Anthology of Russian Absurdism,* Northwestern University Press (Evanston, IL), 2006.

Contributor to books, including *Best American Poetry 2005* and *The PIP Gertrude Stein Awards in Innovative Poetry in English,* Green Integer (Los Angeles, CA), 2007. Contributor to periodicals, including *Jubilat, Fence, American Poetry Review, Conjunctions,* and *Boston Review.*

SIDELIGHTS: Eugene Ostashevsky is a Russian-born and Brooklyn-raised poet and scholar. While pursuing a doctoral degree from Stanford University, Ostashevsky cofounded 9x9 Industries, a San Francisco writers' consortium. He then returned to New York City after spending time in Turkey and became an instructor in the general studies department at New York University. His poetry collections include *Off-Centaur* and *Iterature.*

Ostashevky's poetry has earned commendations for its wit, humor, and skillful use of rhyme. In a review for *Octopus Magazine,* Mathias Svalina wrote that *Iterature* is "an amazing display of dedication to and exploration of a personal style. Ostashevsky pushes all of his language and ideas out, seemingly as quickly and nakedly as possible. His absurdism manifests itself in drastic jumps in ideas, the following of language into cul de sacs of meaning, a mixture of bravado and self deprecation and ubiquitous, devious humor." Svalina further remarked: "Ostashevsky employs the rhyming couplet as his controlling agent and this formal element is what I find most compelling in his work." A *Publishers Weekly* reviewer commented: "Few recent books of verse are as consistently funny and surprising."

BIOGRAPHICAL AND CRITICAL SOURCES:

PERIODICALS

Publishers Weekly, January 23, 2006, review of *Iterature,* p. 189.

ONLINE

Octopus Magazine, http://www.octopusmagazine.com/ (July 24, 2007), Mathias Svalina, review of *Iterature.*

*   *   *

OURS, Dorothy

PERSONAL: Female.

ADDRESSES: E-mail—DorothyOurs@aol.com.

CAREER: National Museum of Racing and Hall of Fame, Saratoga Springs, NY, staff member, 1998-2005.

WRITINGS:

Man o' War: A Legend Like Lightning, St. Martin's Press (New York, NY), 2006.

SIDELIGHTS: Dorothy Ours first became fascinated by horses and horse racing when she was a child. She would watch the thoroughbred races on television, and became particularly interested in Man o' War after watching Secretariat. She began to research the horse's history and career in her spare time and eventually, while working at the National Museum of Racing and Hall of Fame in Saratoga Springs, New York, gained access to many original sources. Ours's debut book, *Man o' War: A Legend Like Lightning,* addresses all the details of this remarkable horse and the people involved in his life. She includes information about his pedigree, owner, jockey, and trainer, and the history of the various races he won, looking at how he eventually became unbeatable because few owners were willing to pit their horses against such a legendary champion. A reviewer for *Horse-Races.net* noted: "Clearly, this is the most comprehensive work on Man o' War ever seen. Ours' research is thorough, in-depth and no stone was left unturned." Comparing Ours's effort to a 2001 best-selling biography of Seabiscuit by Laura Hillenbrand, *Booklist* critic Dennis Dodge stated: "Very much to her credit, Ours meets Hillenbrand's standard in her exhaustively researched account of the career and human connections of Man o' War."

BIOGRAPHICAL AND CRITICAL SOURCES:

PERIODICALS

Biography, summer, 2006, Bill Barich, review of *Man o' War: A Legend Like Lightning.*
Booklist, April 15, 2006, Dennis Dodge, review of *Man o' War,* p. 20.
Books, May 7, 2006, Elizabeth Mitchell, "Tracking Down Some Legends," review of *Man o' War,* p. 1.
Kirkus Reviews, March 15, 2006, review of *Man o' War,* p. 278.
Library Journal, April 1, 2006, Patsy Gray, review of *Man o' War,* p. 102.

ONLINE

Dorothy Ours Home Page, http://www.dorothyours. com (May 15, 2007).
Horse-Races.net, http://www.horse-races.net/ (May 15, 2007), review of *Man o' War.**

P

PARKINSON, Heather 1974-

PERSONAL: Born 1974. *Education:* Graduated from Williamette College; also attended Boise State University.

ADDRESSES: Home—ID.

CAREER: Author. *Boise Weekly,* Boise, ID, former journalist.

AWARDS, HONORS: Received Carson research grant.

WRITINGS:

Across Open Ground: A Novel, Bloomsbury (New York, NY), 2002.

SIDELIGHTS: Heather Parkinson's *Across Open Ground: A Novel* tells a story of frontier life at the beginning of the twentieth century, at a time when the outside world was beginning to impinge on the lives of western families. The novel focuses on the life of sheepherder Walter Pascoe, who "in 1917 leaves his parents for the open-air life herding sheep in and around the Wood River Valley," Adam Tanous stated in the *Idaho Mountain Express.* "It is a life of comfortable routine until he meets and falls in love with a trapper named Trina Ivy. With the outbreak of World War I, Pascoe is drafted and must leave his new love. While they are reunited after the war, much has transpired to alter their relationship." For one thing,

the war has hardened Pascoe. When he learns that local thug Joe Moran has beaten Trina to the point that she has lost the unborn child she conceived with Pascoe, he sets out for revenge. The question for both Walter and Trina is, will they still care for one another after having experienced such violence?

Critical praise for Parkinson often singled out her lyrical use of language as reminiscent of other writers who portray the natural wonders of America. The novelist's prose, a contributor to *Kirkus Reviews* wrote, "elevates [the story] from a mere herder's tale into a kind of ballad to the American landscape." "The vivid picture Parkinson paints of the western prairie and of youthful longing will strike a chord" with fans of Ivan Doig and Claire Davis, Peggy Barber said in her *Booklist* review. "Parkinson's homage to [Cormac] McCarthy," declared a *Publishers Weekly* reviewer, "is especially graceful and poignant in her writing about the land, sheep herding and the animals."

BIOGRAPHICAL AND CRITICAL SOURCES:

PERIODICALS

Booklist, May 1, 2002, Peggy Barber, review of *Across Open Ground: A Novel,* p. 1509.
Kirkus Reviews, April 1, 2002, review of *Across Open Ground,* p. 448.
Library Journal, May 15, 2002, Jack Hafer, review of *Across Open Ground,* p. 127.
New York Times Book Review, June 9, 2002, Will Blythe, review of *Across Open Ground,* p. 13.

Publishers Weekly, March 25, 2002, review of *Across Open Ground,* p. 39.

ONLINE

Idaho Mountain Express, http://www.mtexpress.com/ (May 29, 2002), Adam Tanous, review of *Across Open Ground.*

Salt Lake Tribune Online, http://www.sltrib.co/ (April 14, 2002), Martin Naparsteck, review of *Across Open Ground.**

*　　*　　*

PARSE, Rosemarie R.
See PARSE, Rosemarie Rizzo

*　　*　　*

PARSE, Rosemarie Rizzo
(Rosemarie R. Parse)

PERSONAL: Education: Duquesne University, B.S.N., University of Pittsburg, M.S.N.Ed., Ph.D.

ADDRESSES: Office—Discovery International, Inc. and Institute of Human Becoming, 320 Fort Duquesne Blvd., Ste. 25-J, Pittsburgh, PA 15222, fax: 412-391-8458. *E-mail*—rparse@luc.edu; r.parse@verizon.net.

CAREER: City University of New York, professor and coordinator of the Center for Nursing Research at Hunter College, 1983-1993; Loyola University Chicago, Chicago, IL, professor and Niehoff Chair, 1996-2003, distinguished professor emeritus, 2003—. Also served as faculty member, University of Pittsburg, Pittsburg, PA, and dean of the Nursing School, Duquesne University, Pittsburg. Institute of Human Becoming, Pittsburg, founder and instructor; *Nursing Science Quarterly,* founder and editor; Discovery International, Inc. (nursing organization), president; presenter at numerous conferences.

MEMBER: American Academy of Nursing, American Nurses Association, National League for Nursing, Sigma Theta Tau Internationa; Civic Light Opera Advisory Committee.

AWARDS, HONORS: Sigma Theta Tau and Doody Publishing's Best Picks list in nursing theory book category, 1998, for *The Human Becoming School of Thought: A Perspective for Nurses and Other Health Professionals,* and 1999, for *Hope: An International Human Becoming Perspective;* Lifetime Achievement Award, Unitary Research Section of the Midwest Nursing Research Society, 2001.

WRITINGS:

EDITOR; NONFICTION

Nursing Science: Major Paradigms, Theories, and Critiques, Saunders (Philadelphia, PA), 1987.

Illuminations: The Human Becoming Theory in Practice and Research, National League for Nursing Press (New York, NY), 1995.

Hope: An International Human Becoming Perspective, Jones & Bartlett Publishers (Sudbury, MA), 1999.

NONFICTION

Nursing Fundamentals, Medical Examination Publishing (Flushing, NY), 1974.

Man-Living-Health: A Theory of Nursing, Wiley (New York, NY), 1981.

(With A. Barbara Coyne and Mary Jane Smith) *Nursing Research: Qualitative Methods,* Brady Communications (Bowie, MD), 1985.

The Human Becoming School of Thought: A Perspective for Nurses and Other Health Professionals, Sage Publications (Thousand Oaks, CA), 1998.

Qualitative Inquiry: The Path of Sciencing, Jones & Bartlett Publishers (Boston, MA), 2001.

Community: A Human Becoming Perspective, Jones & Bartlett Publishers (Boston, MA), 2003.

Contributor of essays to books, including *The Language of Nursing Theory and Metatheory,* edited by J. Fawcett and I.M. King, Sigma Theta Tau (Indianapolis, IN), 1997; and *Nursing Theories and Nursing Practice,* edited by M.E. Parker, F.A. Davis, (Philadelphia, PA), 2001. Contributor of articles to periodicals, including *Nursing Science Quarterly, Journal of Advanced Nursing,* and *Visions.* Author's works have been translated into Danish, Finnish, French, German, Italian, Japanese, Spanish, Swedish, Taiwanese, and Korean.

BIOGRAPHICAL AND CRITICAL SOURCES:

PERIODICALS

ANNA Journal, August 1, 1999, review of *The Human Becoming School of Thought: A Perspective for Nurses and Other Health Professionals,* p. 444.
Choice: Current Reviews for Academic Libraries, July 1, 1998, review of *The Human Becoming School of Thought,* p. 1885; May 1, 2000, review of *Hope: An International Human Becoming Perspective,* p. HS20.
SciTech Book News, June 1, 1998, review of *The Human Becoming School of Thought,* p. 100; June 1, 1999, review of *Hope,* p. 131; December 1, 2001, review of *Qualitative Inquiry: The Path of Sciencing,* p. 128; September 1, 2003, review of *Community: A Human Becoming Perspective,* p. 137.

ONLINE

International Consortium of Parse's Scholars Home Page, http://www.luc.edu/ (May 14, 2007).
Loyola University Chicago Web site, http://www.luc.edu/ (May 14, 2007), faculty profile of author.*

*   *   *

PASSANANTE, Joy 1947-
(Joy Cathey Passanante)

PERSONAL: Born April 18, 1947, in St. Louis, MO; daughter of Bart Michael and Alberta Passanante; married Gary Williams, June 13, 1970; children: Liza Bryn, Emily Caterina. *Education:* Attended Sarah Lawrence College, 1965-67; Washington University, St. Louis, MO, A.B., 1969; Cornell University, M.A.T., 1971.

ADDRESSES: Office—University of Idaho, Moscow, ID 83844-0001. *E-mail*—joy@uidaho.edu.

CAREER: High school English teacher in Homer, NY, 1971-73; freelance writer and editor, 1975—; University of Idaho, Moscow, member of English department faculty, 1977-83, 1988—, communications specialist in College of Business and Economics,

1983-90, currently associate director of creative writing. Consultant to Educational Testing Service, Princeton, NJ, 1991—; mentor, Moscow High School, 1992—; academic adviser to Alpha Phi, Moscow, beginning 1997. Member, Northern Idaho Council on English.

MEMBER: Athena, Phi Beta Kappa (vice president of Idaho chapter, 1994-95; president, 1995-97), Academy of American Poets.

AWARDS, HONORS: Fellowship in fiction, Idaho Commission on the Arts, 1990; Outstanding Faculty Award, University of Idaho Interfraternity Council, 1993; QuickArts grant for poetry, 1997; Teaching Excellence Award, University of Idaho, 2001; Fellowship in poetry, Idaho Commission on the Arts, 2001; *ForeWord Magazine* Award finalist for best fiction, 2002, for *My Mother's Lovers;* Mayor's Arts Award, Moscow Arts Comission, 2004; research fellowship, Idaho Humanities Council, 2005; four Pushcart Prize nominations, for essays and stories.

WRITINGS:

Writing Guidelines, 1991.
Sinning in Italy (poetry), Limberlost Press, 1999.
My Mother's Lovers (novel), University of Nevada Press (Reno, NV), 2002.
The Art of Absence: Stories, Lost Horse Press (Sandpoint, ID), 2004.

Contributor of essays, fiction, and poetry to periodicals, including *Alaska Quarterly, Short Story, College English, Gettysburg Review, Georgia Review, Shenandoah,* and *Xavier Review.* Advisory editor, *Frontiers: A Journal of Women Studies,* 1996—.

SIDELIGHTS: In Joy Passanante's first novel, *My Mother's Lovers,* she tells the tale of a young girl growing up the child of unconventional parents who came of age in the radical Sixties. In her early teens, Lake Rose Davis is finding it harder and harder to cope with her parents—and especially with her mother, the exhibitionist painter Mimi. "In a series of discomfiting revelations," wrote a *Publishers Weekly* reviewer, "Lake discovers herself by learning the truth about Mimi, whose exhibitionism hides as much as it reveals." Further revelations come after Lake develops a serious illness and travels to her grandparents' home in St. Louis, Missouri, to recuperate. "As Lake recuperates, then stays on after a tragic accident," declared a contributor to *Kirkus Reviews,* "she learns more about her family, Mimi, and the binding ties of love as she chases her own dreams."

Each story in Passanante's collection *The Art of Absence: Stories* centers on the theme of the loss of love and the failure of relationships. Reviewers celebrated the author's command of language and her restrained approach to these volatile subjects. "Passanante," declared Nathan Leslie in *Pedestal Magazine,* "tends to write in two directions at once—while the subject matter of her stories gravitates towards emotional extremes, the prose is discreet, carefully controlled, burnished." "Passanante's vision is bleak, her eye trained on loss," Danielle LaVaque-Manty stated in her *NewPages.com* review of the volume. "These stories don't lead to despair, however, but rather to recognition of the ways in which our lives remain rich despite the absences that shape them."

BIOGRAPHICAL AND CRITICAL SOURCES:

PERIODICALS

Kirkus Reviews, January 15, 2002, review of *My Mother's Lovers,* p. 69.
Publishers Weekly, February 11, 2002, review of *My Mother's Lovers,* p. 161.

ONLINE

NewPages.com, http://newpages.com/ (May 2, 2007), Danielle LaVaque-Manty, review of *The Art of Absence: Stories.*
Pedestal Magazine, http://www.thepedestalmagazine.com/ (May 2, 2007), Nathan Leslie, review of *The Art of Absence.*

*   *   *

PASSANANTE, Joy Cathey
See PASSANANTE, Joy

PASSARO, Vince

PERSONAL: Married Beth Stolz; separated; children: John, James, Paul. *Education:* Columbia College, graduated, 1979; Columbia University, M.F.A., 1988.

ADDRESSES: Office—Corporation of Yaddo, 630 9th Ave., Ste. 701, New York, NY 10036. *E-mail*—vpassaro@yaddo.org.

CAREER: Author. City University of New York, Baruch College, New York, NY, director of public relations; Corporation of Yaddo, Saratoga Springs, NY, and New York, NY, director of foundation and corporate relations.

WRITINGS:

Violence, Nudity, Adult Content: A Novel, Simon & Schuster (New York, NY), 2002.

Work represented in anthologies, including *Best of the West,* W.W. Norton (New York, NY), 1992; and *Lust, Violence, Sin, Magic,* Atlantic Monthly Press (New York, NY), 1993. Contributor to periodicals and Web sites, including *Nation, New York Times Magazine, Harper's, New York,* and *Salon.com.*

SIDELIGHTS: "Vince Passaro's lacerating debut," entitled *Violence, Nudity, Adult Content: A Novel,* wrote *New York Times* contributor Janet Maslin, ". . . is about a New York lawyer named Will Riordan." Passaro, a widely published essayist and commentator, gives Will's story its own special New York edge: while the destruction of Will's modern marriage and his soul-staining job are relatively commonplace in modern literature, the novel gains power from the protagonist's tart observations about life and from the matter-of-fact violence that pursues Will in both his private life and at work. "While his family implodes," a *Kirkus Reviews* contributor stated, "Riordan broods about his life—a passage about his rage-filled alcoholic father and an entire generation of postwar dads is nothing short of brilliant—and about the city around him." Added to this is the fact that one of his clients, the victim of a gang rape, is also an avant-garde artist who deluges him with e-mails expressing her extremely personal views on the way her case is conducted. The novel, declared Christine Perkins in her *Library Journal* review, becomes a "scorching commentary on office politics and sexual mores." "On another level," Perkins continued, "it's about the dehumanizing effects of rape." The author "has a superb feeling for the city's beauty and banality—indeed, the 'addictive swirl of money and subjugation' that Will observes in a Manhattan strip club seems endemic to all five boroughs," declared *New York Times Book Review* contributor James Marcus. "Passaro is equally good at conveying the crazy compression of Manhattan life, where the verdict on people, places and things tends to be delivered instantaneously." "Throwing legal-thriller curve balls and narrating near cinematic personal struggles," concluded a *Publishers Weekly* reviewer, "Passaro imbues the novel with mesmerizing suspense, leading the reader through a labyrinth to an unexpectedly upbeat finale."

BIOGRAPHICAL AND CRITICAL SOURCES:

PERIODICALS

Book, January-February, 2002, Kevin Greenberg, review of *Violence, Nudity, Adult Content: A Novel,* p. 74.

Booklist, December 15, 2001, Connie Fletcher, review of *Violence, Nudity, Adult Content,* p. 707.

Kirkus Reviews, November 15, 2001, review of *Violence, Nudity, Adult Content,* p. 1572.

Library Journal, December, 2001, Christine Perkins, review of *Violence, Nudity, Adult Content,* p. 174.

New York Times, February 18, 2002, Janet Maslin, review of *Violence, Nudity, Adult Content,* p. B14.

New York Times Book Review, March 10, 2002, James Marcus, review of *Violence, Nudity, Adult Content,* p. 18.

Publishers Weekly, December 24, 2001, review of *Violence, Nudity, Adult Content,* p. 39.

ONLINE

Columbia College Today Online, http://www.college. columbia.edu/ (January, 2003), Justine Bleu, interview with Passaro.

Free Williamsburg, http://www.freewilliamsburg.com/ (April, 2002), J. Stefan Cole, review of *Violence, Nudity, Adult Content.*

Salon.com, http://www.salon.com/ (March 21, 2002), Andrew O'Hehir, review of *Violence, Nudity, Adult Content.*

*   *   *

PEGG, Bruce

PERSONAL: Born in Leicester, England; immigrated to the United States, 1981. *Education:* Loughborough University, Leicestershire, England, B.A.; State University of New York, Brockport, M.A.

ADDRESSES: Home—NY. *E-mail*—bruce.pegg@ sunyit.edu; peggb@herkimer.edu.

CAREER: Held positions as assistant director of writing center, writing center administrator, and writing consultant, Syracuse University Writing Program, Syracuse, NY, 2000-2003; Herkimer County Community College, Herkimer, NY, associate dean of academic affairs, humanities division, 2006; previously taught at Colgate University.

WRITINGS:

Brown Eyed Handsome Man: The Life and Hard Times of Chuck Berry, Routledge (New York, NY), 2002.

SIDELIGHTS: Bruce Pegg has written a biography of rock 'n' roll legend Chuck Berry that, while unauthorized, has been considered by some as the definitive work on the singer's life and career. Berry, who invented rock music as a form, wrote his autobiography in the mid-1980s, but Pegg's volume is a far more comprehensive work, illuminating the darker side of Berry's life that the singer edited out of his own book. Pegg's efforts are fair and balanced, however, revealing him to be both a fan and an unbiased observer of Berry's career and experiences. In *Brown Eyed Handsome Man: The Life and Hard Times of Chuck Berry,* Pegg chronicles Berry's rise to stardom with his series of catchy, new tunes that mixed blues, jazz, and hillbilly music into a fresh format that set the standard for rock music going forward. He also delves into Berry's childhood growing up in segregated St. Louis, and his more questionable exploits as an adult, including his jail sentence for tax evasion and an arrest for allegedly having sex with a minor. Pegg reveals not only Berry's talent as a singer and musician, but as a successful businessman, while being upfront about Berry's failures as well, and includes details gleaned from various interviews with the singer's friends and peers. In a review for *Library Journal,* Henry L. Carrigan, Jr., remarked that "Pegg alternates between hagiography and harsh judgments of Berry, making the book feel off-balance," but ultimately found the biography to be "an often-engaging portrait" of Berry. Tony Glover, writing for the *Blues on Stage* Web site, called Pegg's effort "a quite readable entry into the life and times of a gifted, but fatefully flawed musician."

BIOGRAPHICAL AND CRITICAL SOURCES:

PERIODICALS

American Studies, spring, 2004, Glenn C. Altschurer, review of *Brown Eyed Handsome Man: The Life and Hard Times of Chuck Berry,* pp. 169-170.

Biography, spring, 2003, Jeff Turrentine, review of *Brown Eyed Handsome Man,* p. 348.

Boston Herald, November 10, 2002, Marc Flores, review of *Brown Eyed Handsome Man,* p. 60.

Gazette (Montreal, Quebec, Canada), December 7, 2002, Ian McGillis, review of *Brown Eyed Handsome Man,* p. H4.

Library Journal, October 1, 2002, Henry L. Carrigan, Jr., review of *Brown Eyed Handsome Man,* p. 97.

Post-Standard (Syracuse, NY), March 23, 2003, Mark Bialczak, "Pinmonkey Blends Music Styles," p. 13.

Riverfront Times (St. Louis, MO), May 14, 2003, J. Konkel, review of *Brown Eyed Handsome Man.*

ONLINE

Blues on Stage, http://www.mnblues.com/ (April 27, 2007), Tony Glover, review of *Brown Eyed Handsome Man.*

OneidaDispatch.com, http://www.oneidadispatch.com/ (September 25, 2002), Alex Bonafice, review of *Brown Eyed Handsome Man.**

PELLA, Judith

PERSONAL: Married. *Education:* Attended college. *Hobbies and other interests:* Sailing, quilting, collecting things for her dollhouse, reading.

ADDRESSES: Home—OR.

CAREER: Writer. worked previously as a nurse and an elementary school teacher.

WRITINGS:

NOVELS

Frontier Lady, Bethany House Publishers (Minneapolis, MN), 1993.

Heirs of the Motherland, Bethany House Publishers (Minneapolis, MN), 1993.

Stoner's Crossing, Bethany House Publishers (Minneapolis, MN), 1994.

The Dawning of Deliverance, Bethany House Publishers (Minneapolis, MN), 1995.

Warrior's Song, Bethany House Publishers (Minneapolis, MN), 1996.

Blind Faith, Bethany House Publishers (Minneapolis, MN), 1996.

White Nights, Red Morning, Bethany House Publishers (Minneapolis, MN), 1996.

Passage into Light, Bethany House Publishers (Minneapolis, MN), 1998.

Beloved Stranger, Bethany House Publishers (Minneapolis, MN), 1998.

Texas Angel, Bethany House (Minneapolis, MN), 1999.

Heaven's Road, Bethany House (Minneapolis, MN), 2000.

Written on the Wind, Bethany House Publishers (Minneapolis, MN), 2002.

Somewhere a Song, Bethany House Publishers (Minneapolis, MN), 2002.

Toward the Sunrise, Bethany House (Minneapolis, MN), 2003.

Homeward My Heart, Bethany House Publishers (Minneapolis, MN), 2004.

Mark of the Cross, Bethany House Publishers (Bloomington, MN), 2006.

Bachelor's Puzzle, Bethany House (Minneapolis, MN), 2007.

WITH MICHAEL PHILLIPS; NOVELS

The Heather Hills of Stonewycke, Bethany House Publishers (Minneapolis, MN), 1985.

Flight from Stonewycke, Bethany House Publishers (Minneapolis, MN), 1985.

The Lady of Stonewycke, Bethany House Publishers (Minneapolis, MN), 1986.

Jamie MacLeod, Highland Lass, Bethany House Publishers (Minneapolis, MN), 1987.

Robbie Taggart, Highland Sailor, Bethany House Publishers (Minneapolis, MN), 1987.

Stranger at Stonewycke, Bethany House (Minneapolis, MN), 1987.

Shadows over Stonewycke, Bethany House (Minneapolis, MN), 1988.

Treasure of Stonewycke, Bethany House (Minneapolis, MN), 1988.

My Father's World, Bethany House Publishers (Minneapolis, MN), 1990.

Daughter of Grace, Bethany House Publishers (Minneapolis, MN), 1990.

The Crown and the Crucible, Bethany House (Minneapolis, MN), 1991.

A Place in the Sun, Bethany House Publishers (Minneapolis, MN), 1991.

On the Trail of the Truth, Bethany House Publishers (Minneapolis, MN), 1991.

Travail and Triumph, Bethany House (Minneapolis, MN), 1992.

A House Divided, Bethany House Publishers (Minneapolis, MN), 1992.

The Stonewycke Legacy, Bethany House (Minneapolis, MN), 2000.

The Stonewycke Trilogy, Bethany House (Minneapolis, MN), 2000.

WITH TRACIE PETERSON; NOVELS

Distant Dreams, Bethany House (Minneapolis, MN), 1997.

A Hope Beyond, Bethany House (Minneapolis, MN), 1997.

Westward the Dream, Bethany House Publishers (Minneapolis, MN), 1998.

A Promise for Tomorrow, Bethany House Publishers (Minneapolis, MN), 1998.

Separate Roads, Bethany House Publishers (Minneapolis, MN), 1999.

Ties That Bind, Bethany House (Minneapolis, MN), 2000.

SIDELIGHTS: Judith Pella fell in love with storytelling as a child and began to experiment with writing herself. But as she grew older, she pursued other types of work, spending time as a nurse and then as an elementary school teacher. Eventually, she shared some of her writing with good friend and published writer Michael Phillips. Phillips was very encouraging and suggested Pella might collaborate on an upcoming project with him, as he did not feel he had sufficient time to devote to it. The result was Pella's first published book, *The Heather Hills of Stonewycke.* So began the first series Pella was to write with Phillips and a writing partnership that would continue to thrive for more than two decades. Pella also writes in partnership with Tracie Peterson, and on her own.

Pella's books are classified as Christian fiction and focus primarily on individuals struggling to find love and redemption in the eyes of God. Her settings range from Scotland to the Old West, providing a backdrop for stories that aim to inspire and exude hope. In *Written on the Wind,* the first in her World War II, "Daughters of Fortune" series, is about three sisters living in California at the start of the war. They struggle to please their tough, entrepreneurial father, who publishes a major Los Angeles newspaper. Each daughter attempts to gain her father's favor, and the results are a series of romances and adventures that take place over the course of the book. A *Publishers Weekly* reviewer remarked that the novel "offers some humorous touches and fine descriptive detail, though Pella spends too much time telling rather than showing." Though John Mort, writing for *Booklist,* criticized some of Pella's modern language as inappropriate for the setting, he noted that "her story does come to life in wartime Yugoslavia, Egypt, and especially the Soviet Union."

Mark of the Cross offers readers a medieval romance, set in thirteenth-century Europe, between the noble Beatrice and Philip, an illegitimate son. When Philip is accused of murder and banished from the country, the romance appears more hopeless than ever, but Beatrice's faith leads them back together in the end. Marty Medley, in a review for *Armchair Interviews,* remarked: "The author fills in the history [of] that era quite nicely—adding to the story rather than distracting in its complexity."

BIOGRAPHICAL AND CRITICAL SOURCES:

PERIODICALS

Booklist, October 1, 2001, John Mort, review of *Heaven's Road,* p. 335; January 1, 2002, John Mort, review of *Written on the Wind,* p. 804; April 15, 2006, John Mort, review of *Mark of the Cross,* p. 28.

Library Journal, April 1, 1995, Henry Carrigan, review of *The Dawning of Deliverance,* p. 82; February 1, 1996, Henry Carrigan, review of *Warrior's Song,* p. 66; November 1, 1996, Melissa Hudak, review of *Blind Faith,* p. 54; February 1, 1997, Melissa Hudak, review of *White Nights, Red Mornings,* p. 68; April 1, 1997, Melissa Hudak, review of *Distant Dreams,* p. 80; April 1, 1998, Melissa Hudak, review of *A Promise for Tomorrow,* p. 78; November 1, 1998, Melissa Hudak, review of *Passage into Light,* p. 66; November 15, 1998, Kristin Ramsdell, review of *Westward the Dream,* p. 56; November 1, 1999, review of *Separate Roads,* p. 68; November 1, 1999, Melanie C. Duncan, review of *Texas Angel,* p. 68; April 1, 2000, Melanie C. Duncan, review of *Ties That Bind,* p. 84.

MBR Bookwatch, January 1, 2005, Harriet Klausner, review of *Homeward My Heart.*

Publishers Weekly, October 22, 2001, review of *Written on the Wind,* p. 42.

School Library Journal, September 1, 1997, Janice DeLong, review of *Distant Dreams,* p. 239.

Voice of Youth Advocates, December 1, 1994, review of *Stoner's Crossing,* p. 278.

ONLINE

Armchair Interviews, http://www.armchairinterviews. com/ (May 15, 2007), Marty Medley, review of *Mark of the Cross.*

Curled Up with a Good Book, http://www.curledup. com/ (May 15, 2007), Deanna Couras Goodson, review of *Mark of the Cross.*

Judith Pella Home Page, http://www.judithpella.com (May 15, 2007).*

*   *   *

PERIL, Lynn 1961-

PERSONAL: Born 1961, in Milwaukee, WI; married Johnny Bartlett. *Education:* San Francisco State University, M.A., 1995.

ADDRESSES: Home—Oakland, CA. *E-mail*—peril@ pinkthink.com.

CAREER: Founder and editor of *Mystery Date* (Internet magazine).

AWARDS, HONORS: Pushcart Prize nomination.

WRITINGS:

Pink Think: Becoming a Woman in Many Uneasy Lessons, W.W. Norton (New York, NY), 2002.
College Girls: Bluestockings, Sex Kittens, and Coeds, Then and Now, W.W. Norton (New York, NY), 2006.

Contributor to periodicals, including the London *Guardian, San Francisco Bay Guardian,* and *Hermenaut.* Author of column "The Museum of Femoribilia" for *Bust* magazine.

SIDELIGHTS: Lynn Peril has drawn on her interest in popular culture to produce books, a column, and a magazine. Specifically, Peril is fascinated by sex and dating manuals, etiquette and self-help books, and health, beauty and fashion guides from the 1940s to 1970s. In her first book, *Pink Think: Becoming a Woman in Many Uneasy Lessons,* Peril examines how society in the form of advertisements and advice booklets proposed a skewered, male-oriented view of the "ideal" woman. From advertisements touting Lysol as a product for feminine hygiene to printed advice from a Catholic priest on menstruation, the author provides numerous examples of what she calls "Pink Think" and "femoribilia," that is a host of products such as books, magazines, and even board games that reflect societal standards concerning women.

"The great strength of the book is its sheer exhaustive scope, asserted Barbara Shubinski in *Winterthur Portfolio.* "Peril has a sharp eye for the ironic or ludicrous example and a witty sense of the patronizing, chauvinistic, heterosexist mentality driving the advertisements and advice texts with which she is so clearly fascinated." A *Publishers Weekly* contributor called *Pink Think* "hilariously entertaining." Although other reviewers similarly commented on the author's humorous writing style, many also noted that the book is more than just a fun look at outdated modes of thinking about women. Writing in *Herizons,* Jennifer O'Connor felt that the author "has turned her affection for daisy razors and ads for Serena sanitary pads into a thoughtful analysis of how femininity was, and is, constructed." Emily Toth concluded in the *Women's Review of Books* that "Peril writes about all this in a lively, breezy style that makes for easy, uncluttered reading."

College Girls: Bluestockings, Sex Kittens, and Coeds, Then and Now provides an historical look of women in American colleges primarily through materials such as advice booklets, advertisements, and various other writings. Peril includes such items as an 1830's newspaper editorial that berated a new women's college and suggested the creation of degrees such as M.D.N. (Mistress of the Darning Needle). The author also examines how the idea of whether or not women should attend college and receive the same education as men was a fiercely debated issue in the 1950s; she comments, too, on how a "women's curriculum" designed to make women good homemakers was proposed by some in academia following World War II.

College Girls received praise from many critics. "Researchers and pleasure readers alike will find a great deal to appreciate in Peril's fresh and engaging work," attested Colleen Mondor in *Booklist.* Once again, the critics noted the author's ability to provide sociological insights with humor. A *Publishers Weekly* contributor wrote that the author's "witty, irreverent style, her generous use of old advertisements and photos and her careful footnotes make this text unusually user-friendly." *Library Journal* reviewer Elizabeth M. Wavle called *College Girls,* a "fun, informative, and insightful read."

BIOGRAPHICAL AND CRITICAL SOURCES:

PERIODICALS

Booklist, July 1, 2006, Colleen Mondor, review of *College Girls: Bluestockings, Sex Kittens, and Coeds, Then and Now,* p. 14.
Herizons, winter, 2003, Jennifer O'Connor, review of *Pink Think: Becoming a Woman in Many Uneasy Lessons,* p. 22.

Iris: A Journal about Women, spring-summer, 2004, Marisa Hoheb, review of *Pink Think,* p. 81.
Kirkus Reviews, August 1, 2002, review of *Pink Think,* p. 1104.
Library Journal, August 1, 2006, Elizabeth M. Wavle, review of *College Girls,* p. 110.
New York Times Book Review, October 1, 2006, Jennifer Schuessler, review of *College Girls.*
Publishers Weekly, July 22, 2002, review of *Pink Think,* pp. 164-165; May 29, 2006, review of *College Girls,* p. 49.
Reference & Research Book News, November, 2006, review of *College Girls.*
Winterthur Portfolio, winter, 2002, Barbara Shubinski, review of *Pink Think,* p. 278.
Women's Review of Books, January, 2003, Emily Toth, review of *Pink Think,* p. 13.

ONLINE

Atlantic Online, http://www.theatlantic.com/ (March 6, 2007), Katie Bacon, "Girls Gone Studious," interview with Lynn Peril.
Atomic Magazine, http://www.atomicmag.com/ (April 23, 2007), Dixie Feldman, review of *Pink Think.*
Brooklyn Rail, http://www.brooklynrail.org/ (April 23, 2007), Erica Wetter, review of *College Girls.*
Lynn Peril Home Page, http://www.pinkthink.com (September 18, 2004).
Lynn Peril MySpace.com Page, http://www.myspace.com/lperil (April 23, 2007).
Morphizim, http://www.morphizm.com/ (November 30, 2002), Sandra Fu, "Pink Peril: An Interview with Lynn Peril, *Pink Think.*"
Research Publications, http://www.researchpubs.com/ (September 18, 2004), interview with Lynn Peril.
Zinebook.com, http://www.zinebook.com/ (April 23, 2007), brief interview with Lynn Peril.

*   *   *

PETERS, Christoph 1966-

PERSONAL: Born 1966, in Kalkar, Germany. *Education:* Studied painting at the National Academy of Arts, Karlsruhe, Germany, 1988-94.

ADDRESSES: *Home*—Berlin, Germany.

CAREER: Freelance writer. Worked as an aircraft passenger tester, Frankfurt, Germany, 1995-99.

AWARDS, HONORS: "Aspekte" Prize for the best German-language literary debut, 1999.

WRITINGS:

NOVELS

Stadt, Land, Fluss (title means "Town, Country, River"), Frankfurter Verlagsanstalt (Frankfurt, Germany), 1999.
Das Tuch Aus Nacht, btb (Munich, Germany), 2003, translated by John Cullen as *The Fabric of Night,* Nan A. Talese Books (New York, NY), 2007.
Ein Zimmer im Haus Des Krieges, btb (Munich, Germany), 2006.

OTHER

Kommen und Gehen, Manchmal Bleiben: 14 Geschichten (short stories), Frankfurter Verlagsanstalt (Frankfurt, Germany), 2001.
Heinrich Grewents Arbeit und Liebe: Eine Erzählung, btb (Munich, Germany), 2004.

SIDELIGHTS: German-born writer Christoph Peters began his career as an art student, studying painting at the National Academy of Arts at Karlsruhe. When he became a writer, Peters translated his artist's precision into careful and exact word choice. The protagonist of his first novel, *Stadt, Land, Fluss,* is an art history student who falls in love with and marries his dentist, Hanna. Hanna mysteriously disappears, and Peters traces the man's resulting decline. The book was critically acclaimed upon publication, and went on to win the Aspekte Prize, awarded each year for the best German-language literary debut. Peters has written several other books and a collection of short stories, but *Das Tuch Aus Nacht* is the first to be published in English translation, released in 2007 as *The Fabric of Night.* The book tells the story of a German-born sculptor—again revisiting Peters's early artistic experiences—named Albin Kranz, who is on vacation with his girlfriend in Istanbul. Albin drinks too much and his relationship is in a precarious place, but he notices very little of this because he believes he has witnessed a murder; the only problem is that no one is willing to acknowledge the crime, or even that the victim in question ever existed. Dennis Drabelle, writing for *Book World,* remarked: "This novel breaks rules and gets away with it. It looks like a thriller, acts like a character study and leaves the reader pondering its own narrative structure." He went on to note that, ultimately, Peters focuses more on "depicting the heroism and hubris of trying to penetrate a foreign nation's criminal milieu, than in spinning a puzzle-plot," but despite this variance from standard mystery structure, he found the book "absorbing and strangely satisfying." A contributor for *Kirkus Reviews* wrote: "Confusing at times, disturbing at others, Peters's work rewards the challenge of reading with lasting, moody reflections."

BIOGRAPHICAL AND CRITICAL SOURCES:

PERIODICALS

Book World, January 28, 2007, Dennis Drabelle, "Death in Istanbul: A Tourist Sees a Murder, but No One Believes Him—And There's No Body," review of *The Fabric of Night,* p. 6.
Booklist, November 15, 2003, review of *Kommen und Gehen, Manchmal Bleiben: 14 Geschichten,* p. 590.
Economist, April 15, 2000, "Recent Fiction from Germany," review of *Stadt, Land, Fluss,* p. 14.
Kirkus Reviews, October 1, 2006, review of *The Fabric of Night,* p. 983.
Library Journal, November 15, 2006, Joy Humphrey, review of *The Fabric of Night,* p. 59.
Publishers Weekly, October 30, 2006, review of *The Fabric of Night,* p. 37.
Times Literary Supplement, October 8, 1999, review of *Stadt, Land, Fluss,* p. 7.
World Literature Today, summer-autumn, 2002, Elizabeth Powers, review of *Kommen und Gehen, Manchmal Bleiben,* p. 119.

ONLINE

SFGate.com, http://sfgate.com/ (April 27, 2007), Christine Thomas, "Student Seeks Art, Finds Murder Instead," review of *The Fabric of Night.*

PETERS, Karl E. 1939-

PERSONAL: Born 1939.

ADDRESSES: Home—CT.

CAREER: Rollins College, Winter Park, FL, professor emeritus of philosophy and religion; Hartford College, Hartford, CT, adjunct professor of philosophy; Center for Advanced Study in Religion and Science, president.

MEMBER: University Unitarian Universalist Society (founder, organizer, first president), Institute on Religion in an Age of Science (past president).

WRITINGS:

Dancing with the Sacred: Evolution, Ecology, and God, Trinity Press International (Harrisburg, PA), 2002.

Editor of *Zygon: Journal of Religion and Science.* American Association for the Advancement of Science, editorial advisor.

SIDELIGHTS: Karl E. Peters is an educator and philosopher whose primary area of research interest is the point at which science and religion connect. He is the founder and first president of the University Unitarian Universalist Society, and has worked for both the American Association for the Advancement of Science and the Center for Advanced Study in Religion and Science. Peters's book, *Dancing with the Sacred: Evolution, Ecology, and God,* looks at the place of religion in a life that shows the proof of more scientific explanations behind the workings of the universe. The dance described in the title refers to the dance of life itself, and how people can embrace the sacred concepts of religion without clinging to the traditional personifications used to explain the broad concepts. Peters offers the book as a primer to the idea of naturalistic theism. Steve Young, in a review for *Library Journal,* acknowledged that much of Peters's book covers territory previously explained by various theologians, but concluded that, even so, "Peters's vibrant optimism and joy of life comes ringing forth from his science-based spirituality." Frank R. Hensley,

writing in *Interpretation,* objected to Peters's basic premise and so found himself unable to agree with the book on the whole, but he noted that "anyone who cannot conceive of how to find meaning, morality, and the sacred apart from a personal God may find this book intellectually stimulating." Roger E. Timm, in a review for *Currents in Theology and Mission,* commented that he found the book "helpful, stimulating, and challenging, especially for those concerned for the intersection of faith and science," and *Theological Studies* contributor James F. Salmon wrote: "This clearly written book offers the finest personal exposition of the school of naturalist theism that dominates the writings of many contemporary intellectuals and scientists."

BIOGRAPHICAL AND CRITICAL SOURCES:

PERIODICALS

Booklist, August 1, 2002, Steven Schroeder, review of *Dancing with the Sacred: Evolution, Ecology, and God,* p. 104.
Choice, April, 2003, D.E. Burton-Christie, review of *Dancing with the Sacred,* p. 1381.
Currents in Theology and Mission, April, 2004, Roger E. Timm, review of *Dancing with the Sacred,* p. 127; April, 2005, Antje Jackelen, review of *Dancing with the Sacred,* p. 145.
Interpretation, January, 2004, Frank R. Hensley, review of *Dancing with the Sacred,* p. 101.
Library Journal, August, 2002, Steve Young, review of *Dancing with the Sacred.*
Theological Studies, September, 2004, James F. Salmon, review of *Dancing with the Sacred,* p. 681.
Theology Today, April, 2003, John F. Haught, review of *Dancing with the Sacred,* p. 144.*

*   *   *

PILLSBURY, Joanne

PERSONAL: Education: University of California, Berkeley, B.A., 1982; Columbia University, M.A., 1986, M.Phil., 1987, Ph.D., 1993.

ADDRESSES: Home—MD. *Office*—Department of Art History and Archaeology, 4206 Art/Sociology Bldg., University of Maryland, College Park, MD 20742-1335. *E-mail*—jp297@umail.umd.edu; pillsbury@doaks.org.

CAREER: Art historian, archaeologist. Center for Advanced Study in the Visual Arts, National Gallery of Art, Washington, DC, assistant dean; Sainsbury Research Unit for the Arts of Africa, Oceania, and the Americas, University of East Anglia, Norwich, England, lecturer, 1991—; University of Maryland, College Park, professor of Andean art and archaeology; Dumbarton Oaks, Washington, DC, professor of pre-Columbian studies. Johns Hopkins University, visiting professor, 1998, 1999.

MEMBER: Association for Latin American Art (president), Institute of Andean Studies, Society for American Archaeology, American Association of University Women.

AWARDS, HONORS: Dumbarton Oaks fellow, 1989-90; Samuel H. Kress Foundation grant, 1990; Fulbright scholarship, 1990-91; Andrew W. Mellon grant, 1994-95; Royal Anthropological Institute, fellow.

WRITINGS:

(Editor) *Moche Art and Archaeology in Ancient Peru,* Yale University Press (New Haven, CT), 2001.
(Editor, with Susan Toby Evans) *Palaces of the Ancient New World: A Symposium at Dumbarton Oaks, 10th and 11th October, 1998,* Dumbarton Oaks Research Library and Collection (Washington, DC), 2004.
(General editor, with Jeffrey Quilter) *Variations in the Expression of Inka Power: A Symposium at Dumbarton Oaks, 18 and 19 October, 1997,* Dumbarton Oaks Research Library and Collection (Washington, DC), 2007.
(Editor) *Guide to Documentary Sources for Andean Studies, 1530-1900,* University of Oklahoma Press (Norman, OK), 2008.

Contributor to books by others, including *The Dictionary of Art,* edited by Jane Shoaf Turner, Macmillan (New York, NY), 1996; and *The Spirit of Ancient Peru: Treasures from the Mudeo Arqueologico Rafael Larco Herrera,* edited by Kathleen Berrin, Fine Arts Museums of San Francisco (San Francisco, CA), 1997.

SIDELIGHTS: Joanne Pillsbury is a professor of Andean Art and Archeology. Her primary areas of research interest include ancient American art and archeology with a focus on the Andean art of South America and the archeology of Peru's pre-Hispanic empires. She has participated in various archeological investigations of the region, including a trip to the site at Chan Chan, the capital of the kingdom of Chimor where the Inkas overthrew the ruling society in the 1600s. The project resulted in a range of historical discoveries pertaining to art, architecture, and biology, among other disciplines. Pillsbury has collected a number of the findings with coeditor Susan Toby Evans in the book, *Palaces of the Ancient New World: A Symposium at Dumbarton Oaks, 10th and 11th October, 1998.* George Lau, in a review for *Antiquity,* questioned the use of the term "palace" in the reference work, remarking "Andeanists, generally a conservative lot, have been reluctant to use 'palace' because it would ascribe function to a given context while there may still be reasonable uncertainty."

Pillsbury has also edited *Moche Art and Archaeology in Ancient Peru,* a collection of papers that were presented at a Center for Advanced Study in the Visual Arts symposium at the National Gallery of Art, for which she also provided an introduction. The papers proposed to analyze the relationship between visual arts and archeological representation in early Peruvian Moche culture. In a review for the *Journal of the Royal Anthropological Institute,* George Bankes wrote: "Pillsbury's introduction outlines very well the current state of Moche studies, emphasizing how recent archaeological excavations and icono-graphic studies have refuted earlier unitary models of the Moche."

BIOGRAPHICAL AND CRITICAL SOURCES:

PERIODICALS

Americas: A Quarterly Review of Inter-American Cultural History, Ryan Mongelluzzo, review of *Palaces of the Ancient New World: A Symposium at Dumbarton Oaks, 10th and 11th October, 1998,* p. 151.
Antiquity, December, 2002, Penelope Z. Dransart, review of *Moche Art and Archeology in Ancient Peru,* p. 1158; September, 2006, George Lau, "Ancient Andean Space and Architecture: New Syntheses and Debates," review of *Palaces of the Ancient New World,* p. 720.

Archeology, July 1, 2002, review of *Moche Art and Archeology in Ancient Peru,* p. 61.

Choice, November, 2002, J.B. Richardson III, review of *Moche Art and Archeology in Ancient Peru,* p. 513; October, 2006, M. Watson, review of *Moche Art and Archeology in Ancient Peru,* p. 287.

Journal of the Royal Anthropological Institute, March, 2003, George Bankes, review of *Moche Art and Archaeology in Ancient Peru,* p. 166.

Library Journal, May 1, 2002, Sylvia Andrews, review of *Moche Art and Archeology in Ancient Peru,* p. 98.

Times Literary Supplement, December 20, 2002, Norman Hammond, review of *Moche Art and Archeology in Ancient Peru,* p. 17.

ONLINE

Smith College Web site, http://www.smith.edu/ (April 30, 2007), listing of past officers of Association for Latin American Art.

University of Maryland Web site, http://www.umd.edu/ (April 30, 2007), faculty biography.*

*   *   *

PITTALWALA, Iqbal

PERSONAL: Born in Bombay, India; immigrated to the United States, 1985. *Education:* State University of New York at Stony Brook, Ph.D.; Iowa Writers Workshop, M.F.A., 1995.

ADDRESSES: Home—CA. *Office*—University of California, Irvine, Irvine, CA 92692.

CAREER: University of California, Riverside, campus communications officer, Riverside Extension, creative writing teacher; University of California, Irvine, assistant director of science and technology communications.

WRITINGS:

Dear Paramount Pictures: Stories, Southern Methodist University Press (Dallas, TX), 2002.

Contributor of short fiction to a number of journals, including *Seattle Review, Blue Mesa Review, Trikone,* and *Confrontation.*

SIDELIGHTS: Born and raised in Bombay, India, Iqbal Pittalwala initially moved to the United States in order to pursue a doctorate in atmospheric sciences at the State University of New York at Stony Brook. Purely by chance, he signed up for a writing class in an attempt to work through his writer's block regarding his dissertation, unaware that the class was in fiction writing. He soon discovered both an affinity and a love for the new type of writing, and eventually went on to attend the prestigious Iowa Writers Workshop at the University of Iowa. Pittalwala has written a number of short stories that have been published in journals, including the *Seattle Review* and *Blue Mesa Review,* and have been published as a collection, *Dear Paramount Pictures: Stories.* The book went on to earn a nomination for the Pushcart Prize for Fiction. Pittalwala's stories include both the flavor of his native India and of his adopted country, the United States. In the title story, an elderly woman in Bombay is convinced that the American movie actor James Dean has been reincarnated as Nuruddin All Ahmed, and writes to Paramount Studios in Los Angeles to inform them. In another story, a boy's classmate informs him that his father is having an affair, while in another, a Pakistani woman marries an American only to find he is really homosexual. The stories illuminate a variety of facets of human emotion and experience, from loneliness to the sudden shock of revelation. A writer for *Kirkus Reviews* commented that "the narrative techniques here are mostly trite, and ethnic tags are thought to suffice in spots where, in literature, beauty and artfulness might otherwise reside." However, in a review for the *Antioch Review,* contributor Kyle Minor remarked on Pittalwala's deference to his themes, stating that he "handles them throughout with a delicate hand, good humor, and a remarkable insight into the human condition."

BIOGRAPHICAL AND CRITICAL SOURCES:

PERIODICALS

Antioch Review, September 22, 2003, Kyle Minor, review of *Dear Paramount Pictures: Stories,* p. 787.

Georgia Review, fall, 2003, Kathleen Snodgrass, "Attention Must Be Paid," review of *Dear Paramount Pictures,* pp. 642-653.

Kirkus Reviews, September 1, 2002, review of *Dear Paramount Pictures,* p. 1258.

Virginia Quarterly Review, winter, 2003, review of *Dear Paramount Pictures,* p. 22.

ONLINE

Texas A&M University Press Web site, http://www.tamu.edu/ (April 30, 2007), author biography.

University of California at Riverside Faculty Home Page, http://staffassembly.ucr.edu/ (April 30, 2007), faculty biography.

University of California at Riverside Library Web site, http://library.ucr.edu/ (April 30, 2007), faculty biography.*

* * *

POPE, Francis
  See POPE, Frank

* * *

POPE, Frank 1973-
  (Francis Pope)

PERSONAL: Born May 13, 1973, in Oxford, England; son of Maurice Pope (a classicist and decipherer of ancient texts); married Saba Douglas-Hamilton, 2006. *Education:* University of Edinburgh, B.S.

ADDRESSES: Home—London, England; and Nairobi, Kenya.

CAREER: Maritime archaeologist under the auspices of Oxford University Maritime Archaeological Research and Excavation (MARE), Oxford, England, 1992—.

WRITINGS:

Dragon Sea: A True Tale of Treasure, Archeology, and Greed off the Coast of Vietnam, Harcourt (Orlando, FL), 2007.

SIDELIGHTS: Frank Pope credits his father, Maurice, a classicist and a scholar and translator of ancient texts, for his own interest in academic shipwreck exploration. Maurice Pope had participated in the first such project in 1953 off the Greek island of Chios, and although Pope studied zoology at the University of Edinburgh and went to Belize as part of a conservation effort, he was soon drawn into the line of work his father helped to inaugurate. Pope has participated in a number of projects as a maritime archaeologist, including investigating the wreck of the HMS *Agamemnon,* Lord Nelson's flagship that went down off the coast of Uruguay. In *Dragon Sea: A True Tale of Treasure, Archeology, and Greed off the Coast of Vietnam,* Pope chronicles his experiences excavating the wreck of the *Hoi An,* which sank off Vietnam in the mid-1400s carrying a cargo of valuable ceramics. Oxford don Mensun Bound, who hosts a television program on lost ships, and Malaysian businessman Ong Soo Hin, who had a financial interest in the recovery of the cargo, joined forces to explore the wreck and retrieve its contents. Pope, who has often worked with Bound, recounts the differences in opinion that arose between the scholar and the financial backer as the project progressed, while chronicling the historic excavation, the deepest attempted to that point. A *Publishers Weekly* critic felt that "Pope's strength in detailing the *Hoi An* story comes from his fascinating in-depth portraits of the main players," while Melissa Aho, writing for *Library Journal,* commented that the book "defines the environments, personalities, and dangers that now accompany underwater archaeology."

BIOGRAPHICAL AND CRITICAL SOURCES:

PERIODICALS

Kirkus Reviews, October 1, 2006, review of *Dragon Sea: A True Tale of Treasure, Archeology, and Greed off the Coast of Vietnam,* p. 1003.

Library Journal, November 15, 2006, Melissa Aho, review of *Dragon Sea.*

Publishers Weekly, October 23, 2006, review of *Dragon Sea,* p. 44.

Science News, February 17, 2007, review of *Dragon Sea,* p. 111.

ONLINE

Dragon Sea Web site, http://www.dragon-sea.com (May 7, 2007).

New York Times Book Review Online, http://www.nytimes.com/ (January 28, 2007) Holly Morris, "What Lies Beneath," review of *Dragon Sea;* (February 25, 2007), Richard B. Woodward, "Armchair Traveler," review of *Dragon Sea.**

*   *   *

PORTNOY, Alisse 1969-

PERSONAL: Born 1969. *Education:* Cornell University, B.A., 1990; University of Maryland, M.A., 1993, Ph.D., 1999.

ADDRESSES: Office—Department of English Language and Literature, University of Michigan, 3187 Angell Hall, Ann Arbor, MI 48109-1003. *E-mail*—alisse@umich.edu.

CAREER: University of Michigan, Ann Arbor, assistant professor, 1999-2005, associate professor of English, 2005—, faculty associate of Program in American Culture, 2000—.

MEMBER: American Studies Association, Modern Language Association, National Communication Association, National Council of Teachers of English, Organization of American Historians, Rhetoric Society of America (board of directors, 2002-05), Golden Key International Honour Society (honorary member of University of Michigan chapter).

AWARDS, HONORS: Cornell Tradition fellow, Cornell University, 1989-90; Curriculum Infusion Grant, University of Maryland, 1994-95; Media Union Resource Grant, University of Michigan, 1999-2000; Carl Bode Prize for Outstanding Dissertation in American Literature, University of Maryland, 2000; Rackham Summer Interdisciplinary fellowship, University of Michigan, 2000; First-Year Seminar Arts and Cultural Funding Grants, University of Michigan, 2000, 2003, 2005; Horace H. Rackham School of Graduate Studies Research Grants, University of Michigan, 2001, 2003, and summer research fellowship, 2001; Center for the Education of Women Faculty Research Grant, University of Michigan, 2002-03; Multimedia Teaching Grant, University of Michigan, 2005; Reicker Undergraduate Research Fund grant, University of Michigan, 2005.

WRITINGS:

Their Right to Speak: Women's Activism in the Indian and Slave Debates, Harvard University Press (Cambridge, MA), 2005.

Also contributor of articles to professional journals, including *Journal of the Early Republic, Philosophy and Rhetoric,* and *Rhetoric and Public Affairs.* Managing editor, *Teaching and Learning News,* 1992-99.

SIDELIGHTS: In *Their Right to Speak: Women's Activism in the Indian and Slave Debates,* Alisse Portnoy examines the ways in which American women explored a public persona during the controversial decades of the mid-nineteenth century. Although some prominent women of the Revolutionary period (including Abigail Adams and Mercy Otis Warren) had urged action on granting public rights to women, such as the right to vote, it was not until the mid-nineteenth century that a women's rights movement gained momentum in the United States. Women saw themselves as part of the larger political community and drew on enhanced resources, such as the widespread availability of newspapers and near universal literacy, to make their views public. "Alisse Portnoy's analysis of the rhetoric of European American women in the debates of the 1830s over the forced removal of Native Americans from the South, the abolition of slavery, and the colonization of free African Americans in Africa," stated *Women's Review of Books* contributor Jacqueline Bacon, ". . . will compel others to rethink the much-studied histories of abolition and of nineteenth-century women's rhetorical efforts."

One of the strengths of Portnoy's work, Bacon noted, is its understanding of the importance of the ways in which different groups influenced one another in the great debates of the nineteenth century. "Portnoy's convincing demonstration that 'one of discourse's most powerful functions is the constitution of political agency,'" Bacon concluded, "should generate a renewed and invigorated interest in rhetoric among scholars studying women from various disciplinary perspectives."

BIOGRAPHICAL AND CRITICAL SOURCES:

PERIODICALS

American Historical Review, December, 2006, Beth A. Salerno, review of *Their Right to Speak: Women's Activism in the Indian and Slave Debates,* p. 1514.

Journal of American History, September, 2006, Mary Hershberger, review of *Their Right to Speak,* p. 528.

Journal of the Early Republic, fall, 2006, Michael D. Pierson, review of *Their Right to Speak,* p. 502.

Women's Review of Books, July 1, 2006, Jacqueline Bacon, "Gender and Everything Else," p. 24.*

*   *   *

POULSON-BRYANT, Scott 1966-

PERSONAL: Born 1966, in Long Island, NY. *Education:* Attended Brown University. *Hobbies and other interests:* Music, baseball, books, theater.

ADDRESSES: Home—New York, NY, and Miami, FL. *E-mail*—TheSPBQ@aol.com.

CAREER: Writer and editor. *Vibe* magazine, New York, NY, founding editor, 1993; *America* magazine, senior editor; *Giant* magazine, New York, NY, editorial director, 2006—.

WRITINGS:

(With Smokey D. Fontaine) *What's Your Hi-fi Q? From Prince to Puff Daddy, Thirty Years of Black Music Trivia,* Simon & Schuster (New York, NY), 2002.

Hung: A Meditation on the Measure of Black Men in America, Doubleday (New York, NY), 2005.

Also author of the blog *The SPB Q,* and the online novella *Classic 6.* Author of "Dream America," a column for *Spin.* Contributor of articles and reviews to periodicals, including *Rolling Stone, Village Voice, New York Times, Source, Essence, New York, Guardian,* and the *Face.*

SIDELIGHTS: Scott Poulson-Bryant, a founding editor of *Vibe* magazine and a former columnist for *Spin,* is the author of *Hung: A Meditation on the Measure of Black Men in America,* "an entertaining book devoted to the myth, stereotypes, and hype surrounding black men and their penis size," according to *Black Issues Book Review* contributor Jonathan Luckett. "Writing *Hung* gave me a chance to talk to a lot of peeps about their innermost feelings about the subject," Poulson-Bryant told *Backlist* interviewer Felicia Pride. "Of course, it made some people uncomfortable, but others were so excited to chill and talk that I knew I was on to something that had some cultural significance."

In *Hung,* Poulson-Bryant examines the role of black male sexuality in sports, literature, film, music, and other forms of pop culture. "Using tongue-in-cheek chapter headings such as 'Measuring Up,' 'The Long and Short of It,' and 'How's It Hanging in Hollywood,' Poulson-Bryant untangles the intersections of race, gender, and class, myth and fact," noted Deborah Bolling in the *Women's Review of Books.* "A seasoned guide, he knowledgeably steers the reader through all manner of male sexuality, examining even deep-seated racist sexual mores with humor." According to Gerard Martinez, writing in the *Daily Texan Online,* "All this is preliminary to the true agenda of the book, which is to illustrate the uncertainty that all Americans are experiencing, and have experienced for many decades, by trying to fully identify black men within the larger context of society." "*Hung* is a treatise not only on the black penis and black male sexual prowess and self-image, but also on how black men in America measure up when it comes to political, economic, and cultural power in a white-dominated society," noted Charles Michael Smith in *Gay & Lesbian Review Worldwide.* "Clearly, there are elements of both fear and envy in this comparison." As Poulson-Bryant remarked to Pride, "The myth of the over-sexualized Black man is based, I think, on the fact that American culture needed a scapegoat for its own twisted history. That's the kind of work myths do, they give people space to invent scapegoats or create reasons for thinking the way that they do." Noting that Black males have themselves perpetuated the myth, Poulson-Bryant added: "It's as if there's this acknowledged agreement between the races that white men have the brains and Black men have the brawn, the strength—physically and sexually. There's a certain power that comes along with that, but what kind of power is it truly? It's not political, social, or financial power. White men keep that but anoint us—and we allow ourselves to be anointed—by this lesser thing."

A controversial work, *Hung* nevertheless garnered strong reviews. Poulson-Bryant "irreverently illuminates his theory of male member obsession," Bolling commented. "The book is both a hilarious expose that pokes fun at the precious penis and a chilling commentary on what men truly desire: sexual dominance among themselves." "In the end, the book that Bryant has put together is, in fact, a meditation," wrote Andre Banks in *Colorlines.* "He tells us in his voice, and in those of his peers, that the myth of the hung Black man is alive and well. And in the process inspires a dialogue that is desperately needed, and perhaps more importantly, a possibility that a myth created by racism might some day be destroyed."

BIOGRAPHICAL AND CRITICAL SOURCES:

PERIODICALS

Black Issues Book Review, May 1, 2002, "More Music," review of *What's Your Hi-fi Q? From Prince to Puff Daddy, Thirty Years of Black Music Trivia,* p. 32; March 1, 2006, Jonathan Luckett, review of *Hung: A Meditation on the Measure of Black Men in America,* p. 29.
Colorlines, December 22, 2005, Andre Banks, review of *Hung,* p. 55.
Gay & Lesbian Review Worldwide, January-February, 2006, Charles Michael Smith, "The Politics of Penis Size," review of *Hung,* p. 38.
Kirkus Reviews, July 15, 2005, review of *Hung,* p. 781.
New York, October 24, 2005, Brian Keith Jackson, "Hung Up on Size," review of *Hung.*
New York Times, November 6, 2005, E. Lynn Harris, "Private Parts," review of *Hung.*

Women's Review of Books, July-August, 2006, "The Male Obsession," p. 21.

ONLINE

African American Literature Book Club, http://aalbc. com/ (April 15, 2007), Kam Williams, review of *Hung.*
Backlist, http://www.thebacklist.net/ (April 15, 2007), Felicia Pride, "Getting Raw with Scott Poulson-Bryant, author of *Hung.*"
Daily Texan Online, http://media.www.dailytexan online.com/ (September 21, 2005), Gerard Martinez, "Essay on African-American Culture and Sexuality Measures Up," review of *Hung.*
Hung Web site, http://myspace.com/ruhung (April 15, 2007).*

*   *   *

PRADA, Roberta

PERSONAL: Born in the United States; daughter of Israel and Teddy Josephs; divorced; children: Francesca, John. *Education:* Graduated from Wellesley College, Instituto Superior de Arte del Teatro, Buenos Aires, Argentina, and other institutions. *Hobbies and other interests:* Collecting prints and mid-century modern furniture.

ADDRESSES: Office—Vox Mentor, 343 E. 30th St., Ste. 12M, New York, NY 10016.

CAREER: Professional opera singer (contralto), performing throughout North and South America, Europe, and the United Kingdom; Vox Mentor, New York, NY, president, vocal coach and trainer using the Tomatis method, and publisher; *Vocal Images* (Internet magazine), owner, writer, and translator. Also videographer and editor.

MEMBER: American Guild of Musical Artists, National Association of Teachers of Singing, Wellesley College Alumnae Association, International Listening Association.

AWARDS, HONORS: Barrington Prize in Music; William Matteus Sullivan grant.

WRITINGS:

(Translator and editor, with Francis Keeping and Pierre Sollier) A.A. Tomatis, *The Ear and the Voice,* Scarecrow Press (Lanham, MD), 2004.

(Editor, with Francis Keeping, and translator) J. Faure, *The Voice and Singing,* Vox Mentor (New York, NY), 2005.

SIDELIGHTS: Roberta Prada told *CA:* "I am not what I call 'a natural' writer. It is the compelling nature of the information, which I believe to be of great value for the English-speaking public, that caused me to begin this journey. I have translated two books from French and rewritten them extensively. I also did fact-checking. Dr. Tomatis's book needed that. Anatomy, physiology and other topics were checked with a doctor, a Tomatis practitioner, an ear, nose, and throat specialist, an occupational therapist, and one chapter by one of Caruso's biographers. I threw out a good bit of material that was erroneous, corrected redundancy, and threw out excessively provocative statements, all the while preserving the tone of the original. I wrote about six drafts, and the final work was four years in the making! The Faure book is a bit more modern in tone, but preserves faithfully the original, which was a delightful gem as originally written in 1886. It took two drafts or so and two years to produce. Francis Keeping's work on the music files is a major contribution of this book, and the bulk of its pages.

"I am intuitive by nature, and the writing of nonfiction is very challenging to me. My aim is to make complex material easy to read. I presuppose an audience that is intelligent but new to the material.

"I do not write easily. My high school and prep school English teachers, Anna Shaughnessy and Dorothy Peckham, trained me rigorously in writing. The material itself teaches me. The process of translating is challenging because we do not always think along parallel tracks in different languages, so the translation process brings not only new ideas, but new ways of thinking.

"The need to bring evidence of important ideas concerning what music means to our health, creativity, and the development of society inspires me to continue bringing this information to the public. This is difficult work, and I do it because of a sense of mission, rather than for any intrinsic pleasure."

BIOGRAPHICAL AND CRITICAL SOURCES:

ONLINE

Vocal Images, http://www.vocalimagea.com (April 5, 2007).

Vox Mentor Web site, http://www.voxmentor.com (April 5, 2007).

*   *   *

PRELINGER, Elizabeth

PERSONAL: Education: Harvard University, A.B., A.M., Ph.D.

ADDRESSES: Office—Georgetown University, 102-e Walsh, 37th and O Streets N.W., Washington, DC 20057.

CAREER: Art historian. Georgetown University, Washington, DC, assistant professor of fine arts, became Keyser Family Professor of Art History.

WRITINGS:

NONFICTION

Edvard Munch, Master Printmaker: An Examination the Artist's Work and Techniques Based on the Philip and Lynn Straus Collection, W.W. Norton (New York, NY), 1983.

Käthe Kollwitz, National Gallery of Art (Washington, DC), 1992.

(With Michael Parke-Taylor) *The Symbolist Prints of Edvard Munch: The Vivian and David Campbell Collection,* Yale University Press (New Haven, CT), 1996.

After the Scream: The Late Paintings of Edvard Munch, High Museum of Art (Atlanta, GA)/Yale University Press (New Haven, CT), 2001.

"TREASURES FROM THE SMITHSONIAN AMERICAN ART MUSEUM" SERIES

The Gilded Age, Watson-Guptill (New York, NY), Smithsonian Art Museum (Washington, DC), 2000.

American Impressionism, Watson-Guptill (New York, NY), Smithsonian Art Museum (Washington, DC), 2000.

Scenes of American Life, Watson-Guptill (New York, NY), Smithsonian Art Museum (Washington, DC), 2001.

Contributor to books, including *The Nabis and the Parisian Avant-Garde,* edited by Patricia Eckert Boyer, Rutgers University Press (New Brunswick, NJ), 1988.

SIDELIGHTS: Art historian Elizabeth Prelinger is the author of a number of works about celebrated Norwegian printmaker and painter Edvard Munch, best known for his iconic 1893 work *The Scream.* Deemed "an attractive and thoughtful consideration of early prints" by *Library Journal* contributor Jack Perry Brown, *The Symbolist Prints of Edvard Munch: The Vivian and David Campbell Collection* discusses Munch's background as a graphic artist, describes his innovative printmaking techniques, and examines his Symbolist themes. The work contains fifty-eight reproductions of the artist's prints, including most of his major works. In *After the Scream: The Late Paintings of Edvard Munch,* Prelinger examines more than sixty of the artist's works completed in the latter part of his life, in which he adopted a looser, more vibrant painting style.

In *Käthe Kollwitz,* a catalogue that accompanied a 1992 exhibition of the German sculptor and printmaker's work, Prelinger offers "an interesting and much needed overview of the artist's graphic techniques," stated *Burlington Magazine* contributor Colin Rhodes. According to Carol Small, writing in the *Woman's Art Journal,* Prelinger "emphasizes Kollwitz's extraordinary inventiveness and technical achievements."

Prelinger has also published a number of works in the "Treasures from the Smithsonian American Art Museum" series. *The Gilded Age* presents works by Winslow Homer, Cecilia Beaux, John Singer Sargent, Thomas Eakins, Mary Cassatt, and other notable American artists. *American Impressionism* features paintings by American artists who were influenced by European Impressionism, including James McNeill Whistler and Maurice Prendergast. In *Scenes of American Life,* a "nicely illustrated" work, according to *Library Journal* critic Douglas F. Smith, Prelinger focuses on Depression-era paintings and murals.

BIOGRAPHICAL AND CRITICAL SOURCES:

PERIODICALS

Belles Lettres, winter, 1992, Nancy Derr, review of *Käthe Kollwitz,* pp. 4-5.

Burlington Magazine, April, 1993, Colin Rhodes, review of *Käthe Kollwitz,* pp. 284-285.

Choice, February, 1984, review of *Edvard Munch, Master Printmaker: An Examination the Artist's Work and Techniques Based on the Philip and Lynn Straus Collection,* p. 814; November, 1992, J.A. Day, review of *Käthe Kollwitz,* p. 456; June, 1997, J.G. Holland, review of *The Symbolist Prints of Edvard Munch: The Vivian and David Campbell Collection,* p. 1652.

Hudson Review, autumn, 1992, John Loughery, review of *Käthe Kollwitz,* pp. 445-451.

Kliatt, July, 2001, Paula Rohrlick, review of *Scenes of American Life,* p. 41.

Library Journal, December 1, 1983, Douglas G. Campbell, review of *Edvard Munch, Master Printmaker,* p. 2245; June 15, 1997, Jack Perry Brown, review of *The Symbolist Prints of Edvard Munch,* p. 65; June 1, 2000, Jack Perry Brown, review of *The Gilded Age* and *American Impressionism,* p. 122; July, 2001, Douglas F. Smith, review of *Scenes of American Life,* p. 84.

London Review of Books, September 17, 1984, review of *Edvard Munch, Master Printmaker,* p. 2.

New York Times Book Review, July 19, 1992, Mignon Nixon, review of *Käthe Kollwitz,* p. 20; April 27, 1997, Robin Lippincott, review of *The Symbolist Prints of Edvard Munch,* p. 24.

Quill & Quire, April, 1997, Christopher Hume, review of *The Symbolist Prints of Edvard Munch,* p. 33.

School Arts, September, 2000, Kent Anderson, review of *American Impressionism,* p. 60; March, 2001, Kent Anderson, review of *The Gilded Age,* p. 54.

Times Literary Supplement, March 22, 1985, Roger Cardinal, review of *Edvard Munch, Master Printmaker,* p. 320; April 12, 2002, Chase Madar, review of *After the Scream: The Late Paintings of Edvard Munch,* p. 30.

Woman's Art Journal, spring-summer, 1994, Carol Small, review of *Käthe Kollwitz,* pp. 44-47.

Women's Review of Books, December, 1992, Karen Malpede, review of *Käthe Kollwitz,* p. 5.

ONLINE

Georgetown University Web site, http://www. georgetown.edu/ (April 15, 2007), "Elizabeth Prelinger."*

Q-R

QUESTIER, Michael
See QUESTIER, Michael C.

*   *   *

QUESTIER, Michael C.
(Michael Questier)

PERSONAL: Education: Sussex University, D.Phil., 1991.

ADDRESSES: Office—Department of History, Queen Mary, University of London, Mile End Rd., London E1 4NS, England. *E-mail*—m.c.questier@qmul.ac.uk.

CAREER: Queen Mary, University of London, England, lecturer in early modern British and European history, 2002—. Also served as senior research fellow at Worcester College, Oxford. Previously taught at London University.

WRITINGS:

NONFICTION

Conversion, Politics, and Religion in England, 1580-1625, Cambridge University Press (New York, NY), 1996.
(Editor and author of introduction) *Newsletters from the Archpresbyterate of George Birkhead,* Cambridge University Press (New York, NY), 1998.

(As Michael Questier; editor and contributor, with Peter Lake) *Conformity and Orthodoxy in the English Church, c. 1560-1660,* Boydell Press (Rochester, NY), 2000.
(As Michael Questier; with Peter Lake) *The Antichrist's Lewd Hat: Protestants, Papists, and Players in Post-Reformation England,* Yale University Press (New Haven, CT), 2002.
(Editor) *Newsletters from the Caroline Court, 1631-1638: Catholicism and the Politics of the Personal Rule,* Cambridge University Press (New York, NY), 2005.
Catholicism and Community in Early Modern England: Politics, Aristocratic Patronage and Religion, c. 1550-1640, Cambridge University Press (New York, NY), 2006.

SIDELIGHTS: Michael C. Questier, a lecturer in history at Queen Mary, University of London, publishes widely on sixteenth-and seventeenth-century British politics and religion. In *Conversion, Politics, and Religion in England, 1580-1625,* Questier examines the political and spiritual motives of Catholic and Protestant converts during the English Reformation. "By careful attention to the writings both of proselytizing clerics and the converts themselves," wrote *Journal of Church and State* contributor Rachel Weil, "Questier manages to explain how religious experience might at once transcend the Catholic/Protestant divide (evangelical Catholics and evangelical Protestants uncannily resembled one another), and yet be expressed through and shaped at every turn by the existence of that divide." According to John Spurr, writing in the *Journal of Modern History,* "The great virtue and originality of this book is that Questier steps outside existing debates, not simply refusing to take sides with Catholics or Protestants but refusing the very terms of debate between contemporary polemicists. So he rejects the notion that conversion is simply a matter of leaving one church and joining another and challenges the state's definition of conformity as tantamount to conversion." "Conversion, Questier insists, had a deeper dimension, an inner evangelical core," noted Alexandra Walsham in the *Journal of Ecclesiastical History.* "It was the function of a personal experience of regeneration and spiritual grace which could be mapped on to the public ideological conflict between the two Churches, but which ultimately transcended it."

Newsletters from the Archpresbyterate of George Birkhead contains a series of fifty-six newsletters written by European Catholic priests between 1609 and 1614. "Questier's extensive annotations, the fruit of some impressive historical detective work, are an invaluable aid to unravelling the allusive meaning of this difficult material, as is his lucid and discerning introduction," noted Walsham. In *Newsletters from the Caroline Court, 1631-1638: Catholicism and the Politics of the Personal Rule,* Questier collects ninety-seven newsletters that reveal conflict among English Catholics. "For historians interested in 'the news' in early modern Britain, these newsletters provide a fascinating insight into the workings of the English Catholic community, its concerns, and its religious and political aspirations," remarked Amos Tubb in *History.*

With Peter Lake, Questier edited *Conformity and Orthodoxy in the English Church, c. 1560-1660,* a collection of ten essays about doctrinal orthodoxy, disciplinary conformity, and Catholicism in post-Reformation England. "All the essays are interesting and important, and all relate, more or less, to the theme of shifts in orthodoxies and modes of conformity," noted Christopher Haigh in the *English Historical Review.* "The strength of this collection is to be found not only in its essays but also in its editorial shaping," wrote *Church History* reviewer Lori Anne Ferrell, who added: "This sectioning serves to fashion a disparate collection into a thesis, the architecture of which demonstrates the power of antitype." In the words of *Journal of Ecclesiastical History* reviewer Arnold Hunt, the volume "is one of the most important contributions to the history of the early modern Church of England to have appeared for a long time."

BIOGRAPHICAL AND CRITICAL SOURCES:

PERIODICALS

Albion, spring, 2002, Michael L. Carrafiello, review of *Newsletters from the Archpresbyterate of George Birkhead,* pp. 104-105; summer, 2003, Susan Wabuda, review of *The Antichrist's Lewd Hat: Protestants, Papists, and Players in Post-Reformation England,* p. 280.

American Historical Review, Roger B. Manning, review of *Conversion, Politics, and Religion in England, 1580-1625,* pp. 505-506.

Catholic Historical Review, October, 2000, Albert J. Loomie, review of *Newsletters from the Archpresbyterate of George Birkhead,* p. 686.

Choice, November, 2002, A. Kugler, review of *The Antichrist's Lewd Hat,* p. 542.

Church History, June, 1998, Alana Cain Scott, review of *Conversion, Politics, and Religion in England, 1580-1625,* pp. 388-389; December, 2002, Lori Anne Ferrell, review of *Conformity and Orthodoxy in the English Church, c. 1560-1660,* p. 899.

English Historical Review, November, 1998, Eric Josef Carlson, review of *Conversion, Politics, and Religion in England, 1580-1625,* p. 1302; June, 2002, Christopher Haigh, review of *Conformity and Orthodoxy in the English Church, c. 1560-1660,* p. 703; February, 2003, Christopher Haigh, review of *The Antichrist's Lewd Hat,* p. 147.

History, January, 2007, Amos Tubb, review of *Newsletters from the Caroline Court, 1631-1638: Catholicism and the Politics of the Personal Rule,* pp. 119-120.

History Today, November, 1997, A.G.R. Smith, review of *Conversion, Politics, and Religion in England, 1580-1625,* p. 57; December, 2002, David G. Chandler, review of *The Antichrist's Lewd Hat,* p. 54.

Journal of British Studies, October 1, 2004, Leah S. Marcus, "At the Boundaries," review of *The Antichrist's Lewd Hat.*

Journal of Church and State, autumn, 1998, Rachel Weil, review of *Conversion, Politics, and Religion in England, 1580-1625,* p. 902.

Journal of Ecclesiastical History, October, 1997, Alexandra Walsham, review of *Conversion, Politics, and Religion in England, 1580-1625,* p. 779; October, 2000, Alexandra Walsham, review of

Newsletters from the Archpresbyterate of George Birkhead, p. 809; July, 2002, Arnold Hunt, review of *Conformity and Orthodoxy in the English Church, c. 1560-1660,* p. 609; October, 2006, Thomas M. McCoog, review of *Newsletters from the Caroline Court, 1631-1638,* p. 782.

Journal of Modern History, September, 1998, John Spurr, review of *Conversion, Politics, and Religion in England, 1580-1625,* p. 675.

London Review of Books, September, 2002, Patrick Collinson, review of *The Antichrist's Lewd Hat,* pp. 15-16.

Renaissance Quarterly, autumn, 2002, Stephen L. Collins, review of *Conformity and Orthodoxy in the English Church, c. 1560-1660,* pp. 1102-1106.

Sixteenth Century Journal, summer, 1997, Erick Kelemen, review of *Conversion, Politics, and Religion in England, 1580-1625,* pp. 527-529; autumn, 2001, Dale Walden Johnson, review of *Conformity and Orthodoxy in the English Church, c. 1560-1660,* pp. 797-798.

Times Literary Supplement, July 5, 2002, Euan Cameron, review of *The Antichrist's Lewd Hat,* p. 32; March 24, 2006, Kevin Sharpe, review of *Newsletters from the Caroline Court, 1631-1638,* p. 33.

ONLINE

Queen Mary, University of London Web site, http://www.history.qmul.ac.uk/ (April 15, 2007), "Michael Questier."*

* * *

QUINLAN, Red
See QUINLAN, Sterling C.

* * *

QUINLAN, Sterling C. 1916-2007
(Red Quinlan, Sterling Carroll Quinlan)

OBITUARY NOTICE— See index for *CA* sketch: Born October 23, 1916, in Maquoketa, IA; died of respiratory failure, March 11, 2007, in Chicago, IL. Television executive and author. Considered a pioneer in Chicago television, Quinlan was credited with discovering such talent as comedian Bob Newhart and director William Friedkin. He dropped out of high school in Chicago to try and make his way in radio and newspapers. Meeting with little luck at first, he spent several years riding the rails. Quinlan later regaled audiences with these adventures on a WMAQ serial called *The Open Road,* and in 1994 he published a collection of stories based on these experiences called *Something in Between.* Eventually, he returned home and worked for community newspapers in Chicago in 1930. He then moved to Gary, Indiana, where he hosted "The Boy Reporter and His Community" on radio station WIND. During the mid-1930s, he worked as a writer for the National Broadcasting Company, and then turned to acting. Quinlan acted in both Chicago and Hollywood in the late 1930s before settling down in Chicago. World War II found him enlisting in the U.S. Navy, for which he served in Brazil and in Mississippi. Afterwards, WBKB radio hired him in Chicago, and he worked his way up the ladder to general manager and, from 1953 to 1967, vice president; he was also vice president of the American Broadcasting Company from 1953 to 1964 and president of Field Communications Corporation until 1967. During this time, he became an important figure in local television, helping the careers of talk-show host Lee Phillip Bell, news anchor Frank Reynolds, and comedian Bob Newhart. William Friedkin, who went on to direct such films as *The French Connection* and *The Exorcist,* credited Quinlan with starting his career when the executive backed his efforts to make a documentary about death-row inmate Paul Crump. The first general manager of Chicago's WFLD-TV, Quinlan was president of Field Enterprises from 1965 to 1968. He spent his last career years as a communications consultant for IDC Services in Chicago, until retiring in 1989. As a writer, Quinlan published the nonfiction *The Hundred Million Dollar Lunch* (1974), *Inside ABC: American Broadcasting Company's Rise to Power* (1979) and *Quinlan's Key: How You Too Can Become an Exemplary H.A.* (1984), and he also penned fiction. Inspired in his early years by Russian novelists such as Tolstoy, he published the novel *Jugger* in 1960 and also wrote a play, *The Day the Sun Caught Cold.* During his later years, Quinlan, always a champion of his home town, worked hard to keep his city's film industry alive. Among his many honors, Quinlan was named Chicagoan of the Year in 1964 and Man of the Year by Facets Multimedia in 1981. He was given the Governor's Award from the Chicago Television Academy in 1981, the Vincent

Wasilewski Award from the Illinois Broadcasters Association in 1987, and the Distinguished Service award from the Off the Street Club in 1988.

OBITUARIES AND OTHER SOURCES:

PERIODICALS

Chicago Tribune, March 13, 2007, Section 2, p. 9.

*　　*　　*

QUINLAN, Sterling Carroll
　　See QUINLAN, Sterling C.

*　　*　　*

RAS, Barbara 1949-

PERSONAL: Born 1949, in New Bedford, MA; married; children: one daughter. *Education:* Simmons College, B.A.

ADDRESSES: Home—San Antonio, TX. *Office*—Coates Maddux Library, Trinity University, 1 Trinity Pl., Rm. 325 E, San Antonio, TX 78212-7200. *E-mail*—Barbara.Ras@trinity.edu.

CAREER: Poet. Editor for North Point Press, Wesleyan University Press, University Press of New England, and Sierra Club Books; University of Georgia Press, Athens, assistant director and executive editor; Trinity University Press, San Antonio, TX, director, 2002—. Instructor for Warren Wilson MFA Program for Writers.

AWARDS, HONORS: Kate Tufts Discovery Award, Walt Whitman Award, American Academy of Poets, 1997, and Georgia Author of the Year Award for poetry, 1999, all for *Bite Every Sorrow;* Ascher Montandon Award; has received honors from the National Writers Union, Villa Montalvo, San Jose Poetry Center, and *Spoon River Poetry Review.*

WRITINGS:

(Editor) *Costa Rica: A Traveler's Literary Companion,* foreword by Oscar Arias, Whereabouts Press (San Francisco, CA), 1994.

Bite Every Sorrow (poems), Louisiana State University Press (Baton Rouge, LA), 1998.
One Hidden Stuff (poems), Penguin (New York, NY), 2006.

Contributor to *Between Heaven and Texas,* edited by Naomi Shihab Nye, University of Texas Press (Austin, TX), 2006. Contributor to poetry and literary journals, including *Massachusetts Review, Salmagundi, Orion, Gulf Coast, Prairie Schooner, TriQuarterly, American Scholar,* and *Boulevard.*

SIDELIGHTS: Barbara Ras is the author of the critically acclaimed poetry collections *Bite Every Sorrow* and *One Hidden Stuff.* Ras has traveled extensively in Latin America and lived for a time in Colombia and Costa Rica. In 1994 she edited *Costa Rica: A Traveler's Literary Companion,* a collection of twenty-six stories organized by the geographical regions in which they are set. Among the contributors are José Léon Sánchez, Yolanda Oreamuno, and Carlos Salazar Herrara. According to Diane C. Donovan, writing in *MBR Bookwatch,* the "excellent narrative stories bring to life the underlying nuances of the country's experience as no ordinary travel guide could accomplish." A contributor in the *Economist* similarly noted: "If advice on whether to boil the water or cover your head in holy buildings is what you are after, this is not your book; if you want to make inroads into the Costa Rican imagination, it is a must-read."

The author's debut poetry collection, *Bite Every Sorrow,* appeared in 1998. In the work, Ras examines the details of everyday life, reflecting on marriage, motherhood, work, and family. "Everything she witnesses, overhears, ingests, and touches is a catalyst for her penetrating imagination," noted *Booklist* critic Donna Seaman. Ras garnered the Walt Whitman Award from the Academy of American Poets in 1997 for *Bite Every Sorrow.* C.K. Williams, who judged the award, stated on *Poets.org:* "What's most immediately striking about her work, and what continues to gratify in it, is its sheer human amplitude: her poems are rich with life-matter, with incisive perceptions and acute experiential insight; they're plotted with a wide-ranging self-consciousness and informed by a metaphysically erudite and whimsical exuberance." Williams offered special praise for the opening poem, "You Can't Have It All," which begins: "But you can have the fig tree and its fat leaves like clown hands / gloved with green.

You can have the touch of a single eleven-year-old finger / on your cheek, waking you at one a.m. to say the hamster is back." "There are many such moments in the book," Williams observed, "situations of precisely observed and movingly rendered gesture, in which the domestic, the seemingly ordinary, is exalted by imaginative intensity and sympathy to something beyond itself." According to *Library Journal* contributor Frank Allen, in *Bite Every Sorrow* Ras illustrates "how ordinary personal memories grow into a beautiful 'life of the mind' that transcends selfhood."

Ras's second collection of poems, the 2006 work *One Hidden Stuff,* "is an entertaining and at times very moving . . . effort, which pays attention to life's small pleasures and subtle difficulties," observed a *Publishers Weekly* reviewer. Written primarily in free verse, Ras's poems explore a range of subjects, from dreams and war to dogs barking and the Texas sky. "Propelled by alliteration, assonance, consonance, and exquisite verbs, the poems have a breathless tone," wrote Diane Scharper in *Library Journal,* and Seaman commented in another *Booklist* review that the poet's "bittersweet, immediate, and wise lyrics are long-lined and punctuated with glissandos and unexpected leaps." *One Hidden Stuff* "reveals the confidence and skill of a fine writer who is willing to take risks as she brings the reader along on a quest for the world's one hidden stuff—a venture uniquely appropriate for poetry," concluded John Hammond on *MySanAntonio.com.*

BIOGRAPHICAL AND CRITICAL SOURCES:

PERIODICALS

Booklist, April, 1998, Donna Seaman, review of *Bite Every Sorrow,* p. 1295; September, 2006, Donna Seaman, review of *One Hidden Stuff,* p. 39.

Economist, April 30, 1994, review of *Costa Rica: A Traveler's Literary Companion,* p. 100.

Library Journal, March 1, 1998, Frank Allen, review of *Bite Every Sorrow,* p. 92; November 15, 2006, Diane Scharper, review of *One Hidden Stuff,* p. 75.

MBR Bookwatch, October, 2005, Diane C. Donovan, review of *Costa Rica.*

Publishers Weekly, July 1, 2002, Bob Summer, "Trinity U. to Revive Press," p. 15; September 18, 2006, review of *One Hidden Stuff,* p. 38.

ONLINE

MySanAntonio.com, http://www.mysanantonio.com/ (December 1, 2006), John Hammond, "Poet Looks at Substance That Ties All Together in Life," review of *One Hidden Stuff.*

Poets.org, http://www.poets.org/ (April 15, 2007), "C.K. Williams on Barbara Ras's *Bite Every Sorrow.*"

SouthCoast Today, http://archive.southcoasttoday.com/ (October 17, 1998), Robert Lovinger, "New Bedford Native Earns Poetry Award."*

*　　　*　　　*

REA, Tom 1950-

PERSONAL: Born 1950, in Pittsburgh, PA; married.

ADDRESSES: Home—Casper, WY.

CAREER: Author. Formerly a reporter for the *Casper Star-Tribune,* Casper, WY; founder of Dooryard Press, Story, WY.

AWARDS, HONORS: Spur Award, 2002, for *Bone Wars: The Excavation and Celebrity of Andrew Carnegie's Dinosaur.*

WRITINGS:

Man in a Rowboat (poems), Copper Canyon Press (Port Townsend, WA), 1977.

Smith and Other Poems, Dooryard Press (Story, WY), 1985.

Bone Wars: The Excavation and Celebrity of Andrew Carnegie's Dinosaur (nonfiction), University of Pittsburgh Press (Pittsburgh, PA), 2001.

Devil's Gate: Owning the Land, Owning the Story (nonfiction), University of Oklahoma Press (Norman, OK), 2006.

Contributor to anthologies, including *What Have You Lost?,* Greenwillow Books, 1999.

SIDELIGHTS: Tom Rea is the author of *Bone Wars: The Excavation and Celebrity of Andrew Carnegie's Dinosaur,* "a gripping account of the early evolution of dinosaur study," observed Phil Roberts in *Ohio Valley History.* The work concerns the efforts of steel tycoon and philanthropist Carnegie to obtain the fossilized remains of a dinosaur for his newly-built Carnegie Museum of Natural History in Pittsburgh, Pennsylvania. When he learned that a gigantic sauropod skeleton had been discovered in the Wyoming badlands in 1899, Carnegie assigned museum curator William Holland, a self-taught paleontologist, to purchase the rights, despite the objections of trustees from the University of Wyoming. The creature, named *Diplodocus carnegii* in honor of the wealthy industrialist, proved so popular that plaster casts were made of its bones and shipped to national museums across the globe, including England, Germany, France, and Argentina.

Bone Wars garnered strong reviews. "The cast includes several self-made men, including Carnegie himself, in an age of strong egos and great ambitions," noted John J. Ernissee in *Rocks & Minerals.* Ernissee added, "It is the personalities that Rea brings to life that make this book so rewarding." "As Rea describes it, the dinosaur-hunting business created intense competition among American universities and museums," Roberts stated, adding: "Rea's book does an excellent job of identifying the key players and explaining their motivations."

BIOGRAPHICAL AND CRITICAL SOURCES:

PERIODICALS

Booklist, December 1, 2001, Gavin Quinn, review of *Bone Wars: The Excavation and Celebrity of Andrew Carnegie's Dinosaur,* p. 620.
Choice, May, 2002, T.J. Kroeger, review of *Bone Wars,* p. 1615.
Isis, December, 2002, Dennis R. Dean, review of *Bone Wars,* p. 722.
Library Journal, January, 2002, Amy Brunvand, review of *Bone Wars,* p. 147.
Midwest Book Review, July, 2005, review of *Bone Wars.*
Ohio Valley History, fall, 2005, Phil Roberts, review of *Bone Wars,* pp. 97-98.
Reference & Research Book News, February, 2007, review of *Devil's Gate: Owning the Land, Owning the Story.*

Kit Reed

Rocks & Minerals, July-August, 2003, John J. Ernissee, review of *Bone Wars,* p. 279.
Small Press Review, May, 1986, Patricia Keuning, review of *Smith and Other Poems,* p. 1.
Times Literary Supplement, March 22, 2002, Michael J. Benton, review of *Bone Wars,* pp. 4-5.
True West, March, 2007, Chuck Lewis, review of *Devil's Gate.**

*　　　*　　　*

REED, Kit 1932-
(Kit Craig, Shelley Hyde)

PERSONAL: Born June 7, 1932, in San Diego, CA; daughter of John Rich (a lieutenant commander in the U.S. Navy) and Lillian Craig; married Joseph Wayne Reed, Jr. (a writer, painter, printmaker, and professor), December 10, 1955; children: Joseph McKean, John Craig, Katherine Hyde. *Education:* College of Notre Dame of Maryland, B.A., 1954.

ADDRESSES: Home—Middletown, CT. *Agent*—Charlotte Sheedy Literary Agency, 65 Bleecker Street, New York, NY 10012.

CAREER: St. Petersburg Times, St. Petersburg, FL, reporter and television editor, 1954-55; *Hamden Chronicle,* Hamden, CT, reporter, 1956; *New Haven Register,* New Haven, CT, reporter, 1956-59. Book reviewer for *Hartford Courant* and *St. Petersburg Times;* freelance author of fiction. Visiting writer in India, 1974; Wesleyan University, Middletown, CT, visiting professor of English, then adjunct professor of English, 1974-2007. American Coordinator, Indo-U.S. writers exchange, 1990—; speaker, First Mussoorie International Writers' Festival, U.A., India, 2007.

MEMBER: Writers Guild, PEN, National Book Critics Circle (board member, 1991-95), Authors League Fund (board member).

AWARDS, HONORS: Named New England Newspaper Woman of the Year, New England Women's Press Association, 1958 and 1959; Abraham Woursell Foundation literary grant, 1965-70; Guggenheim fellowships, 1964-65 and 1968; Rockefeller fellow, Aspen Institute, 1976; *The Ballad of T. Rantula* was named to the Best Books for Young Adults list by the American Library Association, 1979; Best Catholic Short Story of the Year Award, Catholic Press Association; Alex Award, American Library Association, for *Thinner Than Thou*; James W. Tiptree Award finalist, for *Little Sisters of the Apocalypse* and *Weird Women, Wired Women.*

WRITINGS:

NOVELS

Mother Isn't Dead, She's Only Sleeping (young adult), Houghton Mifflin (Boston, MA), 1961.
At War as Children, Farrar, Straus (New York, NY), 1964.
The Better Part (young adult), Farrar, Straus (New York, NY), 1967.
Armed Camps (science fiction), Faber & Faber (London, England), 1969, Dutton (New York City), 1970.
Cry of the Daughter, Dutton (New York, NY), 1971.
Tiger Rag, Dutton (New York, NY), 1973.
Captain Grownup (adult), Dutton (New York, NY), 1976.
The Ballad of T. Rantula, Little, Brown (Boston, MA), 1979.

Magic Time (science fiction), Berkley (New York, NY), 1980.
(Under pseudonym Shelley Hyde) *Blood Fever* (science fiction), Pocket Books (New York, NY), 1982.
Fort Privilege (science fiction), Doubleday (Garden City, NY), 1985.
Catholic Girls, Donald I. Fine (New York, NY), 1987.
Little Sister of the Apocalypse (science fiction), Fiction Collective Two (Boulder, CO), 1994.
J. Eden, University Press of New England (Hanover, NH), 1996.
@expectations, Forge (New York, NY), 2000.
Thinner than Thou, Tor (New York, NY), 2004.
Bronze: A Tale of Terror, Night Shade Books (San Francisco, CA), 2005.
The Baby Merchant, Tor (New York, NY), 2006.

Also author, as Kit Craig, of the psychothriller *Gone,* 1992, *Twice Burned,* and four other psychological thrillers published in England.

SHORT STORIES

Mister Da V. and Other Stories (science fiction), Faber & Faber (London, England), 1967, Berkley (New York, NY), 1973.
The Killer Mice (science fiction; young adult), Gollancz (London, England), 1976.
Other Stories and . . . The Attack of the Giant Baby (science fiction), Berkley (New York, NY), 1981.
The Revenge of the Senior Citizens plus a Short Story Collection (science fiction novella and sixteen stories), Doubleday (New York, NY), 1986.
Thief of Lives, University of Missouri Press (Columbia, MO), 1992.
Weird Women, Wired Women, University Press of New England (Hanover, NH), 1998.
Seven for the Apocalypse, University Press of New England, 1999.
Dogs of Truth: New and Uncollected Stories, Tor (New York, NY), 2005.

Contributor of short stories to more than sixty anthologies in the United States, Great Britain, Italy, and France, including *Winter's Tales,* and *Norton Anthology of Contemporary Fiction.* Contributor of short fiction to *Yale Review, Transatlantic Review, Cosmopolitan, Journal, Missouri Review, Magazine of Fantasy and Science Fiction, Redbook, Tampa Review, Texas Review, Voice Literary Supplement, Omni, Nova, Argosy, Town,* and *She.*

OTHER

When We Dream (for children), illustrated by Yutaka Sugita, first published in 1965, first English language edition, Hawthorne (New York, NY), 1966.

(Compiler) *Fat* (anthology), Bobbs-Merrill (Indianapolis, IN), 1974.

The Bathyscaphe (radio play), National Public Radio, 1979.

(Under pseudonym Shelley Hyde) *Blood Fever,* Pocket Books, 1982.

Story First: The Writer as Insider (textbook; contains exercises by husband, Joseph W. Reed), Prentice-Hall (Englewood Cliffs, NJ), 1982, revised edition published as *Mastering Fiction Writing,* Writer's Digest (Cincinnati, OH), 1991.

George Orwell's 1984, Barron's Book Notes (Woodbury, NY), 1984.

Revision, Writer's Digest, 1989.

SIDELIGHTS: Kit Reed's publications are of interest to both adults and teenage readers. As the author once said, "Although I write primarily for adult readers, a great many teens seem to wander into my novels, perhaps because I do not believe there is an enormous difference between adults and young people." Reed's writing falls into a variety of categories: "Some of her stories are realistic, some impressionistic, some fantasy, some science fiction," indicated C.W. Sullivan III in the *St. James Guide to Science Fiction Writers.* "Reed does not write hard, or technologically oriented, science fiction," explained Sullivan. Instead, "Reed seems to deal primarily with the people and to use the science fiction elements as another writer might use a car or truck—as a detail necessary to the story. . . . The two main themes of her work [are] the impact of technology on people's lives and the plight of senior citizens." Sullivan, who noted that "one of [Reed's] strongest pieces of social criticism is 'Golden Acres,' about a home for the elderly," commented that in "the final analysis, it is Reed's characters that carry her fiction—science fiction, fantasy, or mainstream. To be sure, the other aspects of her writing are not found wanting, but her characters—especially the women struggling to find themselves in an indifferent or hostile society, or struggling against various institutions—remain in the reader's mind."

Reed described her genre-crossing writing this way: "Most people write what they want to read. In my case this mean[t] a lot of early science fiction because, starting with the Oz books, I loved stories that departed from reality. Now I am more interested in what seems real. Sometimes I go for reality in a completely everyday way, as in *Captain Grownup* and *The Ballad of T. Rantula,* and at other times as in *Magic Time,* from a position halfway up the wall. The work that pleases me most combines both elements." She also commented about her tendency to write in many genres to Gwyneth Jones of the *Infinity Plus* Web site, writing "I'm easily bored. . . . Brian Aldiss said I was a 'psychological novelist,' if that helps . . . As in, my central concern is why and how we are the way we are." As she commented to Matthew Cheney of *SF Site,* "Both agents and editors will tell me after the fact that a book is satirical or socially concerned or . . . or . . . In fact, all I know about it is whether whatever drove me in the first place has gotten the novel to where it's going."

The Ballad of T. Rantula, which was named to the Best Books for Young Adults list by the American Library Association, deals with the thirteen-year-old hero's attempts to come to terms with the fact of his parents' divorce. According to Anne Tyler in the *New York Times Book Review,* the character is "a stable, honest, earnest human being, the living center of a richly satisfying book." In "an era rampant with novels on marital bustups, Kit Reed's comes as refreshingly different, bringing with it a new point of view," claimed a *West Coast Review of Books* critic. "Told through the eyes of young Fred (Futch) during his last year at elementary school, the narrative avoids the cute and the obvious, rather it is brilliantly, uncannily accurate."

Captain Grownup is an adult novel about a newspaper reporter experiencing a midlife crisis. After his wife kicks him out of their house, he gives up his job to become an English teacher in a small-town high school. Perceiving himself as a person who can help bring out young talent, he becomes platonically involved with a female student. Tyler calls the book "a wry story about a 41-year-old man still trying to take the final steps to adulthood."

During the 1990s Reed released a number of works, including her 1996 *J. Eden,* a novel that "shows us the extent to which people can hurt one another and still be loved and go on," related Molly E. Rauch in the

Nation. The "cleverly assembled and often insightful" story portrays "four New York families shar[ing] a milestone summer in a New England country farmhouse," related a *Publishers Weekly* critic who complimented Reed's dialogue but noted that "some readers may find that the bulk of the novel meanders too slowly through predictable lives." Calling *J. Eden* the "most ambitious . . . [and] slowest" novel by Reed, a *Kirkus Reviews* writer stated that the tale's "suspense hangs on the question of who's sleeping with whom and what everyone is thinking about aging, parenthood, mortality, etc." Telling the story from ten different viewpoints "gets us through in one piece," determined Rauch, who believed that "the sustained hatred and doubt would be devastating otherwise." *Entertainment Weekly* critic Suzanne Ruta similarly praised Reed for getting her readers to empathize with the story's "self-absorbed boomers and their desperately precocious offspring."

A veteran of online communication, Reed, who teaches classes online, tells the tale of a woman whose Internet life becomes more real and important to her than her daily existence in *@expectations*. Jenny is a devoted wife, stepmother, and successful therapist. But she is plagued by dissatisfaction and troubles, and she sheds them when she goes online and becomes Zan, a resident of the resort StElene. She consorts with her online lover, "Reverdy," and tries to provide support to nineteen-year-old "Lark"; when Reverby disappears, she and Lark embark on a real world journey to find him. "Reed makes Jenny's slide into an online world seem nearly plausible in this up-to-the-minute alternative love story," wrote a *Publishers Weekly* contributor. Though noting the sudden haste of action toward the end of the novel, *New York Times Book Review* contributor J.D. Biersdorfer felt, "Reed manages to make a success of *@expectations* by zeroing in on that fascinating feeling one can get when leaving a mundane life to recreate the self in an alternative reality."

Though Reed isn't one to get on "the soapbox, tub-thumping political aspect" of issues she cares about, as she explained to Jones on the *Infinity Plus* Web site, her novels and stories often contain some social criticism. Many of her short stories have been considered feminist by critics (though Reed herself prefers the term "womanist"), and her novel *Thinner Than Thou* is direct commentary on the worship of body image embraced in the United States. Reed made it very clear

to Jones that the issue is not just obesity: "There's a thread about Annie, the anorectic girl and one about Marg, who's facing her first facelift and another about Gloria and the other oldsters who look unsightly to body-conscious Americans who don't want to see ugly people walking around," she wrote. In the novel, an order of nuns known as the Dedicated Sisters, are a sort of body police who take people to their convent in order for them to heal; strangely associated Reverend Earl runs a supposed luxury spa that is, in reality, a prison camp for the obese, those who have eating disorders, or other body issues. "Reed provides much food for thought and reaffirms her position as one of our brightest cultural commentators," wrote a *Publishers Weekly* contributor of the novel. A *Kirkus Reviews* contributor called the novel, "unsettling, sometimes appalling: satire edging remorselessly toward reality." Owen McNally of the *Hartford Courant* wrote of Reed's prose, "Always, her prose is lean, fat-free and frequently seasoned with zesty turns of phrase. . . . Reed serves a feast of entertaining food for thought."

In *The Baby Merchant,* extremely likeable Tom Starbird is extremely good at his job: he kidnaps "unwanted" children and places them in loving families. Jake Zorn, a newsman, comes to Starbird for a child, but instead of business as usual, he threatens to ruin Starbird if he doesn't come through on his end of the deal. When Starbird's chosen unwed mother, Sasha, runs away from the group home where she's been living, Starbird has to revise his plans. "Reed writes a fast-paced thriller with a consummate sense of style," wrote Regina Schroeder in *Booklist.* Of the role of Sasha, Collette Bancroft of the *St. Petersburg Times* wrote, "Trust Kit Reed to break the mold for an action hero. In *The Baby Merchant,* hers is a nine-months-pregnant graduate student on the run from a man whose business is stealing babies."

Along with her novels, Reed has also published collections of short fiction. *Weird Women, Wired Women,* is a 1998 collection of nineteen short stories focusing on women—particularly their mother-daughter relationships and their role in an American male-dominated society. "Covering more than 30 years of her darkly speculative fiction. . . . the volume offers a definitive, indispensable sampling of Reed in top form," reported a *Kirkus Reviews* contributor. "Anger, resentment, love, and obligation blur in tales that blend pathos and irony with the downright weird," summarized *Library Journal* contributor Eleanor J. Bader. Crediting the "unique blend of humor" of this "versatile" and "prolific" author, Ted Leventhal believed the collection of "humorous, ironic prose . . . [in] surreal short stories" was undoubtedly "a worthwhile read," however, a *Booklist* critic contended *Weird Women, Wired Women* "suffers from repetition [of theme]." The "crisp and to the point" text in the "impressive . . . [but] somewhat cold" collection contains "unrelenting obsessiveness," determined a *Publishers Weekly* reviewer who similarly concluded that the "lack of contrast to offset the prevailing darkness becomes unnerving." In contrast, Bader judged the perspectives Reed presents to be "fresh" and "refreshing."

Like her previous collections, *Seven for the Apocalpyse* is a mix of science fiction, mainstream, and "womanist" writings, "sometimes all these things at once," according to Roberta Johnson in *Booklist*. In the longest story, "The Little Sisters of the Apocalypse," Reed depicts motorcycle-riding nuns, protecting a group of women abandoned by their men when the men went to war. When the men return, the women must consider whether or not they want them back. Other tales feature a home security device in love with her owner, a man coping with his wife's Alzheimer's disease, a penal colony disguised as a living history tourist trap, and a retelling of the old fairy tale, "The Juniper Tree," retitled "The Singing Marine." According to a *Publishers Weekly* contributor, "Reed's stories are strikingly imagined and tautly written." Of the last story in the collection, Elizabeth Hand, writing in the *Magazine of Science Fiction and Fantasy,* wrote, "It leaves the reader thirsty for more, which is a good way, maybe the best way, to end any book." Reed's subsequent collection, *Dogs of Truth: New and Uncollected Stories,* which *Booklist* contributor Regina Schroeder considered "a set of marvelous glimpses of the darker side of everything." Many of the dystopian tales feature scary children and teenagers: one couple is stalked by a baby stroller, and in another tale, high schoolers revolt against their almost military enclosure of a high school—until they get bored and their revolt trails off. "Reed's humor is as sharp and cool as the edge of an icicle. These *Dogs of Truth* have bite," wrote Colette Bancroft in the *St. Petersburg Times.*

When discussing her writing process with Matthew Cheney of *SF Site,* Reed described, "I've always been a visceral writer, as in, I don't have an intellectual ap-

Kit at age three

proach, twelve steps or twelve things you need to put in to make a story, any of that; I sit down in the morning most days and do what I have to do, whatever that is." Rob Bedford of *SFF World Web site* asked Reed what drew her to become a writer, and she answered, "I've been telling stories since I was four and a half; it's all I ever wanted to do; by the time I was in first grade I was writing them instead of dictating to my mother. It's who I am."

AUTOBIOGRAPHICAL ESSAY: Kit Reed contributed the following autobiographical essay to *CA:*

At three I got lost at an intersection in downtown San Francisco, but only for a minute. Crossing the street, my panicky parents looked back and saw me planted on the curb. Adults streamed past on either side as I sat there, resolutely trying to jam an object into a box that was too small for it.

It's the story of my life.

A lifetime later a friend saw me reviving a defunct coffee maker. He suggested gently that it was beyond hope. I stopped long enough to say, "I never give up."

Then I admitted, "Sometimes you get tired of being the kind of person who never gives up."

It is, on the other hand, the engine that drives my work. For a writer, talent is only the beginning. Writers have to be tough, persistent and alert to the world outside their heads.

Mine changed constantly. We moved a dozen times before I finished college.

I was born in San Diego, California, but I'm not from anywhere. The Naval officer's tour of duty was about two years—until war changed everything. I used to think it was the ideal way to live. If life in a given place went sour, the inconvenience was only temporary. Soon enough, there would be crates in the living room. A new school in a new place.

I used to wonder whether I'd be any good at living in the same town for long. Where I come from, if things aren't going right you can always move.

We had moved from California to Honolulu, to New London and back to Honolulu by the time I was four. Landscapes changed all the time. My parents and the Navy were the constants in my life: Mummy and Daddy and Harbor Wilson, the plush Easter bunny who started my career.

Wherever we moved certain objects followed, to be uncrated and set up in living rooms from Honolulu to Washington, DC, to Panama and later to St. Petersburg, Florida, and on and on. These were the treasures Naval officers' families shored up against their ruin: camphor wood chest, chow bench, brass table; the Chinese rug and the teakwood desk.

There were treasures just like them in hundreds of other Navy living rooms. Come into one of our houses anywhere and you were at home. I still have some of these loyal objects. More important, Harbor sits in state in our upstairs hall. She is wearing three medals that followed her starring role in my first novel: one

an American Library Association award for *Thinner Than Thou,* two from the New England Newspaperwomen's Association for work I did for the *New Haven Register.*

In Honolulu, we lived in a bungalow perched on a mountainside. We had a Japanese maid. Daddy built me a playhouse out of a furniture crate. I sat my mother down and dictated my first novel. She printed it on paper folded to make a book. I was four and a half. She read it back, including a (parenthetical) question I had asked, which she had dutifully transcribed. I told her it didn't belong and covered the erasure with a drawing of Harbor and her friend Bobby Jones. I titled the book "Harbor Plots Her Plans."

Four other bunnies, Bobby, Miz, Peter, and Pitty Pat, ended up somewhere on the road down Diamond Head; they fell off the running board where I'd lined them up before my father left for the base at Pearl Harbor, where the USS *Neches* was docked. Later he was detached and sent to the Navy Department, which gave us two years of ordinary American life in Washington, DC.

I fell in love with Mikey in first grade. The big kids made me walk on flypaper in Helen Simmel's tent. My mother lost a baby, not the first and not the last. The RH factor was still a problem waiting to be solved. I wrote and illustrated the second Harbor book. My father was crestfallen because instead of waiting to be read to, I read the next "Oz" book to myself. I read *Beowulf* in the bathroom one long night while a gullible babysitter waited for me to come out.

Daddy and I went for a walk on Thanksgiving, just the two of us, in the snow. He took me for my first haircut, freeing me from the bondage of my mother's laboriously tended Shirley Temple curls, and he probably sat me on the roving photographer's pony when he took my picture in front of our neat little house. When my new kitten gave Daddy hives they bought me a Scottie; I wanted a dog just like Fala. I had an accordion I didn't want to play, a bunny fur coat with matching muff.

In DC, I was bowled over by *The Spirit.* Comics! Big Little Books. My mother's anxieties were catching. Radio accounts of bubonic plague and black widow

Kit with her parents, Lillian and John Craig, adorned with leis in Honolulu, 1939

spiders left me feeling my armpits for buboes, looking for spiders marked by the red hourglass and, incidentally, worrying about appendicitis. My mother subscribed to a religious newsletter, perhaps looking for a cure to ailments she could not name. I loved the gruesome details of all those heinous afflictions miraculously cured by St. Anne de Beaupré.

Ordinary wasn't quite ordinary, although I didn't know it; one day Daddy came home and destroyed all the toys marked MADE IN JAPAN. We were about to move.

In a childhood marked by frequent moves and changing scenery, there was another constant: the long-running story inside my head.

We were still in Honolulu when I began it, after my parents had turned out the lights and closed the door. It took the sting out of being put to bed. My story

featured blond twins just about my age named Dick and Daisy, who lived on a ranch. It continued night after night until the three of us were old enough to start thinking about sex. One of us wasn't ready to be that person, and the stories stopped. The cast included Brad and Brenda, who had dark hair. Then I added red-headed Rusty; I was in love with him.

By that time we were back in to snowy New London, where my father took command of the R-17. An aspiring flier who washed out at Pensacola, he turned to what the Navy called the Silent Service: submarines. The adventures of Harbor escalated. In "Harbor and Shamrock Wilson," Harbor's plane crashed in the jungle and she met her colored sister, a tribal princess. Together, they came back to America and became best friends. We moved to Panama and then, abruptly, back to New London before Christmas. That was the year I started over in St. Joseph's in New London twice, at a nuns' school in Panama and in St. Paul's school in Florida—all in fourth grade.

I asked for a gaudy Carmen Miranda doll that Christmas, but found the economy model stashed in a closet early that December. On Sunday morning the phone rang. Daddy answered it. Japanese planes had bombed Pearl Harbor and his brother Jimmy, an officer on the *Pennsylvania,* was dead. If I'd known enough to *worry,* I thought, none of this would have happened. Things would work out, as long as I had a plan. If they attacked New London I would crouch by the stairs and bash them with my alarm clock as they came in. On our last Christmas together, Santa brought the big Carmen Miranda doll instead.

By January the three of us and Toughy, the Scottie, were on our way to St. Petersburg, Florida, the safe place my father had chosen for my mother to sit out the war. Where I was used to hills, Florida was dauntingly flat, with staggering 360-degree skies. Spongy Bermuda grass battled for survival in sandy gray dirt. Sand spurs scratched my ankles and stuck in Toughy's paws. It was like landing on Mars. I used to stare out at sunny winter landscapes, praying for snow.

We said goodbye to Daddy at the Atlantic Coast Line station in downtown St. Petersburg—one of those wide places in the road where trains stopped on their way back to the real world. I remember hugging him and turning away stoically because in a life of change there was yet another constant: officers' children don't cry.

They think. And they worry. And they plan. God, do they plan. Do this right next time, or do it differently; expect the worst and the worst won't happen; watch out what you trust in and the next time, there won't be a war.

A Naval Academy graduate from Jacksonville, Florida, John R. Craig went where the Navy sent him, right up to the end. He went to the Pacific as skipper of the USS *Grampus,* a submarine that landed coast watchers during World War Two and destroyed several enemy ships in the Coral Sea. I still have his Navy Cross and his Bronze Star. Chief (VADM K.S.) Masterson, an Academy classmate and one of my first adult friends, told me years later that he and his wife, Charlotte, saw Jack for the last time in San Francisco the night before he shipped out. I can't bear to look at his letters home from that period but I cherish his exit line:

"If you see me lying drunk in the gutter turn me over. I don't want them to see the brass buttons on the uniform."

He was a gentle, funny man who used what spare time he had making intricate ship models, an inlaid cribbage board, a record cabinet, a teakwood album that he filled with snapshots lovingly captioned in white ink. He subscribed to *Popular Mechanics,* which I loved, and until I protested that I could read the next "Oz" book faster by myself, he read to me. I often wonder what I would have been like if he had lived.

Jack was one of three children, the second son born to James E. Craig and Clara Belle Rich Craig, who was—literally—the first white child born in Deland, the Florida town her parents founded in 1874. I imagine that going South, Union Army Captain John Rich invited a few freemen and their families along to help him settle the new land. Interesting that the Deland Web site revises history, calling Grandmother the "first child" born there. Widowed by the time I knew her well, my grandmother Craig was smart, funny, and tough as nails. Contemporary photos indicate that as a girl, she was also beautiful.

She rated films for the Florida State Board of Censors and was—I fear—a leader in the DAR. But she was kind and she cooked, and, in sharp contrast to my mother, she loved to do it. Role model? Probably. Except for the DAR.

Jack Craig was a small man, neatly put together and, according to his superior officers, one who could be counted on to deliver the message to Garcia verbatim, and under fire. As an ensign he met and married a Jacksonville girl, Lillian Hyde. She was brought up in a tradition that died before she came of age: ladies talked in euphemisms. And ladies didn't work, although when Jack met her she was teaching school. The Hydes grew up in their own little Tara with white columns on the big front porch and servants' quarters behind the house; a bronze nymph raised a lamp high above the newel post in the front hall. There were nine children if you counted Uncle LeRoy, who burned to a cinder playing with matches under the back porch.

The family had pretensions. Because some America-bound ancestor had missed his tax bill, my mother said, his property in central London was "escheated to the crown." Hyde Park. She spent years scouring libraries for proof that she was descended from the patroon of Staten Island. After she died I handed her burden off to the archivist at the University of Florida.

Marie, the oldest sister, made her debut in Charleston at the St. Cecelia's Ball, well before the family lost its money in the 1923 Florida real estate crash. Older brothers moved on before I was old enough to visit the house, leaving behind three single sisters and Marie's orphaned daughter in a house full of hotly contested furniture.

The street had gone downhill since the glory days when, my mother reported glowingly, "John [the cook] said, 'Miss Lillian, you're poor to carry' and cut me an extra piece of pie," and, "Nurse used to take us out in the pony cart. People would say, 'I just know you're Forrest Hyde's children. I can tell by the eyes.'" For her, 553 May Street was always "home"—unlike anyplace she lived afterward, with what remained of our shrinking nuclear family.

Interesting, that she idealized an experience that must have been miserable. Lillian was the shy one, who only got attention when she was sick. She didn't much like her siblings, whom I was expected to love. Except for a few ceremonial visits when I was small, we avoided Jacksonville until my mother was widowed.

Later she felt guilty because the night the telegram came ("missing in action and presumed lost") she told me it was from her brother Forrest, and sent me back to bed. The next morning she broke the news—and put me to bed. The day after, we got up and got dressed and carried on as if everything was going to be all right (they'd find him) and nothing had changed. It was what you did. The alternatives were too grim.

At school, however, I was marked. The only kid without a father. As though it was something I did. Every time a new boy came into the class I studied him greedily, hoping he was like me. A former neighbor greeted me in tears, "Oh you poor child, you have lost your father." I despised the old lady for treating me like an aberration when I was working hard to be just like everybody else.

For the survivors, Missing in Action is both better and worse than dead. For a long time I imagined Daddy was a prisoner, or marooned on a desert island; as an adult I wondered what would happen if, mysteriously, he came back. What would he be like? Would he be proud of me? When my mother died I found letters of inquiry to the Navy Department, to Academy classmates. She tracked down leads well into the 1960s. Like me, she never gave up—on that, at least.

We moved into a room in somebody else's house. Later we had two rooms in a larger house, and next, a garage apartment. Toughy went with us. Harbor and my other stuffed rabbits did too. Made from cartons, their houses lined the sidewalk wherever we moved. Their town was named Bunny Ridge. "Harbor Comics" replaced the Harbor books.

Finally my mother went against the advice of crusty Forrest the financier and went into capital, what little there was. She bought us a house and saw it through renovation. It was necessary, to give me an apparently normal life.

We went to the christening of the USS *John R. Craig,* DD 885. Instead of a father, I had a ship.

It was probably good for me to grow up with an anxious hypochondriac. A cough bought me freedom for days. A polio scare kept me home for most of sixth grade, and I loved it. I read through the "Oz" books for the dozenth time, hung on the radio, wrote ("good heavens, Deanna ejaculated") and drew, all in the comfort and security of my very own bed.

I already knew that the solution to life's problems was *not* lying down. Except when sidelined by childbirth or major surgery, I have never spent a day in bed.

I also learned, by negative example, that it did *not* matter what people said about what you wore or what you did. With her social aspirations, my mother taught me the converse: to value meritocracy. You are what you achieve. Poor little only mother, bringing up an only child. She was a mass of social anxieties. She never outgrew her fear that I would mortify her. "You can't go out wearing/saying/doing that," she'd say, guaranteeing that I would do anything to prove her wrong. "What will people think?"

When my bio turned up in *Who's Who,* she assumed it was only for that year. When I juggled work and family, she was afraid I'd "overdo." Ladies didn't work.

I should, however, add that she was essentially sweet, good at turning my anger into laughter. She had a formidable vocabulary. In her own tentative, frightened way, she was strong. When I got thrown from a horse in summer camp she engineered riding lessons. During the war she drove us up and down the Eastern Seaboard to see relatives in Jacksonville and Bronxville—and in Washington, the Mastersons, whose sons were the nearest things to siblings that I had. She managed our finances so carefully that I was a senior in college before I learned how tight things were.

She believed certain material wasn't suitable for children. Just as well she didn't know what I read, from her Book of the Month Club selections to *Forever Amber* and other parents' sex manuals—on the sly at the houses of friends. At twelve I went to the first movie I'd been allowed to see where everything did *not* come out all right in the end. Watching Gary Cooper fight to the death as Dr. Wassell, I understood for the first time that if heroes could die on the screen, then my father might not come back.

Walking to school behind the big kids, I heard a boy telling a story—*a story!*—about something that had happened. It was better than radio. He did all the voices. Rapt, I thought: *I want to be that person.*

In the new house I began a novel about a girl and a horse. By then I was writing flap copy for the book I expected to publish, and soon. "Kitten Craig is twelve years old and has her own horse."

I did. My mother bought me an old cow pony with a sagging lip; until zoning caught up with us, he lived in the garage. Phlegmatic Satin was replaced by Rex, a skittish five-gaited horse with a barbwire scar on his haunch.

The visits to Jacksonville accelerated. I thanked God for the Craigs. Grandmother expected me to be tough. She had to be, with both sons killed in the war. Aunt Lydia was thirteen years younger than my father, and I saw him in her face. She was an air-traffic controller when women weren't accepted. Being with them was an emotional boot camp: shape up or ship out. It was good for me. Great Aunt Ruth Rich was a journalist who kept on typing after she went blind. I re-read "Oz" books at their house; I read condensed novels in Grandmother's Omnibook; I read anything I found in every house we stayed in.

The Hydes were another story, one I transformed in my fourth novel, *Cry of the Daughter.* They were indeed a southern novel, just not that one. Fuse Faulkner at tremendous speeds with *Gone with the Wind* and you get the idea. On May Street I read books my aunts had on hand, including *Native Son* and *Scarlet Sister Mary,* which I hid under a sofa cushion so I wouldn't get caught.

Even without the Navy to prod her, my mother moved us to Parris Island, South Carolina, the summer I turned fifteen. She may have bought into the myth— that the right move would change her life. Or, she sometimes thought, the right operation: for the deviated septum, the defective toe joint, the malady she could not diagnose and would never cure—depression, because she never stopped grieving for him.

I fell in love with the Carolina landscape—dense marsh grass in the Inland Waterway; magnificent live-oaks shrouded in Spanish moss. I fell in love with the human landscape: desperate Marine recruits running the obstacle course behind the Officers' Guest House where we lived; public high school, that microcosm of aspiration and politics, sex and violence. Classes were mediocre but going to Beaufort High was a powerful lesson in life.

To survive, a military kid learns to look and listen. Walk the walk and talk the talk or the pack will find out you are different and turn on you. Going into each new place, I learned to absorb social configurations without being told, move fast and join in conversations that had been going on for years. "Hey," I said in Beaufort, with its tidewater vocabulary and country cadences; it was never "Hi." Constant moves sharpened my ear for dialogue. It serves me to this day. I hear my characters coming before I see them.

At Beaufort High I blended—for a while.

We lived on the base, where my mother managed the Officers' Club until she declared for the last time, "This job is untenable," and quit. By then she and a boy from Wilder's stable had driven to St. Petersburg with a horse trailer to bring Rex back: five-foot woman, loading a horse that stood fifteen and a half hands high.

Life on the base was exciting. Privileged. There were free movies at the Odeon, where dependents sat in a special section behind platoons of boots with shaved heads. There was a bowling alley. There was the club. I could swim in the pool all weekend, flirt with junior officers at dinner, sign a chit for apple pie for breakfast on Mondays before I left for school. In splendid isolation, seven of us rode the forty-five minutes from the base to Beaufort on a city bus painted regulation green. I never stopped reading, but in Beaufort, I wrote only for class.

"Oh," Mrs. Combs said, delivering Part One of the Chinese curse: "You are so fa-*ceel."*

I had two boyfriends—the first an incipient stalker and the second a country boy who dumped me because I wouldn't put out. At the time I thought it was because I was funny, too brash. Also true. Lesson taken: don't let them know you're smart.

It was harder to hide the fact that I couldn't hit the ball. On the third strike Coach Askew loomed, drawling, "Gurl, ain't yew got no screw-ples?" Probably not.

We spent an extra year in Beaufort because after years of repression in parochial schools, I was out riding around in cars with boys and for a while, at least, they thought I was cute.

We lived on Federal Street in the town where Captain John Rich and his wife, Clara, buried their first baby before they went south. By that time the local kids were on to me. I was the same stupid, vulnerable stiff who didn't belong anywhere.

I read lurid historical novels in that house, and during study halls I raced through the library's run of Edna Ferber, a crash course in construction and suspense. Book reviews in *Time Magazine* opened a new world to me. There were dozens of new novels every month. I wanted to read them all—and write about them. Imagine. I was sixteen.

My cousin Marie came to live with us, toting a baby of her own, and in her own wonderful, easygoing way, she put certain things in perspective. "You know, sometimes your mother can be a bitch." Decades later my daughter alleviated years of filial guilt by suggesting Marie was right.

I fell into a posture of rebellion; it was time. I was an adult with a family of my own when my mother's best friend told me, "Your mother was very brave, letting you live your own life instead of hanging on to you." That too.

Maybe that's why we moved back to Washington at the end of my junior year at Beaufort High. Unless she feared the impossible, that her clueless, virginal daughter was having sex. Mystified, I found out by accident why I had been hauled into the base dispensary. The doctor reassured her and sent us home.

Although I hadn't thought about getting into college, my mother had. The formidable Sister Mary Leonard let me into Georgetown Visitation Convent in Washington, and from a world of boys who might—just might—fall in love with me, I moved into a girls' boarding school where Dobermans were posted at the bottom of the stairs every night, although it was never clear whether they were to keep out intruders, or keep us in. Reading *The Count of Monte Cristo*, I felt like Edmund Dantes, jailed in the Chateau d'If.

I knew we'd have to leave the horse behind when we left Beaufort. We left my dog!

Visitation was good for me, but not the way my mother hoped. Instead of polishing my manners, the school encouraged me to let the people know I had brains. Once again I came late to the feast; the boarders had been together for years. It went better for me than for the colonel's daughter, who claimed the Virgin came to her in the chapel with orders for the nuns to send her back to Colorado, where she belonged.

On weekends, my mother and I went calling on my father's classmates in their snug houses with their complete families: parents, children. Intact. They were generous when we came to call.

One day the senior class got on a bus and went to National Cathedral School to take SATs. In vocabulary, I score in the ninety-ninth percentile—I just do, but there was a hitch. Leonard looked down her aristocratic nose. "My dear, with your math scores, you'll be fortunate if you get into any college at all." Mandatory GREs two years later confirmed it. In math I scored in the fourth percentile.

The College of Notre Dame in Baltimore was kind enough to take me. Later, Sister Maura Eichner let me submit short stories in lieu of a footnoted thesis. I roomed with the talented, temperamental daughter of the *Washington Post*'s answer to Ann Landers. In a conventional college we found the outsider culture, along with another good friend who later became a nun.

With meals and housekeeping taken care of, the sisters thought women could do anything: be scientists, scholars, artists. My favorite was the incendiary Sister Ignatius, who moderated the college paper. Her temper was like the weather. Violent, unpredictable. We asked survivors: "How is she today?"

The Ig was a precisionist, tougher than any city editor. She chose me to edit the yearbook, not the obvious A student. When the creator of *Pogo* came to speak I did the interview. The clipping got me my first job.

As freshmen, we were bussed to Annapolis for tea fights at the Naval Academy. I was in love with the Navy, from the craggy bust of Tecumseh to the photo of my father's gym team enshrined in Dahlgren Hall. I could show you the exact location of the initialed brick among thousands in front of Bancroft Hall. I went to hops with sons of my father's classmates. I thought I'd marry into the Navy. It was home.

But meanwhile. Meanwhile! The house in St. Petersburg was between tenants and needed work the summer after my freshman year. I was painting kitchen cabinets when my mother's college roommate invited us to dinner. Her son Jimmy had a hot date, but his

"In senior year I knitted a Dramat muffler for Joe," Baltimore, Maryland, 1954 Bill Rettberg Photography

mother barred the door. "You have to get a date for Kitten too." He dug up a high school classmate, a scholarship student at Yale who was, I was warned, "smart." I imagined a weedy character with glasses. He produced Joe Reed.

Attacking *War and Peace* that summer, I had read as far as the Battle of Austerlitz. I never finished the book.

We went dancing at the Bath Club where as a kid I'd been watched over by the club's fatherly headwaiter, B.C. A dance band played on the terrace by the pool.

Joe and I danced well together; we still do. On the way home one of us quoted T.S. Eliot's sober instructions about wiping your hand across the mouth. . . . In a flash the other provided the second line, and it is significant that I don't remember who said which.

Jimmy never scored with that hot girl, but Joe and I were bonded for life. We had just turned nineteen.

The next summer my mother pushed me into typing school—liberating for someone whose wretched handwriting could never keep pace with her thoughts. They taught me how to type.

Joe gave me the Modern Library Faulkner. He introduced me to *Vile Bodies.* Along with Scott Fitzgerald and Graham Greene, William Faulkner and Evelyn Waugh taught me how to write.

Decades later I marveled. "How did we find each other?"

He said, "How do two giraffes find each other in a field of zebras?"

My mother noted mildly that we might not have much in common, all we ever did was go to the movies, but she reckoned without the hours we spent parked on the Vinoy fill or in front of the house. There have been thousands of movies since, and in spite of her fears, we never run out of things to talk about.

His mother, I learned later, didn't approve of me. Where she wanted him to marry up, a Catholic girl would burden him with babies. I could only drag him down. She'd have moved heaven and earth to stop the wedding, but she couldn't budge Joe.

My mother worried because we fought. We fight like tigers. Growing up with a woman who would brood until I begged her to tell me what I'd done wrong, I vowed to get it out and get it over with. Fight. Negotiate. Resolve.

Being a long-distance landlord tired my mother, who had quit the government job that brought her to Washington. She'd tried selling insurance and real estate without success. It wasn't hard to convince her to move back to St. Petersburg. Friends lived there. So did the Reeds.

College life went on, but with a difference. There were the letters, days that there weren't letters, weeks of saving up for trips. Days at Notre Dame unfolded in black-and-white. The movie turned to Technicolor the minute I got off the train in New Haven. Although he was an English major whose work-study job put him to work for the noted Boswell scholar Frederick A. Pottle, Joe's life revolved around the Dramat, center of the outsider culture at Yale. He loved building sets and he loved running things. He was president in his senior year.

I went to every show. At the parties afterward, there was the ritual. Sam Pottle played mad piano while people sang drunken, outrageous songs. We were nothing like the preppy drunks going past outside on Fraternity Row with girls from Wellesley/Vassar/Smith with their cashmere sweaters and perfect hair.

It was a good fit for a Navy junior who didn't belong anywhere.

Compared to childhood, adult life is a dream. Unlike children, grownups make the decisions. Adults are in control of what they do, and what comes next. While Joe joined the USS *Macon* as an ensign in the reserve, I applied to the *St. Petersburg Times.* I got to the heart of the personality test, choosing answers that made me look inventive, creative, aggressive, naturally curious. All true.

Outside the Society department, which was its own kind of ghetto, there were five women—a record for newspapers in those days. Lorna Carroll, the religion editor, was an ex-showgirl. Assigned to a story about a crop duster, she cried, "Lash me to the plane." A neophyte who never went to journalism school, I was hired to answer the phone.

I loved it. I was being paid for what I did! I went into the newsroom on my days off for the sheer pleasure of hanging out with people who, like me, observed and recorded details about a world where they didn't necessarily belong.

Soon I was editing copy. I "enterprised" a feature about a sidewalk bank teller—my first. I convinced the desk to let me review new television shows. In short order I was a TV columnist. Unthinkable now, but nobody did it on a regular basis then.

Chick Ober was city editor, stern and businesslike. With work, I could make him smile. The newsroom was dominated by men, all busy and obviously more important than I could hope to be, pounding on klunky standard typewriters. I would have done anything to impress those guys.

I wrote well but moved too fast; after I overlooked a writ in Circuit Court I ended up on Obits, where I spent six dismal weeks phoning funeral homes. Lorna went on a two-week vacation and I dummied and wrote headlines and most of the copy for the weekly church page. I chose a pseudonym: Fidelia Kirk. In the composing room, I threw out blocks of hot type and rearranged columns with the best of them. I learned to read in reverse.

"Well," said my boss on the project, "you just passed Journalism 101." Sandy Stiles took notice and had me design and write for the TV section in his new Sunday magazine. From answering the phone, I had moved up fast. By that time I had inherited Great Aunt Ruth's typewriter. I remember starting and abandoning one short story at home.

I read C.S. Lewis's theological science fiction trilogy, starting with *Out of the Silent Planet.* For a child who grew up on the "Oz" books, SF was the route into imaginary adult worlds. It fed my appetite for the weird.

A year later Joe came home on leave and we were engaged. Back on the *Macon,* he broke the news to his skipper, then-Captian Vernon L. Lowrance. When he told my father's classmate that he was marrying Jack Craig's daughter, Rebel laughed. "Get out of here, you make me feel old." Although Joe's mother is not smiling in the wedding photos, we were married that December. We moved to Great Lakes Naval Training Center for his last six months in the service.

Bottom line? I lost my job.

Kit and Joe leave the Sunset Country Club after their wedding, December 10, 1955 Graham Photography

I went from struggling star, still rising, at the country's best independent newspaper to the editorship of the District Public Works Office house organ, *The Right Angle*. I didn't know it was the ideal career move. With a job I could do in two days and a month of eight-hour work days to do it in, I wrote.

What was I reading? I remember *Miss Lonelyhearts*, which I read standing up in a drugstore because I couldn't afford the paperback. Shirley Jackson. J.D. Salinger. I remember an early fight over what belonged on our first bookshelf. I held out for my favorites, no matter how battered. Joe was a bindings snob. We split the difference.

I wrote a dozen stories in that period, sent them out to a pay-by-the-read "literary agent" and discovered that the operation was a scam. Ten dollars for the reading. If you wanted further notes on your story, you paid more. Life was too short. Joe pointed me to two amazing details in Herodotus. I wrote a story called "To Be Taken in a Strange Country."

My mother met a writer at the Bath Club. She said, "Oh, my daughter's a writer too." He offered to put me in touch with his agent at Curtis Brown. Emilie Jacobson liked my work but thought "To Be Taken" was too strange to show. She asked to see more. It would be a while.

We were moving to New Haven. Joe was preparing for graduate school at Yale. I was never happier to lose a job. After three tense months on area weeklies owned by the spoiled son of a St. Louis newspaper scion, I moved to the *New Haven Register*. In a newsroom with exactly one other woman, I was hired to answer the phone. But not for long. I did rewrites. Then I did a couple of obits. I did a story. Then I did another one.

I followed a visiting nurse through her day in the poorest neighborhood in New Haven. With a photographer riding post, I covered a drug bust. I was learning how a city works.

Whenever an author came to town, I did the interview. I went in without an agenda. After the first question, I built questions on their answers. Avid for any detail that would help me become a writer, I took notes. With my head bent over the notebook, I was invisible. They opened up as if to their psychiatrists.

Composing on the typewriter taught me discipline. There was a lot of tearing out and crumpling pages and starting over from the top. As I hammered away at the lead, the rest of the story organized itself. Fiction unfolds for me in the same way. Writing and rewriting, I discover the tone, the point of view, the cadences of my characters. I find out what I'm doing in the process of getting it down, and getting it *right*.

I learned more from crusty newsmen than any writing program could teach. Precision and accuracy were the rule. There was no place in the newsroom for prima donnas. Excel and Chick or Bart or Al might mutter, "Good story." High praise. At the *Register*, Charlie McQueeney pulled me into the composing room, where the clatter of the Mergenthalers would keep the news that he was giving me a raise from reaching his staff.

Perhaps the most valuable lesson was in working on deadline. Now I work according to deadlines I set for myself.

Interviewing the news editor's wife, Kaatje Hurlbut, who had just sold her first short story to *Mademoiselle,* I learned that she'd been writing for eight hours a day for fifteen years. Inspired, I came home and pulled out "To Be Taken in a Strange Country." Bob Mills at *Venture* rejected it but sent me to Anthony Boucher at *The Magazine of Fantasy and Science Fiction,* who took it. That first sale was like a dealer's sample of a powerful drug. With no time to write, I finished long days in the newsroom and wrote short stories at night.

In the era of the happy housewife, Joe and I had agreed that a woman with a career was more interesting than one without. I put him through graduate school; since then he has supported my work, whether or not it pays. As resident critic, he reads every line of fiction I write.

At work, I was covering Juvenile Court. We were the first paper to do it. Assistant managing editor Al Sizer made an arrangement with the judge, agreeing to mask the young offenders' identities. Again, I was the invisible reporter: observing, recording, astonished by how many cases were custody matters placing children when there were no responsible adults. Many ended up in the state school, batched with serious offenders. My third novel, *The Better Part,* reflects some of what I learned.

Four boys from the projects mugged and murdered an old man for a watch and some pocket change. Al assigned me to an in-depth series. I talked to families, to police and social workers, trying to find out what turned them into killers. The New England Newspaperwomen of America named me best reporter of the year. Picking up my second medal the following May, I asked about the last year's winner. "Died in childbirth," I was told. I was pregnant, although it didn't show.

One week in August, I interviewed Cary Grant and covered a talk by Eleanor Roosevelt. That Friday Charlie said he was afraid I'd deliver in the newsroom and sent me home. The guys in the newsroom took up a collection for a farewell present. I bought a desk. I thought I had a week to get ready, but that night I went to the hospital and by Saturday night, Joe and I had a boy.

Once more, I was out of a job.

In my life as a novelist, I have honored a tacit agreement that I will never write about my children, but it's important to name them here. We have three, Joseph McKean Reed, John Craig Reed, and Katherine Hyde Reed. We used to come home early from parties because they were more fun to hang out with than most adults. They are grown now, pair-bonded in much the same way we are, Mack to Kristina Reed, John to Germàn Angulo-Salom and Katy to Ko Maruyama; Cooper and Miranda Reed and Jack and Reed Maruyama complete the group. Our joy is that our adult children are friends and colleagues who still like to hang out with us.

After five years in newsrooms, however, motherhood came as a shock. Where other Yale wives were getting together over morning coffee, I had been at work. Dumped into the new world with nothing to steer by but a copy of *Dr. Spock.* I was in culture shock. For the first time ever, I was physically weak. I had this small person to take care of, I hurt all over *and* I lost my job.

Recovery was swift after my mother left for home; she was intent on housekeeping, when all I wanted to do was sleep. The baby's schedule arranged itself and set my work times. After the morning bath, he slept for at least two hours. At four weeks I wrote a short story and (thanks Mom, for sewing lessons when I was twelve) made a skirt. At six weeks I started a novel and made a suit.

I read through Lawrence Durrell's *Alexandria Quartet* during that period. I discovered Ray Bradbury and Theodore Sturgeon and Ian Fleming; I read *Jude the Obscure* and A.E. Ellis's response to *The Magic Mountain,* a scorching novel called *The Rack.* I was reviewing fiction for the *Register* in exchange for the book.

As a reporter committed to accuracy, I used to lie awake worrying. Had I gotten the facts wrong, had I misquoted a source? Fiction opened the door to freedom. As Joe's mentor at Yale, Frederick Hilles, said cheerily, "You don't have to worry. You can make it all up."

Examining life, I could shape lives on the page. Writing was my way of making life make sense. What's more, I could invent. Emmy Jacobson had no interest in weirdness, but sold my more reality-driven stories to *Redbook* and *Cosmopolitan*. The others, I sent out on my own.

Developing writers often write what they like to read. I was torn between Waugh and Faulkner, Fitzgerald and Salinger—and SF. Speculative fiction let me learn how to write without touching my central material. I mailed dozens of stories to genre magazines. My favorite rejection came from H.L. Gold, who in response to my question, "How does this grab you?" wrote back, "Right down the throat and by the lunch." My second favorite came from Emmy, who said of my story "Winter," "If you can sell this I'll pin a medal on you."

"Winter" appeared in MacMillan of London's *Winter's Tales* along with pieces by Ted Hughes and Sylvia Plath. It has been widely anthologized, most recently in *The Norton Anthology of Contemporary Literature*.

Peter Parsons, who edited a town-gown issue of the *Yale Literary Magazine* used a story. Mimicking author notes I'd read, I said it was part of a novel. Peter thought his uncle, a publisher, might want to see it. How much did I have? I wrote five chapters and an outline on Aunt Ruth's plum-colored Smith Corona, tapping away on a card table in the front hall. I entered the Houghton Mifflin contest. Robert Stone won, but I got a contract for *Mother Isn't Dead She's Only Sleeping*. By the time we arrived at Wesleyan for Joe's first job, the manuscript was done.

A dramatic change after Yale and New Haven, the small-town campus looked like a magazine cover by Norman Rockwell. Wholesome youths in Zelan windbreakers gathered around pep-rally bonfires across the street from our house. The first of our student roomers-cum-babysitters demonstrated that they were more interesting than they looked.

Infant naptimes eroded and we paid a local woman to watch the baby five mornings a week. It set my work schedule: work mornings, Monday through Friday. Take nights and weekends off. Routine serves me well. Sit down at the same time every day and sooner or later, something will happen. Now work time expands into the afternoons.

Transatlantic Review took two stories during this period, but I was also selling to *The Magazine of Fantasy and Science Fiction*. I was either blessed or cursed by a darker imagination than most and then and now, I am like the witch on the weather house. Sometimes the sensitive realist comes out; sometimes it's the witch. All my life I have worked to prove that they are the same person, but in publishing, you go where they take you. Editors of speculative fiction have always welcomed me.

At a party for my second novel, a faculty wife told my friend Jessie that it was obscene for me to be locked away upstairs working while downstairs, another woman watched my son. She was telling the wrong person: a mother of three who is also an M.D.

I was never cut out to be a housewife. I did what I did, took care of my baby and kept to myself. I rewrote the Ilg/Ames child-care columns for the Hall Syndicate. I interviewed Richard Wilbur and Paul Horgan and John Cage for the *Register*. Dick was taken aback by the pace of the questions. "When you're interviewing, you turn into somebody else."

The dean's wife looked hurt when I shrugged off the faculty wives' club; the chaplain's wife eyed me suspiciously: *Are you going to write about us?* Years later a religionist's unhappy wife confessed, "We thought you were crazy, sitting up there typing while we were outside with our babies, but. . . " Sigh. "Now you're *somebody* and I'm not."

A friend told us we had arrived "in the year of dancing and petty flirtation." The year before, an irate speech teacher had tried to kill an innocent professor who happened to look like the man who had seduced his wife. A member of the Dutch Resistance in World War Two, the wife of the real culprit had turned the cuckold with the pistol away from the door by implicating the wrong man.

Wow, *this* was interesting.

Throughout the Sixties and Seventies the college community lived out its own comic strip, writing new chapters every day. People went running down the

Young parents Kit and Joe, with son Jeseph McKean "Mack," 1960 Graham Photography

street with children, pounding on windows of houses from which they had been exiled. I was told that our next-door neighbor, who happened to be Joe's boss, resented me because I wouldn't flirt. He was a ludicrous popinjay, flaunting his key to the Playboy Bunny Club. Joe got tenure anyway.

Faculty parties were a revelation; turn a corner at any gathering and find somebody surprising rubbing up against somebody they weren't married to. Didn't they know how silly they looked? Marriages crumbled, or cracked and got glued back together, but for us it was a remarkable spectator sport.

In more than one way, novelist and historian Paul Horgan was the saving grace. As director of the Center for

Advanced Studies, he brought Jean Stafford and Herbert Reed to town, Martin D'Arcy, Frank Kermode and Daniel Patrick Moynihan. Faculty seemed uneasy with eminent outsiders. At Paul's behest, we entertained them all in our half of a college duplex. Edmund Wilson came to dinner and seemed delighted and grateful to be sitting down with us, even though we were only kids.

With his style and humor, Paul made clear that there was a whole world beyond the small academic community with its feverish attempts at festivity. He liked us. He liked my work.

After *Mother Isn't Dead She's Only Sleeping,* Houghton Mifflin wanted to send me to Bread Loaf to network. There were two drawbacks. First, I didn't want to go away to write; I worked at home. Second, I was pregnant again.

I turned in *At War as Children,* my elegiac response to my childhood and to the suicide of Switch Masterson. Houghton Mifflin expected a second comic novel. Rejecting the manuscript, my editor wrote, "I predict a long and interesting career."

Part Two of the Chinese curse slid into place.

I've never written the same thing twice, a problem in a publishing world where readers like to know what they're getting when they buy a book. I am too easily bored.

Paul liked the manuscript and took *At War as Children* to Bob Giroux of Farrar, Straus, who published the book. When galleys came I discovered that a pushy copy editor had inserted her own word choices and arbitrary punctuation into my text. In the days of hot type, corrections on proofs were expensive. The author was usually billed. To Bob's credit, the house covered the cost of restoring my copy.

As a precisionist, I care passionately about the way the text looks on the page. Every line has been through several drafts and I resent the outsider who, on the basis of one reading, decides that I'd prefer their changes to my careful work.

Except for one poisonous review, good things followed the publication of *At War:* a Guggenheim, a paperback sale, the knowledge that there were more books to come. In the realm of Chinese curses, I was my own self-fulfilling prophecy. I disappointed Bob with a collection of SF short stories under the title *Mr. Da V.*

After a Guggenheim trip to South Carolina, we settled in for a summer taking care of the Pottles' house. A painter who has had shows in New York, Washington and New Delhi, Joe got his start there. He painted a pair of herbals for the bathroom we redecorated for the Pottles as a thank-you gift.

I broke my heart over a long, complex novel nobody wanted to publish and on the rebound wrote *The Better Part.* A reviewer said it "made Holden Caulfield

sound like Little Lord Fauntleroy." We took our two little boys to London. By the time Farrar, Straus engineered my invitation to a party for "cool people under 35," I was too pregnant to go. Our daughter came that May. At Paul's Center dinner that night, Joe says, fellows Stephen Spender and Frank Kermode toasted her.

On that first trip to London, I met Hilary Rubinstein of A.P. Watt, who took Joe and me to lunch at Simpson's in the Strand and in the most gentlemanly way possible, talked about how we might make money together. He sold *Mr. Da V.* and *Armed Camps,* my fourth novel, to Charles Monteith at Faber and Faber, the house where T.S. Eliot had worked.

Although *Armed Camps* satisfied Faber, my version of *Why Are We in Vietnam* didn't sit well with the Farrar, Straus image of the sensitive literary writer, Kit Reed. It was time to reinvent myself. Agent Carl Brandt helped me do the job, convincing John MacRae of Dutton to buy *Armed Camps* and *Cry of the Daughter.* He would go on to publish *Tiger Rag* and *Captain Grownup* before we parted ways.

Friends from New York came to the house with their children—the nearest thing to cousins that our children have. Bob Giroux and Charlie Reilly came. Piers Paul Read and his wife came, as did Joan and Harry Harrison. Students who would become friends came.

We went: to Boston, to upstate New York, to Manhattan and Washington.

Nicholas Ray came to the house, half-blind and lugging cans of film documenting the trial of the Chicago Seven. He imagined a movie of *The Better Part* would bring Oscar nominations like his picture, *Rebel without a Cause.* We heard Nick on the wall phone in our kitchen, desperately trying to reach his money. His money refused to pick up the phone.

Fred Pottle came into the Boswell office where Joe was working on Volume Ten of the papers and said he'd nominated me for an award. The letter came in German. The Abraham Woursell Foundation gave five-year literary grants; I was the first American grantee.

We bought a new car. We got a Scottie. We made the down payment on a house. The woman who never belonged anywhere has lived at the same address since 1971.

Meanwhile Wesleyan was in flux. In the wake of the first Kennedy assassination, the Sixties had rolled in like an eighteen-wheeler, carrying every drug in the pharmacy and a new kind of student. Creative. Inventive. Unconventional. People like us. Someone said, "You attract the arties," and we did, although we said no thank you when they came bearing drugs. Postrevolution Wesleyan brought us friends like television director Alan Metzger, who shot the first student film made at Wesleyan; Internet guru John Perry Barlow; producer Laurence Mark.

After the Kent State shootings, previously square faculty members let their hair grow and donned flashy flares. The women's revolution gathered force. At consciousness-raising sessions, faculty wives vented about their lives. I was too busy with career and family to take the time.

Our friends outside Wesleyan were in flux too. As the country moved into the *Ice Storm* era, marriages we believed in started busting up. When these things happened we felt like the kids in the sad song where the folks sit them down to break the bad news. Baffled. Maybe we were the only people around who were surprised.

The year our daughter was born I stood in for a writing teacher sidelined by a heart attack. I taught his class in my living room with Joe standing by, in case. He was, after all, the teacher. I'd never done it before. In the mid-Seventies the college wanted a writer to teach one class a year. They turned to me. Sure, I said. I didn't mind doing it, but just until my ship came in.

I've been teaching ever since. Stephen Alter and I cooked an Indian dinner when Hilary and Helge Rubinstein came from London; Hilary sold Steve's first novel to Diana Athill at Cape. Other students who are friends and colleagues include Peter Blauner and Suzanne Berne, Daniel Handler, Cheryl Sucher and Matt Tyrnauer, Alisa Kwitney and Alexander Chee. There are more, just beginning to publish.

My first class was coming up when Pat Moynihan phoned from India, where he was ambassador, to find out whether Joe and I would come, but there was no splitting the job of cultural attaché. We chose the short visit, a USIS lecture tour, and went for three weeks. Ignoring our bank balance, we bought tickets for the children. Joe was chairing the English department. I was recovering from the non-response to *Tiger Rag.* Time to reinvent myself. I began my second comic novel, *Captain Grownup,* on our return. Peter Prescott, who later became a dear friend, called to tell me *Newsweek* was reviewing the novel. I said, "Thank God." I knew the movie deal wouldn't work out when I found out the producers wanted my male reporter to be a photographer, played by Diane Keaton.

The following summer we were Mellon fellows at the Aspen Institute. Everybody went except the Scottie. In one seminar an oil executive asked me how much I made. I told him, not admitting that most of it came from teaching. The next question staggered me. "Writing," he asked, "is this a hobby with you?"

It's my *life.*

Meanwhile, friends' marriages were crumbling all around us, a complex problem I addressed first in *The Ballad of T. Rantula,* published by Genevieve Young at Little, Brown in 1979. It was a good year for me. Carl convinced David Hartwell at Berkley to buy a collection and a novel. John Madden directed an adaptation of my story "Pilots of the Purple Twilight" on National Public Radio.

In movies, there is a unit called The Last Good Time. As our sons entered college, I plunged into yet another long, complicated novel that nobody would buy. In the Eighties I kept a morbid journal of submissions: short stories sent out and accepted, and novels and short stories returned. I remember one page marked: ZERO YEAR. Doubleday published two books in the Eighties but to cut costs, never produced bound galleys.

Wesleyan offered a special deal on computers to faculty. Joe was buying one. Like most writers at the time, I thought the "word processor" was a monstrosity. It would only ruin my work. As part of an MIT project involving playwrights, Arthur Kopit became a

Boarding the ferry to Robben Island in Cape Town, South Africa, 2006: Joe and Kit with German Angulo-Salom and son John

cyber-evangelist. Clare Brandt sat us down at her Kaypro. It looked easy enough. Born competitive, I knew that if Joe had a computer, to save our marriage, I had to get one too. Our Digital Rainbows came with inscrutable instructions. We were like gorillas, trying to figure out how to open our coconuts.

By the time computer classes started a week later, I had written a short story. I went from composing on a Royal Standard office model typewriter to the fluidity of a computer, but it didn't change the way I work. I don't work any faster. Spared the mechanical effort of throwing the carriage, I don't declare a passage is finished because I'm exhausted. Instead of making eleven or twelve passes, I can keep going until I have it right.

Editors admired my big novel, but nobody made an offer. Once again, it was time to reinvent myself. I wrote my third comic novel, *Catholic Girls.* It came

out in 1987, the year my mother began the downhill slide into death. The next five years were punctuated by trips to Florida, where I wove a few lines of personal history into *Little Sisters of the Apocalypse,* an SF novel about biker nuns.

The phrase "track record" crept into my conversations with Carl. I was having what a friend called "a midlist crisis." I began a psychological thriller about a submariner's widow who vanishes one day. I was writing to save my life. In 1990 Carl and I had what Clare called "the friendliest divorce I've ever seen." They are still dear friends. Richard Pine masterminded my reincarnation, selling *Gone* under my maiden name.

Between foreign, paperback, and film rights, Kit Craig made more money than all those years of Kit Reed put together. A second thriller followed. A six-figure offer for two more. But. But . . . I was deep in yet another

The Reed and Maruyama families, 2007: (standing) the author's daughter-in-law, Kristina Reed, with son Mack; son-in-law Ko Maruyama, with daughter, Kate; (sitting) Kit and Joe, with grandchildren Cooper Reed, Jack Maruyama, Kit Reed, Joseph Reed, Miranda Reed, and Reed Maruyama

long, complex novel that may never be published. Remember the Chinese curse. I declined.

Four more thrillers appeared in the U.K. before I closed the door on that chapter. *J. Eden,* the long, complex novel I began in the late Eighties came out in 1996 from the University Press of New England. As a regular reviewer for *The Hartford Courant,* I joined the National Books Critic Circle, and for four years, served on the board.

Meanwhile, I was leading a double life. My friend Stew the nun had plumbed the Internet. She gave me the Telnet address of an amazing place: an online gathering place for some 9,000 people from all over the world. I got a character on LambdaMOO, the text-

based grandfather of Second Life. Although the community is dwindling, I'm still there.

I needed time off from Wesleyan. I was granted a year to design an online writing course. Patterned after LambdaMOO, my little virtual community allows student writers to workshop stories in a real-time, text-based environment where nobody knows what they look like and nobody can see them blush. Until the last class at my house, they don't know who each other are.

It seemed logical to write about the cyber-life. Fascinated by the power of text and performative utterance, I began *@expectations,* published in 2000. Two more novels followed, both departures from the

Kit and Joe Reed, 2005

expected and both billed as SF. At this writing, *The Baby Merchant* is the most recent, unfolding in a near future that is, essentially, already here.

Beginning this summary of a long career, I talked about anxieties and planning ahead, both essential to my survival. In college, where I was labeled an underachiever, a clueless teacher asked me to summarize my philosophy of life. It was an outrageous request. I didn't have one, at least nothing I could articulate, but I can say this.

As a fatherless kid reared by an anxious mother, I dealt in worst-case scenarios. If X happened, I could always do Y. I think of it as protective pessimism. The protective pessimist is always prepared, never disappointed and often pleasantly surprised. Like Paul Horgan, I always have a work in progress by the time a novel

comes out. For a writer, this is essential. Whatever happens, it won't be so bad if you have a backup plan.

Like everything that has ever happened to me, thinking in worst-case scenarios taught me how to write. My fiction grows out of a profusion of *what-ifs*. What if X happened to this character? What would I do in his place?

To finish a biography neatly, the obliging subject needs to rise to fame—or die. I haven't accomplished the first and am not about to try the second. At this writing, I am beginning a new novel. The work goes on.

BIOGRAPHICAL AND CRITICAL SOURCES:

BOOKS

St. James Guide to Science Fiction Writers, 4th edition, St. James Press (Detroit, MI), 1996.

PERIODICALS

Best Sellers, July 1, 1970; April 1, 1971.

Booklist, June 1, 1986; March 15, 1998, Ted Leventhal, review of *Weird Women, Wired Women,* p. 1203; May 15, 1999, Roberta Johnson, review of *Seven for the Apocalypse,* p. 1682; August, 2000, Whitney Scott, review of *@expectations,* p. 2108; June 1, 2004, Paula Leudtke, review of *Thinner Than Thou,* p. 1713; April 1, 2005, Gillian Engberg, "The Alex Awards, 2005," p. 1355; September 1, 2005, Regina Schroeder, review of *Dogs of Truth: New and Uncollected Stories,* p. 76; April 1, 2006, review of *The Baby Merchant,* p. 29.

Books and Bookmen, March, 1968.

Book World, July 5, 1970.

Entertainment Weekly, March 15, 1996, p. 59.

Hartford Courant (Hartford, CT), June 9, 2004, Owen McNally, "The Land of Bodily Bliss."

Kirkus Reviews, July 15, 1987; September 1, 1992; July 1, 1994; January 15, 1996; February 1, 1998; April 15, 2004, review of *Thinner Than Thou,* p. 368.

Library Journal, August, 1987; October 15, 1992; February 1, 1998, Eleanor J. Bader, review of *Weird Women, Wired Women,* p. 115; June 15, 2004, Jackie Cassada, review of *Thinner Than Thou,* p. 62.

Listener, September 18, 1969.

Locus, May, 1989; November, 1993.

Los Angeles Times Book Review, April 21, 1996.

Magazine of Science Fiction and Fantasy, September, 1999, Elizabeth Hand, review of *Seven for the Apocalypse,* p. 30.

Nation, April 22, 1996, p. 36.

New York Times, April 12, 1976.

New York Times Book Review, March 8, 1964; July 4, 1976; June 17, 1979; March 8, 1981; November 1, 1987; January 17, 1993; April 21, 1996; October 29, 2000, J.D. Biersdorfer, "You've Got Males," p. 38; January 1, 2006, Sarah Ferguson, "Fiction Chronicle," p. 17.

Observer, October 5, 1969.

People, July 5, 2004, Lynn Andriani, review of *Thinner Than Thou,* p. 47.

Philadelphia Inquirer (Philadelphia, PA), August 16, 2006, Martha Woodall, review of *The Baby Merchant.*

Publishers Weekly, July 24, 1987; August 17, 1992; July 25, 1994; December 18, 1995, p. 39; February 9, 1998, review of *Weird Women, Wired Women,* p. 75; May 24, 1999, review of *Seven for the Apocalypse,* p. 65; July 31, 2000, review of *@expectations,* p. 67; May 10, 2004, review of *Thinner Than Thou,* p. 41, and Melissa Mia Hall, "Abandon Flesh All Ye Who Enter Here," p. 42; July 25, 2005, review of *The Dogs of Truth,* p. 53; September 12, 2005, review of *Bronze: A Tale of Terror,* p. 46; March 13, 2006, review of *The Baby Merchant,* p. 46.

Review of Contemporary Fiction, spring, 1999, Irving Malin, review of *Weird Women, Wired Women,* p. 199.

School Library Journal, January, 1992.

Sewanee Review, July, 1990; October, 1992.

St. Petersburg Times (St. Petersburg, FL), September 11, 2005, Colette Bancroft, "Stories with Teeth," p. 7P; June 11, 2006, Colette Bancroft, "Fiction That Feels Like Foreshadowing," p. 6P.

Times Literary Supplement, October 16, 1969.

Voice of Youth Advocates, August, 1985; August, 1986.

Washington Post Book World, August 30, 1981; April 28, 1985; May 25, 1986.

West Coast Review of Books, September, 1979.

Womens Review of Books, July, 1995.

ONLINE

Infinity Plus, http://www.infinityplus.co.uk/nonfiction/intkr.htm (May 18, 2007), Gwyneth Jones, interview with Reed.

Kit Reed's Home Page, http://www.kitreed.net (May 18, 2007).

Ohio History Central Online Encyclopedia, http://www.ohiohistorycentral.org/entry.php?rec=1769 (May 18, 2007), profile of Kit Reed.

SFF World Web site, http://www.sffworld.com/interview/188p0.html (May 25, 2006), Rob Bedford, "Interview with Kit Reed."

SF Site, http://www.sfsite.com/07a/kr227.htm (May 18, 2007), Matthew Cheney, "A Conversation with Kit Reed."

Wesleyan University Web site, http://www.wesleyan.edu/wesmaps/course9900/faculty/reed497.htm (May 18, 2007), profile of Reed.

RENSTROM, Christopher

PERSONAL: Born in Menlo Park, CA. *Education:* Attended Juilliard School of Drama for one year; privately trained in astrology by Zoltan Mason.

ADDRESSES: E-mail—ruleplanets@aol.com.

CAREER: Astrologer, writer, playwright. Astrologer in private practice, New York, NY, 1985—. Creator of Condé Nast's 900 Astrology phone line for *Allure*, 1996; creator of *Renstrom's Horoscopes* for nGames. Lecturer at the Learning Annex, New York, NY.

WRITINGS:

Ruling Planets: Your Astrological Guide to Life's Ups and Downs, HarperResource (New York, NY), 2002.

Also author of four plays produced Off-Off-Broadway. Author of daily horoscope column for *Allure*, 1991—, *San Francisco Chronicle,*1997—, and *SFGate.com.*

SIDELIGHTS: Christopher Renstrom is a nationally known astrologer who has been in private practice since 1985. "I basically see myself as a cosmic weatherman," Renstrom told Jeff Belanger in an interview on *GhostVillage.com.* In addition, Renstrom serves as the astrologist for *Allure* magazine and the *San Francisco Chronicle,* and he is the author of *Ruling Planets: Your Astrological Guide to Life's Ups and Downs.*

Though astrology dates to Babylonian times, Renstrom told Belanger, it didn't become popular in the United States until the early twentieth century. "The contribution America made that no one else did was psychological astrology," Renstrom stated. "America was the first country to really wed astrology to someone's psychology and use it to understand your behavior and potential as a person and use it to better yourself." In *Ruling Planets,* Renstrom explains that an individual's personality traits are based on one's ruling planet and not one's zodiac sign. Traditionally, Renstrom notes, people identified themselves as a "child of Mars" rather than an Aries; the practice of using zodiac signs originated in Great Britain in the 1930s. "Renstrom

tells us that the original emphasis on a 'ruling planet' (which is continually in motion) is missing from today's astrology texts," stated Hilary Williamson on the *BookLoons* Web site. In the work, Renstrom shows readers how to determine their ruling planet, discusses the characteristics associated with that planet, and offers a compatibility analysis. "Rich illustrations and very witty and warm text make this book a keeper," noted a contributor on the *Cafe Astrology* Web site.

BIOGRAPHICAL AND CRITICAL SOURCES:

PERIODICALS

Library Journal, November 1, 2002, Marija Sanderling, review of *Ruling Planets: Your Astrological Guide to Life's Ups and Downs,* p. 109.

ONLINE

BookLoons, http://www.bookloons.com/ (April 15, 2007), Hilary Williamson, review of *Ruling Planets.*
Cafe Astrology, http://www.cafeastrology.com/ (April 15, 2007), review of *Ruling Planets.*
eMuse, http://emuse.tms.tribune.com/ (October 7, 2004), biography of Christopher Renstrom.
GhostVillage.com, http://www.ghostvillage.com/ (July 12, 2003), Jeff Belanger, "What's Your Sign?," review of *Ruling Planets.*
HarperCollins Web site, http://www.harpercollins.com/ (April 15, 2007), biography of Christopher Renstrom.*

*   *   *

RICHARDSON, Scott
See MILLIONAIRE, Tony

*   *   *

RICHARDSON, Tim 1968-

PERSONAL: Born 1968.

CAREER: Writer.

WRITINGS:

Sweets: A History of Temptation, Bloomsbury (New York, NY), 2002.

(Editor) *The Vanguard Landscapes and Gardens of Martha Schwartz,* Thames & Hudson (New York, NY), 2004.

(With Noel Kingsbury) *Vista: The Culture and Politics of Gardens,* Frances Lincoln (London, England), 2005.

English Gardens of the Twentieth Century: From the Archives of "Country Life," Aurum Press (London, England), 2005.

SIDELIGHTS: In *Sweets: A History of Temptation,* self-styled "international confectionery historian" Tim Richardson "thoroughly examines candy history, tracing its journey from East to West," observed a critic in *Publishers Weekly.* In the work, Richardson chronicles the origins of many types of candies, such as marzipan and chewing gum, and looks at the evolution of the modern candy industry. The author, whose grandfather worked for a toffee company, researched his book by sampling numerous treats and touring confectionery plants and factories around the globe, including Hershey's Chocolate World in Pennsylvania and the Haribo plant in England, which manufactures gummy bears. "The writing in general is light and tongue-in-cheek, scattered with some truly dreadful puns, though clearly well-researched and factually accurate," noted Stephanie Perry on the *Steph's Book Reviews* Web site. Perry added that the author "retains an admirably well-adjusted view of the cosmic importance of his scholarly focus, and steers clear of academic pomposity. If anything, the writing is perhaps a little too jolly or chummy, but then, we are talking about a history of candy here—it's hard to take any of this too seriously, which seems to be exactly Richardson's point." According to Tom Jaine, reviewing *Sweets* on the *Guardian Unlimited* Web site. "Richardson has pulled countless plums out of this lucky dip of a subject." Jaine concluded, "His enthusiasm is boundless, his love of sugar knows no limit."

BIOGRAPHICAL AND CRITICAL SOURCES:

PERIODICALS

Booklist, December 1, 2002, Mark Knoblauch, review of *Sweets: A History of Temptation,* p. 633.

Library Journal, November 1, 2002, John Charles, review of *Sweets,* p. 123; September 1, 2004, Valerie Nye, review of *The Vanguard Landscapes and Gardens of Martha Schwartz,* p. 147; November 1, 2005, Phillip Oliver, review of *English Gardens in the Twentieth Century: From the Archives of "Country Life,"* p. 105.

Los Angeles Times, December 2, 2002, Merle Rubin, review of *Sweets,* p. E11.

New York Times Book Review, December 8, 2002, Jane and Michael Stern, review of *Sweets,* p. 6.

People, November 25, 2002, Lan N. Nguyen, review of *Sweets,* p. 47.

Publishers Weekly, October 14, 2002, review of *Sweets,* p. 77.

ONLINE

Guardian Unlimited, http://books.guardian.co.uk/ (October 12, 2002), Tom Jaine, "La Dolce Vita," review of *Sweets.*

Steph's Book Reviews, http://www.stephsbookreviews. com/ (February 3, 2003), Stephanie Perry, review of *Sweets.**

* * *

RIECKHOFF, Paul 1975-

PERSONAL: Born 1975; son of an electrician and a nurse. *Education:* Amherst College, B.A., 1998.

ADDRESSES: Home—New York, NY. *E-mail*—info@ iava.com.

CAREER: Writer, soldier, activist, educator, television and radio commentator, film producer, investment banker, coach, and administrator. Iraq and Afghanistan Veterans of America (IAVA), founder and executive director; Operation Truth, founder. JP Morgan, investment banking analyst, 1999-2001. Worked as a high school football coach. Coproducer of documentary, *When I Came Home;* executive producer of *The Wolf,* Los Angeles, CA. Frequent guest on radio and television stations and networks, including *The Week with George Stephanopoulos,* ABC, *Hannity & Colmes,* Fox News Channel, *NBC Nightly News, 60 Minutes II,* CBS, *Paula Zahn Now,* CNN, *World News Tonight,*

ABC, *Al Franken Show,* Air America, and *All Things Considered,* National Public Radio. *Military service:* Enlisted in U.S. Army Reserves, 1998; served with 812th Military Police Company; served as an infantry officer with the 3rd Infantry and 1st Armored Divisions in Iraq, 2001-04; first lieutenant in New York Army National Guard, 2004—.

WRITINGS:

Chasing Ghosts: A Soldier's Fight for America from Baghdad to Washington, NAL Caliber (New York, NY), 2006.

Contributor to periodicals, including *AlterNet* and the *International Herald Tribune.*

SIDELIGHTS: Paul Rieckhoff is a writer, activist, and former Army infantry officer who served a ten-month tour of duty in some of the more dangerous areas of Iraq. A former investment banker on Wall Street, Rieckhoff left that job a few days before the September 11th terrorist attacks. Later, he spent several weeks working as a volunteer in the rescue effort at ground zero. Rieckhoff volunteered for duty in Iraq, and in 2003, he was deployed there with the 3rd Infantry Division. As a platoon leader, he commanded hundreds of combat patrols in the Adamiyah section of Baghdad. Although the thirty-eight soldiers under his command did sustain some injuries, they all returned alive. Rieckhoff was released from active duty in March, 2004, and currently serves as an infantry officer in the New York Army National Guard.

While in Iraq, Rieckhoff experienced firsthand the conditions under which American soldiers have been expected to operate. He observed the poor planning, lack of material support, and inadequate mission goals, as well as the insufficient number of troops available to make operations in Iraq work properly. Above all, he saw how the deficiencies in American foreign policy in Iraq only made matters worse in a volatile environment where Americans have sometimes been seen as invaders rather than liberators.

When he returned to civilian life after active duty, Rieckhoff knew that the military service members needed a voice outside of government, one that had

direct experience and knew what was needed to make their mission safer and more successful. As an advocate for the soldiers who have served in the Middle East, Rieckhoff founded and serves as the executive director of Iraq and Afghanistan Veterans of America (IAVA), an organization dedicated to the needs of veterans who have been involved in the War on Terror. He is also the founder of Operation Truth, an organization designed "to advocate for better pay, family support, equipment and counseling for current and former soldiers—and to provide a forum for veterans to discuss what went right, and what went wrong, in Afghanistan and Iraq," noted Jennifer Barrett Ozols in an article on *MSNBC.com.*

In *Chasing Ghosts: A Soldier's Fight for America from Baghdad to Washington,* Rieckhoff tells the story of his military and combat experience in Iraq and the problems he experienced there. He recounts in detail the combat operations, the constant worry about attack, the tense relationship between the American military and the Iraqi citizenry, and the supremely frustrating attempts to fight an insurgency that appeared to have the ability to appear and disappear at will like the ghosts in the book's title. His work also showcases his attempts to connect with members of both the Republican and Democrat parties in order to improve conditions for soldiers in Iraq. *Booklist* reviewer Frieda Murray called Rieckhoff's book "a most commendable eyewitness report on Iraq." Nancy Larrabee, writing in the *Library Journal,* observed that *Chasing Ghosts* is a "somewhat angry but undeniably proud narrative" presented with the intent to illustrate "circumstances in Iraq from a soldier's perspective."

BIOGRAPHICAL AND CRITICAL SOURCES:

PERIODICALS

Booklist, May 15, 2006, Frieda Murray, review of *Chasing Ghosts: A Soldier's Fight for America from Baghdad to Washington,* p. 20.

Book World, July 16, 2006, Stephanie Giry, "Beyond Our Borders," review of *Chasing Ghosts,* p. 13.

Library Journal, May 1, 2006, Nancy Larrabee, review of *Chasing Ghosts,* p. 103.

Mother Jones, August 14, 2005, biography of Paul Rieckhoff.

New York Times, May 1, 2004, Carl Hulse, "Iraq Veteran Will Deliver War Critique for Democrats," p. A11; May 2, 2004, Anthony

Ramirez, "National Guard Officer Offers Criticism of Bush's Iraq Plans," p. A16; October 29, 2004, Lynda Richardson, "Back from Iraq, and Fighting for Soldiers," profile of Paul Rieckhoff, p. B2.

Publishers Weekly, March 27, 2006, review of *Chasing Ghosts,* p. 75.

ONLINE

MSNBC.com, http://www.msnbc.com/ (August 6, 2004), Jennifer Barrett Ozols, "Q&A: A Soldier Seeks the Truth about Iraq," interview with Paul Rieckhoff.

Paul Rieckhoff Home Page, http://www.paulrieckhoff. com (May 14, 2007).

Paul Rieckhoff MySpace page, http://www.myspace. com/paulrieckhoff (May 24, 2007).

PBS Now, http://www.pbs.org/now/ (June 30, 2006), "Murder amidst War: Interview with Paul Rieckhoff."*

*   *   *

ROBERTS, David 1944-

PERSONAL: Born 1944; married.

ADDRESSES: Agent—The Andrew Lownie Literary Agency Ltd., 17 Sutherland St., London SW1V 4JU, England. *E-mail*—dr@lordedwardcorinth.co.uk.

CAREER: Former editor for publishing company Chatto & Windus; former editorial director, Weidenfeld & Nicolson; former partner, Michael O'Mara Books; full-time writer, 2000—.

WRITINGS:

"EDWARD CORINTH AND VERITY BROWN" SERIES

Sweet Poison, Carroll & Graf Publishers (New York, NY), 2001.

Bones of the Buried, Constable (London, England), 2001.

Hollow Crown, Carroll & Graf Publishers (New York, NY), 2002.

Dangerous Sea, Carroll & Graf Publishers (New York, NY), 2003.

The More Deceived, Constable (London, England), 2004.

A Grave Man, Constable (London, England), 2005.

The Quality of Mercy, Carroll & Graf Publishers (New York, NY), 2006.

SIDELIGHTS: David Roberts's mystery series featuring English nobleman Lord Edward Corinth and communist journalist Verity Brown has frequently been compared to the Lord Peter Wimsey books by Dorothy L. Sayers. Set in the 1930s, the novels mix mystery and political intrigue with the burgeoning romance between seemingly opposite personalities. The romance and banter between Edward and Verity add some levity to the stories. Critics often compliment the author on his ability to capture the angst of the time, as well as the attitudes of England's upper class, in a world increasingly threatened by the rising Nazi menace.

The main characters are introduced in *Sweet Poison.* The year is 1935, and when an English general, the Duke of Mersham, is poisoned at a dinner party, there are many suspects. Among them are a German diplomat and an Englishman who held the victim responsible for his brother's death in World War I. Edward happens to be the duke's younger brother, and he sets out to find the killer, aided by reporter Brown. "Readers waiting for another Christie redux will find great pleasure in this thoroughly enjoyable first novel," predicted George Needham in *Booklist,* while Rex E. Klett declared it a "finely tuned historical" in his *Library Journal* review.

Brown is in Spain during the months before the civil war there in *Bones of the Buried,* and she contacts Corinth for help when a fellow communist—and former lover—David Griffiths-Jones is imprisoned on false murder charges. While Lord Edward quickly shows that the accused is innocent, he later suspects connections between the deaths of several Eton alumni, including the man Griffiths-Jones had supposedly murdered. "Not much for Verity to do here except be duped," remarked a *Kirkus Reviews* writer, "but Roberts provides a solid primer on Eton society." Although a *Publishers Weekly* critic called the tale "intriguing," the reviewer felt that "a few logical inconsistencies . . . undercut a compelling historical." *Booklist* contributor David Pitt, however, complimented the author's accurate historical detail in a novel "ideal for fans of politically charged period yarns."

With *Hollow Crown* and *Dangerous Sea,* critics found Roberts achieving his stride. Lord Edward's skills are increasingly being sought after by England's Foreign Office for various sensitive matters, and with *Hollow Crown,* the sensitive materials are potentially embarrassing love letters written by King Edward VIII. In *Dangerous Sea,* he is asked to help protect Lord Benyon during a sea voyage. Naturally, mysterious murders occur in both books that Edward must deal with, and Verity lends her aid, as well. With *Hollow Crown,* a *Publishers Weekly* critic complimented the "telling period detail and an intelligent portrayal of the political issues behind the Abdication Crisis." The romance between Edward and Verity, whose attraction for one another intermittently outweighs their political differences, finally achieves consummation in a book that is a "solid entry in [Roberts's] stylish cozy series," according to a *Publishers Weekly* reviewer.

Roberts occasionally brings real historical people into his novels, as he does in *The More Deceived,* in which Winston Churchill makes an appearance. Verity, unfortunately, does not like Churchill at first, a fact that causes a rift in her relationship with Edward. In later installments, however, the famous British leader begins to grow on her, despite her views on politics. Meanwhile, *The More Deceived* has Lord Edward helping the Foreign Office investigate sources providing Churchill with information about the Nazis. Killings within the Foreign Office set off an investigation in this "cleverly plotted whodunnit," remarked Margaret Flanagan in *Booklist,* who also called Edward and Verity "two charming romantic foils." "Roberts adroitly combines engaging lessons on the politics of the day with a compelling, well-paced story," reported a *Publishers Weekly* critic.

Attention turns increasingly from the war in Spain to Nazi Germany with *A Grave Man* and *The Quality of Mercy.* Some critics of these novels felt that Roberts struggles a bit with his characters, who are having trouble with their relationship in *A Grave Man.* A number of reviewers also believed that overly complicated plotting in the novel proves problematic. The former mystery has the pair investigating the murder of a famous archaeologist, while in *The Quality of Mercy,* they each aid in the escape of Jewish refugees from the impending invasion of Austria by Germany. A *Publishers Weekly* writer remarked that in *A Grave Man,* "Roberts does a fine job of elucidating the politics of the period," but the souring relationship between the main characters "puts a definite damper" on the story. A *Kirkus Reviews* contributor considered all the political intrigue "a little too complicated" but in this case felt that the "sleuths complement each other well." Michele Leber asserted in the *Library Journal,* though, that *A Grave Man* is "just the ticket for Dorothy Sayers fans." Reviewing *The Quality of Mercy,* a *Publishers Weekly* contributor reported that this seventh installment "falls short of the high standard" of the previous books, but that the carefully described setting "adds luster to the story." Sarah Abel, writing for *Shots Magazine,* went further, stating that "David Roberts weaves an abundance of historical detail into his story giving the reader a rich flavour of a world on the edge of war," and that "*The Quality of Mercy* is a substantial, intelligent read peppered with artistic references, literary quotes and fascinating snippets of history."

BIOGRAPHICAL AND CRITICAL SOURCES:

PERIODICALS

Booklist, May 1, 2000, GraceAnne A. DeCandido, review of *Sweet Poison,* p. 1599; November 15, 2000, review of *Sweet Poison,* p. 623; September 15, 2001, David Pitt, review of *Bones of the Buried,* p. 200; November 15, 2004, Margaret Flanagan, review of *The More Deceived,* p. 566; November 15, 2006, Steve Weinberg, review of *The Quality of Mercy,* p. 36.

Drood Review of Mystery, November 1, 2000, review of *Sweet Poison,* p. 18.

Kirkus Reviews, August 15, 2001, review of *Bones of the Buried,* p. 1172; November 15, 2002, review of *Hollow Crown,* p. 1660; October 15, 2003, review of *Dangerous Sea,* p. 1255; November 1, 2005, review of *A Grave Man,* p. 1166; October 15, 2006, review of *The Quality of Mercy,* p. 1049.

Library Journal, December 1, 2000, Rex Klett, review of *Sweet Poison,* p. 195; November 1, 2004, Rex E. Klett, review of *The More Deceived,* p. 62; December 1, 2005, Michele Leber, review of *A Grave Man,* p. 103.

Publishers Weekly, September 3, 2001, review of *Bones of the Buried,* p. 66; December 16, 2002, review of *Hollow Crown,* p. 48; November 24,

2003, review of *Dangerous Sea,* p. 45; October 11, 2004, review of *More Deceived,* p. 59; November 14, 2005, review of *A Grave Man,* p. 48; October 16, 2006, review of *The Quality of Mercy,* p. 37.

Reference & Research Book News, February 1, 2000, review of *Sweet Poison,* p. 175.

ONLINE

Andrew Lownie Literary Agency Web site, http://www.andrewlownie.co.uk/ (April 1, 2006), description of David Roberts's detective series and brief biography of the author.

Shots Magazine Online, http://www.shotsmag.co.uk/ (October 1, 2006), Sarah Abel, review of *The Quality of Mercy;* (November 1, 2006), Catherine Hunt, review of *A Grave Man.**

*   *   *

ROBERTS, Mark D. 1957(?)-

PERSONAL: Born c. 1957; married; wife's name Linda; children: two. *Education:* Harvard University, B.A. (magna cum laude), 1979, M.A., 1984, Ph.D., 1992.

ADDRESSES: Home—CA. *Office*—Irvine Presbyterian Church, 4445 Alton Pkwy., Irvine, CA 92604. *E-mail*—roberts@irvinepres.com.

CAREER: Harvard University, Cambridge, MA, teaching fellow, 1980-83; Hollywood Presbyterian Church, Hollywood, CA, associate pastor of education, 1987-91; Irvine Presbyterian Church, Irvine, CA, senior pastor, 1991—; Fuller Theological Seminary, Pasadena, CA, adjunct assistant professor, 1994—; San Francisco Theological Seminary, Pasadena, CA, adjunct instructor, 1995-2001.

MEMBER: Phi Beta Kappa.

AWARDS, HONORS: Danforth Fellowship, Harvard University.

WRITINGS:

The Communicator's Commentary: Ezra, Nehemiah, Esther, Word Books, 1993.

After "I Believe": Experiencing Authentic Christian Living, Baker Books (Grand Rapids, MI), 2002.

Jesus Revealed: Know Him Better to Love Him Better, WaterBrook Press (Colorado Springs, CO), 2002.

Dare to Be True: Living in the Freedom of Complete Honesty, WaterBrook Press (Colorado Springs, CO), 2003.

No Holds Barred: Wrestling with God in Prayer, WaterBrook Press (Colorado Springs, CO), 2005.

Can We Trust the Gospels? Investigating the Reliability of Matthew, Mark, Luke, and John, Crossway Books (Wheaton, IL), 2007.

Contributor, editorial board member, and author of "Lyrical Poetry" column for *Worship Leader.*

SIDELIGHTS: Mark D. Roberts is a pastor who has written numerous books on religion and faith. He has particularly been interested in the place of religion in modern society and how faith can be incorporated into a person's real life. In *Jesus Revealed: Know Him Better to Love Him Better,* Roberts addresses what he explains as the general lack of knowledge about Jesus Christ among most Christians. While Roberts acknowledges that Christians understand the basic tenets of their faith, he states that they do not delve deeper into the complexities of the man behind the religion. He seeks to uncover these layers, describing Christ as both man and God, rabbi, prophet, and savior. A reviewer for *Publishers Weekly* remarked that "the prose is not lively enough to capture and maintain the attention required for such a multifaceted, in-depth study," but nevertheless felt the book should prove a useful tool for anyone looking for details about Christ.

No Holds Barred: Wrestling with God in Prayer takes a close look at the Psalms, both as prayer and as emotional links to God. Roberts notes that the Presbyterian denomination has a reputation of conservatism that often seems in conflict with more emotionally charged prayer. He claims, though, that to truly embrace religion it is important to understand God's attitude toward all facets of life, and that many of those areas touch on very deep emotions, all of which have a place in the human psyche. A *Publishers Weekly* contributor remarked that Roberts "skillfully dissects the Psalms and pleads for fellow believers to step alongside him."

BIOGRAPHICAL AND CRITICAL SOURCES:

PERIODICALS

Publishers Weekly, July 15, 2002, review of *Jesus Revealed: Know Him Better to Love Him Better,* p. 69; February 28, 2005, review of *No Holds Barred: Wrestling with God in Prayer,* p. 62.

ONLINE

Central Park Bench Blog, http://centralparkbench. blogspot.com/ (September 20, 2005), review of *No Holds Barred.*
Daily Psalm, http://www.thedailypsalm.com (April 30, 2007), Mark D. Robert's devotional Web site.
Law Religion Culture Review Blog, http:// lawreligionculturereview.blogspot.com/ (March 9, 2005), review of *Jesus Revealed.*
Mark D. Roberts Home Page, http://www.markd roberts.com (September 19, 2004).*

*   *   *

ROBINSON, Elizabeth 1961-

PERSONAL: Born 1961. *Education:* Bard College, B.A., 1984; Brown University, M.A., 1987; Pacific School of Religion, M.Div., 1995, M.A., 1999.

ADDRESSES: Home—CO. *E-mail*—elzarob@comcast. net.

CAREER: Has taught at University of Colorado, Boulder.

AWARDS, HONORS: Gertrude Stein Awards in Innovative Poetry, 1993-1994, 1994-1995, 2004-2005; National Poetry Series Award, for *Pure Descent,* 2001; Fence Modern Poets Prize, 2002, for *Apprehend.*

WRITINGS:

POETRY

In the Sequence of Falling Things, Paradigm Press (Sausalito, CA), 1990.

Bed of Lists, Kelsey St. Press (Berkeley, CA), 1990.
House Made of Silver, Kelsey St. Press (Berkeley, CA), 2000.
Harrow, Omnidawn (Richmond, CA), 2001.
Apprehend, Fence Books (New York, NY), 2003.
Pure Descent, Sun & Moon Press 2003.
Apostrophe, Apogee Press (Berkeley, CA), 2006.
Under That Silky Roof, Burning Deck (Providence RI), 2006.

POETRY CHAPBOOKS

My Name Happens Also, Burning Deck Press, 1987.
Nearings, Leave Press, 1991.
String, French Bread Press, 1992.
Iemanje, Meow Press, 1993.
Eight Etudes, Paradigm Press, 1998.
Other Veins, Absent Roots, Instress, 1998.
As Betokening, Quarry Press, 1998.
Lodger, Arcturus Editions, 1999.
Refractory Responses, Seeing Eye Books, 2003.
The End of the World, Left Hand Books, 2005.
Exequey, Furniture Press, 2006.
The Golem, Phylum Press, 2006.
Murderous Secrets, Wintered Series, 2006.
Carrington, Hot Whiskey Press, 2006.

Contributor to anthologies, including *49+1, Nouveaux Poetes Americains,* Editions Royaumont, 1991; *Writing from the New Coast,* Oblek Editions, 1993; *The Gertrude Stein Awards in Innovative American Poetry,* Sun & Moon Press, 1993-94; *Primary Trouble,* Talisman House, 1995; *American Poetry: The Next Generation,* Carnegie Mellon Press, 2000; *The Best American Poetry of 2002,* Scribner Poetry, 2003; *The Grand Permission: Essays on Motherhood and Poetics,* Wesleyan University Press, 2003; *Enough: Poems in Protest of the War,* O Books, 2003; and *Isn't It Romantic,* Verse Press, 2005. Contributor to periodicals, including *Alice Blue, Antennae, Bird Dog, Boomerang, Chase Park, Colorado Review, Conjunctions, Copper Nickel, Denver Quarterly, Dislocate, Epoch, Fracture, Fence, Germ, In Tense, Ixnay, Kenning, New American Writing, New Review, Nocturnes, Parthenon West, Poetry Salzburg Review, Pool, Small Town, Sulfur, Third Bed, Transmission, Untitled, Ur Vox, Volt,* and *Women's Studies Quarterly.* Coeditor, *26* (magazine) and of "EtherDome" (chapbook series).

SIDELIGHTS: Elizabeth Robinson developed her love of poetry at a young age. Her family attended church regularly, and she recalls memorizing Bible verses as a child. In an interview for the *Here Comes Everybody* blog, Robinson remarked: "I remember especially liking Job, and the beginning of the gospel of John, with all its braiding of phrases." She also enjoyed poems such as Edward Lear's "The Owl and the Pussycat" and Robert Louis Stevenson's "At the Seaside," as well as the works of Emily Dickinson. Her interest was solidified in college, where she encountered a broader range of poets. However, she went on to study philosophy and ethics, and eventually religion, all of which provides fodder for her own poetry. As she told *Here Comes Everybody:* "I think that philosophical thinking can be similar to poetic thinking, in terms of recreating logic and offering intellectual and creative permissions."

Robinson has written numerous volumes of poems, and has won an assortment of accolades and prizes. In addition, she serves as a coeditor of the literary magazine *26* and the "EtherDome" series of chapbooks, the latter of which strives to promote the work of emerging women poets. But it is her own work for which she is best known and critically acclaimed. Patrick Pritchett, in a review of *Apprehend* for the *Jacket* Web site, wrote that Robinson "over the last few years has quietly, but unmistakably, emerged as the one of the finest poets of her generation." Of the collection, which focuses primarily on spiritual desire and the crises to which it sometimes leads, the critic remarked: "Robinson's wisdom is to acknowledge that what we ask of the poem, as of the fairy tale, is that it affirms for us that yes, the world is broken, but that nevertheless, we are somehow safe inside of it."

BIOGRAPHICAL AND CRITICAL SOURCES:

PERIODICALS

Publishers Weekly, October 16, 2000, review of *House Made of Silver,* p. 67; July 31, 2006, review of *Under That Silky Roof,* p. 55.
World Literature Today, January 1, 1992, review of *Bed of Lists,* p. 140.

ONLINE

Here Comes Everybody Blog, http://herecomes everybody.blogspot.com/ (April 19, 2005), interview with Elizabeth Robinson.

Jacket, http://jacketmagazine.com/ (April 30, 2007), Patrick Pritchett, review of *Apprehend.*
Small Press Traffic, http://www.sptraffic.org/ (April 30, 2007), Sarah Anne Cox, review of *Harrow.*

*   *   *

ROFFEY, Monique 1965-

PERSONAL: Born 1965, in Port of Spain, Trinidad. *Education:* Holds a degree from University of East Anglia; Lancaster University, M.A. (with distinction), doctoral studies.

ADDRESSES: Home—London, England. *E-mail*—M.Roffey@sussex.ac.uk.

CAREER: Amnesty International, human rights activist; Arvon Foundation, Devon, England, codirector of Totleigh Barton Centre, 2002-06; University of Sussex, Sussex, England, Royal Literary Fund fellow and writer in residence, 2006—.

WRITINGS:

Sun Dog (novel), Scribner (London, England), 2002, published as *August Frost,* Atlantic Monthly Press (New York, NY), 2003.

Contributor of short fiction to journals, including *New Writing 13* and *Matter.*

SIDELIGHTS: Monique Roffey was born in Port of Spain, Trinidad, and later moved to England, where she attended Lancaster University and worked as a journalist and human rights activist. Her debut novel, *Sun Dog,* published as *August Frost* in the United States, was critically well received. The book combines the qualities of fantasy and fable in a realistic framework, chronicling the journey of August, a Londoner in his thirties whose body suffers strange alterations according to the seasons. August goes in search of his birth father, whom he hopes can provide him with answers regarding his peculiar physical traits. A contributor to *Kirkus Reviews* found the book to be "an oddly moving and poignant tale, unfortunately marred by an amorphous beginning and a pace far too leisurely." On the other hand, a *Publishers Weekly* reviewer described the book as "mournful, quietly suspenseful and gently surreal," and, while noting that the pace might have been swifter at times, concluded that it "marks the arrival of a talented newcomer." *New York Times Book Review* contributor Kate Bolick felt that "the themes of identity, self-acceptance, belonging and love are made mawkish by too much vague, florid language," while *Booklist* critic Kevin Canfield called Roffey's debut "rich and layered and sophisticated in a way that not enough novels are."

BIOGRAPHICAL AND CRITICAL SOURCES:

PERIODICALS

Booklist, January 1, 2003, Kevin Canfield, review of *August Frost,* p. 851.

Kirkus Reviews, December 1, 2002, review of *August Frost,* p. 1727.

New York Times Book Review, April 6, 2003, Kate Bolick, review of *August Frost,* p. 24.

Publishers Weekly, March 3, 2003, review of *August Frost,* p. 55.

ONLINE

Spannered.org, http://www.spannered.org/ (April 30, 2007), review of *Sun Dog.*

*　　　*　　　*

ROGAL, Stan 1950-
(Stanley William Rogal)

PERSONAL: Born March 5, 1950, in Vancouver, British Columbia, Canada. *Education:* Simon Fraser University, B.A., 1982; York University, M.A., 1988.

ADDRESSES: *Home*—Toronto, Ontario, Canada.

CAREER: Actor, director, and poet. Idler Pub, Toronto, Ontario, Canada, ran reading series for ten years; Bald Ego Theatre, Toronto, former cofounder and artistic director; Bulletproof Theatre, Toronto, artistic director. Actor in stage productions, including *The Day Room, Sleepers Awake,* and *Care Naked.*

MEMBER: League of Canadian Poets, Playwrights Union.

AWARDS, HONORS: Poetry award, Toronto Arts Council, 1990; Canada Council grant, 1997; fiction award, Toronto Arts Council, 1998.

WRITINGS:

POETRY

Sweet Betsy from Pike, Wolsak & Wynn (Toronto, Ontario, Canada), 1992.

The Imaginary Museum, ECW (Toronto, Ontario, Canada), 1993.

Geometry of the Odd, Wolsak & Wynn (Toronto, Ontario, Canada), 1999.

Lines of Embarkation, Coach House (Toronto, Ontario, Canada), 1999.

Sub Rosa, Wolsak & Wynn (Toronto, Ontario, Canada), 2003.

All Watched Over by Machines of Loving Grace, Above/Ground Press (Ottawa, Ontario, Canada), 2004.

In Search of the Emerald City, Seraphim Editions (Toronto, Ontario, Canada), 2004.

Fabulous Freaks, Wolsak & Wynn (Toronto, Ontario, Canada), 2005.

FICTION

What Passes for Love (short stories), Insomniac Press (Toronto, Ontario, Canada), 1996.

Personations (short stories), Exile Editions (Toronto, Ontario, Canada), 1997.

Restless (short stories), Insomniac Press (Toronto, Ontario, Canada), 1998.

The Long Drive Home (novel), Insomniac Press (Toronto, Ontario, Canada), 1999.

Bafflegab (novel), Insomniac Press (Toronto, Ontario, Canada), 2001.

Tell Him You're Married (short stories), Insomniac Press (Toronto, Ontario, Canada), 2002.

Also author of plays, including: (and director) *Sunny Boy Recites,* produced in Toronto, Ontario, Canada; *Blood Suit;* (and director) *Portrait of Ophelia, Drowned; Orpheus,* produced in Toronto; (and director) *Gulf,* produced in Toronto; (and director) *Dick and Dick Do America;* and *The Threepenny EPIC Cabaret,* produced in Toronto. Work represented in anthologies, including *The Last Word,* Insomniac Press (Toronto, Ontario, Canada), 1995; *Carnival,* Insomniac Press, 1996; and *Vintage '96,* Quarry Press, 1997.

SIDELIGHTS: Canadian Stan Rogal works across a broad range of genres, including fiction, poetry, and plays. He began his career as an actor and director in Toronto, Ontario, where he has served as cofounder and artistic director of the Bald Ego Theatre, and was also artistic director of the Bulletproof Theatre. But Rogal's writing expanded beyond theater to include short stories, novels, and poetry collections. His first book, *Sweet Betsy from Pike,* includes a series of poems that relate to the exploits of a Canadian woman traveling west. His next collection of poems, *The Imaginary Museum,* was called "a compelling journey through a talented and serious poet's mind" by *Canadian Book Review Annual* critic Peter Baltensperger. The book drew a qualified response from *Books in Canada* contributor Margaret Sweatman, who lamented Rogal's alleged "aesthetic posture" but acknowledged his "stylish and courageous language."

Rogal's next effort, *What Passes for Love,* is a collection of short stories described by *Quill & Quire* contributor Peter Rudd as "dense sketches." Among the tales in this collection are "Skin Deep," in which a woman, to the consternation of her husband, slowly mutates—body part by body part—into another person; "Home after All," wherein a couple make some surprising discoveries about their apartment; and "A Taste of Apricots," wherein a nameless protagonist reflects on his relationships and his identity. Discussing "A Taste of Apricots" in a *Books in Canada* interview with Judith Fitzgerald, Rogal acknowledged the story's "dreamlike quality, its weirdness." Speaking of the entire volume, Rogal told Fitzgerald: "I wanted to play with different forms, voices, tenses, echoes, and approaches, so I wasn't just writing the same story over and over again. I also wanted to make sure the stories were linked in terms of their thematic coherence." Fitzgerald observed that the stories in *What Passes for Love* "take issue with adultery,

betrayal, passion, obsession . . . , forgiveness, and the painful paradoxes of pleasure, while blending lyrical substance and a crisp, uncluttered, and often colloquial style with a gritty . . . approach that belies [Rogal's] disarming propriety concerning what does, in fact, pass for love." Rudd, meanwhile, felt that the various tales "are fun to read," and he characterized Rogal's voice as "immediately familiar and appealing."

The Long Drive Home also relates unlikely events. In this novel two professional killers—both middle-aged, both plagued with exhausting family duties and troublesome prostate glands—and an unscrupulous contractor, whose problems include an alcoholic girlfriend and a moronic daughter, all find themselves conducting various duties in rural French Canada. "Don't be surprised," concluded *Booklist* reviewer Whitney Scott, "if *The Long Drive Home* becomes a fine film directed, for course, by [Robert] Altman or [Quentin] Tarantino." Nathaniel George Moore likewise remarked in *Half Empty* on the novel's suitability for film adaptation, commenting that it is "broken up into almost cinematic styled clips" and has an "almost road movie style."

The same year that *The Long Ride Home* was published, Rogal also released two poetry collections: *Lines of Embarkation* and *Geometry of the Odd.* Moore, in his *Half Empty* review, compared *Lines of Embarkation* to Rogal's earlier verse collections and declared that the latter volume "seems a lot more logical and tighter." The critic added that Rogal's poetics "use logic as humour . . . , taking away the muse, or taking the muse hostage, silencing the predictable nature of the reader to the page, disengaging them from the cinematic spoon-fed familiar traits of language." Devin Crawley, writing for *Quill & Quire,* remarked that the poems in *Geometry of the Odd* "reward multiple readings with their subtle, latent imagery and repeated phrases that resonate elegantly." Crawley also felt that "Rogal's intellect bores into the world and manufactures startling conceits."

Rogal's novel *Bafflegab* is a disjointed work that remarks upon the nature and conditions of writing. Shane Neilson, writing in the *Danforth Review,* compared it to "a fragmented, dark, antiheroic ramble of a novel—akin to Dostoevsky's 'Notes from Underground.'" Structurally, the book is less novelistic in form and more similar to a play, complete with dialogue that has been read aloud on a Toronto radio station. Neilson went on to state: "This novel attempts something grand and doesn't achieve it," adding: "It's too easy to skewer the masses, much more difficult to prod them into metamorphosis—and that's what Rogal is trying to do in this novel." The critic did, however, remark upon the musicality and rhythm of Rogal's writing that contributes to the reader's desire to vocalize the dialogue aloud. Stephen Guy-Bray, in a review for *Canadian Literature,* found the book to be "always interesting, often very funny, and sometimes lyrical."

BIOGRAPHICAL AND CRITICAL SOURCES:

PERIODICALS

ARC, Dec 22, 2004, review of *Sub Rosa,* p. 105.

Booklist, February 1, 1993, review of *Sweet Betsy from Pike,* p. 52; September 1, 1999, Whitney Scott, review of *The Long Drive Home,* p. 69.

Books in Canada, April 1, 1994, Margaret Sweatman, review of *The Imaginary Museum,* p. 48; November 1, 1996, Judith Fitzgerald, "There Really Is Something Called Love," review of *What Passes for Love,* pp. 15-17; May 1, 2003, review of *Tell Him You're Married,* p. 18.

Canadian Book Review Annual, January 1, 1994, Peter Baltensperger, review of *The Imaginary Museum,* p. 218; January 1, 1997, Louise E. Allin, review of *What Passes for Love,* pp. 212-213; January 1, 1999, review of *The Long Drive Home,* p. 184; January 1, 2002, review of *Bafflegab,* p. 180; January 1, 2004, Bert Almon, review of *Sub Rosa,* p. 244.

Canadian Literature, March 22, 1994, Lesley D. Clement, "Journeys and Returns," review of *Sweet Betsy from Pike,* p. 141; March 22, 2003, Stephen Guy-Bray, "Short Pieces," review of *Bafflegab,* pp. 141-142.

Malahat Review, September 22, 2004, Tanis MacDonald, review of *Sub Rosa,* p. 88.

Matrix, January 1, 2001, review of *Bafflegab,* pp. 85-86.

Quill & Quire, April 1, 1996, Peter Rudd, review of *What Passes for Love,* p. 31; October 1, 1999, Devin Crawley, review of *Geometry of the Odd,* p. 40; December 1, 2000, review of *Bafflegab,* pp. 27-28.

ONLINE

Canadian Literature, http://www.canlit.ca/ (April 30, 2007), Eva-Marie Kröller, "Faux Fifties," review of *Restless.*

Danforth Review, http://www.danforthreview.com/ (April 30, 2007), Shane Neilson, review of *Bafflegab.*

Half Empty, http://www.articles.halfempty.com/ (January 16, 2000), Nathaniel George Moore, "Stan Rogal: The Imaginary Muse."

This, http://dev.thismagazine.com/ (April 30, 2007), Chris Chambers, "Words Are Not Enough," review of *In Search of the Emerald City.**

*   *   *

ROGAL, Stanley William
See ROGAL, Stan

*   *   *

ROONEY, Kathleen 1980-

PERSONAL: Born March 2, 1980, in Beckley, WV; married Martin Seay (a bookseller and writer), August 13, 2005. *Education:* George Washington University, B.A., 2002; Emerson College, M.F.A., 2005. *Politics:* Democrat. *Religion:* Roman Catholic.

ADDRESSES: E-mail—kathleenmrooney@gmail.com.

CAREER: Pacific Lutheran University, Tacoma, WA, visiting assistant professor of English, 2006-07. Cofounder and copublisher of the blog *Rose Metal Press,* 2006—.

WRITINGS:

Reading with Oprah, University of Arkansas Press (Fayetteville, AR), 2005.

Twentysomething Essays by Twentysomething Writers, Random House (New York, NY), 2006.

(Editor, with Abigail Beckel) *Brevity and Echo* (short fiction), Rose Metal Press (Boston, MA), 2006.

Contributor of poetry, with Elisa Gabert, to *MiPOesias, Otoliths, Sawbuck, 21 Stars Review, Cohncher, Dusie,* and *Past Simple.* Contributor of essays and reviews to periodicals, including *Gulf Coast, Another*

Chicago Magazine, Western Humanities Revew, Ninth Letter, Contemporary Poetry Review, Nation, New Hampshire Review, Boston Review, and *Octopus.*

*   *   *

ROOSEVELT, David B. 1942-

PERSONAL: Born 1942, in Fort Worth, TX; son of Elliot and Ruth Roosevelt; grandson of Franklin D. Roosevelt (former president) and Eleanor Roosevelt. *Education:* Texas Christian University, B.A.

CAREER: Philanthropist, consultant, lecturer. Chemical Bank, New York, NY, former executive; Greater Cedar Rapids Community Foundation, Cedar Rapids, IA, chief executive officer, 1996-2003; Netherland-America Foundation, executive director, 2003—. Founding executive director, Arkansas Community Foundation; served on the boards and as a fund-raiser for various charities, including AmeriCorps and the Franklin Delano Roosevelt Memorial fundraising committee.

WRITINGS:

(With Manuela Dunn-Mascetti) *Grandmère: A Personal History of Eleanor Roosevelt* (memoir), introduction by Mike Wallace, Warner Books (New York, NY), 2002.

SIDELIGHTS: David B. Roosevelt is the grandson of former U.S. President Franklin D. Roosevelt and his wife, Eleanor. A philanthropist and frequent lecturer on the history of the Roosevelt family, he is also the author of *Grandmère: A Personal History of Eleanor Roosevelt.* The book includes Roosevelt's own personal memories of his grandmother from his childhood up until her death when he was twenty years old. He was close to his grandmother and spent most of his summers at Val-Kill, her cottage in Hyde Park, New York, with his siblings and cousins. In addition to his own experiences, Roosevelt provides a history of his grandmother's own childhood and upbringing, as well as her fifty-plus-year marriage and life as the wife of a career politician. He provides access to information garnered from family papers, letters, and interviews. A contributor to *Kirkus Reviews* called the book "a lov-

ing tribute distinguished more by the many hitherto unseen family photographs than by the familiar memories." In *Publishers Weekly* a writer labeled Roosevelt's effort "a touching, human-size account of a woman who seemed larger than life." Brenda Hyde, in a review for *Seeds of Knowledge,* found the book to be "an inspiring tale of a woman who doesn't come into her own until she sees her inner beauty and talents and acts upon them."

BIOGRAPHICAL AND CRITICAL SOURCES:

BOOKS

Roosevelt, David B., and Manuela Dunn-Mascetti, *Grandmère: A Personal History of Eleanor Roosevelt,* Warner Books (New York, NY), 2002.

PERIODICALS

Chronicle of Philanthropy, March 20, 2003, Jeffrey Klineman, "New Director's Lineage Is a Bonus," interview with David B. Roosevelt.
Kirkus Reviews, August 1, 2002, review of *Grandmère,* p. 1108.
M2 Best Books, April 8, 2003, Ian Sanderson, review of *Grandmère.*
Publishers Weekly, August 5, 2002, review of *Grandmère,* p. 61.

ONLINE

BookLoons, http://www.bookloons.com/ (May 1, 2007), Hilary Williamsom, review of *Grandmère.*
BookPage, http://www.bookpage.com/ (May 1, 2007), Edward Morris, review of *Grandmère.*
Feminenza Community Web site, http://community.feminenza.org/ (February 10, 2007), R. Weber, review of *Grandmère.*
Seeds of Knowledge, http://www.seedsofknowledge.com/ (May 1, 2007), Brenda Hyde, review of *Grandmère.*

OTHER

CNN Larry King Live, Cable News Network, aired November 28, 2002, interview with David B. Roosevelt and Mike Wallace.*

ROOTS, Garrison 1952-

PERSONAL: Born June 25, 1952, in Abilene, TX. *Education:* Massachusetts College of Art, B.F.A., 1979; Washington University School of Fine Arts, M.F.A., 1981.

ADDRESSES: Office—Sibell-Wolle Fine Arts Building, Campus Box 318, University of Colorado, Boulder, CO 80309-0318.

CAREER: Sculptor, educator. Swain School of Design, New Bedford, MA, instructor, 1981-1982; University of Colorado, Boulder, assistant professor, 1982-89, associate professor, 1989-97, professor of fine arts, 1997—, area coordinator of sculpture, 1982—, department chair and associate chair of graduate studies. Founding member of FUSE Exhibitions and ART-NAUTS (international artists organization); serves on professional panels and on boards of directors, including the Boulder Center for the Visual Arts.

Exhibitions: Solo exhibitions include University Gallery, University of Texas, Arlington, 1979; Merrimac Gallery, St. Louis Community College, St. Louis, MO, 1980; Washington University, St. Louis, MO, 1981; Crapo Gallery, Swain School of Design, New Bedford, MA, 1981; ARC/Raw Space Gallery, Chicago, IL, 1982; Center for Idea Art, Denver, CO, 1983; Los Angeles Institute of Contemporary Art, Los Angeles, CA, 1983; Fort Worth Art Museum, Fort Worth, TX, 1984; Contemporary Arts Center, New Orleans, LA, 1984; Arvada Center for the Arts, Arvada, CO, 1984; Alternative Museum, New York, NY, 1986; University of Colorado Art Galleries, Boulder, 1987; Cincinnati Artists Group Effort, Cincinnati, OH, 1989; Spaces, Cleveland, OH, 1991; Institute for Design and Experimental Art, Sacramento, CA, 1992; University of Colorado Art Galleries, Boulder, 1993; Southwest China Normal University, Sichuan, China, 1993; Laumeier Sculpture Park and Museum, St. Louis, MO, 1996; Bemis Center for Contemporary Art, Omaha, NE, 1999; Dairy Center for the Arts, Boulder, CO, 2003; public commissions at Memphis/Shelby County Public Library, Memphis, TN, Miami International Airport North Terminal, Miami, FL, Dallas Convention Center, Dallas, TX, and Denver Center for the Performing Arts, Denver, CO; work represented in group exhibitions in the United States, Mexico, Peru, Russia, Spain, and Chile.

MEMBER: College Art Association.

AWARDS, HONORS: Grants from the National Endowment for the Arts, 1982, 1984, Colorado Council on the Arts, 1986, 1994, University of Colorado, Boulder, 1992, 1993 (three), 1994, 1996, 1997, 1998, 2003; New Forms regional grant, 1993; WESTAF/NEA fellowship, 1995; Art Institute fellow, University of Wisconsin, Madison, 2004.

WRITINGS:

Designing the World's Best Public Art, Images Publishing Group (Mulgrave, Victoria, Australia), 2002.

Editor of exhibition catalogs.

BIOGRAPHICAL AND CRITICAL SOURCES:

PERIODICALS

Library Journal, September 15, 2002, Michael Dashkin, review of *Designing the World's Best Public Art,* p. 60.

ONLINE

Garrison Roots Home Page, http://www.garrisonroots. com (September 26, 2004).
University of Colorado Web site, http://www.colorado. com/ (May 14, 2007), faculty profile of author.*

*   *   *

ROUNTREE, Helen C. 1944-

PERSONAL: Born October 8, 1944, in Camp LeJeune, NC; daughter of Henning Ainsworth, Jr., and Mildred Ellen Rountree. *Education:* College of William and Mary, A.B, 1966; University of Utah, M.A, 1968; University of Wisconsin, Milwaukee, Ph.D, 1973. *Politics:* Democrat. *Religion:* Episcopalian. *Hobbies and other interests:* Landscape photography, designing and making tapestry afghans, choir singing.

ADDRESSES: Office—Department of Sociology, Old Dominion University, Norfolk, VA, 23529.

CAREER: Old Dominion University, Norfolk, VA, instructor in sociology, 1968-73, assistant professor of anthropology, 1973-80, associate professor, 1980-91, professor of anthropology, 1991-99, professor emerita of anthropology, 1999—. Consultant to Jamestown Settlement Museum, Williamsburg, VA, 1986; Virginia Council on Indians, Richmond, 1993; and Maryland Commission on Indian Affairs, Annapolis, 1995.

MEMBER: Society for Applied Anthropology (fellow), American Anthropological Association (life member), American Society for Ethnohistory (president, 1993-94), Royal Anthropological Institute of Great Britain and Ireland (overseas member).

AWARDS, HONORS: Outstanding Faculty award, State Council of Higher Education for Virginia, 1995.

WRITINGS:

The Powhatan Indians of Virginia: Their Traditional Culture, University of Oklahoma Press (Norman, OK), 1989.

Pocahontas's People: The Powhatan Indians of Virginia through Four Centuries, University of Oklahoma Press (Norman, OK), 1990.

(Editor) *Powhatan Foreign Relations, 1500-1722,* University Press of Virginia (Charlottesville, VA), 1993.

Young Pocahontas in the Indian World, [Yorktown, VA], 1995.

(With Thomas E. Davidson) *Eastern Shore Indians of Virginia and Maryland,* University Press of Virginia (Charlottesville, VA), 1997.

(With E. Randolph Turner III) *Before and after Jamestown: Virginia's Powhatans and Their Predecessors,* foreword by Jerald T. Milanich, University Press of Florida (Gainesville, FL), 2002.

Pocahontas, Powhatan, Opechancanough: Three Indian Lives Changed by Jamestown, University of Virginia Press (Charlottesville, VA), 2005.

(With Wayne E. Clark and Kent Mountford) *John Smith's Chesapeake Voyages, 1607-1609,* University of Virginia Press (Charlottesville, VA), 2007.

SIDELIGHTS: Helen C. Rountree is widely regarded as a leading researcher and writer on Virginia's Native American people and has been made an honorary member of the Nansemond and Upper Mattaponi tribes. She is also the author and editor numerous books focusing on Eastern American Indian tribes, primarily the Powhatans. For example, she served as editor of *Powhatan Foreign Relations, 1500-1722.* In this book, Rountree presents nine essays that examine the relationships that the Powhatan Indians had with other tribes and the newly arrived Europeans. The essays cover a wide range of topics, from physical characteristics of the Indians to their subsistence living. The various authors also examine how the Europeans and the Powhatans viewed each other. Raymond Wilson, writing in the *Journal of American Ethnic History,* commented that the "authors offer a comprehensive look at the thirty Algonquian-speaking tribes collectively known as the Powhatan."

In their book *Eastern Shore Indians of Virginia and Maryland,* Rountree and Thomas E. Davidson delve into the tribes of Virginia and Maryland's Eastern Shore Indians from approximately the year 800 C.E. They provide information on each tribe's characteristics and traditions and also explore the plants and animals that the Indians lived with and used. The authors examine how ecological and geographical difference and changes affected the tribes' various cultures and everyday lives. "With the publication of *Eastern Shore Indians,* anthropologist Helen Rountree coauthors her most compelling work to date," according to Edward Ragan in the *American Indian Quarterly.* "Once again, she enriches our understanding of Native culture in the Chesapeake Bay."

Rountree collaborated with E. Randolph Turner III to write *Before and after Jamestown: Virginia's Powhatans and Their Predecessors.* This general history of the tribe traces their origins back to 900 C.E. and follows the tribes' fortunes to current times. "As a popular history, the work has many strengths," wrote April L. Hatfield in the *Journal of Southern History.* "Its introduction offers a clear and, indeed, interesting primer on the kinds of sources available for studying Indians in both pre-historical and historical periods." Hatfield went on to comment that the book "represents an important synthesis of archaeological, anthropological, and historical material that will interest many general readers."

In her 2005 book, *Pocahontas, Powhatan, Opechancanough: Three Indian Lives Changed by Jamestown,* the author provides a Native American perspective of the settlement of Jamestown and, in the process, includes biographies of Pocahontas, her father Chief Powhatan, and Chief Opechancanough, who captured Captain John Smith. Michael D. Green, writing in *Southern Cultures*, remarked that "if anyone can write a history of the encounter between them and the English at Jamestown from their point of view, it is" Roundtree. Green also wrote that the author "has done a marvelous job in producing a readable, believable book that readers, particularly nonspecialists, should love." Virginia Historical Society Web site contributor Alexander B. Haskell felt that the author "brings to the book a wealth of understanding about seventeenth-century Powhatan culture."

BIOGRAPHICAL AND CRITICAL SOURCES:

PERIODICALS

American Anthropologist, March 1, 1999, review of *Eastern Shore Indians of Virginia and Maryland,* p. 195.

American Historical Review, December 1, 1990, review of *The Powhatan Indians of Virginia: Their Traditional Culture,* p. 1618; June 1, 2006, review of *Pocahontas, Powhatan, and Opechancanough: Three Indian Lives Changed by Jamestown,* p. 821.

American Indian Culture and Research Journal, March 22, 2003, review of *Before and after Jamestown: Virginia's Powhatans and their Predecessors,* p. 106; June 22, 2005, review of *Pocahontas, Powhatan, Opechancanough,* p. 162.

American Indian Quarterly, September 22, 1990, review of *The Powhatan Indians of Virginia,* p. 418; fall, 1998, Edward Ragan, review of *Eastern Shore Indians of Virginia and Maryland,* p. 501.

American Studies International, April 1, 1995, review of *The Powhatan Indians of Virginia,* p. 137.

Choice: Current Reviews for Academic Libraries, September 1, 1993, review of *Powhatan: Foreign Relations, 1500-1722,* p. 206; June 1, 1998, review of *Eastern Shore Indians of Virginia and Maryland,* p. 1752; February 1, 2003, review of *Before and after Jamestown,* p. 1045; March 1, 2006, review of *Pocahontas, Powhatan, Opechancanough,* p. 1290.

Ethnohistory, June 22, 1991, review of *The Powhatan Indians of Virginia,* p. 336; September 22, 1992, review of *Pocahontas's People: The Powhatan Indians of Virginia through Four Centuries,* p. 517; June 22, 1999, review of *Eastern Shore Indians of Virginia and Maryland,* p. 623.

Historical Archaeology, September 22, 1997, review of *Powhatan Foreign Relations, 1500-1722,* p. 122.

Journal of American Ethnic History, January 1, 1992, review of *The Powhatan Indians of Virginia,* p. 77; June 22, 1993, review of *Pocahontas's People,* p. 75; Raymond Wilson, summer, 1997, review of *Powhatan Foreign Relations, 1500-1722,* p. 89.

Journal of American Folklore, June 22, 1993, review of *The Powhatan Indians of Virginia,* p. 373.

Journal of American History, June 1, 1990, review of *The Powhatan Indians of Virginia,* p. 279; December 1, 1991, review of *Pocahontas's People,* p. 1046; September 1, 1994, review of *Powhatan Foreign Relations, 1500-1722,* p. 639; March 1, 1999, review of *Eastern Shore Indians of Virginia and Maryland,* p. 1571; September 1, 2006, review of *Pocahontas, Powhatan, Opechancanough,* p. 494.

Journal of Anthropological Research, March 22, 1999, review of *Eastern Shore Indians of Virginia and Maryland,* p. 172.

Journal of Interdisciplinary History, March 22, 1995, review of *Powhatan Foreign Relations, 1500-1722,* p. 716.

Journal of Southern History, May 1, 1991, reviews of *Pocahontas's People* and *Powhatan Indians of Virginia,* p. 300; August 1, 1994, review of *Powhatan Foreign Relations, 1500-1722,* p. 553; May 1, 1999, review of *Eastern Shore Indians of Virginia and Maryland,* p. 380; November 1, 2003, April L. Hatfield, review of *Before and after Jamestown,* p. 863.

Journal of the West, October 1, 1990, review of *The Powhatan Indians of Virginia,* p. 107.

Library Journal, October 1, 1990, review of *Pocahontas's People,* p. 102.

Mississippi Quarterly, September 22, 1991, review of *Pocahontas's People,* p. 505.

Pacific Historical Review, August 1, 1992, review of *Pocahontas's People,* p. 417.

Quest, fall, 2005, "Helen Clark Rountree," profile of the author.

Reference & Research Book News, August 1, 1989, review of *The Powhatan Indians of Virginia,* p. 8; June 1, 1993, review of *Powhatan Foreign Relations, 1500-1722,* p. 12; May 1, 1998, review of *Eastern Shore Indians of Virginia and Maryland,*

p. 39; August 1, 2005, review of *Pocahontas, Powhatan, Opechancanough,* p. 59.

Southern Cultures, Michael D. Green, summer, 2006, review of *Pocahontas, Powhatan, Opechancanough,* p. 94.

Virginia Magazine of History and Biography, January 1, 1990, review of *The Powhatan Indians of Virginia,* p. 103; April 1, 1991, review of *Pocahontas's People,* p. 204; January 1, 1994, review of *Powhatan Foreign Relations, 1500-1722,* p. 103; June 22, 2002, review of *Before and after Jamestown,* p. 399; March 22, 2006, review of *Pocahontas, Powhatan, Opechancanough,* p. 292.

Virginia Quarterly Review, January 1, 2003, review of *Before and after Jamestown,* p. 9.

Western Historical Quarterly, May 1, 1990, review of *The Powhatan Indians of Virginia,* p. 233; November 1, 1991, review of *Pocahontas's People,* p. 492.

William and Mary Quarterly, April 1, 1990, review of *The Powhatan Indians of Virginia,* p. 303; January 1, 1994, review of *Powhatan Foreign Relations, 1500-1722,* p. 125; July 1, 1999, review of *Eastern Shore Indians of Virginia and Maryland,* p. 633; October 1, 2005, review of *Pocahontas, Powhatan, Opechancanough,* p. 774.

ONLINE

Virginia Historical Society Web site, http://www.vahistorical.org/ (April 23, 2007), Alexander B. Haskell, review of *Pocahontas, Powhatan, Opechancanough.*

Virginia Libraries Web site, http://scholar.lib.vt.edu/ (April 23, 2007), Patricia F. Watkinson, review of *Pocahontas, Powhatan, Opechancanough.**

*   *   *

RUBIN, Aviel 1967-

PERSONAL: Born November 8, 1967, in Manhattan, KS. *Education:* University of Michigan, B.S., 1989, M.S.E., 1991, Ph.D., 1994. *Hobbies and other interests:* Pool, golf, tennis, soccer, photography, piano, playing with his kids.

ADDRESSES: Home—Owing Mills, MD. *E-mail*—rubin@jhu.edu; avi@rubin.net.

CAREER: University of Michigan, Ann Arbor, teaching assistant, 1988-93; IBM, Poughkeepsie, NY, programmer, 1989; Great Lakes Software Co., Howell, MI, programmer, 1990; cryptology and network security research for Bellcore (now Telcordia), 1994-96; New York University, New York, NY, adjunct professor, 1995-99; secure systems researcher for AT&T Labs, 1997-2002; Johns Hopkins University, Baltimore, MD, associate professor, 2003-04, professor of computer science, 2004—, technical director of Information Security Institute, 2003—. Cofounder, Independent Security Evaluators (computer security consulting firm). Visiting professor, École Normale Supérieure, Paris, France, 1999. Director, USENIX Organization, 2000-04.

AWARDS, HONORS: Branstom Prize, University of Michigan, 1986; National Science Foundation fellowship, 1992; Baltimorean of the Year, *Baltimore,* 2003; Pioneer Award, Electronic Frontiers Foundation, 2004.

WRITINGS:

(With Daniel Greer and Marcus J. Ranum) *Web Security Sourcebook,* Wiley Computer (New York, NY), 1997.

White-Hat Security Arsenal: Tackling the Threats, foreword by William R. Cheswick, Addison-Wesley (Boston, MA), 2001.

(With William R. Cheswick and Stephen M. Bellovin) *Firewalls and Internet Security: Repelling the Wily Hacker,* 2nd edition, Addison-Wesley (Boston, MA), 2003.

Brave New Ballot: The Battle to Safeguard Democracy in the Age of Electronic Voting, Morgan Road Books (New York, NY), 2006.

Contributor to books, including, with Marc Waldman and Lorrie Faith Cranor, *Peer to Peer,* O'Reilly & Associates, 2001; and *Communications Policy and Information Technology: Promises, Problems, Prospects,* edited by Lorrie Faith Cranor and Shane Mitchell Greenstein, MIT Press, 2002. Contributor to journals, including *Electronic Commerce Research Journal, Communications of the ACM, Computer Networks, IEEE Internet Computing, Journal of Computer Systems,* and *Computer Communications.* Associate editor, *Electronic Commerce Research Journal,* 1999-2002, *ACM Transactions on Internet Tech-*

nology, 2002-05, *IEEE Securtiy & Privacy Magazine,* 2003—, and *IEEE Transactions on Software Engineering,* 2005-06. Coeditor, *Electronic Newsletter of the IEEE Technical Committee on Security & Privacy,* 1998. Member of editorial board, *Journal of Privacy Technology,* 2004-06; member of editorial and advisory board, *International Journal of Information and Computer Security,* 2004-06.

SIDELIGHTS: Aviel Rubin is a computer science professor and computer network security specialist. He is well known and highly regarded in the field of computer security, particularly with regard to his work to secure the national elections system and to ensure the validity of the voting process. Following the drawn-out U.S. presidential elections of 2000, along with its hanging chad issues, many states attempted to implement a new electronic voting system—the Diebold electronic voting technology. The new process proved to be insecure, however, and Rubin made national news with his investigation into the issue. In his book *Brave New Ballot: The Battle to Safeguard Democracy in the Age of Electronic Voting,* Rubin explains how he and two graduate students revealed the safety issues, and the political upheaval that followed as various government officials refused to accept his evidence, claiming he was attempting to undermine the electoral process. The issue was further complicated by Rubin's own ties to a company that produced voting software. In a review for the *Washington Monthly,* Phil Keisling felt that "Rubin has written an engaging memoir of his three years in the vortex of electronic voting controversy." Vanessa Bush, writing in *Booklist,* called Rubin's effort "an absorbing account of how his involvement in the e-voting controversy affected his life and career."

Rubin has also written several other books on computer network and Internet security, including an update of *Firewalls and Internet Security: Repelling the Wily Hacker,* which he wrote with William R. Cheswick and Stephen M. Bellovin, the authors of the original edition. The book takes the approach to security that, rather than providing your network with an impenetrable firewall, it is preferable to build a filter or gatekeeping system that allows only certain information through, dependent on the wishes of the network owner. Patrick Mueller remarked in *Information Security Online:* "Despite a few hiccups, *Firewalls and Internet Security* will rightly join its predecessor as an instant security classic."

BIOGRAPHICAL AND CRITICAL SOURCES:

BOOKS

Rubin, Aviel, *Brave New Ballot: The Battle to Safeguard Democracy in the Age of Electronic Voting,* Morgan Road Books (New York, NY), 2006.

PERIODICALS

Booklist, September 1, 2006, Vanessa Bush, review of *Brave New Ballot,* p. 29.
Campaigns & Elections, October-November, 2006, review of *Brave New Ballot,* p. 62.
IEEE Micro, September-October, 2003, Richard Mateosian, review of *Firewalls and Internet Security: Repelling the Wily Hacker,* p. 6.
Publishers Weekly, July 31, 2006, review of *Brave New Ballot,* p. 71.
Washington Monthly, December 1, 2006, Phil Keisling, "Election Fraud, American Style: The Most Effective Voter Suppression Tool Is the Polling Booth Itself," review of *Brave New Ballot,* p. 46.

ONLINE

Aviel Rubin Blog, http://avi-rubin.blogspot.com (May 7, 2007).
Aviel Rubin Home Page, http://avirubin.com (May 1, 2007).
Brave New Ballot Web site, http://www.bravenew ballot.com (May 1, 2007).
Help Net Security Web site, http://www.net-security. org/ (February 26, 2003), Mirko Zorz, interview with Aviel Rubin.
Information Security Online, http://infosecuritymag. techtarget.com/ (May 1, 2007), Patrick Mueller, "Secure Reads," review of *Firewalls and Internet Security.**

*   *   *

RUBIN, Michael B. 1972-

PERSONAL: Born 1972; married; children: one daughter. *Education:* University of Michigan, bachelor's degree; Northwestern University, M.B.A.

ADDRESSES: *Home*—Portsmouth, NH. *Office*—Total Candor LLC, P.O. Box 4283, Porstmouth, NH 03802-4283. *E-mail*—Michael@totalcandor.com.

CAREER: Certified public accountant, financial planner, speaker, and author. Total Candor LLC (financial planning education company), Portsmouth, NH, founder; Toys "R" Us, Inc., Wayne, NJ, new venture executive. Also worked in personal financial services divisions of Arthur Andersen and Coopers & Lybrand.

WRITINGS:

Beyond Paycheck to Paycheck: A Conversation about Income, Wealth, and the Steps in Between, Wachtel & Martin (Portsmouth, NH), 2007.

SIDELIGHTS: Michael B. Rubin told *CA:* "Although I wish I'd had the foresight to intentionally take advantage of the enhanced readability of dialogue, I never intended to write *Beyond Paycheck to Paycheck: A Conversation about Income, Wealth, and the Steps in Between* as a true conversation. But shortly after I began writing, I began hearing people with questions. Since I didn't have any significant mental problems I was aware of, I decided to—quite literally—include those questions.

"It is because I've had so many money-related conversations that I knew what most readers' follow-up questions would be. So rather than just continuing by providing the answers, I showed the questions too, in everyday language. This allows people to gain comfort in the knowledge that they are not alone in pursuing true understanding.

"I've also talked with and been disappointed by the many people who've been taken advantage of by others. Some people came to me knowing they'd been had and wanting me to both explain and lessen the damage. Other folks were quite surprised to learn they had been given poor advice. Still others remain in denial to this day. It is critically important to understand that not every financial services professional has your best interest at heart. As a result, I created Gary, who embodies all that can go wrong with a financial advisor. He lacks ethics and is amazingly sly. To be truly educated, you must know he's out there. Far better for

you to meet him in *Beyond Paycheck to Paycheck,* than at the golf course. You need to know what he says, the way he says it, and be able to ask the right questions in order to identify him.

"We all learn from Gary, since it's as important to be knowledgeable about what not to do and who not to trust as it is to achieve awareness about what to do and who to trust. The financial advisors you want to work with would all agree passionately. After all, Garys make such advisors look even better."

BIOGRAPHICAL AND CRITICAL SOURCES:

PERIODICALS

Republican (Springfield, MA), March 25, 2007, Bea O'Quinn Dewberry, "Women Bank on Money Advice."

ONLINE

Total Candor Web site, http://www.totalcandor.com/ (May 14, 2007), profile of author.

*   *   *

RUDALEVIGE, Andrew 1968-

PERSONAL: Born 1968, in Watertown, MA. *Education:* University of Chicago, B.A., 1989; Harvard University, M.A., 1997, Ph.D., 2000.

ADDRESSES: *Office*—Carlisle, PA. *E-mail*—rudaleva@dickinson.edu.

CAREER: Legislative assistant to Massachusetts State Senator Michael J. Barrett, 1989-91, chief of staff, 1991-94; town councilor for Watertown, MA, 1994-96, and charter commissioner, 1997; Harvard University, Cambridge, MA, teaching fellow, 1996-2000; Dickinson College, Carlisle, PA, assistant professor, 2000-04, associate professor of political science, 2004—, department chair, 2006—. Visiting scholar, Princeton University Center for the Study of Democratic Politics, 2004-05.

MEMBER: Phi Beta Kappa.

AWARDS, HONORS: Moody Fellowship, Lyndon Baines Johnson Foundation, 1998; Mellon Foundation dissertation research fellowship, 1998, and dissertation completion fellowship, 1999; research grant, Harvard University, 1999; research grant, Gerald R. Ford Foundation, 1999; Student Marshal and National Merit Scholar, University of Chicago; Toppan Prize, Harvard University, 1999, for the best dissertation in political science; research grant, Harry S. Truman Institute, 2001; Presidency Research Group Founders' Prizes for best paper on the presidency, American Political Science Association, 2003, 2006; Richard E. Neustadt Award for the Best Book on the Presidency of 2002, American Political Science Association, 2003, for *Managing the Presidents Program: Presidential Leadership and Legislative Policy Formation;* research grant, Franklin and Eleanor Roosevelt Institute, 2004; Outstanding Academic Title, *Choice,* 2006, for *The New Imperial Presidency.*

WRITINGS:

Managing the President's Program: Presidential Leadership and Legislative Policy Formulation, Princeton University Press (Princeton, NJ), 2002.
The New Imperial Presidency: Renewing Presidential Power after Watergate, University of Michigan Press (Ann Arbor, MI), 2005.

Contributor to books, including *Debating the Presidency: Conflicting Perspectives on the American Executive,* edited by Richard Ellis and Michael Nelson, Congressional Quarterly Press, 2006; *The Second Term of George W. Bush: Prospects and Perils,* edited by Douglas M. Brateebo, Robert Maranto, and Tom Lansford, Palgrave Macmillan, 2006; *School Money Trials: The Legal Pursuit of Educational Adequacy,* edited by Martin R. West and Paul E. Peterson, Brookings Institution Press, 2007; *Footing the Tuition Bill,* edited by Rick Hess, American Enterprise Institute Press; *CQ's Guide to the Presidency,* 4th edition, edited by Michael Nelson, Congressional Quarterly Press; and *Formative Acts: American Politics in the Making,* edited by Stephen Skowronek and Matthew Glassman, University of Pennsylvania Press. Contributor to periodicals, including *Congress and the Presidency, Presidential Studies Quarterly, Political Science*

Quarterly, American Politics Research, American Political Science Review, and *Journal of Public Administration Research and Theory.*

SIDELIGHTS: Andrew Rudalevige is a political scientist who is well respected as an expert on the uses of presidential power. He has written extensively regarding the presidency of George W. Bush with regard to his shift towards what Rudalevige considers an "imperial presidency." His book *The New Imperial Presidency: Renewing Presidential Power after Watergate* refers back to an earlier volume by Arthur M. Schlesinger, Jr., who discussed President Nixon's expansion of the role of the president in blatant disregard of the three-branch system of leadership set down by the U.S. Constitution. Rudalevige analyzes the ways in which President George W. Bush has similarly exceeded the powers delegated to him by his position. Russell Muirhead, writing for the *Political Science Quarterly,* remarked: "This book should help awaken both the electorate and its leaders to the urgency of a subject long at the heart of constitutional government," calling it "gracefully written, [and] sparkling with vivid quotations and insightful analysis." Writing in the *Presidential Studies Quarterly,* Nancy V. Baker called Rudalevige's effort "an important and ambitious work."

Rudalevige's earlier book, *Managing the President's Program: Presidential Leadership and Legislative Policy Formulation,* takes a broader look at the role of the president. In particular, Rudalevige addresses what leadership qualities are vital for a good president and the tasks necessary for an individual attempting to coexist with the other branches of the U.S. government. In a review in the *Political Science Quarterly,* Shirley Anne Warshaw asserted: "This well-written and well-researched study substantially adds to the body of literature on presidential leadership, broadening our knowledge of how the White House staff can be most effectively used for moving the president's policy agenda forward in the legislative arena."

BIOGRAPHICAL AND CRITICAL SOURCES:

PERIODICALS

Choice: Current Reviews for Academic Libraries, April 1, 2006, M.J. Rozell, review of *The New Imperial Presidency: Renewing Presidential Power after Watergate,* p. 1482.

Political Science Quarterly, summer, 2003, Shirley Anne Warshaw, review of *Managing the President's Program: Presidential Leadership and Legislative Policy Formation,* p. 323; fall, 2006, Russell Muirhead, review of *The New Imperial Presidency,* p. 519.

Prairie Schooner, June 22, 2003, review of *Managing the President's Program,* p. 323.

Presidential Studies Quarterly, September 1, 2006, Nancy V. Baker, review of *The New Imperial Presidency.*

Reference & Research Book News, February 1, 2006, review of *The New Imperial Presidency.*

ONLINE

Dickinson University Faculty Web site, http://users. dickinson.edu/ (May 1, 2007), curriculum vitae for Andrew Rudalevige.

*   *   *

RYAN, Teresa LeYung

PERSONAL: Born in Hong Kong, China; immigrated to the United States.

ADDRESSES: *Home*—Berkeley, CA. *E-mail*—info@ lovemadeofheart.com.

CAREER: Author. Has worked as a secretary.

MEMBER: California Writers Club, San Francisco/ Peninsula branch (board member), Women's National Book Association (San Francisco chapter; board member), Northern California Independent Booksellers Association, Pacific Northwest Booksellers Association, Chinese Historical Society of America, Association for Asian American Studies.

WRITINGS:

Love Made of Heart, Kensington Books (New York, NY), 2002.

BIOGRAPHICAL AND CRITICAL SOURCES:

PERIODICALS

Publishers Weekly, September 23, 2002, review of *Love Made of Heart,* p. 51.

ONLINE

Teresa LeYung Ryan Home Page, http://www.love madeofheart.com (September 25, 2004).*

S

SACUTA, Norman 1962-

PERSONAL: Born 1962. *Education:* University of Alberta, M.A., 1987; University of British Columbia, M.F.A., 1988; also studied at the University of Sussex.

ADDRESSES: Home—Edmonton, Alberta, Canada.

CAREER: University of Alberta, Edmonton, Alberta, Canada, instructor, 1990s.

AWARDS, HONORS: New playwright award, Alberta Culture Playwriting Competition, 1990, for *Ismay: A Play about the Titanic;* Canada Council for the Arts grant, 1997-98.

WRITINGS:

Garments of the Known (poems), Nightwood Editions (Robert Creek, British Columbia, Canada), 2001.

Also author of *Ismay: A Play about the Titanic.* Work represented in anthologies, including *Threshold: An Anthology of Contemporary Writing from Alberta.* Contributor to periodicals, including *Antigonish Review, Dandelion, Grain, Matrix, Edmonton Journal, NeWest Review, Canadian Forum,* and *Outlooks.*

SIDELIGHTS: Norman Sacuta produces work that appears to invite an analysis of contradictions. Often about rural Alberta, his poems set up opposing themes of light and darkness, that which is clear versus that which is hidden, and images of roughnecks and other "real" men juxtaposed against homoeroticism and scenes of domesticity. The verses also hint at the political revelations that Sacuta experienced while attending the Sexual Dissidence and Cultural Change Program at the University of Sussex in England during the 1990s. His first collection, *Garments of the Known,* is a slim book of poems ranging from sonnets to experimental forms. The unifying focus of the work is the idea that there is an ever-widening gap between the things people feel and the things they are willing to admit aloud. In a review for the *Lambda Book Report,* Jonathan Alexander remarked that "Sacuta's verse plays on our emotions to remind us—again— that not all desire is sanctioned, not all love so easily rendered in couplets, quatrains, and sonnets," adding that he "dwells, as much as he can, in describing the situation of the inarticulate." Alex Boyd, writing for the *Danforth Review,* commented that Sacuta's debut effort "shows promise even as it is a frustrating mixture of clarity and obscurity." Boyd added that his ideas "cover a variety of landscapes and situations, and I wanted to read the poems without guessing at his meaning."

BIOGRAPHICAL AND CRITICAL SOURCES:

PERIODICALS

ARC, December 22, 2002, review of *Garments of the Known,* pp. 103-104.
Books in Canada, March, 2003, Robert Moore, "Truths Told Slant," review of *Garments of the Known.*

Canadian Book Review Annual, January 1, 2002, review of *Garments of the Known,* p. 221.

Lambda Book Report, April, 2002, Jonathan Alexander, review of *Garments of the Known,* p. 20.

ONLINE

Danforth Review, http://www.danforthreview.com/ (May 1, 2007), Alex Boyd, review of *Garments of the Known.*

Norman Sacuta Home Page, http://www.normsacuta. com (September 25, 2004).

*   *   *

SAKEY, Marcus

PERSONAL: Born in Flint, MI; married. *Education:* University of Michigan, graduated.

ADDRESSES: Home—Chicago, IL. *Agent*—Scott Miller, Trident Media Group, 41 Madison Ave., 36th Fl., New York, NY 10010. *E-mail*—msakey@rcn.com.

CAREER: Writer. Has worked in advertising for ten years.

WRITINGS:

The Blade Itself (novel), St. Martin's Minotaur (New York, NY), 2007.

SIDELIGHTS: Marcus Sakey spent ten years working in the advertising and marketing industry, a career foundation that he credits for his ability to write fiction about thieves and killers. His love of crime novels has also influenced him, and he cites Dennis Lehane, Elmore Leonard, and James Ellroy—all of whom he has been compared to—as some of his favorite authors. For his first novel, the critically well-received *The Blade Itself,* Sakey conducted extensive research, spending time with homicide detectives and learning how to pick a dead bolt. The book follows the exploits of retired thief Danny Carter, who has become a respectable businessman. He discovers, though, that leaving his past behind is not as easy as

he had hoped when his former partner in crime, Evan McGann, is released from prison. *Library Journal* critic Teresa L. Jacobsen remarked that "Sakey's insights into Danny's struggles to maintain a decent, honest life truly make the story stand out." A *Publishers Weekly* contributor called the book a "brilliant debut," and "a must read." *New York Times Book Review* writer Marilyn Stasio commented of Sakey's effort: "The narrative drive of this white-knuckle story owes everything to the raw tension between virtuous Danny and evil Evan." In a review for the *Washington Post,* Patrick Anderson noted that "Sakey does the big things right but sometimes stumbles on small things. His novel is fast-moving and suspenseful, but it can be touchy-feely." However, Anderson went on to praise Sakey's writing overall, calling the book "an impressive start to his career."

BIOGRAPHICAL AND CRITICAL SOURCES:

PERIODICALS

Booklist, October 15, 2006, Sue O'Brien, review of *The Blade Itself,* p. 33.

Chicago Tribune Books, January 14, 2007, Dick Adler, review of *The Blade Itself,* p. 8.

Kirkus Reviews, October 1, 2006, review of *The Blade Itself,* p. 984.

Library Journal, October 15, 2006, Teresa L. Jacobsen, review of *The Blade Itself,* p. 57.

New York Times Book Review, January 14, 2007, Marilyn Stasio, "Rookie Blues," review of *The Blade Itself,* p. 23.

Publishers Weekly, October 2, 2006, review of *The Blade Itself,* p. 38; November 6, 2006, Robert C. Hahn, "PW talks with Marcus Sakey: A Sharp Debut," p. 35.

Washington Post, January 15, 2007, Patrick Anderson, "Cold Evil in the Windy City," review of *The Blade Itself,* p. C3.

ONLINE

Bookreporter.com, http://www.bookreporter.com/ (May 1, 2007), Joe Hartlaub, review of *The Blade Itself.*

January, http://www.januarymagazine.com/ (May 1, 2007), David Thayer, "Partners in Crime," review of *The Blade Itself.*

Marcus Sakey Home Page, http://marcussakey.com (May 7, 2007).

Pop Syndicate, http://www.popsyndicate.com/ (January 25, 2007), review of *The Blade Itself.*

*   *   *

SALEM, Salwa 1940-1992

PERSONAL: Born 1940, in Kafr Zib^d, Palestine; died of cancer, 1992, in Parma, Italy; married; husband's name Muhammad. *Education:* Attended University of Damascus.

CAREER: Activist and educator. Taught school in Kuwait.

WRITINGS:

(With Laura Maritano) *The Wind in My Hair* (memoir), translated by Yvonne Freccero, Interlink Books (Northampton, MA), 2007.

SIDELIGHTS: Born in Palestine, Salwa Salem fled her childhood home after the Arab-Israeli War of 1948 and began a life of nomadic exile, journeying to Kuwait and Austria before settling in Italy. In her posthumously published memoir *The Wind in My Hair,* dictated while she was dying of cancer, Salem "skillfully interweaves a history of the Palestinian longing for nationhood and a personal story of a courageous Arab woman activist," observed *Library Journal* contributor Elizabeth R. Hayford.

Salem grew up in a prosperous family in Jaffa, but when the violence started her father relocated the family to Nablus, where they lived under Jordanian rule. "Salem became very politically active as a schoolgirl, officially joining the outlawed Ba'ath party at the age of 15," noted Maureen Clare Murphy on the *Electronic Intifada* Web site. "Influenced by her intellectual and politically savvy brother Adnan, Salem devoured every book she had access to, and organized subversive actions with her fellow students against the Jordanian government authorities." She later traveled to Kuwait where she worked as a teacher and met her husband, Muhammad, with whom she moved to Vienna.

The Six-Day War of 1967, during which Israel captured the Sinai Peninsula, Golan Heights, Gaza Strip, and West Bank, proved devastating to the Palestinians. Discussing the lasting effects of that war in *The Wind in My Hair,* Salem writes: "As for us, we had so many dreams, so many words and ideologies. We believed in socialism and in pan-Arabism. Today everything is different." Salem and her family moved to Parma, Italy, in part to escape the racism they faced in Austria. Murphy stated that although "Salem writes of feeling more content while in Italy, she was still disturbed by the repressive measures imposed on her family back in Nablus, where she could travel only with an Israeli-issued visitor's permit. Additionally, she writes of her regret that her children did not know of the warm extended family that she so enjoyed as a child."

The Wind in My Hair received strong reviews. A critic in *Kirkus Reviews* deemed the work "evocative and discomforting" and remarked that "much of the prose is direct, spare and stirring in its simplicity," and Murphy noted that the author's experiences "give a window into that of a generation of Palestinians born into dispossession."

BIOGRAPHICAL AND CRITICAL SOURCES:

BOOKS

Salem, Salwa, and Laura Maritano, *The Wind in My Hair,* translated by Yvonne Freccero, Interlink Books (Northampton, MA), 2007.

PERIODICALS

Kirkus Reviews, October 1, 2004, review of *The Wind in My Hair,* p. 1004.
Library Journal, February 15, 2007, Elizabeth R. Hayford, review of *The Wind in My Hair,* p. 127.
Reference & Research Book News, February, 2007, review of *The Wind in My Hair.*

ONLINE

Electronic Intifada, http://electronicintifada.net/ (February 18, 2007), Maureen Clare Murphy, "Two Palestinian Women Recall Their Lives in Exile," review of *The Wind in My Hair.**

SAMPSON, Kevin

PERSONAL: Born in Liverpool, England.

ADDRESSES: Agent—Jago Irwin, PFD, Drury House, 34-43 Russell St., London WC2B 5HA, England.

CAREER: Author. *Mail on Sunday,* London, England, features writer; Channel Four, London, assistant youth editor, 1987-88; Kinesis Films (production company), founder, 1988-90; The Farm (band), Liverpool, England, manager, 1990-95.

AWARDS, HONORS: Named young writer of the year, *Cosmopolitan,* 1986.

WRITINGS:

NOVELS

Awaydays, Jonathan Cape (London, England), 1998.
Powder: A Rock 'n' Roll Novel, Jonathan Cape (London, England), 1999.
Leisure, Jonathan Cape (London, England), 2000.
Outlaws, Jonathan Cape (London, England), 2001.
Clubland, Jonathan Cape (London, England), 2002.
Freshers, Jonathan Cape (London, England), 2003.
Stars Are Stars, Jonathan Cape (London, England), 2006.

OTHER

Extra Time: A Season in the Life of a Football Fan, Jonathan Cape (London, England), 1998.

Author of the screenplays *Clubland,* World Productions, *Higher Than the Sun,* World Productions, and *Surveillance,* Fulcrum. Contributor to *Vox'n'Roll,* an anthology edited by Richard Thomas. Contributor of reviews to *New Music Express, The Face,* and *Sounds.*

SIDELIGHTS: British writer Kevin Sampson, a former rock critic and band manager, is the author of the semiautobiographical tale *Powder: A Rock 'n' Roll Novel.* In the work, Sampson details the rise and fall of The Grams, an alternative rock band from Liver-

pool, England. In an interview with Anna Battista on the *Erasing Clouds* Web site, Sampson remarked: "*Powder* was a huge success: people are fascinated by the excesses of famous people, especially actors and rock stars, and this confirmed their worst fears!"

Sampson found early success in music journalism, publishing his first review at the age of eighteen. He wrote for such publications as *New Music Express* and founded his own film production company before serving as manager of The Farm, a Liverpool-based band, from 1990 to 1995. In *Powder,* Sampson looks at the music industry through the eyes of Keva McCluskey, lead singer and songwriter of The Grams, his hedonistic bandmates, their manager Wheezer Finlay, and wealthy producer Guy de Burret. According to Sia Michel, writing in the *New York Times Book Review,* the author "skewers British musicians as lazy and naïve, but he sympathizes with them when it comes to the destructive effects the music business has on their creativity and morale." "As a whole *Powder* is an endless entertaining journey through the world of rock'n'roll, highly detailed, full of crazed humanity and debauched fooleries, two characteristics proper to human beings, but also full of immorality and demented excess, two characteristics typical of any band on this planet," observed Battista.

BIOGRAPHICAL AND CRITICAL SOURCES:

PERIODICALS

Books, autumn, 1999, Ralph Baxter, review of *Powder: A Rock 'n' Roll Novel,* p. 10.
Independent, July 3, 1999, Ben Thompson, review of *Powder,* p. 9.
Kirkus Reviews, August 15, 2002, review of *Powder,* p. 1173.
Library Journal, August, 2002, Heather McCormack, review of *Powder,* p. 146.
New York Times Book Review, November 3, 2002, Sia Michel, "Meet the Grams," review of *Powder,* p. 23.
Publishers Weekly, October 9, 2000, review of *Powder,* p. 71; July 8, 2002, review of *Powder,* p. 28.
Times Educational Supplement, September 5, 2003, review of *Freshers,* p. 17.

ONLINE

BBC Collective, http://www.bbc.co.uk/ (September 12, 2003), Laura Bushell, review of *Freshers.*

Erasing Clouds, http://www.erasingclouds.com/ (May 13, 2007), Anna Battista, "Scoring for Liverpool: Interview with Writer Kevin Sampson"; (May 13, 2007), Anna Battista, "Of Freshers and Men: An Interview with Kevin Sampson."*

*   *   *

SCHMID, Hillel 1944-

PERSONAL: Born July 11, 1944, in Palestine (now Israel); son of Israel (a municipal mayor) and Yehudith (a homemaker) Schmid; married September 3, 1967; wife's name Tikva (a teacher); children: Yaron, Michel, Noam. *Ethnicity:* "Jewish." *Education:* Trained at Hebrew University of Jerusalem. *Religion:* Jewish.

ADDRESSES: Home—Mevasseret Zion, Israel. *Office*—Center for the Study of Philanthropy in Israel, Hebrew University of Jerusalem, Mt. Scopus, Jerusalem 91905, Israel. *E-mail*—hillels@mscc.huji.ac.il.

CAREER: Hebrew University of Jerusalem, Jerusalem, Israel, professor, 1980—, and director of Center for the Study of Philanthropy in Israel, also former dean of School of Social Work and Social Welfare. Israeli Federation of Community Centers, president. *Military service:* Israel Defense Forces, served in infantry and in a mental health services unit.

WRITINGS:

(Editor, with David Bargal) *Organizational Change and Development in Human Service Organizations,* Haworth Press (Binghamton, NY), 1992.
Neighborhood Self-Management Experiments in Civil Society, Kluwer Academic (New York, NY), 2001.
(Editor) *Organizational and Structural Dilemmas in Nonprofit Human Service Organizations,* Haworth Press (Binghamton, NY), 2004.

Also author of books published in Hebrew. Contributor to professional journals.

SIDELIGHTS: Hillel Schmid told *CA:* "My primary motivation for writing is to share with the academic and real world the research findings, conclusions, and implications for the improvement of services and quality of life for the millions of people who need help, love, empathy, and support. I want to contribute to theories on the management of nonprofit human service organizations, to get better understanding of their ways of operation in both formal and informal settings. I am inspired by my studies, my concerns, and my desire for personal development."

*   *   *

SCHOCH, Robert M. 1957-
(Robert Milton Schoch)

PERSONAL: Born March 30, 1957, in Washington, DC; son of Milton Ralph and Cornelia Alicia Schoch. *Education:* George Washington University, B.A., 1979, B.S., 1979; Yale University, M.Phil., 1981, Ph.D., 1983.

ADDRESSES: Office—College of General Studies, Boston University, 871 Commonwealth Ave., Boston, MA 02215. *E-mail*—schoch@bu.edu.

CAREER: Peabody Museum of Natural History, Yale University, New Haven, CT, curatorial assistant, 1982-83, research assistant, 1983-84, curatorial affiliate, 1985-1990; Schiele Museum of Natural History, Gastonia, NC, research associate, 1984-1999; Boston University, Boston, MA, assistant professor in division of science, 1984-90, assistant professor of geology, 1985-88; associate professor of natural science, 1990—.

MEMBER: Paleontology Society, Society of Vertebrate Paleontology, Geological Society of America, Sigma Xi.

AWARDS, HONORS: National Science Foundation grant, 1979-84; Peyton Richter Award for interdisciplinary teaching, Boston University, 1990.

WRITINGS:

(With Spencer G. Lucas) *A New Species of Conoryctella (Mammalia, Taeniodonta) from the Paleocene of the San Juan Basin, New Mexico, and a*

Revision of the Genus ("Postilla" series), Peabody Museum of Natural History/Yale University (New Haven, CT), 1981.

A New Species of Isectolophus (Mammalia, Tapiroidea) from the Middle Eocene of Wyoming ("Postilla" series), Peabody Museum of Natural History/Yale University (New Haven, CT), 1983.

Tanyops undans Marsh, 1894, a Junior Subjective Synonym of Protapirus obliquidens Wortman and Earle, 1893 (Mammalia, Perissodactyla) ("Postilla" series), Peabody Museum of Natural History/Yale University (New Haven, CT), 1983.

(With J.D. Archibald and J.K. Rigby, Jr.) *A New Subfamily, Conacodontinae, and New Species, Conacodon kohlbergeri, of the Periptychidae (Condylarthra, Mammalia)* ("Postilla" series), Peabody Museum of Natural History/Yale University (New Haven, CT), 1983.

(Editor) *Vertebrate Paleontology* ("Benchmark Papers in Geology" series), Van Nostrand Reinhold (New York, NY), 1984.

Revision of Metacheiromys Wortman, 1903 and a Review of the Palaeanodonta ("Postilla" series), Peabody Museum of Natural History/Yale University (New Haven, CT), 1984.

Two Unusual Specimens of Helaletes in the Yale Peabody Museum Collections, and Some Comments on the Ancestry of the Tapiridae (Perissodactyla, Mammalia) ("Postilla" series), Peabody Museum of Natural History/Yale University (New Haven, CT), 1984.

Notes on the Type Specimens of Pteranodon and Nyctosaurus (Pterosauria, Pteranodontidae) in the Yale Peabody Museum Collections ("Postilla" series), Peabody Museum of Natural History/Yale University (New Haven, CT), 1984.

The Type Specimens of Tapiravus validus and Tapiravus rarus (Mammalia, Perissodactyla), with a Review of the Genus, and a New Report of Miotapirus (Miotapirus marslandensis Schoch and Prins, New Species) from Nebraska ("Postilla" series), Peabody Museum of Natural History/Yale University (New Haven, CT), 1984.

Preliminary Description of a New Late Paleocene Land Mammal Fauna from South Carolina, U.S.A. ("Postilla" series), Peabody Museum of Natural History/Yale University (New Haven, CT), 1985.

Phylogeny Reconstruction in Paleontology, Van Nostrand Reinhold (New York, NY), 1986.

Systematics, Functional Morphology, and Macroevolution of the Extinct Mammalian Order Taeniodonta ("Bulletin" series), Peabody Museum of Natural History/Yale University (New Haven, CT), 1986.

Stratigraphy: Principles and Methods, Van Nostrand Reinhold (New York, NY), 1989.

(Editor, with Donald R. Prothero) *The Evolution of Perissodactyls* ("Oxford Monographs on Geology and Geophysics" series), Oxford University Press (New York, NY), 1989.

Case Studies in Environmental Science, West Publishing (Minneapolis/St. Paul, MN), 1996.

(With Michael L. McKinney) *Environmental Science: Systems and Solutions,* West Publishing (Minneapolis/St. Paul, MN), 1996, 4th edition, with Michael L. McKinney and Logan Yonavjak, Jones & Bartlett Publishers (Sudbury, MA), 2007.

(With Robert Aquinas McNally) *Voices of the Rocks: A Scientist Looks at Catastrophes and Ancient Civilizations,* Harmony Books (New York, NY), 1999.

(With Donald R. Prothero) *Horns, Tusks, and Flippers: The Evolution of Hoofed Mammals,* Johns Hopkins University Press (Baltimore, MD), 2002.

(With Robert Aquinas McNally) *Voyages of the Pyramid Builders: The True Origins of the Pyramids, from Lost Egypt to Ancient America,* Jeremy P. Tarcher (New York, NY), 2003.

(With Robert Aquinas McNally) *Pyramid Quest: Secrets of the Great Pyramid and the Dawn of Civilization,* Jeremy P. Tarcher/Penguin (New York, NY), 2005.

Contributor to journals, including *A Modern Journal of Ancient Egypt, Geoarchaeology, Chroniques des Civilsations Disparues, Pre-Columbiana,* and *Atlantis Rising.* Editor, *Vertebrate Paleontology,* 1984. Schoch's books have been translated into foreign languages.

SIDELIGHTS: Especially known for his research on the pyramids of Egypt, Robert M. Schoch is a geologist whose interests also include paleontology, evolution, environmental science, geoarchaeology, and the world's prehistoric and ancient cultures. In 1993 the new genus *Schochia,* an extinct group of mammals, was named in his honor. Schoch is also the author and editor of numerous books focusing on his various areas of interest. He collaborated, for example, with science writer Robert Aquinas McNally to write *Voices of the Rocks: A Scientist Looks at Catastrophes and Ancient Civilizations.* The authors investigate numerous questions surrounding ancient civilizations, such as the common story of a "great flood" and the existence of the city of Atlantis. They also explore the potential role that natural disasters played in creating and destroying civilizations. Jean E. Crampon reported in the *Library Journal* that "Schoch does a very good job of explaining technical terms . . . so that they are comprehensible to the nonscientist."

Horns, Tusks, and Flippers: The Evolution of Hoofed Mammals, which Schoch wrote with Donald R. Prothero, provides an up-to-date account of scientific knowledge concerning the history of hoofed mammals. "What could be a rather dull exposition of a parade of different mammals is saved . . . [by] interspersed interesting historical information and anecdotes about the early work on these groups," according to J. David Archibald in the *Quarterly Review of Biology.*

In his second book with McNally, *Voyages of the Pyramid Builders: The True Origins of the Pyramids, from Lost Egypt to Ancient America,* Schoch explores his theory that ancient pyramids are found throughout the world because they are the result of prehistoric societies that spread their cultures around the globe. "His case . . . is carefully crafted," wrote a *Kirkus Reviews* contributor, who called *Voyages of the Pyramid Builders* "gee-whiz industriously wrapped in solid science." A *Publishers Weekly* reviewer commented that "Schoch's evocation of the pyramids forcefully reminds us of their enduring power as monuments to the spirit of human creativity."

Schoch collaborated for a third time with McNally for the 2005 book *Pyramid Quest: Secrets of the Great Pyramid and the Dawn of Civilization.* Here, the authors go against the popularly held archaeological viewpoint that the Great Pyramid was built in a relatively short time during the reign of one pharaoh around 2551-2528 B.C.E. Instead, the authors present their case that the foundations for building the pyramid go back some thousands of years earlier to 7000-5000 B.C.E. They also discuss their belief that the Great Pyramid was probably not a tomb but had some other social significance. "One need know very little about ancient history or Egyptology to be drawn into their revisionist argument," commented a *Krikus Reviews* contributor. The reviewer went on to call *Pyramid Quest* "very readable intrigue, bolstered by logic and calculations." Another *Publishers Weekly* contributor noted that the authors include so much "information . . . that it may be the only guide to the Great Pyramid most readers will ever need."

BIOGRAPHICAL AND CRITICAL SOURCES:

PERIODICALS

Choice: Current Reviews for Academic Libraries, November 1, 1999, review of *Voices of the Rocks: A Scientist Looks at Catastrophes and Ancient Civilizations,* p. 572; October 1, 2003, review of *Voyages of the Pyramid Builders: The True Origins of the Pyramids, from Lost Egypt to Ancient America,* p. 392.

Civil Engineering, December 1, 2005, review of *Pyramid Quest: Secrets of the Great Pyramid and the Dawn of Civilization,* p. 67.

Kirkus Reviews, December 1, 2002, review of *Voyages of the Pyramid Builders,* p. 1757; April 15, 2005, review of *Pyramid Quest,* p. 464.

Library Journal, June 1, 1999, Jean E. Crampon, review of *Voices of the Rocks,* p. 164.

Los Angeles Times, October 23, 1991, "Sphinx's New Riddle—Is It Older Than Experts Say?," p. A1.

Nature, October 19, 1989, review of *Stratigraphy: Principles and Methods,* p. 579.

New Scientist, April 28, 1990, review of *Stratigraphy,* p. 78; April 5, 2003, Peter James, "Bricks and Mortals," review of *Voyages of the Pyramid Builders,* p. 51.

New York Times, October 24, 1991, "Science's Newest Riddle: How Old Is Sphinx," p. A15; October 25, 1991, "A Very Old Sphinx May Be Older Yet; Scientist Says Erosion Rate Doubles Monument's Age—So Who Built It?," p. A13.

Publishers Weekly, April 26, 1999, review of *Voices of the Rocks,* p. 70; January 13, 2003, review of *Voyages of the Pyramid Builders,* p. 51; May 23, 2005, review of *Pyramid Quest,* p. 74.

Quarterly Review of Biology, J. David Archibald, December 1, 2003, review of *Horns, Tusks, and Flippers: The Evolution of Hoofed Mammals,* p. 483.

Science, February 6, 1987, Andrew B. Smith, review of *Phylogeny Reconstruction in Paleontology,* p. 696.

Science Books & Films, March 1, 2000, review of *Voices of the Rocks,* p. 73.

ONLINE

Boston University's College of General Studies Web site, http://www.bu.edu/cgs/ (April 23, 2007), faculty profile of Robert M. Schoch.

Daily Grail, http://www.dailygrail.com/ (February 10, 2006), "Schoch to the System—An Interview with Robert Schoch."

Robert M. Schoch Home Page, http://www.robertschoch.net (April 23, 2007).

*   *   *

SCHOCH, Robert Milton
See SCHOCH, Robert M.

*   *   *

SCHWARTZ, Joanne M. 1960-

PERSONAL: Born January 1, 1960, in San Francisco, CA; daughter of Joseph (an accountant) and Juanita (a homemaker) Geraci; married Robert N. Schwartz (a nurse), June 4, 1988; children: Harrison. *Ethnicity:* "Caucasian." *Education:* Santa Clara University, B.S., 1982, M.B.A., 1985. *Politics:* Independent. *Religion:* Roman Catholic. *Hobbies and other interests:* Collecting charms and other vintage jewelry.

ADDRESSES: Home—San Jose, CA. *Office*—Agilent Technologies, 5301 Stevens Creek Blvd., Santa Clara, CA 95051. *E-mail*—schwartznet@sbcglobal.net.

CAREER: Agilent Technologies, Santa Clara, CA, legal operations manager, 1987—.

WRITINGS:

Charms and Charm Bracelets: The Complete Guide, Schiffer Publishing (Atglen, PA), 2004.

SIDELIGHTS: Joanne M. Schwartz told *CA:* "I write to inform and entertain—both my readers and myself. I enjoy collecting original source material, particularly vintage catalogs and magazines. My goal with *Charms and Charm Bracelets: The Complete Guide* was to produce an informative yet readable book. I wrote the book to protect others from being taken advantage of. What I call 'Internet alchemy' seemingly transforms oft-repeated errors into truth. I find it gratifying that many online auction listings cite my book."

SCOTT, Jessica
See De WIRE, Elinor

*   *   *

SCOTT-WARREN, Jason

PERSONAL: Married Mary Laven (a professor); children: Daniel, Benjamin. *Education:* Jesus College, Cambridge, graduated, 1989.

ADDRESSES: Office—Department of English, University of York, Heslington, York YO10 5DD, England. *E-mail*—jesw1@york.ac.uk.

CAREER: Department of English and Related Literature, University of York, York, England, lecturer in English. Has lectured at Cambridge University.

WRITINGS:

Sir John Harington and the Book as Gift, Oxford University Press (New York, NY), 2001.
(Editor, with Lloyd Kermode and Martine van Elk) *Tudor Drama before Shakespeare, 1485-1590: New Directions for Research, Criticism, and Pedagogy,* Palgrave Macmillan (New York, NY), 2004.
Early Modern English Literature, Polity (Malden, MA), 2005.

SIDELIGHTS: Jason Scott-Warren is the author of *Sir John Harington and the Book as Gift* and coeditor of *Tudor Drama before Shakespeare, 1485-1590: New Directions for Research, Criticism, and Pedagogy.* In *Sir John Harington and the Book as Gift,* Scott-Warren profiles the colorful Elizabethan courtier, translator, and author. During his lifetime, Harington produced a wide range of writings, including a translation of Ariosto's *Orlando Furioso* and the satiric work *Metamorphosis of Ajax,* designed primarily as gifts. He distributed the works to such individuals as Prince Henry, King James VI, and his own mother-in-law. "As Scott-Warren argues, these gifts were seldom gratuitous," observed Steven W. May in the *Renaissance Quarterly.* "Harington used them for a variety of purposes: to generate and modulate his public image, to advertise his eligibility for office, and to advocate public policy." May added that Scott-Warren "presents Harington as a tireless author who wrote and disseminated his works steadily from 1591 until his death in December 1612. The analysis of Harington, who is invariably pigeonholed among the Elizabethans, as an active author during the early Stuart period is one of the most original and illuminating aspects of this soundly researched book."

BIOGRAPHICAL AND CRITICAL SOURCES:

PERIODICALS

Cambridge Quarterly, June, 2003, Alison Shell, review of *Sir John Harington and the Book as Gift,* p. 185.
Clio, fall, 2006, Peter C. Herman, review of *Tudor Drama before Shakespeare, 1485-1590: New Directions for Research, Criticism, and Pedagogy,* p. 107.
English Historical Review, June, 2002, Katherine Duncan-Jones, review of *Sir John Harington and the Book as Gift,* p. 700.
Medieval Review, March, 2006, Ineke Murakami, review of *Tudor Drama before Shakespeare, 1485-1590.*
Renaissance Quarterly, winter, 2002, Steven W. May, review of *Sir John Harington and the Book as Gift,* p. 1451; summer, 2006, review of *Tudor Drama before Shakespeare, 1485-1590,* p. 631.
Review of English Studies, September, 2003, Mike Pincombe, review of *Sir John Harington and the Book as Gift,* p. 528.
Sixteenth Century Journal, spring, 2003, review of *Sir John Harington and the Book as Gift,* p. 246.
Times Literary Supplement, December 28, 2001, Harold Love, "Book Tokens," review of *Sir John Harington and the Book as Gift,* pp. 23-24.*

*   *   *

SEIDMAN, Anthony 1973-

PERSONAL: Born 1973, in Los Angeles, CA; married; children: one. *Education:* Syracuse University, B.A.; University of Texas at El Paso, M.F.A.

CAREER: Worked as an English instructor at Autonomous University of Ciudad Juarez, Chihuahua, Mexico.

WRITINGS:

On Carbon-Dating Hunger, Bitter Oleander Press (Fayetteville, NY), 2000.
Where Thirsts Intersect, Bitter Oleander Press (Fayetteville, NY), 2006.

Contributor of poetry to *Corresponding Voices,* Syracuse University Press (Syracuse, NY), 2003. Contributor of poetry to periodicals, including *Bitter Oleander, Pearl, Rattle, Borderlands, The Bloomsbury Review, Luna, Hunger, Sulphur River Literary Review, Tierra Adentro, Steaua, Códice, La Reforma,* and *Hunger.* The author's poems have been translated into Spanish.*

*   *   *

SENSTAD, Susan Schwartz 1945-

PERSONAL: Born 1945; married. *Education:* Earned M.A. and M.F.A.; received training in voice dialogue from Dr. Sidra Stone and Dr. Hal Stone.

ADDRESSES: Home—Oslo, Norway. *E-mail*—sss@ ideamos.net.

CAREER: Family therapist.

AWARDS, HONORS: Charles Angoff Award, for *Music for the Third Ear.*

WRITINGS:

Music for the Third Ear (novel), Picador USA (New York, NY), 2001.

Contributor to *Literary Review.*

SIDELIGHTS: Susan Schwartz Senstad, a family therapist living in Norway, is the author of *Music for the Third Ear,* "a piercing portrait of desperate lives," observed Martin Wilson in the *Austin Chronicle*. The novel centers on Mette and Hans Olav Kaldstad, a Norwegian couple who agree to take in a pair of refugees fleeing the Bosnian war. Mesud Nadarevic, a Muslim who bears the scars of torture, and his wife, Zheljka, a Croatian Catholic who was gang-raped by Serbian soldiers, are angry and hostile, and they soon leave. A disappointed Mette tracks down Zheljka, who reveals that she became pregnant by one of the rapists and gave birth to a son whom she named Zero and, at Mesud's insistence, gave up for adoption. When the childless Mette, the daughter of Holocaust survivors, intercepts a letter from the adoptive father, she decides to bring the boy to Norway. "Senstad tells the story in a tightly constructed jigsaw of shifting points of view, with real compassion for almost all the characters," wrote *New York Times Book Review* contributor George Robinson.

Music for the Third Ear, Senstad's debut work, received largely positive reviews. The author's "strongest writing comes in the story of Zheljka," commented Richard Eder in the *New York Times Book Review*. "The repeated rapes are described with details that manage to be horrifying and exalted, as if great suffering merited a great voice." "Without becoming didactic, Senstad examines the poisonous consequences of wartime atrocities—the Holocaust, the Yugoslav conflict—upon the lives of individuals thrown together in their aftermath," noted a critic in *Publishers Weekly*.

BIOGRAPHICAL AND CRITICAL SOURCES:

PERIODICALS

Austin Chronicle, April 27, 2001, Martin Wilson, review of *Music for the Third Ear*.

Booklist, January 1, 2001, Kristine Huntley, review of *Music for the Third Ear*, p. 922.

Library Journal, January 1, 2001, Molly Abramowitz, review of *Music for the Third Ear*, p. 157.

New York Times Book Review, February 23, 2001, Richard Eder, "The Anguish of Souls Echoes across an Era," review of *Music for the Third Ear*; March 18, 2001, George Robinson, review of *Music for the Third Ear*.

Publishers Weekly, December 11, 2000, review of *Music for the Third Ear*, p. 64.

Times Literary Supplement, April 21, 2000, review of *Music for the Third Ear*, p. 23.

Tribune Books (Chicago, IL), March 31, 2002, review of *Music for the Third Ear*, p. 7.

Washington Post Book World, February 4, 2001, Laura Beers, "Stories of War, Remembrance and Other Brutalities, from El Salvador to Norway," review of *Music for the Third Ear*, p. 7.*

*   *   *

SENTELL, Todd 1961-

PERSONAL: Born July, 1961, in Atlanta, GA. *Hobbies and other interests:* Golf, running, Muay Thai kick boxing, boxing.

ADDRESSES: Home—GA.

CAREER: Writer. Teaches learning-disabled students in Atlanta, GA. Has worked as a television sports photographer, reporter, and anchor in SC; former director of sales and marketing for The Golf Club of Georgia.

MEMBER: Golf Writers Association of America, United States Track & Field Association, Atlanta Track Club.

AWARDS, HONORS: Magazine Association of Georgia award for "Georgia Boys, Masterful Men."

WRITINGS:

Toonamint of Champions: How Lajuanita Mumps Got to Join Augusta National Golf Club Real Easy, Kunati Books (Largo, FL), 2007.

Editor of *Southern Literary Review*, 2007—. Columnist for *Golf Georgia*. Contributor to periodicals, including *Fairways & Greens*, *GolfStyles Atlanta*, *Golf Illustrated*, *Golf News*, *Fore! Georgia*, *Orlando GolfLife*, and *Atlanta GolfLife*.

SIDELIGHTS: Todd Sentell, a highly regarded golf writer, is the author of the comic novel *Toonamint of Champions: How Lajuanita Mumps Got to Join*

Augusta National Golf Club Real Easy. "When you grow up in the sixties and seventies in Austell, Georgia, you may find your literary influences to be a funny bunch: Lewis Grizzard, Woody Allen, Monty Python, *M*A*S*H*," Sentell remarked on the Kunati Books Web site. "In other words, I'm not afraid to tell you that it wasn't the ancient masters that got me all riled up about good writing, but people and shows and scenes and characters that proved to me you could get real, real funny and still send an important message."

Toonamint of Champions follows the efforts of Georgia bank teller Waymon Poodle to fulfill his lifelong dream: playing a round of golf at legendary Augusta National Golf Club, the home of the annual Masters Tournament. Even Waymon's long-suffering girlfriend, Lajuanita Mumps, takes a backseat to his quest, which involves such colorful characters as accountant Emiglio Rafsooliwicki and Augusta chairman Leonard 'Huge Pecker' Leboeuf. The author's experience "as 'the director of sales and marketing for an ootsie-tootsie private golf club' gives him the background material for carving up golf's sacred rituals and icons of the greens," observed M. Wayne Cunningham in *ForeWord Magazine.* "His expertise as an established humorist has him operating with wit and polish."

BIOGRAPHICAL AND CRITICAL SOURCES:

PERIODICALS

Booklist, December 15, 2006, Bill Ott, review of *Toonamint of Champions: How Lajuanita Mumps Got to Join Augusta National Golf Club Real Easy,* p. 24.
Kirkus Reviews, October 1, 2006, review of *Toonamint of Champions,* p. 985.

ONLINE

ForeWord Magazine, http://www.forewordmagazine. com/ (April 20, 2007), M. Wayne Cunningham, review of *Toonamint of Champions.*
Kunati Books Web site, http://www.kunati.com/ (November 16, 2006), "Meet Todd Sentell . . . In His Own Words."*

SHACKLEFORD, John M. 1929-

PERSONAL: Born December 22, 1929, in Mobile, AL; son of Robert and Myrtice Shackleford; married October 1, 1954; wife's name Jeanne; children: Jeanne Marie Shackleford Freeman, Petronella Shackleford Schnormeier. *Ethnicity:* "White." *Education:* Spring Hill College, B.S., 1957; University of Alabama, Ph.D., 1961; earned M.A., 1992. *Politics:* Independent. *Religion:* Roman Catholic. *Hobbies and other interests:* Reading, chamber music.

ADDRESSES: Home—Mobile, AL. *E-mail*—jshackleford@zebra.net.

CAREER: University of Alabama, College of Medicine, Birmingham, associate professor of anatomy, 1961-72; University of South Alabama, Mobile, professor of anatomy and department chair, 1972-90; worked as instructor in theology, 1993-2001. University of Oslo, visiting associate professor, 1963. Also served on the board of directors for the Alabama Department of Rehabilitation Services.

AWARDS, HONORS: Gold Award, Alabama Easter Seals.

WRITINGS:

The Biblical Heart, Factor Press (Mobile, AL), 1996.
Biblical Body Language: The Figurative Face of Scripture, University Press of America (Lanham, MD), 2000.
Science and Religion: Expelling the Demons from the Marriage Bed, Factor Press (Mobile, AL), 2001.
God as Symbol: What Our Beliefs Tell Us, University Press of America (Lanham, MD), 2004.
Faith Seeking Understanding: Approaching God through Science, Paulist Press (Mahwah, NJ), 2007.

Contributor of about forty articles to scientific journals.

SIDELIGHTS: John M. Shackleford told *CA:* "I was injured in 1949 and have been in a wheelchair since then. I received the major portion of my education following my injury. After retiring in 1990 from my position as an anatomist, I returned to college and earned an M.A. in theology. My books are related to my scientific background in combination with my theological efforts. Science and religion are my principal interests at the present time."

*　　*　　*

SHANNONHOUSE, Rebecca

PERSONAL: Female.

ADDRESSES: Home—New York, NY.

CAREER: Freelance writer and editor.

WRITINGS:

(Editor) *Out of Her Mind: Women Writing on Madness,* Modern Library (New York, NY), 2000.
(Editor) *Under the Influence: The Literature of Addiction,* foreword by Pete Hamill, Modern Library (New York, NY), 2003.

Contributor to periodicals, including the *New York Times, San Francisco Chronicle,* and *USA Today.*

SIDELIGHTS: Freelance writer Rebecca Shannonhouse is the editor of *Out of Her Mind: Women Writing on Madness* and *Under the Influence: The Literature of Addiction.* In *Out of Her Mind,* Shannonhouse offers a selection of writings about mental illness, including Charlotte Perkins Gilman's *The Yellow Wallpaper,* Sylvia Plath's *The Bell Jar,* and Susanna Kaysen's *Girl, Interrupted.* "*Out of Her Mind* is a chic, slim, utterly tasteful volume, light enough for your purse but heavy enough—in subject matter—to be worth reading," remarked Charity Vogel in the *Buffalo News.* According to a contributor on the *Sundress Publications* Web site, "Each essay is unique, offering both first person and indirect accounts of 'madness,' making the book a valuable resource for those interested in psychology and women's writing."

Under the Influence, a look at substance abuse, gambling, and sexual addiction, contains essays, stories, and excerpts from longer works, including

Confessions of an Opium-Eater by Thomas De Quincey, *The Doors of Perception* by Aldous Huxley, and *Love Sick* by Sue Silverman. Writing in the *Boston Phoenix,* Richard C. Walls stated that *Under the Influence* "does establish a pedigree for drug-related writing," and a critic in *Kirkus Reviews* remarked that the volume offers "a nice variety of perspectives on the pleasures and perils of excess."

BIOGRAPHICAL AND CRITICAL SOURCES:

PERIODICALS

Boston Phoenix, March 27-April 3, 2003, Richard C. Walls, review of *Out of Her Mind: Women Writing on Madness.*
Buffalo News (Buffalo, NY), April 16, 2000, Charity Vogel, "Collection Is Lightweight Yet Provocative," review of *Out of Her Mind,* p. F6.
Kirkus Reviews, December 1, 1999, review of *Out of Her Mind,* p. 1870; December 1, 2002, review of *Under the Influence: The Literature of Addiction,* p. 1757.
Library Journal, January, 2000, Angela M. Weiler, review of *Out of Her Mind,* p. 137.
New Yorker, March 13, 2000, review of *Out of Her Mind,* p. 22.
Tribune Books (Chicago, IL), February 9, 2003, review of *Under the Influence,* p. 6; March 23, 2003, review of *Out of Her Mind,* p. 6.

ONLINE

Sundress Publications, http://www.sundress.net/ (April 20, 2007), review of *Out of Her Mind.**

*　　*　　*

SHAPELL, Nathan 1922-2007

OBITUARY NOTICE— See index for *CA* sketch: Born March 6, 1922, in Sosnowitz, Poland; died March 11, 2007. Builder and author. A Holocaust survivor who immigrated to California, Shapell became a prominent commercial and home developer. He was born Natan Schapelski and was just a teenager when the Nazis invaded and sent his mother to a ghetto. For some time he smuggled Jews out of Poland until he was captured and sent to Auschwitz. His brother-in-law Max Webb was there and, along with help from others, hid Shapell from the Nazi guards, thus saving his life. Shapell would eventually spend time in two other concentration camps until the Allies liberated them. After the war, he lived in Munchberg, where he helped build houses for homeless Jewish refugees. After marrying, he moved to Los Angeles in 1952, changed his last name, and established a construction business in Beverly Hills with Webb and his brother David. The company prospered, and over the next decades Shapell Industries built communities all up and down the California coastline. They specialized in high-quality homes, including those on the former Metro-Goldwyn-Mayer ranch in Thousand Oaks. In addition to this business, he served for many years on the Little Hoover Commission, which worked to reform nursing home standards and education spending, and to lower taxes. He chaired the commission from 1979 until 1997. He also served on other state and local advisory boards, as well as on the board of nonprofit organizations, such as Project Hope and the Jewish Federation Council. Shapell wrote about his wartime experiences in *Witness to the Truth* (1974). He passed away while on a ship heading home to San Pedro, California.

OBITUARIES AND OTHER SOURCES:

BOOKS

Shapell, Nathan, *Witness to the Truth,* McKay, 1974.

PERIODICALS

Los Angeles Times, March 13, 2007, p. B8.

*   *   *

SHAW, June

PERSONAL: Married (husband deceased); children: five. *Education:* B.A. *Hobbies and other interests:* Swimming, fishing, dancing, flower gardening.

ADDRESSES: Home—LA.

CAREER: Writer. Former teacher.

MEMBER: Mystery Writers of America, Romance Writers of America, Sisters in Crime.

AWARDS, HONORS: Grants from Louisiana Division of the Arts.

WRITINGS:

Relative Danger (mystery novel), Five Star (Detroit, MI), 2006.

Also author of one-act plays produced Off-Off-Broadway. Author of *Attacked,* a screenplay. Contributor to periodicals.

SIDELIGHTS: June Shaw is the author of the mystery novel *Relative Danger,* featuring widowed business owner Cealie Gunther. Shaw, who raised five children, earned a college degree, and became a teacher after her own husband passed away, has published a number of short stories, completed a screenplay, and had two plays produced Off-Off-Broadway.

In *Relative Danger,* Cealie arrives in the Chicago suburbs to visit her granddaughter, Kat, an honor student who is about to graduate from high school. A dark cloud falls over the upcoming ceremony when a school custodian, Mr. Labruzzo, is found dead in the auditorium, having fallen from a balcony. Police soon rule the death a murder, however, and one of Kat's favorite teachers, Miss Hernandez, who has become a mother figure to the motherless girl, becomes the chief suspect. A distraught Kat refuses to go back to class, though it means she will miss final exams and graduation. In an effort to solve the crime and get Kat back in class, Cealie takes a job as a substitute teacher at the school, where she encounters unruly students and eccentric colleagues. Shaw's debut novel received generally strong reviews. "*Relative Danger* has lots going for it: a likeable heroine, a bit of romance and a sense of humor," noted a contributor on the *Cozy Library* Web site. A *Publishers Weekly* critic observed that "humorous dialogue, a suspenseful climax and good character development should please . . . fans."

Shaw told *CA:* "I'm thrilled to be included in *Contemporary Authors,* first of all because it affirms that I've fulfilled my childhood dream of becoming an author! I'm also excited because as a student, I often did research for school reports in *Contemporary Authors.*

"My dream started in ninth grade. My English teacher told me to write a paragraph about a splinter to practice writing for an upcoming literary rally. I described a sliver of wood and he said, 'No, like this.' And then he wrote 'Ouch!' He told me to take it from the splinter's point of view. Someone just sat on him. That was it—my inspiration for becoming a writer. Before that I thought all authors were old men who'd died in Europe. I had no idea that a writer could create a thing or person who did and said what the author wanted the character to do.

"I was busy in school and soon afterward, with getting married and having five children close together. My husband died while they were young. Besides the emotional turmoil, I knew I had to earn a living. I wanted to write—but my silly children wanted to wear shoes and eat. I finished college and then taught English to teenagers while I raised my own and sold a few short pieces to periodicals. I've retired now, and my sweet children have given me eight terrific grandkids. And I sold my debut novel!

"I enjoy numerous authors, especially the humor and pace of the 'Stephanie Plum' books by Janet Evanovitch. I feel truly honored to have some readers compare my work to hers.

"I also feel successful because many readers tell me *Relative Danger* made them fear, laugh, and cry. Their feedback makes believe I've done my job of being entertaining. I hope I'll be able to entertain readers for many more years."

BIOGRAPHICAL AND CRITICAL SOURCES:

PERIODICALS

Kirkus Reviews, October 1, 2006, review of *Relative Danger,* p. 993.
Publishers Weekly, October 30, 2006, review of *Relative Danger,* p. 41.

ONLINE

Cozy Library, http://www.cozylibrary.com/ (September 13, 2006), review of *Relative Danger.*

June Shaw Home Page, http://www.juneshaw.com (April 20, 2007).
Spinetingler Magazine, http://www.spinetinglermag.com/ (January 2, 2007), Dawn Dowdle, review of *Relative Danger.*

*   *   *

SHERMAN, David J. 1966-

PERSONAL: Born 1966, in Racine, WI; married; children: one daughter.

ADDRESSES: Home—CA.

CAREER: Writer, 1998—. Worked variously as a computer programmer, warehouse manager, truck driver, dispatcher, safety consultant, and record store owner.

MEMBER: National Writers Union, Mystery Writers of America, Sisters in Crime, Private Eye Writers of America, American Crime Writers League.

WRITINGS:

The Dark Side: A Jack Murphy Novel, Bloody Mist Press (Las Vegas, NV), 2002.

Also author of poems and short stories.

SIDELIGHTS: David J. Sherman is the author of *The Dark Side: A Jack Murphy Novel.* "My style of writing is hardboiled PI, kick-ass partner, guns, drugs, crimes, killings and the loss of a kneecap or two," Sherman told Jon Jordan on the *Books 'n' Bytes* Web site. Citing his influences as Raymond Chandler, Robert B. Parker, Robert Crais, and Dennis Lehane, Sherman added: "All I try to do when I write is be real. I view myself as a storyteller, not an English major."

In *The Dark Side,* Sherman introduces Jack Murphy, a former small-town police officer turned private investigator who lives in Los Angeles. Murphy, who specializes in tracking down deadbeat dads and cheating husbands, is hired by Raymond Sanders to locate his sixteen-year-old daughter, Carrie. Though Sanders reveals that the first detective he hired was killed under mysterious circumstances, it doesn't prevent Murphy from taking the case. With the help of his sidekick Arturo, a former gang member and ex-convict, and his resourceful secretary Nadia, Murphy enters the seedy world of child pornography and prostitution. "Sherman writes with class," Robin Glazer wrote on *Myshelf.com.* "His violent scenes are never gratuitous and always expertly done." In his debut novel, Sherman "combines a mystery-noir prose style with a vividly contemporary setting," noted *Booklist* reviewer David Pitt.

BIOGRAPHICAL AND CRITICAL SOURCES:

PERIODICALS

Booklist, October 1, 2002, David Pitt, review of *The Dark Side: A Jack Murphy Novel,* p. 305.

ONLINE

Books 'n' Bytes, http://www.booksnbytes.com/ (May 14, 2007), Jon Jordan, "Interview with David J. Sherman."

David J. Sherman Home Page, http://www.davidjsherman.com (September 26, 2004).

Myshelf.com, http://www.myshelf.com/ (April 20, 2007), Robin Glazer, review of *The Dark Side.*

Mystery Morgue, http://breakthroughpromotions.com/mysterymorgue/ (May 14, 2007), Dawn McKinney, review of *The Dark Side.*

Reviewing the Evidence, http://www.reviewingthe evidence.com/ (November 2, 2002), Angel L. Soto, review of *The Dark Side.**

*   *   *

SHOOLERY, Judith L.

PERSONAL: Married. *Education:* Kalamazoo College, graduated, 1957.

ADDRESSES: Home—Half Moon Bay, CA.

CAREER: Former science teacher; Hoover Institution, Stanford University, Stanford, CA, book editor, 1979-1990.

WRITINGS:

(With Edward Teller) *Memoirs: A Twentieth-Century Journey in Science and Politics,* Perseus (Cambridge, MA), 2001.

SIDELIGHTS: Judith L. Shoolery is a former science teacher who became a writer and editor. She collaborated with the late physicist Edward Teller to write *Memoirs: A Twentieth-Century Journey in Science and Politics.* The book recounts Teller's controversial career and life with a focus on the connection between science and politics, especially in relation to Teller's work on nuclear weapons with J. Robert Oppenheimer and others. The book includes Teller's views about many modern-day scientific advances, as well as a thirty-page appendix of transcripts outlining why Teller testified against Oppenheimer in a 1954 congressional hearing. "Curiosity will impel even his harshest critics into these memoirs," wrote Bryce Christensen in *Booklist.* Richard Rhodes noted in the *New York Times Book Review:* "Edward Teller has published other memoirs, but none has been so comprehensive as this presumably final statement." Although reviewers observed that much of Teller's views about science, politics, and his role in nuclear arms development appear egocentric, many critics also commented that Teller and Shoolery provide an honest and heartfelt look at Teller's youth and early career. A *Kirkus Reviews* contributor, for example, stated that the "narrative has many fine moments," adding that the book's authors write "affectingly of his youth in a Hungary, and later Germany, in which anti-Semitism was on the rise." In *Commentary,* Dan Seligman called the book "a terrific read," adding: "Its up-close portraits of the scientific luminaries who created nuclear weapons ring true."

BIOGRAPHICAL AND CRITICAL SOURCES:

PERIODICALS

Booklist, October 15, 2001, Bryce Christensen, review of *Memoirs: A Twentieth-Century Journey in Science and Politics,* p. 364.

Bulletin of the Atomic Scientists, January-February, 2002, Mary Palevsky, review of *Memoirs,* p. 64.

Choice, April, 2002, N. Sadanand, review of *Memoirs,* p. 1443.

Commentary, November, 2001, Dan Seligman, review of *Memoirs,* p. 69.

Isis, June, 2003, Zuoyue Wang, review of *Memoirs,* p. 419.

Journal of Military History, April, 2002, Frank Settle, review of *Memoirs,* p. 635.

Kirkus Reviews, September 1, 2001, review of *Memoirs,* p. 1278.

National Interest, spring, 2002, Adam Schulman, review of *Memoirs,* p. 130.

Nature, February 14, 2002, review of *Memoirs,* p. 735.

New York Times Book Review, November 25, 2001, Richard Rhodes, review of *Memoirs,* p. 15.

Times Literary Supplement, June 28, 2002, Brian Pippard, review of *Memoirs,* p. 28.

Wall Street Journal, October 30, 2001, Gabriel Schoenfeld, review of *Memoirs,* p. A21.

Washington Post, January 6, 2002, review of *Memoirs,* p. T06.

Wilson Quarterly, winter, 2002, Kai Bird, review of *Memoirs,* p. 109.

ONLINE

Christian Science Monitor Online, http://www.csmonitor.com/ (November 8, 2001), Robert C. Cowen, review of *Memoirs.*

JewishPress.com, http://www.thejewishpress.com/ (July 24, 2002), Michael Skakun, review of *Memoirs.*

Physics Today Online, http://www.aip.org/ (September 20, 2004), Hans A. Bethe, review of *Memoirs.*

Texas Observer Online, http://www.texasobserver.org/ (July 5, 2002), Anna Mayo, review of *Memoirs.*

USA Today Online, http://www.usatoday.com/ (January 11, 2002), Susan Page, "Teller Has No Apologies for His Cold War Role," interview with Judith L. Shoolery.*

* * *

SINGH, Sonia

PERSONAL: Born in CA. *Education:* California State University at Fullerton, bachelor's degree.

CAREER: Writer. Previously worked in India writing for a television soap opera.

WRITINGS:

NOVELS

Goddess for Hire, Avon Trade (New York, NY), 2004.

Bollywood Confidential, Avon Books (New York, NY), 2005.

Ghost, Interrupted, Avon Trade (New York, NY), 2007.

SIDELIGHTS: Sonia Singh is a first-generation Indo-American whose novels provide a humorous look at both American and Indian cultures. Her first novel, *Goddess for Hire,* features Maya, an Indian-American woman who at thirty is single and not a doctor, which is a great disappointment to the rest of family, who are all doctors. In a strange turn of events, Maya is kidnapped by two men who say that she is the host for the return of the dark goddess Kali. They inform her that it is her duty to fight evil. In the meantime, Maya must deal with a fanatic trying to find Kali and kill Maya in the process. She is also dealing with her feelings about Tahir, an Indian man picked by Maya's aunt for an arranged marriage. *Library Journal* contributor Beth Gibbs remarked that the author's "descriptions of her [Maya's] lifestyle and her traditional family . . . are quite humorous." In a review on the *Crescent Blues Book Views* Web site, Kathryn Yelinek similarly observed that the author "writes with a witty, minimalist style."

Singh's second novel, *Bollywood Confidential,* tells the story of Raveena Rai, who is finding it tough to break into Hollywood films. She takes a role in a Bollywood film in India, looking at the project as an opportunity to also explore her Indian heritage. When she arrives in India, Raveena meets her Uncle Heeru, who lives with pigeons. Raveena, who ends up fighting off the advances of a Bollywood director, then meets the Bollywood superstar Siddharth and begins a torrid romance. Calling the novel a "zany, laugh-out-loud romp," Jenny McLarin added in *Booklist* that the author "provides a compelling description of Bombay." A *Publishers Weekly* contributor referred to *Bollywood Confidential* as a "snappy overseas romp."

Ghost, Interrupted features the members of the Cold Spot ghost-hunting firm: Scott Wilder, a former stockbroker with no paranormal powers; Anjali Kumar, an Indian-American psychic Scott hires to work for him; and Coulter Marshal, who uses telekinesis to move things with his mind. The novel revolves around the group's efforts to rid upscale homes of the ghosts that haunt them; Anjali's affairs with her two coworkers also occupy much of the plot. Eventually, the group finds itself in competition with a similar organization headed by Scott's ex-girlfriend as both groups try to rid a military base of a tortured dead soldier's ghost. In her review in *Library Journal,* Nanette Donohue wrote that "the result is fast paced and clever, and it works." Several reviewers also appreciated the author's ability to create interesting characters. For example, a *Publishers Weekly* contributor wrote that "the book's unlikely heroes make for pleasant company." *Booklist* contributor Kristine Huntley called *Ghost, Interrupted* "out-of-this-world fun . . . with a compelling cast."

BIOGRAPHICAL AND CRITICAL SOURCES:

PERIODICALS

Booklist, July, 2005, Jenny McLarin, review of *Bollywood Confidential,* p. 1902; December 1, 2006, Kristine Huntley, review of *Ghost, Interrupted,* p. 33.

Kirkus Reviews, May 15, 2004, review of *Goddess for Hire,* p. 468; October 15, 2006, review of *Ghost, Interrupted,* p. 1043.

Library Journal, July, 2004, Beth Gibbs, review of *Goddess for Hire,* p. 74; December 1, 2006, Nanette Donohue, review of *Ghost, Interrupted,* p. 116.

Publishers Weekly, May 23, 2005, review of *Bollywood Confidential,* p. 56; October 23, 2006, review of *Ghost, Interrupted,* p. 33.

ONLINE

Crescent Blues Book Views, http://www.crescentblues.com/ (April 24, 2007), Kathryn Yelinek, review of *Goddess for Hire.*

DesiLit Daily, http://www.desilit.org/ (May 10, 2005), Pooja Makhijani, review of *Bollywood Confidential.*

Reeta.sawf.org, http://reeta.sawf.org/ (April 24, 2007), review of *Goddess for Hire.*

Sawnet, http://www.sawnet.org/ (April 24, 2007), Reeta Sinha, review of *Goddess for Hire.*

Sonia Singh Home Page, http://www.soniasingh.com (April 24, 2007).*

* * *

SIZEMORE, Susan

PERSONAL: Hobbies and other interests: Knitting, collecting art glass, reading, watching basketball.

ADDRESSES: E-mail—sgsizemore@msn.com.

CAREER: Has worked as an editor for Spec Press, as a chef, and an anthropologist.

AWARDS, HONORS: Golden Heart Award, Romance Writers of America for *Wings of the Storm;* Sapphire Award, for a short story.

WRITINGS:

ROMANCE NOVELS

Wings of the Storm, Harper Monogram (New York, NY), 1992.

My First Duchess, Harper Monogram (New York, NY), 1993.

My Own True Love, Harper Monogram (New York, NY), 1994.

In My Dreams, Harper Monogram (New York, NY), 1994.

Nothing Else Matters, Harper Monogram (New York, NY), 1995.

After the Storm, Harper Monogram (New York, NY), 1996.

The Autumn Lord, Harper Monogram (New York, NY), 1996.

One of These Nights, Harper Monogram (New York, NY), 1997.

Stranger by Her Side, Silhouette (New York, NY), 1997.

The Price of Innocence, Avon Books (New York, NY), 1999.

His Last Best Hope, Silhouette (New York, NY), 2000.

On a Long Ago Night, Avon Books (New York, NY), 2000.

The Price of Passion, Avon Books (New York, NY), 2001.

Too Wicked to Marry, Avon Books (New York, NY), 2002.

Captured Innocence, Avon Books (New York, NY), 2003.

Scandalous Miranda, Avon Books (New York, NY), 2005.

"LAWS OF THE BLOOD" SERIES; FANTASY NOVELS

The Hunt, Ace Books (New York, NY), 1999.

Partners, Ace Books (New York, NY), 2000.

Companions, Ace Books (New York, NY), 2001.

Deceptions, Ace Books (New York, NY), 2002.

Heroes, Ace Books (New York, NY), 2003.

"PRIMES UNIVERSE" SERIES; PARANORMAL ROMANCE NOVELS

I Burn for You, Pocket Star Books (New York, NY), 2003.

I Thirst for You, Pocket Star Books (New York, NY), 2003.

I Hunger for You, Pocket Star Books (New York, NY), 2004.

(With Christine Feehan) *The Shadows of Christmas Past: Two Novellas,* Pocket Star Books (New York, NY), 2004.

Crave the Night (omnibus; include the novels *I Burn for You, I Hunger for You,* and *I Thirst for You*), Pocket Books (New York, NY), 2005.

Master of Darkness, Pocket Star Books (New York, NY), 2006.

Primal Heat, Pocket Books (New York, NY), 2006.

OTHER

Gates of Hell, Speculation Press (Kingston, IL), 2000.

(With Marguerite Krause) *Moons' Dreaming* ("Children of the Rock" series), Five Star (Waterville, ME), 2003.

(With Marguerite Krause) *Moons' Dancing* ("Children of the Rock" series), Five Star (Waterville, ME), 2004.

Also author of the blog *Susan Sizemore's Space.* Work represented in anthologies, including *Vengeance Fantastic,* DAW, 2002; *Pharaoh Fantastic,* DAW, 2002; and *The Magic Shop,* DAW, 2004.

SIDELIGHTS: Susan Sizemore is the author of romance novels, historical romances, fantasy, science fiction, and contemporary suspense. For example, her "Laws of the Blood" series is about the culture of vampirism in modern America. In her first book in the series, *The Hunt,* the author introduces readers to this modern vampire society, including its internal conflicts. On the one side are those vampires who want to keep the vampire laws designed to protect both them and humans; the other vampires want to forget about the laws. In this installment, Selim is an Enforcer located in Los Angeles who must contend with a group of vampires who want to hunt without restraint. "The characterizations are excellent, the plot strong and the pace well implemented," reported Steve Lazarowitz on the *SF Site.*

Partners continues the series and features Char, an Enforcer vampire whose job it is to keep vampires in line and their presence hidden from the normal humans. When Char discovers a cult in Seattle that threatens both vampires and humans, she must set out to destroy them while battling her own inner demons in the process. Lazarowitz, writing again on the *SF Site,* noted that the author "gives us a cast of memorable characters that are realistic, entertaining and interesting," adding: "Her descriptions are wonderful." In *Companions,* Selena Crawford is a homicide detective who is also the human companion of the vampire Istvan. Despite Selena's efforts to resist her attraction to Istvan, the two are soon working together on a case involving the mutilated corpses of vampires. Kristina Huntley, writing in *Booklist,* referred to *Companions* as "a rousing adventure."

The next book in the series, *Deceptions,* focuses on Olympias, an Enforcer vampire who tries to rid the Washington, DC, area of certain nests of vampires. However, Olympias raises the ire of her fellow vampires when she becomes attracted to a human, Mike Falconer, whom another vampire wants for a mate. Further complicating the issue is the fact that Mike is part of a secret government project that may have discovered the existence of vampires. Writing in *Booklist,* Huntley called the novel a "thrilling, sexually charged yarn." The fifth installment in the "Laws of the Blood" series, *Heroes,* finds vampires vacationing in Las Vegas. Charlotte has a human lover, Jebel, who is reluctant to let Charlotte turn him into a vampire. Also on hand is an Enforcer named Ben, who is out to uphold the vampire laws, and a group of vampires determined to bring down all of the Enforcers. *Booklist* critic Huntley wrote that the novel "opens up intriguing possibilities for future installments."

Sizemore is also the author of the "Primes Universe" paranormal romance series. Much like her "Laws of the Blood" series, these books present a modern-day vampire culture made up of various clans, including the Clan Primes, a group of vampires whose job it is to protect humans. However, the bulk of the stories focus on the paranormal romance element. For example, in *I Burn for You,* the first novel in the series, Alex Reynard of the Reynard Clan is undergoing an experiment to allow him to go out into the daylight. Working as a bodyguard, Reynard meets his soul mate, Domini Lancer, a mortal bodyguard who is nevertheless being hunted by fanatical vampire slayers. "This is definitely a book for readers who like romance novels that have a strong alpha male hero," according to a contributor to the *Love Vampires* Web site.

In the second book in the series, *I Thirst for You,* the author introduces the vampire Marcus Cage, who has escaped from medical scientists experimenting on him. He quickly comes across Jo Elliot, whom he recognizes as his soul mate. He drinks her blood and turns her into a vampire. However, Jo does not realize what has happened to her as she and Marcus hide from Marcus's former captors. Kristin Ramsdell, writing in the *Library Journal,* noted that the book "will appeal to fans who like their vampire heroes hot, sexy."

In addition to writing more mainstream romances such as the historical romance *Scandalous Miranda,* the author has also penned science fiction romances, such as *The Gates of Hell.* This novel revolves around the Sagouran plague, which threatens to wipe out every civilization it infects. Roxanne is a physician and a member of the most revered race in the universe, known as the healers of Kiltirah. Because of her healing abilities, she is sought after by several civilizations

in crisis. As each group tries to get to her, intrigue and murder results. Roxanne is eventually kidnapped by space pirate Pyr. Despite Pyr's nasty reputation, the two develop a romance. "Sizemore's characters are strongly drawn and interesting," reported Lisa Du-Mond on the *SF Site.*

BIOGRAPHICAL AND CRITICAL SOURCES:

PERIODICALS

Booklist, September 15, 2001, Kristine Huntley, review of *Companions,* p. 201; October 15, 2002, Kristine Huntley, review of *Deceptions,* p. 396; October 1, 2003, Nina C. Davis, review of *I Burn for You,* p. 307; October 15, 2003, Kristine Huntley, review of *Heroes,* p. 400.
California Bookwatch, November, 2006, review of *Primal Heat.*
Kliatt, January, 2000, Joseph R. DeMarco, review of *The Hunt,* p. 24.
Library Journal, May 15, 2000, Kristin Ramsdell, review of *On a Long Ago Night,* p. 78; February 15, 2001, Kristin Ramsdell, review of *The Price of Passion,* p. 154; May 15, 2004, Kristin Ramsdell, review of *I Thirst for You,* p. 71; November 25, 2004, Kristen Ramsdell, review of *The Shadows of Christmas Past: Two Novellas,* p. 47.
MBR Bookwatch, May 1, 2005, review of *I Hunger for You.*
Publishers Weekly, November 1, 2004, review of *The Shadows of Christmas Past,* p. 49.
Voice of Youth Advocates, April, 2000, Shari Fesko, review of *The Hunt,* p. 50; June 1, 2003, review of *Deceptions,* p. 152.

ONLINE

All about Romance, http://www.likesbooks.com/ (September 20, 2004), Blythe Barnhill, review of *On a Long Ago Night,* Colleen McMahon, review of *Partners,* Rachel Potter, review of *Companions,* Liz Zink, review of *Deceptions,* Heidi L. Haglin, review of *Too Wicked to Marry,* and Rachel Potter, review of *Captured Innocence.*
Best Reviews, http://thebestreviews.com/ (September 11, 2001), Harriet Klausner, review of *Companions;* (November 5, 2001), Harriet Klausner, review of *Gates of Hell;* (December 1, 2001),

Harriet Klausner, review of *Too Wicked to Marry;* (September 15, 2002), Harriet Klausner, review of *Deceptions;* (December 13, 2002), Harriet Klausner, review of *Captured Innocence.*

Crescent Blues Book Views, http://www.crescentblues. com/ (September 20, 2004), Jean Marie Ward, review of *The Gates of Hell;* (April 24, 2007), Jean Marie Ward, "Susan Sizemore: Multiple Mythos," interview with the author.

Love Vampires, http://www.lovevampires.com/ (April 24, 2007), reviews of *Master of Darkness, I Hunger for Your, I Thirst for You,* and *I Burn for You.*

ParaNormal Romance Reviews, http://pnr. thebestreviews.com/ (April 24, 2007), brief profile of Susan Sizemore.

Romance Reader, http://www.theromancereader.com/ (January 5, 1999), Thea Davis, review of *His Last Best Hope;* (June 12, 2000), Cathy Sova, review of *On a Long Ago Night;* (February 3, 2001), Wilda Turner, review of *The Price of Passion;* (January 21, 2002), Jean Mason, review of *Too Wicked to Marry;* (September 20, 2004), Cathy Sova, review of *The Price of Innocence.*

SF Site, http://www.sfsite.com/ (April 24, 2007), Steve Lazarowitz, reviews of *Partners* and *The Hunt,* Lisa DuMond, review of *The Gates of Hell,* and Cindy Lynn Speer, review of *Deceptions.*

SFFWorld.com, http://www.sffworld.com/ (December 1, 1999), interview with Susan Sizemore.

Susan Sizemore Home Page, http://www. susansizemore.com (September 20, 2004).

Vampire Genre, http://www.vampiregenre.com/ (January 29, 2006), review of *Master of Darkness;* (July 25, 2006), Vicky London, review of *Primal Heat.*

We Really Dig Romance Novels, http://www. wereallydig.com/ (April 24, 2007), "Interview with Romance Author Susan Sizemore."

Writing-World.com, http://www.writing-world.com/ (April 24, 2007), Moira Allen, "Writing with Bite: An Interview with Susan Sizemore."*

*   *   *

SLATER, Susan 1942-

PERSONAL: Born 1942.

CAREER: Writer. Has worked for a government contractor, and as a human resources director, creative writing instructor, corporate trainer, technical editor,

and human resource manager. Has also taught English as second language (ESL) and English as a foreign language (EFL) in Mexico and Central America.

WRITINGS:

Flash Flood (mystery novel), Poisoned Pen Press (Scottsdale, AZ), 2003.
Five o'Clock Shadow (mystery novel), Poisoned Pen Press (Scottsdale, AZ), 2004.

"BEN PECOS" SERIES; MYSTERY NOVELS

The Pumpkin Seed Massacre, Intrigue Press (Angel Fire, NM), 1999.
Yellow Lies, Intrigue Press (Philadelphia, PA), 2000.
Thunderbird, Intrigue Press (Philadelphia, PA), 2002.

Work represented in anthologies, including *Crooks, Crimes, and Christmas,* Worldwide Library, 2003.

SIDELIGHTS: Susan Slater is a writer and author of the "Ben Pecos" mystery series. The series features a young Tewa Pueblo Indian who is a psychologist and medical investigator working on a Pueblo Indian reservation. In the first novel in the series, *The Pumpkin Seed Massacre,* Ben investigates a mysterious and deadly epidemic. Although a Pueblo by birth, Ben knows little about his people's ways, which is hindering him in his investigation since he thinks that something in the Pueblo folk practices may be causing the epidemic. *Booklist* critic John Rowen observed that Slater's debut features a "brisk pace, well-rendered New Mexico landscape, and challenging plot." Susan A. Zappia wrote in the *Library Journal* that the author "successfully taps into the complex issues facing Native American communities in this dynamic mystery."

Yellow Lies finds Ben Pecos and his fiancée, Julie Conlin, dealing with a corpse that mysteriously appears at Ben's boardinghouse. It turns out that Hawiuh artist and con man Salvador Zuni previously found the body in the trunk of his car, from which it later disappeared. Rowen, writing again in *Booklist,* noted that the novel features "dry humor; crackling suspense; and a surprise ending." According to Rita Ratacheck on *MurderEx-*

press.net, Slater has produced "a good story and a mystic atmosphere sprinkled with tribal rituals and unanswered questions."

Thunderbird features policeman Tommy Spottedhorse and Ben Pecos working on a case involving UFO sightings and mutilated livestock. When Tommy's love interest, Brenda Begay, disappears, the investigation turns more serious as Tommy traces the UFO sightings to an army stealth airplane crash. Writing in *Booklist,* Jenny McLarin remarked that the author "effectively develops the mystery elements of her story." In a review in the *Library Journal,* Rex Klett praised the novel for its "suspenseful narrative and colorful glimpses of Native American life."

Slater has also written other mystery novels, including *Flash Flood,* which features private investigator Dan Mahoney working for an insurance company on an investigation into the deaths of three prize-winning cattle. The cattle belonged to Billy Roland Edklund, who wants the insurance company to pay compensation in the area of six figures. The apparently simple case turns complicated with the death of an ex-con and his girlfriend. Dan, meanwhile, has affair with Professor Elaine Linden; although Dan wants to quickly end the affair, he is badgered by the FBI to continue the relationship as part of an investigation they are conducting. A *Kirkus Reviews* contributor called the mystery a "lively, surprising, overstuffed case." A *Publishers Weekly* critic commented that "Dan Mahoney is an appealingly resilient character."

In *Five o'Clock Shadow* Pauly Caton witnesses her husband's death in a ballooning accident in the New Mexico desert. Strangely, she also sees a small naked boy running from the crash site and finds another man at the site who has been shot in the head. An autopsy of her husband reveals that he had a vasectomy. Pauly, who had been discussing having children, was unaware of her husband's operation. As she investigates her husband's past, she discovers that he is not the man she thought he was and may even have been a pedophile. "From the book's devastating opening to its chilling climax, readers will be captivated by Slater's fresh, gutsy heroine," asserted a *Publishers Weekly* contributor.

Slater told *CA:* "Reading is what first got me interested in writing. I try to learn from every writer I read. There is such talent out there. For example, Craig Johnson's beginnings and endings are inspiring!

"I treat writing like any job . . . nine to five daily, weekends off. Vacations only if I earn them!

"The most surprising thing I have learned as a writer is that writing is very, very hard work; but somehow frustratingly rewarding—I can't imagine doing anything else! But I did think that each book would get easier!"

When asked which of her books is her favorite, Slater said: "Can a 'mother' really play favorites? Well, if I have to . . . I like the 'Ben Pecos' series because it's nicely crafted, and *Flash Flood* as a stand alone because I made a convoluted plot make sense!

"I would like to think that the 'Ben Pecos' series will introduce readers to the beauty and mystique of the Southwest. I live in a rich part of the United States. Other than that, I just want to entertain—provide a good read and maybe be a little thought provoking."

BIOGRAPHICAL AND CRITICAL SOURCES:

PERIODICALS

Booklist, September 1, 1999, John Rowen, review of *The Pumpkin Seed Massacre,* p. 73; August, 2000, John Rowen, review of *Yellow Lies,* p. 2122; January 1, 2002, Jenny McLarin, review of *Thunderbird,* p. 820; February 15, 2004, Jenny McLarin, review of *Five o'Clock Shadow,* p. 1044.

Bookwatch, April 1, 2004, review of *Five o'Clock Shadow,* p. 10.

Drood Review of Mystery, January 1, 2002, review of *Thunderbird,* p. 11.

Kirkus Reviews, November 15, 2002, review of *Flash Flood,* p. 1661.

Library Journal, September 1, 1999, Susan A. Zappia, review of *The Pumpkin Seed Massacre,* p. 237; January, 2002, Rex Klett, review of *Thunderbird,* p. 157; January, 2003, Rex E. Klett, review of *Flash Flood,* p. 162.

Publishers Weekly, September 27, 1999, review of *The Pumpkin Seed Massacre,* p. 77; July 31, 2000, review of *Yellow Lies,* p. 76; January 14, 2002, review of *Thunderbird,* p. 44; December 9, 2002, review of *Flash Flood,* p. 66; January 19, 2004, review of *Five o'Clock Shadow,* p. 57.

ONLINE

Books 'n' Bytes, http://www.booksnbytes.com/ (September 26, 2004), Harriet Klausner, reviews of *The Pumpkin Seed Massacre, Yellow Lies, Flash Flood,* and *Five o'Clock Shadow.*

Crescent Blues Book Views, http://www.crescentblues. com/ (April 24, 2007), Ceridwen Lewin, review of *Five o'Clock Shadow.*

MurderExpress.net, http://www.murderexpress.net/ (April 24, 2007), Rita Ratacheck, review of *Yellow Lies.*

Mystery Reader, http://www.themysteryreader.com/ (September 26, 2004), Judith Flavell, review of *Flash Flood.*

Susan Slater Home Page, http://www.susanslater.com (April 24, 2007).

*   *   *

SMALL, Karna
   See BODMAN, Karna Small

*   *   *

SMITH, Tom 1953-

PERSONAL: Born 1953, in CT. *Education:* Attended Elmira College and the University of Exeter; Drew University, B.A., 1975; Southern Connecticut State University, M.A., 1977.

ADDRESSES: *E-mail*—ccl1891@crescentcity lynchings. com.

CAREER: Freelance researcher, writer, and editor. Associate writer and columnist for *New Haven Advocate* and *Fairfield Advocate* newspapers, 1978-87. Has also worked as a professional musician, justice of the peace, assistant registrar of voters, fine arts appraiser, and auction runner.

MEMBER: Authors Guild.

WRITINGS:

Discovery of the Americas, 1492-1800 ("Discovery and Exploration" series), Facts on File (New York, NY), 2003.

The Crescent City Lynchings: The Murder of Chief Hennessy, the New Orleans "Mafia" Trials, and the Parish Prison Mob, Lyons Press (Guilford, CT), 2007.

Contributor to books, including *Great American Trials,* Visible Ink Press (Detroit, MI), 1993; *Sex, Sin & Mayhem: Notorious Trials of the 1990s,* Visible Ink Press (Detroit, MI), 1995; *Great World Trials,* Visible Ink Press (Detroit, MI), 1997; *Famous First Facts about the Environment,* H.W. Wilson (New York, NY), 2002; *The American West,* Wiley (New York, NY), 2003; and *Exploration in the World of the Middle Ages, 500-1500,* Facts on File (New York, NY), 2005. Contributor to periodicals, including *Spin, New Times Connecticut,* and *Living Blues.* Contributor of reviews to *Record Roundup,* 1984-94; columnist and contributor for *CT Life,* 1993-97.

SIDELIGHTS: Tom Smith is the author of *The Crescent City Lynchings: The Murder of Chief Hennessy, the New Orleans "Mafia" Trials, and the Parish Prison Mob,* "an engrossing examination of a crime that rocked late-19th-century Louisiana," observed a *Kirkus Reviews* contributor. In October 1890, New Orleans police chief David Hennessy was gunned down while walking home; as he lay dying, Henness y blamed the shooting on Italians. Mass arrests followed, and police eventually charged nineteen Italian and Italian American men with conspiring to murder the chief. At the first of two trials, nine of the defendants were acquitted, prompting charges of jury tampering. An outraged mob stormed the Orleans Parish Prison and lynched eleven of the men, creating a diplomatic crisis between the United States and Italy. "Quoting heavily from newspaper accounts, Smith is able to bring a local and timely flavor" to his work, noted a critic in *Publishers Weekly.* "In *The Crescent City Lynchings,*" wrote New Orleans *Times-Picayne* contributor Michael A. Ross, "Smith rejects the approach of previous historians, and instead lets the reader decide whether the jury's verdict in the Hennessy case was just. Although some readers may get bogged down in the welter of witnesses, conflicting testimony and legal maneuvering, Smith's account will appeal to those who want to know exactly what evidence the jury heard." *Booklist* reviewer Mike Tribby also offered praise for Smith's work, calling it "a rich, insightful slice of Americana."

BIOGRAPHICAL AND CRITICAL SOURCES:

PERIODICALS

Booklist, November 15, 2006, Mike Tribby, review of *The Crescent City Lynchings: The Murder of Chief Hennessy, the New Orleans "Mafia" Trials, and the Parish Prison Mob,* p. 11.
Kirkus Reviews, October 1, 2006, review of *The Crescent City Lynchings,* p. 1005.
Publishers Weekly, November 20, 2006, review of *The Crescent City Lynchings,* p. 55.
Times-Picayne (New Orleans, LA), March 11, 2007, Michael A. Ross, review of *The Crescent City Lynchings.*

ONLINE

BlogCritics Online, http://blogcritics.org/ (February 3, 2007), Simon Barrett, review of *The Crescent City Lynchings;* (February 5, 2007), Simon Barrett, "An Interview with Tom Smith, Author of *The Crescent City Lynchings.*"
Clews, http://laurajames.typepad.com/ (February 21, 2007) Laura James, "*Clews* Interviews True Crime Author Tom Smith."
Tom Smith Home Page, http://www.crescentcity lynchings.com (April 20, 2007).*

*   *   *

SOLDEN, Sari

PERSONAL: Education: Graduate of University of Michigan; California State University, M.A.

ADDRESSES: Home and office—Ann Arbor, MI.

CAREER: Psychotherapist and marriage and family counselor, Ann Arbor, MI. Public speaker and consultant to mental health professionals on the topic of adult Attention-Deficit/Hyperactivity Disorder (AD/HD). Former consultant to counseling program for adults with learning disabilities at California's Marin County Family Service Agency.

MEMBER: National Attention Deficit Disorder Association, Children and Adults with AD/HD (CHADD), American Counseling Association, California Association for Marriage and Family Therapists, American Association for Marriage and Family Therapists.

AWARDS, HONORS: National Attention Deficit Disorder Association award for outstanding service by a helping professional, 1996.

WRITINGS:

Women with Attention Deficit Disorder: Embracing Disorganization at Home and in the Workplace, Underwood Books (Grass Valley, CA), 1995, revised 10th anniversary edition published as *Women with Attention Deficit Disorder: Embrace Your Differences and Transform Your Life,* Underwood Books (Nevada City, CA), 2005.
Journeys through ADDulthood: Discover a New Sense of Identity and Meaning While Living with Attention Deficit Disorder, Walker (New York, NY), 2002.

SIDELIGHTS: Sari Solden, a psychotherapist who specializes in treating individuals with attention-deficit/hyperactivity disorder, is the author of *Women with Attention Deficit Disorder: Embrace Your Differences and Transform Your Life.* In the work, Solden, who herself has Attention Deficit Disorder (ADD), discusses the symptoms of the condition, examines available treatments, and presents strategies for living a productive life. "Solden's own journey, plus the case histories she records, are painful yet powerful insights to the world of a disorder which can lead to creative problem solving and a compassion for others with ADD," observed a contributor in *Herizons.*

In *Journeys through ADDulthood: Discover a New Sense of Identity and Meaning While Living with Attention Deficit Disorder,* Solden outlines a three-step approach to leading a fulfilling life for adults with ADD. The author contends that individuals must first understand the disorder, then discover and accept one's true identity, and finally learn to connect with others. "The ADHD adult has to separate themselves and their self-worth from the symptoms of ADHD," wrote Lew Mills on the CHADD of Northern California Web site.

"Solden emphasizes reconnecting with the dreams that unexplained ADHD symptoms may have prematurely cut off." "Perhaps most useful are the dialogues that are included to help readers handle situations that have been problematic in the past," noted a *Publishers Weekly* reviewer. *Library Journal* contributor Dale Farris praised *Journeys through ADDulthood* "for its focus on adults and the author's emphasis on learning how to come to terms with and live comfortably with the disease."

Solden told *CA:* "I have been writing all my life, mostly poetic prose, but these are my first books from a therapist's point of view. Even though these books were written from my mental health professional perspective, I was able to infuse my own authentic voice into the material. This was very important to my goal of connecting to my readers and allowing them to discover themselves in the characters I used to bring the material to life.

"My writing process is unusual in that I have organizational problems and am very creative, so I create a huge amount of writing based on several years of work and then I try and pare it down—more like Michelangelo sculpting out of stone rather than starting from scratch and building up. I put everything I have thought or created or written during several years on a subject and whittle it down to the essence. So I have to go very wide first in order to go deep in the end.

"What I have learned as a writer is how to work with editors—what to insist on in order to keep your voice in tact but when to let go and let someone else objectively help you cut."

When asked to identify which of her books is her favorite, Solden said: "I guess I will always have a special place in my heart for *Women with ADD* because when it first came out, no one else had written on the subject. It healed so many women around the world who saw their experiences described and for the first time knew they were not alone in what they had been experiencing.

"I once read a line that said the best part about writing a book is that 'it brings your tribe to you.' I have made so many wonderful connections and relationships with people who are my 'tribe' all around the world as result of this first book, and I think that has been the best part of all."

BIOGRAPHICAL AND CRITICAL SOURCES:

PERIODICALS

Herizons, summer, 1997, review of *Women with Attention Deficit Disorder: Embracing Disorganization at Home and in the Workplace,* p. 39.

Library Journal, September 15, 2002, Dale Farris, review of *Journeys through ADDulthood: Discover a New Sense of Identity and Meaning While Living with Attention Deficit Disorder,* p. 79.

Publishers Weekly, August 19, 2002, review of *Journeys through ADDulthood,* p. 85.

Small Press Bookwatch, November, 2006, review of *Women with Attention Deficit Disorder: Embrace Your Differences and Transform Your Life.*

ONLINE

CHADD of Northern California, http://www.chaddnorcal.org/Books/Recs.htm/ (April 20, 2007), Lew Mills, review of *Journeys through ADDulthood.*

Sari Solden Home Page, http://www.sarisolden.com (September 27, 2004).

*   *   *

SOROKIN, Vladimir 1955-
(Vladimir Georgievich Sorokin)

PERSONAL: Born August 7, 1955, in Bykovo, Russia; married; children: twin daughters. *Education:* Moscow Institute of Oil and Gas, graduated, 1977.

ADDRESSES: Home—Moscow, Russia.

CAREER: Writer, playwright, illustrator, and artist.

MEMBER: Russian PEN club.

AWARDS, HONORS: National Booker Award, 2001; Award of Andrey Beliy, 2001, for outstanding contributions to Russian literature.

WRITINGS:

Ochered (novel), Sintaksis (Parizh, Russia), 1985, translated, and with an introduction, by Sally Laird as *The Queue,* Readers International (New York, NY), 1988.

Roman, Tri Kita (Moscow, Russia), 1994.

Norma (title means "The Norm"), Tri Kita (Moscow, Russia), 1994.

Tridtsataialiubov' Mariny (title means "Marina's Thirtieth Love"), Izd. R. Eálinina (Moscow, Russia), 1995.

Sobranie Sochinenii v Dvukh Tomakh, Ad Marginem (Moscow, Russia), 1998.

Goluboe Salo (novel; title means "Blue Fat" or "Blue Lard"), Ad Marginem (Moscow, Russia), 1999.

Serdtsa chetyrekh (title means "Four Stout Hearts"), Ad Marginem (Moscow, Russia), 2001.

Pir (title means "The Feast"), Ad Marginem (Moscow, Russia), 2001.

Pervyi Subbotnik: Rasskazy (short stories; title means "The First Saturday Workday"), Ad Marginem (Moscow, Russia), 2001.

Lëd (novel), Ad Marginem (Moscow, Russia), 2002.

ËPS, ZebraE (Moscow, Russia), 2002.

Utro Snaipera, Ad Marginem (Moscow, Russia), 2002.

Put' Bro (novel; title means "Bros Way"), Zakharov (Moscow, Russia), 2004.

Russkii Rasskaz XX Veka, Zakharov (Moscow, Russia), 2005.

Den' Oprichnika, Zakharov (Moscow, Russia), 2006.

Ice, translated by Jamey Gambrell, New York Review Books (New York, NY), 2007.

PLAYS

Pelmeni, first produced 1984.

Zemlyanka (title means "The Hut," or "Earth-House"), 1985.

Russkaya Babushka (title means "Russian Grandmother"), 1988.

Doverie (title means "Confidence"), 1989.

Dismorphomania, 1990.

Yubiley (title means "Anniversary"), 1993.

Hochzeitreise (title means "The Post-Nuptual Journey"), c. 1994.

Shchi (title means "Cabbage Soup"), c. 1995.

Dostoevsky-Trip, 1997.

S Novym Godom (title means "Happy New Year"), 1998.

MOVIE SCREENPLAYS

Bezumny Fritz (title means "Mad Fritz"), 1994.

Moskva (title means "Moscow"), Ad Marginem (Moscow, Russia), 2001.

Kopeyka (title means "Kopeck"), 2002.

4, Zakharov (Moscow, Russia), 2005.

Also author of scripts *Veshch* ("Thing") and *Cashfire.*

Also author of *V Glub' Rossii* (photograph album; title means "In the Depths of Russia"), with Oleg Kulik; and *Deti Rozentalya* (opera libretto; title means "Rosenthal's Children"). Contributor to periodicals, including *A-Ya, Tretya Modernizatsiya, Mitin, Konets Veka, Vestnik Novoy Literatury,* and *Rodnik.* Books have been translated into English, French, German, Dutch, Finnish, Swedish, Italian, Polish, Japanese, and Korean.

SIDELIGHTS: Although he went to college to become an engineer, Vladimir Sorokin instead turned his talents to illustrating books and then to writing them. Since that time, he has become a prolific author of novels, short stories, plays, and screenplays. Sorokin often writes in the fantasy-science fiction genre, but with an ulterior motive. Writing in *World Literature Today,* Tatiana Nazarenko commented that Sorokin has a "well-established practice of deconstructing ideological, mythological, and discursive clichés of totalitarian power." For example, in his satirical and allegorical novel *Norma,* the author tells the story of a prestigious food, "Norm," wanted by all Soviet citizens despite the fact that it is disgusting in odor and taste. "'Norm' becomes a grotesque embodiment of the uniformity of Soviet life, devoid of any individuality that could escape 'norm,'" explained Juri Talvet in *World Literature Today.* "It is not tasty or attractive, but everybody is made to believe that accepting it is the only way to exist." Talvet went on to call the novel "a skillfully constructed and bitingly witty narrative."

Pervyi Subbotnik: Rasskazy is a collection of twenty-nine of the author's short stories that parody Russian culture, society, and politics. For example, in "Sergei Andreevich" the author tells a story of a Russian field trip led by a beloved teacher who inspires one of his students to perform a grotesque act. Writing in *World*

Literature Today, Joseph P. Mozur, Jr., referred to the short story as a "devastating parody of the mentor-protege relationship so prominent in the didactic world of socialist realism." Mozur went on to write that the short-story collection is "strong medicine for readers in a country reared on socialist realism."

In his first novel translated into English, *Ice,* Sorokin tells the strange story of young Muscovites with blonde hair and blue eyes who are being kidnapped and having their chests cracked open with hammers made of ice from outer space. If their hearts are silent, they are left to die; but if the hearts utter some words from a mysterious "heart language" the young men and women are trained to become "heart speakers." The novel revolves around three such survivors and their mentor, who trains them to work towards the apocalyptic destruction of humans. Referring to *Ice* as "a truly thrilling postmodern thriller" in *Library Journal,* Jim Dwyer went on to call the novel "a cautionary tale about totalitarianism, bigotry, elitism, and fundamentalism." Commenting that the novel "provides a head-scratching pleasure and deceptive quickness," Jon Fasman claimed in a *Los Angeles Times* review that "Sorokin is that most dreaded of creatures—an experimental author—but he wears this mantle lightly."

In 2002, Sorokin faced criminal charges for distributing pornography in the form of his novel *Goluboe Salo.* The book contains a homosexual sex scene between the former Soviet Leaders Joseph Stalin and Nikita Khrushchev. Though the charges were eventually dropped, Sorokin's work remains highly controversial in Russia.

BIOGRAPHICAL AND CRITICAL SOURCES:

BOOKS

Vladimir Sorokin, Russlit (Moscow, Russia), 1992.

PERIODICALS

Booklist, December 1, 2006, Micahel Gannon, review of *Ice,* p. 23.

Current Digest of the Post-Soviet Press, August 14, 2002, "Pornography Case Opens against Novelist Sorokin," p. 1.

Economist, August 17, 2002, "Hardly Worth the Trouble; Destroying Books in Russia."

Entertainment Weekly, January 26, 2007, "Robots, Re-boots, and Superhero Shrinks," includes review of *Ice,* p. 75.

IPR Strategic Business Information Database, August 5, 2002, "Russia: Walking Together Leader Justifies Accusations"; August 5, 2002, "Russia: Public Rushes to Read Beleaguered Author"; August 5, 2002, "Russia: Prosecutor Files Charges"; August 5, 2002, "Russia: Culture Ministry Speaks Out against Sorokin Investigation"; September 9, 2002, Russia Court Denies Avant-Garde Writer's Suit"; September 17, 2002, "Russia: Bomb Rocks Walking Together Headqurters"; October 7, 2002, "Russia: Embattled Writer Shortlisted for Presitigous Prize"; October 10, 2002, "Russia: Bookstore Owner Complains of Persecution"; May 4, 2003, "Russia: Pornography Charges Droopped against Avant-Garde Writer"; March 13, 2005, "Russia: Avant Garde Writer at Center of another Controversy."

Index on Censorship, April 1, 2003, "Trick Lard," p. 202.

Kirkus Reviews, October 15, 2006, review of *Ice,* p. 1043.

Library Journal, June 15, 1988, review of *The Queue,* p. 69; November 15, 2006, Jim Dwyer, review of *Ice,* p. 60.

Los Angeles Times, July 12, 2002, "The World: Russia Targets Writer in Porn Investigation," p. A3; January 7, 2007, Jon Fasman, review of *Ice.*

M2 Best Books, August 6, 2002, "Russian Author Refuses to Give Evidence"; July 23, 2002, "Russian Author Charged with Distributing Pornography"; September 2, 2002, "Controversial Writer Loses Copyright Battle"; October 9, 2002, "Anti-Pornography Campaign in Russia Targets another Author."

Moscow News, October 18, 1992, "Playing with Cultural Space," p. 15; April 22, 1994, "They Did Not Write Like This Before," p. 12; December 30, 1994, "At Last, Vladimir Sorokin Receives His Due," p. 10; September 6, 2000, "Literature Is a Battle of the Writer's Psychic States . . . ," p. 11; December 8, 2006, "The Big Three?," p. 13.

New York Review of Books, December 16, 2004, "Subversive Activities," p. 65.

New York Times, July 12, 2002, "Russia: Novelist Faces Pornography Charge," pp. A6, A8; July 19, 2002, "What They're Reading about in Moscow," p. A21.

New York Times Book Review, October 2, 1988, review of *The Queue,* p. 26.

Publishers Weekly, May 13, 1988, review of *The Queue,* p. 269; October 2, 2006, review of *Ice,* p. 38.

Russian Life, November 1, 2002, "Sound Familiar?," p. 7.

Times Literary Supplement, June 24, 1988, review of *The Queue,* p. 698; December 4, 1992, "A Month in Dachau," p. 10.

Wall Street Journal, March 17, 1987, "Spy Story: How the FBI, Tipped by a Russian, Tracked an Intelligence Leak; Agency Found an Old Tape of Ron Pelton's First Call to Soviets 7 Years Ago; A Missed Summons to Vienna," p. 1; July 12, 2002, "Russian Police Probe Novelist's Work," p. A6; July 12, 2002, "A Literary Spring in Russia: After Decade of Uncertainty, Writers Are Again Popular—and Controversial," p. A14.

Washington Post, July 12, 2002, review of *Ice,* p. A14.

World Literature Today, March 22, 1989, review of *The Queue,* p. 329; spring, 2002, Joseph P. Mozur, Jr., review of *Pervyi subbotnik: Rasskazy,* p. 225; October 1, 2002, "Books: Russian Literary Salons," p. 42; October-December, 2003, Tatiana Nazarenko, review of *Led,* p. 133; October-December 1, 2003, Juri Talvet, review of *Norma,* p. 134.

ONLINE

Spiegel Online, http://www.spiegel.de/(February 2, 2007), Martin Doerry and Matthias Schepp, "Spiegel Interview with Author Vladimir Sorokin."

Vladimir Sorokin's Home Page, http://www.srkn.ru/english (April 25, 2007).

Waggish Blog, http://www.waggish.org/ (February 17, 2007), review of *Ice.*

*   *   *

SOROKIN, Vladimir Georgievich
    See SOROKIN, Vladimir

SORYO, Fuyumi 1959-

PERSONAL: Born January 6, 1959, in Beppu, Japan.

ADDRESSES: E-mail—souryoufuyumi@hotmail.com.

CAREER: Manga artist and comics creator.

AWARDS, HONORS: Shogakukan Manga Award, 1998, for *Boyfriend.*

WRITINGS:

"MARS" MANGA SERIES

Mars, Volume 1, TokyoPop (Los Angeles, CA), 2002.
Mars, Volume 2, TokyoPop (Los Angeles, CA), 2002.
Mars, Volume 3, TokyoPop (Los Angeles, CA), 2002.
Mars, Volume 4, TokyoPop (Los Angeles, CA), 2002.
Mars, Volume 5, TokyoPop (Los Angeles, CA), 2002.
Mars, Volume 6, TokyoPop (Los Angeles, CA), 2002.
Mars, Volume 7, TokyoPop (Los Angeles, CA), 2002.
Mars, Volume 8, TokyoPop (Los Angeles, CA), 2003.
Mars, Volume 9, TokyoPop (Los Angeles, CA), 2003.
Mars, Volume 10, TokyoPop (Los Angeles, CA), 2003.
Mars, Volume 11, TokyoPop (Los Angeles, CA), 2003.
Mars, Volume 12, TokyoPop (Los Angeles, CA), 2003.
Mars, Volume 13, TokyoPop (Los Angeles, CA), 2003.
Mars, Volume 14, TokyoPop (Los Angeles, CA), 2003.
Mars, Volume 15, TokyoPop (Los Angeles, CA), 2003.
Mars: Horse with No Name, TokyoPop (Los Angeles, CA), 2004.

"ETERNAL SABBATH" MANGA SERIES

ES: Eternal Sabbath, Volume 1, Del Rey (New York, NY) 2006.
ES: Eternal Sabbath, Volume 2, Del Rey (New York, NY) 2006.
ES: Eternal Sabbath, Volume 3, Del Rey (New York, NY) 2006.
ES: Eternal Sabbath, Volume 4, Del Rey (New York, NY) 2007.
ES: Eternal Sabbath, Volume 5, Del Rey (New York, NY) 2007.

ES: Eternal Sabbath, Volume 6, Del Rey (New York, NY) 2007.

ES: Eternal Sabbath, Volume 7, Del Rey (New York, NY) 2007.

OTHER

Doll, Kodansha (Tokyo, Japan) 1996.

Taiyo no Ijiwaru, Kodansha (Tokyo, Japan) 2002.

Also author of *Boyfriend,* Shogakukan Productions; *Three,* Shogakukan Productions; and *Tennen no Musume-san,* Kodansha.

SIDELIGHTS: Fuyumi Soryo is the author and illustrator of the popular "Mars" and "Eternal Sabbath" manga series. In the "Mars" series, Soryo chronicles the unlikely relationship between a pair of Japanese teenagers: Kira Aso, an intensely shy but gifted artist, and Kashino Rei, a handsome motorcycle racer with a mysterious past. Although *Library Journal* critic Steve Raiteri felt that "Mars" will appeal especially to teenage girls, he noted that the series "has the depth and quality to interest older comics readers also."

The "Eternal Sabbath" series concerns Dr. Mine Kujyou, a brilliant neuroscience researcher who discovers a pair of genetically engineered clones with the ability to control people's minds. Though Shuro chooses to live in harmony with human society, Isaac is bent on destruction, using his powers to commit a series of brutal murders. "Soryo's thriller is a well-paced, meticulously drawn manga that reads like a movie," observed a critic in a *Publishers Weekly* review of *ES: Eternal Sabbath, Volume 2. Anime News Network* contributor Carlos Santos remarked that the series has "all the good things you want in a suspense thriller—strong-willed characters, twist-a-minute plotting, and a premise that keeps things teetering on the brink between life and death." Santos also praised the artwork in "Eternal Sabbath," commenting: "It seems that Fuyumi Soryo has never doubted where to draw a line; the sharp, precise style is a perfect match for the analytical (yet intense) mood of the story."

BIOGRAPHICAL AND CRITICAL SOURCES:

PERIODICALS

Library Journal, January, 2003, Steve Raiteri, review of *Mars, Volume 4,* p. 84.

Publishers Weekly, September 4, 2006, review of *ES: Eternal Sabbath, Volume 2,* p. 45.

School Library Journal, September 1, 2006, Lisa Goldstein, review of *ES: Eternal Sabbath, Volume 1,* p. 244.

ONLINE

Anime News Network, http://www.animenewsnetwork. com/ (March 20, 2007), Carlos Santos, review of *ES: Eternal Sabbath, Volume 2.**

*   *   *

SPARLING, Ken 1959-

PERSONAL: Born 1959, in Canada; married; wife's name Mary; children: Mark, Stephen.

ADDRESSES: *Home*—Richmond Hill, Ontario, Canada. *Office*—Marketing and Communications, Toronto Public Library, 789 Yonge St., Toronto, Ontario M2N 5N9, Canada.

CAREER: Writer, editor, and librarian. North York Public Library, Toronto, Ontario, Canada, librarian; Gutter Press Publications, Toronto, editor.

WRITINGS:

NOVELS

Dad Says He Saw You at the Mall, Knopf (New York, NY), 1996.

Hush Up and Listen Stinky Poo Butt, self-published, 2000.

[untitled], Pedlar Press (Toronto, Ontario, Canada), 2003.

For Those Whom God Has Blessed with Fingers, Pedlar Press (Toronto, Ontario, Canada), 2005.

NONFICTION

Michael Schumacher: Living on the Limit, Warwick Publishing (Toronto, Ontario, Canada), 1999.

Jacques Villeneuve, Warwick Publishing (Toronto, Ontario, Canada), 1999.

Venus and Serena Williams, Warwick Publishing (Toronto, Ontario, Canada), 2000.

Jeff Gordon, Warwick Publishing (Toronto, Ontario, Canada), 2001.

Contributor of short stories to *The Quarterly, New York Tyrant,* and *Land-Grant College Review.* Former fiction editor of *Blood & Aphorisms.*

SIDELIGHTS: Ken Sparling, a writer, editor, and communications officer at the Toronto Public Library, is the author of *Dad Says He Saw You at the Mall,* [*untitled*], and other experimental works. "In a market ruled by long, historical fiction tomes, he keeps putting out slim, fragmented—some might call them postmodern—anti-narrative 'novels,'" observed Micah Toub in *Quill & Quire.* "In fact, Sparling may just be one of the least careerist authors working in Canada today."

In his debut work, *Dad Says He Saw You at the Mall,* Sparling serves as both author and subject, examining the minutia of everyday life. According to *Eye Weekly* contributor Hal Niedzviecki, Sparling's prose "subverts traditional narrative. This novel has no plot, only a series of sprawling observations focused around the narrator's relationship with his wife and son. The family does things that almost every family does, but Sparling relives these events as if they were singular, revealing experiments concerning the nature of suburban existence." "The voice is 'minimalist,' but not flat," observed *Elimae* Web site contributor B. Renner. "Sparling's narration is sly, affecting, laugh-out-loud funny, sometimes in the same paragraph."

Sparling's self-published work *Hush Up and Listen Stinky Poo Butt,* assembled with duct tape and the shells of abandoned library books, also concerns the life of a suburban husband and father. "*Stinky Poo* is about being caught in the middle of things," Niedzviecki wrote in *This Magazine.* "It's about stasis, about denial and acceptance, about a new way to live life to the absolute limit—not through extreme adventure, but through extreme mundanity." [*untitled*] features only Sparling's name and the publisher's logo on its cover. "This novel doesn't seem to have limitations," Andy Devine commented on the *Elimae* Web site. "It isn't limited by plot or by character description. The next word in the sentence could be any word, the next sentence any sentence."

Like the author's previous works, *For Those Whom God Has Blessed with Fingers* employs a nonlinear narrative. "Without the force of forward linear progression, reading becomes a quieter, slower, more visceral activity," noted Rebecca Silver Slayter on the *Rabble.ca* Web site. "And in *For Those Whom God Has Blessed with Fingers,* what remains, beyond the detritus of narrative convention, is a lovely, graceful, and sometimes savage thing."

Sparling told *CA:* "I started writing because, when I was a child, people seemed never to hear me when I spoke to them, but they sometimes paid attention to what I wrote.

"I think music has a big influence on what I write—all kinds of music from folk/roots to prog[ressive] rock to 'Over the Rainbow.' When I write, I seem to be trying to drive away the meaning of individual words in order to come upon a deeper (more felt?) meaning, the way music sometimes does (at least for me).

"Of all my books, I most love *Hush Up and Listen Stinky Poo Butt.* Besides having the power to startle and delight me when I go back and browse through it, the book pleases me because I wrote it, laid it out, and bound it myself, with the help of a few good people: my friend and editor, Derek McCormack; my wife, Mary, who sewed the pages of the book; and my sons, Mark and Stephen, who made the cover art."

BIOGRAPHICAL AND CRITICAL SOURCES:

PERIODICALS

Books in Canada, October, 1996, review of *Dad Says He Saw You at the Mall,* p. 40; summer, 2003, Nathan Whitlock, "Twisting One's Own Arm to Write Fiction," review of [*untitled*], p. 3.

Canadian Literature, spring, 1999, review of *Dad Says He Saw You at the Mall,* p. 161.

Canadian Review of Materials, June 9, 2000, review of *Michael Schumacher: Living on the Limit.*

Eye Weekly, April 25, 1996, Hal Niedzviecki, review of *Dad Says He Saw You at the Mall.*

Library Journal, March 1, 1996, review of *Dad Says He Saw You at the Mall,* p. 106.

Publishers Weekly, January 29, 1996, review of *Dad Says He Saw You at the Mall,* p. 85.

Quill & Quire, April, 1996, Ann Ireland, review of *Dad Says He Saw You at the Mall,* p. 30; March, 1999, review of *Michael Schumacher,* p. 58; November, 2005, Micah Toub, "Breaking Every Rule."

This Magazine, May-June, 2001, Nal Niedzviecki, "Anti-novelist: Ken Sparling Is Faced with an Interesting Dilemma," pp. 13-15

ONLINE

Elimae, http://www.elimae.com/ (April 20, 2007), B. Renner, review of *Dad Says He Saw You at the Mall,* and Andy Devine, review of *[untitled].*

Rabble.ca, http://www.rabble.ca/ (April 20, 2007), Rebecca Silver Slayter, review of *For Those Whom God Has Blessed with Fingers.*

TDR: The Danforth Review Online, http://www.danforthreview.com/ (May 14, 2007), Michael Bryson, "TDR Interview: Ken Sparling."

*　　*　　*

STAM, Allan C.

PERSONAL: Education: Cornell University, B.A., 1988; University of Michigan, M.A., 1991, Ph.D., 1993.

ADDRESSES: Home—Lyme, NH. *Office*—Department of Government, Dartmouth College, Hanover, NH 03755.

CAREER: American University, Washington, DC, assistant professor of international service, 1993-96; Yale University, New Haven, CT, assistant professor of political science, 1996-2000, junior faculty fellow, 1998; Dartmouth College, Hanover, NH, associate professor, 2000-04, professor of government, 2004-05, Daniel Webster Professor, 2005—, Elizabeth R. and Robert A. Jeffe fellow, 2004-05. Harvard University, faculty associate of Olin Institute for Strategic Studies, 2000—, visiting associate professor, 2004; guest speaker at other institutions, including University of Rwanda, University of Cork, National Chengchi University, University of Girona, Columbia University, Princeton University, Duke University, and University of California, Los Angeles; conference participant.

MEMBER: American Political Science association (council member, 1998-2001), Council on Foreign Relations, Midwest Political Science Association.

AWARDS, HONORS: National Science Foundation grants, 1996-98, 1999-2002, 2003-06; award for best research software, Computers and Multimedia Section, American Political Science Association, 1998; Karl Deutsch Award, International Studies Association, 2004; fellowship, Center for Advanced Study in the Behavioral Sciences, Stanford, CA, 2004.

WRITINGS:

Win, Lose, or Draw: Domestic Politics and the Crucible of War, University of Michigan Press (Ann Arbor, MI), 1996.

(With Jacek Kugler, Douglas Lemke, and Ronald L. Tammen) *Power Transitions: Strategies for the 21st Century,* Chatham Press (New York, NY), 2001.

(With Dan Reiter) *Democracies at War,* Princeton University Press (Princeton, NJ), 2002.

(With D. Scott Bennett) *The Behavioral Origins of War,* University of Michigan Press (Ann Arbor, MI), 2004.

Contributor to books, including *Dissolving Boundaries,* edited by Suzanne Werner, David Davis, and Bruce Bueno de Mesquita, Blackwell Publishers (Malden, MA), 2003; and *New Direction for International Relations,* edited by Alex Mintz and Bruce Russett, Lexington Books, 2005. Contributor of articles and reviews to periodicals, including *Journal of Conflict Resolution, Foreign Policy Analysis, International Studies Perspectives, International Security, International Interactions, Political Science Quarterly, British Journal of Political Sciences,* and *American Political Science Review. Journal of Conflict Resolution,* member of editorial board.

SIDELIGHTS: Allan C. Stam told *CA:* "Writing is something that scratches a number of itches. First, I write because I enjoy writing. If given a choice I would rather write, and rewrite, than read. Of course there's a symbiotic relationship between the two, but the creative aspect of writing is more engaging for me than the more passive process of reading.

"The topics I work on tend to be inspired by empirical puzzles or contradictions in existing work, or else by issues we don't understand well. I typically spend a lot of time thinking it all through, then I basically purge my thoughts into the computer, which then kicks off the (seemingly) endless rewriting."

Stam added: "Michael Herron and I are assembling the data necessary to test competing claims about the source of Islamic fundamentalist enmity toward the United States and the West. One story focuses on U.S. policies and terrorists' instrumental responses. Another story emphasizes the expressive nature of religiously motivated violence. By assembling multidimensional indicators of policies toward the Middle East, political and personal freedoms, and economic globalization and commercialism, we hope to shed light on what factors best predict which states are most likely to become targets of extremist groups. In doing so we hope to be able to adjudicate what has become an important public policy debate in the context of the Bush administration's 'War on Terrorism.' I am also working on a book-length project on surrender, desertion, and world politics, in which I investigate the limits of rationality during times of war. I demonstrate how states systematically manipulate the preferences of their citizens and the soldiers on the opposing side, and how this affects soldier reliability and, in turn, battlefield outcomes and world politics."

*   *   *

STAMAN, A. Louise

PERSONAL: Married E. Michael Staman (a professor); children: Laura, Karen, Jeanette. *Education:* Kent State University, B.A.; University of Illinois, M.A. (French); Old Dominion University, M.A. (humanities); also studied in Paris, France, Montreal, Quebec, Canada, and Neuchâtel, Switzerland.

ADDRESSES: Home—Macon, GA. *E-mail*—lousie. staman@maconstate.edu.

CAREER: Writer, editor, and researcher. Has also taught college-level French and served as a tutor.

AWARDS, HONORS: Grand prize winner, Jekyll Island Millennium Time Capsule Contest, for the poem "Future, Past and Present"; Illuminati Press of

Miami University of Middletown Writing Competition winner, 2006, for poem "Clippings"; Honorable Mention, William Faulkner-William Wisdom Creative Writing Competition, 2006, for poem "My Five Breasts"; Eric Hoffer Award for Books, and Gold in Regional Award, "IPPY" Independent Publisher Book Awards, both 2007, both for *Loosening Corsets: The Heroic Life of Georgia's Feisty Mrs. Felton, First Woman Senator of the United States.*

WRITINGS:

With the Stroke of a Pen: A Story of Ambition, Greed, Infidelity, and the Murder of French Publisher Robert Denoël, Thomas Dunne Books (New York, NY), 2002.
Loosening Corsets: The Heroic Life of Georgia's Feisty Mrs. Felton, First Woman Senator of the United States, Tiger Iron Press (Macon, GA), 2006.
Rupert and the Bag (children's book), illustrated by Rich Adams, Tiger Iron Press (Macon, GA), 2006.

With the Stroke of a Pen has been translated into French.

Also author of *Home Grown Georgia Poems.* Contributor to *Under My Skin,* a poetry anthology.

SIDELIGHTS: A. Louise Staman is the author of *With the Stroke of a Pen: A Story of Ambition, Greed, Infidelity, and the Murder of French Publisher Robert Denoël.* Using personal papers, court documents, and archival materials unsealed by the French government, Staman traces the life of the Belgian-born Denoël, who arrived in Paris in 1926 and opened his publishing house two years later. He recruited some of the finest writers of the era, including Louis-Ferdinand Celine, Antonin Artaud, and Jean Genet. When the Nazis occupied France, Denoël began publishing anti-Semitic works while also promoting the efforts of Elsa Triolet, a Jewish author who won the Prix Goncourt. Denoël was shot to death on December 2, 1945; the crime was never officially solved, although robbery did appear to be the motive. According to *Library Journal* critic Mary Salony, "Staman's report of the investigation reveals a tale of crime, betrayal, and coverup," and a *Kirkus Reviews* contributor noted that the author "makes a convincing argument that Denoel was killed by intimates who wanted both to gain his publishing house and shut his mouth for good." In the words of *Booklist* critic Elsa Gaztambide, *With the Stroke of a Pen* "is a spectacular example of riveting research."

Staman is also the author of *Loosening Corsets: The Heroic Life of Georgia's Feisty Mrs. Felton, First Woman Senator of the United States,* a biography of Rebecca Latimer Felton, a journalist, suffragist, and reformer who was sworn in to the U.S. Senate in 1922 at the age of eighty-seven.

BIOGRAPHICAL AND CRITICAL SOURCES:

PERIODICALS

Booklist, November 15, 2002, Elsa Gaztambide, review of *With the Stroke of a Pen: A Story of Ambition, Greed, Infidelity, and the Murder of French Publisher Robert Denoël,* p. 550.
Kirkus Reviews, September 1, 2002, review of *With the Stroke of a Pen,* p. 1290.
Library Journal, October 1, 2002, Mary Salony, review of *With the Stroke of a Pen,* p. 114.
Publishers Weekly, October 28, 2002, review of *With the Stroke of a Pen,* p. 61.

ONLINE

A. Louise Staman Home Page, http://www.alouisestaman.com (April 20, 2007).
Sweet Briar College, http://www.sbc.edu/ (February 22, 2007), Jennifer McManamay, "Biographer Brings Remarkable Story of First Woman in U.S. Senate to Sweet Briar."

*   *   *

STEINHARDT, Arnold 1937-

PERSONAL: Born 1937, in Los Angeles, CA. *Education:* Attended Curtis Institute of Music; privately trained.

ADDRESSES: E-mail—mail@arnoldsteinhardt.com.

CAREER: Violinist. Made debut at the age of fourteen as guest soloist with Los Angeles Philharmonic Orchestra; Guarneri String Quartet, founding member and first violinist, 1964—; recitalist and soloist with orchestras, including the New York Philharmonic, Detroit Symphony, and Cleveland Orchestra; has recorded albums for RCA Victor, Philips, Arabesque, Sheffield Lab, Biddolph Records, Town Hall, and Surrounded by Entertainment. Professor of Violin at University of Maryland, Rutgers University, Bard College, and Curtis Institute of Music.

AWARDS, HONORS: Philadelphia Youth Competition winner, 1957; Leventritt Award, 1958; Queen Elizabeth International Violin Competition, bronze medalist, 1963; honorary doctorates from University of South Florida and Harpur College. The Guarneri Quartet has received numerous honors, including the New York Seal of Recognition, 1982; Award of Merit, Association of Performing Arts Presenters, 1992; Richard J. Bogomolny National Service Award, Chamber Music America, 2004; and Ford Honors Award, from the University Musical Society of the University of Michigan, 2005.

WRITINGS:

Indivisible by Four: A String Quartet in Pursuit of Harmony (memoir), Farrar, Straus & Giroux (New York, NY), 1998.
Violin Dreams (memoir), with compact disc recording by Steinhardt, Houghton Mifflin (Boston, MA), 2006.

Contributor to periodicals, including *Chamber Music America, Musical America,* and *Keynote.*

SIDELIGHTS: Arnold Steinhardt, an accomplished violinist and a founding member of the esteemed Guarneri String Quartet, is the author of *Indivisible by Four: A String Quartet in Pursuit of Harmony* and *Violin Dreams. Indivisible by Four* chronicles Steinhardt's solo career as well as his decades-long association with violinist John Dalley, violist Michael Tree, and cellist David Soyer. "Musicians' memoirs are rarely addressed to other musicians: instead they are meant for the authors and their fans, as a sort of interior investigation," observed *New York Times Book Review* critic Benjamin Ivry. "At its best, the musical memoir can try to address the question of how the artist did it. This is what Steinhardt accomplishes in a satisfying way." Describing *Indivisible by Four* as a "cheerful, informative chronicle," *Library Journal* contributor Bonnie Jo Dopp noted that the work "will be welcomed by all who know and love their work."

In *Violin Dreams,* Steinhardt traces his rise as a professional musician, offers a history of the world's finest violin makers, and discusses his fondness for Johann Sebastian Bach's *Chaconne,* a long piece for solo violin. Steinhardt "shapes his story with a series of almost mythical odysseys and visions that parallel his technical and intellectual progress," remarked a *Publishers Weekly* contributor, and a critic in *Kirkus Reviews* noted that the violinist's "passion is undeniably contagious; even the uninitiated will savor the technical sections for their revelations about the relationship between career performer and instrument."

Steinhardt told *CA:* "I began to write about my profession primarily because people seemed so curious about such basic questions as: what does it entail to learn an instrument, how does one study music, and what is the interaction between musicians in the learning process like?

"I am surprised at how much the act of writing resembles practicing music. Whether working obsessively on a paragraph or a musical phrase, the hope is to make it detailed, clear, effortless, and uplifting. My model, my inspiration is the writings of E.B. White.

"My wish is that my writing will inform, entertain, and uplift readers."

BIOGRAPHICAL AND CRITICAL SOURCES:

BOOKS

Blum, David, *The Art of Quartet Playing: The Guarneri in Conversation with David Blum,* Knopf (New York, NY), 1986.
Ruttencutter, Helen Drees, *Quartet: A Profile of the Guarneri Quartet,* Lippincott & Crowell (New York, NY), 1980.
Steinhardt, Arnold, *Indivisible by Four: A String Quartet in Pursuit of Harmony,* Farrar, Straus & Giroux (New York, NY), 1998.

Steinhardt, Arnold, *Violin Dreams,* Houghton Mifflin (Boston, MA), 2006.

PERIODICALS

Booklist, November 1, 1998, Alan Hirsch, review of *Indivisible by Four,* p. 462.
California Bookwatch, December 1, 2006, review of *Violin Dreams.*
Choice, May, 1999, E. Gaub, review of *Indivisible by Four,* p. 1629.
High Fidelity, November, 1986, Thomas Willis, "The Art of Quartet Playing," p. 15.
Kirkus Reviews, August 1, 2006, review of *Violin Dreams,* p. 774.
Library Journal, November 15, 1998, Bonnie Jo Dopp, review of *Indivisible by Four,* p. 70.
New Yorker, January 25, 1999, review of *Indivisible by Four,* p. 93.
New York Times, February 24, 1985, Bernard Holland, "Guarneri Stands for Durability," p. H27.
New York Times Book Review, November 29, 1998, Benjamin Ivry, "Fab Four," review of *Indivisible by Four.*
Publishers Weekly, September 21, 1998, *Indivisible by Four,* p. 36; July 31, 2006, review of *Violin Dreams,* p. 62.
Reference & Research Book News, February, 1999, review of *Indivisible by Four,* p. 141.

ONLINE

Arnold Steinhardt Home Page, http://www. arnoldsteinhardt.com (April 20, 2007).

OTHER

High Fidelity: The Guarneri String Quartet (documentary film), Four Oaks Foundation, 1989.

*   *   *

STEPHEN, Lynn

PERSONAL: Born in Chicago, IL. *Education:* Carleton College, B.A. (magna cum laude), 1979; Brandeis University, Ph.D., 1987.

ADDRESSES: Office—Department of Anthropology, 1218 University of Oregon, Eugene, OR 97401-1218. *E-mail*—stephenl@oregon.uoregon.edu.

CAREER: Brandeis University, Waltham, MA, teaching assistant, 1983, 1986; Tufts University, Medford, MA, lecturer, 1983; Massachusetts Institute of Technology, Cambridge, MA, lecturer, 1984, 1986-87, visiting scholar, 1987; Northeastern University, Boston, MA, assistant professor, 1987-92, associate professor, 1992-97, professor of anthropology, 1997-98, director of Latin American and Caribbean Studies, 1995-97; University of Oregon, Eugene, professor of anthropology, 1998—, distinguished professor of arts and sciences, 2003—, chair of anthropology department, 2001-04. Visiting faculty member at Radcliffe College, 1994, 1996.

AWARDS, HONORS: Grants and fellowships from National Science Foundation, 1993-95, University of California, 1994-95, 1996, 2002-03 (declined), Wenner-Gren Foundation, 1994-95, 1997-98, Center for U.S. Mexican Studies, 1995, and National Endowment for the Humanities, 1999-2000; Radcliffe Institute fellow, 2004-05.

WRITINGS:

(Editor, with James Dow) *Class, Politics, and Popular Religion in Mexico and Central America,* Society for Latin American Anthropology (Washington, DC), 1990.

Zapotec Women, University of Texas Press (Austin, TX), 1991, 2nd edition published as *Zapotec Women: Gender, Class, and Ethnicity in Globalized Oaxaca,* Duke University Press (Durham, NC), 2005.

(Editor and translator) Maria Teresa Tula, *Hear My Testimony: Maria Teresa Tula, Human Rights Activist of El Salvador,* South End Press (Boston, MA), 1994.

Women and Social Movements in Latin America: Power from Below, University of Texas Press (Austin, TX), 1997.

Zapata Lives! Histories and Cultural Politics in Southern Mexico, University of California Press (Berkeley, CA), 2002.

(Editor, with others) *The Americas Reader: Culture, History, and Representation,* Blackwell (London, England), 2002.

(Editor, with Matthew C. Gutmann, Felix V. Matos Rodriguez, and Patricia Zavella) *Perspectives on Las Américas: A Reader in Culture, History, and Representation,* Blackwell (London, England), 2003.

(Editor, with Shannon Speed and R. Aída Hernández Castillo) *Dissident Women: Gender and Cultural Politics in Chiapas,* University of Texas Press (Austin, TX), 2006.

Transborder Lives: Indigenous Oaxacans in Mexico, California, and Oregon, Duke University Press (Durham, NC), 2007.

Contributor to books, including *Women's Participation in Mexican Political Life,* edited by Victoria Rodriguez, Westview Press (Boulder, CO), 1998; and *Women and Civil War: Impact, Organizations, and Action,* edited by Krishna Kumar, Lynne Reinner Press (Boulder, CO), 2001. Contributor to journals, including the *Journal of Latin American Anthropology, Latin American Perspectives, American Ethnologist, Latin American Research Review,* and *Latino Studies Journal.*

SIDELIGHTS: Lynn Stephen is an archaeologist whose primary interest is the intersection of culture and politics with a focus on issues such as ethnicity, gender, class, and nationalism in Latin America. Stephens interviewed women activists from El Salvador, Mexico, Brazil, and Chile for her book *Women and Social Movements in Latin America: Power from Below.* Through these interviews and various case studies the author provides a look at women's ability to organize grassroots political organizations. She also explores the influence of a machismo society on the ability of its women to be politically active. James D. Hurtig, writing in *Economic Development & Cultural Change,* noted of the book: "In each case the woman's personal life history is interwoven with her insights into the basis for women's struggles and effective strategies for change. These accounts are compelling in their intimacy, and several tell stories of suffering, sacrifice, and commitment that are profoundly moving." In the *Historian,* Susan K. Besse predicted: "This book should be of great interest to students seeking to understand the lived reality of poor Latin American women, as well as to political activists and feminist theorists striving to imagine and implement new, more globally relevant feminist practices."

Zapata Lives! Histories and Cultural Politics in Southern Mexico explores how those involved in the

Zapatista rebellion in Chiapas, Mexico, in 1994 used the political symbolism of the famous early twentieth-century Mexican revolutionary Emiliano Zapata for their rebellion against globalization. Stephen also discusses how the Mexican government itself has used a similar Zapata-based symbolism to try to unite the country—once in the 1930s and again in the 1990s—when the government sought to gain support for the North American Free Trade Association treaty. Thomas Benjamin, writing in *History: Review of New Books,* referred to the book as "a product of careful and intelligent investigation, combining both anthropological fieldwork and historical research." *Latin American Politics and Society* contributor Stephen Lewis noted that the author's "exploration of the role of women in contemporary Zapatismo is a major contribution." Lewis went on to call *Zapata Lives!* "an ambitious, well-executed study that speaks to a broad audience."

Stephen is also author of *Zapotec Women,* first published in 1991 with a second edition appearing in 2005 as *Zapotec Women: Gender, Class, and Ethnicity in Globalized Oaxaca.* The book focuses on the lives of women living in the Zapotec community of Teotitlan del Valle in Oaxaca, Mexico. The author is largely interested in documenting how these women transformed their lives and attained a degree of entrepreneurial success in a worldwide capitalistic market through their rug-weaving enterprises. "Stephen's book banishes stereotypes of the 'from traditional to modern' process to provide the reader with a nuanced understanding of a Oaxacan context of daily life," reported Sandra Niessen in *Man.* Niessen added: "The current volume is well-constructed through an elegant interweaving of individual voices in narrative transcription, with explanatory descriptions of the conditions—historical, political, economic, social—which have shaped those voices."

Stephen has also served as editor or coeditor of several books, including Maria Teresa Tula's *Hear My Testimony: Maria Teresa Tula, Human Rights Activist of El Salvador,* which Stephen edited and translated. This book features Tula's testimony about the victims of human rights abuses in El Salvador. According to Kathleen Logan in the *Latin American Research Review,* Stephen also writes of her "close collaboration with . . . Tula in all aspects of the production of the final work, including the contestation, altering of worldviews, and friendship that developed from their collaboration." In *Perspectives on Las Américas: A*

Reader in Culture, History, and Representation, Stephen and fellow editors Matthew C. Gutmann, Felix V. Matos Rodriguez, and Patricia Zavella bring together previously published articles on a variety of topics focusing on Latin American life and culture, from farm workers to Latin American artists. "As a work designed for students *Perspectives on Las Américas* has proved itself a success," concluded Rebecca Earle in the *Journal of Latin American Studies.*

BIOGRAPHICAL AND CRITICAL SOURCES:

PERIODICALS

American Anthropologist, September, 1992, John M. Watanabe, review of *Class, Politics, and Popular Religion in Mexico and Central America,* pp. 714-715; September, 1998, Lisa Baldez, review of *Women and Social Movements in Latin America: Power from Below,* p. 785.

American Ethnologist, November, 1994, Michael B. Whiteford, review of *Class, Politics, and Popular Religion in Mexico and Central America,* pp. 1074-1075; August, 1995, Karen Brodkin Sacks, review of *Hear My Testimony: Maria Teresa Tula, Human Rights Activist of El Salvador,* p. 670; May, 1999, Joann Martin, review of *Women and Social Movements in Latin America,* p. 482.

American Historical Review, April, 2003, David Carey, Jr., review of *Zapata Lives! Histories and Cultural Politics in Southern Mexico,* pp. 550-551.

Americas: A Quarterly Review of Inter-American Cultural History, October, 1993, Florence E. Babb, review of *Zapotec Women,* pp. 276-277; October, 1998, Heidi Tinsman, review of *Women and Social Movements in Latin America,* p. 324; January, 2003, Arthur Schmidt, review of *Zapata Lives!,* p. 441.

Choice, October, 1992, E. Bastida, review of *Zapotec Women,* p. 366; July-August, 1995, W.Q. Morales, review of *Hear My Testimony,* pp. 1795-1796; March, 1998, review of *Women and Social Movements in Latin America,* p. 1281; September, 2002, P.R. Sullivan, review of *Zapata Lives!,* p. 166.

Economic Development & Cultural Change, July, 1999, Janise D. Hurtig, review of *Women and Social Movements in Latin America,* p. 899.

Hispanic American Historical Review, August, 2004, Samuel Brunk, review of *Zapata Lives!,* p. 550.

Historian, summer, 1999, Susan K. Besse, review of *Women and Social Movements in Latin America,* p. 924.

History: Review of New Books, Thomas Benjamin, spring, 2002, review of *Zapata Lives!,* p. 104.

Journal of Interamerican Studies and World Affairs, fall, 1999, Philip Oxhorn, review of *Women and Social Movements in Latin America,* p. 129.

Journal of Latin American Anthropology, November, 2006, Michael James Higgins, review of *Zapotec Women: Gender, Class, and Ethnicity in Globalized Oaxaca,* p. 453.

Journal of Latin American Studies, May, 1999, Maxine Molyneux, review of *Women and Social Movements in Latin America,* p. 535; August, 2003, Shannan L. Mattiace, review of *Zapata Lives!,* p. 641; November, 2004, Rebecca Earle, review of *Perspectives on Las Américas: A Reader in Culture, History and Representation,* p. 809.

Latin American Politics and Society, summer, 2003, Stephen Lewis, review of *Zapata Lives!,* p. 185.

Latin American Research Review, winter, 1997, Kathleen Logan, review of *Hear My Testimony,* p. 199; spring, 2000, Tracy Fitzsimmons, review of *Women and Social Movements in Latin America,* p. 216.

Library Journal, May 1, 1994, Louise Leonard, review of *Hear My Testimony,* p. 126.

Man, June, 1994, Sandra Niessen, review of *Zapotec Women,* p. 533.

Mexican Studies-Estudios Mexicanos, summer, 1993, Scott Cook, review of *Zapotec Women,* p. 303.

Reviews in Anthropology, February, 1996, Martha Woodson Rees, review of *Zapotec Women,* pp. 107-123.

Signs, spring, 2001, Sarah A. Radcliffe, review of *Women and Social Movements in Latin America,* p. 905.

Times Literary Supplement, May 10, 2002, Benjamin Smith, review of *Zapata Lives!,* p. 31.

ONLINE

Radcliffe University Web site, http://www.radcliffe.edu/ (April 24, 2007), profile of Lynn Stephen.

University of Oregon Web site, http://darkwing. uoregon.edu/ (April 24, 2007), faculty profile of Lynn Stephen.*

STIEFEL, Vicki

PERSONAL: Married William G. Tapply (a writer); children: Blake, Ben; stepchildren: Mike, Melissa, Sarah. *Education:* Ithaca College, B.A. *Hobbies and other interests:* Scuba diving, fly fishing, digital imagery, photography, singing.

ADDRESSES: Home—Hancock, NH. *E-mail*—vs@ vickistiefel.com.

CAREER: Novelist and journalist. *Dive Training,* contributing editor; *Worcester Magazine,* film critic, columnist, and feature writer; The Meetings Group/ Primedia Business Magazines & Media, special sections editor. Has worked as an assistant producer for a stock company, professional photographer, high school drama and English teacher, hamburger cook, scuba diving shop manager, editor, and adolescent counselor, and has worked with law enforcement professionals.

WRITINGS:

CRIME NOVELS

Body Parts, Dorchester Publishing (New York, NY), 2004.

The Dead Stone, Dorchester Publishing (New York, NY), 2005.

The Grief Shop, Leisure Books (New York, NY), 2006.

The Bone Man, Leisure Books (New York, NY), 2007.

Contributor to magazines, including *New Woman, Harvard Post, Alert Diver,* and *Improper Bostonian.*

SIDELIGHTS: Vicki Stiefel's popular crime novels feature protagonist Tally Whyte, a homicide counselor in Massachusetts who works with police officers and lawyers. In the first installment in the series, *Body Parts,* Tally confronts a vicious serial killer who is known as "the Harvester" because of his habit of collecting a body part from each of his female victims. Convinced that the cops have arrested the wrong man, Tally decides to find the real Harvester herself, finally coming face to face with the killer in a finale that a *Publishers Weekly* reviewer described as "shocking and gruesome." Comparing Stiefel's work to that of veteran mystery writers Mary Higgins Clark and Sue Grafton, the reviewer concluded that Tally is a "tenacious but vulnerable" and admirably credible character.

Tally returns to her home town in rural Maine to clear up some ugly rumors about her father's alleged real-estate theft in *The Dead Stone*. However, before Tally can get very far, her best friend's sister is murdered, and Tally again finds herself in the role of detective. Harriet Klausner, writing on the *Books 'n' Bytes* Web site, praised the book's complex and intriguing plot and observed that Stiefel is a "talented writer of psychological suspense."

In *The Grief Shop*, Tally faces the horrible possibility that one of her colleagues may be a murderer. The plot begins when the body of a little girl is dumped inside the office of the chief medical examiner where Tally works. Because no one can enter the building without security clearance, investigators suspect that someone in the department must be involved. As Tally sets out to find the killer, she must also deal with the kidnapping of her boss (who is also her stepmother). A contributor to *Publishers Weekly* considered Tally a "compelling protagonist," and observed that Stiefel "can hold her own against genre heavy-weights like John Sanford and Patricia Cornwell."

BIOGRAPHICAL AND CRITICAL SOURCES:

PERIODICALS

Publishers Weekly, December 15, 2003, review of *Body Parts*, p. 59; July 31, 2006, review of *The Grief Shop*, p. 59.

ONLINE

Books 'n' Bytes, http://www.booksnbytes.com/ (April 23, 2007), Harriet Klausner, reviews of *Body Parts* and *The Grief Shop*.
MBR Bookwatch, http://www.midwestbookreview.com/ (March 1, 2005), Harriet Klausner, review of *The Dead Stone*.
New Mystery Reader Magazine, http://www.newmysteryreader.com/ (April 23, 2007), Stephanie Padilla, review of *The Grief Shop*.

STODDARD, Grant

PERSONAL: Born in Thurrock, Essex, England. *Education:* Attended Thames Valley University.

ADDRESSES: Home—New York, NY. *E-mail*—grantstoddard@hotmail.com.

CAREER: Journalist. *Nerve.com,* columnist.

WRITINGS:

Working Stiff: The Misadventures of an Accidental Sexpert (memoir), HarperPerennial (New York, NY), 2007.

Contributor to periodicals, including *Men's Health, Glamour, British GQ,* and *New York.*

SIDELIGHTS: When Grant Stoddard moved from England to the United States at age twenty-one, he wanted only to find a girlfriend and a job. Unlucky in love, he ended up writing the "I Did It for Science" column for *Nerve.com.* The job required him to participate in, and then write about, a wide range of offbeat sexual activities, which eventually made him into a self-described "sexpert." Stoddard's unusual job provides the foundation for his memoir, *Working Stiff: The Misadventures of an Accidental Sexpert.* In addition to anecdotes about Stoddard's sexual adventures, including being shrink-wrapped in plastic and participating in orgies, the book chronicles his earlier life in England, where he had been a painfully shy student. "I spent my time repelling women in droves," he said in remarks quoted by London *Times Online* contributor Fleur Britten. "I was hobbit-like in appearance and world view." Despite this acute lack of confidence, Stoddard found that he could do just about anything involving sex if it was part of his work. As he explained to *Advocate* writer David Jay Lasky, "I felt like a guinea pig, really. I had no control over what I did."

While acknowledging the explicit material in *Working Stiff,* many critics found the most enjoyable feature of the book to be its humor. A writer for *Publishers Weekly* considered the book "consistently hilarious" and "appealing." In *Booklist,* Joanne Wilkinson praised its "self-deprecating wit" and "surprising sweetness." Steve Almond, writing in the *Los Angeles Times Book Review Online,* expressed a different view, arguing that, for all its detailed descriptions of sex, *Working Stiff* is mostly a book about "immigrant yearning." Observing that Stoddard writes best when he "runs up against his own vulnerability" and honestly explores his emotions, Almond concluded that *Working Stiff* does not include enough of such insights, making the book "the literary equivalent of a quickie." *Pop Matters* contributor Jason B. Jones also noted the book's lack of emotional reflection, but nevertheless found the book funny and sweet. Observing that Stoddard comes off in the book "as a man full of vulnerability," Lasky called *Working Stiff* "one of the best works of creative nonfiction since Joan Didion's *Slouching Towards Bethlehem.*"

BIOGRAPHICAL AND CRITICAL SOURCES:

BOOKS

Stoddard, Grant, *Working Stiff: The Misadventures of an Accidental Sexpert,* HarperPerennial (New York, NY), 2007.

PERIODICALS

Advocate, February 27, 2007, David Jay Lasky, "Working Boy: Premier New York City Sex Columnist Grant Stoddard Explored America's Sexual Underworld and Lived to Tell about It," p. 58.
Booklist, November 1, 2006, Joanne Wilkinson, review of *Working Stiff,* p. 10.
Hollywood Reporter, March 7, 2007, Nicole Sperling, "Vantage Buys into 'Stiff' Sentences," p. 4.
Kirkus Reviews, October 1, 2006, review of *Working Stiff,* p. 1005.
Publishers Weekly, December 19, 2005, "Sex-capades of an Expat," p. 8; October 9, 2006, review of *Working Stiff,* p. 45.

ONLINE

Los Angeles Times Book Review Online, http://www.calendarlive.com/ (April 23, 2007), Steve Almond, review of *Working Stiff.*

PopMatters, http://www.popmatters.com/ (April 23, 2007), Jason B. Jones, "The Sexual Tastes of Urbanites, and the Transplanted Englishman Who Loved Them."
Times Online (London, England), http://www.women.timesonline.co.uk/ (Marcy 25, 2007), Fleur Britten, "The Accidental Sexpert."*

*   *   *

SULLIVAN, Russell

PERSONAL: Male.

ADDRESSES: Home—Boston, MA.

CAREER: Writer. Linkage, Inc., Burlington, MA, senior vice president and general counsel.

WRITINGS:

(With Philip J. Harkins and Stephen M. Brown) *Outsourcing and Human Resources: Trends, Models, and Guidelines,* LER Press (Lexington, MA), 1996.
Rocky Marciano: The Rock of His Times ("Sport and Society" series), University of Illinois Press (Urbana, IL), 2002.

SIDELIGHTS: Russell Sullivan writes from the perspective of a dedicated sports fan in *Rocky Marciano: The Rock of His Times,* a biography of the only heavyweight boxing champion to retire undefeated. Marciano, who reigned from 1952 to 1956, did not fight with finesse; though he retained a perfect record, his legacy has fallen into relative obscurity. Sullivan's book aims to restore Marciano's reputation as a great champion. His account of the boxer's life and career, critics noted, is thorough and scholarly. A reviewer for *Publishers Weekly* particularly appreciated the historical context that Sullivan provides about the boxing world in the 1950s, when superficial social conformity often hid darker realities such as racism. John Green, writing in *Booklist,* also praised the book's "broad scope." *New York Times Book Review* contributor Dave Anderson noted that "Sullivan does not pretend to be a boxing expert" and "wisely leans on the words of the best sportswriters of Marciano's era." The result, in Anderson's view, is a book that is "much more than a fan's adoring recital of Marciano's big fights." In addition to chronicling the highlights of the boxer's career, the book also reveals Marciano's flaws, including his marital infidelities and his cheapness with money. "More than anything else," Anderson concluded, "the book assesses Marciano in the context of his times."

BIOGRAPHICAL AND CRITICAL SOURCES:

PERIODICALS

Biography, spring, 2003, Gordon Marino, review of *Rocky Marciano: The Rock of His Times,* p. 372.
Booklist, September 1, 2002, John Green, review of *Rocky Marciano,* p. 46.
Library Journal, August, 2002, Jim Burns, review of *Rocky Marciano,* p. 107.
New York Times Book Review, September 15, 2002, Dave Anderson, review of *Rocky Marciano,* p. 21.
Publishers Weekly, July 29, 2002, review of *Rocky Marciano,* p. 65.*

*   *   *

SWOFFORD, Anthony 1970(?)-

PERSONAL: Born c. 1970, in Fairfield, CA. *Education:* Attended American River College, Sacramento, CA, the University of California at Davis, and the Iowa Writer's Workshop.

ADDRESSES: Home—New York, NY. *E-mail*—anthony@anthonyswofford.com.

CAREER: Lewis & Clark College, Portland, OR, adjunct professor of humanities, until 2003; St. Mary's College, Moraga, CA, assistant professor of English, 2003-04. University of Iowa, Iowa City, IA, teaching-writing fellow; Yaddo, Saratoga Springs, NY, writer in residence, 2002. *Military service:* U.S. Marines, 1990-1991; served in the Gulf War in a Surveillance and Target Acquisition/Scout-Sniper platoon.

AWARDS, HONORS: Michener-Copernicus Fellowship.

WRITINGS:

Jarhead: A Marine's Chronicle of the Gulf War and Other Battles, Scribner (New York, NY), 2003.
Exit A (novel), Scribner (New York, NY), 2007.

Contributor of nonfiction to periodicals, including the *New York Times, Harper's, Men's Journal,* and the *Iowa Review.* Columnist for *Details* magazine.

ADAPTATIONS: Jarhead has been adapted as a film and as an audiobook.

SIDELIGHTS: Anthony Swofford was born into a military family and joined the U.S. Marines. He served in the Gulf War in 1991 as part of the Surveillance and Target Acquisition/Scout-Sniper platoon. Swofford's first book, *Jarhead: A Marine's Chronicle of the Gulf War and Other Battles,* recounts his service during that war. The book, which was also adapted as a major motion picture, begins with Swofford's basic training, describing the usual tough drill instructor and soldiers' escapades drinking, fighting, and hunting for prostitutes. Once their Marine platoon dispatches to the Middle East, however, Swofford and his mates deal more with military brass infighting and dysentery rather than with the enemy Iraqi army. Nevertheless, Swofford and another Marine sniper are sent out on a mission to kill enemy officers only to have the mission halted when they get their targets in their sights.

Many critics praised Swofford's memoir. Noting that "there's not a clichéd moment in this rueful account of a Marine's life," a *Kirkus Reviews* contributor reported that *Jarhead* is "full of insight into the minds and rucksacks of our latter-day warriors." A *Publishers Weekly* critic commented that the author provides "an unflinching portrayal of the loneliness and brutality of modern warfare and sophisticated analyses of—and visceral reactions to—its politics." Several reviewers commented on the author's ability to combine the usual soldier's boasting with humor and a clear analysis of the horrors of war, even one that was easily won. "Although Swofford is not shy relating his various exploits in graphic words and scenes, there is more to this memoir than bravado," according to Peter Gilmore in the *U.S. Catholic.* Gilmore further observed: "Near the end of this memoir he pens the shortest of chapters with the deepest of feeling and insight."

Swofford turns from fact to fiction with his debut novel, *Exit A*. In an interview with Rachel Deahl for *Publishers Weekly,* Swofford related that he always considered himself a fiction writer and had previously written short stories. "Content dictates form for me, and also genre, and the story of my time in the Marine Corps and at war needed to be told as nonfiction," Swofford explained. The author added that the memoir "was simply the book I needed to write at that time." As for the novel, Swofford told Jay MacDonald in an interview on the *BookPage* Web site: "I wanted to capture these fascinating years, 17 and 18, where there is a lot of anxiety about what one is going to do in the world and what one's place is. And there is the anxiety and excitement of leaving home and the influence of your parents."

Exit A tells the story of Severin Boxx, a seventeen-year-old "military brat" who is living at the Yokota air base outside of Tokyo in 1989. A football player on his high school team, Severin strives for the typical American life and has a crush on Virginia Kindwall, who is half Japanese and the daughter of his football coach. However, Virginia has joined a Japanese robbery gang. As she tries to live out her hero-outlaw fantasies, she convinces Severin to also participate. Their escapades lead to severe consequences for both them. The novel then jumps ahead fifteen years. Severin has a Ph.D. and is unhappily married when his former coach, now the dying General Kindwall, asks Severin to help find his daughter, who is living in Japan with her own daughter and has cut off all ties to the general.

"Exit A (the title refers to the way out of the subway station near the air base) is at its best when Swofford describes the surreal netherworld created by the grafting of American military culture on to a strange and largely hostile land," wrote Stephen Amidon in the *New Statesman.* Keir Graff stated in *Booklist:* "The book starts off strongly, setting Severin's dilemma against the uneasy, and vividly depicted, symbiosis between base and city." Some reviewers commented that the author handled the first half of his story depicting the teenager years ably but felt that he was less successful with the second half of the book dealing with his protagonists' adult lives. However, a *Kirkus Reviews* contributor called *Exit A* "a well-rounded tale."

BIOGRAPHICAL AND CRITICAL SOURCES:

BOOKS

Swofford, Anthony, *Jarhead: A Marine's Chronicle of the Gulf War and Other Battles,* Scribner (New York, NY), 2003.

PERIODICALS

Armor, July-August, 2004, Kevin Benson, review of *Jarhead,* p. 83.

Book, May-June, 2003, James Sullivan, review of *Jarhead,* p. 83.

Booklist, January 1, 2003, Gilbert Taylor, review of *Jarhead,* p. 842; October 1, 2003, Jeanette Larson, review of *Jarhead,* p. 340; August 1, 2006, Keir Graff, review of *Exit A,* p. 8.

Bookseller, September 13, 2002, Nicolette Jones, "The Philosophical Detective: Nicolette Jones on an Unusual Crime Series, A Novel from Pile and Other Recent Acquisitions," p. 28.

Business Week Online, April 1, 2003, Thane Peterson, review of *Jarhead.*

Christian Science Monitor, March 20, 2003, review of *Jarhead,* p. 19; November 25, 2003, review of *Jarhead,* p. B4.

Commonweal, December 1, 2006, Keith C. Burris, review of *Jarhead,* p. 23.

DAV, May-June, 2006, "'Jarhead' Author Speaks Out for Disabled Veterans," p. 14.

Entertainment Weekly, March 14, 2003, Chris Nashawaty, review of *Jarhead,* p. 70; December 19, 2003, review of *Jarhead,* p. 83; January 12, 2007, Gregory Kirschling, review of *Exit A,* p. 83.

Harper's, November, 2005, Lawrence Weschler, "Valkyries over Iraq," p. 65.

Kirkus Reviews, December 15, 2002, review of *Jarhead,* p. 1822; October 15, 2006, review of *Exit A,* p. 1043.

Library Journal, January, 2003, Edwin B. Burgess, review of *Jarhead,* p. 126; January, 2004, Don Wismer, review of *Jarhead,* p. 183.

Los Angeles Times, March 30, 2003, Gloria Emerson, review of *Jarhead,* p. R8; January 14, 2007, Art Winslow, review of *Exit A.*

New Statesman, April 28, 2003, Maurice Walsh, review of *Jarhead,* p. 48; February 12, 2007, Stephen Amidon, review of *Exit A,* p. 60.

Newsweek, March 3, 2003, Malcolm Jones, review of *Jarhead,* p. 59.

New York Times, February 19, 2003, review of *Jarhead,* p. E1; March 17, 2003, Dinitia Smith, review of *Jarhead,* p. E1.

New York Times Book Review, March 2, 2003, Mark Bowden, review of *Jarhead,* p. 8; December 28, 2003, Scott Veale, review of *Jarhead,* p. 16; January 14, 2007, William T. Vollmann, review of *Exit A,* p. 14.

Publishers Weekly, December 2, 2002, review of *Jarhead,* p. 41; March 31, 2003, Edward Nawotka, "On the Hells of 'Jarhead': What Does Anthony Swofford's Breakout Memoir Suggest about Wartime Reading Tastes?," p. 20; October 2, 2006, review of *Exit A,* p. 37; October 2, 2006, "This Will All End in Tears," p. 46; November 20, 2006, Rachel Deahl, "Beating the Literary Drums of War," interview with Anthony Swofford, p. 29.

Reviewer's Bookwatch, November, 2004, Betty Winslow, review of *Jarhead.*

Sabretache, September, 2003, Syd Wigzell, review of *Jarhead,* p. 50.

Spectator, March 22, 2003, Jonathan Mirsky, review of *Jarhead,* p. 38.

Times Literary Supplement, August 22, 2003, Christopher Coker, review of *Jarhead,* p. 22.

U.S. Catholic, November, 2003, Peter Gilmour, review of *Jarhead,* p. 32.

U.S. News & World Report, March 24, 2003, Justin Ewers, review of *Jarhead,* p. 52.

Wall Street Journal, April 30, 2003, Bing West, review of *Jarhead,* p. D8.

ONLINE

BookPage, http://www.bookpage.com/ (April 25, 2007), Jay MacDonald, "'Jarhead' Author Takes a New Direction in Debut Novel," interview with Anthony Swofford.

Bookslut, http://www.bookslut.com/ (July 11, 2003), William O. Pate II, review of *Jarhead.*

Combustible Celluloid, http://www.combustible celluloid.com/ (October 24, 2005), Jeffrey M. Anderson, "Interview with Anthony Swofford."

Esquire Online, http://www.esquire.com/ (July 11, 2003), Adrienne Miller, review of *Jarhead.*

Findlaw's Writ, http://writ.news.findlaw.com/ (April 18, 2003), Sam Williamson, review of *Jarhead.*

Guardian Online, http://books.guardian.co.uk/ (March 23, 2003), Tim Adams, review of *Jarhead.*

Houston Chronicle Online http://www.chron.com/ (February 28, 2003), Fritz Lanham, review of *Jarhead.*

Independent Online, http://enjoyment.independent.co.uk/ (March 15, 2007), Victoria James, review of *Exit A.*

Onion A.V. Club, http://www.theonionavclub.com/ (January 29, 2003), Scott Tobias, review of *Jarhead.*

Powell's Web site, http://www.powells.com/ (July 11, 2003), Dave Weich, "Anthony Swofford Opens His Jar: Buzz Spreads Far and Wide."

Salon.com, http://www.salon.com/ (March 10, 2003), Laura Miller, review of *Jarhead.*

St. Mary's College Web site, http://www.stmarys-ca.edu/ (September 27, 2004), faculty profile of Anthony Swofford.

USA Today Online, http://www.usatoday.com/ (March 12, 2003), J. Ford Huffman, review of *Jarhead.*

Washington Post Online, http://discuss.washingtonpost.com/ (March 21, 2003), "Confronting Iraq: A Marine Chronicle."

T

TADA, Joni Eareckson 1949-

PERSONAL: Born 1949; married Ken Tada (a retired teacher), 1982. *Hobbies and other interests:* Painting.

ADDRESSES: Office—Agoura Hills, CA.

CAREER: Founder and chief executive officer, Joni and Friends (Christian ministry), Agoura Hills, CA, 1979—, and of the Joni and Friends International Disability Center. Served on National Council on Disability; senior associate, Disability Concerns for the Lausanne Committee for World Evangelization; board member, Christian Writers Guild, Christian Medical and Dental Society, and New Europe Communications; honorary cochair, Presidential Prayer Team; member, Disability Advisory Committee, U.S. State Department, 2005—. Advisor to National Institute on Learning Disabilities, American Leprosy Mission, Christian Blind Mission International, and Love and Action.

AWARDS, HONORS: Golden Plate Award, American Academy of Achievement; Courage Award, Courage Rehabilitation Center; Award of Excellence, Patricia Neal Rehabilitation Center; Victory Award, National Rehabilitation Hospital; Golden Word Award, International Bible Society; Layperson of the Year, National Association of Evangelicals; Churchwoman of the Year, Religious Heritage Foundation, 1993; Gold Medallion, Evangelical Publishers' Association, 1997, for *Tell Me the Promises,* 1998, for *Tell Me the Truth;* Silver Medal, C.S. Lewis Awards, 1997, for *Tell Me the Promises;* William Ayer Award, National Religious Broadcasters' Association, 2002; Golden Medallion Award, 2003, for *When God Weeps,* 2004, for *Hymns for a Kid's Heart,* Volume 1; Golden Medallion Lifetime Achievement Award, Evangelical Christian Publishers Association, 2003; inducted into the Christian Booksellers Association Hall of Fame. Honorary bachelor's degree, Western Maryland College; doctor of humanities, Gordon College; D.H.L., Columbia International University; doctor of divinity, Westminster Theological Seminary and Lancaster Bible College.

WRITINGS:

(With Joe Musser) *Joni,* Zondervan (Grand Rapids, MI), 1976, published as *Joni Eareckson Tada: Her Story,* Inspirational Press (New York, NY), 1994, twentieth anniversary edition published as *Joni: An Unforgettable Story,* Zondervan (Grand Rapids, MI), 1996.

(With Steve Estes, and illustrator) *A Step Further,* Zondervan (Grand Rapids, MI), 1978, updated and expanded edition, 1990.

Choices, Changes, Zondervan (Grand Rapids, MI), 1986.

(With Gene Newman) *All God's Children: Ministry to the Disabled,* Ministry Resources Library (Grand Rapids, MI), 1987, revised edition, Zondervan (Grand Rapids, MI), 1993.

(With Bev Singleton) *Friendship Unlimited: How You Can Help a Disabled Friend,* H. Shaw Publishers (Wheaton, IL), 1987.

Jeremy, Barnabas, and the Wonderful Dream, illustrated by Ann Neilsen, Chariot Books (Elgin, IL), 1987.

Meet My Friends, D.C. Cook (Elgin, IL), 1987.

Darcy, Chariot Books (Elgin, IL), 1988.

Ryan and the Circus Wheels, illustrated by Norman McGary, Chariot Books (Elgin, IL), 1988.

Secret Strength: For Those Who Search, Multnomah (Portland, OR), 1988.

Glorious Intruder: God's Presence in Life's Chaos, Multnomah (Portland, OR), 1989.

Let God Be God, edited by Bryce Inman, transcribed by Bryce Inman and Jerry Cleveland, Word Music (Irving, TX), 1989.

A Christmas Longing, Multnomah (Portland, OR), 1990.

Seeking God: My Journey of Prayer and Praise, Wolgemuth & Hyatt (Brentwood, TN), 1991.

(With Joe Musser and Linda Lee Maifair) *Joni's Story,* Zondervan (Grand Rapids, MI), 1992.

When Is It Right to Die? Suicide, Euthanasia, Suffering, Mercy, foreword by C. Everett Koop, Zondervan (Grand Rapids, MI), 1992.

(With Steve Jensen) *Darcy and the Meanest Teacher in the World,* Chariot Books (Elgin, IL), 1993.

Diamonds in the Dust: 366 Sparkling Devotions, Zondervan (Grand Rapids, MI), 1993.

(With others) *Flights of Angels: Selections from Billy Graham, Joni Eareckson Tada, Helen Steiner Rice & Others,* Dimensions for Living (Nashville, TN), 1994.

(With Steve Jensen) *Darcy's Dog Dilemma,* Chariot Books (Elgin, IL), 1994.

(With Steve Jensen) *Darcy's Great Expectations,* Chariot Books (Elgin, IL), 1994.

Heaven: Your Real Home, Zondervan (Grand Rapid, MI), 1995.

The Life and Death Dilemma: Families Facing Health Care Choices, revised edition, Zondervan (Grand Rapids, MI), 1995.

A Christmas Longing, Multnomah Books (Portland, OR), 1996.

(With Steve Jensen) *Tell Me the Promises: A Family Covenant for Eternity,* illustrated by Ron DiCianni, Crossway Books (Wheaton, IL), 1996.

(With Steve Jensen) *Barrier-free Friendships: Bridging the Distance between You and Friends with Disabilities,* revised edition, Zondervan (Grand Rapids, MI), 1997.

(With Steve Jensen) *Tell Me the Truth: God's Eternal Truths for Families,* illustrated by Ron DiCianni, Crossway Books (Wheaton, IL), 1997.

(With Steve Estes) *When God Weeps: Why Our Sufferings Matter to the Almighty,* Zondervan (Grand Rapids, MI), 1997.

God's Precious Love, Zondervan (Grand Rapids, MI), 1998.

I'll Be with You Always, illustrated by Craig Nelson, Crossway Books (Wheaton, IL), 1998.

More Precious Than Silver: 366 Daily Devotional Readings, Zondervan (Grand Rapids, MI), 1998.

Heaven: What Will It Be Like?, Marshall Pickering (London, England), 1999.

Holiness in Hidden Places, Countryman (Nashville, TN), 1999.

You've Got a Friend, illustrated by Jeff Meyer, Crossway Books (Wheaton, IL), 1999.

(With Steve Jensen) *The Amazing Secret,* Crossway Books (Wheaton, IL), 2000.

(With Melody Carlson) *Forever Friends,* Crossway Books (Wheaton, IL), 2000.

(With Steve Jensen) *The Unforgettable Summer,* Crossway Books (Wheaton, IL), 2000.

The Incredible Discovery of Lindsey Renee, illustrated by Irena Roman, Crossway Books (Wheaton, IL), 2001.

(With Steve Jensen) *The Mission Adventure,* Crossway Books (Wheaton, IL), 2001.

(With Kay Strom) *Ordinary People, Extraordinary Faith,* T. Nelson (Nashville, TN), 2001.

(Compiler, with others) *What Wondrous Love Is This? Hymns of Wonder and Worship to Remember His Love* (includes sound disc), Crossway Books (Wheaton, IL), 2002.

(With others) *When Morning Gilds the Skies: Hymns of Heaven and Our Eternal Hope,* Crossway Books (Wheaton, IL), 2002.

On the Wings of the West Wind, illustrated by Michael Steirnagle, Crossway Books (Wheaton, IL), 2002.

God's Tender Care, Inspirio (Grand Rapids, MI), 2002.

The God I Love: A Lifetime of Walking with Jesus (memoir), Zondervan (Grand Rapids, MI), 2003.

(With Bobbie Wolgemuth) *Hymns for a Kid's Heart,* illustrated by Sergio Martinez, Crossway Books (Wheaton, IL), 2003.

31 Days toward Intimacy with God, Multnomah Publishers (Sisters, OR), 2005.

(With Dave and Jan Dravecky) *365 Days of Hope,* Authentic Media (Waynesboro, GA), 2005.

A Father's Touch, illustrated by Craig Nelson, Crossway Books (Wheaton, IL), 2005.

31 Days toward Overcoming Adversity, Multnomah Publishers (Sisters, OR), 2006.

(With Nigel M. de S. Cameron) *How to Be a Christian in a Brave New World,* Zondervan (Grand Rapids, MI), 2006.

Pearls of Great Price: 366 Daily Devotional Readings, Zondervan (Grand Rapids, MI), 2006.

31 Days toward Passionate Faith, Multnomah Publishers (Colorado Springs, CO), 2007.

Author of foreword, *Pursued: A True Story of Crime, Faith, and Family,* by Donald Smarto, InterVarsity Press (Downers Grove, IL), 1990; *Just Like Everybody Else,* by Jim Pierson, illustrated by Kathy Parks, Standard (Cincinnati, OH), 1993; *Harps & Halos: Songs about Heaven,* Everland Entertainment: Word Records & Music (Nashville, TN), 1994; *Acres of Hope: The Miraculous Story of One Family's Gift of Love to Children without Hope,* by Patty Anglin and Joe Musser, Promise Press (Uhrichsville, OH), 1999; author of introduction, *Hand That Paints the Sky: Delighting in the Creator's Canvas,* special message from artist/composer Cindy Morgan, New Leaf Press (Green Forest, AR), 2003. General editor with Dave and Jan Dravecky, *NIV Encouragement Bible: New International Version,* Zondervan (Grand Rapids, MI), 2001. Contributor to *O Come, All Ye Faithful: Hymns of Adoration to Celebrate His Birth,* Crossway. Contributor to periodicals, including *Christianity Today, War Cry,* and *Today's Christian Woman.*

SOUND RECORDINGS

Joni's Song, Word (Waco, TX), 1981.

Spirit Wings, Word (Waco, TX), 1982.

Lord of Love, Word Records (Waco, Texas), 1984.

I've Got Wheels!, Word Records (Waco, TX), 1985.

Let God Be God, Word (Dallas, TX), 1989.

When Is It Right to Die? Suicide, Euthanasia, Suffering, Mercy (sound recording), Zondervan (Grand Rapids, MI), 1992.

Joni, Zondervan Audio Pages (Grand Rapids, MI), 2001.

(Narrator) Stephen Elkins, *The Great Adventure: A Very Special Story for Children* (includes sound disc), illustrated by Ellie Colton, Broadman & Holman Publishers (Nashville, TN), 2001.

God's Precious Love, Inspirio (Grand Rapids, MI), 2002.

God's Tender Care, Inspirio (Grand Rapids, MI), 2002.

When Morning Gildes the Skies, Great Hymns of Our Faith, Crossway Books (Wheaton, IL), 2002.

Choose Life!, Focus on the Family (Colorado Springs, CO), 2004.

ADAPTATIONS: Joni was adapted as a feature film.

SIDELIGHTS: An athletic teenager who loved to swim and ride horses, Joni Eareckson Tada had her life changed forever when she was seventeen. She dived into the shallow end of a pool and broke her neck in 1967. Paralyzed, she has been a quadriplegic ever since, a disability that severely tested her Christian beliefs. She seriously contemplated suicide, as she told an interviewer on the *Notes in the Key of Life* Web site: "I was so depressed, so discouraged . . . and when I was even brave enough to think about living life sitting in a wheelchair for the rest of my life, without use of my hands, I begged my friends to aid me in suicide. I asked them to bring in their mothers' sleeping pills, their father's razor blades, anything to put me out of my misery." Tada eventually found the strength to go on with her life through her religious faith. Seeking to inspire others with disabilities, she founded the ministry Joni and Friends. The organization serves the public in many ways. For example, they refurbish thousands of wheelchairs and distribute them to the needy worldwide, they aid hundreds of families whose members have special needs, and they provide educational and religious support through publications, organized retreats, radio broadcasts, and more.

Tada has written dozens of inspirational books, too, for both adults and children, including her autobiographical books *Joni: An Unforgettable Story* and *The God I Love: A Lifetime of Walking with Jesus.* The former was later republished as *Joni* and has been adapted as an inspirational film. A *Publishers Weekly* critic said of the autobiography that "Christian readers should appreciate this mature, absorbing reminiscence of a remarkable life," while *Booklist* reviewer Donna Chavez called it a "moving, well-told memoir."

Others with her disability have supported such causes as assisted suicide and stem cell research, positions that Tada has said her Christian beliefs do not allow her to support. Contrary to the position taken by the late actor Christopher Reeve, who supported the use of embryonic cells to repair nerve damage, Tada has felt that such research cheapens human dignity and the human soul. In *How to Be a Christian in a Brave New World,* which she cowrote, Tada addresses stem cell research, as well as other issues involving medical ethics, such as cloning, in vitro fertilization, and euthanasia. Graham Christian stated in his *Library Journal* review that the book is "thoughtfully argued."

Assisted suicide is the topic of Tada's *When Is It Right to Die? Suicide, Euthanasia, Suffering, Mercy.* This is a subject that the author knows very well, and her conclusion that killing oneself is not the right choice thus bears considerable weight. Instead, she counsels those who are suffering to seek hospice care and to find comfort in the words of the Bible. Tada "delivers an eloquent, persuasive testimony," according to one *Publishers Weekly* reviewer. A writer for *Issues in Law & Medicine* concluded: "It presents a reasoned argument—including moral, emotional, philosophical, and spiritual aspects—to an issue society will increasingly face."

BIOGRAPHICAL AND CRITICAL SOURCES:

BOOKS

Tada, Joni Eareckson, and Joe Musser, *Joni: An Unforgettable Story,* Zondervan (Grand Rapids, MI), 1996.

Tada, Joni Eareckson, *The God I Love: A Lifetime of Walking with Jesus,* Zondervan (Grand Rapids, MI), 2003.

PERIODICALS

Booklist, October 1, 1996, review of *Joni,* p. 308; July 1, 2003, Donna Chavez, review of *The God I Love,* p. 1849; October 15, 1992, "When Is It Right to Die?," p. 385.

Christianity Today, March 1, 2003, Joni Eareckson Tada, "Threat of Biotech: Joni Eareckson Tada Responds to Christopher Reeve and Others," p. 60; August 1, 2003, review of *The God I Love,* p. 58.

Issues in Law & Medicine, December 22, 1992, "When Is It Right to Die?," p. 419.

Library Journal, September 15, 1992, review of *When Is It Right to Die? Suicide, Euthanasia, Suffering, Mercy,* p. 80; May 1, 2006, Graham Christian, review of *How to Be a Christian in a Brave New World,* p. 91.

Publishers Weekly, October 26, 1992, review of *When Is It Right to Die?,* p. 51; November 9, 1998, review of *More Precious Than Silver: 366 Daily Devotional Readings,* p. 72; September 24, 2001, review of "How to Be Santa Claus," p. 61; February 18, 2002, review of *What Wondrous Love Is*

This: Hymns of Wonder and Worship to Remember His Love, p. 64; June 16, 2003, review of *The God I Love,* p. 65; April 3, 2006, review of *How to Be a Christian in a Brave New World,* p. 65.

School Library Journal, May 1, 1993, "Joni's Story," p. 112.

ONLINE

Armchair Interviews, http://www.armchairinterviews. com/ (May 15, 2007), Brenda A. Snodgrass, review of *31 Days toward Passionate Faith.*

BBC Web site, http://www.bbc.co.uk (May 15, 2007), interview with Joni Eareckson Tada.

Joni and Friends, http://www.joniandfriends.org (May 15, 2007).

Notes in the Key of Life, http://cindyswanslife. blogspot.com/ (February 3, 2005), interview with Joni Eareckson Tada.*

*   *   *

TARASSOFF, Lev
See TROYAT, Henri

*   *   *

TARDI, Alan 1956-

PERSONAL: Born 1956, in Chicago, IL. *Education:* Attended San Francisco Conservatory of Music; earned B.A.

ADDRESSES: Home—New York, NY, and Castiglione Falletto, Italy. *E-mail*—alan@alantardi.com.

CAREER: Freelance writer and restaurant consultant. Chef at restaurants, including Chantrelle and Lafayette, both New York, NY; owner and chef, Follonico, New York, NY, 1992-2001.

WRITINGS:

Romancing the Vine: Life, Love and Transformation in the Vineyards of Barolo (memoir), St. Martin's Press (New York, NY), 2006.

SIDELIGHTS: After a long and varied career as a restaurateur, Alan Tardi closed his successful Follonico restaurant in New York City and traveled to the Piedmont region of Italy, where he fell in love with the slower pace of a life centered around local foods and wines. He describes his experiences in his new Italian home in his memoir, *Romancing the Vine: Life, Love and Transformation in the Vineyards of Barolo.* The book recounts Tardi's growing affection for the village of Castiglione Falletto, in Italy's famed Barolo wine region, and his love for Ivana, the woman who inspired his move and whose family vineyards he helps to restore. It also contains twenty-five recipes from the region. According to a contributor to *Publishers Weekly, Romancing the Vine* offers many of the pleasures that are expected in the genre of food and wine writing, but noted that Tardi's "take on the healing powers of old-fashioned hard work and his guidance into his lifestyle is comforting and satisfying." June Sawyers, writing in the *Chicago Tribune,* observed that the book is "more complicated and sophisticated" than typical memoirs of disaffected Americans finding their bliss in charming Old World locales. In Sawyers's view, Tardi's emphasis on the history and process of Italian wine making gives his book particular appeal.

Tardi told *CA:* "I have always enjoyed telling stories and relating experiences. My professional writing is an outgrowth of that. The process is fairly straightforward: In the natural course of my life I have certain experiences which I think might be of interest and/or value to others. I then try to relate them in the most articulate way possible, using words as a vehicle for trying to recapture and relay these experiences.

"I hope that my experiences—and my writing about them—will provide insight and enjoyment."

BIOGRAPHICAL AND CRITICAL SOURCES:

BOOKS

Tardi, Alan, *Romancing the Vine: Life, Love and Transformation in the Vineyards of Barolo,* St. Martin's Press (New York, NY), 2006.

PERIODICALS

Chicago Tribune, December 24, 2006, June Sawyers, "The Resourceful Traveler," review of *Romancing the Vine.*

Publishers Weekly, October 9, 2006, review of *Romancing the Vine,* p. 51.

ONLINE

Alan Tardi Home Page, http://www.alantardi.com (April 24, 2007).

*   *   *

TAYLOR, Carole Anne 1943-

PERSONAL: Born 1943. *Education:* Reed College, B.A., 1965, M.A.T., 1967; Harvard University, Ph.D., 1978.

ADDRESSES: E-mail—ctaylor@bates.edu.

CAREER: Cleveland High School, Portland, OR, teacher of English, 1966-67; Riverdale Country School, Bronx, NY, teacher of English and advanced placement, 1967-71; The Concord School, Sandridge, Hertfordshire, England, teacher of English and American literature, and department chair, 1971-73; Harvard University, teaching fellow (expositor writing), 1973-74, (history and literature), 1974-77; Bates College, Lewiston, ME, chair, American Cultural Studies, 1992-94, assistant professor of English, 1978-85, associate professor, 1985-92, professor of English and African American/American cultural studies, 1993—, founding member, 1990-91, and chair, 1991-93, of Committee on African American Studies and American Cultural Studies, chair, department of English, 1996-2000.

MEMBER: The Maine People's Alliance (state board, 1997-99), Maine Rural Workers' Coalition (state board, 1998-2003), Community ERA (founding member, 1994), The Many and One Coalition, Lewiston, Center for Justice, Equality, and Democracy (advisory board, 2002—), Phi Beta Kappa.

AWARDS, HONORS: Reed College Creative Scholarship, summer, 1964; Susan Anthony Potter Prize in Comparative Literature, Harvard University, 1975; Whiting Foundation Graduate Fellowship in the Humanities, Harvard University, 1977-78; Fulbright

Foundation Fellowship, National Taiwan University, Taiwan, 1985-86; Robert H. Kroepsch Award for Excellence in Teaching, Bates College, 1987; Project Mentor, National Council for the Humanities, 1989-90; Project Humanist, Metropolitan Life Multicultural Grant to the Olin Museum of Art, Bates College, 1992-93; Project Humanist, Project on National Healthcare, National Endowment for the Humanities, Program Committee 1999-2001; Robert H. Kroepsch Award for Excellence in Teaching, Bates College, 2002.

WRITINGS:

Roland Barthes, a Bibliographical Reader's Guide, Garland Publishing (New York, NY), 1983.
A Poetics of Seeing: The Implications of Visual Form in Modern Poetry, Garland Publishing (New York, NY), 1985.
The Tragedy and Comedy of Resistance: Reading Modernity through Black Women's Fiction, University of Pennsylvania Press (Philadelphia, PA), 2000.

SIDELIGHTS: In *The Tragedy and Comedy of Resistance: Reading Modernity through Black Women's Fiction,* Carole Anne Taylor challenges traditional literary theories about genre in order to situate black women's writing at the center of critical theory. Focusing on novels by Toni Morrison, Alice Walker, and Gloria Naylor, she argues that their writing possesses a theory of resistance and struggle that is not found in liberal critical theory. For example, black women's writing disrupts traditional views of comedy and tragedy by an awareness of their intersubjectivities. As *Rocky Mountain Review of Language and Literature* contributor Doreen Alvarez Saar explained, black women writers know that "Tragedy requires a 'witnessing' of the great wrongs implicit in all social interaction while the comedy relief of shared laughter ultimately coexists with the deep understanding of that tragedy." This differs from liberal theory, which is premised on the role of the reader as a sympathetic viewer of the tragedy, not as an actor who participates in the struggle against whatever injustice has created the tragic conditions.

While agreeing with much of Taylor's argument, Erik Dussere, writing in the *Novel: A Forum on Fiction,* observed that a weakness in her analysis is that "it requires Taylor to treat the contemporary novels as didactic and prescriptive theoretical works, rather than as nuanced, open-ended literary texts." Still, Dussere concluded that "Taylor's project of reading against the grain of literary influence is a strong one, and does much to question the admittedly questionable traditions within which modernism has been categorized and canonized." Saar called *The Tragedy and Comedy of Resistance* an "ambitious and heartfelt project" enhanced by a "cogent" analysis.

BIOGRAPHICAL AND CRITICAL SOURCES:

PERIODICALS

Choice, April, 2000, J. Tharp, review of *The Tragedy and Comedy of Resistance: Reading Modernity through Black Women's Fiction,* p. 1470.
Modern Fiction Studies, January, 2000, Kimberly D. Blockett, review of *The Tragedy and Comedy of Resistance,* p. 1039.
Novel: A Forum on Fiction, fall, 1999, Erik Dussere, "Intercultural Transmission," p. 138.
Rocky Mountain Review of Language and Literature, Volume 59, number 1, 2005, Doreen Alvarez Saar, review of *The Tragedy and Comedy of Resistance,* pp. 74-75.

ONLINE

Bates College Web site, http://www.bates.edu/ (April 24, 2007), faculty profile of author.*

*   *   *

TAYLOR, Kim

PERSONAL: Born in Denver, CO. *Education:* University of California, Irvine, B.A.; California State University, Los Angeles, M.A.

ADDRESSES: Home and office—Salinas, CA. *E-mail*—kimtaylor@kimtaylor.net.

CAREER: Educator and author. Heald College, Salinas, CA, instructor; RISE (nonprofit job-training program), lead faculty member. Singular Productions, Los Angeles, CA, former actor and founding member.

AWARDS, HONORS: Willa Literary Award for Best Young Adult Novel, Women Writing the West, 2002, for *Cissy Funk.*

WRITINGS:

Cissy Funk (young-adult fiction), HarperCollins (New York, NY), 2001.
Bowery Girl (young-adult novel), Viking (New York, NY), 2006.

Also author of two-act play *Not So Quiet,* adapted from the novel by Helen Zenna Smith.

SIDELIGHTS: In addition to teaching at the college level, Kim Taylor is the author of several young-adult novels and a stage adaptation of Helen Zenna Smith's World War I novel *Not So Quiet. Cissy Funk,* which earned Taylor the 2002 Willa Cather Award from Women Writing the West, is set in Colorado during the Depression years of the 1930s, and follows a fourteen-year-old girl as she copes with an abusive mother, a runaway father, and the loving aunt who attempts to rescue her. Taylor's second novel, *Bowery Girl,* was inspired by the author's love of history and her reading of Jacob Riis's famous 1890 social documentary history *How the Other Half Lives: Studies among the Tenements of New York.*

Set in the late nineteenth century, *Bowery Girl* shows teen readers that the modern realities of city life—gang violence, crime, unplanned pregnancy, and poverty—are nothing new: they were shared by teens of previous generations. In the novel, street-smart, sixteen-year-old Mollie Flynn relies on her wits and thieving ways to survive in nineteenth-century Manhattan. Dreaming of the better life that she might have across the newly erected Brooklyn Bridge, Molly and her roommate, Annabelle, decide to save up enough money to make this shared dream a reality. However, Annabelle works as a prostitute, and when she winds up pregnant the dream is threatened. Hoping to find a way to keep their plan alive, the teens enroll in a series of self-improvement classes, despite the pressure of those around them to accept their station as Bowery dwellers. In *Kliatt,* Janis Flint-Ferguson called *Bowery Girl* "a gritty, realistic look" at life in the nineteenth century, while Jennifer Mattson commented in *Booklist* that the author "allows her characters to behave mostly

unhampered" by any overarching message. In *Voice of Youth Advocates,* Mary E. Heslin called Taylor's young characters "complex" and concluded that *Bowery Girl* "is not just fine historical fiction; it is also splendid writing with mega teen appeal."

For Taylor, the research she did while writing *Bowery Girl* was one of the most compelling parts of the writing process. As she noted on her home page: "To research 1883 Manhattan is to conjure ghosts, to dig through contemporary and historical accounts that sometimes glorify and exaggerate both rich and poor, both goodness and evil. The specifics in research, beyond dates and places and streets, came from studying the photographs of the time. To look for the dimness of the gaslights, the children playing in a street and blithely unaware of the dead horse laying ten feet away, the thick layer of grease on a tenement wall, a momentary smile. To walk, for a moment, with two young women who wanted only a bit of sunshine and a chance for something better."

BIOGRAPHICAL AND CRITICAL SOURCES:

PERIODICALS

Booklist, August, 2001, Frances Bradburn, review of *Cissy Funk,* p. 2109; March 1, 2006, Jennifer Mattson, review of *Bowery Girl,* p. 83.
Bulletin of the Center for Children's Books, May, 2001, review of *Cissy Funk,* p. 354; May, 2006, Elizabeth Bush, review of *Bowery Girl,* p. 425.
Journal of Adolescent & Adult Literacy, October, 2006, Judith A. Hayn, review of *Bowery Girl,* p. 159.
Kirkus Reviews, April 1, 2006, review of *Bowery Girl,* p. 358.
Kliatt, March, 2006, Janis Flint-Ferguson, review of *Bowery Girl,* p. 17.
Publishers Weekly, May 28, 2001, review of *Cissy Funk,* p. 89.
School Library Journal, May, 2001, Cindy Darling Codell, review of *Cissy Funk,* p. 160; March, 2006, Kelly Czarnecki, review of *Bowery Girl,* p. 230.
Voice of Youth Advocates, August, 2001, review of *Cissy Funk,* p. 207; April, 2006, Mary E. Heslin, review of *Bowery Girl,* p. 52.

ONLINE

Kim Taylor Home Page, http://www.kimtaylor.net (May 16, 2007).

TAYLOR, Russell 1960(?)-

PERSONAL: Born c. 1960, in York, England. *Education:* Attended Oxford University.

ADDRESSES: Home—London, England.

CAREER: Journalist, writer, composer. Writer for the "Alex" comic strip in *Daily Telegraph* and other British newspapers, 1987—; has composed music for television and films, including *Kids behind Bars* and *The Dying Rooms.*

AWARDS, HONORS: Member of the Order of the British Empire, awarded 2003; Best Cartoon Strip of the Year, Cartoon Art Trust, 2003, for "Alex."

WRITINGS:

"ALEX" COLLECTIONS; WITH CHARLES PEATTIE

Alex, Penguin Books (London, England), 1987.
The Unabashed Alex, Penguin Books (London, England), 1988.
Alex II: Magnum Force, Penguin Books (London, England), 1989.
Alex III: Son of Alex, Penguin Books (London, England), 1990.
Alex IV: The Man with the Golden Handshake, Penguin Books (London, England), 1991.
Alex V: For the Love of Alex, Penguin Books (London, England), 1992.
Alex Calls the Shots, Headline (London, England), 1993.
The Alex Omnibus, Penguin Books (London, England), 1993.
Alex Plays the Game, Headline (London, England), 1994.
Alex Knows the Score, Headline (London, England), 1995.
Alex Sweeps the Board, Headline (London, England), 1996.
Alex Feels the Pinch, Headline (London, England), 1997.
The Full Alex Omnibus: Collected Strips 1987-1998, Headline (London, England), 1998.
The Alex Technique: On Jobs in the City, Headline (London, England), 1999.

The Best of Alex 1998-2001, Carlton Books (London, England), 2001,
The Best of Alex 2002, Carlton Books (London, England), 2002.
The Best of Alex 2003, Carlton Books (London, England), 2003.
The Best of Alex 2004, Prion Books (London, England), 2004.

OTHER

(With Marc Polonsky) *U.S.S.R.—From an Original Idea by Karl Marx,* illustrated by Kirill Miller, Faber & Faber (London, England), 1986.
The Looniness of the Long Distance Runner: An Unfit Londoner's Attempt to Run the New York City Marathon from Scratch, Carlton Books (London, England), 2003.

ADAPTATIONS: Russell Taylor and Charles Peattie adapted "Alex" for a stage play, 2003.

SIDELIGHTS: Though he has never bought a stock share or even worked in an office, Russell Taylor, with artist partner Charles Peattie, created a cartoon strip character that York *Evening Press* contributor Chris Titley called "Britain's most famous stockbroker." Alex Masterley, wearing what Titley described as a "pin-stripe suit and permanent sneer," starred in the comic strip "Alex," which enjoyed an immensely popular sixteen-year run in major British newspapers, starting with the London *Daily News* and then going to the *Independent* and the *Daily Telegraph.* Taylor and Peattie, who drew the cartoon, created more than 4,000 strips which have been collected in some seventeen "Alex" books.

Taylor knew from an early age that he was good at writing jokes, having created his own humor magazine in school and, later, publishing a satirical travelogue about his post-university visit to the Soviet Union, *U.S.S.R.—From an Original Idea by Karl Marx,* which he wrote with Marc Polonsky. When Taylor met Peattie, a former portrait painter, at a party in London, the two decided to become partners on a comic strip—though Taylor had never tried his hand at cartoon writing. "I wanted a strip about people living in London," Taylor explained to Titley. "Back in the Eighties, yuppies were the big thing, so we decided we would make him a yuppie. He had a yuppie mobile phone before most people had mobile phones, he drove a BMW, had a lovely home and girlfriend, and was quite objectionable."

Though he is best known for creating "Alex," Taylor has also received glowing reviews for *The Looniness of the Long Distance Runner: An Unfit Londoner's Attempt to Run the New York City Marathon from Scratch.* As its title suggests, the book chronicles Taylor's experiences training for and running the New York City marathon—a formidable challenge for a confirmed nonathlete, who ended up finishing 7,659th out of 32,000 entrants. London *Sunday Times* writer Frank Graham chose *The Looniness of the Long Distance Runner* as "book of the week," calling it a "remarkable triumph" that is "unremitting[ly] witty and amusing." Emily Melton, writing in *Booklist,* commended Taylor for avoiding potentially tedious details about training regimens and making his book "howlingly funny" throughout.

BIOGRAPHICAL AND CRITICAL SOURCES:

PERIODICALS

Booklist, October 1, 2002, Emily Melton, review of *The Looniness of the Long Distance Runner: An Unfit Londoner's Attempt to Run the New York City Marathon from Scratch,* p. 296.
Daily Telegraph (London, England), December 31, 2002, Becky Barrow, "Years of City Lunches Earn Alex Tea at the Palace"; February 26, 2003, Adam Jay, "Russelled Up a Princely Way with Protocol"; November 27, 2003, Danielle Rossingh, "Off the Page and on the Stage"; December 4, 2003, Simon Goodley, "After Careers Perfecting. . . . "
Evening Press (York, England), January 17, 2003, "Why I Axed Alex, the Smug City Slicker."
Financial News (London, England), November 17, 2002, "Alex Acts as a Guide for Us All."
Mirror (London, England), February 1, 2003, Andrea Henry, review of *The Looniness of the Long Distance Runner,* p. 56.
Sunday Times (London, England), February 23, 2003, Frank Graham, review of *The Looniness of the Long Distance Runner.*

ONLINE

Alex Comic Strip Books Gallery, http://www.tonystrading.co.uk/ (September 22, 2004).*

TENTLER, Leslie Woodcock 1945-

PERSONAL: Born February 20, 1945, in Muskegon, MI; daughter of Leonard (a labor leader and diplomat) and Loula (a medical technologist and administrator) Woodcock; married Thomas N. Tentler (a professor of history), September 2, 1971; children: Sarah Margaret, Gregory John, Daniel Leonard. *Ethnicity:* "Anglo/Irish-American." *Education:* University of Michigan, B.A., 1967, Ph.D., 1975. *Politics:* Democrat. *Religion:* Roman Catholic.

ADDRESSES: Home—Washington, DC. *Office*—Department of History, Catholic University of America, Washington, DC 20003. *E-mail*—tentler@cua.edu.

CAREER: University of Michigan—Dearborn, began as assistant professor, became professor of history, 1974-98; Catholic University of America, Washington, DC, professor of history, 1998—.

MEMBER: American Historical Association, American Catholic Historical Association.

WRITINGS:

Wage-Earning Women, Oxford University Press (New York, NY), 1979.
Seasons of Grace (nonfiction), Wayne State University Press (Detroit, MI), 1990.
Catholics and Contraception: An American History, Cornell University Press (Ithaca, NY), 2004.

*   *   *

TEWKSBURY, Henry 1923-2003

(Henry the Cheese Man, Henry Peter Tewksbury, Peter Tewksbury)

PERSONAL: Born 1923, in Cleveland, OH; died February 20, 2003, in Brattleboro, VT; married Kathleen Willoughby (divorced); married Ann Schuyler; children: two from first marriage, four from second marriage.

CAREER: Brattleboro Food Co-op, Brattleboro, VT, cheese department manager. Former film director and television producer and writer; wrote episodes for *My Three Sons* and *Alcoa Premier,* produced the television series *Father Knows Best.* Worked as school administrator, voice actor for cartoons, cattle farmer, radio sportscaster, and furniture salesman.

AWARDS, HONORS: Emmy Award, best direction for a single program of a comedy series, for episode "Medal for Margaret," *Father Knows Best,* 1959.

WRITINGS:

The Cheeses of Vermont: A Gourmet Guide to Vermont's Artisanal Cheesemakers, Countryman Press (Woodstock, VT), 2002.

SIDELIGHTS: One of the pioneers of the artisanal cheese movement in Vermont in the early 1990s, Henry Tewksbury wrote the well-received *The Cheeses of Vermont: A Gourmet Guide to Vermont's Artisanal Cheesemakers.* The book explains the history and techniques of cheesemaking, and also lists cheesemakers by region. Reviewers and cheese enthusiasts welcomed the book as a well-written and informative guide by a figure who was highly esteemed among artisan farmers and did much to promote the role of cheesemaking in Vermont's economy. As Tewksbury explained to *Boston Globe* writer William A. Davis in 2000, many Vermont cheeses can compete with the best cheeses in the world. "High-quality farmstead cheeses," he pointed out, "are helping save the Vermont family farm and preserve the Vermont landscape." Farmstead cheese, he went on to say, "is made at a farm from the milk of animals—cows, goats, or sheep—that are also raised and milked there. This means the cheese has a unique flavor with subtle seasonal and annual differences, just like wine from a vineyard."

Though he became best-known as "Henry the Cheeseman," Tewksbury had enjoyed a distinguished earlier career as a producer, director, and writer of films and television series. Despite the success he found in Hollywood, including three Emmy nominations and one award, Tewksbury grew dissatisfied with this competitive lifestyle and moved to Vermont. As a cheesemaker and worker at the Brattleboro Food Co-

op, he lived so unassumingly that his associates and neighbors were stunned to discover that he had once made major deals in Hollywood.

BIOGRAPHICAL AND CRITICAL SOURCES:

PERIODICALS

Bloomsbury Review, July-August, 2002, Greg Kirrish, review of *The Cheeses of Vermont: A Gourmet Guide to Vermont's Artisanal Cheesemakers.*
Boston Globe, June 21, 2000, William A. Davis, review of *The Cheeses of Vermont,* p. F8.
Gourmet Retailer, July, 2002, review of *The Cheeses of Vermont,* p. 46.
Publishers Weekly, March 4, 2002, review of *The Cheeses of Vermont,* p. 77.

ONLINE

Internet Movie Database, http://www.imdb.com/ (May 14, 2007), "Peter Tewksbury."*

*   *   *

**TEWKSBURY, Henry Peter
    See TEWKSBURY, Henry**

*   *   *

**TEWKSBURY, Peter
    See TEWKSBURY, Henry**

*   *   *

**TINTORI, Karen
    (Jillian Karr, a joint pseudonym, Karen A. Katz)**

PERSONAL: Married; children: two. *Education:* Wayne State University, B.A.

ADDRESSES: Home—MI. *Agent*—Sally Wofford-Girand, Sally Wofford-Girand Literary Agency, Brickhouse Literary Agents, 80 5th Ave., Ste. 1101-03, New York, NY 10011.

CAREER: Has worked for *New York* (magazine), as an assistant editor for the *FTD Florist* (magazine), and in public relations.

WRITINGS:

(As Karen A. Katz, with E.B. Freedman and Jan Greenberg) *What Does Being Jewish Mean: Read-Aloud Responses to Questions Jewish Children Ask about History, Culture, and Religion,* Prentice Hall Press (New York, NY), 1991.

Trapped: The 1909 Cherry Mine Disaster, Atria Books (New York, NY), 2002.

(With Jill Gregory) *The Book of Names* (novel), St. Martin's Press (New York, NY), 2007.

Unto the Daughters: The Legacy of an Honor Killing in a Sicilian-American Family (memoir), St. Martin's Press (New York, NY), 2007.

MYSTERY NOVELS; WITH JILL GREGORY; UNDER JOINT PSEUDONYM JILLIAN KARR

Something Borrowed, Something Blue, Doubleday (New York, NY), 1993.

Catch Me If You Can, Avon Books (New York, NY), 1996.

ADAPTATIONS: Something Borrowed, Something Blue was made into a CBS-TV movie.

SIDELIGHTS: Karen Tintori is an author who has also written as Karen A. Katz, and under the joint pseudonym Jillian Karr with her friend and collaborator, Jill Gregory. In her nonfiction book *Trapped: The 1909 Cherry Mine Disaster,* Tintori tells the story of 480 coal miners trapped in a 1909 Illinois mine disaster resulting from the worst coal mine fire in the history of the United States. Tintori has a special association with the disaster because her grandfather should have died in the fire but stayed home because he had a hangover. The author explores how the miners, who included both men and young boys, fought to survive, focusing primarily on twenty-one survivors who were sealed off in another part of the mine in attempt to put the fire out. Also examined is the horrendous suffering of the dead miners' surviving families, who were unable to recover the bodies until the following spring. "Tintori's graphic account of this tragedy is a sad but gripping story," reported George Cohen in *Booklist.* In the *Library Journal* Daniel Liestman felt that the author "has presented a very accessible and gripping account of a human tragedy."

Tintori teamed with Jill Gregory to write *The Book of Names.* The novel revolves around David Shepard, who has a near-death experience that leads to his suddenly thinking about various names. He begins writing the names down, and before long he has a list of thousands of names. However, when his stepdaughter's name appears on the list David decides to investigate what this strange phenomenon is all about. Eventually, he encounters a mysterious and malevolent cult called Gnoseos, which kills certain people to make sure that the world remains unbalanced. Their devious plot is based on the Jewish tradition that thirty-six people are born during each generation to help support the universal laws. David realizes that the names he has written down are the cult's victims or victims-to-come. He then joins archaeologist Yael HarPaz to fight the group and try to save his stepdaughter. "Convincing characters and a rapidly moving plot combine to create an enjoyable religious thriller," wrote Joy St. John in her *Library Journal* assessment. Several reviewers also commented on the authors' ability to create a fascinating mystery. For example, a *Kirkus Reviews* contributor wrote: "Attentive readers will particularly relish the crossword-puzzle aspect of the denouement." A contributor to the *Economist* concluded that "*The Book of Names* self-assuredly fulfills the requirements of the religious thriller in terms of characterisation, plot and pace."

BIOGRAPHICAL AND CRITICAL SOURCES:

BOOKS

Tintori, Karen, *Unto the Daughters: The Legacy of an Honor Killing in a Sicilian-American Family,* St. Martin's Press (New York, NY), 2007.

PERIODICALS

American History, February 1, 2003, review of *Trapped: The 1909 Cherry Mine Disaster,* p. 61.

Booklist, September 1, 2002, George Cohen, review of *Trapped,* p. 52; December 15, 2006, Ilene Cooper, review of *The Book of Names,* p. 25.

Books, February 4, 2007, review of *The Book of Names,* p. 8.

Chicago Sun Times, February 4, 2007, Cathleen Falsani, "Spiritual Thriller Flying off Shelves; Da Vinci Code-esque Novel Has Local Ties."

Economist, January 13, 2007, "Watch Out Dan Brown; New Fiction 3," review of *The Book of Names,* p. 76.

Kirkus Reviews, July 15, 2002, review of *Trapped,* p. 1020; October 1, 2006, review of *The Book of Names,* p. 978.

Library Journal, August, 2002, Daniel Liestman, review of *Trapped,* p. 119; October 15, 2006, Joy St. John, review of *The Book of Names,* p. 51.

Publishers Weekly, July 8, 2002, review of *Trapped,* p. 42; October 16, 2006, review of *The Book of Names,* p. 33.

Tribune Books (Chicago, IL), April 27, 2003, review of *Trapped,* p. 3.

ONLINE

Karen Tintori Home Page, http://www.karentintori. com (April 25, 2007).*

*   *   *

TIRRELL, Art 1941-

PERSONAL: Born May 27, 1941; children: Cayleen (daughter). *Hobbies and other interests:* Sailing.

ADDRESSES: Home—Oswego, NY *E-mail*—atirrel@ twcny.rr.com.

CAREER: Tirrell's Appliance Company, Oswego, NY, founder, 1974—; novelist.

AWARDS, HONORS: United States Yacht Racing Union Sportsman of the Year; honorary member, Oswego High School Sailing Club.

WRITINGS:

The Secret Ever Keeps (novel), Kunati Inc. (Largo, FL), 2007.

SIDELIGHTS: Art Tirrell draws on the adventure-filled history of the Lake Ontario region in his first novel, *The Secret Ever Keeps.* Set near Oswego, New York, on the southern shore of Lake Ontario, the book combines a contemporary love story with a plot that features Prohibition-era smuggling, treasure hunting, and the 1780 wreck of a British warship that may implicate George Washington in a scandal. Real events, according to Tirrell, provided all the inspiration he could want for a tale of intrigue. "Oswego has an incredibly rich history," he told Steve Yablonski in the *Oswego Daily News.* "Amazing things happened here during Prohibition. I'm surprised more writers aren't taking advantage."

A lifelong resident of the Oswego area and an accomplished sailor, Tirrell wanted to become a writer ever since his eighth-grade teacher praised his talent with words. But Tirrell did not begin writing seriously until 1997, when he could take time away from running his successful appliance dealership. Joining an online writing group, he learned the craft of writing fiction and completed the manuscript of *The Secret Ever Keeps.* The book, according to Yablonski, is "brimming with the flavor of local history." Carol Haggas, writing in *Foreword Magazine,* praised the novel's intricate plotting and sympathetically drawn characters, and deemed the book "an accomplished and assured fictional debut."

Tirrell told *CA:* "My goal as a writer is to perfect my craft and entertain the reader. If occasionally from these efforts a moment of deeper understanding arises, it's all the better, then, isn't it?"

BIOGRAPHICAL AND CRITICAL SOURCES:

PERIODICALS

Foreword Magazine, March, 2007, Carol Haggas, review of *The Secret Ever Keeps,* p. 54.

Kirkus Reviews, October 1, 2006, review of *The Secret Ever Keeps,* p. 986.

Oswego Daily News, March 30, 2007, Steve Yablonski, "Oswego Businessman Begins New Career as Author."

ONLINE

Art Tirrell Home Page, http://arttirrell.com (April 25, 2007).

Kunati Books Home Page, http://www.kunati.com (May 31, 2007), profile of author.

* * *

TROYAT, Henri 1911-2007
[A pseudonym]
(Lev Tarassoff)

OBITUARY NOTICE— See index for *CA* sketch: Born November 1, 1911, in Moscow, Russia; died March 4 (some sources say March 2), 2007, in Paris, France. Author. Troyat was an award-winning and prolific novelist who was beloved for his lengthy historical sagas. Although born in Russia, he learned to speak fluent French from his Swiss governess. When his family fled the country because of the Russian Revolution, it was thus easy for him to adapt to their new home in Paris. Here he changed his name from Lev Aslanovitch Tarassoff to Henri Troyat, attended the Lycee Pasteur, and earned a law degree. He worked for the local government prefecture in the late 1930s, while composing his early novels. His first, *Faux Jour* (1935), which was actually written while he was serving in the French military, won the Prix Populiste; his fourth novel, *L'Araigne* (1938; translated as *The Web* in 1984), earned the prestigious Prix Goncourt. Quitting his day job in 1942, Troyat devoted himself to writing and would go on to pen over one hundred novels, short-story collections, biographies, travelogues, and other works. He won the Prix Louis Barthou from the French Academy in 1938 and the Grand Prix Litteraire de Monaco in 1952 for *La neige en deuil.* Because of his clear, direct writing style, Troyat was not always a favorite of literary critics, but he was extremely popular among general readers. He loved to write multivolume sagas about families surviving difficult historical times, sometimes drawing from his own experiences in Russia and France. His lucid writing style also made his biographies popular, and he typically wrote about literary and political giants from Russian history, such as Dostoyevsky, Tolstoy, Chekov, Catherine the Great, and Ivan the Terrible; he also wrote about important French writers, including Flaubert and Balzac. A biography he wrote about Juliette Drouet, however, got him into legal trouble when in 2003 he was found guilty of plagiarism. Other than this dark chapter, Troyat enjoyed a distinguished career. He was elected to the French Academy in 1959; in addition, he was appointed Commandeur de l'Ordre National du Merité, Commandeur des Arts et des Lettres, and Grandcroix of the Legion d'Honneur. He published his autobiography, *Un si long chemin,* in 1976.

OBITUARIES AND OTHER SOURCES:

BOOKS

Troyat, Henri, *Un si long chemin,* Stock (Paris, France), 1976.

PERIODICALS

Los Angeles Times, March 7, 2007, p. B11.
New York Times, March 6, 2007, p. C13.
Times (London, England), March 6, 2007, p. 54.
Washington Post, March 6, 2007, p. B8.

U-V

UNDERHILL, Robert 1931-

PERSONAL: Born 1931.

ADDRESSES: Home—MI.

CAREER: Psychiatrist.

WRITINGS:

Strawberry Moon (mystery novel), Arbutus Press (Traverse City, MI), 2006.

SIDELIGHTS: Robert Underhill is the author of the novel *Strawberry Moon,* a mystery concerning the disappearance of Dr. Barbara Wilson. At first it is assumed that Dr. Wilson was carjacked, but later her body is discovered in the woods near her truck. She has been strangled and scalped, giving Sheriff Hoss Davis the impression that local troublemaker Harry Swifthawk might be involved. Over the course of his investigation, Davis deals with the politics of both tribal leaders and the FBI, as he attempts to narrow his list of suspects. A critic for *Hidden Staircase Mystery Books Reviews* called Underhill's effort "intricately plotted" and "all very well done up to a point," but noted that "several key plot elements remain unresolved at the end of the book." A contributor for *Heartland Reviews,* on the other hand, praised the novel for its "excellent red herrings and relationship foibles thrown in to keep the reader guessing." Jo Ann Vicarel, writing for *Library Journal,* considered the book to be "a winner, especially for readers who like tales set in rural America or having Native American elements."

BIOGRAPHICAL AND CRITICAL SOURCES:

PERIODICALS

Library Journal, April 1, 2006, Jo Ann Vicarel, "Mystery," review of *Strawberry Moon,* p. 68.

ONLINE

Heartland Reviews, http://www.heartlandreviews.com/ (May 23, 2007), review of *Strawberry Moon.*
Hidden Staircase Mystery Books Reviews, http://mysteriousreviews.hiddenstaircasemysterybooks.com/ (May 23, 2007), review of *Strawberry Moon.*

*   *   *

VAN HEEMST, David B. 1966-

PERSONAL: Born March 12, 1966, in Paterson, NJ; son of Henry Peter and Julia Margaret (a homemaker) Van Heemst; married April Michelle Cordes (a teacher), July 1, 1995; children: Maggie and Ellie (twins). *Ethnicity:* "Caucasian." *Education:* Dordt College, B.A., 1988; American University, M.A., 1990; University of Virginia, Ph.D., 1993; Olivet

Nazarene University, M.P.L., 1995, M.A., 1998. *Religion:* Christian. *Hobbies and other interests:* Long-distance running, family activities, reading.

ADDRESSES: Home—IL. *Office*—Olivet Nazarene University, 1 University Ave., Bourbonnais, IL 60914. *E-mail*—dvh@olivet.edu.

CAREER: Olivet Nazarene University, Bourbonnais, IL, professor of political science, 1993—. Also community volunteer.

MEMBER: American Political Science Association, American Counseling Association, National Political Science Honor Society, National Counseling Honor Society, Center for Public Justice.

WRITINGS:

Empowering the Poor: Why Justice Requires School Choice, Rowman & Littlefield Education (Lanham, MD), 2004.

Herman Dooyeweerd and Eric Voegelin: A Comparative Study, Edwin Mellen Press (Lewiston, NY), 2005.

(With Bob Goudzwaard and Mark Vander Vennen) *Hope in Troubled Times: A New Vision for Confronting Global Crises,* Baker Academic (Grand Rapids, MI), 2007.

SIDELIGHTS: David B. Van Heemst told *CA:* "All of my writing emerges from this single passion: a desire to seek justice for those who are suffering the most. My first book paints a vision of justice for socioeconomically disadvantaged children in the United States. My second book fleshes out a philosophical conception of justice. My third book looks at how we might begin to seek justice for the economically disadvantaged throughout the world. My hope is that my writing may advance the cause of justice for those who are presently suffering so that they might suffer no more.

"I remember one of the moments that first inspired me. I was serving as a group therapist at a school in a very poor school district, and I looked into the eyes of an eight-year-old who had the sadness in her eyes of some eighty-year-olds. I thought to myself, I've got to do something to help her. Writing became my way of helping.

"The most significant influences on my work are the philosophies of Herman Dooyeweerd and Eric Voegelin.

"I like to write when I have huge chunks of time. I like to close myself off and become engaged with the texts themselves. The most surprising thing I've learned as a writer is that it's hard work!

"It might be hard for me to pick a favorite because all [of my books] are expressions of my soul.

"My deepest hope is that my work may be one small part of seeking justice for those who today have no justice."

*　　*　　*

VARELA, Barry

PERSONAL: Married Fiona Morgan (a professional writer and reporter); children: two daughters. *Education:* Grinnell College, B.A.

ADDRESSES: Home and office—Durham, NC.

CAREER: Author and editor. Former editor for Harper & Row, Random House, and Henry Holt publishers, New York, NY; Early Intervention Training Center for Infants and Toddlers with Visual Impairments, editor; freelance writer.

WRITINGS:

Palmers Gate, Roaring Brook Press (New Milford, CT), 2006.

Gizmo, Roaring Brook Press (New Milford, CT), 2007.

Coauthor and ghost writer for books, mainly in the field of children's literature.

SIDELIGHTS: Before penning his first young-adult novel, *Palmers Gate,* Barry Varela coauthored a variety of books within the genre of children's literature, sometimes as a ghost writer. Varela's debut novel deals with the difficult issue of sexual abuse, interweaving it within the confines of a unique friendship between a young boy and his next-door neighbor. The novel's lead character is Robbie, a pretty typical ten-year-old boy who lives with his single mom. Things drastically change, however, when a new family moves next door and Robbie begins to notice strange things about his new neighbors. The boy is especially confounded by the family's daughter, Colleen, a classmate of Robbie's. In class, Colleen is unusually quiet and she wears outdated clothes, and she quickly becomes the target of classroom taunting. Knowing that Colleen has family issues, Robbie begins to feel protective of her and they soon develop a secret friendship. When rumors about Colleen's bizarre behavior begin to circulate, Robbie ultimately sacrifices his own future in order to save that of his friend.

Critics have been divided in their assessment of Varela's unique tale that insinuates the difficult issue of sexual abuse. A critic for *Kirkus Reviews* noted that while the novel's ending is abrupt, *Palmers Gate* presents "a well-constructed portrait of a confused child." A *Publishers Weekly* reviewer described the book as a "strange and moving novella," and, in addition to being "gracefully written," it "unfolds with excellent pacing."

BIOGRAPHICAL AND CRITICAL SOURCES:

PERIODICALS

Bulletin of the Center for Children's Books, July-August, 2006, Deborah Stevenson, review of *Palmers Gate,* p. 520.
Kirkus Reviews, May 1, 2006, review of *Palmers Gate,* p. 469.
Library Media Connection, November-December, 2006, Barbara J. McKee, review of *Palmers Gate,* p. 76.

Publishers Weekly, June 26, 2006, review of *Palmers Gate,* p. 52.
School Library Journal, July, 2006, Carolyn Lehman, review of *Palmers Gate,* p. 114.

ONLINE

Barry Varela Home Page, http://www.barryvarela.com (May 1, 2007)*.

*   *   *

VELDOF, Jerilyn R. 1968(?)-

PERSONAL: Born c. 1968. *Education:* Attended the School for International Training, Experiment in International Living Coastal Studies Program, Kenya, East Africa, fall, 1989; Ithaca College, B.A. (magna cum laude), 1990; State University of New York at Buffalo, M.L.S., 1994.

ADDRESSES: Office—University of Minnesota Libraries, 243 Walter Library, 117 Pleasant Ave. S.E., Minneapolis, MN 55455. *E-mail*—jveldof@umn.edu.

CAREER: University of Arizona Libraries, Tucson, assistant librarian, 1994-98; University of Minnesota Libraries, Minneapolis, assistant librarian, 1998-2002, associate librarian, 2003—.

MEMBER: American Library Association (Library and Information Technology Association division).

WRITINGS:

Creating the One-Shot Library Workshop: A Step-by-Step Guide, American Library Association (Chicago, IL), 2006.

Contributor to books, including *Information Imagineering: Meeting at the Interface,* edited by Milton T. Wolf, Pat Ensor, and Mary Augusta Thomas, American Library Association, 1998; *Integrating Information Literacy into the College Experience,* by Julia K. Nims and others, Pierian Press, 2003; and *Developing Web-based Instruction: Planning, Designing, Managing and Evaluating the Results,* edited by Elizabeth A. Dupuis, Neal-Schuman Publishers, 2003. Contributor of book reviews to *Library Journal;* contributor of scholarly articles to journals, including *Academic Exchange Quarterly, Research Strategies, Journal of Library Administration, Library and Information Science Research, Internet Reference Services Quarterly,* and *Cultural Diversity at Work.*

SIDELIGHTS: Jerilyn R. Veldof is an expert on library organization and cataloging. Her first book, *Creating the One-Shot Library Workshop: A Step-by-Step Guide,* offers readers a guide to teaching research skills during a short workshop session of approximately fifty minutes, with a focus on the skills needed by students, employees, and patrons. The book includes such helpful details as reminders, a check list, and guidelines for evaluation, and is heavily based on Veldof's own experiences as a coordinator of user education and distance learning earlier in her career at the University of Minnesota Libraries. *Library Journal* contributor Betty J. Glass called Veldof's effort "a timely, assessment-conscious, 20-step guide for a rigorous instructional design process." James Bierman noted in the *Reference & User Services Quarterly* that while the subject matter has the potential to be extremely boring, "Veldof is quick to establish an informal, friendly, even conspiratorial tone," concluding that the book is "an accessible, well-articulated work that provides an unusually thorough treatment of the instructional design process."

BIOGRAPHICAL AND CRITICAL SOURCES:

PERIODICALS

American Libraries, August 1, 2006, "Stepping up to Instruction," review of *Creating the One-Shot Library Workshop: A Step-by-Step Guide,* p. 80.
Library Journal, September 15, 2006, Betty J. Glass, "One-Shot Instruction," review of *Creating the One-Shot Library Workshop,* p. 92.
Reference & Research Book News, August 1, 2006, review of *Creating the One-Shot Library Workshop.*

Reference & User Services Quarterly, winter, 2006, James Bierman, review of *Creating the One-Shot Library Workshop.*

ONLINE

University of Minnesota Libraries Web site, http://www.lib.umn.edu/ (May 23, 2007), career information on Jerilyn R. Veldof.*

*   *   *

VENKATESH, Sudhir Alladi

PERSONAL: Education: University of California at San Diego, B.A., 1988; University of Chicago, M.A., 1992, Ph.D., 1997.

ADDRESSES: Office—Department of Sociology, Columbia University, 413 Fayerweather Hall, New York, NY 10027. *E-mail*—sv185@columbia.edu.

CAREER: Columbia University, New York, NY, assistant professor of sociology and African American studies, and director of research at Institute for Research in African-American Studies, 1999—. Codirector, Youth and Globalization Research Network, Social Science Research Council. Documentary filmmaker, including *Dislocation,* broadcast on Chicago PBS affiliate WTTW, 2005, and of film *Abhidya.*

AWARDS, HONORS: Century Scholarship, University of Chicago, 1989-90; Foreign Language and Area Studies fellowship, University of Chicago, 1990-91; Patricia Lynn Baker Prize, University of Chicago, 1993; dissertation fellowship, Chapin Hall Center at the University of Chicago, 1993-95; Dissertation Research Grant, Johann Jacobs Foundation, 1994; John D. and Catherine T. MacArthur Foundation grant, 1995; junior fellowship, Society of Fellows at Harvard University, 1997-99; Young and Mid-Career Child and Family Scholars Award, Institute of Medicine, National Academy of Sciences, 1997-98; American Bar Foundation grant, 1998-2000; Graham Foundation for Advanced Studies in the Fine Arts grant, 1999; Joint Center of Poverty Research and

Department of Health and Human Services grant, 2000; National Science Foundation CAREER Award for Young Investigators, 2000-04.

WRITINGS:

American Project: The Rise and Fall of a Modern Ghetto, Harvard University Press (Cambridge, MA), 2000.

Off the Books: The Underground Economy of the Urban Poor, Harvard University Press (Cambridge, MA), 2006.

(Editor, with Ronald Kassimir) *Youth, Globalization, and the Law,* Stanford University Press (Stanford, CA), 2007.

Contributor to books, including *Children and Their Families in Big Cities: Strategies for Service Reform,* edited by Alfred J. Kahn and Sheila B. Kamerman, Columbia University, 1996; *Sociological Studies of Children,* Volume 8, edited by David Kinney, JAI Press, 2000; and *Alternate Perspectives on Gangs and Communities,* edited by Louis Kontos, David Brotherton, and Luis Barrios, Columbia University Press. Contributor to periodicals, including *Social Science History, Theory and Society, Journal of Sociology, Journal of Community Psychology, Signs: A Journal of Women in Culture and Society, Social Services Review, American Prospect, Sociological Perspectives, Le Monde Diplomatique, Il Manifesto, Public Culture, Law and Social Inquiry, American Journal of Sociology, Contemporary Sociology,* and *Journal of Economics.*

SIDELIGHTS: Sociologist Sudhir Alladi Venkatesh is primarily interested in studying the urban living conditions of the poor. Both his *American Project: The Rise and Fall of a Modern Ghetto* and *Off the Books: The Underground Economy of the Urban Poor* aim to dispel some preconceptions and myths of life in ghettos and housing projects in his native Chicago. The former book is an examination of the Robert Taylor Homes project, which was completed in 1962 and once had 27,000 residents. In decline now, the buildings are being torn down and only a few residents remain. Primarily through interviews with current and former residents, Venkatesh tries to explain why the huge project failed. "The result is a fascinating study

of community dynamics between various groups of tenants, including leaders and members of the Black Kings gang, and how they created and lived what Venkatesh refers to as an 'ordered environment'—against incredible odds," according to Adele Oltman in a *Nation* review. Venkatesh describes the underground economy that evolved at Robert Taylor and how tenant leaders bribed police to keep authorities away while residents created under-the-table businesses such as car repair shops and salons to survive. The decline of the project occurred for several reasons, including the Chicago Housing Authority's inability to keep up with repairs, which made the buildings hazardous to live in, and because of increasingly violent drug gangs that wrested power away from tenant leaders.

Despite this dangerous turn of events, Venkatesh portrays the community as being populated with basically good people struggling against impossible circumstances. "Venkatesh is to be commended for rejecting the perception of the black ghetto as a morally deficient space," insisted Oltman, "and for letting the voices of the tenants be heard. The result is a rich account of the political lives of the leaders and some of its residents." Some critics, including Oltman, however, felt that *American Project* would have been a more valuable book had the author put his subject within a broader political and social context. "As an ethnography, *American Project* is an innovative, insightful and valuable examination of internal project politics," concluded Oltman, adding: "As a history that attempts to explain the failure of the projects, however, it is incomplete." Similarly, *Christian Century* reviewer Robert Westbrook stated: "If Venkatesh gives a full hearing to the tenants . . . his ethnography suffers from an inattentiveness to the wider context for project living." With a mixed reaction, David P. Varady wrote in the *Journal of the American Planning Association:* "While the book adds to our understanding of the strengths and weaknesses of community-based organizations in public housing, it offers few useful suggestions for America's public housing policy, and more specifically, it says almost nothing about how to improve HUD's HOPE VI program." Nevertheless, in *American Prospect,* Alexander von Hoffman concluded: "The brilliance of the author's approach is that he listens sympathetically to the people who lived and worked in this massive public housing development, yet he remains scrupulously objective."

Off the Books is a work similar in some ways to *American Project,* but this time Venkatesh examines the impoverished Marquis Park neighborhood of Chicago. The focus here is on the underground economy, and how criminals, gangs, and respectable citizens have formed a type of symbiotic relationship in order to provide each other with services that government has failed to supply. Police and politicians are often involved in the subterfuge as well, while clergy leaders take on liaison roles to keep the community together. The author again draws heavily on interviews with his subjects. "If Venkatesh's picture of the ghetto is accurate," remarked Kerry Howley in *Reason,* "the task is not to change the people within its borders, as conservatives would have it, or to ply them with subsidies, as their liberal counterparts would. Ending the isolation of Marquis Park means allowing its bustling informal economy to join the wider network of formal exchange." "Although the book's academic tenor is occasionally wearying, Venkatesh keeps his work vital and poignant," reported a *Publishers Weekly* critic, who described *Off the Books* as a "revealing study."

BIOGRAPHICAL AND CRITICAL SOURCES:

PERIODICALS

American Prospect, April 9, 2001, Alexander von Hoffman, review of *American Project: The Rise and Fall of a Modern Ghetto,* p. 40.

Christian Century, July 4, 2001, Robert Westbrook, review of *American Project,* p. 26.

Journal of Negro History, January 1, 2001, review of *American Project,* p. 65.

Journal of the American Planning Association, March 22, 2002, review of *American Project,* p. 210.

Library Journal, September 15, 2000, Paula R. Dempsey, review of *American Project,* p. 104; September 15, 2006, Ellen D. Gilbert, review of *Off the Books: The Underground Economy of the Urban Poor,* p. 78.

Nation, June 4, 2001, Adele Oltman, "Sub-Urban Planning," review of *American Project,* p. 30.

Publishers Weekly, September 4, 2006, review of *Off the Books,* p. 56.

Reason, May, 2007, Kerry Howley, "Ghetto Capitalists," review of *Off the Books.*

Social Service Review, September 1, 2001, review of *American Project,* p. 532.

ONLINE

Harvard University Press Web site, http://www.hup.harvard.edu/ (May 15, 2007), interview with Sudhir Alladi Venkatesh.

Joint Center for Poverty Research, http://www.jcpr.org/ (May 15, 2007), curriculum vitae for Sudhir Alladi Venkatesh.

Prospect Magazine Online, http://www.prospect-magazine.co.uk/ (May 15, 2007), Diane Coyle, "The South Side's Dark Side," review of *Off the Books.*

Slate, http://www.slate.com/ (December 8, 2006), Patrick Radden Keefe, "Jurisprudence: Ghetto Capitalism," review of *Off the Books.**

*   *   *

VINEN, Richard

PERSONAL: Male.

ADDRESSES: Office—Department of History, King's College, London WC2R 2LS, England. *E-mail*—richard.vinen@kcl.ac.uk.

CAREER: University of London, Queen Mary-Westfield College, London, England, former lecturer; Cambridge University, Trinity College, Cambridge, England, former fellow; University of London, King's College, London, reader in modern European history, 1991—.

WRITINGS:

The Politics of French Business: 1936-1945, Cambridge University Press (New York, NY), 1991, new edition, 2002.

Bourgeois Politics in France, 1945-1951, Cambridge University Press (New York, NY), 1995, new edition, 2002.

France, 1934-1970, St. Martin's Press (New York, NY), 1996.

A History in Fragments: Europe in the Twentieth Century, Da Capo Press (Cambridge, MA), 2001.

The Unfree French: Life under the Occupation, Yale University Press (New Haven, CT), 2006.

SIDELIGHTS: Historian Richard Vinen is best known for his studies of life in France during and immediately after World War II. His books seek to dispel what he feels are the many myths that have survived, often at the hands of other historians, about this period. In *The Politics of French Business: 1936-1945,* for example, he argues against the popular belief that big businesses in France collaborated with the puppet Vichy government, while in *The Unfree French: Life under the Occupation,* he paints an unflattering picture of French citizens who, often starving, frequently cooperated with the Germans. Vinen's revisionist histories have been praised for their research and for illuminating neglected aspects of French history. Sometimes he has shown that the past was less noble than hoped, while in other cases he has explained that criticism of the French has been misguided.

In *The Politics of French Business,* Vinen counters charges that French businesses supported the collaborationist Vichy government and the German occupiers. "Vinen has produced a well written book, useful in demolishing certain myths," concluded David Johnson in *Business History.* Naomi Hyamson added in a *History Today* article that "scholars will welcome this detailed analysis of extensive documents that have recently become available." Moving on to the period just after World War II, Vinen wrote *Bourgeois Politics in France, 1945-1951,* which "challenges the perception that [the Fourth Republic's] . . . politics was synonymous with failure," reported Samir Saul in the *Canadian Journal of History.* Vinen shows that the bourgeoisie tried to preserve economic order and the status quo, and that these attempts should not be regarded as failures to reform the economy during the late 1940s. Saul considered Vinen's effort "well researched, tightly constructed and interspersed with profound insights, [while] the general thesis is more baffling than convincing." Martin Thomas, writing in the *English Historical Review,* felt the history fails somewhat in portraying the political context of the times, but asserted that the book is "a challenging and well-crafted piece of work. Vinen's awareness of the unique nature of multi-party politics in the early years of France's Fourth Republic is nicely combined with a refreshing willingness to evaluate this period on its own terms."

Vinen sought to dispel more myths with his *The Unfree French.* Rather than portraying the supposed glories of the French Resistance, the historian reveals that most French, demoralized by their devastating defeat in 1940, were mostly preoccupied with simply trying to go about their daily lives. This was a challenge, though, because the German occupiers either consumed or shipped out most of their food and other resources. French citizens, therefore, often cooperated with the enemy in sometimes horrible ways just to get enough food to eat. Vinen discusses how, with the exception of the Jewish French, most French were relatively well treated by the Germans; he details the "often surprisingly courteous relations that the Wehrmacht had with the conquered people," remarked Simon Heffer in the *Literary Review,* describing the history as an "immaculately researched, well-written and original book." Some critics, such as *Independent* contributor Kenneth O. Morgan, felt that the one-sidedness of a history that barely mentions the Resistance poses a problem, while still adding that "as a social history of wartime, this is a valuable work. It strips away the stereotypes and lays bare the painful choices for a nation defiantly singing the Marseillaise to cover its defeat." An *Economist* critic, however, called *The Unfree French* "eminently balanced," especially on such topics as the fate of the Jews, eighty percent of whom survived the occupation and many of whom found refuge in hilltop villages that the Germans could not reach. *Atlantic Monthly* contributor Benjamin Schwartz declared it an "exceptionally well-written book [that] looks at the lives of ordinary people throughout France during that low, dishonest half decade."

BIOGRAPHICAL AND CRITICAL SOURCES:

PERIODICALS

Atlantic Monthly, October 1, 2006, Benjamin Schwarz, "Path of Least Resistance: What to Read This Month," review of *The Unfree French: Life under the Occupation,* p. 107.
Booklist, October 1, 2006, Gilbert Taylor, review of *The Unfree French,* p. 23.
Business History, October 1, 1992, David Johnson, *The Politics of French Business: 1936-1945,* p. 115.
Canadian Journal of History, August 1, 1996, Samir Saul, review of *Bourgeois Politics in France, 1945-1951,* p. 322.

Economist, April 15, 2006, "Not a Good Time to Be Hungry; France during the Second World War," review of *The Unfree French,* p. 84.

English Historical Review, November 1, 1994, Richard McAllister, review of *The Politics of French Business,* p. 1339; June 1, 1997, Martin Thomas, review of *Bourgeois Politics in France, 1945-1951,* p. 816.

History Today, December 1, 1993, Naomi Hyamson, review of *The Politics of French Business,* p. 58.

Library Journal, November 1, 2001, Robert J. Andrews, review of *A History in Fragments: Europe in the Twentieth Century,* p. 111; September 15, 2006, Marie Marmo Mullaney, review of *The Unfree French,* p. 74.

Spectator, April 29, 2006, Frederic Raphael, "Making the Best of Defeat," review of *The Unfree French.*

ONLINE

French Culture, http://www.frenchculture.org/ (May 15, 2007), review of *The Unfree French.*

Independent Online, http://enjoyment.independent.co.uk/ (June 9, 2006), Kenneth O. Morgan, "Ordeals and Deals of a Land in Chains," review of *The Unfree French.*

King's College London Web site, http://www.kcl.ac.uk/ (May 15, 2007), faculty profile of Richard Vinen.

Literary Review Online, http://www.literaryreview.co.uk/ (May 15, 2007), Simon Heffer, "Swept under the Carpet," review of *The Unfree French.*

New York Books, http://www.nybooks.com/ (May 15, 2007), Robert O. Paxton, "The Jew Hater," review of *The Unfree French.**

W

WATERS, Michael R. 1955-

PERSONAL: Born April 9, 1955, in National City, CA; married; children: one. *Ethnicity:* "White." *Education:* University of Arizona, B.S. (with honors), 1977, M.S., 1980, Ph.D., 1983.

ADDRESSES: *Office*—Department of Anthropology, Texas A&M University, Box 4352, College Station, TX 77843-4352; fax: 979-845-4070.

CAREER: Archaeological field assistant, 1971-78; archaeological consultant for projects in California and Arizona, 1978-86; Texas A&M University, College Station, assistant professor, 1986-91, associate professor, 1991-98, professor of anthropology and geography, 1998—, Fallon-Marshall Lecturer, 2005, holder of endowed chair in First American studies and executive director of North Star Archaeological Research Program, 2002—, and director of Center for the Study of the First Americans, 2005—. University of Leeds, distinguished international visiting scholar, 2000; guest lecturer at other institutions. Geoarchaeologist for field projects in the United States, Yemen, Jamaica, and Russia, 1979-96.

MEMBER: Society for American Archaeology, American Quaternary Association, Geological Society of America (fellow), Sigma Xi.

AWARDS, HONORS: Rip Rapp Archaeological Geology Award and Kirk Bryan Award, both Geological Society of America, 2004; grants from Geological Society of America, Great Basin Foundation, Wenner-Gren Foundation for Anthropological Research, Texas Historical Commission, International Research and Exchanges Board, National Geographic Society, and National Science Foundation.

WRITINGS:

Principles of Geoarchaeology: A North American Perspective, University of Arizona Press (Tucson, AZ), 1992.

Lone Star Stalag: German Prisoners of War at Camp Hearne, Texas A&M University Press (College Station, TX), 2004.

(Editor, with R. Bonnichsen, B.T. Lepper, and D, Stanford) *Paleoamerican Origins: Beyond Clovis,* Center for the Study of the First Americans, Texas A&M University (College Station, TX), 2005.

(Editor, with J.C. Ravesloot and J.A. Darling, and contributor) *Indigenous Ecologies and Sustainability: Humans and Landscape Past and Present,* University of Arizona Press (Tucson, AZ), 2006.

Also creator of several geologic maps. Contributor to books, including *Hohokam and Patayan: Prehistory of Southwestern Arizona,* edited by R.H. McGuire and M.B. Schiffer, Academic Press (New York, NY), 1982; *Environments and Extinctions: Man in Late Glacial North America,* edited by J.I. Mead and D. Meltzer, Center for the Study of Early Man, University of Maine (Orono, ME), 1985; and *Environmental Change and Human Adaptation in the Ancient American Southwest,* edited by D.E. Doyel and J.S. Dean, University of New Mexico Press (Albuquerque, NM), 2006.

Contributor of more than sixty articles and reviews to scientific journals and popular magazines, including *Nature, Journal of Field Archaeology, Geoarchaeology: An International Journal, Science, American Antiquity, Geology, Asian Perspectives, Pacific Coast Archaeological Quarterly, Plains Anthropologist,* and *American Anthropologist.*

* * *

WATZLAWICK, Paul 1921-2007

OBITUARY NOTICE— See index for *CA* sketch: Born July 25, 1921, in Villach, Austria; died of cardiac arrest, March 31, 2007, in Palo Alto, CA. Psychologist, educator, and author. Watzlawick was a pioneering family therapist who emphasized effective communications as more valuable to improved mental health than Freudian psychoanalysis. A graduate of the University of Venice, where he earned a Ph.D. in 1949, he studied psychology at the C.G. Jung Institute for Analytical Psychology in Zurich. He earned his diploma in 1954 and went into private practice. During the late-1950s, he taught at the University of El Salvador, and he was a researcher at Temple University in 1960. That year, he joined the Mental Research Institute in Palo Alto. He developed his MRI Brief Therapy approach, which emphasized communication as vital to improving mental well being. He then began teaching in 1967, when he joined the Stanford University faculty as a clinical instructor; he remained there until his retirement as clinical professor emeritus. Watzlawick was the author of over a dozen books; most are for professionals and some are in German, but he also wrote books for general readers that have a lightly humorous edge. Among these are *The Situation Is Hopeless, but Not Serious: The Pursuit of Unhappiness* (1983) and *Ultra-Solutions; or, How to Fail Most Successfully* (1988). Other works by Watzlawick include *How Real Is Real?* (1976) and *Munchhausen's Pigtail; or, Psychotherapy and "Reality": Essays and Lectures* (1990).

OBITUARIES AND OTHER SOURCES:

PERIODICALS

Los Angeles Times, April 6, 2007, p. B8.

WAUGH, Colin M. 1955-

PERSONAL: Born September 25, 1955, in Edinburgh, Scotland. *Education:* University of Aberdeen, M.A.; additional graduate study at London School of Economics and Political Science, London. *Politics:* Liberal Democrat (British party).

ADDRESSES: Office—303 Park Ave. S., Ste. 1164, New York, NY 10010. *E-mail*—colinwaugh@btinternet.com.

CAREER: Writer.

WRITINGS:

Paul Kagame and Rwanda, McFarland (Jefferson, NC), 2004.

Contributor to the book *Intelligent Commodity Investing,* Risk Books (London, England), 2007.

SIDELIGHTS: Colin M. Waugh told *CA:* "In setting out to write an African political narrative, I had to choose which of the countries I had come to know was the one with the most worthwhile story to tell and the most potent message to deliver. The experience of the genocide makes Rwanda unique, at least in terms of modern history. Genocide is a particularly atrocious form of violence, a repugnant crime, an extreme form of persecution, and an act of mass murder all rolled into one horror story to whet the appetites of the most compulsive of audiences. Yet, while the European wars, the Nazi genocide against the Jews, or more recently the struggle for power in Vietnam have absorbed those with a fascination for humanity's darker side, somehow when it comes to Africa, everyone turns the other way.

"My book, however, is not principally about the genocide, although the events surrounding the tragic months of 1994 in Rwanda inevitably occupy a prominent place in any account of the country's modern political era. It is also about the alteration of Rwandan politics from the accepted norm of post-conflict recovery and development in Africa that this unusual country represents. Rwanda is run according to a formula that doesn't quite fit the usual mold for the western reader with a passing interest in sub-Saharan Africa. In addition to civil war, poverty, and disease, the next thing that novice western readers associate with African societies is corruption. In this respect, Rwanda begins to break away from the conventional model. Corruption is not endemic in Rwanda in the way that it is in much of the rest of the world.

"I recall an incident in 1995 when, driving northward from Kigali on a Sunday afternoon with a colleague, and having just completed an illegal shortcut, I was stopped by a Rwandan officer who had observed the maneuver. After checking my license he informed me that I would have to come back to the police station the following day to retrieve my documents, quite an inconvenience as I had by now driven far from my base. I told him that I could not agree to this demand and a standoff then ensued. Remaining patiently seated in the car, I talked to the soldier about our respective home towns, sports, languages, and the like, while he held on to my license and I declined to agree to returning later to retrieve it. My colleague suggested a small bribe to break the impasse, which I at first resisted, then later agreed to, offering perhaps a day's pay to the young serviceman. As I anticipated, he rejected the offer and proceeded to carry on the conservation for another fifteen minutes. The light was fading and our urge to capitulate mounted by the minute. Suddenly when it seemed that only our surrender could break the deadlock, the officer leaned closer toward the car and looked straight at me, saying: 'You know, you are very disciplined,' and handed me back my license without emotion. I later learned that this was a fair compliment from a young member of Rwanda's armed forces who had just refused to be bought. The intrinsically ordered nature of Rwandan society stems in part from the tradition and history of its people, but also in recent times it is in good measure due to a leadership that has reinforced a natural tendency through authority as well as example.

"The story of Paul Kagame's ascent from junior officer in a foreign guerrilla army to the presidency of Rwanda is the story of how this leadership, this authority, and this reassertion of tradition came about in a country that had known only fear, division, and clan-based nepotism for many years. The personality of Paul Kagame and his centrality to the evolution of a different type of modern African state is another reason for my choice of modern Rwanda as the subject of my book.

"Kagame's story is also that of a battlefield general and latterly a politician who was often described in the past as secretive or mysterious, and who was given to neither public displays of emotion nor unnecessary discussions with members of the foreign media. I wanted to ensure that Kagame's views, often contested, were as much part of this record as the descriptions and conclusions that I came to through my own reading, research, or listening to the opinions of others. Being neither an accredited journalist from a major news organization nor an insider with Rwandan connections, for me the process of arranging interviews with President Kagame was a lengthy and frustrating one. Nevertheless, with a measure of persistence some helping hands were finally extended, and soon the formalities toward arranging my presidential encounter were underway.

"Once focused on the idea of my project, the president participated in the interview process with remarkable relish, particularly when the opportunity arose to recount experiences from the early days of his career. Advisors who were present at the sessions commented afterward that they too had been made aware of new details from their chief executive's early life that came as revelations about the person to whose service they consecrated most of their daylight hours.

"While much of the early work for this book was carried out in libraries, through consulting Internet archives, and talking to people living outside Rwanda, the journals kept from my visits during the 1990s are the source of much of the anecdotal material that is included. While avoiding personal references in the text itself, I nevertheless tried to open up a number of topics with relevance beyond the Rwandan experience for the reader's reflection."

*   *   *

WEINSTEIN, David M. 1967-

PERSONAL: Born January 10, 1967, in Long Island, NY; married July 1, 2001; wife's name Rachel; children: Sara, Ellie. *Ethnicity:* "White." *Education:* Brandeis University, B.A., 1989; University of Maryland, Ph.D., 1997.

ADDRESSES: Office—National Endowment for the Humanities, 1100 Pennsylvania Ave. N.W., Washington, DC 20506. *E-mail*—davidrachel2001@ hotmail.com.

CAREER: George Mason University, Fairfax, VA, visiting assistant professor, 1998-2000; National Endowment for the Humanities, Washington, DC, senior program officer, 2000—.

WRITINGS:

The Forgotten Network: DuMont and the Birth of American Television, Temple University Press (Philadelphia, PA), 2004.

* * *

WEISSBERGER, Barbara F. 1946-

PERSONAL: Born May 31, 1946, in Waltham, MA; children: David, Michael. *Education:* Indiana University, B.A., 1966; New York University, M.A., 1967; Harvard University, Ph.D., 1976.

ADDRESSES: Office—Department of Spanish and Portuguese Studies, University of Minnesota—Twin Cities, 51 Folwell Hall, 9 Pleasant St. S.E., Minneapolis, MN 55455. *E-mail*—weiss046@umn.edu.

CAREER: Brown University, Providence, RI, assistant professor of Spanish, 1979-83; Randolph-Macon College, Ashland, VA, assistant professor of Spanish, 1983-85; Old Dominion University, Norfolk, VA, associate professor of Spanish, 1985-2001; University of Minnesota—Twin Cities, Minneapolis, associate professor of Spanish, 2001—.

WRITINGS:

Isabel Rules: Constructing Queenship, Wielding Power, University of Minnesota Press (Minneapolis, MN), 2004.

* * *

WHITE, Mel 1940-

PERSONAL: Born 1940; married; wife's name Lyla (divorced); partner of Gary Nixon. *Education:* Warner Pacific College, B.A., 1962; University of Portland, M.A., 1963; Fuller Theological Seminary, Ph.D.; attended University of Southern California, University of California at Los Angeles, and Harvard University.

ADDRESSES: Home—Lynchburg, VA.

CAREER: Mel White Productions, Los Angeles, CA, founder, beginning 1965; First Covenant Church, Pasadena, CA, senior pastor, beginning 1973; Cathedral of Hope Metropolitan Community Church, Dallas, TX, dean, beginning 1993; Universal Fellowship of Metropolitan Community Churches, national minister of justice, beginning 1995.

MEMBER: Soulforce (founder), 1998.

AWARDS, HONORS: Rockefeller grant, for religious studies.

WRITINGS:

(With Howard Rutledge, Phyllis Rutledge, and Lyla White) *In the Presence of Mine Enemies, 1965-1973: A Prisoner of War,* illustrated by Gerald Coffee, Revell (Old Tappan, NJ), 1973.

(With Merrill Womach, Virginia Womach, and Lyla White) *Tested by Fire,* Revell (Old Tappan, NJ), 1976.

Lust: The Other Side of Love, Revell (Old Tappan, NJ), 1978.

(With Paul Scotchmer and Marguerite Shuster) *Deceived,* Spire Books (Old Tappan, NJ), 1979.

Margaret of Molokai, Word Books (Waco, TX), 1981.

Mike Douglas—When the Going Gets Tough (biography), Word Books (Waco, TX), 1982.

(With Marie Rothenberg) *David,* Revell (Old Tappan, NJ), 1985.

(With Tony Melendez) *A Gift of Hope: The Tony Melendez Story,* Harper & Row (San Francisco, CA), 1989.

Aquino (biography), Word (Dallas, TX), 1989.

Stranger at the Gate: To Be Gay and Christian in America, Simon & Schuster (New York, NY), 1994.

"Pat Robertson—Preaching Politics," *Biography,* (teleplay), A&E Television Network, 1996.

Religion Gone Bad: The Hidden Dangers of the Christian Right, J.P. Tarcher/Penguin (New York, NY), 2006.

Has ghostwritten works for Billy Graham, Oliver North, D. James Kennedy, Jerry Falwell, and Pat Robertson.

ADAPTATIONS: David was adapted as a television movie, National Broadcasting Company, 1988; *Stranger at the Gate* was adapted as a sound recording, Simon & Schuster, 1994.

SIDELIGHTS: Mel White has had an eclectic career, starting with decades in Hollywood as a television and film producer under the blanket of Mel White Productions, which he founded in 1965. He is the author of numerous books on a number of subjects, including the best seller *David,* which recounts the true story of David Rothenberg, the boy who was burned by his father; a biography of talk-show host Mike Douglas, *Mike Douglas—When the Going Gets Tough;* and *Aquino,* a biography of the president of the Philippines. He also became an ordained minister and was an important leader in the rise of evangelical Christianity from the 1960s into the early 1990s, serving as a pastor for several California churches. Despite a long-term marriage and his involvement in the church, White was struggling with his homosexuality, and eventually, after years of torment, determined it was time to come out of the closet. He divorced and moved in with his partner, Gary Nixon. He went on to become a vocal advocate for acceptance of gay and lesbian lifestyles within the folds of Christianity. As part of his stance, White founded Soulforce, an organization based on the tenets of civil disobedience and inspired by the teachings of Mahatma Gandhi and Martin Luther King, Jr. White has taken on the Christian right, standing up to such leaders as Pat Robertson and demanding tolerance and acceptance and an end to violence and prejudicial behavior against homosexuals. White has spent time in jail due to his beliefs and has written several books that preach tolerance and address what he feels is part of the true nature of Christianity—acceptance despite sexual orientation.

In *Stranger at the Gate: To Be Gay and Christian in America,* White offers readers the story of his early adult life as a closeted gay man, his struggles during the course of his career in Hollywood, his marriage to his former wife, Lyla White, his thoughts of suicide, and the extreme measures he took in an attempt to end his supposedly unnatural attraction to other men. The book includes his coming out and the way he has begun to look at Christianity and the structure of the church's teachings in relation to his own lifestyle. Bob Davies, in a review for *Christianity Today,* sympathized with White's difficulties, even if he did not condone

his more extreme methods of protest. The critic remarked that the book "reveals the personal agony that can result from unloving attitudes—still all-too-common in some Christian circles—toward those who battle homosexual desires," concluding that "the church can do a much better job dealing with the issue of homosexuality without going down the path Mel White encourages us to take."

Religion Gone Bad: The Hidden Dangers of the Christian Right offers an insider's view of Christian fundamentalist ideas. White uses his decades of church participation to illustrate just how negative and intolerant the beliefs are with regard to homosexuality and the gay and lesbian community. A contributor to *Kirkus Reviews* considered the book to be an "effective mobilization tool for those who share the author's mindset, but too narrow in its focus to garner much appeal to readers of other persuasions."

BIOGRAPHICAL AND CRITICAL SOURCES:

BOOKS

White, Mel, *Stranger at the Gate: To Be Gay and Christian in America,* Simon & Schuster (New York, NY), 1994.

PERIODICALS

Christian Century, January 18, 1995, Sally B. Geis, "A Place at the Table: The Gay Individual in American Society," review of *Stranger at the Gate,* p. 55.
Christianity Today, June 20, 1994, Bob Davies, review of *Stranger at the Gate,* p. 35.
Kirkus Reviews, August 1, 2006, review of *Religion Gone Bad: The Hidden Dangers of the Christian Right,* p. 777.
Library Journal, October 1, 2006, James A. Overbeck, review of *Religion Gone Bad,* p. 82.
National Review, June 27, 1994, William Murchison, review of *Stranger at the Gate,* p. 65.
Publishers Weekly, March 28, 1994, review of *Stranger at the Gate,* p. 78.

ONLINE

Harvard University Office of News and Public Affairs, http://www.hno.harvard.edu/ (May 23, 2007), Wendy McDowell, "White Makes Case for Gay Marriage."

Mel White Home Page, http://www.melwhite.org (May 23, 2007).

Oasis, http://www.oasismag.com/ (May 23, 2007), Jeff Walsh, "One Gay Man's Journey to Find God, and Himself."

Southern Poverty Law Center, http://www.splcenter. org/ (May 23, 2007), "A Thorn in Their Side."*

*   *   *

WILDE, Lori 1968-
(Laura Anthony)

PERSONAL: Born 1968. *Education:* Received degree in nursing.

ADDRESSES: E-mail—lori@loriwilde.com.

CAREER: Author and registered nurse.

WRITINGS:

ROMANCE NOVELS

License to Thrill, Warner Books (New York, NY), 2003.

Packed with Pleasure, Harlequin (New York, NY), 2003.

As You Like It, Harlequin (New York, NY), 2004.

Charmed and Dangerous, Warner Books (New York, NY), 2004.

Gotta Have It, Harlequin (New York, NY), 2004.

Racing against the Clock, Silhouette Books (New York, NY), 2004.

Mission: Irresistible, Warner Books (New York, NY), 2005.

Saving Allegheny Green, Harlequin (New York, NY), 2005.

Shockingly Sensual, Harlequin (New York, NY), 2005.

Destiny's Hand, Harlequin (New York, NY), 2006.

Angels and Outlaws, Harlequin (New York, NY), 2006.

You Only Love Twice, Warner Books (New York, NY), 2006.

There Goes the Bride, Warner Books (New York, NY), 2007.

Has also written six books for Harlequin Duets under the pseudonym Laura Anthony.

SIDELIGHTS: Lori Wilde is known for writing fast-paced thriller romances with a generous dash of humor. Her heroines often prove themselves smart and funny even as they get themselves in outrageous situations. Wilde's debut novel, *License to Thrill,* is "equal parts silliness and innovation," according to Wendy Crutcher in the *Romance Review.* The story features a Las Vegas private investigator named Charlee Champagne, who gets involved with banker Mason Gentry. It seems that Mason's grandfather might be in cahoots with Charlee's grandmother in the theft of half a million dollars. The two set out to find the truth, with much of the humor coming from the contrast between the staid Mason and the wilder Charlee. *Booklist* contributor Shelley Mosley called it a "sassy, in-your-face style, reminiscent of Janet Evanovich, Wilde has created an unforgettable heroine." Crutcher appreciated the well-rounded characters and fun heroine, and although the reviewer noted "some wackiness toward the end of the book" that made it difficult to suspend disbelief, the critic praised Wilde for giving "the reader something different."

Charmed and Dangerous features a former Olympic athlete named Maddie Cooper, whose twin, Cassie, supposedly is involved in an art theft being investigated by FBI agent David Marshall. Maddie seeks to clear her sister's name. "There's nothing subtle or surprising about Wilde's plot and characterizations," reported a *Publishers Weekly* critic, who nevertheless admitted the story has "its witty moments." On the other hand, Rashmi Srinivas asserted in a *BookLoons* review that "Lori Wilde once again delights her growing fan base with an emotional roller-coaster of an adventure that's as hot as it is romantic!" *Mission: Irresistible* has Cassie as the heroine this time. Cassie is a public relations specialist for a museum when a valuable Egyptian amulet goes missing. *Novel Talk* writer Lucele Coutts asserted that with this novel, "Lori Wilde cleverly fits the pieces of this puzzle together with humor, charm, and tension, including lots of surprises."

More recent offerings by Wilde include such novels as *Saving Allegheny Green* and *Shockingly Sensual.* The protagonist of the former story is a nurse who supports her mother, aunt, and troubled sister. Trouble ensues after Allegheny's sister shoots her no-good, drug-addicted husband in the foot. The book is full of quirky characters, including an evangelist neighbor and a suspicious deputy sheriff. While enjoying the "quirky and offbeat backdrop" of the story, a *Paperback Reader* contributor felt that the heroine's "perpetual state of sacrifice grows monotonous and her viewpoint falters from a lack of depth." With *Shockingly Sensual,* Wilde returned to her more typically humorous romantic adventures. A shock jock named Callie Ryder has received threats after writing a titillating book and Luke Cardasian is hired by Callie's agent to protect her. What results is a predictable conflict of personalities in what an *MBR Bookwatch* writer described as an "amusing contemporary romance."

Wilde's 2006 tale *You Only Love Twice* is a quirky adventure about comic-book writer Marlie Montague. Marlie is the author of the "Angelina Adventure" series about a heroine who fights against government conspiracies. When one of Marlie's plots too closely resembles reality, however, she becomes a target of secretive forces and must hire a bodyguard to protect her. Although a *Publishers Weekly* critic noted the lack of emotional depth to the story, the reviewer predicted that "readers will be too busy laughing at the shenanigans to mind." Martina Bexte, writing on *BookLoons,* admitted the plot of the novel is too bizarre to be believed, but added: "I had so much fun reading this story, I didn't care how out there the plot was."

BIOGRAPHICAL AND CRITICAL SOURCES:

PERIODICALS

Booklist, January 1, 2004, Shelley Mosley, review of *License to Thrill,* p. 835; May 15, 2005, Shelley Mosley, review of *Mission: Irresistible,* p. 1642; February 15, 2006, Shelley Mosley, review of *You Only Love Twice,* p. 54; March 15, 2007, "There Goes the Bride," p. 32.
Cosmopolitan, January 1, 2004, "A Night of Five-Star Sex: From the Steamy New Novel *License to Thrill,* by Lori Wilde," excerpt from the novel, p. 180.
MBR Bookwatch, April 1, 2005, review of *Shockingly Sensual.*
Publishers Weekly, June 14, 2004, review of *Charmed and Dangerous,* p. 50; April 18, 2005, review of *Mission: Irresistible,* p. 49; January 23, 2006, review of *You Only Love Twice,* p. 192.

ONLINE

All Readers, http://www.allreaders.com/ (May 15, 2007), Harriet Klausner, review of *Charmed and Dangerous.*
Armchair Interviews, http://www.armchairinterviews. com/ (May 15, 2007), Yuka Mizushima, review of *There Goes the Bride.*
Best Reviews, http://thebestreviews.com/ (April 22, 2003), Beatrice Sigman, "Double the Trouble with These Hot Alaskan Men"; (January 15, 2006), Harriet Klausner, "Interesting Police Procedural Romance," review of *Angels and Outlaws.*
BookLoons, http://www.bookloons.com/ (May 15, 2007), Martina Bexte, review of *You Only Love Twice,* Marie Hashima Lofton, review of *Mission: Irresistible,* and Rashmi Srinivas, review of *Charmed and Dangerous.*
Contemporary Romance Writers, http://www. contemporaryromancewriters.com/ (May 15, 2007), review of *There Goes the Bride.*
Lori Wilde Home Page, http://www.loriwilde.com (May 15, 2007).
My Shelf, http://www.myshelf.com/ (May 15, 2007), review of *License to Thrill.*
Novel Talk, http://www.noveltalk.com/ (March 29, 2005), Lucele Coutts, review of *Mission: Irresistible.*
Paperback Reader, http://www.paperbackreader.net/ (October 1, 2005), review of *Saving Allegheny Green.*
Romance Reader, http://www.theromancereader.com/ (May 15, 2007), Wendy Crutcher, review of *License to Thrill.**

                            *   *   *

WILKINS, Rose

PERSONAL: Daughter of an artist. *Education:* Graduate of Bristol University; Oxford University, M.A.

ADDRESSES: Home and office—London, England.

CAREER: Author and editor, working in London, England.

WRITINGS:

So Super Starry, Dial Books (New York, NY), 2004.

So Super Stylish, Macmillan Children's Books (London, England), 2005, Dial Books (New York, NY), 2006.

I Love Genie . . . Wishful Thinking, Macmillan Children's Books (London, England), 2007.

SIDELIGHTS: Since she is the great-great niece of British author Charles Kingsley, it was only natural for Rose Wilkins to enter a literary profession. Wilkins did not originally intend to pursue a novel-writing career, however; in fact, she wrote the initial draft of her first novel on a dare. As she explained in an online interview with *Word Mavericks:* "One night I was joking to my friends that I should start a romance novel. . . . I made a bet to write the opening chapter of a 'snogbuster' for teens within a week, but I found I was enjoying myself so much I didn't stop there." A publishing house eventually bought the rights to Wilkins's draft and in 2004 *So Super Starry* was published.

So Super Starry centers on Octavia, the daughter of a film producer and actress. Tired of being in the spotlight that shines on her parents, she prefers to remain low key and avoids the other celebrity offspring attending her elite private school. Citing Wilkins's humorous tone, a *Publishers Weekly* writer deemed *So Super Starry* an "entertaining debut." A sequel, *So Super Stylish,* continues to follow the trials and tribulations of Octavia. In an attempt to live a more normal life, the teen transfers from her private school to a public school, hoping to fit in. Unfortunately, she soon finds herself in a predicament as a result of the media blitz that erupts when her actress mom is accused of having an affair with a well-known television executive. *Kliatt* reviewer Claire Rosser noted that Wilkins controls her sequel's eventful plotline "with finesse."

In her *Word Mavericks* interview, Wilkins advised aspiring writers to "read masses of everything." "Also," she suggested "keeping the diary—it will get you into the habit of writing in a disciplined manner and putting thoughts into words."

BIOGRAPHICAL AND CRITICAL SOURCES:

PERIODICALS

Booklist, October 15, 2004, Cindy Welch, review of *So Super Starry,* p. 399; February 15, 2006, Debbie Carton, review of *So Super Stylish,* p. 92.

Bulletin of the Center for Children's Books, November, 2004, Deborah Stevenson, review of *So Super Starry,* p. 151.

Kliatt, March, 2006, Claire Rosser, review of *So Super Starry,* p. 18.

Publishers Weekly, November 22, 2004, review of *So Super Starry,* p. 61.

School Library Journal, December, 2004, Tina Zuback, review of *So Super Starry,* p. 154; March, 2006, Heather E. Miller, review of *So Super Stylish,* p. 233.

Times Educational Supplement, May 21, 2004, Adèle Geras, "Pretty in Pink," p. C19; May 13, 2005, Adèle Geras, review of *So Super Stylish,* p. 25.

Voice of Youth Advocates, December, 2004, review of *So Super Starry,* p. 397; April, 2006, Angelica Delgado, review of *So Super Stylish,* p. 55.

ONLINE

Pan MacMillan Web site, http://www.panmacmillan. com/ (May 1, 2007), "Rose Wilkins."

Word Mavericks Web site, http://www.wordmavericks. com/ (May 1, 2007), interview with Wilkins.*

*   *   *

WILLIAMS, Laura E.

(L.E. Williams, Laura Ellen Williams)

PERSONAL: Born in Korea. *Education:* Earned college degree.

ADDRESSES: *Home*—Hartford, CT.

CAREER: Children's book writer. Manchester High School, Manchester, CT, English teacher.

WRITINGS:

FOR CHILDREN

The Long Silk Strand: A Grandmother's Legacy to Her Granddaughter, illustrated by Grayce Bochak, Boyds Mills Press (Honesdale, PA), 1995.

Behind the Bedroom Wall, illustrated by A. Nancy Goldstein, Milkweed Editions (Minneapolis, MN), 1996.

Torch Fishing with the Sun, illustrated by Fabricio Vanden Broeck, Boyds Mills Press (Honesdale, PA), 1999.

The Spider's Web, illustrated by Erica Magnus, Milkweed Editions (Minneapolis, MN), 1999.

The Ghost Stallion, Holt (New York, NY), 1999.

Up a Creek, Holt (New York, NY), 2000.

The Executioner's Daughter, Holt (New York, NY), 2000.

(And photographer) *ABC Kids,* Philomel (New York, NY), 2000.

(Editor) *Unexpected: Eleven Mysterious Stories,* Scholastic (New York, NY), 2005.

The Best Winds, illustrated by Eujin Kim Neiland, Boyds Mills Press (Honesdale, PA), 2006.

"MAGIC ATTIC CLUB" SERIES; UNDER NAME L.E. WILLIAMS

Rose Faces the Music, illustrated by Bill Dodge, Magic Attic Press (Portland, ME), 1997.

Cheyenne Rose, illustrated by Dan Burr, Magic Attic Press (Portland, ME), 1997.

Island Rose, illustrated by Tony Meers, Magic Attic Press (Portland, ME), 1998.

Champion Rose, illustrated by Bill Dodge, Magic Attic Press (Portland, ME), 1999.

"MYSTIC LIGHTHOUSE" MYSTERY SERIES

The Mystery of the Dark Lighthouse, Scholastic (New York, NY), 2000.

The Mystery of Dead Man's Curve, Scholastic (New York, NY), 2000.

The Mystery of the Bad Luck Curse, Scholastic (New York, NY), 2001.

The Mystery of the Haunted Playhouse, Scholastic (New York, NY), 2001.

The Mystery of the Phantom Ship, Scholastic (New York, NY), 2001.

The Mystery of the Missing Tiger, Scholastic (New York, NY), 2002.

Also author of books in "Let's Have a Party" series.

SIDELIGHTS: Multicultural and multigenerational stories as well as mysteries and young-adult novels are among the books written by Laura E. Williams.

Inspired by her own travels—born in Korea, she has also lived in Belgium and on the island of Hawaii—Williams began her writing career crafting original folk tales, as in her debut, *The Long Silk Thread: A Grandmother's Legacy to Her Granddaughter,* as well as *The Best Winds* and *Torch Fishing with the Sun.* Another picture book, *ABC Kids,* is self-illustrated and features what *School Library Journal* contributor Linda Ludke described as "stunning close-up photography" of young children at play. Williams's middle-grade novels *Behind the Wall* and *The Spider's Web* deal with the power of prejudice, both in World War II Germany and among modern neo-Nazis, while the quandary of a modern teen and an environmentalist parent are the focus of *Up the Creek.*

A "graceful story" in the opinion of a *Publishers Weekly* contributor, *The Long Silk Thread* draws young readers back to ancient Japan and into a family tradition. As young Yasuyo listens, her beloved grandmother tells the stories of her long life while winding a ball from tied-together strands of silk. When the elderly woman dies, Yasuyo climbs the silk up to heaven, but learns that her true place is on earth with those who love her. In *Torch Fishing with the Sun,* Williams crafts what a *Publishers Weekly* contributor described as "an affectionate original folktale" about a Hawaiian boy named Makoa who looks forward to being entrusted with an important task: like his grandfather, he will learn to capture the sun so that, unlike the other men of his village, he can fish without torchlight during the dark of night. In *Booklist,* Lauren Peterson praised *Torch Fishing with the Sun* as "both appealing and timeless," while in *Booklist,* Ilene Cooper noted of *The Long Silk Thread* that Williams's "telling is stately but is also full of warmth."

Another multigenerational picture book, *The Best Winds* focuses on Jinho, a boy who is frustrated by his immigrant grandfather's determination to retain his Korean ways. Ignoring the advice the man shares while the two are constructing a kite together, the boy decides to fly the kite on his own, before the weather is appropriate. When it is damaged due to his inability to direct it, Jinho realizes that there is much he can learn from the elderly man; making a new kite, the two work together to make it take flight. In *School Library Journal,* Amanda Conover Le praised *The Best Winds* as "a heartwarming tale," and *Booklist* contributor Kay Weisman deemed it a "great choice for spring story hours."

Moving to an older audience, Williams focuses on life in the Middle Ages in *The Executioner's Daughter*. Here readers meet Lily, a shy girl whose father is the village executioner. When other children shun her, Lily turns to the forest animals, and begins to care for those that are injured. After his wife dies, Lily's father asks that she take her mother's place as his assistant, which forces the girl to face the horrors of her father's job and the ironies of her age. Reviewing *The Executioner's Daughter* for *School Library Journal*, Bruce Ann Shook praised the story's "strong, insightful" heroine and called Williams's novel a "well-written story" that serves as "an excellent vehicle for demonstrating the harsh realities of life" in mid-fifteenth-century England.

In the middle-grade novel *Up a Creek*, Williams introduces thirteen-year-old Starshine Bott and her single mother, Miracle. Involved in activist causes, mother and daughter live in a small Louisiana town with Starshine's grandmother. When Miracle's involvement in saving a stand of old oak trees from destruction prevents her from caring for her hospitalized mother, Starshine must reexamine the values and choices she had formerly accepted without question. Praised by *School Library Journal* contributor Shawn Brommer as "a celebration of family and feminine strength," *Up a Creek* features "characters [that] are well realized and multidimensional." While noting that Williams "takes on momentous issues with mixed results," a *Publishers Weekly* contributor predicted that *Up a Creek* will inspire "budding environmentalists." In the view of *Booklist* critic Karen Hutt, the novel will "appeal to girls struggling to define themselves and their relationships with their mothers.

In addition to standalone novels, Williams has also contributed to several novel series. In her "Mystic Lighthouse" mysteries, which includes *The Mystery of Dead Man's Curve, The Mystery of the Bad Luck Curse,* and *The Mystery of the Haunted Playhouse,* Zeke and Jen are living with their Aunt Bee in Maine, and their home is an old lighthouse. During the series, the siblings encounter ghostly visits, strange curses, phantom ships, and suspicious accidents, and ferret out each mystery with Aunt Bee's help. The "Mystic Lighthouse" books include a removable fill-in-the-blank page on which junior sleuths can record notes as each story unfolds.

BIOGRAPHICAL AND CRITICAL SOURCES:

PERIODICALS

Booklist, February 1, 1996, Ilene Cooper, review of *The Long Silk Thread: A Grandmother's Legacy to Her Granddaughter,* p. 940; August, 1996, Hazel Rochman, review of *Behind the Bedroom Wall,* p. 1900; March 15, 1999, Lauren Peterson, review of *Torch Fishing with the Sun,* p. 1336; June 1, 1999, Hazel Rochman, review of *The Spider's Web,* p. 1832; July, 2000, review of *ABC Kids,* p. 2044; January 1, 2001, Karen Hutt, review of *Up a Creek,* p. 941; April 1, 2006, Kay Weisman, review of *The Best Winds,* p. 49.

Bulletin of the Center for Children's Books, May, 2000, review of *The Executioner's Daughter,* p. 340; October, 2000, review of *ABC Kids,* p. 87; February, 2001, review of *Up a Creek,* p. 240.

Five Owls (annual), 2003, review of *The Executioner's Daughter,* p. 30.

Horn Book, January-February, 1997, Hannah B. Zeiger, review of *Behind the Bedroom Wall,* p. 69.

Kirkus Reviews, January 1, 2006, review of *The Best Winds,* p. 47.

New York Times Book Review, June 18, 2000, review of *The Executioner's Daughter,* p. 25.

Publishers Weekly, July 10, 1995, review of *The Long Silk Thread,* p. 57; June 17, 1996, review of *Behind the Bedroom Wall,* p. 66; February 15, 1999, review of *Torch Fishing with the Sun,* p. 107; December 11, 2000, review of *Up a Creek,* p. 85.

School Library Journal, September, 1996, Amy Kellman, review of *Behind the Bedroom Wall,* p. 208; June, 1999, Steven Englefried, review of *Torch Fishing with the Sun,* p. 108; November, 1999, review of *The Ghost Stallion,* p. 166; December, 1999, review of *The Spider's Web,* p. 144; June, 2000, Linda Ludke, review of *ABC Kids,* p. 137, and Bruce Anne Shook, review of *The Executioner's Daughter,* p. 156; January, 2001, Shawn Brommer, review of *Up a Creek,* p. 135; January, 2006, Adrienne Furness, review of *Unexpected: Eleven Mysterious Stories,* p. 145; March, 2006, Amanda Conover Le, review of *The Best Winds,* p. 204.

Voice of Youth Advocates, February, 2000, review of *The Ghost Stallion,* p. 412; October, 2000, review of *The Executioner's Daughter,* p. 272; April, 2001, review of *Up a Creek,* p. 47.

WILLIAMS, Laura Ellen
     See WILLIAMS, Laura E.

*   *   *

WILLIAMS, L.E.
     See WILLIAMS, Laura E.

*   *   *

WILSON, Howard

PERSONAL: Married; children: two sons. *Education:* Northwestern University, graduated.

ADDRESSES: Home—Kyoto, Japan. *E-mail*—manyoan@kyoto.email.ne.jp.

CAREER: Writer. Worked as speechwriter, copywriter, advertising writer, and lecturer on comparative religions.

WRITINGS:

Take the Cash and Run (novel), Trafford Publishing (Victoria, British Columbia, Canada), 2006.

Author of several other books.

*   *   *

WINSON, Anthony 1952-

PERSONAL: Born October 15, 1952, in Quebec, Canada; son of Robert William and Dorothy Eileen Winson; children: Devin William. *Ethnicity:* "Anglo." *Education:* University of Western Ontario, B.A. (hons.), 1975; University of Toronto, M.A., 1976, Ph.D., 1982.

ADDRESSES: Home—Guelph, Ontario, Canada. *Office*—Department of Sociology and Anthropology, University of Guelph, Guelph, Ontario N1G 2W1, Canada.

CAREER: Saint Mary's University, Halifax, Nova Scotia, Canada, research director for Gorsebrook Research Institute, 1982-85; University of Western Ontario, London, Ontario, Canada, assistant professor, 1985-86; University of Guelph, Guelph, Ontario, professor of sociology, 1986—.

MEMBER: Canadian Sociology and Anthropology Association, Canadian Association of Food Studies, Rural Sociological Association (United States).

AWARDS, HONORS: John Porter Book Prize, Canadian Sociology and Anthropology Association, 2003, for *Contingent Work, Disrupted Lives.*

WRITINGS:

Coffee and Democracy in Modern Costa Rica, Macmillan (New York, NY), 1989.
The Intimate Commodity, Greenwood Press (Westport, CT), 1993.
Contingent Work, Disrupted Lives, University of Toronto Press (Toronto, Ontario, Canada), 2002.

SIDELIGHTS: Anthony Winson told *CA:* "I am primarily motivated to write by a desire to put what creative energies I have to some positive purpose in changing this world for the better. As it turns out I have found that writing is the way I can most effectively express my creativity. My work has been influenced by an upbringing in remote rural communities and environments, both in Canada and southern Africa, and by experience as an adult living, working, and traveling in Latin America. This experience has motivated me to write on themes related to rural peoples, environments, agrarian social structures, and the process of social change in the countryside in both Latin America and Canada."

*   *   *

WORTHEN, Dennis B. 1945-
     (Dennis Brent Worthen)

PERSONAL: Born June 3, 1945, in Wilmington, DE; son of Charles S. and Mary Katherine Worthen; married Patricia L. Urban (an accountant), May 1, 1965; children: David B., Daniel B. *Education:* North

Central Michigan College, A.B.A., 1963; University of Michigan, B.A., 1964; Case Western Reserve University, M.S. in L.S., 1973, M.S., 1974, Ph.D., 1976.

ADDRESSES: Home—Loveland, OH. Office—Lloyd Library and Museum, 917 Plum St., Cincinnati, OH 45202. E-mail—dbworthen@lloydlibrary.org.

CAREER: Kroger Co., Livonia, MI, manager, 1965-66; E.R. Squibb and Sons, Inc., Rolling Meadows, IL, medical sales representative, 1966-72; Case Western Reserve University, Cleveland, OH, instructor in library science and coordinator of Clinical Drug Information Program, 1974-76; Norwich Eaton Pharmaceuticals, Inc., Norwich, NY, chief of information services section, 1976-85, manager of formularies and reimbursement, 1986-88, director of pharmacy and government relations, 1988-92; Procter & Gamble Pharmaceuticals, Norwich, director of pharmacy affairs, 1992-94; Procter & Gamble Health Care, Cincinnati, OH, director of pharmacy affairs, 1994-99; Lloyd Library and Museum, Cincinnati, executive director, 1999-2001, research scholar, 2001—. Queen's University of Belfast, Allied Irish Banks Visiting Professor, annually 1986-89; adjunct professor at University of Mississippi, 1987-99, University of South Carolina, 1990-99, Ohio State University, 1994-99, University of Cincinnati, 1999—, and University of Illinois at Chicago Circle, 2005-06; Massachusetts College of Pharmacy and Health Sciences, William E. Hassan, Jr., Distinguished Rho Chi Memorial Lecturer, 2000; University of Pittsburgh, Tucci Lecturer, 2005; University of the Sciences in Philadelphia, Misher Lecturer, 2005; guest lecturer at other institutions, including Southern Illinois University, University of North Carolina at Chapel Hill, University of West Virginia, and Ohio Northern University; also conference presenter and symposium chair.

MEMBER: American Institute of the History of Pharmacy (council member, 2000-03; member of board of directors, 2005-08), American Association of Colleges of Pharmacy (chair of industry advisory committee, 1990-93), American Pharmacists Association (member of foundation board of directors, 2005-08; vice president, 2006), George F. Archambault Foundation (member of board of directors, 2006—). American Association for the History of Medicine, Beta Phi Mu, Phi Lambda Sigma.

AWARDS, HONORS: Grant from National Library of Medicine, 1984-86; distinguished service awards from College of Pharmacy, University of South Carolina, 1991, and board of directors, American Association of Colleges of Pharmacy, 1994; Fischelis grants, American Institute of the History of Pharmacy, 1996, 2003; meritorious service award, Southern School of Pharmacy, Mercer University, 1998; National Pharmacy Leadership Award, Phi Lambda Sigma, 1998; named Linwood F. Tice Friend of the American Pharmaceutical Association, 1998; certificate of recognition, Phi Lambda Sigma, 1999; elected to the International Academy of the History of Pharmacy.

WRITINGS:

(Compiler, with J.R. Lorimer) Enteral Hyperalimentation with Chemically Defined Elemental Diets: A Source Book, Norwich Eaton Pharmaceuticals (Norwich, NY), 1978, 2nd edition, 1979.

(Editor) Procter & Gamble Pharmacist's Handbook, Technomic Press (Lancaster, PA), 1998, 2nd edition, 2001.

(Editor and contributor) A Road Map to a Profession's Future: The Mills Study Commission on Pharmacy, Gordon & Breach (Amsterdam, Netherlands), 1999, published as The Mills Study Commission on Pharmacy: A Road Map to a Profession's Future, Pharmaceutical Products Press (New York, NY), 2006.

(With M.A. Flannery) Pharmaceutical Education in the Queen City: 150 Years of Service, 1850-2000, Haworth Press (Binghamton, NY), 2001.

(Editor, with G. Griffenhagen, G. Bowers, and R. Penna) Reflections on Pharmacy by the Remington Medalists, 1919-2003, 2nd edition, American Pharmacists Association (Washington, DC), 2004.

Pharmacy in World War II, Haworth Press (Binghamton, NY), 2004.

(Editor in chief) Dictionary of Pharmacy, Pharmaceutical Products Press (New York, NY), 2004.

Author of curriculum materials. Contributor to books, including American Pharmacy: A Collection of Historical Essays, edited by G. Higby, American Institute of the History of Pharmacy (Madison, WI), 2005; and Leadership and Advocacy for Pharmacy, edited by C.J. Boyle and others, American Pharmacists Association (Washington, DC), 2007. Senior editor,

"Pharmaceutical Heritage: Pharmaceutical Care through History" series, Haworth Press (Binghamton, NY), 1998—. Author of "Profiles of Excellence," in *Journal of Pharmacy Teaching,* 1999-2003; "Compounding in History," *International Journal of Pharmaceutical Compounding,* 2000-05; "Wish You Were Here," *International Journal of Pharmaceutical Compounding,* 2001-02; "Heroes of Pharmacy," *Journal of the American Pharmaceutical Association,* 2001—; and "Pharmaceutical Heritage," *Pharmacy Practice News,* 2006—. Editor of "From the Drug Information Centres," in *Journal of Clinical Pharmacy and Therapeutics,* 1987-94. Contributor of articles and reviews to professional journals, including *Pharmacy in History, Journal of Pharmaceutical Marketing and Management, Journal of Pharmaceutical Education, Journal for the American Society of Information Science,* and *Ethics in Science and Medicine.* Editor, *Lloydiana: Publications of the Lloyd Library and Museum,* 1999-2001. Contributing editor, *Pharmacy Times,* 1990-96, and *U.S. Pharmacist,* 1997-99; book review editor, *Journal of Pharmacoepidemiology.* Member of editorial board, *Journal of Clinical Pharmacy and Therapeutics,* 1987-94, and *Journal of Research in Pharmaceutical Economics;* member of editorial advisory board, *Journal of the American Pharmaceutical Association,* 1999-2001, *Journal of Pharmacy Teaching,* 1999-2004; member of editorial advisory board, Pharmaceutical Products Press.

*   *   *

WORTHEN, Dennis Brent
   See WORTHEN, Dennis B.

*   *   *

WRIGHT, Edward

PERSONAL: Education: Attended Hendrix College; graduated from Vanderbilt University (with honors); Northwestern University, M.A.

ADDRESSES: Agent—Jane Conway-Gordon, Jane Conway-Gordon Ltd., 1 Old Compton St., London W1D 5JA, England.

CAREER: Journalist and writer. *Chicago Tribune,* Chicago, IL, editor; *Los Angeles Times,* Los Angeles,

CA, senior editor. *Military service:* U.S. Navy, served as an officer for three years.

AWARDS, HONORS: Debut Dagger Award, for *Clea's Moon;* Shamus Award, 2005, for *While I Disappear;* best hardcover mystery novel of the year, Southern California Booksellers, for *While I Disappear;* Ellis Peters Historical Crime Award, Crime Writers' Association of Great Britain, 2006, for *Red Sky Lament.*

WRITINGS:

The Great Bicycle Caper: Across America on a Ten Speed, Ageless Adventures (Albuquerque, NM), 1993.
The Great River Caper: Down the Mississippi Head to Toe, Ageless Adventures (Albuquerque, NM), 1995.
Damnation Falls, Orion Books (London, England), 2007.

"JOHN RAY HORN" MYSTERY SERIES

Clea's Moon, Putnam (New York, NY), 2003.
While I Disappear, Putnam (New York, NY), 2004.
Red Sky Lament, Orion Books (London, England), 2006.

Also wrote the travel advisory column for the *Los Angeles Times.*

SIDELIGHTS: Edward Wright was raised in Arkansas and moved to Tennessee to finish his undergraduate studies at Vanderbilt University. Upon graduation he joined the U.S. Navy and served for three years as an officer on destroyers, mainly in the Caribbean during the Vietnam War. He returned to academia, receiving a graduate degree in journalism from Northwestern University to assist in a career move into the publishing industry. He worked as an editor for the *Chicago Tribune* and *Los Angeles Times,* focusing primarily on Middle East affairs. In the early 1990s, Wright got the idea that he wanted to pursue fiction writing and started writing his first novel in the "John Ray Horn" series, *Clea's Moon.*

Clea's Moon is set in post-WWII Los Angeles and features John Ray Horn, a former B-movie western actor. Recently out of prison for an assault charge, Horn makes a living as a debt collector for a casino-owner friend, Joseph Mad Crow. Not long a free man, Horn gets involved in a mystery involving his friend's murdered son, his missing stepdaughter, and a child pornography ring, and pieces together the holes in the story. Connie Fletcher, writing in *Booklist,* called the novel "a well-paced mystery." A contributor to *Kirkus Reviews* stated: "If the build-up landed like the fade-out, this one would be headed for Hollywood. Alas, it's not a wrap." Fletcher, however, praised Wright for his use of WWII details, adding that it is "just the kind of first novel that makes you hope for more."

In *While I Disappear,* Horn's past resurfaces when a former costar, Rose Galen, comes back into his life. Like Horn, she is living a rough life, oftentimes on the wrong side of the law. When Horn decides he will help her get back on her feet, Galen is found strangled in her bed. Horn investigates with the help of Mad Crow and his daughter, but face difficulty from a tough detective. A contributor to *Kirkus Reviews* called the prose "melancholy" and "evocative" and thought that the subplots "effectively create split-level nostalgia." A reviewer in *Publishers Weekly* called this book "stronger" than the first, noting that "Wright does a superb job of integrating a fair-play whodunit plot into a hardboiled setting rife with personal and official corruption." Bill Ott, in a *Booklist* review, remarked that the "characters evoke an era, but they also feel pain, the timeless kind, and their problems don't go away when the credits roll."

The third book in the series, *Red Sky Lament,* details the communist manhunt that was let loose by overzealous figures in Hollywood on their rivals. Horn, reluctant to get involved, does so at the request of a friend and serial star, Laura Lee Paisley. Paisley's father, a Hollywood screenwriter, was accused of being a communist sympathizer. However, when he ends up dead, Horn has to deal with more than just Holly-

wood rumors. In *Shots,* Catherine Hunt called it "a crime book that you know you will keep on your shelves and read again." Writing on the *Armchair Interviews* Web site, Connie Anderson praised the tense atmosphere of that period, adding: "You can feel the fear that maybe 'today's the day my name' will be given." Concluding a *Booklist* review, Ott remarked that the series is "a must for noir fans with a sense of irony."

BIOGRAPHICAL AND CRITICAL SOURCES:

PERIODICALS

Booklist, May 1, 2003, Connie Fletcher, review of *Clea's Moon,* p. 1555; May 1, 2004, Bill Ott, review of *While I Disappear,* p. 1519; August 1, 2006, Bill Ott, review of *Red Sky Lament,* p. 53.
Kirkus Reviews, May 1, 2003, review of *Clea's Moon,* p. 641; March 15, 2004, review of *While I Disappear,* p. 252; August 1, 2006, review of *Red Sky Lament,* p. 759.
Library Journal, May 1, 2004, Rex E. Klett, review of *While I Disappear,* p. 143.
Publishers Weekly, April 26, 2004, review of *While I Disappear,* p. 45.
Shots, February, 2006, Catherine Hunt, review of *Red Sky Lament.*

ONLINE

Armchair Interviews, http://www.armchairinterviews. com/ (May 20, 2007), Connie Anderson, review of *Red Sky Lament.*
Edward Wright Home Page, http://www.edward wrightbooks.com (May 20, 2007), author biography.
Gumshoe Review, http://www.gumshoereview.com/ (April 1, 2007), Ernest Lilley, author interview.*

Y-Z

YOST, Mark 1962-

PERSONAL: Born 1962; married; wife's name Leslie; children: George.

ADDRESSES: Home—Lake Elmo, MN.

CAREER: Journalist. Dow Jones Newswire, New York, NY, journalist, then Detroit bureau chief; *Wall Street Journal,* New York, NY, and Brussels, Belgium, editorial page, for five years.

WRITINGS:

Tailgating, Sacks, and Salary Caps: How the NFL Became the Most Successful Sports League in History, Kaplan (Chicago, IL), 2006.
The 200-mph Billboard: The Inside Story of How Big Money Changed NASCAR, MBI (St. Paul, MN), 2007.

Contributor to periodicals, including *New York Times, Philadelphia Inquirer, American Spectator,* and the *Wall Street Journal.*

SIDELIGHTS: Mark Yost began his career in business and sports journalism in the 1980s and worked for a number of prestigious periodicals. Yost made his start in New York, with the Dow Jones Newswire. His performance there helped land him the position of Detroit bureau chief, covering the country's automo-tive industry. Yost also worked for five years on the editorial page of the *Wall Street Journal,* both in New York and Brussels, Belgium. Yost contributes regularly to top echelon periodicals, including the *New York Times, Philadelphia Inquirer,* and the *Wall Street Journal.*

In 2006 Yost published his first book, titled *Tailgating, Sacks, and Salary Caps: How the NFL Became the Most Successful Sports League in History.* In it Yost gives the reader a history of the business aspect of the National Football League from the days when television rights were negotiated individually to 2006, when the League has become a six-billion-dollar venture. Among the many topics covered, Yost highlights the shared-revenue concept pioneered by former commissioner Pete Rozelle, merchandising rights, pan-gender appeal, and the rising popularity and profitability of fantasy football. A contributor to *Sports Illustrated* noted that "there's little unfamiliar or earth-shattering in the tale Yost tells, but his solidly packaged overview is educational for the fan who has mostly concerned himself . . . with the action on the field." Wes Lukowsky, writing in *Booklist,* summarized the book as "a fascinating financial history of the league," adding that "it will fascinate virtually any NFL watcher" and those interested in the business side of the game.

BIOGRAPHICAL AND CRITICAL SOURCES:

PERIODICALS

Booklist, September 1, 2006, Wes Lukowsky, review of *Tailgating, Sacks, and Salary Caps: How the*

NFL Became the Most Successful Sports League in History, p. 50.

Money, October 1, 2006, review of *Tailgating, Sacks, and Salary Caps.*

Sports Illustrated, August 23, 2006, review of *Tailgating, Sacks, and Salary Caps.*

ONLINE

St. Petersburg Times Festival of Reading, http://www.festivalofreading.com/ (May 21, 2007), author profile.*

*   *   *

ZAPPA, Ahmet 1974-
(Ahmet Emuukha Rodan Zappa)

PERSONAL: Born May 15, 1974, in Los Angeles, CA; son of Frank Zappa (a musician) and Gail Sloatman (a businesswoman); married Selma Blair (an actress), June, 2004 (divorced, June, 2006); children.

ADDRESSES: Home and office—Los Angeles, CA.

CAREER: Musician, actor, and writer. Member of band "Z"; performed with father, Frank Zappa, and brother, Dweezil Zappa, on recordings *Shampoo Horn* and *Music for Pets,* and with Leather Dynamite. Host of television programs, including *Based On, But Can They Sing?, webRIOT,* and *Robotica.* Actor in film and television, including *Roseanne, Mad TV, Children of the Corn V, Too Pure, Jack Frost, Grown Ups,* and *Ready to Rumble;* voice actor on *Powder: Up Here* and *Gen 13.* Executive producer of film *Fraggle Rock.*

WRITINGS:

(Self-illustrated) *The Monstrous Memoirs of a Mighty McFearless,* Random House (New York, NY), 2006.

ADAPTATIONS: The Monstrous Memoirs of a Mighty McFearless was adapted for film by Disney Studios.

SIDELIGHTS: Ahmet Zappa's childhood in the home of legendary rocker Frank Zappa was unconventional in many ways, and finding time to watch monster movies was a pastime shared by father and son. For the impressionable young Ahmet, such imaginative viewing made a strong impression. "As a child, what Ahmet desperately needed was an advice book on how to repel monsters, say, when they emerged from under your bed and announced they were about to eat you," reported Sharon Krum in the London *Guardian.* Drawing on his childhood memories, the musician and actor wrote and illustrated *The Monstrous Memoirs of a Mighty McFearless,* his first novel for young readers. "I wanted to create a book that would have been very useful to me as a child," Zappa told Katherine Rushton of the *Bookseller,* recalling his own elaborate nighttime rituals to ward off monsters. "This is me celebrating my life. I'm writing what I know."

The Monstrous Memoirs of a Mighty McFearless takes readers into the lives of Max and Minerva, the children of a "monsterminator." As they help their father fight monsters, they are guided by an encyclopedia-with-attitude named Ms. Monstranomicon. When their father is captured, Max and Minerva set out to rescue him using a bag of tricks that includes concoctions made of cat hair, coffee grounds, and toilet water. While noting that Zappa incorporates some obvious gags, such as naming a castle "Doominstinkinfart," a *Kirkus Reviews* contributor concluded that "the lighthearted gross-out humor, lavishly illustrated with photographs and childlike drawings, will provide plenty of silly entertainment." Diana Tixier Herald, writing in *Booklist,* wrote that "Lemony Snicket fans who relish the strange and yucky will find Zappa's barf-filled romp . . . monstrously entertaining."

Zappa struggled with learning disabilities as a child, and as an author he has made it one of his goals to create a text that is accessible to reluctant readers. To raise the interest level, he includes illustrations that depict monsters of all sorts, as well as brief bites of "factual" information about the monster world. In fact, Zappa originally conceived *The Monstrous Memoirs of a Mighty McFearless* as a series of illustrations rather than a novel; when his publisher told him they would only accept the illustrations if there was a story to go along with them, he pressed onward. The resulting text, according to Rushton, is three times longer than that Zappa was required to write. According to a *Publishers Weekly* contributor, "Zappa's lively monster doodles and photo-illustrations of the main characters . . . add kooky, creepy graphic appeal" to the novel.

Of his literary goals, Zappa stated on his home page: "My simplest wish was to be able write a book that everyone would enjoy, but more specifically, I wanted to write a book that would empower children to overcome their fears and inspire those who have suffered similar learning disabilities as mine to realize just how wonderful reading a book can be."

BIOGRAPHICAL AND CRITICAL SOURCES:

PERIODICALS

Booklist, May 15, 2006, Diana Tixier Herald, review of *The Monstrous Memoirs of a Mighty McFearless,* p. 59.

Bookseller, June 30, 2006, Katherine Rushton, "Monstrous Parenting," p. 23.

Guardian (London, England), July 29, 2006, Sharon Krum, interview with Zappa.

Kirkus Reviews, June 15, 2006, review of *The Monstrous Memoirs of a Mighty McFearless,* p. 639.

Library Media Connection, October, 2006, Betsy Ruffin, review of *The Monstrous Memoirs of a Mighty McFearless,* p. 73.

People, February 9, 2004, "Blair Hitch Project," p. 22.

Publishers Weekly, June 26, 2006, review of *The Monstrous Memoirs of a Mighty McFearless,* p. 52.

School Library Journal, July, 2006, Walter Minkel, review of *The Monstrous Memoirs of a Mighty McFearless,* p. 116.

Time, April 19, 1993, Sophfronia Scott Gregory, "Making Brotherly Music," p. 73.

ONLINE

Ahmet Zappa Home Page, http://www.ahmetzappa. com (April 28, 2007).*

*   *   *

ZAPPA, Ahmet Emuukha Rodan
    See ZAPPA, Ahmet

ZEITLIN, Michael 1957-

PERSONAL: Born January 30, 1957, in Detroit, MI; son of Irving M. (a professor) and Esther (a painter and sculptor) Zeitlin; married Deborah Dunne (divorced); married Denyse Wilson (an actress); children: Isaiah, Daniel, Jonathan. *Ethnicity:* "Jewish." *Education:* University of Toronto, B.A., 1979, M.A., 1980, Ph.D., 1988.

ADDRESSES: Home—Vancouver, British Columbia, Canada. *Office*—University of British Columbia, 1873 East Mall, Ste. 397, Vancouver, British Columbia V6T 1Z1, Canada. *E-mail*—mzeitlin@interchange.ubc.ca.

CAREER: University of British Columbia, Vancouver, British Columbia, Canada, associate professor, 1990—.

WRITINGS:

(Editor, with Paul Budra) *Soldier Talk: The Vietnam War in Oral Narrative,* Indiana University Press (Bloomington, IN), 2004.

(Editor) *Méconnaissance, Race, and the Real in Faulkner's Fiction,* Presses Universitaires de Rennes (Rennes, France), 2004.

Work represented in anthologies. Contributor to scholarly journals.

*   *   *

ZHUK, Sergei I. 1958-

PERSONAL: Born December 18, 1958, in Valutino, U.S.S.R. (now Ukraine); son of Ivan (an engineer) and Valentina (a librarian) Zhuk; married Irina Kozintseva (an interpreter), February 5, 1981; children: Andrey S. *Ethnicity:* "Ukrainian." *Education:* Institute of World History of the U.S.S.R., Ph.D., 1987; Dniepropetrovsk University, doctorate, 1996; Johns Hopkins University, Ph.D., 2002. *Politics:* Liberal. *Religion:* Orthodox Christian.

ADDRESSES: Home—Muncie, IN. *Office*—Department of History, Ball State University, Muncie, IN 67306. *E-mail*—sizhuk@bsu.edu.

CAREER: Dniepropetrovsk University, Dniepropetrovsk, Ukraine, associate professor of history, 1989-97; Ball State University, Muncie, IN, assistant professor of history, 2003—.

MEMBER: American Historical Association, Organization of American Historians, American Association for the Advancement of Slavic Studies.

WRITINGS:

Russia's Lost Reformation, Woodrow Wilson Center Press (Washington, DC), 2004.

SIDELIGHTS: Sergei I. Zhuk told *CA:* "I write because I love history and I like to tell stories about history."